John Constable's Skies

To

Geoff & Maureen

Merry Christmas 1999

'we see nothing truly till we understand it'

Lots of love

John, Lynn, Jacob, Tobias
& Gabriel

xxxxx

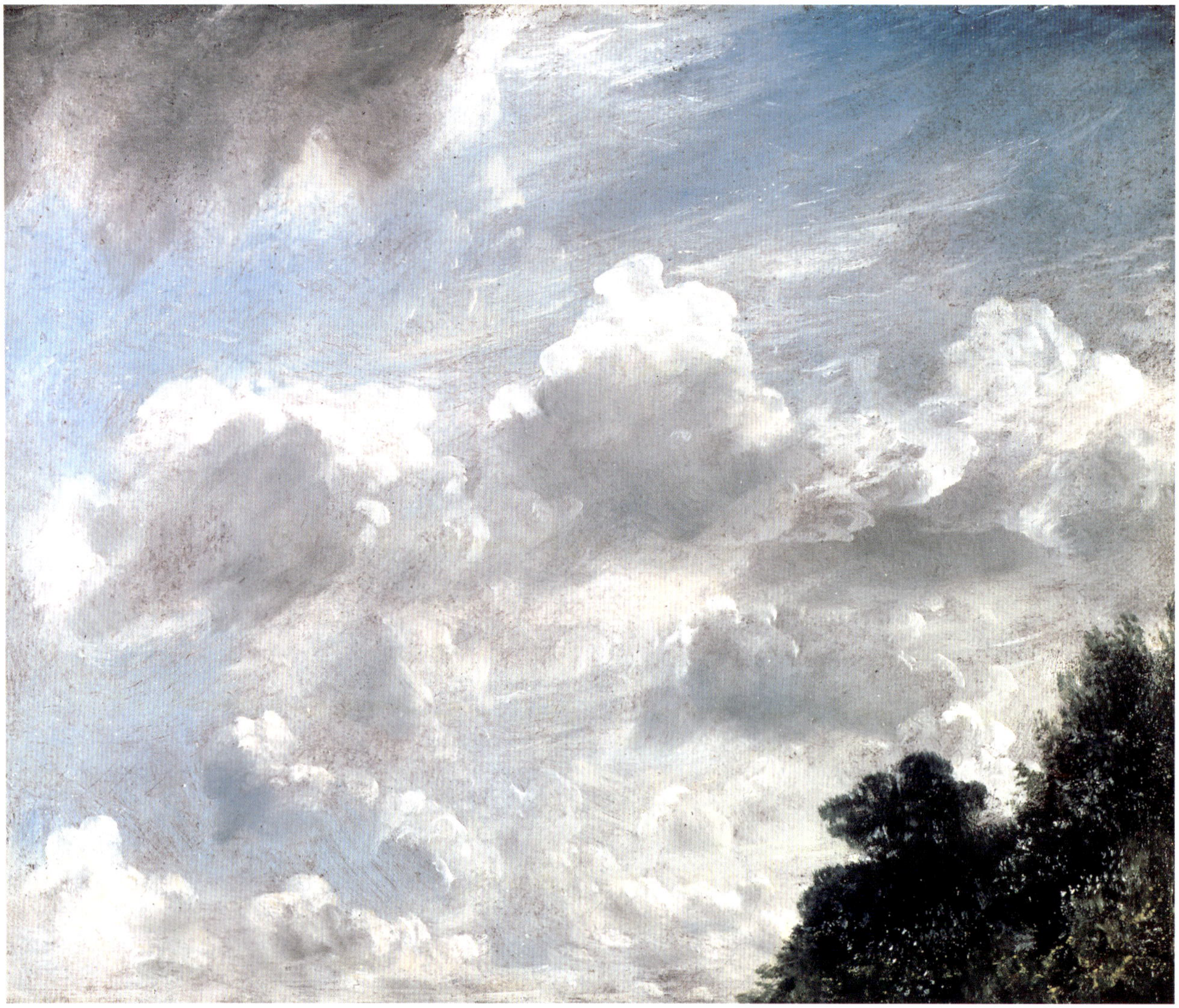

'Hampstead, Sepr 11, 1821. 10. to 11. Morning under the sun – Clouds silvery grey, on warm ground Sultry. Light wind to the S.W. fine all day – but rain in the night following.'

John Constable, *Cloud Study, Hampstead; Tree at Right*, 11 September 1821. Royal Academy of Arts, London

John Constable's Skies

A Fusion of Art and Science

John E. Thornes

Director of the Atmospheric Impacts Research Group,
School of Geography and Environmental Sciences, University of Birmingham

THE UNIVERSITY
OF BIRMINGHAM

UNIVERSITY PRESS

First published in the United Kingdom by The University of Birmingham Press,
Edgbaston, Birmingham, B15 2TT, UK

ISBN 1-902459-02-4

British Library Cataloguing in Publication data
A CIP catalogue record for this book is available from the British Library

Designed and produced by Production Line, Minster Lovell, Oxford
Printed in Great Britain by Butler & Tanner Ltd, Frome, Somerset

Contents

Acknowledgements 8
List of tables 9
List of figures 11
List of plates 12
Introduction 17

Chapter 1 Landscape meteorology 21

1.1 The imitation of nature 21
1.2 The sky 24
1.3 The atmosphere 28
1.3.1 Visibility 29
1.3.2 Aerial perspective 29
1.3.3 The impact of climate change 31
1.3.4 The impact of air pollution 33
1.4 Clouds and weather 36
1.4.1 A brief history of cloud classification 37
1.4.2 The colour of clouds 39
1.4.3 Cloud perspective 40
1.4.4 Influence of weather on sky and landscape colours 41
1.4.5 The portrayal of wind 42
1.5 Light, the sun, rainbows and other optical effects 43
1.5.1 Sunlight and the colour of the sun 44
1.5.2 Light and other optical effects 44
1.5.3 The rainbow 46
1.6 Of truth of skies 48

Chapter 2 John Constable's meteorological understanding 51

2.1 Constable's art and science 51

2.2 Weather in Constable's skies 52

2.3 Constable's training as a windmiller 53

2.4 Hampstead Heath 55

2.5 Constable's letters 56

2.6 The inscriptions to the sky studies of 1820/22 58

2.6.1 The month of painting 59
2.6.2 The hour of painting 64
2.6.3 References to past weather 65
2.6.4 References to future weather 65
2.6.5 Quoted wind direction 66
2.6.6 Quoted wind speed 66
2.6.7 Quoted direction of view 66
2.6.8 Summary of interpretations of the 1820/22 sky study weather inscriptions 67

2.7 Constable's annotations to Forster's book 68

2.8 Copies of Cozens' skies and other drawings 79

2.9 Constable's enigmatic rainbow 80

2.10 *English Landscape Scenery* 89

Chapter 3 Evolution of the skies in Constable's art 93

3.1 Dawn in the valley 1776–98: calm 95

3.2 Sunrise 1799–1812: light air 95

3.3 Morning 1812–16: slight breeze 103

3.4 Late morning 1817–20: gentle breeze 109

3.5 High noon 1821–22: moderate breeze 116

3.6 Afternoon 1823–28: fresh breeze 126

3.7 Sunset 1829–32: strong breeze 136

3.8 The valley in shadow 1833–37: near gale 143

Chapter 4 The influence of art and science on Constable's skies 153

4.1 A brief history of skies in landscape art 154

4.2 From the beginnings of art to the end of the sixteenth century 154

4.3 The painted skies of the seventeenth century 161

4.3.1 Peter Paul Rubens (1577–1640) 162
4.3.2 Nicolas Poussin (1594–1665) 164
4.3.3 Claude Lorrain (1600–82) 166
4.3.4 Rembrandt (Harmensz van Rijn) (1606-69) 168
4.3.5 Salvator Rosa (1615–73) 169
4.3.6 Aelbert Cuyp (1620–91) 170
4.3.7 Jacob van Ruisdael (1628/29–82) 170
4.3.8 Philips Koninck (1619–88), Meyndert Hobbema (1638–1709) and Willem van de Velde (1633–1707) 175

4.4 Eighteenth-century skies in England
Richard Wilson (1713/14–82), Alexander Cozens (1717–86), Thomas Gainsborough (1727–88) and Thomas Girtin (1775–1802) 176

4.5 Nineteenth-century skies
Joseph Mallord William Turner (1775–1851) 179

4.6 Johan Christian Dahl (1788–1857) and the Dresden School 184

4.7 Landscape painting, artistic style, science and skies 185

4.8 Meteorological science through the eyes of Luke Howard 188

4.9 John Ruskin and the role of skies in landscape painting 191

Chapter 5 A fusion of art and science 202

Appendix 1 Towards an accurate dating of certain of John Constable's sky studies 1820/22 202

Appendix 2 Sky studies without weather inscriptions attributed to John Constable 275

Appendix 3 Transcript of the letter from John Constable to the Revd. John Fisher, 23 October 1821 278

Bibliography 283

Index 286

Acknowledgements

The idea for this book came out of the 1991 Constable Exhibition at the Tate Gallery. I was approached by the late Ian Fleming-Williams and David Thomson to update a paper I wrote in 1978 entitled *The Accurate Dating of Certain of John Constable's Cloud Studies 1821/22 Using Historical Weather Records*. Ian Fleming-Williams gave me great encouragement and his enthusiasm was infectious. It is very sad that he will not see the final product of his nurturing. David Thomson has been a rock of support and has always responded positively to my requests for advice. I must also thank him for his generous financial support towards the illustrations and provision of access to his own considerable Constable collection.

For my wife Lynn and my three boys Jacob, Tobias and Gabriel: I thank them for all their patient hours whilst I have been locked in my study. I hope the production of this book will encourage them to believe that they will see more of me from now on. Lynn's continuing love of art and me has been inspirational.

I must thank my parents for their endless support. Tragically my father died when the book was just underway and he did not get to read any of it. However he is there on every page and the book is written for him.

Many others have helped and encouraged in the laborious task of turning a first draft into a finished book. I would like especially to thank Brian Allen for his endless guidance and encouragement and the Paul Mellon Centre for their generous financial support towards the illustrations. Vicki Whittaker has done a wonderful and patient job as editor; her tactful suggestions have always improved my prose considerably. The School of Geography and Environmental Sciences at the University of Birmingham provided generous financial support for this project. Many others have helped over the years, both intentionally and unintentionally, and I wish to thank you all: Kevin Burkhill, Dennis Cosgrove, Sarah Cove, Steve Daniels, Steve Ellis, Stan Gedzelman, James Hamilton, Charlotte Klonk, Anne Lyles, Edward Morris, Leslie Parris, Geoff Petts, Bill Pike, Hugh Prince, Brenda Renwick, Graham Reynolds, Peter (Sid) Sollis, Paul Spencer-Longhurst, Julia Thomas, Charlie Webster and Shearer West.

Every effort has been made to trace the copyright holders of all copyright material reproduced in this book. If a copyright holder has been inadvertantly overlooked, they are asked to contact the publisher at their earliest convenience.

List of Tables

Table 1	The international classification of visibility	29
Table 2	Relative frequencies (%) of cloud families for different regional schools of painting	31
Table 3	Relative frequencies (%) of cloudiness for different regional schools of painting	31
Table 4	Average cloudiness (C) of sky area shown in paintings of all schools (%), and total number of coastal floods and severe freezes (F) in Europe by 50-year epochs	32
Table 5	Major volcanic eruptions that coloured the skies of England during Constable's lifetime (1776–1837)	33
Table 6	Landmarks in cloud classification	37
Table 7	The international cloud classification	38
Table 8	Effect of scattering, reflection, refraction and diffraction on light as it passes through the atmosphere	44
Table 9	Droplet size and rainbow colours	47
Table 10	Dated sky studies and weather inscriptions 1820–22	60
Table 11	Analysis of the fifty-four dated sky studies 1820–22	62
Table 12	Analysis of weather inscriptions on fifty-one sky studies	63
Table 13	Mean monthly air temperature at Somerset House, London 1820–22	64
Table 14	Wind directions at Stratford recorded by Howard	66
Table 15	Direction of view versus wind direction	67
Table 16	Approximate height of rainbow at noon for different months and latitudes	84
Table 17	Lamarck's cloud classification	189
Table 18	The dating of fifteen sky studies with incomplete dates	205
Table 19	Date and size of each sky study classified into 'sky and landscape' or 'pure sky'	206

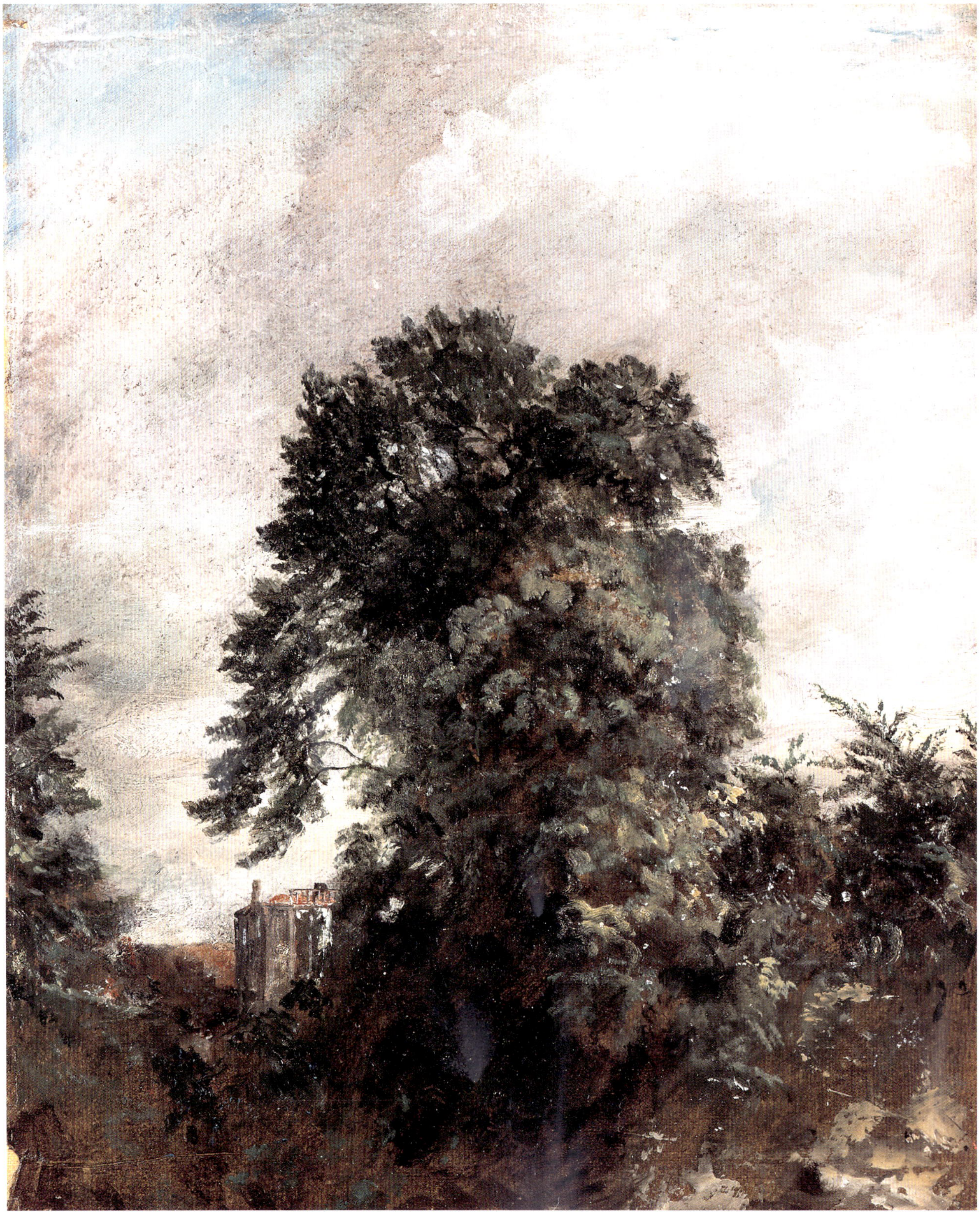

'29th July 1822 looking east 10 in the morning – silvery clouds'
John Constable, *Landscape Study: Tree and Corner House*, 29 July 1822. Royal Academy of Arts, London

List of Figures

Figure 1	The electromagnetic spectrum	23
Figure 2	Light scattered to the eye by the atmosphere	24
Figure 3	Depth of atmosphere to the eye from the horizon	25
Figure 4	Composition of light coming from a small volume of air lying at various distances from the eye	25
Figure 5	Ratio of frequencies of pale-blue skies to deep-blue skies in the paintings of different European countries	27
Figure 6	Average % visibility for different regional schools of painting	30
Figure 7	Overall % cloudiness for different regional schools of painting	32
Figure 8	Number of foggy days each year in London since the seventeenth century	36
Figure 9	Light and shadow on cumulus clouds	38
Figure 10	The refraction of starlight	45
Figure 11	Geometry of a rainbow	46
Figure 12	Path of light through a raindrop	46
Figure 13	Rainbow angle from Constable's *Salisbury Cathedral from the Meadows*, 1831	83
Figure 14	Constable's rainbow diagrams – recto of sheet A	87
Figure 15	Constable's rainbow diagrams – verso of sheet A	87
Figure 16	Constable's rainbow diagrams – recto of sheet B	87
Figure 17	Constable's rainbow diagrams – verso of sheet B	87
Figure 18	Sheet of paper cut by Constable for sky studies	121
Figure 19	Ruskin's rectilinear cloud perspective	194
Figure 20	Ruskin's curvilinear cloud perspective	195
Figure 21	Historical weather record sites (1820–22) in relation to Hampstead Heath	203
Figure 22	Extract from Luke Howard's weather observations (October 1821 – Stratford, London)	207

List of Plates

Plate 1	Richard Wilson, *The River Dee, near Eaton Hall*	26
Plate 2	Claude Monet, *Impression, Soleil levant* (Impression, Sunrise)	34
Plate 3	Claude Monet, *View of Houses of Parliament*	35
Plate 4	Luke Howard, *Cloud Sketches (Cirrus, Cumulus and Stratus)*	37
Plate 5	David Cox, *Sun, Wind and Rain*	42
Plate 6	David Lucas, John Constable's *Spring. East Bergholt Common, Hail Squalls – Noon*	43
Plate 7	John Constable, *Hampstead Heath with the House called 'The Salt Box'*	58
Plate 8	Cloud studies by Thomas Forster	74
Plate 9	Cloud studies by Thomas Forster	74
Plate 10	Stratocumulus from spreading out of cumulus	75
Plate 11	Cumulonimbus with anvil	75
Plate 12	John Constable, *Seven Cloud Studies after Alexander Cozens*	79
Plate 13	John Constable, Sketch accompanying passage from Robert Bloomfield's *The Farmer's Boy*	81
Plate 14	David Lucas, John Constable's *Stoke by Neyland*, Suffolk.	84
Plate 15	John Constable, *Dedham Vale*, 1802	97
Plate 16	John Constable, *Stour Valley*	98
Plate 17	John Constable, *Derwentwater*	98
Plate 18	John Constable, *Borrowdale, Twilight*	101
Plate 19	John Constable, *Dedham Vale*, 1810	101
Plate 20	John Constable, *The River Stour at Sunset*	101
Plate 21	John Constable, *The Valley of the Stour, Sunset*	102
Plate 22	John Constable, *Landscape with Double Rainbow*	104
Plate 23	John Constable, *A Lock on the Stour*	104
Plate 24	John Constable, *Malthouse Field, East Bergholt*	105
Plate 25	John Constable, *Golding Constable's Kitchen Garden*	106
Plate 26	John Constable, *Stoke by Nayland*	107
Plate 27	John Constable, *Wivenhoe Park*	107
Plate 28	John Constable, *Weymouth Bay, with Jordan Hill*	108

Plate 29	John Constable, *Scene on a Navigable River (Flatford Mill)*	108
Plate 30	John Constable, *A Cottage in a Cornfield*, 1817	110
Plate 31	John Constable, *A Cottage in a Cornfield*, 1833	111
Plate 32	John Constable, *Dedham Lock and Mill*, 1819[?]	112
Plate 33	John Constable, *Dedham Lock and Mill*, 1819[?] (another version)	112
Plate 34	John Constable, *The White Horse*	113
Plate 35	John Constable, *Branch Hill Pond*	114
Plate 36	John Constable, *Stratford Mill*	115
Plate 37	John Constable, *Harwich Lighthouse*	116
Plate 38	John Constable, *The Hay Wain*	118
Plate 39	John Constable, Sketch for *The Hay Wain*	120
Plate 40	John Constable, *Study of Cirrus Clouds*	123
Plate 41	John Constable, *View on the Stour near Dedham*	125
Plate 42	John Constable, *Salisbury Cathedral from the Bishop's Grounds*	126
Plate 43	John Constable, *Salisbury Cathedral*	127
Plate 44	John Constable, *Seascape Study with Rain Clouds*	129
Plate 45	John Constable, *Brighton Beach with Colliers*	129
Plate 46	John Constable, *The Leaping Horse*	130
Plate 47	John Constable, *Branch Hill Pond, Hampstead Heath*	131
Plate 48	John Constable, *The Cornfield*	132
Plate 49	John Constable, *Vale of Dedham*	133
Plate 50	John Constable, *A Boat Passing a Lock*	134
Plate 51	John Constable, *The Chain Pier Brighton*	135
Plate 52	John Constable, *Sky Study with Rainbow*	136
Plate 53	John Constable, *Hampstead Heath: Branch Hill Pond*	137
Plate 54	John Constable, *Hadleigh Castle*	137
Plate 55	John Constable, *The Close, Salisbury*	138
Plate 56	David Lucas, John Constable's *Lock on the Stour*	140
Plate 57	John Constable, *Old Sarum*, 1829	140
Plate 58	John Constable, *Hampstead Heath*	141
Plate 59	John Constable, *Salisbury Cathedral from the Meadows*	143
Plate 60	John Constable, *The Opening of Waterloo Bridge*	144
Plate 61	John Constable, *London from Hampstead with a Double Rainbow*	144
Plate 62	John Constable, *Old Sarum*, 1834	146
Plate 63	John Constable, *Stonehenge*	146
Plate 64	John Constable, *Hampstead Heath with a Rainbow*	147
Plate 65	John Constable, *Cottage, East Bergholt*	148
Plate 66	Attributed to Jacopo di Cione, *The Crucifixion*	155
Plate 67	Giovanni Bellini, *Madonna of the Meadow*	156

Plate 68	Jan van Eyck, *The Crucifixion*	157
Plate 69	Giorgione, *La Tempesta*	159
Plate 70	Pieter Bruegel, *Hunters in the Snow*	161
Plate 71	Peter Paul Rubens, *An Autumn Landscape*	162
Plate 72	Peter Paul Rubens, *Landscape with a Rainbow*	163
Plate 73	Nicolas Poussin, *Landscape with Man Washing his Feet at a Fountain*	165
Plate 74	Nicolas Poussin, *L'Hiver ou le Déluge*	166
Plate 75	Claude Lorrain, *The Embarkation of Saint Ursala*	167
Plate 76	Rembrandt, *The Mill*	168
Plate 77	Salvator Rosa, *Landscape with Tobias and the Angel*	170
Plate 78	Aelbert Cuyp, *Thunderstorm over Dordrecht*	171
Plate 79	Jacob Ruisdael, *Vessels in a Breeze*	173
Plate 80	Jacob Ruisdael, *Winter Landscape*	174
Plate 81	Philips Koninck, *Landscape with a Road by a River*	176
Plate 82	Alexander Cozens, *After Rain*	178
Plate 83	Thomas Gainsborough, *Mr and Mrs Andrews*	178
Plate 84	Joseph Mallord William Turner, *Snow Storm: Hannibal and his Army Crossing the Alps*	181
Plate 85	Joseph Mallord William Turner, *Raby Castle*	182
Plate 86	Joseph Mallord WilliamTurner, *Coventry*	183
Plate 87	Johan Christian Dahl, *Cloud Study*	185
Plate 88	John Constable, *Sketch at Hampstead: Stormy Sunset*	210
Plate 89	John Constable, *View of Hampstead Heath Looking Towards Harrow*	211
Plate 90	John Constable, *Sketch at Hampstead: Evening*	212
Plate 91	John Constable, *Landscape Study: Hampstead Looking West*	215
Plate 92	John Constable, *Cloud Study, Early Morning, Looking East from Hampstead*	217
Plate 93	John Constable, *View from Hampstead Heath Looking Towards Harrow*	219
Plate 94	John Constable, *Study of Sky and Trees*	221
Plate 95	John Constable, *Cloud Study with Treetops and Building*	223
Plate 96	John Constable, *Cloud Study, Hampstead; Tree at Right*	225
Plate 97	John Constable, *Study of Sky and Trees, with a Red House, at Hampstead*	226
Plate 98	John Constable, *Hampstead Heath, Sun Setting over Harrow*	227
Plate 99	John Constable, *Cloud Study*	229
Plate 100	John Constable, *Study of Sky and Trees*	231
Plate 101	John Constable, *Cloud Study*	233
Plate 102	John Constable, *Cloud Study with Trees*	234
Plate 103	John Constable, *Cloud Study: Horizon of Trees*	235
Plate 104	John Constable, *Landscape Study: Hampstead Heath Looking Towards Harrow*	237
Plate 105	John Constable, *Cloud Study*	239

Plate 106	John Constable, *Study of Sky and Trees at Hampstead*	241
Plate 107	John Constable, *Hampstead Heath: Branch Hill Pond*	244
Plate 108	John Constable, *A View on Hampstead Heath with Figures in the Foreground*	247
Plate 109	John Constable, *A Sandbank at Hampstead Heath*	249
Plate 110	John Constable, *Clouds above Hampstead Heath*	251
Plate 111	John Constable, *Landscape Study: Tree and Corner House*	253
Plate 112	John Constable, *The Road to the Spaniards, Hampstead*	254
Plate 113	John Constable, *A View on Hampstead Heath*	255
Plate 114	John Constable, *A View at Hampstead: Evening*	256
Plate 115	John Constable, *Hampstead Heath: Stormy Sunset*	257
Plate 116	John Constable, *Study of Cumulus Clouds*	258
Plate 117	John Constable, *Cloud Study*	263
Plate 118	John Constable, *Study of Clouds*	264
Plate 119	John Constable, *Clouds*	265
Plate 120	John Constable, *Cloud Study*	266
Plate 121	John Constable, *Cloud Study*	267
Plate 122	John Constable, *Cloud Study*	268
Plate 123	John Constable, *Study of Cumulus Clouds*	269
Plate 124	John Constable, *Cloud Study*	271
Plate 125	John Constable, *Cloud Study*	273

Introduction

The sky is a finely tuned paradigm of the alliance between art and science. In that mutable void, the landscape artist's concerns – poetic, ideal and symbolic, empirical and scientific – were sharpened rather than blurred. As the source of light, spiritual as well as secular, the sky relieved absolutism with infinite moods, unchanging ideals with endless process. No wonder the artists fixed their particular attention on those moist cargoes that described the void in brief but repeated compositions: clouds.[1]

As a trained meteorologist I have been used to observing the sky all my life. I can remember, as a boy, helping my father to take weather observations in our garden in Batley, Yorkshire. However I was taught at school and university that meteorology was a science and that my observations of the atmosphere were part of a positivistic process of the examination of theories and models. In 1975 I reluctantly allowed myself to be dragged along by a friend to the Turner exhibition at the Royal Academy.[2] I could not believe my eyes. There was canvas upon canvas of weather and atmosphere and sunlight and clouds. A microcosm of meteorology. The very next week I set my students an essay on the effect of weather on landscape appreciation. They were back within days to complain that they couldn't find a single reference on the subject. Astonished, I went to the university library and could only find a handful of references myself. This was the start of an exciting period in my life when I began to explore the literature on landscape painting. I discovered that, although there was a small but fascinating literature on landscape meteorology written by meteorologists, art historians, with a few notable exceptions, appeared mostly to have ignored the sky. By the time of the Constable exhibition of 1976 at the Tate Gallery[3] I was already intrigued and fascinated by Constable's skies.

I had soon discovered Badt's classic series of essays, published in 1950, entitled *John Constable's Clouds*, in which he puts forward the hypothesis that John Constable's remarkable cloud studies of 1821/22 may, indeed must, have been inspired by Luke Howard's cloud classification.[4] This simple hypothesis was then used by Badt to examine the relationships between art and science at the beginning of the nineteenth century, which led me on to John Ruskin, whose brilliant word paintings of the sky and clouds are still unsurpassed.

This book, written nearly half a century after Badt's, is an attempt to reassess Constable's skies from a meteorological point of view, taking into account the large volume of Constable material that has come to light in that time. It aims to provide a meteorological framework for the appreciation of John Constable's skies, as well as providing a comprehensive catalogue of his cloud and sky studies. This will, I hope, enable the reader to understand why Constable's skies are so memorable, as well as giving some insight into how to appreciate, interpret and compare his skies with those of other landscape artists.

In writing a text such as this, as a meteorologist I have felt daunted by the sheer volume of art history relating to Constable and landscape art in the first half of the nineteenth century. Badt's brilliant little book is a hard act to follow. Nevertheless I have striven to answer some of the following questions that sprang to mind before I wrote this book: Has Badt's hypothesis been strengthened or weakened by the passage of time? How did contemporary meteorology influence Constable's works? How much meteorology did Constable understand? How do Constable's skies stand up to a critical analysis made more than 150 years after his death? How do Constable's skies compare with Turner's and other landscape artists before and during his lifetime? Can Constable be considered as the greatest sky painter of all time?

The atmosphere is an integral part of every landscape – we see and hear everything through it – and yet the links between meteorology and painting are still relatively unexplored. Certainly many of the general public, and also a considerable number of artists and critics, have a very simple view of landscape meteorology: the sky is blue, the clouds are white, the atmosphere is invisible, the sun is yellow and rainbow colours are remembered as Richard Of York Gained Battles In Vain. But to myself and others, including Constable, the atmosphere is a source of infinite moods, divine inspiration, naive wonderment and a ceaseless physical and dynamic process.

Meteorology and art

The atmosphere is the most valuable resource on earth: without air to breath we could not survive for more than a few minutes. Attempts to understand how the atmosphere has evolved, how it functions, its impact on the development of society, and society's impact on the atmosphere itself, have been studied under the banner of meteorology since Aristotle wrote his classic text *Meteorologica* in about 350 BC.[5] Traditionally meteorology has been regarded as a 'pure' science, the invisible atmosphere given over to mathematics, physics and chemistry. Observations of the atmosphere and equations of state and motion are fed into ever more powerful computers from which weather and climate forecasts emerge. Adiabatic lapse rates, coriolis forces, entropy, gravity waves, chaos theory – it all sounds very scientific; and yet meteorologists still talk of 'the *art* of weather forecasting'. The output of the numerical weather prediction models is on a large scale of tens of kilometres, yet this still has to be interpreted by a human being to forecast the likely weather at a particular place. This requires local geographical knowledge and experience – something that is very difficult to program into a computer.

The role of meteorology in the advancement of science, religion and art is as yet poorly documented. To most people the workings of the atmosphere are just as mysterious today as they were for Aristotle and the Greeks over 2000 years ago. Despite its familiarity the atmosphere has always presented a number of mysteries and contradictions. For instance, a typical cumulus cloud can weigh several thousand tonnes, and a thunder cloud (cumulonimbus) upwards of 100 000 tonnes. How can a cloud stay aloft when water is 1000 times denser than air at typical cloud heights? Up to the nineteenth century cloud droplets were called 'vesicules', and were thought to contain a vacuum which enabled them to float in the atmosphere. In fact cloud droplets are composed of ordinary water (ice in cirrus clouds) and are falling continuously under the force of gravity. Small droplets fall at such a slow rate that they do not appear to be moving. There are many other atmospheric puzzles that present themselves to the astute observer, not all of which have yet found full scientific explanation. Some of these will be examined in Chapter 1 – for instance why the sky appears blue and rarely green, and why a rainbow cannot be seen at noon in summer in England.

The artistic side of atmospheric studies has been largely ignored by meteorologists. This is surprising because the atmosphere presents such lavish natural beauty. 'Sometimes gentle, sometimes capricious, sometimes awful, never the same for two moments together; almost human in its passions, almost spiritual in its tenderness, almost divine in its infinity.'[6] This is not to say that meteorologists and climatologists are unaware of atmospheric beauty in nature, but that they have failed to realise the academic and practical value of studying the aesthetics of the atmosphere. The intellectual appeal of atmospheric studies has suffered as a consequence, with the atmosphere seemingly regarded by many meteorologists as an invisible fluid that inhabits their super-computers.

Bonacina, in 1939, was the first meteorologist to stress the importance of an artistic as well as a scientific approach to the atmosphere. He defined the term 'landscape meteorology' to be 'those scenic influences of sky, atmosphere, weather and climate which form part of our natural human environment ... whether the natural scenery is merely received and carefully stored in memory, or is photographed, painted or described.'[7] Landscape meteorology is part of the broader field of atmospheric perception which encompasses all our sensual interactions with the atmosphere. A howling gale; a blinding flash of lightning followed by a heart-stopping, explosive, rippling crack of thunder; the delicious smell of country air; the taste and smell of smoking summer rain or the burning heat of the summer sun; all these moods of the atmosphere control our own moods and feelings, often without our realising it. The atmosphere has also always been a rich source of vocabulary for expressing human and animal moods and feelings: *you could cut the atmosphere with a knife; in the current economic climate*; *it never rains but it pours; she said, with a note of thunder in her voice.* Atmospheric perception involves an appreciation of how we consciously and unconsciously interact with our atmospheric environment. Conscious responses such as unfurling an umbrella or changing our clothes are everyday events, whilst others such as the painting of a cloud are less common. Unconscious responses, which we often take for granted, include the simple act of breathing about 14kg of air every day; our body's usually successful attempts to maintain its core temperature at 37°C; and the sense of well-being we experience on a bright sunny morning.

Our weather and climate are studied in a less academic but much more practical way by farmers, pilots, sailors, builders and gardeners, and, of course, artists. Art of all forms is affected and influenced by the atmosphere. The musical note is carried to our ear by the atmosphere, the sculpture or the painting is usually lit by the sky both in its production and in its viewing. Yet few artists have made the sky one of their principal themes. Wagner, Beethoven and Debussy have painted musical skies, but none are instantly associated with them. Aristophanes, Thomson, Shelley, and Ruskin have written about skies but they are not labelled by them. But in landscape art there is one artist who is inextricably linked with his skies – the landscape artist John Constable. Turner, Cox, Monet, Magritte and others have painted wonderful skies but they are all primarily known for other stylistic features. Constable was fascinated by the sky and its associated weather, and one particular annotation, a line down the margin, in his copy of Thomas Forster's book *Researches about Atmospheric Phaenomena*, first published in 1813, shows that he perhaps shared Forster's view that

> *Meteorology considered as a subject of amusement seems to have some advantages over many other pursuits; inasmuch as it may be studied and will afford interest in places unfavourable to the cultivation of other sciences.... The atmosphere and its phaenomena are every where, and thunder rolls, and rainbows glitter in all conceivable situations.*[8]

To fully appreciate the beauty and power of the atmosphere we have to be taught to understand it. As John Constable said: 'we see nothing truly till we understand it'.[9] This is a theme that we shall examine throughout this book. We cannot see the sky 'truly' until we understand how it functions. The first chapter of this book therefore attempts to give the reader a basic scientific understanding of skies, so that it should then be possible to fully appreciate both the real sky and the sky of any landscape painting. Chapter 2 examines all the direct evidence available that enables an assessment of Constable's meteorological understanding. Chapter 3 unravels the almost linear evolution of the skies in Constable's works and their increasing windiness. Chapter 4 attempts to set his skies in context by examining the skies of other artists and the state of landscape art and meteorological science at the beginning of the nineteenth century. Chapter 5 summarises all the direct and indirect evidence to assess whether or not Constable's skies are the most scientifically accurate of all landscape art. Appendix 1 contains a complete catalogue of fifty-four of Constable's dated sky studies painted between October 1820 and October 1822 and uses contemporary weather records to date certain studies more accurately. Appendix 2 lists another sixty-eight sky studies that have been attributed to Constable but are not dated. Appendix 3 is a transcript of Constable's important letter to the Reverend John Fisher of 23 October 1821.

Notes

1 B. Novak, *Nature and Culture* (London: Thames and Hudson, 1980), p. 78, quoted whilst discussing mid nineteenth-century American landscape artists, but applies equally well to British landscape artists of the first half of the nineteenth century.

2 Turner (1775–1851), Bicentenary Exhibition, The Royal Academy of Arts, London, November–March 1974/75.

3 Constable (1776–1837), Bicentenary Exhibition, The Tate Gallery, London, February–April 1976.

4 K. Badt, *John Constable's Clouds* (London: Routledge & Kegan Paul, 1950).

5 Aristotle, *Meteorologica*, ~350 BC (London: Loeb Classical Library, 1962).

6 J. Ruskin, *Moderns Painters I*. In *The Works of John Ruskin*, edited by E. T. Cook and A. Wedderburn, 39 vols. (London: Library Edition: 1903–12), *Works III*, part II, section 3, entitled 'Of Truth of Skies', p. 344.

7 L. C. W. Bonacina, 'Landscape meteorology and its reflection in art and literature', *Quarterly Journal of the Royal Meteorological Society,* 65 (1939): 485–97.

8 T. Forster, *Researches about Atmospheric Phaenomena* (London: Baldwin, Cradock & Joy, 1815), preface to the second edition, p. vii.

9 From Constable's third lecture at the Royal Institution in 1836. See C. R. Leslie, *Memoirs of the Life of John Constable*, 2nd edn (London: Longman's, Brown, Green and Longman's, 1845), p. 350.

CHAPTER ONE

Landscape meteorology

For almost five hundred years the central goal of European painting was the imitation of nature. Many artists and theorists, believing that imitation must be based on scientific principles, found inspiration or guidance in two branches of optics – the geometrical science of perspective and the physical science of colour.[1]

1.1 The imitation of nature

The imitation of nature did not normally mean the representation of real views of nature; the scene had to be out of the artist's imagination. Thus the painted skies of 'old masters' such as Claude, Poussin, Salvator Rosa, and the Dutch and Flemish seventeenth-century artists such as Ruisdael and Rubens, were not copied directly from nature but were created in the studio. The sky was used as a 'backdrop' to the scene enacted in the landscape. As Constable wrote in his famous letter to Fisher on 23 October 1821: 'I have often been advised to consider my sky as *a white sheet drawn behind the objects*.'[2]

There were few scientific principles about the atmosphere to help artists imitate the sky until Luke Howard's cloud classification was published in 1803.[3] The lighting of the landscape was usually considered independently from that of the sky, which seems almost incomprehensible today. The transition from ideal landscapes to real landscapes took place gradually but the sky was rarely painted for its own sake. As late as 1871 Ruskin wrote: 'A cloud, looked at as a cloud only, is no more a subject for painting than so much feculence in dirty water.... That it is worthy of being painted at all depends upon it being the means of nourishment and chastisement to men, or the dwelling place of imaginary Gods.'[4] Yet Ruskin had already written in 1856 in *Modern Painters III*: 'if a general and characteristic name were needed for modern landscape art, none better could be invented than "the service of clouds"'.[5]

The first half of the nineteenth century, principally illustrated through the paintings of Turner and Constable, saw the sky dominating landscape art. Yet of all the aspects of nature that artists have tried to imitate throughout the ages the sky has been the most neglected and poorly executed from a scientific point of view. In far too many landscape paintings there is no harmony between the lighting of the sky and the landscape, and the clouds are often unrealistic in form and totally wrong in terms of perspective. The sky is probably the most difficult part of nature to imitate because of its ephemeral character, and there has been virtually nothing useful written for artists on the perspective and colour of skies. Artists, therefore, have been able to rely little on any literature for inspiration and guidance. Instead they have had to rely on their own observations, unless they have had the confidence and ability to delve into the scientific literature, which has had much to say about the colour, but virtually nothing to say about the perspective, of skies. Similarly, art critics have largely ignored the skies in their analysis of paintings and have rather taken the sky for granted when looking at a landscape painting.

It is very important to remember, as John Constable reminds us, that 'the sky is the source of light in nature – and governs everything',[6] including the colour of the landscape. How uninteresting it would be if the lighting of the landscape was the same all the time – for instance if the sun shone continuously from the same position and there was no weather. It is the changing sky that vitalises the landscape, both practically through the light, the warmth and the water that it brings to the vegetation and soil, and spiritually through its limitless moods. In view of the fact that the atmosphere and sky are seemingly abstract and infinite and yet are often taken for granted, it is important to present the reader, right at the beginning of this book, with a simple framework to enable an appreciation of skies. Having read this chapter it is hoped that the reader will be able to appreciate form, light, colour and process in the atmosphere and sky, and then apply this knowledge when looking at a landscape painting.

It is sometimes convenient to call the area of sky above the landscape in a picture the 'skyscape'. Later in this book I shall use the term 'skyscape' to refer to paintings and sketches in which almost 100 per cent of the picture is sky. Very few artists have painted skyscapes for their own sake. Vanderveldt was quoted by Gilpin as having made many excursions up and down the Thames to study the sky: 'These expeditions Vanderveldt called ... going a skoying.'[7] (Constable also used the term 'skying' in his famous letter to Fisher of 23 October 1821, as will be discussed in Chapter 2.) The vast majority of artists however have not engaged in 'skying', although most must have sketched sky effects at some time. Probably the first English artist to draw a range of skies was Alexander Cozens, who published a set of fictional skies around 1785 for artists to copy onto their landscapes.[8] The fact that these skies were published by Cozens shows how difficult contemporary artists must have found the painting of the sky. Chapter 4 traces in detail the portrayal of skies in the landscape painting of artists who may have influenced the skies of Constable's art.

When looking at the sky, or the sky in a landscape painting, it is useful to have a mental checklist to remind oneself of the components that make up the whole skyscape. Obviously the landscape painter may not always be trying to recreate a 'realistic' sky, but may be trying to give an overall impression of the sky without identifiable features. Nevertheless, it is useful to see what level of detail the artist has achieved. Over the years art historians and art critics, with the exception of Ruskin, have spent little time examining the 'truth' of the skies of landscape paintings. Ruskin, in *Modern Painters I*, outlined his own checklist for the appreciation of all paintings:

> *I think that all the sources of pleasure, or of any other good, to be derived from works of art, may be referred to five distinct heads.*
>
> I. *Ideas of Power. – The perception or conception of the mental or bodily powers by which the work has been produced.*
> II. *Ideas of Imitation. – The perception that the thing produced resembles something else.*
> III. *Ideas of Truth. – The perception of faithfulness in a statement of facts by the thing produced.*
> IV. *Ideas of Beauty. – The perception of beauty, either in the thing produced, or in what it suggests or resembles.*
> V. *Ideas of Relation. – The perception of intellectual relations in the thing produced, or in what it suggests or resembles.*[9]

This chapter is concerned mostly with what Ruskin called 'Ideas of Imitation and Truth' as applied to the sky. Ruskin devotes a whole section of *Modern Painters* to the discussion of skies.[10] His discussion of clouds is fascinating but rather dated, as will be discussed in Chapter 4. However he is correct when he writes:

I shall enter upon the examination of what is true in sky at greater length, because it is the only part of a picture of which all, if they will, may be competent judges. What I may have to assert respecting the rocks of Salvator, or the boughs of Claude, I can scarcely prove.... But what I say of the sky can be brought to an immediate test by all.[11]

For our purpose we can divide our analysis of the 'skyscape' into four more detailed components. When looking at the sky of a landscape painting it is proposed that each of these components should be considered in turn, in the order shown.

1. The sky – form, light and colour
2. The atmosphere – visible colours and form, or invisible?
3. The clouds and weather – form, light, colour and process
4. The sun, sunlight, rainbows and other optical effects – form, light, colour and process

Strictly speaking the term 'sky' just refers to the scattered light that reaches our eyes from the sun. However in discussing the skies of John Constable I am including all the atmospheric phenomena in his paintings, be it clouds, wind, dew, rain or sunshine.

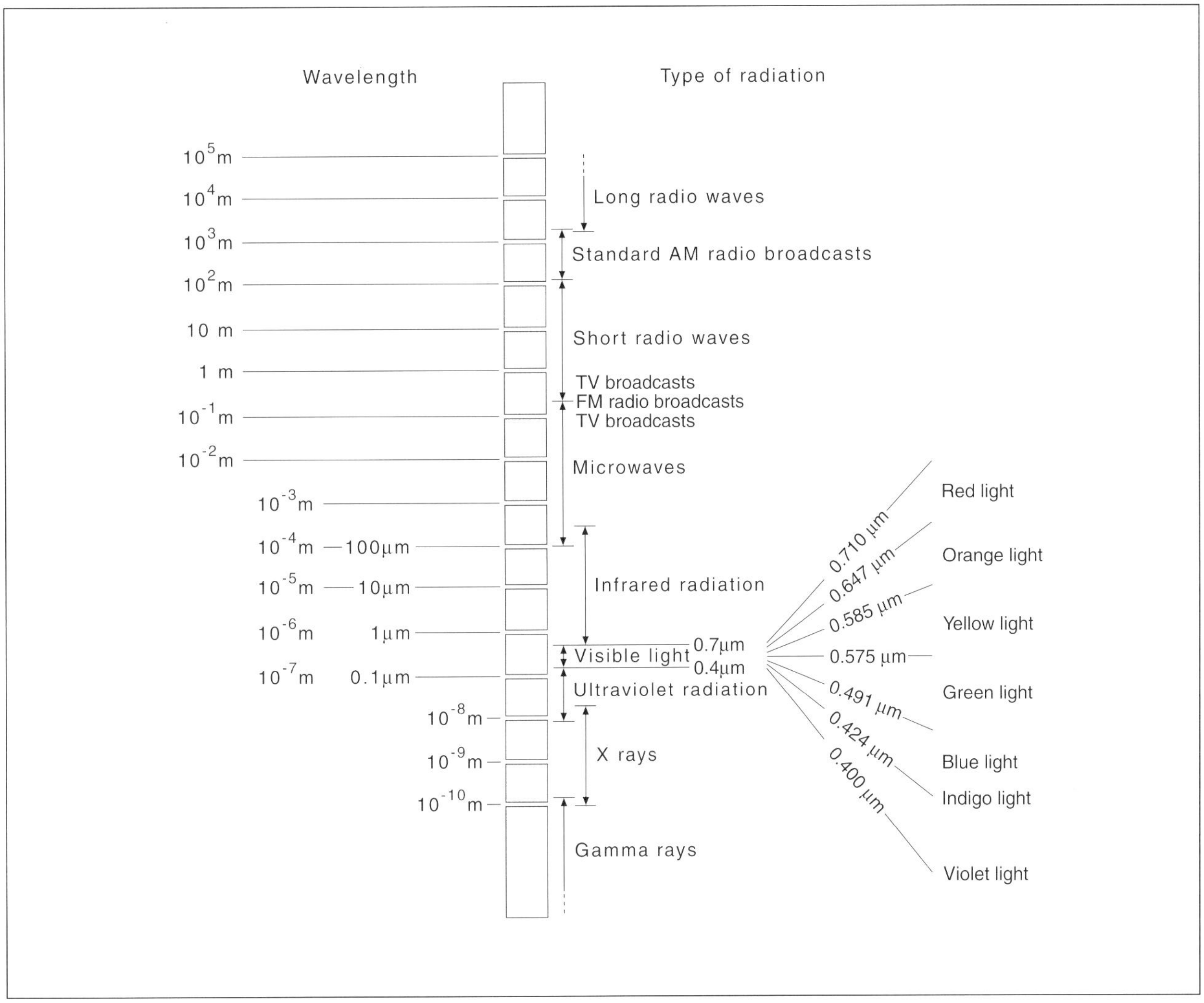

Figure 1 The electromagnetic spectrum

1.2 The sky

From sunrise to sunset, at any place in the landscape, one can imagine a huge blue dome of sky that arches overhead from horizon to horizon in all directions. The sky is ephemeral. On a cloudless day it quivers above us and then is transformed completely at night. 'In unending beauty the blue sky spans the Earth. It is as if this blue were fathomless, as if its very depth were [in]palpable. The variety of its tints is infinite; it changes from day to day, from one point of the sky to the other.'[12]

Of course the sky does not exist as such; it has no physical reality but is a display of sunlight scattered to our eyes by the air molecules that make up the atmosphere. The human eye has evolved to be sensitive to a small part of the electromagnetic spectrum that we call light – the visible part of the spectrum which corresponds to the peak emission of our sun as shown in Figure 1. The colours of the sky and the atmosphere are directly affected by this visible part of the spectrum. Colours, like light, can be explained scientifically but human perception also plays an important role. For the purposes of this chapter light and colour will be discussed in their simple scientific form.

Figure 2 shows that the reason we see the sky is because the air molecules scatter a small proportion of the sunlight that passes through them in all directions, some of which reaches our eyes. Sunlight is thought to be made up of the seven basic colours that we know so well from the rainbow sequence: red, orange, yellow, green, blue, indigo, and violet. Each of these colours has a characteristic wavelength as shown in Figure 1. As the sunlight passes down through the atmosphere these quanta of light encounter the tiny air molecules that make up the atmosphere. The air molecules are about a thousand times smaller than these quanta of coloured light, and it was shown by Lord Rayleigh towards the end of the nineteenth century that the amount of scattering by the air molecules is different for distinct colours.[13] The shorter wavelengths are scattered more by the air molecules than the longer wavelengths because the air molecules are proportionally larger in relation to them. Thus the atmosphere scatters more of the shorter wavelength violet-blue light than it does of the longer wavelength red-yellow light, and hence the sky appears blue because that is the dominant wavelength reaching our eye. (The shortest wavelength is actually violet and indeed more violet than blue normally reaches our eyes, but our eyes are not very sensitive to violet.) The sky-blue colour we see is a mixture of blue, with some green, yellow, orange and red. The overall amount of scattering is small, but strong enough to light the sky in a layer of atmosphere many miles deep.

When wavelengths of all colours are present in roughly equal amounts then the sky appears white. If, during the day, we look towards the sky just above the horizon our eyes are receiving scattered light from a great depth of atmosphere, so the sky appears white because it is a mixture of all wavelengths. When small particles of dust and salt are present the colour of the sky changes from blue to a milky white. This is called 'Mie scattering' and gives the sky a 'hazy' appearance. If the humidity is high enough then soluble condensation nuclei will take up water molecules and form small droplets in the atmosphere, which will also cause scattering of all wavelengths. Again the sky will appear hazy and white.

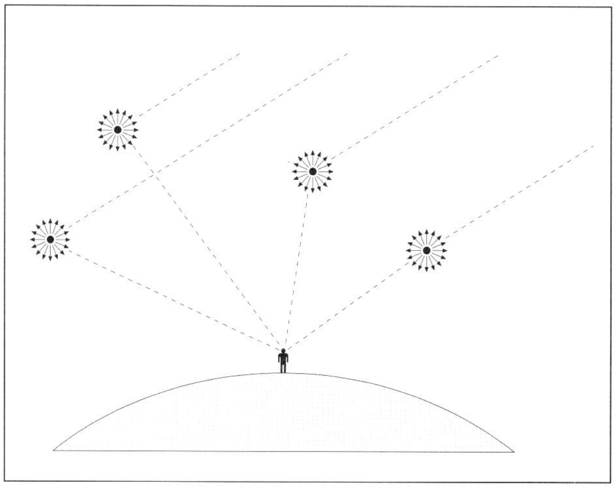

Figure 2
Light scattered to the eye by the atmosphere

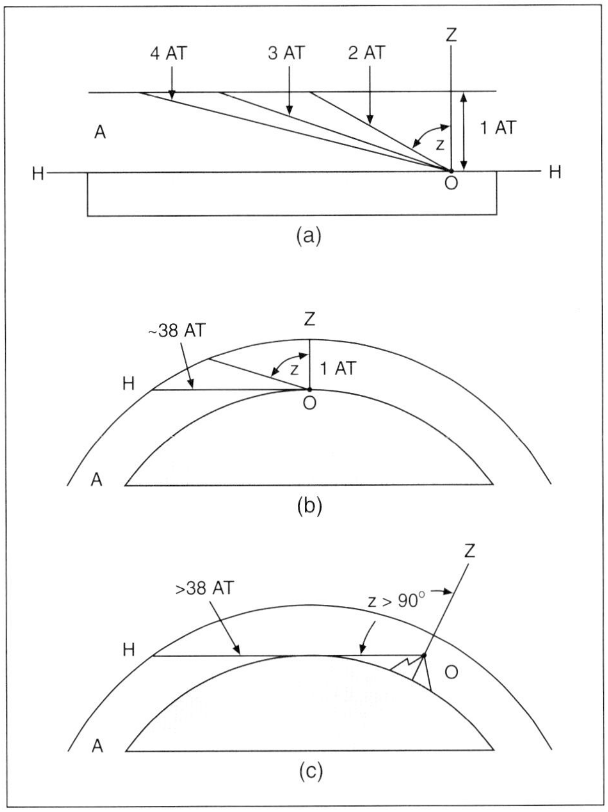

Figure 3
Depth of atmosphere to the eye from the horizon (Adapted from D. K. Lynch and W. Livingston, *Color and Light in Nature*)

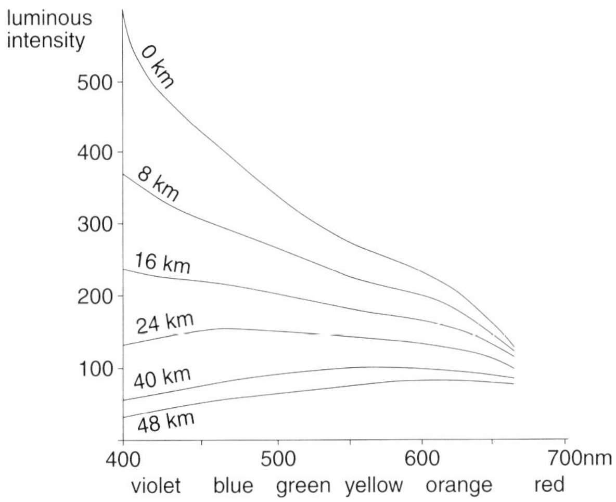

Figure 4
Composition of light coming from a small volume of air lying at various distances from the eye (Adapted from M. Minnaert, *Light and Colour in the Open Air*)

Figure 3 shows that, due to the curvature of the earth's surface, if we assume that the atmosphere is about 100km deep, then light reaching our eye horizontally, as at sunrise or sunset, has to traverse a distance equivalent to 3800km of atmosphere. If one is looking at the far horizon from the top of a mountain then the depth is even greater. Figure 4 shows the composition of light coming from a small volume of air lying at various distances from the eye. The flatness of the curve at about 32km when green is the dominant colour explains why green is rarely seen as a sky colour. Most of the other colours are also present which means that a very pale green is all that is likely to be seen.

The sky is by no means a uniform shade of blue. The deepest blue is at an angle of about ninety degrees from the sun to our eyes to the sky. Thus there is a bright region around the sun and opposite it. The shades of blue vary daily according to the amount of dust and water in the air. Indeed the colour of the sky has been used to estimate the turbidity or dust content of the air. The cleanest, deepest blue occurs after rain when the atmosphere has been cleansed of dust particles. The palest, whitest blues occur when cirrus clouds develop, or when hot dry climates have their deep blue skies whitened by the dust particles thrown up into the sky by the wind. During the day the sky is at its bluest at sunrise and sunset when the dome of the sky is at ninety degrees to the sun. Other beautiful colours can be seen in the sky, such as the purple of twilight, which Minnaert says is strongest in late summer and autumn.[14]

The blueness of the sky varies from day to day and from place to place. When assessing the accuracy of the colour of the sky in a landscape painting one should take into account from the scene depicted the time of day (is it noon or sunset?); the time of year (winter or summer?); the location (England or Italy?); the weather conditions (recent rain or dry and dusty?) and the part of the sky visible (are we near the horizon?). Wilson, who is known as the father of British landscape painting, returning to Britain from an extensive stay in Italy, brought back with him the blue Italian

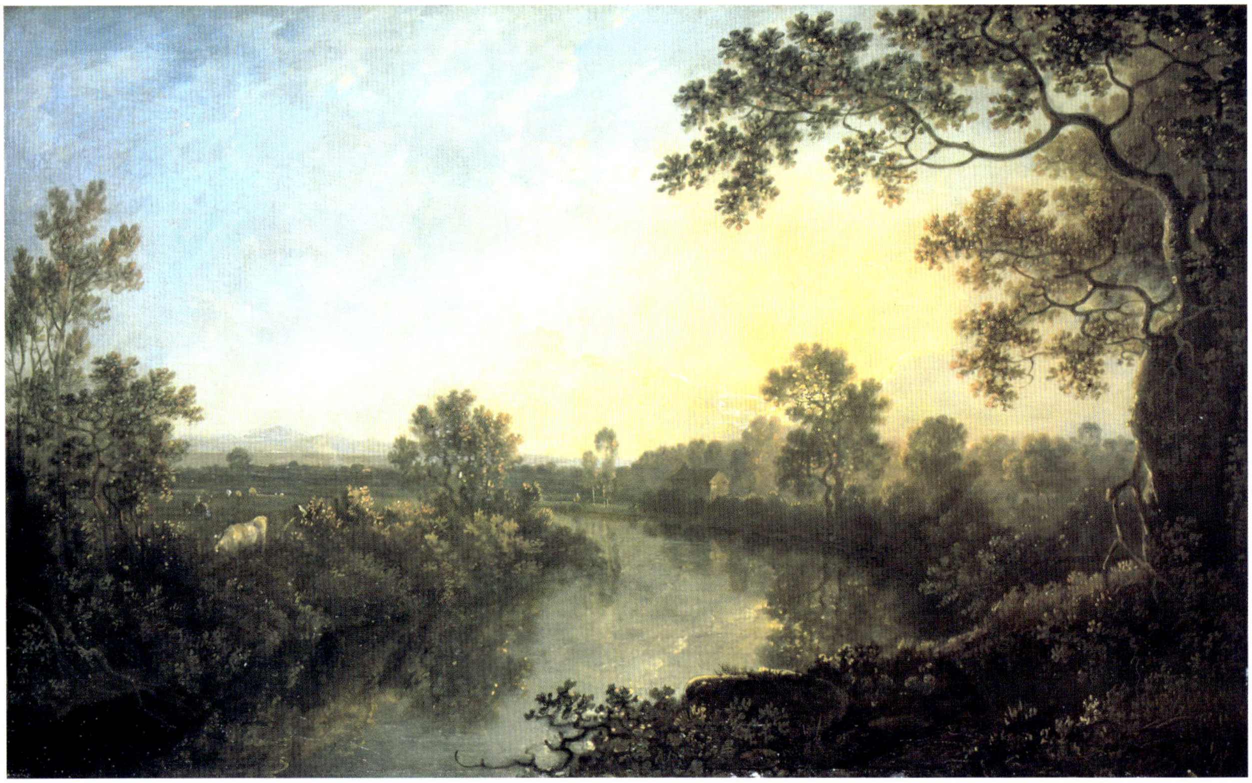

Plate 1 Richard Wilson, *The River Dee, near Eaton Hall*, c.1759–60. Barber Institute of Fine Arts, University of Birmingham/Bridgeman Art Library, London/New York

sky and golden Mediterranean light that look rather incongruous in some of his British landscapes such as *The River Dee, near Eaton Hall* shown in Plate 1. Whether Wilson was aware that he needed to change his sky palette when returning to Britain, or whether he thought an Italian sky would heighten the effect of his British landscapes we will never know.

Neuberger, an American meteorologist, compared the painted blue skies in 4500 paintings exhibited in galleries in North America and Europe. Figure 5 shows the ratios of frequencies of pale-blue skies to those with deep-blue skies. The British school has the largest number of pale-blue skies with a ratio of 3.1:1 whereas the ratio is much less than 1 in central and southern European schools. There are several explanations for this. The sky appears a deeper blue at lower latitudes because the sun climbs higher in the sky as the day progresses, and the deepest blue is therefore nearer the horizon and more likely to be included in a landscape painting. The observed blueness depends upon the presence of dust particles, and on their size and concentration. This can vary with the prevailing air mass and the direction of the wind which may bring dust or pollution overhead. Water vapour tends to whiten the sky; hence the high humidity in Britain leads to paler skies. The bluer skies of the Mediterranean also reflect off the Mediterranean Sea to make it appear much bluer than the seas off the coasts of England.

A simple instrument used to measure the colour of the sky is a cyanometer. The first scientific attempt to measure the blueness of the sky was made in 1788 by the famous French scientist De Saussure, who developed a colour scale of fifty-three different blue shades ranging from white through blue to black. This type of colour chart was commonly used in the nineteenth century but such measurements are rarely made today. In the past it was customary to make one's own cyanometer:

Mix zinc-white and bistre with Prussian blue or cobalt blue in different proportions. These mixtures do not fade. By painting them on strips of cardboard and numbering them we shall be well equipped for measuring the colour of the sky. This method is still often applied when travelling, and the composition of the light of the different numbers on the scale can be examined colorimetrically later on.... Care should be taken when using these blueness-scales to stand with one's back to the sun and to let it shine on the scale.[15]

The chart was usually circular so that it could easily be rotated to match the colour. It was customary to note the deepest colour of blue at ninety degrees from the sun. Although the scales could be standardised, the observations were usually personal and were not normally exchanged. Attempts to make cyanometry measurements more objective have been made by Linke[16] and Neuberger.[17] The Linke scale consists of eight shades of blue from pure white to ultramarine blue with black. These eight shades are printed on cards and held up to the sky with the sun at one's back. Neuberger suggested a simple seven-step memory scale which had three key points:

1 = very pale blue
4 = medium blue
7 = very dark blue

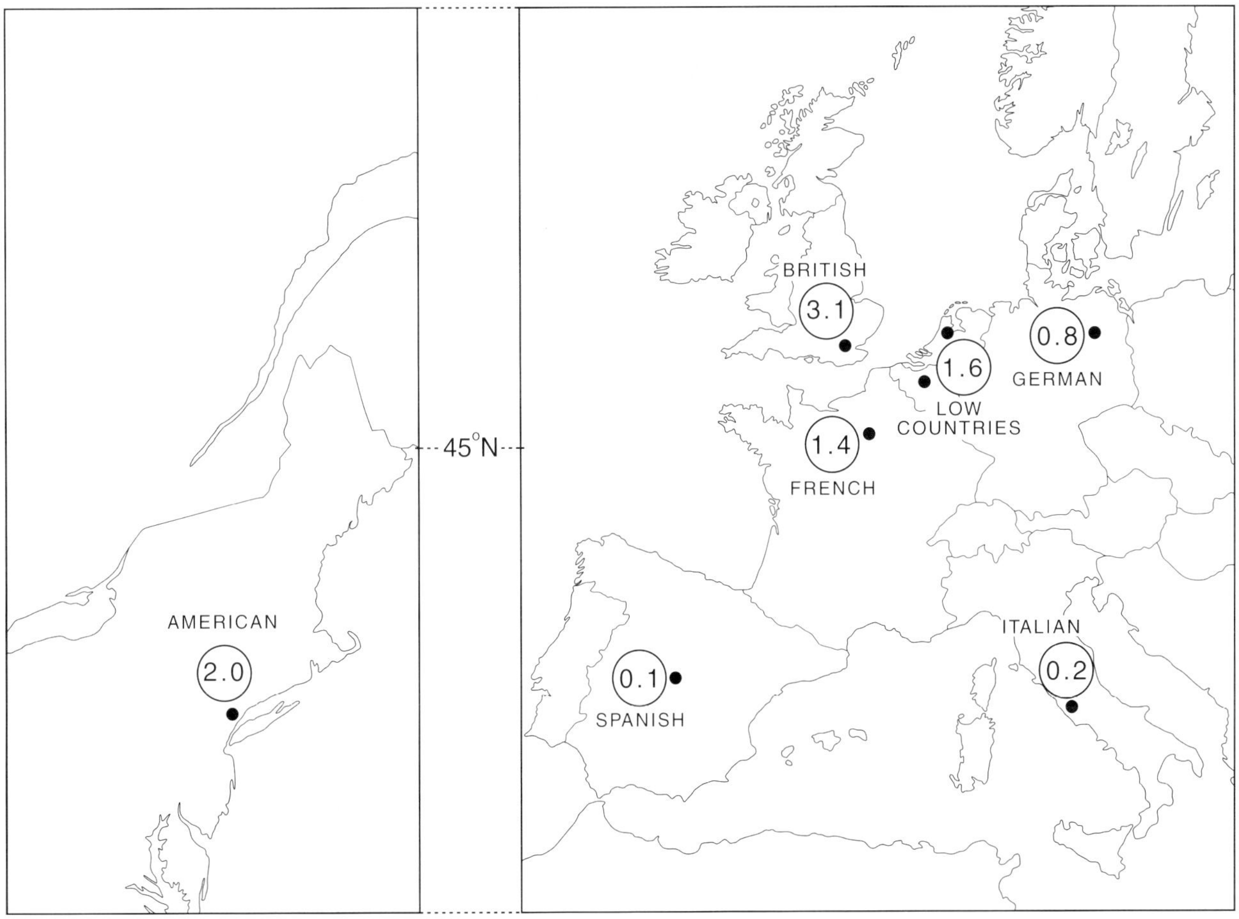

Figure 5 Ratio of frequencies of pale-blue skies to deep-blue skies in the paintings of different European countries (Adapted from H. Neuberger, 'Climate in art')

The intermediate numbers 2, 3, 5 and 6 are used if one cannot decide on one of the key points. Neuberger found an excellent agreement with the Linke scale with the advantage that no colour cards are needed. Nevertheless some training is needed to give examples of the colour of the key points. I have no record of artists using cyanometers or memory scales to record the colour of the sky for their sketches, but it would not be surprising if an artist such as Constable was aware of their existence. However it is likely that artists relied upon their own skill at recording sky colours and therefore many mistakes were made.

Two recent texts by art historians, looking at science and colour in art, have paid little attention to the sky. In his introduction to Part III of *The Science of Art*, entitled 'The Colour of Light', Kemp reminds us forcefully of the difficulties both artists and scientists have had throughout history to marry light and colour successfully. He writes:

> *If there is anything upon which almost all the writers on colour agree, from the time of Aristotle to the present day, it is that colour as seen in nature presents a bewildering variety of kaleidoscope variations – fleeting, fluctuating; and almost infinitely slippery whenever we try to entrap them in a regular net of scientific categories.*[18]

This is certainly very true for the sky and its colours, although Kemp devotes little space to discussing the sky. Despite his detailed discussion of aids for artists there is no mention, for example, of the use of a cyanometer. Gage devotes a chapter of his *Colour and Culture* to 'Unweaving the Rainbow' but he rarely mentions the sky in any other context.[19] The colours of the sky have always attracted attention but have rarely demanded an explanation. The rainbow is the exception and is probably the only icon of the sky that has assumed religious, political and artistic status as well as continuing to attract explanations from science.

1.3 The atmosphere

The atmosphere extends out to about 400km from the earth's surface, and is divided into five different layers: the troposphere, stratosphere, mesosphere, thermosphere and exosphere. Nearly all of our weather takes place in the bottom 10 to 15km, which is called the troposphere. This is a very thin layer compared to the horizontal size of the atmosphere which covers the whole planet. It is as if all our weather takes place within the varnish on a globe. The natural atmosphere is composed of gases and particles that for most of the time appear invisible to the naked eye. A litre of air contains something like 78cc of nitrogen (N_2) and 21cc of oxygen (O_2) and several million 'dust' particles called aerosols. The rest is made up of small amounts of carbon dioxide (CO_2), argon (Ar) and several other mostly inert gases. A litre of air has a fixed composition of gases near the earth's surface, but the amount of water vapour and dust will vary from place to place. It is the relatively small quantities of dust and water vapour in the atmosphere that control the variety of effects that we see, and these quantities will vary with the weather conditions and the proximity to water and sources of natural or anthropogenic pollution. As does the sky, the atmosphere will imbue different places with a distinct character according to the local climate.

The atmosphere controls what is called aerial perspective[20] and therefore the three dimensions of colour – hue, saturation and tone – in a landscape. These three dimensions of colour also control the contrast between objects and their background as discussed in section 1.3.2 below. The distance to the horizon in a flat landscape is only about 15km, although if mountains are present, on a clear day distances of 40km or more can clearly be seen by the eye. Clouds are normally restricted to a maximum height of 10 to 15km and hence the dome of the sky appears to be flattened by clouds. The atmosphere is very important in controlling the visibility within a landscape, from the one extreme of dense fog through to the other extreme of excellent visibility. Visibility can vary from hour to hour, and certainly varies considerably from day to day. Hence a view of a landscape is radically different every day.

1.3.1 Visibility

In meteorology the term 'visibility' (or 'visual range') is used to define the maximum distance from which an object can be distinguished against its background. This distance observed is largely controlled by the quantity of dust, smoke, other pollutants and water vapour present in the atmosphere. (The air molecules also play their part in scattering the light, as already discussed.) Low cloud and fog is also very important in limiting the distance that can be seen. Visibility is not therefore the simple distance to the visible horizon but requires a relatively small object to be identified, whereas merely distinguishing between the whole horizon and the sky does not imply that any features on the horizon need to be identified.[21]

Meteorologists' concerns with visibility are limited to its importance in aviation and for other forms of transport where poor visibility can cause serious problems. Meteorologists are not usually concerned with visible range if it extends beyond several kilometres. Table 1 shows the World Meteorological Organisation's definition of visibility, which highlights the fog end of the spectrum.

Table 1
The international classification of visibility[22]

Visibility	*Description*
Less than 40m	Dense fog
40–200m	Thick fog
200–1000m	Fog
1–2km	Mist (if mainly due to water droplets) Haze (if mainly due to smoke or dust)
2–4km	Poor visibility
4–10km	Moderate visibility
10–40km	Good visibility
Over 40km	Excellent visibility

Visibility has not therefore been defined with landscape meteorology in mind, which would prefer an emphasis upon the more distant visibility. Geographers and artists are concerned with the visible landscape and the way in which that visible landscape changes as the atmosphere changes. Little research has been done in this area – to discover the frequency of different visibilities within a landscape, for example.

Visibility in the British Isles is at its best in sunny anticyclonic (high-pressure) weather, when the airstream is from the north (polar air) and thus contains less dust and water vapour. Wind direction is therefore very important at a particular location. An interesting exercise is to construct a series of lines representing the maximum visibility in different directions for different wind directions and humidities. These will change over time if the amount of visible air pollution changes, as discussed below.

1.3.2 Aerial perspective

In order to achieve in two dimensions an impression of a real three-dimensional landscape the artist uses geometrical perspective. This is not sufficient on its own to convince the eye. Aerial perspective must also be achieved. As well as decreasing in apparent size, a receding object undergoes changes in colour – in hue, saturation, tone and contrast. As already implied there is no one agreed way of measuring colour, but the system most widely used in science and industry is that developed by the Commission Internationale de l'Eclairage (CIE) because it relates light spectra and colour perception mathematically.

The term 'hue' relates to the perceived colour of an object in white light and refers to the normal colour vocabulary of red, blue, green, yellow etc. The term 'saturation' (or 'intensity' or 'purity') represents the percentage of pure hue present. A spectrum colour, or hue, has a purity or saturation of 100 per cent, whilst white's purity/saturation is 0 per cent. The tone of a colour (or its 'luminosity') concerns its relationship to a scale of values from white to black. Thus a red can be made lighter in tone by the addition of white and darker in tone by the addition of black.

Aerial perspective requires that as one looks further and further towards the horizon there is a change of hue towards the blue end of the spectrum, a decrease of saturation, a lighter tone and hence a decrease of contrast between objects and their background. The change of hue towards the blue end of the spectrum can make distant mountains appear blue, such as the Blue Ridge mountains of Virginia and the Blue Mountains of Australia.

As the meteorologist Tyldesley states, all these effects can be achieved in paint to give the required rendering of aerial perspective but there is no one solution for all landscapes:

When we look at an object, the eye receives not only light from the object itself, but also light that has been scattered into the line of sight by the intervening atmosphere. Air molecules and small particles scatter light of short wavelengths preferentially hence the blueness of distance. Larger particles, of size comparable to or larger than the wavelength of light, scatter all wavelengths about equally and cause admixture of white light. All sizes of scattering particle contribute to the decrease of contrast. It is clear then that while the rules of geometrical perspective are invariant with time and space, aerial perspective cannot be laid on mechanically, but must change continually in accordance with the infinite variability of the atmosphere.[23]

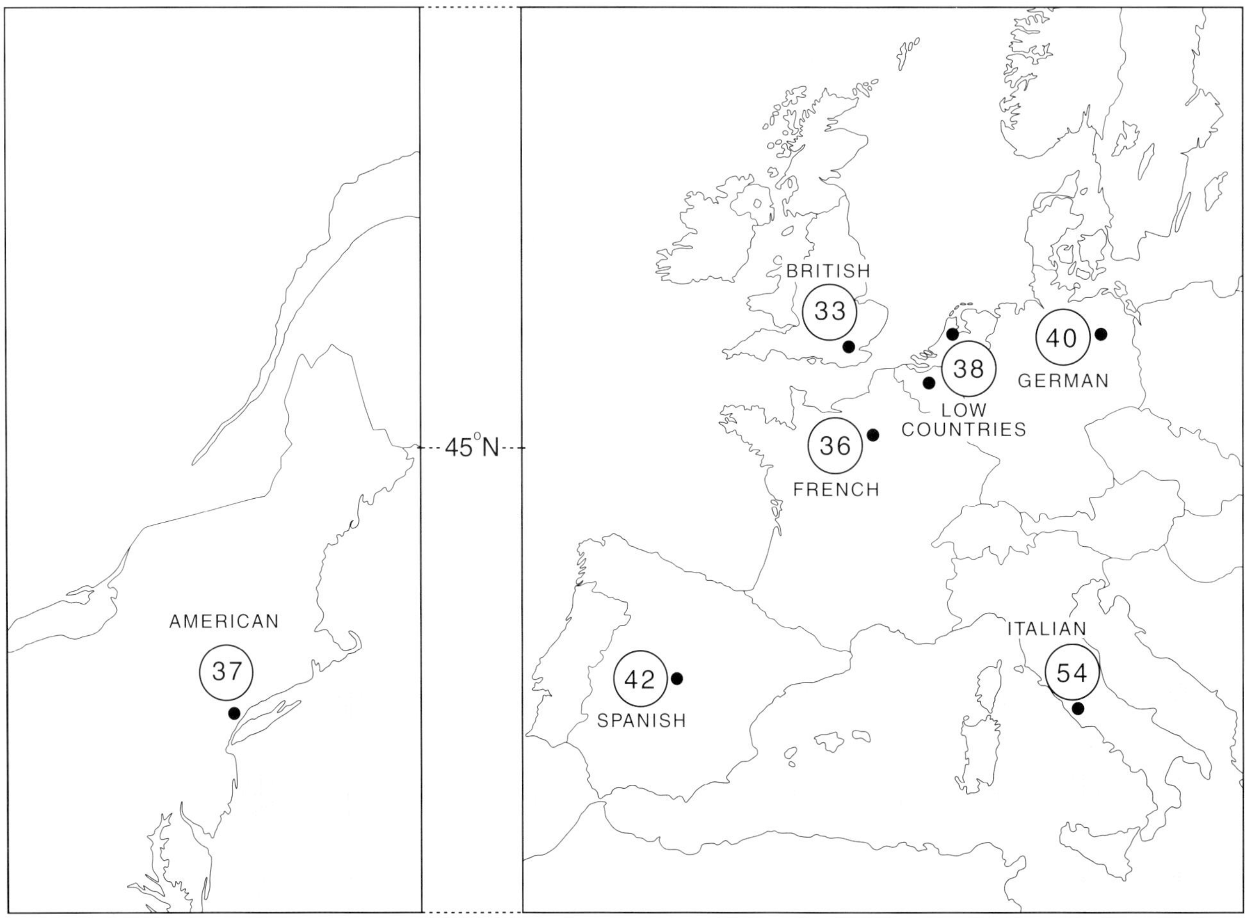

Figure 6 Average % visibility for different regional schools of painting (Adapted from H. Neuberger, 'Climate in art')

When looking at the landscape and following the eye towards the horizon one is looking through the most dense part of the atmosphere – that near the surface. Here light is being scattered or reflected to one's eye not only by objects but also by the molecules of the intervening atmosphere. Dust and smoke are most prevalent in the lower part of the atmosphere as they are mostly produced close to the earth's surface, whether naturally generated (e.g. soil erosion) or man made (e.g. a chimney). Molecules in the atmosphere may produce dramatic effects on the colours the eye perceives; for example, even far away from sources of pollution the formation of a blue haze above the landscape has been observed. It is thought that extremely small particles called terpenes, which are hydrocarbons, are released by vegetation and combine with small amounts of ozone to produce tiny particles that increase the scattering of the blue light.

Hence, although geometrical perspective is fixed for all times and space, aerial perspective varies from day to day and sometimes from hour to hour. Therefore a landscape exhibits infinite moods as each day the atmosphere provides a new configuration.

1.3.3 The impact of climate change

Although the composition of the atmosphere has remained virtually unchanged over the last few hundred years, there have been some significant minor changes. The increase in the amount of carbon dioxide in the atmosphere may have very important consequences for the earth's climate, but has no direct impact on the light and colour of the atmosphere, as carbon dioxide is a colourless gas. Indirectly, however, if the weather and climate at a location is changed then of course it may alter the colour of the sky, the aerial perspective and the visibility.

Neuberger, as already mentioned, in a fascinating survey of more than 12 000 paintings in European and North American art galleries, shows how the weather and climate in different regions might be reflected in the landscapes of artists from different regions in both space and time.[24] Although this is remarkably deterministic, the results from such a large sample are to be believed. Neuberger is aware that changes in artistic taste may be as significant as the climate in determining the colours of the painted skies, but argues also that artistic taste could be influenced by climate. Neuberger's findings on visibility in the painting of different countries is shown in Figure 6 which gives the derived average percentage visibility, and demonstrates that visibility in paintings appears to be worst in British landscapes and best in Italian landscapes. This is probably due to the frequency of low cloud and fog as well as the higher humidity in the British Isles.

Table 2
Relative frequencies (%) of cloud families for different regional schools of painting[25]

	CLOUD FAMILIES			
Schools	*High*	*Middle*	*Low*	*Convective*
American	5	43	30	22
British	5	23	40	32
Low Countries	5	32	27	36
French	9	36	27	28
German	11	33	27	29
Italian	9	43	14	34
Spanish	6	38	28	28
Average	8	35	25	32

Table 3
Relative frequencies (%) of cloudiness for different regional schools of painting[26]

Schools	*Clear*	*Scattered*	*Broken*	*Overcast*
American	5	16	47	32
British	0	4	48	48
Low Countries	7	11	44	38
French	9	10	49	32
German	16	16	42	26
Italian	12	24	42	22
Spanish	13	13	38	36
Average	9	13	44	34

Tables 2 and 3 show the relative frequencies of cloud type and amount for the different regional schools of painting. It can be seen that not a single painting in the British School was observed to be cloudless, and that the British School had the highest frequency of overcast skies. Figure 7 shows the overall percentage cloudiness for each school and again the results indicate that Britain is seen to be the cloudiest.

Neuberger goes on to show that the 'Little Ice Age' that took place between about 1550 and 1850 is evident as an increase in cloudiness in all regional schools. His results are shown in Table 4 which shows that cloudiness in art peaked between 1600 and 1649 when on average 84 per cent of the skies of paintings were covered with cloud.

Neuberger's findings suggest that artists have been subconsciously observant of the general features of the skies around them in terms of cloudiness, visibility, sky colours and so forth.

Table 4
Average cloudiness (C) of sky area shown in paintings of all schools (%), and total number of coastal floods and severe freezes (F) in Europe by 50-year epochs[27]

EPOCH	*C*	*F*
1400–49	29	61
1450–99	37	54
1500–49	50	85
1550–99	77	124
1600–49	84	141
1650–99	79	150
1700–49	77	130
1750–99	74	-
1800–49	65	-
1850–99	70	-
1900–67	74	-

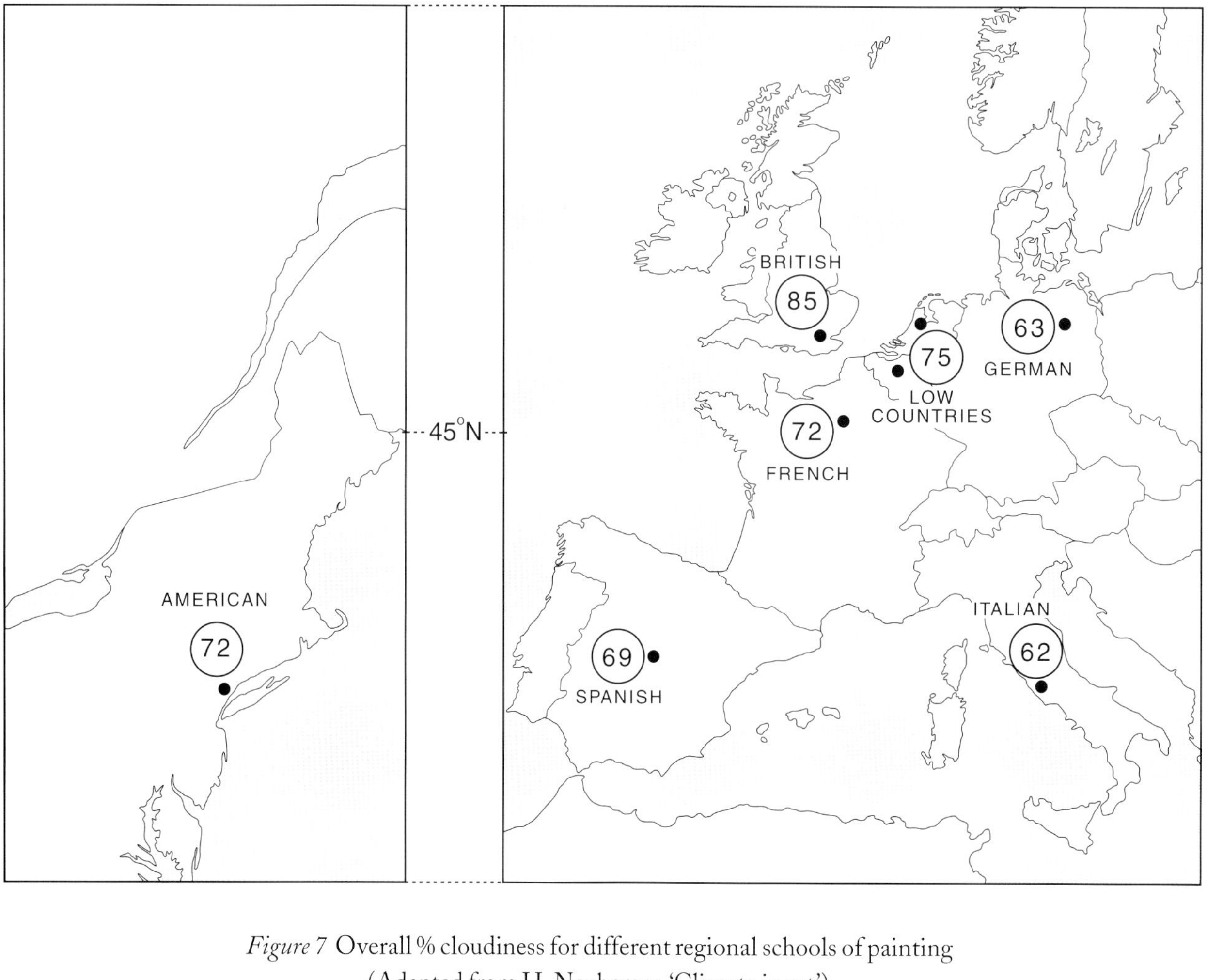

Figure 7 Overall % cloudiness for different regional schools of painting (Adapted from H. Neuberger, 'Climate in art')

Neuberger did not comment on the truth of the skies in individual paintings. He mechanically recorded the content of the painted skies as best he could. We cannot conclude from his findings therefore that artists have conquered the imitation of skies in all their moods. The deterministic approach tells us no more than that artists are generally observant of their natural surroundings, not that they can imitate nature accurately. It is interesting to note however that the skies of artists worked up in studios did apparently reflect the general atmospheric and climatic conditions of the region where the artist lived.

1.3.4 The impact of air pollution

Air pollutants that have had a direct influence on the light and colour of the atmosphere can be divided into two groups. Firstly, and most importantly, there are those associated with smoke; and secondly those associated with photochemical air pollution, such as ozone and nitrogen dioxide. Air pollutants like smoke are present naturally in the atmosphere, for instance from volcanoes and from forest fires caused by lightning. We have already said that natural aerosols in the atmosphere affect the colour of the sky and aerial perspective. Anthropogenic air pollutants have become significant since the Industrial Revolution, particularly in well-populated areas where most people live and work.

Dust particles vary considerably in size. The smallest particles scatter light as do the air molecules, but larger particles scatter all wavelengths equally giving the sky a whiter colour. Smoke particles are usually small and help to scatter out the blue end of the spectrum – sometimes completely, leaving spectacular sunrises and sunsets. This effect can also happen naturally, as illustrated by the colourful skies associated with the smoke of volcanic eruptions, such as Krakatoa in 1883. Table 5 gives a list of the major volcanic eruptions that had an impact on sky colours in England during Constable's lifetime.

Table 5
Major volcanic eruptions that coloured the skies of England during Constable's lifetime (1776–1837)

Year	Eruption	Effect
1783	Eldeyjar, Iceland	Sun coppery coloured in Norfolk
1808	Sao George, Azores	Abnormal brilliance of twilight in London
1809	Etna, Italy	Rose-coloured haze over the sky in London
1811	Sabrina, Azores	Unusually red-coloured skies over London
1811	Vesuvius	Red twilights over London
1812	Vincent, West Indies	Unusually luminous coloured twilights in London
1813	Vesuvius	Orange-red twilights over London
1814	Mayon, Luzon	Lemon surmounted by purple and much orange and rose-red twilight over London
1815	Tambora, Little Sundra Islands	Remarkable sunsets in London
1818	Vesuvius	Richly coloured twilights over London
1821	Kluchev, Kamchatka	Exceptional sunset colours in London
1822	Galunggung, Java	Sunset skies near London very bright and the clouds frequently red
1831	Babujan, Philippine Islands	Remarkably red and yellow skies, and lurid sunsets in England

It is ironic that although the landscape is faded and darkened by smoke and visibility reduced, the colours in the atmosphere are in fact enriched by smoke. Hence when air pollution, due primarily to smoke, was at its worst at the end of the nineteenth century, the sunrises and sunsets were at their most colourful and a blue sky could rarely be seen. Monet's *Impression, Sunrise* (Plate 2) is a glorious reminder of the sort of sunrises we no longer experience in the wake of clean air legislation and the decline in the use of coal as a fuel. The belching chimneys so clearly seen in Monet's picture of Le Havre in 1879, which contribute to the light and colour of the sky, are scarcely commented upon in the huge literature about the painting.

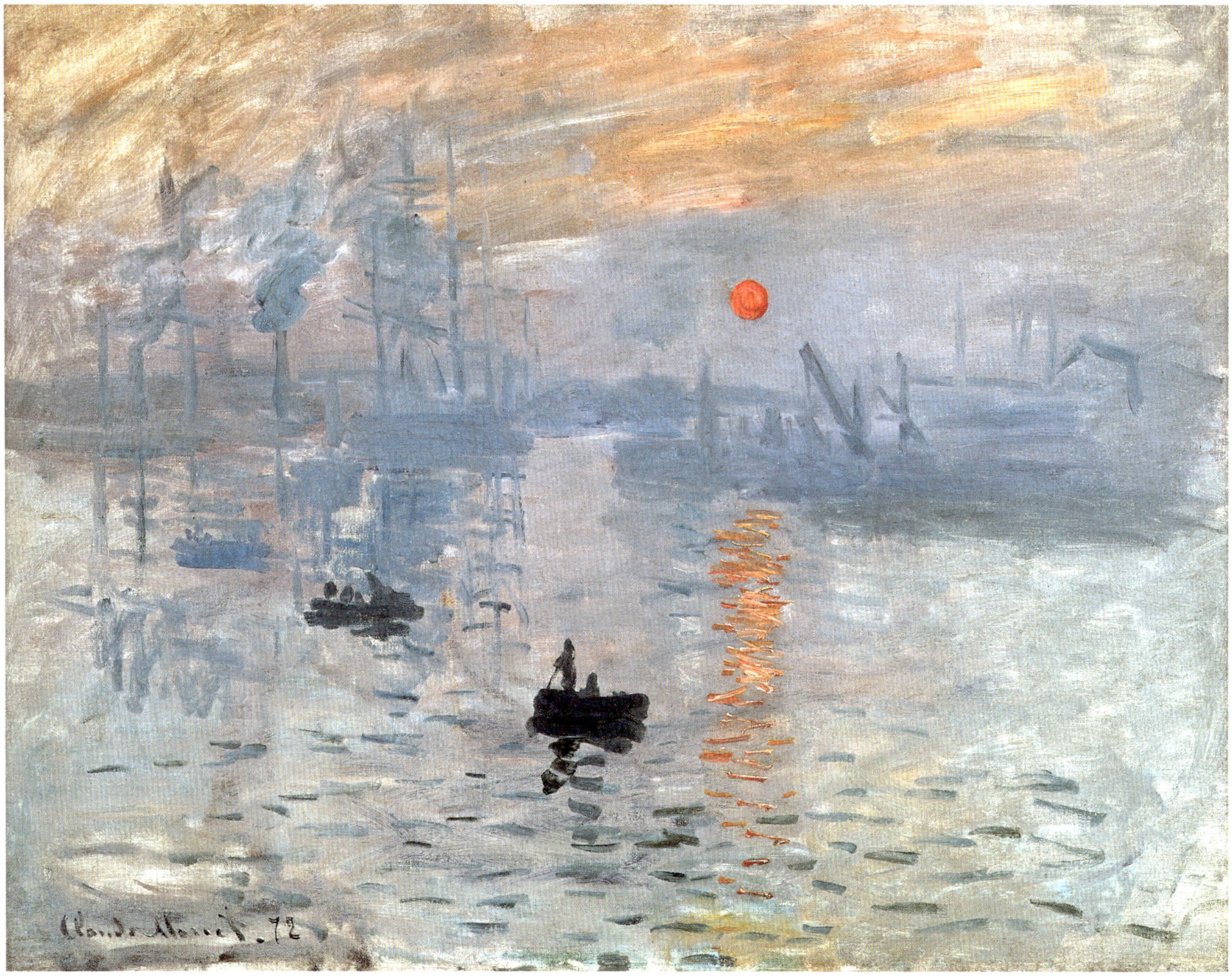

Plate 2 Claude Monet, *Impression, Soleil levant* (Impression, Sunrise), 1872.
Musée Marmottan – Claude Monet, Paris. Copyright Photographie Giraudon

Smoke pollution in the major cities in the nineteenth century could lead to the formation of 'smogs' that hung around for weeks, blocking out the blue sky completely. This led to the landscape being lit by diffuse light rather than by direct sunlight. This is a much softer light that dulls shadows and gives a more uniform effect. Monet's views of London, such as *View of Houses of Parliament*, 1871 (Plate 3), illustrate dramatically how the sky and clouds were hidden by the smoke-filled atmosphere and that the diffuse light was full of colours from the red end of the spectrum, all the blue end having been scattered out by the smoke.

Figure 8 shows how the number of foggy days in London has changed since the seventeenth century. The smoke, and associated fog levels in London (and probably other major European cities like Paris), peaked at the end of the nineteenth century.[28] London became famous for its 'pea-soupers' and visibility was poor throughout the winter months. During a thirty-day survey of the fog in London in the winter of 1900/01 St Paul's Cathedral could not be seen from Westminster, nor Westminster from St Paul's, even though they are only three kilometres apart.

Oscar Wilde recognised that the impressionists were inspired by fog but he went rather overboard, as was his style, when theorising that nature imitates art rather than the other way round:

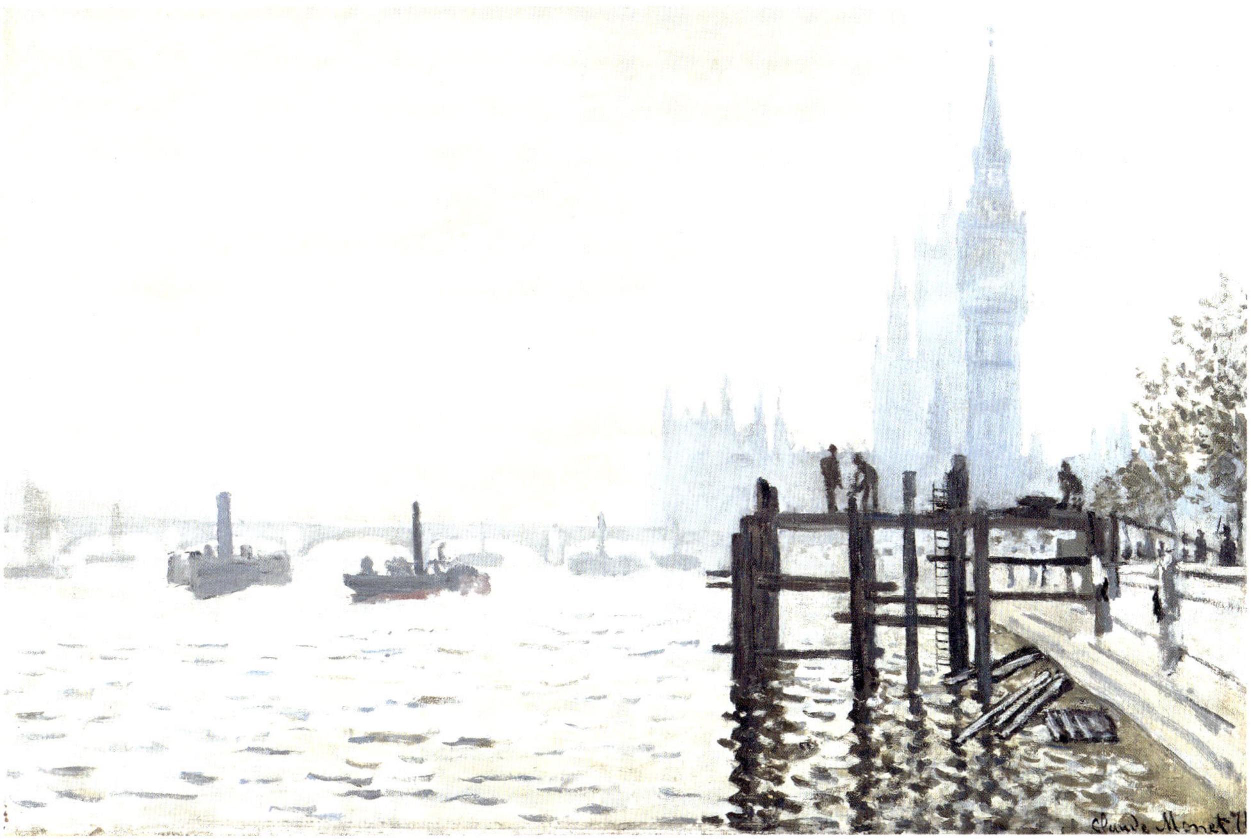

Plate 3 Claude Monet, *View of Houses of Parliament*, 1871. Copyright National Gallery, London

> *Where, if not from the impressionists, do we get those wonderful brown fogs that come creeping down our streets, blurring the gas lamps and changing the houses into monstrous shadows? To whom, if not to them and their master, do we owe the lovely silver mists that brood over our river, and turn to faint forms of fading grace curved bridge and swaying barge. The extraordinary change that has taken place in the climate of London during the last ten years is entirely due to a particular school of Art.... At present people see fogs, not because there are fogs, but because poets and painters have taught them the mysterious loveliness of such effects. There may have been fogs for centuries in London. I dare say there were. But no one saw them, and so we do not know anything about them. They did not exist until Art had invented them. Now, it must be admitted, fogs are carried to excess.*[29]

According to Wilde fogs were 'in', but sunsets were definitely 'out'!

> *Sunsets are quite old-fashioned. They belong to a time when Turner was the last note in art. Upon the other hand they go on. Yesterday evening Mrs Arundel insisted on my going to the window and looking at the glorious sky, as she called it.... And what was it? It was simply a very second-rate Turner, a Turner of a bad period, with all the painter's worst faults exaggerated and over-emphasised.*[30]

Since the turn of the century smoke levels have dropped as coal has became unfashionable and as fuel and clean air legislation has been introduced. With the decline in smoke levels other pollutants have come to the fore, many of which, such as those from motor vehicles, are required to be invisible by law. The term 'smog' (a combination of the words

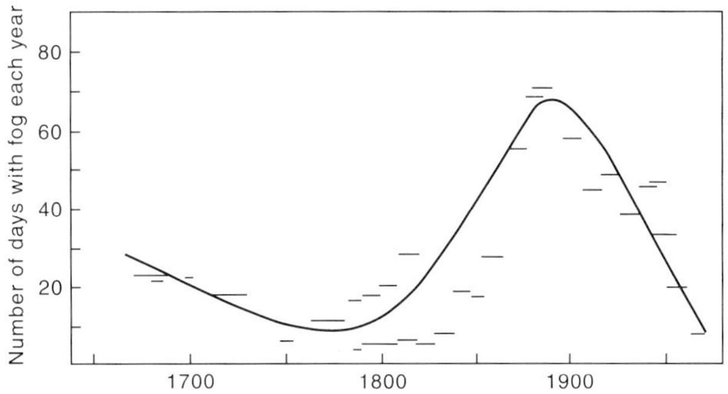

Figure 8 Number of foggy days each year in London since the seventeenth century (Adapted from P. Brimblecombe, 'London air pollution')

'smoke' and 'fog') was first introduced in 1905 to describe the London pea-soupers. It has now taken on a new meaning to describe the photochemical broths of ozone typified by Los Angeles smog. Ozone, nitrogen dioxide and hydrocarbons are the principle chemicals that give photochemical smogs their familiar yellow-brown colour. Visibility is reduced by the hydrocarbons which are particles like smoke. Ozone is a secondary pollutant formed by the action of sunlight on vehicle exhaust gases. This type of smog was first noted in Los Angeles in the mid 1940s. Legislation to reduce vehicle exhaust emissions has not yet eliminated the problem and cities such as Los Angeles, Mexico City and Tokyo still get high levels of ozone. Once formed, the ozone has a lifetime of several days and is carried by the wind into rural areas. Indeed ozone levels may be higher in rural areas than urban areas, and elevated levels can cover huge rural areas, reducing visibility.

The state of the atmosphere therefore determines the distance that we can see through it. The air molecules, water molecules, dust, smoke and other air pollutants provide a constantly changing aerial perspective in both time and space. In the nineteenth century in Europe air pollution had its greatest effect on aerial perspective and the colours of the sky and the atmosphere. Generally speaking Turner's, and other artists', 'phantasmagoria' of atmosphere as it has been called, was heightened by the smoke of the Industrial Revolution, although Turner was also fascinated by the passage of light through any atmosphere. Constable, on the other hand, paid little attention to the atmosphere and air pollution, concentrating on the sky and clouds.

1.4 Clouds and weather

Luke Howard's cloud classification scheme was originally presented as a paper to the Askesian Society sometime in the winter of 1802/03, and was first published in 1803. He muses:

> *If clouds were the mere result of the condensation of vapour in the masses of the atmosphere which they occupy, if their variations were produced by movements in the atmosphere alone, then indeed might the study of them be deemed an useless pursuit of shadows, an attempt to describe forms which, being the sport of winds, must be ever varying, and therefore not to be defined. However ... the case is not so with clouds. They are subject to certain distinct modifications, produced by the general causes which affect all the variations of the atmosphere; they are commonly as good visible indicators of the operation of these causes, as is the countenance of the state of a person's mind or body.*[31]

In other words, clouds reflect the current state of the atmosphere, rather as a person's face reflects their moods. Whereas the atmosphere is often regarded as invisible, the clouds, by their presence or absence, are a constant visible reminder of the state of the weather.

Howard's contribution to both the art and science of meteorology will be discussed in detail in Chapter 4, but his cloud classification, along with that of Lamarck,[32] was an application of the Linnean method of classification to clouds (see section 1.4.1 below). (Howard's classification probably succeeded because it was in Latin, the 'Esperanto' of the intelligentsia of that time, whereas Lamarck's classification was in French.[33]) Plate 4 shows the cloud sketches that Howard

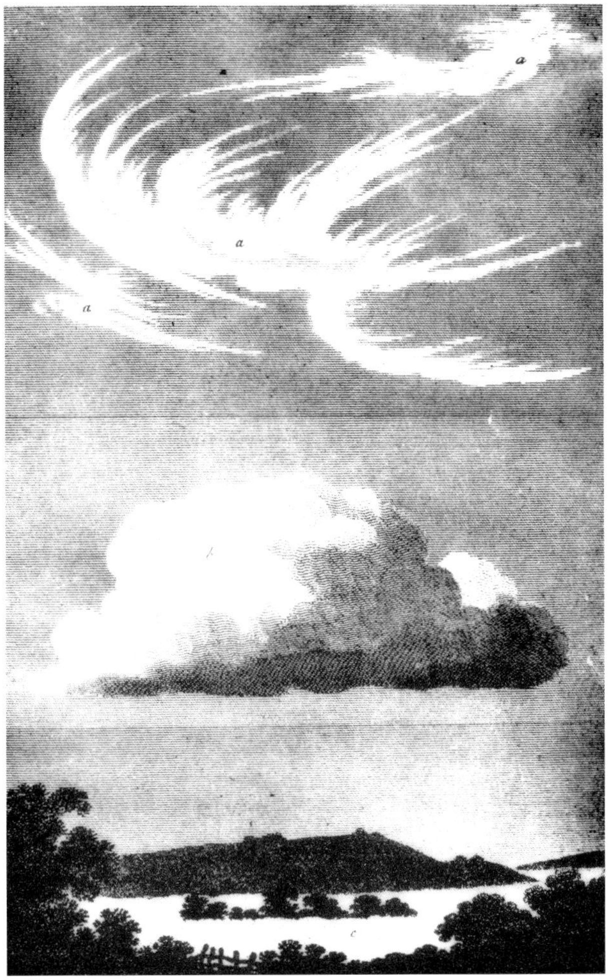

Plate 4 Luke Howard, *Cloud Sketches (Cirrus, Cumulus and Stratus)*, 1803.

included to give examples of stratus, cumulus and cirrus respectively.

Gedzelman[34] points out that before Howard's classification there were few widely used terms for different cloud types, whereas plants and animals have had colloquial names since language began. This is because of the ephemeral nature of clouds, and because a knowledge of process as well as form is required in order to distinguish between the different types.

1.4.1 A brief history of cloud classification

Cloud attributes include colour, brightness, height, size and shape. In order to classify clouds into types (called 'genera') one has to chose visual attributes that are common to all clouds in a type. Colour and brightness will vary with the time of day and season, and therefore height, size and shape are used as benchmarks. Table 6 shows how Howard's original classification has been modified over the years but is still the core of the modern classification system. The current system of classification uses the Linnean binomial system whereby the various cloud forms are grouped into 'genera', while 'species' and 'varieties' also occur (see Table 7a). More than 400 different cloud classifications can now be made, but a knowledge of the ten basic types, as shown in Table 6, is usually sufficient.[35] (Even this seemingly exhaustive system does not enable all clouds to be easily classified as it is based on shape. It is often very difficult to distinguish cloud types from the ground – for instance to distinguish between altostratus and cirrostratus.)

The international cloud classification defines cloud genera as mutually exclusive groups. A cloud can only belong to one genera and further it can

Table 6
Landmarks in cloud classification

1802	Lamarck publishes his classification in French[36]
1802	Howard presents paper on Modification of Clouds, defining four basic cloud genera:

Genera	*Derivatives*
cirrus	cirrocumulus, cirrostratus
cumulus	cumulostratus (only term no longer used)
stratus	
nimbus	

1840	Kaemtz defines stratocumulus
1877	Renou defines altocumulus, altostratus
1880	Weilbach defines cumulonimbus

Thus ten genera of cloud are recognised today:

cirrus (Ci)
cirrocumulus (Cc)
cirrostratus (Cs)
altocumulus (Ac)
altostratus (As)
nimbostratus (Ns)
stratocumulus (Sc)
stratus (St)
cumulus (Cu)
cumulonimbus (Cb)

Table 7
The international cloud classification

Table 7a Subtypes of cloud

Subtype	*Can belong to genus*
Species:	
Fibratus: fibrous	Ci, Cs
Uncinus: hooked	Ci
Spissatus: thick	Ci
Castellanus: turret-like	Ci, Cc, Ac, Sc
Floccus: woolly	Ci, Cc, Ac
Stratiformis: flattened	Cc, Ac, Sc
Nebulosus: misty, nebulous	Cs, St
Lenticularis: lens-shaped	Cc, Ac, Sc
Fractus: broken	St, Cu
Humilis: small-sized	Cu
Mediocris: medium-sized	Cu
Congestus: heaped-up	Cu
Calvus: bald, bared	Cb
Capillatus: hair-like	Cb
Varieties:	
Intortus: twisted	Ci
Duplicatus: repeated	Ci, Cs, Ac, As, Sc
Vertebratus: vertebrae-like	Ci
Translucidus: transparent	Ac, As, Sc, St
Undulatus: wave-like	Cc, Cs, Ac, As, Sc, St
Perlucidus: opaque	Ac, Sc
Radiatus: ray-like	CI, Ac, As, Sc, Cu
Opacus: shadowy or thick	Ac, As, Sc, St
Lacunosus: with holes or furrows	Cc, Ac, Sc

Subtype	*Can belong to genus*
Supplementary features and accessory clouds:	
Incus: anvil-like	Cb
Mamma: udder-like	Ci, Cc, Ac, As, Sc, Cb
Virga: rod or branch-like	Cc, Ac, As, Ns, Sc, Cu, Cb
Praecipitatio: precipice-like	As, Ns, Sc, St, Cu, Cb
Arcus: arch-like	Cu, Cb
Tuba: tube-like	Cu, Cb
Pileus: cap-like	Cu, Cb
Velum: sail-like	Cu, Cb
Pannus: ragged or tattered	As, Ns, Cu, Cb

Table 7b Cloud genera

	Mother Clouds	
Genus	*Genitus*	*Mutatus*
Cirrus (Ci)	Cc, Ac, Cb	Cs
Cirrocumulus (Cc)	Cs, Cb	Ci, Cs, Ac
Cirrostratus (Cs)	Cc, Cb	Ci, Cc, As
Altocumulus (Ac)	Cu, Cb	Cc, As, Ns, Sc
Altostratus (As)	Ac, Cb	Cs, Ns
Nimbostratus (Ns)	Cu, Cb	Ac, As, Sc
Stratocumulus (Sc)	As, Ns, Cu, Cb	Ac, Ns, St
Stratus (St)	Ns, Cu, Cb	Sc
Cumulus (Cu)	Ac, Sc	Sc, St
Cumulonimbus (Cb)	Ac, As, Ns, Sc, Cu	Cu

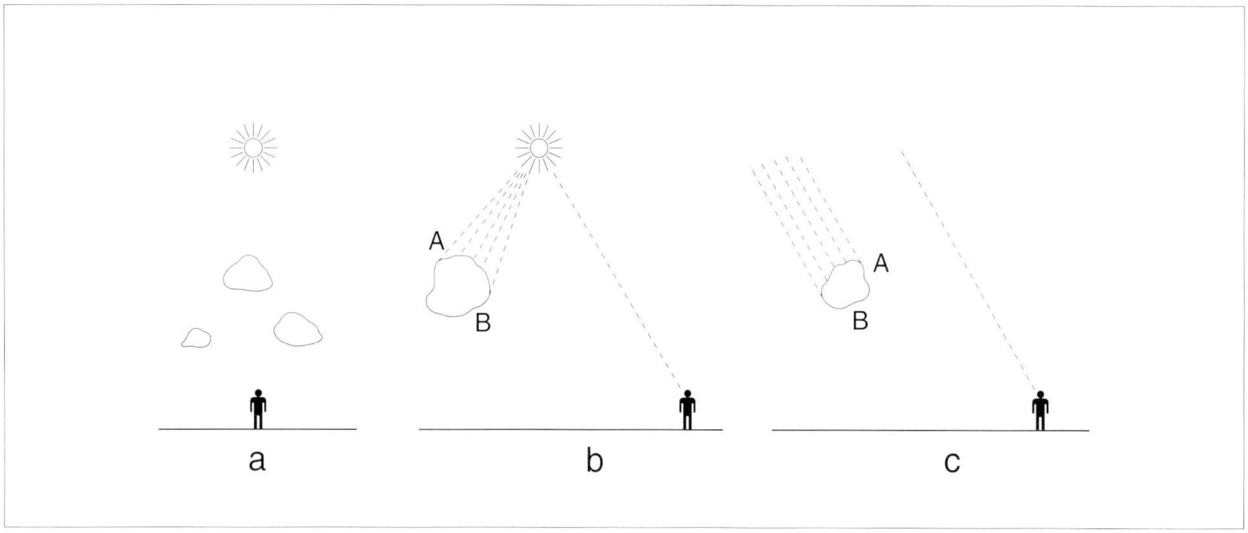

Figure 9 Light and shadow on cumulus clouds (Adapted from M. Minnaert, *Light and Colour in the Open Air*)

only belong to one species within that genera. Cloud varieties and supplementary features and accessories are also defined but can only be linked to certain genera as shown in Table 7a. When naming a cloud, such as *altocumulus stratiformis perlucidus*, the genus is given first followed by the species and then the variety. The classification also takes into account the fact that whilst most clouds develop in clear air some grow out of existing 'mother' clouds. The suffix 'genitus' is added if only a part of the 'mother' cloud changes genus, whereas the suffix 'mutatus' is used if the whole, or virtually the whole, cloud changes genus. This is shown in Table 7b.

1.4.2 The colour of clouds

Most clouds are composed of droplets of water. (Cirrus clouds, however, are composed of crystals of ice.) These droplets and crystals are large in comparison to the wavelength of light and scatter all wavelengths equally. Hence clouds should appear white. However the actual colour perceived by an observer on the ground will depend also upon the position of the sun in the sky, the time of day and the number and size of clouds present.

The clouds are illuminated by direct sunlight, by light reflected from other clouds, and by light from the sky itself. If the cloud is directly illuminated by the sun it will appear white, but the underside of the cloud will appear grey as virtually no light gets through the cloud. (Clouds can be treated as if they are solid, in other words they reflect most of the incident light.) When the sun is high in the sky, such as on a summer's afternoon, it is inevitable that any cloud which is overhead will be a shade of grey because we are looking at the base of the cloud. As we look away, lowering our eyes slowly towards the horizon, we are more likely to see progressively less of the base of the clouds and more of their sides. Thus there is a whitening of the appearance of the clouds away from us. This is limited by a blueing of the clouds with distance as more scattered blue light reaches our eye from the air molecules between us and the cloud.

On a showery summer or autumn day, with cumulus clouds developing and moving quickly across the sky, it is difficult to comprehend the great variety of shades of grey. It is easy to show how our perception of the colours we expect to see can be mistaken. Figure 9 illustrates that due to our great distance from the sun the sun's rays are effectively parallel. This means that clouds that we would expect to appear white (Figures 9b and 9c) actually appear grey. However, it is not possible to explain all the observed cloud colours purely on the basis of sunbeam angles and shadows. The presence or absence of dust and smoke is also important. The colour perceived also depends upon the background colour against which they are viewed.

Clouds of most colours can be observed. Greenler displays colour plates of white, black, green, yellow, red and blue clouds.[37] At sunrise and sunset clouds can have a seemingly infinite range of colours and shapes. Shortly before the sun sets, or just after it has risen, a cloud is illuminated by direct light from the sun, which at sunset becomes gradually yellow, orange and red; and also from the sky, which at sunset is orange-red towards the sun and blue elsewhere. The best sunsets are when the clouds are thin and fragmentary so that the light can get through them and there is little shadow.

The colour and shading of clouds are of great importance to artists but they are by no means easy to represent in a painting. Constable was, of course, aware of these difficulties and tried very hard to overcome them, as will be discussed in detail later. The lighting of clouds was discussed by the meteorologist Thomas Forster in his book *Researches about Atmospheric Phaenomena*, the second edition of which was published in 1815 and was annotated by Constable. Forster wrote: 'All clouds are capable of becoming lighter or darker, according to their relative position with respect to the sun.'[38] Constable encircled this sentence and underlined part of it twice, and in the margin he wrote 'as seen opposite or under the sun'. As Reynolds suggests, Constable was aware that 'any specific effect of lighting on the ground is consistent with one, and only one, distribution of clouds and with one position of the sun in the sky'.[39]

1.4.3 Cloud perspective

Perspective is a way of representing a three-dimensional world onto a two-dimensional medium. Several types of geometrical perspective within a landscape have been discussed. All of them relate only to the earth's surface, but the sky is much more difficult to deal with: one cannot just apply normal methods of perspective to the sky. The vast dome of the sky is much more curved than the earth's surface, which is why the contrails from fighter planes flying in straight lines appear as a 'domed birdcage', whereas parallel railway lines appear to converge towards the horizon.

The subject of cloud perspective remains unresearched: although guidelines for painting the sky and clouds exist (see below), they pay scant attention to perspective. Although meteorological observers have always estimated the amount of sky covered by clouds in eighths (oktas) or tenths, this measurement has always been based on subjective judgement. Recent work has shown that satellite estimates of cloud cover can be significantly different from human observations at ground level. For instance, tall but well-spaced cumulus clouds will seem to merge when viewed from the ground, so that, say, the sky appears to be five oktas covered, whereas a satellite might only see three oktas. Moreover, clouds overhead appear to cover more sky than clouds near the horizon. (Meteorologists are not too worried by this lack of accuracy because human cloud observations are not usually critical for weather forecasting, and satellites can do a much better job for a huge area.)

Stringer, a meteorologist, summarises some of the problems of perspective in relation to the sky.

> *Observation shows that visual space in the atmosphere is not a simple transformation of physical space. This is illustrated by measurement of the apparent shape of the sky. The daytime sky appears to be a flattened vault, which is flattest under cloudy conditions. A moonless night sky, by contrast, appears to be arched.*[40]

Landscape artists have often ignored the crucial importance of cloud perspective. Ruskin makes the only attempt I have ever seen to give guidance in the form of diagrams (Figures 19 and 20) printed in *Modern Painters IV*. These are discussed in Chapter 4. The artist Battershill, in his 1980 book *Painting Skies*, gives little advice other than: 'Clouds diminish in size as they go upwards and towards the horizon ... there is a great deal more to it than that of course ... [but] to begin with, you only need concern yourself with the principle of diminishing perspective to try and get the appearance of clouds going away into the distance.'[41]

Badt reminds us that many Romantic painters of the early part of the nineteenth century were not interested in perspective in their skies:

> *When it came to the sky, they painted atmosphere and light in recollection of the work of Claude. Without bothering themselves with any clear conception of clouds, they made a thoroughgoing use of the circumstance that a cloud seems to be able to assume any form that the painter likes, in order to give their landscapes what they called an 'ideal' atmosphere.*[42]

In a footnote Badt gives a typical example of the sort of rules that were laid down for painting the sky:

> *All over Europe painters had access to rules for doing this, which were clearly laid down. As an example here is a quotation from John Burnet's A Practical Treatise on Painting, London, 1827: 'In compositions constructed on this principle (i.e. the angular composition) particularly where the landscape occupies a large portion, many artists carry the lines of the clouds in a contrary direction to counteract the appearance of all the lines running to a point. Thus using the darks of the clouds, &c., to antagonise, as it is termed, may apparently produce a better equipose, but sacrifices many advantages; for we observe in many of the pictures of Cuyp, Rubens, and Teniers, where the figures,*

landscape, and sky are all on the same side of the composition, that a rich and soft effect is produced.'[43]

Constable obtained copies of two of Burnet's books for his friend Fisher and was therefore likely to be aware of Burnet's advice for the painting of skies, but it is not known if he agreed with such statements.[44] As noted in the introduction to this chapter, Constable said in his letter to Fisher of 23 October 1821: 'I have often been advised to consider my sky as a white sheet drawn behind the objects – certainly if the sky is obtrusive – (as mine are) it is bad, but if they are evaded (as mine are not) it is worse.'[45] In other words, the sky was to be considered almost as the backcloth on a stage, distant and out of the way. Obviously when a landscape artist chooses the effective frame for a painting the amount of sky to be included can vary from all sky to no sky. A skyscape might be defined as a painting with more than 90 per cent of the picture occupied by sky, but even if the skyscape is 100 per cent sky only a small fraction of the visible sky is likely to have been painted. Just as the landscape retreats away from the observer, so the clouds and sky must come overhead. Again how far the clouds, if present, come overhead depends upon the chosen frame of the picture.

Some artists may find that if they are sketching or painting in the open air it is advantageous to paint with their canvases at right angles to the wind if the clouds are in parallel lanes or 'streets'. Otherwise only the base of a cloud street passing overhead will be visible. (This assumes that the clouds are moving in the same direction as the surface wind. If they are not, which is quite common, it may be advantageous to align oneself at right angles to the cloud movement). It is better to look at what is effectively a cross section of the cloud street. Constable often painted at right angles to the wind as discussed in section 2.6.7 below. He also painted into the wind on occasions and in a letter to W. Carpenter, for whom he was retouching a painting, he stated that 'I have now got... some wind in my face'.

On balance, most landscape painters have adopted the Claude approach and created unobtrusive skies in their paintings, partly because of the problems of handling sky and cloud perspective.

1.4.4 Influence of weather on sky and landscape colours

The most obvious weather element that affects the visual range as well as the colour of the sky is precipitation, both as it falls through the atmosphere and also as it covers the ground. Snow alters the colour of the ground completely and can totally transform a landscape. Rain also changes the colour of a surface and makes it darker and warmer – the first drops of rain appear dark on the surface as the light is partly absorbed by the water. Whether or not we can see rain or snow falling from the sky depends upon the relative brightness of the background. Hence it is often difficult to see them against a relatively bright sky, but much easier against darker trees and houses.[46] Heavy rain seen falling from a cloud in parallel streaks seems dark against the lighter background of the sky because the rain is preventing light from the sky behind from reaching our eye. This is beautifully portrayed by Constable in *Seascape Study with Rainclouds* (Plate 44).

Another important form of precipitation is dew and frost formation. Dewdrops and crystals of hoar-frost produce a literal rainbow of colours when light falls on them, and the sparkle of morning dew enhances any scene. Constable delighted in any landscape 'still gemmed with the morning dew'. The dew drops do not wet the surface of a leaf or flower as would rain. Each droplet remains as an individual sphere, often with a thin layer of air separating the droplet from the leaf. This can give grass a greyish tinge as the light is reflected from all the tiny drops.[47]

Another weather phenomenon which affects the colour of the sky is the amount of light which a surface reflects (albedo), which can then be further reflected towards the eye by cloud. If two ground surfaces side by side have very different albedos (e.g. pack ice and sea) this difference will be apparent in the brightness of the sky above.

Eskimos use this phenomena to locate cracks in the sea ice when travelling across it – if there is a crack then they perceive a dark 'water sky' above it. Conversely, when travelling by boat warning of potentially damaging sea ice up ahead can be given by a white 'ice blink'.

1.4.5 The portrayal of wind

The depiction of movement or motion in a painting has fascinated artists for centuries. Landscape artists, like Constable, felt it imperative to portray movement within their paintings. Wind can only be painted indirectly through, for instance, the suggested movement of clouds, the smoke from a chimney, the bending of trees, or the whipping of waves and the full sails of leaning boats. One of the most expressive painters of wind is David Cox, as illustrated by his *Sun, Wind and Rain* (Plate 5). The umbrella pointing into the wind, the slanting rain, the bending trees and vegetation, the blanket on the lady on the horse pulled up around her neck, the soaring birds – all point to a blustery wind. Constable's *Hay Wain* (Plate 38) suggests a gentle westerly airstream with the smoke from Willy Lott's house chimney. (In Chapter 3 I shall demonstrate that, broadly speaking, Constable's paintings became windier as his career and confidence progressed, culminating in the storms of his later years.)

Constable was probably also well aware of 'wind shear' which occurs when the wind carries the clouds in different directions and speeds at different heights in the atmosphere. In the text

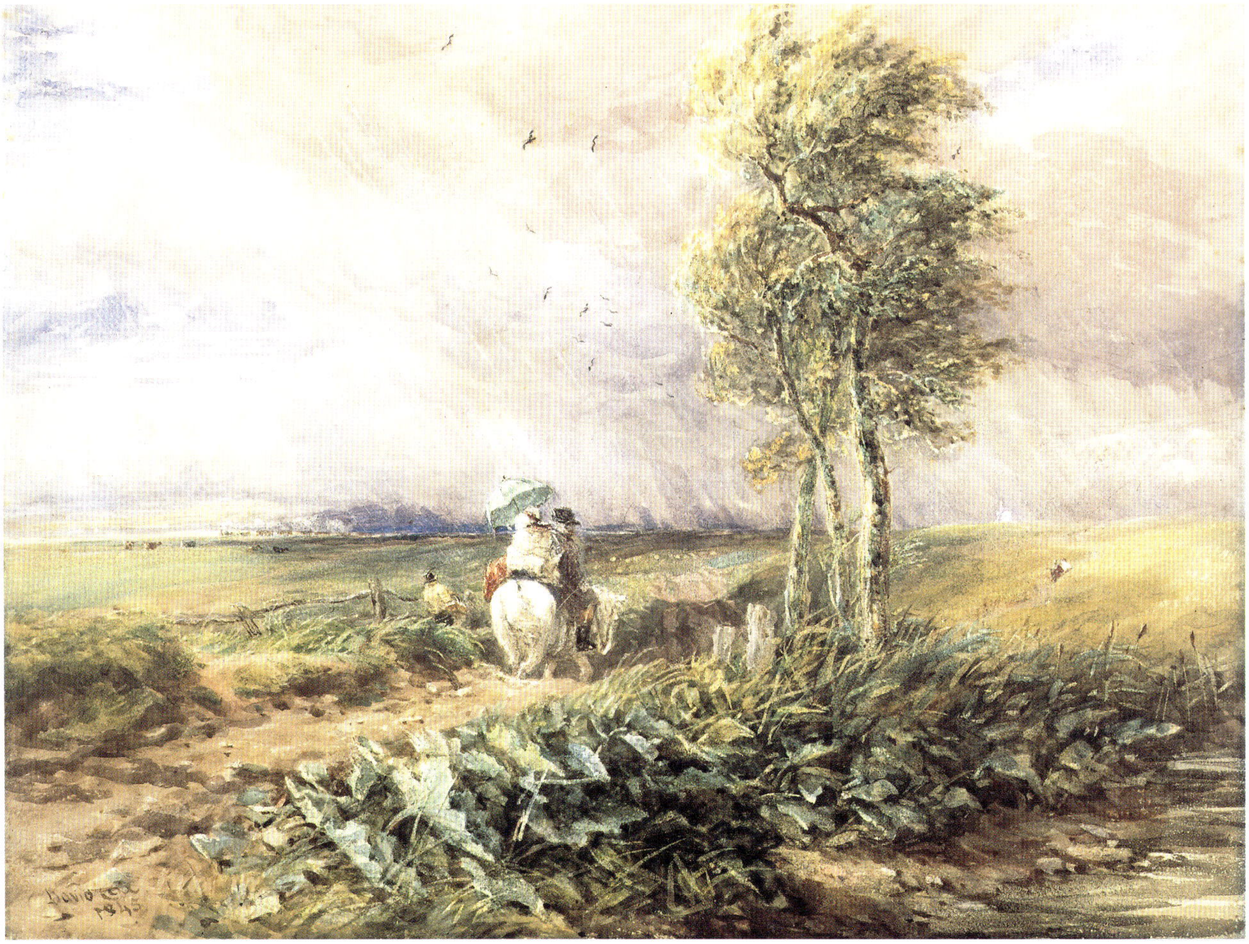

Plate 5 David Cox, *Sun, Wind and Rain*, 1845. Birmingham Museums & Art Gallery

accompanying *Spring. East Bergholt Common, Hail Squalls. – Noon* (Plate 6), the second mezzotint in the 1834 edition of *English Landscape Scenery*, Constable describes how 'messenger' clouds (which we would today call 'scud' clouds or stratus fractus) often move at different levels and speeds below rain clouds.[48]

1.5 Light, the sun, rainbows and other optical effects

> *Just as composers select a specific key to stimulate a particular kind of emotional response, so landscapists use different kinds of light to set the emotional tone of a painting.*[49]

Light, daylight, sunlight, moonlight – whatever we like to call it, landscape painters are really painters of light. The artist uses colour and tone to try to create an effect or mood for the beholder of the picture. (Conversely the portrayal of light can be used by the art critic to interpret the mood of the artist. Constable's stormy skies painted late in his life, such as *Hadleigh Castle* (Plate 54) , *Old Sarum* (Plates 57 and 62) and *Stonehenge* (Plate 63) have often been associated with his frequently depressed state of mind at that time.)

The lighting of a landscape is controlled by the position of the sun in the sky and the position and speed of movement of the clouds. In view of the fact that a landscape painting depicts only a fraction of the potential landscape, light and shade in the landscape of a picture may be controlled by sun and cloud which are outside the frame of the picture; but even when this is the case, the amount of cloud represented should be consistent with the rest of the sky.

Rembrandt used light (and dark) in his paintings to create the necessary mood or atmosphere with almost total disregard to the painted sky (see section 4.3.4). The overall contrast of light and shade was called chiaroscuro by artists, a term which referred to the tone of the colours in a landscape, which is controlled by the amount of light getting through the clouds. Constable regarded chiaroscuro as a vital ingredient of his

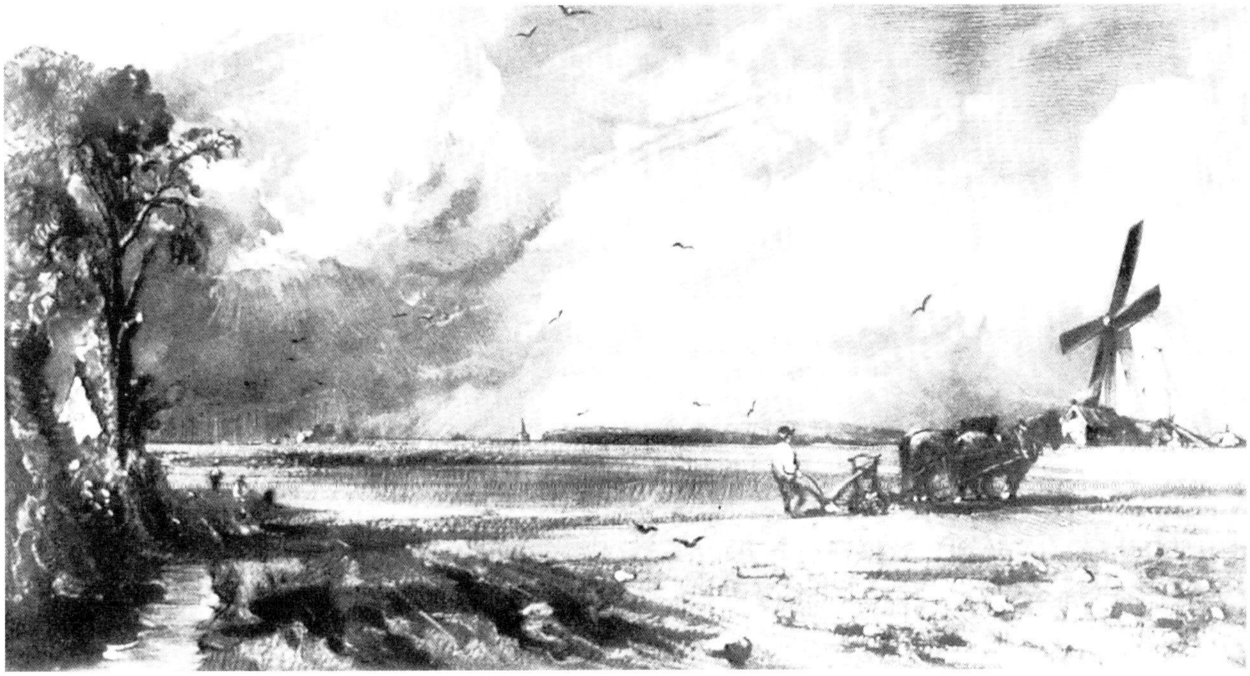

Plate 6 David Lucas, John Constable's *Spring. East Bergholt Common, Hail Squalls – Noon*, 1834. V&A Picture Library

landscapes. The play of cloud shadows on the landscape has always been a popular source of inspiration for artists, especially in Britain.

1.5.1 Sunlight and the colour of the sun

All natural light comes from the sun and about half of the energy that reaches our atmosphere from the sun is in the form of visible light. Whenever we see colour we know that light must be reaching our eyes. The sunlight which comes straight to our eyes from the sun appears pale yellow due to the scattering out of the blue end of the spectrum.

The colour of the sun itself, when it is visible, changes throughout the day. The brightness of the sun is such that we never normally look at it unless it is low in the sky. To the naked eye the sun appears whitish because of the mixture of yellow and blue sky light. The sun's colour as it rises or sets changes every day according to the amount and size of dust particles in the atmosphere. Bright yellow sunsets can only occur if the atmosphere is relatively clean, for instance after recent rain. If there are many small particles scattering the sunlight then the yellow may be scattered out leaving only orange and red. When the atmosphere is well laden with particles then only the red light will get through. Natural 'pollutants' such as sea salt and water vapour can also produce vividly red sunrises and sunsets.

Normally the rising sun is a brighter yellow than the setting sun as the daytime hours produce more anthropogenic pollution and more evaporation. The sun can appear green or blue under certain conditions, as on 26 September 1950, when smoke from a forest fire in Alberta, Canada circled the globe at a height of about 10 to 13km and caused a blue-green sun to be seen over the British Isles.

1.5.2 Light and other optical effects

What our eyes perceive of the landscape depends upon the route by which the light arrives at our eye. As light passes down through the atmosphere it may

Table 8
Effect of scattering, reflection, refraction and diffraction on light as it passes through the atmosphere

Process	*Effect*
Scattering	Blue colour of sky, other colours at sunrise and sunset; white colour of clouds; crepuscular rays; blue moon
Reflection	Rainbows; sun pillars, circles and crosses
Refraction	Rainbows, halos, arcs, spots, mirages, twinkling stars, green flash, twilight, sundogs
Diffraction	corona, glory, brocken bow, cloud iridescence, Bishop's Ring

encounter air molecules, water molecules, water droplets, dust particles or clouds, or it may pass through them all and arrive at the earth's surface unaffected. If the light does directly encounter one of the above obstructions it may be absorbed, scattered, reflected, refracted or diffracted depending upon the obstruction. Few of the visible quanta of light are absorbed but much scattering, reflection and refraction of light takes place. Table 8 shows which atmospheric phenomena are caused by which combination of processes. A very brief discussion of some of these optical phenomena is given below before the rainbow, which is of most interest in relation to Constable's skies, is discussed in more detail.[50] There are many other important properties of light such as interference and polarisation that will not be discussed here, but it is clear that light is just as much a fascinating challenge for science as it is for art.

Landscape artists, over the years, have attempted to paint most of these phenomena, but it is the effects of scattering that are our chief concern when looking at the skies of landscape paintings. Scattering takes place continuously in the atmosphere whereas the other effects are more rare. (Rainbows, for example, only occur on a few days each year but are found in many landscape paintings.) The process of scattering has already been discussed and is caused by the physical barrier of air molecules, dust, air pollution, water droplets and ice crystals to the passage of the light through the atmosphere. Normally we do not see the rays of light that pass down through the atmosphere, but on occasions sunbeams, penetrating through gaps in low cloud, are rendered visible by water or dust particles in the air. These are called crepuscular rays, or are more commonly referred to as Jacob's ladder, or the 'sun drawing water'. Crepuscular rays can also sometimes be seen radiating upwards when the sun is hidden behind a cumulus or cumulonimbus cloud, and also at twilight when they diverge upwards when the sun is below the horizon. Anticrepuscular rays are rarely seen but they are a continuation of crepuscular rays right across the sky to the opposite horizon where they appear to converge.

Reflection takes place off and within water droplets and ice crystals as the path of the light is altered. Light will only enter or leave a droplet or ice crystal if the angle of incidence is steep enough, otherwise it will be reflected.

Refraction is the term for the apparent bending of light when it enters water droplets or ice crystals. It is caused by the differing densities of bodies through which the light passes. Refraction creates the apparent curvature of light through the atmosphere due to the great increase in air density close to the earth's surface. Figure 10 shows how starlight is bent as it passes through the earth's atmosphere. Refraction also causes a distortion of the setting or rising sun and effectively enables us to see over the horizon and to see the setting sun for longer, and the rising sun sooner, than if there were no atmosphere. Refraction also explains the formation of halos and arcs.

Diffraction of light is a consequence of its wavelike properties. Whenever light passes close to an object, such as an ice crystal or water droplet in the atmosphere, the light appears to be deflected by its edge. Again the reasons for this are not understood but experiments have shown that the effect is real. Diffraction explains the corona seen around the sun or moon, cloud iridescence, Bishop's Ring, the spectre of the brocken bow, and the glory.

Another well-known atmospheric phenomenon is the aurora borealis or 'northern lights' which is caused by streams of charged solar particles which collide with atmospheric gases and give off vivid coloured glows with folded shapes. These displays take place at about 100km above the earth's surface and are best seen north of the British Isles. Nevertheless in northern Scotland they can be seen on up to 150 nights of the year, and are visible on average ten nights a year in southern England.

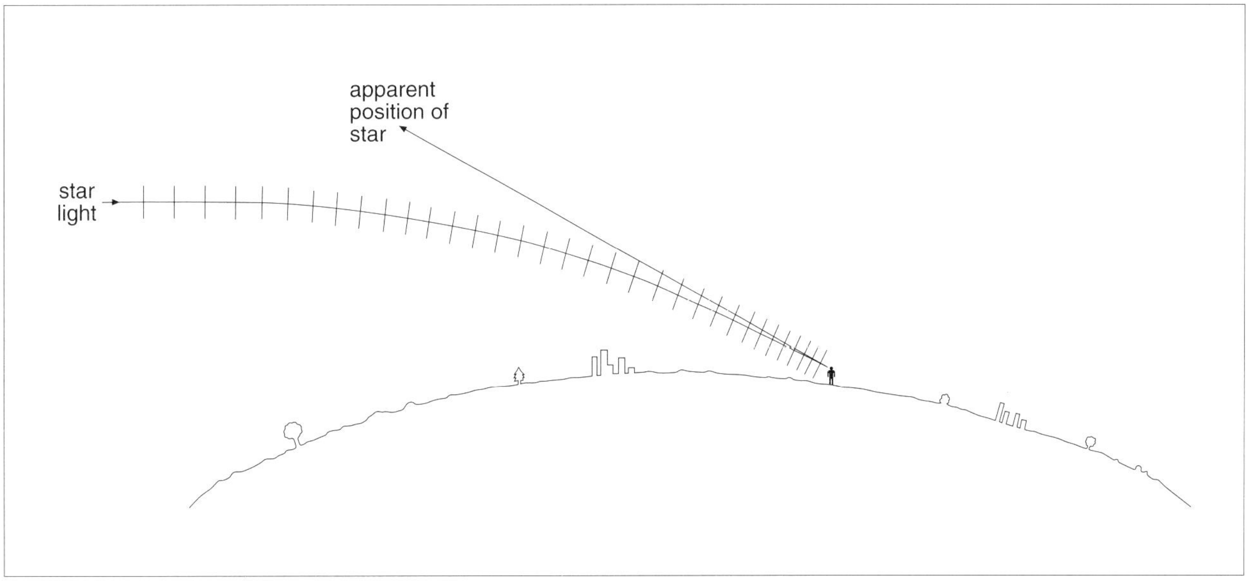

Figure 10 The refraction of starlight

1.5.3 The rainbow

The rainbow is often symbolised as a bridge between art and science. It is by far the most painted optical phenomena apart from the sun itself. Every school child knows the colours of the rainbow but few realise that the colours in what is called the primary bow are reversed in the secondary bow of a double rainbow. Also few people are aware of the supernumerary arcs that sometimes accompany the primary bow. These arcs appear on the lower side of the primary bow as shown in Figure 11. It is these supernumerary arcs that have taken the longest to explain and mathematical models are only just getting close, as discussed by Nussenzveig in his classic paper 'The theory of the rainbow'.[51]

The written history of the understanding of the formation of the rainbow goes back to Aristotle who thought that the rainbow was an unusual reflection of sunlight from clouds. Aristotle succeeded in explaining the shape of the bow, and recognised that a rainbow does not have a distinct location. The angle through which light from the sun is bent to our eye by a rainbow (42 degrees for the primary bow) as shown in Figure 11 was first measured by Roger Bacon in 1266. (The secondary bow subtends an angle of about 50 degrees to the ground.) In 1304 a German monk, Theodoric of Freiberg, rejected Aristotle and wrote that each drop of rain is capable of producing a rainbow. These findings were independently rediscovered by Descartes who showed that the rainbow is made up of rays of light that have undergone one internal reflection within a raindrop as shown in Figure 12. The secondary bow is derived from rays that have undergone two internal reflections. (Note from Figure 12 that refraction is also involved as the light passes from air to water and from water to air. Snell's law, which was formulated in 1621, allows the amount of refraction to be calculated.)

Descartes painstakingly calculated the paths of rays of light through droplets at different angles of incidence. He was able to explain the primary and secondary bows and also what is called Alexander's

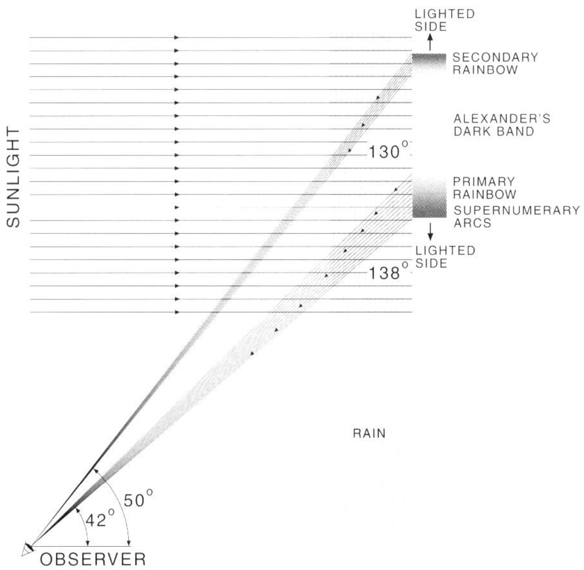

Figure 11
Geometry of a rainbow (Adapted from H. Nussenzveig, 'The theory of the rainbow')

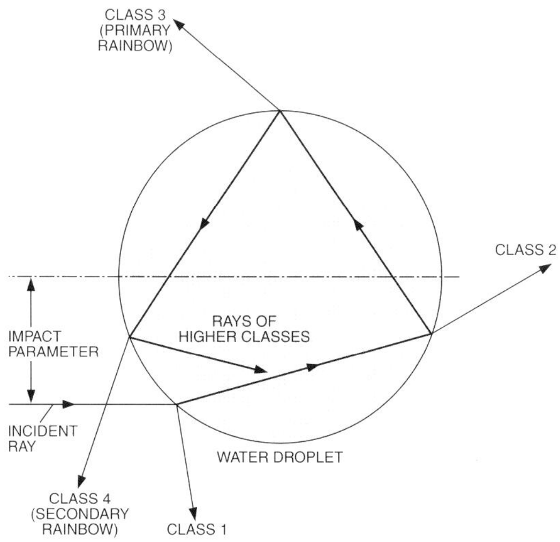

Figure 12
Path of light through a raindrop (Adapted from H. Nussenzveig, 'The theory of the rainbow')

Dark Band (the area between the primary and secondary bows), as illustrated in Figure 11. His theory suggested however that the size of the droplets is not important. If that were the case then all rainbows would look the same. In reality every rainbow is slightly different. The reasons for this were not demonstrated until much later.

The colours of the bow were first explained by Newton in 1666. He showed that white light is a combination of colours and that each colour is refracted slightly differently. Thus a rainbow is really a combination of several individually coloured bows.

Newton and Descartes between them explained all the major features of the bows but could not explain the supernumerary arcs. The optical effect of interference was discovered by Young in 1803 and he applied this to the theory of the rainbow, demonstrating that when rays of light from different sources converge they can either combine to create brighter bands or cancel one another out to give darker bands. He showed that rays of light which came out of the raindrops at the same angle but from different sources were interfering in this manner such that darker and brighter bands could be expected just below the primary bow. The extent of these bows does depend upon droplet size.

Although Young's theory appeared to have solved the one outstanding problem, there was a major snag. According to his results Alexander's Dark Band should be completely dark as no rays of light emerge from the droplets at that angle (see Figure 12). The theory of diffraction is required to show that, in fact, some light will be deflected into this zone. In 1835 Potter pointed out the possible role of caustic curves of light, like the cusp of light formed in a teacup when sunlight is reflected from its inner walls. In 1838 Airy developed a new mathematical function which could describe this process. However the full explanation of the intensity of light from the vicinity of a rainbow took more than another century to develop. Airy's method does show that the droplet size is important in determining how far the individual coloured bows overlap. For a bright rainbow with pure colours droplets of diameter of a few millimetres are needed. If the droplets are very small, of the order of diameter 0.1 mm, then the overlap of colours is so great that the resulting bow is almost white.[52]

The current theory that appears to describe virtually all the features of a rainbow is what is called the complex angular momentum theory. This theory takes into account that quanta of light can be regarded as particles as well as waves. When a quanta of light enters a raindrop it sets off a number of waves around the surface of the droplet that constantly shed radiation, which can interfere with the light emerging from the droplet.

The sun is not a single point in space and therefore the sun's rays are not exactly parallel. This means that there is normally overlap between the colours of the bow. No two bows are ever exactly the same but Minnaert has determined the

Table 9

Droplet size and rainbow colours

Approx. droplet diameter	*Description*
1–2mm	Very bright primary bow with violet, vivid green, and pure red; blue weak. Pink and green supernumerary arcs appear to merge into the primary bow.
0.5mm	Red of primary weak. Fewer supernumeraries.
0.2–0.3mm	Red absent from primary bow, rest of bow is well developed. Supernumerary arcs are pale yellow.
0.1–0.2mm	Gap between primary bow and first supernumerary.
0.08–0.1mm	Primary bow is broad and pale; only the violet component is vivid. First supernumerary arc whitish and well separated from primary bow.
0.06mm	Primary rainbow contains a distinct white stripe.
< 0.06mm	Mistbow, cloudbow or fogbow white, except for a tinge of orange on outside edge and blue on inside edge.

relationship between droplet size and the usual visible colours of the resultant rainbow as shown in Table 9.[53]

We should therefore be wary of criticising the colours of a rainbow in a painting because a wide range of colours is possible. Moreover, because the refractive index of water depends to a slight extent on temperature, droplets of the same size may produce slightly different bows according to the season. A rainbow may also appear slightly disjointed if the droplets causing the top of the bow are of a different temperature to those causing the base of the bow.

The height of a rainbow in the sky depends upon the time of day and the day of the year. The rainbow can be seen as a complete circle if we look at it from the air, for instance from an aeroplane, or if we look at the spray of a waterfall. The tallest rainbows are seen when the sun is close to the horizon and the top of the bow then subtends a maximum angle of 42 degrees to the ground. From the ground it is not possible to see a rainbow at noon in England from the end of March until the middle of September. On 21 June when the sun is at its highest in the sky in England, it is not possible to see a rainbow from about 9.30am until about 4.30pm (British Summer Time).

The width of the secondary bow is about twice that of the primary bow, and the distance between the reds of the two bows is approximately three times the width of the secondary bow. There are further bows created by the droplets but they are virtually impossible to see with the naked eye. Up to thirteen different bows have been detected under laboratory conditions. The third and fourth bows are actually visible looking towards the sun and hence the rain has to be between the observer and the sun, so these are rarely seen. In many situations only fragments of the bow are visible because the shower of rain that is making the rainbow visible is not big enough to cover the area of sky the bow occupies. The apparent size of the bow depends upon how far away the rain is falling. The further away the rain, the bigger the apparent size of the bow.

Each rainbow is unique to each observer and as you move so your rainbow moves with you. The rainbow is always directly opposite the sun. If you move towards it, it will retreat. If you move away from it, it will move with you. If you move sideways it will move with you in the same direction. If the shower of rain that is producing the rainbow just happens to be moving directly away from you opposite the sun, then the rainbow will appear to get slightly bigger. If the shower is moving directly towards you it will appear to get slightly smaller.

This rich variety of features of the rainbow is not readily understood by artists nor by the general public. Even Constable painted summer rainbows at noon, although he knew that this was impossible (as discussed in section 2.9 below).

1.6 Of truth of skies

This chapter has examined the major visual components of the sky that we need to understand before we can attempt an examination of the truth of an artist's skies. It gives us a number of criteria with which we might attempt to judge such skies:

- The perceived shape and colour of the sky;
- The colour of the atmosphere if visible and the portrayal of aerial perspective;
- The colour of the clouds;
- The shape of the clouds – are they identifiable?
- The shading of the landscape with reference to the clouds and perceived position of the sun;
- The perspective of the clouds;
- The perceived wind direction and speed (if applicable);
- The presence or absence of air pollution;

- The proportion of the picture occupied by sky;
- The veracity and position of optical effects e.g. rainbows.

One must be careful not to be over-critical of skies painted in the past. The colours in a painting may have changed with time, the painting may have darkened and require cleaning, and present day knowledge may be very different to perceived knowledge at the time of painting. Nevertheless, armed with this basic knowledge of landscape meteorology we should now be able to objectively compare the skies of John Constable with nature's own and also compare them with the skies of other artists.

Notes

1 M. Kemp, *The Science of Art* (New Haven: Yale University Press, 1990), back cover copy.
2 J. Constable. Taken from a letter to the Reverend John Fisher written on 23 October 1821. See Appendix 3 for a transcription of the original letter.
3 L. Howard, 'On the modification of clouds', *Tilloch's Philosophical Magazine* (1803), published in three parts in vols. XVI: 97–107, 344–57, XVII: 5–11.
4 J. Ruskin, 'Lectures on landscape', delivered at Oxford in the Lent term. In *The Works of John Ruskin*, edited by E. T. Cook and A. Wedderburn, 39 vols. (London: Library Edition, 1903-12), *XXII*: p. 15.
5 Ruskin, *Modern Painters III*, *Works V*, p. 318.
6 J. Constable. Taken from the original letter to Fisher written on 23 October 1821 – see Appendix 3.
7 W. Gilpin, *Three Essays on Picturesque Landscape* (London: R. Blamire, 1792), p. 34.
8 A. Cozens, *A New Method of Assisting the Invention in Drawing Original Compositions of Landscape* (London, c. 1785).
9 Ruskin, *Modern Painters I*, *Works III*, p. 93.
10 Ibid., pp. 343–419. The section is called 'Of Truth of Skies', and has four chapters entitled 'Of the Open Sky', 'Of Truth of Clouds:- First of the Region of the Cirrus', 'Of Truth of Clouds:- Secondly, Of the Central Cloud Region', 'Of Truth of Clouds:- Thirdly, Of the Region of the Rain-Cloud'.
11 Ibid., p. 346.
12 M. Minnaert, *The Nature of Light and Colour in the Open Air* (New York: Dover Publications Inc., 1954), p. 238.
13 Lord Rayleigh, 'On the light from the sky, its polarisation and colour', *Philosophical Magazine* 41 (1871): 107–20, 274–9.
14 M. Minnaert, *Light and Colour in the Open Air*, p. 279.
15 Ibid., p. 244.
16 F. Linke, *Monthly Weather Review* 56 (1928): 224–5.
17 H. and M. Neuberger, 'Color memory in cyanometry', *Bulletin of the American Meteorological Society* 24 (1943): 47–53.
18 M. Kemp, *The Science of Art*, part III, p. 261.
19 J. Gage, *Colour and Culture* (London: Thames and Hudson, 1993).
20 The concept of aerial perspective was probably first referred to by Leonardo da Vinci in his *Treatise on Painting*: 'colours become weaker in proportion to their distance from the person who is looking at them'.
21 *Information about changes in visibility is often of critical significance in aviation, and to geographers and others concerned with the "visible landscape", visual range is the most important of all the meteorological elements.*

Although the curvature of the Earth's surface limits the horizontal distance at which topographical features can be seen from a given point, the normal distances visible at the Earth's surface are very much less than this limiting distance, because of the presence of the atmosphere. The various constituents of the atmosphere, water droplets, dust, smoke and other pollution particles, condensation nuclei, and the air molecules themselves, determine the optical visibility through it. Different airstreams, different air masses, and different topographies, geographical locations, and land uses have characteristic visibility ranges associated with them, depending on the season and time of day.'

(E.T. Stringer, *Techniques of Climatology* (San Francisco: W. H. Freeman & Co., 1972), p. 334)
22 Meteorological Office, *Observer's Handbook* (London: HMSO, 1969), p. 43.
23 J. B. Tyldesley, 'Weather in Constable's paintings', *Weather* 23 (1968): 344–8.
24 H. Neuberger, 'Climate in art', *Weather* 25 (1970): 46–56.
25 Ibid. p. 50.
26 Ibid. p. 50.
27 Ibid. p. 55.
28 P. Brimblecombe, 'London air pollution', *Atmospheric Environment* 11 (1977): 1157–62; and P. Brimblecombe, *The Big Smoke – A history of air pollution in London since medieval times* (London: Routledge, 1987).

29 O. Wilde, 'The decay of lying', in *The Works of Oscar Wilde*, Golden Heritage Series (Leicester: Galley Press, 1987), pp. 909–31.
30 Ibid.
31 L. Howard, 'On the modification of clouds'.
32 J. Lamarck, *Annuaire Météorologique* (Paris, 1802), An. x, 3, p. 149; An. xi, 4, pp. 126, 128; An. xii, 5, p. 159.
33 J. E. Thornes, 'Luke Howard's influence on art and literature in the early nineteenth century', *Weather* 39 (1984): 252–5.
34 S. D. Gedzelman, 'Cloud classification before Luke Howard', *Bulletin of the American Meteorological Society* 70 (1989): 381–95.
35 See Meteorological Office, *Cloud Types for Observers* (London: HMSO, 1962) for basic instructions on cloud identification and observation.
36 L. Howard, 'On the modification of clouds'.
37 R. Greenler, *Rainbows, Halos, and Glories* (Cambridge: Cambridge University Press, 1980), pp. 22–3. See also D. K. Lynch and W. Livingston, *Color and Light in Nature* (Cambridge: Cambridge University Press, 1995).
38 T. Forster, *Researches about Atmospheric Phaenomena*, 2nd edn (London: Baldwin, Cradock & Joy, 1815), p. 19. The annotations made by Constable are discussed in detail in section 2.7 of the present volume.
39 G. Reynolds, *Constable: The Natural Painter* (St. Albans: Panther Books, 1976), p. 83.
40 E. T. Stringer, *Techniques of Climatology*, p. 336.
41 N. Battershill, *Painting Skies* (London: Pitman Publishing, 1980).
42 K. Badt, *John Constable's Clouds* (London: Routledge & Kegan Paul, 1950), p. 22.
43 Ibid.
44 Constable obtained copies of Burnet's books, *Practical Hints on Colour in Painting* (1827) and *Practical Hints on Light and Shade in Painting* (1826), for Fisher – see L. Parris, C. Shields and I. Fleming-Williams (eds), *John Constable: Further Documents & Correspondence*, (London: The Tate Gallery and the Suffolk Records Society, 1975), p. 28.
45 See note 2, above.
46 Minnaert, *Light and Colour in the Open Air*, pp. 260–1 notes that:
It is worth while during a shower to observe in which direction the falling rain is most easily seen. The drops are not visible against the bright sky nor against the ground, but they are against houses and trees. Evidently they can be seen only when they deflect the light from its path and bring brightness where formerly it was dark.... This is an application of the general principle that the eye is sensitive to the ratio of light intensities, not their differences. If light of intensity 100 falls on a drop and the intensity scattered by the drop is 10, then it will show up very well against a dark background of intensity 5, since the ratio of intensities is 2:1. On the other hand, the diminution in intensity of transmitted light from 100 to 90 means that the intensity ratio of the drop seen against the sky is only 10:9, which is scarcely perceptible.
47 Ruskin, *The Art of England*, *Works XXXIII*, p. 386: *you can never see what the colour of a carnation or a wild rose really is till you get the dew on it*. See also Minnaert, *Light and Colour in the Open Air*, p. 38:
The greyish aspect of bedewed grass is due to the reflection of the rays of light in all the tiny drops, inside as well as outside; a great number of the rays do not even touch the blade of grass.
[...]
Let us select one large drop and look at it with one eye, and we shall see colours appear as soon as we observe it in a direction making a sufficiently large angle with the direction of incidence. First we see blue, then green and then, particularly clearly, yellow, orange, red.
48 Taken from D. Hill, *Constable's English Landscape Scenery* (London: The Promotional Reprint Company, 1992), p. 99.
49 B. Jeffares, *Landscape Painting* (Oxford: Phaidon, 1979), p. 11.
50 The reader is referred to the following excellent works for more details: Minnaert, *Light and Colour in the Open Air*; Greenler, *Rainbows, Halos, and Glories*; Lynch and Livingston, *Color and Light in Nature*. Two collections of reprints from Scientific American are also useful: *Light from the Sky* 1980 and *Atmospheric Phenomena* 1980 (Oxford: Freeman)
51 H. Nussenzveig, 'The theory of the rainbow', *Scientific American* (April 1977).
52 Ibid.
53 Taken from Minnaert, *Light and Colour in the Open Air*, p. 178 and F. Schaaf, *Seeing the Sky* (London: John Wiley and Sons, 1990).

Chapter Two

John Constable's meteorological understanding

We see nothing truly till we understand it

2.1 Constable's art and science

Most artists, if asked for what purpose they paint, would say 'to express my feelings'. Constable himself wrote 'Painting is with me but another word for feeling'.[1] This implies that artists' senses are just as, if not more, important to them than current artistic culture and a historical knowledge of art. For most artists a scientific understanding of how nature works is not considered necessary and they believe that their common sense and imagination will tell them all they need to know.

In this context Constable was an exception: he rebelled against the artistic culture that taught artists to use their imagination to compose their pictures rather than nature herself. He respected the 'old masters' but, as Leslie remembers Constable saying, 'When I sit down to make a sketch from nature, the first thing I try to do is to forget that I have ever seen a picture'.[2] He refused to be shackled by convention in his art and, as he observed in 1836 in his first lecture at the Royal Institution, 'I hope to show that ours is a regularly taught profession; that it is *scientific* as well as *poetic*; that imagination alone never did, and never can, produce works that are to stand by a comparison with *realities*.' At the end of his fourth lecture at the Royal Institution he re-emphasised the point: 'Painting is a science, and should be pursued as an inquiry into the laws of nature. Why, then may not landscape painting be considered as a branch of natural philosophy, of which pictures are but the experiments?'[3]

Thus Constable believed that a landscape artist needed a combination of direct observation and experience, imagination and scientific understanding in order to create a painting that could be compared with nature. This combination of observation and explanation took Constable beyond mere description and imitation. Constable regarded his art as a form of experimental science. Charlotte Klonk has suggested the term 'phenomenalism' to describe a period at the end of the eighteenth and beginning of the nineteenth century when both art and science were committed 'to the scrupulous observation of particular phenomena, without making prior assumptions about meaning or underlying causes'.[4] She suggests that phenomenalism is evident in Constable's work up to around 1817 when he exhibited *Flatford Mill* (Plate 29) at the Royal Academy. *Flatford Mill* is static and descriptive. This ties in with the conclusions of the present study that in order to paint realistic skies Constable had to go beyond observation and attempt to understand scientific meteorological theories.

Constable's extensive cloud studies of 1820/22 were certainly experiments in colour, light, and aerial and cloud perspective, as well a testing of Luke Howard's cloud classification. *The Hay Wain* (Plate 38), exhibited in 1821, goes beyond *Flatford Mill* and represents a scientific understanding as well as an artistic interpretation. But how does a scientific understanding help the artist? Keats believed that science was the enemy of poetry. His poem 'Lamia' is an indictment of Newton's scientific explanation of the colours of the rainbow, which he thought robbed the rainbow of its mystery:

> *Philosophy will clip an Angel's wings,*
> *Conquer all mysteries by rule and line,*
> *Empty the haunted air, and gnomed mine-*
> *Unweave a rainbow, as it erewhile made*
> *The tender-person'd Lamia melt into a shade.*

But Keats wrote elsewhere:

> *The difference of high sensations ... with and without knowledge appears to me to be this: in the latter case we are continually falling ten thousand fathoms deep, and being blown up again, without wings, and with all the horror of a bare-shouldered creature: in the former case, our shoulders are fledged, and we go through the same air and space without fear.*[5]

This analogy of being able to fly with knowledge or be blown around uncontrollably without it, is perfect for the sky. How much scientific knowledge is required to enable one to 'fly' is arguable. In Constable's case, was it sufficient for him to understand Luke Howard's cloud classification, or did he need to understand the formation of clouds? Moreover what may be regarded as scientifically true today may be proven to be false tomorrow. Does this matter? Provided the artist has the confidence to 'fly' it probably does not as long as science brings order to chaos.

Science has pervaded art since the invention of perspective by Brunelleschi at the beginning of the fifteenth century, but the dialogue between art and science has waxed and waned over the years. The first half of the nineteenth century is an interesting time for the links between art and science to be examined.[6] The tremendous influence that Howard's cloud classification had on Goethe was picked up by Carl Gustav Carus (1789–1869) who was one of the most cultured men of his age. Carus, a medical scientist and painter, believed that the young landscape painter should be trained in the workings of natural science and 'informed about the peculiar laws of atmospheric phenomena, the different names of clouds, of their formation and dissolution as of their movements.' Goethe implanted in Carus the idea of the 'production of modern art by means of science' leading to art becoming the crown of science. Perhaps Constable's skies can be regarded as the crown of Luke Howard's cloud classification?

2.2 Weather in Constable's skies

The debate as to the influence of meteorological science upon Constable's art, principally through the cloud classification of Luke Howard, was ignited by the fascinating theory of Kurt Badt published in 1950.[7] Badt made much of the possible intellectual stimulus that Howard's cloud classification would have had upon Constable at a time, around 1821, when Constable was struggling to harmonise sky and landscape. The debate was fuelled by Hawes[8] who stressed the environmental influences upon Constable's atmospheric understanding and doubted that Howard's cloud classification would have had much impact in comparison, for instance, with Constable's experiences as a windmiller. (This debate will be examined in detail in Chapter 3.) Through an examination of Constable's annotations to Forster's book, *Researches about Atmospheric Phaenomena,* I have shown elsewhere that Constable was fully aware of Howard's cloud classification, and indeed was sufficiently versed in meteorology to argue with some of Forster's assertions.[9]

This chapter will examine both the direct evidence of Constable's knowledge of meteorology through his writings and annotations and the indirect evidence, such as that provided by the environmental influences of his windmiller days and the 'atmospheric laboratory' of Hampstead Heath. The evidence from Constable's sky studies and their influence on his finished works will be discussed in Chapter 3.

Let us now examine in detail Constable's meteorological knowledge, starting with Constable's training as a windmiller.

2.3 Constable's training as a windmiller

Constable worked for his father for at least a year, when he was a teenager in the late 1780s. This included a time working at the windmill on East Bergholt Common. Normally the eldest son, Golding, would have been trained to take over the family business, but it appears that he was not capable. John was therefore taught the miller's skills but it became increasingly obvious that John's heart was in art, and not in taking over the family business. This responsibility was eventually passed on to the next oldest son, Abram. Nevertheless John's experience as a miller gave him considerable familiarity with the sky and the weather.

The weather is of utmost importance to the operation of a windmill. Constable's father's windmill was a typical 'post windmill', common in the area, and it features in many of Constable's paintings. As with all windmills if the wind is too light then it is impossible to operate, and if the wind is too strong the sails of the mill may be damaged if the sail cloth is not furled in time. As Wailes writes:

> *Each cloth had to be set or furled by hand, one at a time, and for this purpose each sail had to be brought round to the lowest position in turn. It often necessitated breaking the mill in full sail and sometimes stones had to be choked with grain to help the slowing down process for fear of firing the brake. At best it was an unpleasant operation, and often a dangerous job, in wet or stormy weather, and in frosty weather, wet sail cloths would freeze hard as boards.*[10]

In order to plan the day ahead it was important to try to forecast the likely weather and therefore the likely strength and direction of the wind. The mill would have to be turned to face the wind to get maximum speed of rotation and to avoid damage in strong winds, so constant surveillance was required. It was also important to forecast strong winds, particularly those associated with thunderstorms, as they often give little warning, and the wind could change to the opposite direction in minutes. As Wailes confirms:

> *As a storm of this kind moves across the country in a straight line like a wave curling back on itself, the hot air in front of it flows in from the opposite direction, rising to meet the storm. At any point just in front of the line of advance of the storm, therefore, the wind, which will have been blowing in the opposite direction to the storm, will drop and, as the storm sweeps over the spot, will suddenly blow strongly from the opposite direction ... in such a case the miller must turn ... the mill by hand or it will become tail-winded; the cloths or shutters will be blown out of the sails and possibly the mill will be blown over forwards in the case of a post mill.... By quartering the mill (i.e. turning the sails through ninety degrees) the edge of the sails will be presented to the wind and heavy gales have been withstood without serious damage in this way.*[11]

Constable's interest in the weather and ability to forecast the wind speed and direction and the movement of thunderstorms undoubtedly stems from his early experience as a windmiller. No doubt the local weather lore would have been passed on to him by his father or other experienced local millers employed by the family. Windmillers, like shepherds, ploughmen and mariners, were known for their knowledge of the local weather. David Lucas, in a letter written after Constable's death, stated that the artist 'worked as a Miller several Years and here told me that he made his earliest studies and most useful observations on atmospheric effects'.[12]

Leslie writes that Constable performed his duties as a windmiller 'carefully and well' and that he was known locally as the 'handsome miller'.[13] In Constable's description of 'Spring' in *English Landscape Scenery*, he alludes to windmillers recognising what would today be called 'scud' clouds as messengers of bad weather. The engraving 'Spring' (Plate 6 of this volume) contains a windmill and Leslie writes:

> *The windmill in an engraving from one of his sketches entitled 'spring,' is one of those in which he worked; and its outline, with the name of 'John Constable, 1792,' very accurately and neatly carved by him with a penknife, still remains on one of its timbers.... By a wind-miller every change of the sky is watched with peculiar interest; and it will appear from Constable's description of this plate that the time spent as one, was not wholly lost to him as a painter.*[14]

The descriptions of the engravings in *English Landscape Scenery* will be examined for meteorological content in section 2.10, but there is no doubt that Constable admired the sky from an early age.

In Constable's third lecture at the Royal Institution in 1836 he showed considerable working knowledge of windmills when discussing a small evening winter picture by Ruisdael (Plate 80), and further he showed how this knowledge could be used to relate the position of the sails to the future weather in the form of a predicted thaw. Leslie writes:

> *This picture ... represents an approaching thaw. The ground is covered with snow, and the trees are still white; but there are two windmills near the centre; the one has the sails furled, and is turned in the position from which the wind blew when the mill left off work; the other has the canvass on the poles, and is turned another way, which indicates a change in the wind; the clouds are opening in that direction, which appears by the glow in the sky to be the south, (the sun's winter habitation in our hemisphere,) and this change will produce a thaw before the morning. The concurrence of these circumstances shows that Ruisdael understood what he was painting.*[15]

The picture was copied by Constable, who was correct in his supposition that Ruisdael understood the weather in his paintings, and that the snow must have come from the east, the direction in which the first windmill is facing.

Overall Constable's windmiller days undoubtedly provided him with a purpose for watching the sky which then turned into an interest and a fascination. Just as Luke Howard had pondered on his Latin names for clouds as he gazed out of the window as a schoolboy, so Constable learned the ways of the weather and the different cloud types that accompanied different weather conditions at an early age.

We have already discussed how Constable regarded his own sky studies as experiments in science. He also paid tribute to other artists whom he thought had made a breakthrough in natural representation. For instance, Constable described a landscape by Cuyp (Plate 78) as:

> *a truly sublime Cuyp, still and tranquil, the town of Dort is seen with its towers and windmills under the insidious gleam of a feint watery sun, while a horrid rent in the sky almost frightens one, and the lightning descends to the earth over some poor cottages with a glide that is so much like nature that I wish I had seen it before I sent away my 'Salisbury'.*

Gombrich comments on this description:

> *Constable was convinced Cuyp had made a valid discovery. He had examined Cuyp's rendering of lightning and found it like nature.*

> *Not a transcript of course – who could transcribe a flash of lightening, and that in oil paint? – but a configuration which, in the context, became a valid cryptogram for that unpaintable glare. On that point, then, there was no need to experiment any more.... He [Constable] thought, and rightly, that only experimentation can show the artist a way out of the prison of style toward a greater truth. Only through trying out new effects never seen before in paint could he learn about nature.*[16]

As we have seen, Constable went much further than Gombrich suggests – he consulted contemporary science as well as art and nature in his search for the truth in his skies. However such was the fragmentary stage of meteorological science at this time that it could be argued that his experiences as a windmiller were just as valuable to him as his contemporary knowledge of meteorology.

2.4 Hampstead Heath

Hampstead Heath can be regarded as an 'atmospheric laboratory' that had an important influence on Constable's skies. From its elevated position Constable could look down on views in all directions, enhancing the size of the sky. Hampstead was a small village at that time, some seven kilometres north west of the centre of London. Constable first stayed in Hampstead in 1819, renting a house at No. 2 Lower Terrace in Hampstead within a few minutes' walking distance of the Heath. He rented a house in Hampstead every summer from 1819 to 1826, apart from 1824. In 1827 he moved there more permanently leasing No. 6 (now No. 40) Well Walk. If Constable had stayed in central London he would not have observed so easily the changing atmosphere from sunrise to sunset that is so spectacular from the heights of the Heath. If geography is important then so is the weather and climate of the area at that time. It has been taken for granted that Constable's skies are representative of skies to be seen in southern England, particularly the summer and autumn skies displayed in the 1820/22 skying period.[17] (Constable said in his letter to Fisher on 20 September 1821: 'We have had noble clouds and effects of light and dark and colour as is always the case in such seasons as the present.'[18]) The fact that the summer of 1821, when Constable started in earnest his extensive skying period, produced suitable weather conditions – rich selections of cumulus and nimbus, to use Howard's classification – is important. If the summer and autumn sky had remained void of such clouds that year then Constable's sky studies might never have been painted. Indeed 1821 was a remarkable year for weather. Luke Howard wrote:

> *The year [1821] was remarkable for fluctuations in the atmosphere, the length of the spaces described by the curve of the barometrical clock on the scale, amounting to about 100 inches, represents very well the free play of the currents north and south, through the whole of it ... and the result was, that 1821 makes its appearance among the years quite in the wet extreme.*[19]

This moist summer ensured that the grass would be bright green on the Heath and that the ponds would be full. Leslie wrote of this period in Constable's life:

> *Constable's art was never more perfect, perhaps never so perfect, as at this period of his life. I remember being greatly struck by a small picture, a view from Hampstead Heath, which I first saw at Ruysdael House, as Mr Fisher called his residence in Keppel Street. I have before noticed that what are commonly called warm colours are not necessary to produce the impression of warmth in landscape; and this picture affords, to me, the strongest possible proof of this. The sky is of the blue of an English summer day, with large, but not threatening, clouds of a silvery whiteness. The distance is of a deep blue, and the near trees and grass of the freshest green; for Constable could never consent to parch up the verdure of nature to obtain warmth. These tints*

are balanced by a very little warm colour on a road and gravel pit in the foreground, a single house in the middle distance, and the scarlet jacket of a labourer. Yet I know of no picture in which the mid-day heat of Midsummer is so admirably expressed; and were not the eye refreshed by the shade thrown over a great part of the foreground by some young trees, that border the road, and the cool blue of water near it, one would wish, in looking at it, for a parasol, as Fuseli wished for an umbrella when standing before one of Constable's showers. I am writing of this picture, which appears to have been painted in the open air, after an acquaintance with it of five-and-twenty years.[20]

Reynolds confirms that this description is of *Hampstead Heath with the House called 'The Salt Box'* (Plate 7) which he ascribes to 1821, although if Leslie was correct then it must have been painted in 1820.[21] Certainly the wet weather of 1821 may have enhanced the green of the foliage that year. The cumulus and nimbus clouds would have been a frequent occurrence in the summer of 1821 and although this argument is rather deterministic, undeniably the weather did play its part amongst other factors in producing Constable's remarkable skies.

2.5 Constable's letters

Fortunately many of Constable's letters and other writings have survived. His comments on the painting of skies are mostly restricted to the period 1821/22. On 20 September 1821 Constable wrote to his friend Fisher:

I have likewise made many skies and effects – for I wish it could be said of me as Fuselli says of Rembrandt, 'he followed nature in her calmest abodes and could pluck a flower on every hedge – yet he was born to cast a steadfast eye on the bolder phenomena of nature'. We have had noble clouds & effects of light & dark & color – as is always the case in such seasons as the present.[22]

This letter shows Constable's determination to perfect his skies and his understanding of the effects wrought on them by the seasons. The motivation for this sudden burst of sky studies will be discussed in detail later but one of the likely factors was the difficulty that Constable had with the skies of his early 'six-footers', which were considered obtrusive by art critics and others at the time. For instance Fisher relayed criticisms about the sky in *Stratford Mill* (1820) (Plate 36) to Constable in a letter. Leslie reports that:

On the 26th of September [1821], Fisher wrote to tell Constable of objections that were made to the sky in Mr. Tinney's picture, by a 'grand critical party' who had sat in judgement on it. 'After talking in vain for some time,' he continues, 'I brought them out of my portfolio two prints from Wouvermans and a Vander Neer, where the whole stress was laid on the sky, and that silenced them.'[23]

Then follows the famous letter of 23 October 1821 from Constable to Fisher, by which time Constable had completed a comprehensive series of sky studies. His letter confidently declares:

I have not been idle and have made more particular and general study than I have ever done in one summer, but I am most anxious to get into my London painting room, for I do not consider myself at work without I am before a six foot canvas – I have done a good deal of skying – I am determined to conquer all difficulties and that most arduous one among the rest.[24]

This certainly points to a connection between the skies in the six-footers and the sky studies. Constable could not omit or ignore clouds – the 'bolder phenomena of nature' – from his six-footers. They represented a considerable challenge, a challenge that he knew would be very difficult to overcome, and a challenge that he outlined in full in the same letter to Fisher:

That Landscape painter who does not make his skies a very material part of his composition – neglects to avail himself of most of his greatest aids. Sir Joshua speaking of the 'Landscape' of Titian Salvator Claude – says 'Even their skies seem to sympathise with the subject'. I have often been advised to consider my sky as a white sheet drawn behind the objects. Certainly, if the sky is obtrusive, as mine are, it is bad; but if it is evaded, as mine are not, it is worse; they must stand and always shall with me make an effectual part of the composition. It will be difficult to name a class of Landscape – in which the sky is not the 'key note' – the 'standard of scale' – and the chief 'Organ of sentiment'. You may conceive, then, what a white sheet would do for me, impressed as I am with these notions, and they cannot be erroneous. The sky is the source of light in nature and governs everything; even our common observations on the weather of every day are suggested by [it]. The difficulty [of skies] in painting is very great, both as to composition and execution; because with all their brilliancy and consequence, they ought not to come forward, or, indeed, be hardly thought of any more than extreme distances are; but these remarks do not apply to phenomena or accidental effects of sky, because they always attract particularly... I may say all this to you, though you do not want to be told that I know very well what I am about, and that my skies have not been neglected, though they have often failed in execution, no doubt, from an over-anxiety about them, which alone will destroy that easy appearance which Nature always has in all her movements.[25]

This remarkable series of statements confirms Constable's considerable passion for skies, expressing both his anxieties and confidence that he was at last close to being able to 'conquer all difficulties'. Constable's belief that the sky is the 'key note', the 'standard of scale', the 'chief organ of sentiment' and the 'source of light' that governs everything, was a completely new approach to landscape painting which contradicted contemporary wisdom. For most artists the landscape was the keynote, the standard of scale, and the chief organ of sentiment, and the sky and light were used merely to add mood to a picture. This emphasis on the sky was a unique but scientifically correct approach.

As well as wanting to improve the skies of his six-footers Constable was genuinely interested in and fascinated by his 'skying'. The 'pure sky' studies (i.e. there is no visible landscape, only sky), as opposed to the 'sky and landscape' studies, which he made in both 1821 and 1822, show a love of the open air and skies for their own sake. They were experiments in lighting, colour, perspective, cloud form, weather forecasting and in capturing rapidly changing clouds on canvas. Although Constable does not want the skies of his six-footers to be 'obtrusive', a sky can hardly be considered 'obtrusive' in a pure sky study. On 7 October 1822 Constable wrote to Fisher: 'I have made about 50 careful studies of skies tolerably large, to be careful.'[26] (Of these fifty skies we can only identify sixteen with any degree of certainty. See Appendix 1.)

Later in life, in a letter to George Constable on 12 December 1836, Constable wrote:

> *My observations on clouds and skies are on scraps and bits of paper, and I have never yet put them together so as to form a lecture, which I shall do, and probably deliver at Hampstead next summer.... If you want anything more about the atmosphere, and I can help you, write to me. Forster's is the best book – he is far from right, still he has the merit of breaking much ground.*[27]

Thus Constable is sufficiently confident of his knowledge of meteorology to state that 'he is far from right' when recommending Forster's meteorological text. It is a great pity that Constable did not live long enough to give his skies lecture, and of course none of his 'observations on clouds and skies' have survived apart from the annotations to his cloud studies.

2.6 The inscriptions to the sky studies of 1820/22

Constable's first detailed weather inscriptions were on his Lake District sketches of 1806 which are discussed in detail in the next chapter. They show a keen awareness of 'episodes' of weather that he tried to capture in his paintings. The language is very straightforward with virtually no specialist meteorological jargon, apart from the use of the word 'cumulostrati' in his annotations of Forster's book (which is discussed in section 2.7 below) and his apparent use of the Beaufort wind scale particularly in his 1820/22 sky study inscriptions.

Admiral Sir F. Beaufort (1774–1857) devised his famous wind scale, which was used originally with reference to a man-of-war of the period 1800–50, to go from 0 for calm to 12 for a hurricane.[28] The scale was modified in 1926 but the twelve-fold scale remains using the sailor's traditional notation as shown below:

The Beaufort wind scale

Force		*Force*	
0	Calm	6	Strong breeze
1	Light air	7	Near gale
2	Slight breeze	8	Gale
3	Gentle breeze	9	Strong gale
4	Moderate breeze	10	Storm
5	Fresh breeze	11	Violent storm
		12	Hurricane

Constable was aware of such a scale as he used a form of the Beaufort scale in twenty-three of the surviving forty-nine inscribed sky studies as shown in Table 12d. The words 'breeze' and 'wind' are interchangeable. Constable probably learned of the sailors' wind scales when working for his father who used to ship his grain up to London. He also spent nearly a month on board ship in April 1803 with Captain Torin, a friend of his father.

Table 10 gives a complete list of all the known sky studies that have weather notes inscribed on them that are dated between 1820 and 1822. There are fifty-four dated sky studies of which fifty-one

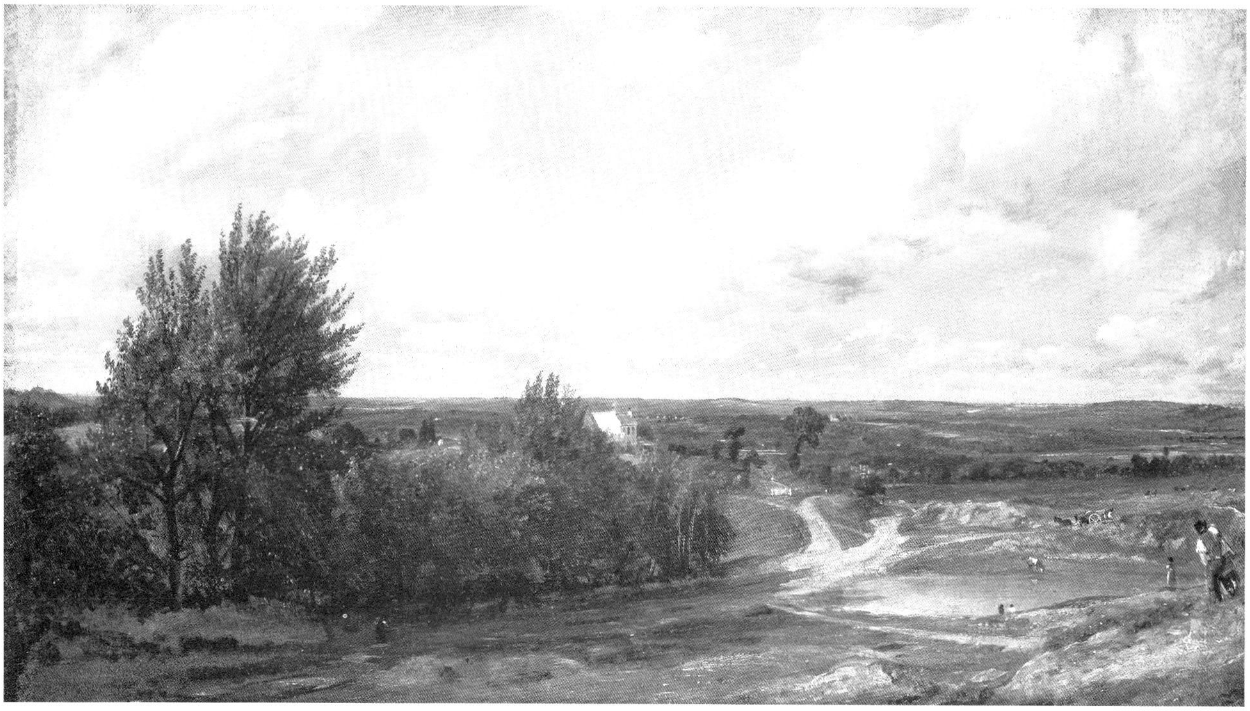

Plate 7 John Constable, *Hampstead Heath with the House called 'The Salt Box'*
Copyright Tate Gallery, London 1998

have weather-related inscriptions. Table 10 shows that of the fifty-one, four have been ascribed to 1820; twenty-six to 1821; and twenty-one to 1822. Of the fifty-four sky studies, nineteen (35 per cent) have been classified as pure sky studies. (For a full discussion of the problems of dating these and other sky studies that do not give the complete date see Appendix 1.)

The Graham Reynolds numbering scheme has been used for convenience in this section and in the tables which follow. Catalogue numbers are expressed as e.g. (R21.53). Reynolds has entries for fifty-one of the fifty-four sky studies in his 1984 catalogue. Three new inscriptions appear in the 1996 Reynolds catalogue relating to entries 20.78, 21.46 and 22.30A.[29]

The inscriptions to the sky studies are extremely revealing of Constable's meteorological understanding and his reasons for producing the sky studies. For instance he often recorded the date, the time of day, the direction he was facing, the wind speed and direction, and the current weather, e.g. '25th. Septr 1821 about from 2 to 3 afternoon looking to the north – Strong Wind at west, bright light coming through the Clouds which were lying one on another' (R21.52). On other occasions Constable goes further and talks of the weather he encountered either before or after he had worked on the painting; for example, on 27 September 1821 he made three different cloud studies at different times, all of which refer to previous rain:

> *Septr 27th 1821 – 10 morning, fine morning after Rainey night [R21.53]*
>
> *Noon 27 Sept very bright after rain / wind West [R21.54]*
>
> *4 afternoon 27 Septr 1821 wood bank of Vale very [?warm] & bright after rain [R21.55]*

Again this suggests that Constable liked to paint after rain, when the grass is moist and green and the leaves are glistening. On other occasions he notes the weather which occurred after his study: 'Septr 13th. one o'clock. Slight wind at North West, which became tempestuous in the afternoon, With Rain all the night following'(R21.50). These comments must have been written on the back of the study the following day, perhaps when it had dried out sufficiently to handle. This is the first pure sky study for which there are records and it has been dated by the present author as 1821.[30] The inscription suggests that Constable's aim in producing a pictorial weather diary was to enable him to produce sky studies which were so realistic that one could forecast the future weather from them. The possible link between wind direction and ensuing rainfall would be familiar to Constable from his windmiller days. Each of the studies listed in Table 10 is examined in detail in Appendix 1, but the data contained in all fifty-one weather inscriptions will now be scrutinised. The fifty-one surviving studies represent a significant sample of probably more than one hundred studies that were produced by Constable during 1820/22. Tables 11 and 12 show a breakdown of seven different aspects of the inscriptions, which are discussed in turn below.

2.6.1 The month of painting (Table 11a)

The first sky study is dated 17 October 1820 and the last 31 September 1822. This last study, dated 31 September 1822, was presumably painted on 1 October. By 7 October 1822 Constable had written to Fisher that he had made about fifty sky studies and he had probably done enough 'skying' by the beginning of October 1822 to satisfy his needs. Also by the middle of October 1822 he had left Hampstead and returned to his home in Charlotte Street. Table 11a shows that most of the 1821 studies were undertaken in September whereas the 1822 studies were mostly painted in July and August. In total, for all three years, September proves the most popular month with more than one third, nineteen (35 per cent), of the fifty-four studies.

The timing of the sky studies reflects the time that Constable was at Hampstead in the summer and autumn months of 1820/22. The days that he chose to paint skies presumably reflected the

Table 10
Dated sky studies and weather inscriptions 1820–22

1820	
(1) 17.10.20	Hampd. 17th October 1820 Stormy Sunset. Wind. W. (R20.77, 127 x 171, 56°F)
(2) 18.10.20	18 Oct 1820 – 4 to 5 1/2/ ... wind north west (R20.78, 197 x 318, 54°F)
(3) 25.10.20	Hampstead Heath – fine evening [...] wind N W October 25 1820. (R20.81, 140 x 245, 52°F)
(4) 28.10.20?	28th Octr. fine Evening Wind Gentle at S.W. (R20.82, 159 x 203, 50°F)
1821	
(5) 14.07.21	Hampstead July 14 1821 6 to 7 p.m. N.W. breeze strong. (R21.37, 254 x 274, 72°F)
(6) 18.07.21	Hampstead Heath from under 'The Terrace'; hot day, noon Painted on the spot 18 July 1821. (R21.38, 75°F)
(7) 19.07.21	1/2p 5 am 19th July looking East. The day beautiful at noon plain blue sky. (R21.39, 145 x 325, 78°F)
(8) 19.07.21	Evening of Coronation July 19. 1821. Westward by North – cloudy and tempestuous looking but did not turn out so. (R21.40, 241 x 292, 78°F)
(9) 25.07.21	July 25. 1821. looking due West Wind to W 5 afternoon sun behind a shower. (R21.41,167 x 222, 72°F)
(10) ?.08.21	5 Oclock afternoon: August 1821 very fine bright & wind after rain slightly in the morning. (R21.44, 250 x 298)
(11) 03.09.21	September 3d. Noon. very sultry. with large drops of Rain falling on my palate light air from S.W. (R21.45, 241 x 298, 78°F)
(12) 10.09.21	Sepr. 10 1821 Eleven o'clock Sultry with warm gentle [?rain] falling large heavy clouds [...] a heavy downpour and thunder. (R21.46, 216 x 292, 70°F)
(13) 10.09.21	Sepr. 10. 1821, Noon. gentle Wind at West. very sultry after a heavy shower with thunder. accumulated thunder clouds passing slowly away to the south East. very bright & hot. all the foliage sparkling [?with the] and wet. (R21.46a, 248 x 302, 70°F)
(14) 11.09.21	Hampstead, Sepr 11, 1821. 10. to 11. Morning under the sun – Clouds silvery grey, on warm ground Sultry. Light wind to the S.W. fine all day – but rain in the night following. (R21.47, 242 x 298, 71°F)
(15) 12.09.21	Sepr. 12. 1821. Noon. Wind fresh at West [...] Sun very Hot. looking southward exceedingly bright vivid & Glowing, very heavy showers in the Afternoon but a fine evening. High wind in the night. (R21.48, 241 x 298, 71°F)
(16) 12.09.21	Sepr 12. 1821. Sun setting over Harrow This appearance of the Evening was [?aft] just after a very heavy rain more rain in the night and a very [?high] wind which continued all the day following – [the 13th] while making this sketch observed the Moon rising very beautifully [?in the] due East over the heavy clouds from which the late showers had fallen., and West gentle [...] increasing from the North west. rather. (R21.49, 241 x 292, 71°F)
(17) ***13.09.21***	***Septr 13th. one o'clock. Slight wind at North West, which became tempestuous in the afternoon, With Rain all the night following. (R21.50, 248 x 303, 66°F)***
(18) 24.09.21	Sept. 24th ... 10 o'clock morning wind S.W. warm & fine till afternoon, when it rained & wind got more to the north. (R21.51, 248 x 305, 66°F)
(19) ***25.09.21***	***25th. Septr 1821 about from 2 to 3 afternoon looking to the north – Strong Wind at west, bright light coming through the Clouds which were lying one on another. (R21.52, 212 x 290, 66°F)***
(20) 27.09.21	Septr 27th 1821 – 10 morning, fine morning after Rainey night. (R21.53, 165 x 310, 63°F)
(21) 27.09.21	Noon 27 Sept very bright after rain wind West. (R21.54, 248 x 292, 63°F)
(22) 27.09.21	4 afternoon 27 Septr 1821 wood bank of Vale very [?warm] & bright after rain. (R21.55, 235 x 286, 63°F)
(23) ***28.09.21***	***Sep. 28 1821 Noon – looking North West windy from the S.W. large bright clouds flying rather fast very stormy night followed. (R21.57, 255 x 305, 65°F)***
(24) 02.10.21	Ocr. 2d. 1821. 8. to 9. very fine still morning. turned out a may day. (R21.58, 245 x 298, 61°F)
(25) 09.10.21	9th Octr 1821 Sun hot Wind southern with mist. (R21.59, 247 x 292, 60°F)
(26) 12.10.21	Very fine evening after a brilliant day, gentle wind South, 12th October, 1821. (R21.60, 247 x 285, 58°F)

Table 10 (continued)
Dated sky sketches and weather inscriptions 1820–22

1821 (continued)	
(27) 13.10.21	Octr-13th. 1821. – 4 to 5 afternoon – very fine with Gentle Wind at N.E. (R21.61, 248 x 298, 60°F)
(28) 30.10.21?	Hampstead Oct. 30th. very fine – gentle wind at south-west. (R21.63, 241 x 266, 57°F)
(29) 31.10.21	Hampstead 31st Oct. 1821. Very fine afternoon of a beautiful day, it began with rain. Wind fresh from West. (R21.64, 260 x 325, 60°F)
(30) 02.11.21	Novr. 2d 1821, Hampstead Heath windy afternoon. (R21.66, 248 x 298, 63°F)
1822	
(31) 18.04.22?	***April 18th [?] Showery Wind N. Easterly (R22.30A, 145 x 220, ?)***
(32) 04.07.22	Hampstead. July 4th, 1822 very fine and hot Wind, W Clouds very high and climbing. (R22.9, 321 x 495, 78°F)
(33) ***28.07.22***	***28th July 12 oclock noon. Very fine day, showery and [?] warm No. West under the sun. (R22.11, 290 x 480, 72°F)***
(34) 29.07.22	29 July 1822 looking east 10 in the morning – silvery clouds. (R22.12, 292 x 241, 74°F)
(35) 29(?).07.22	[Hamp]stead. Monday 2[..] July 1822 looking N E 3 P M [?previous to] a thunder squallwind N West. (R22.10, 311 x 521, 74°F)
(36) 30.07.22	July, 30th 1822. Noon under the Sun. (R22.13, 242 x 298, 67°F)
(37) 31.07.22	Evning, 31st July, 1822 Shower approaching. (R22.14, 165 x 298, 75°F)
(38) 31.07.22	July 31. 1822 Stormy sunset. (R22.15, 162 x 305, 75°F)
(39) ?.07.22	July – noon – Hampstead Heath – looking north – wind South east.(R22.45, 247 x 400)
(40) ***01.08.22***	***Augt 1. 1822 11 o clock A.M. very hot with large climbing Clouds under the Sun. wind westerly. (R22.16, 305 x 508, 68°F)***
(41) ***01.08.22***	***(R22.17, 472 x 584, 68°F)***
(42) ***12.08.22***	***Aug 12. 1822 (R22.18, 254 x 222, 75°F)***
(43) ***18?.08.22***	***Sunday, 11 to 12, very fine hot day, wind light at N.W. climbing electric clouds looking S.W. (R22.66, 80°F)***
(44) 25.08.22	Hampstead Heath. Sunday Augst. 25, 1822 After Sunset. (R22.19, 266 x 482, 70°F)
(45) ***26.08.22***	***August 26th 1822, noon, under the sun, very hot and bright, looking S.W. (R22.20, 70°F)***
(46) ***27.08.22***	***27 augt 11 o'clock Noon looking Eastward large silvery [clouds?] wind Gentle at S West. (R22.21, 475 x 575, 71°F)***
(47) ***31.08.22***	***5 – 6 oclock Eveng Augt 31st 1822. Large clouds to the Eastward – light wind [?West]. (R22.22, 470 x 580, 69°F)***
(48) ***05.09.22***	***5th September 1822, 10 o'clock. Morning looking South-East very brisk wind at West, very bright and fresh grey clouds running very fast over a yellow bed about half-way in the sky. Very appropriate for the coast at Osmington. (R22.23, 370 x 490, 73°F)***
(49) ***05.09.22***	***Sept.5. 1822. looking S.E. noon. Wind very brisk. & fresh. Clouds. moving very fast. with occasional very bright openings to the blue. (R22.24, 298 x 483, 73°F)***
(50) ***06.09.22***	***Sepr. 6. 1822 Noon. Gentle wind at west. hot & fine. (R22.26, 72°F)***
(51) 06.09.22	***Sept. 6th, 1822, looking S.E. – 12 to 1 oclock, wind brisk and west, fresh and bright, between showers, much the look of rain all the morning, with expect. Rain – but very fine, and Grand all the afternoon and sunny. (R22.25, 300 x 500, 72°F)***
(52) ***21.09.22***	***Sepr. 21. 1822. 1/2 pst one o clock, looking south. Wind very fresh at East, but warm. (R22.27, 287 x 483, 65°F)***
(53) ***21.09.22***	***Sepr. 21 1822. looking South brisk Wind at East Warm & fresh. 3 oclo afternoon. (R22.28, 305 x 492, 65°F)***
(54) ***31.09.22***	***31st Sepr 10-11 o'clock morning looking Eastward a gentle wind to East. (R22.30, 480 x 590, 56°F)***

Notes

1 Pure sky studies are denoted in bold italics (No. 23: 28 September 1821 has a very thin strip of landscape at the bottom but is classified as a pure sky study.)

2 The daily maximum temperature is given in degrees Fahrenheit extracted from Howard's *Climate of London* (1833 edition).

3 Three of the above sky studies (41, 42 and 44) only contain information about the date and/or time, but are included as they can still be compared with the historical weather records.

Table 11
Analysis of the fifty-four dated sky studies 1820–22

a) Month of painting

	1820	*1821*	*1822*	*Total*			*Average maximum temperature °F* *1820*	*1821*	*1822*
April			1	1	(2%)				
July		5	8	13	(24%)	J		75	73
August		1	8	9	(17%)	A		-	71
September		13	6	19	(35%)	S		68	70
October	4	6	1	11	(20%)	O	53	60	-
November		1	0	1	(2%)	N		63	

b) Hour of painting

5.30	8.30	10am	10.30	11am	11.30	Noon	12.30	1pm	1.30	2.30	3pm	4pm	4.30	5pm	5.30	6.30	After-noon	Even.	Sunset
21.39	21.58	21.51	21.47	21.46	**22.21**	21.38	**22.25**	**21.50**	**22.27**	**21.52**	22.10	21.55	20.78	21.41	**22.22**	21.37	21.64	20.81	20.77
		21.53	**22.30**	**22.16**	**22.66**	21.45					**22.28**		21.61	21.44			21.66	20.82	21.49
		22.12				21.46a												21.40	22.15
		22.23				21.48												21.60	22.19
						21.54												22.14	
						21.57													
						22.11													
						22.13													
						22.20													
						22.24													
						22.26													
						22.45													

Notes

1 The time of day is mentioned in 48 out of 54 sketches (89%). These 48 can be subdivided as follows: morning = 12 (25%); noon = 12 (25%); afternoon = 15 (31%); evening/sunset = 9 (19%).

2 Numbers refer to Reynolds' 1984 and 1996 Constable catalogues. Those in bold are pure sky studies.

weather conditions and the state of the sky as well as his social diary. However there is evidence that although Constable may have preferred to paint landscape and clouds in the spring because of the heightened contrast between the clouds and the fresh green grass, he appreciated the enhanced beauty of autumnal clouds. Two quotes from his book *English Landscape Scenery* make these points, firstly from the text accompanying 'Spring':

> *This plate may perhaps give some idea of one of those bright and animated days of the early year, when all nature bears so exhilarating an aspect; when at noon large garish clouds, surcharged with hail or sleet, sweep with their broad cool shadows the fields, woods, and hills; and by the contrast of their depths and bloom enhance the value of the vivid greens and yellows, so peculiar to this season.*[31]

The summer and autumn skies are praised in the introduction: 'England, with her climate of more than vernal freshness, and in whose summer skies, and rich autumnal clouds, the observer of Nature may daily watch her endless varieties of effect.'[32]

It was pleasanter to paint in the open air in the summer and early autumn than in spring when the weather is still too cold to keep the fingers nimble. The air temperature in September is usually higher than in April or May. The mean monthly temperatures for Somerset House in London for 1820–22 are given below in degrees Fahrenheit in Table 13.[33]

Table 12
Analysis of weather inscriptions on fifty-one sky studies

a) References to past weather
21.44, 21.46a, 21.49, 21.53, 21.54, 21.55, 21.60, 21.64, **22.25** (9 out of 51 = 18%)

b) References to future weather
21.39, 21.40, 21.47, 21.48, 21.49, **21.50**, 21.51, **21.57**, 21.58, 22.10, **22.25** (11 out of 51 = 22%)

c) Quoted wind direction

N	NE	E	SE	S	SW	W	NW
	21.61	**22.27**	22.45	21.59	20.82	20.77	20.78
	22.30A	**22.28**		21.60	21.45	21.41	20.81
		22.30			21.47	21.46a	21.37
					21.51	21.48	**21.50**
					21.57	21.49	22.10
					21.63	**21.52**	**22.11**
					22.21	21.54	**22.66**
						21.64	
						22.9	
						22.16	
						22.22?	
						22.23	
						22.25	
						22.26	

Note
36 out of 51 (71%) mention the wind direction. 14 out of 36 (39%) mention a west wind and 28 out of 36 a westerly (SW+W+NW) component (78%)

d) Quoted wind speed – a form of the Beaufort scale

Still	**Light air**	**Slight**	**Gentle**	**Moderate**	**Fresh**	**Strong**
Calm	Force 1	Force 2	Force 3	Force 4	Force 5	Force 6
21.58	21.45	21.47	20.82		21.48	21.37
		21.50*	21.46a		21.64	**21.52**
		22.22	21.49		**22.24**	
		22.66	21.60		**22.25**	
			21.61		**22.27**	
			21.63		**22.28**	
			22.21			
			22.26			
			22.30			

Notes
1 Both 'slight' and 'light' have been used for Force 2 in past versions of the Beaufort scale.
2 Other terms used: 'windy' – **21.57**, 21.66; 'very brisk' – **22.23**.
3 26 out of 51 (51%) mention wind speed, of which 23 out of the 26 (88%) use a form of the Beaufort scale.

(continued overleaf)

Table 12 (continued)
Analysis of weather inscriptions on 51 sky studies

e) Quoted direction of view with time and wind direction

N	NE	E	SE	S	SW	W	NW
21.52	22.10	21.39	**22.23**	21.48	**22.20**	21.41	21.40
W 2.30pm	NW 3pm	5.30am	W 10am	W noon	noon	W 5pm	Evening
22.45		**22.12**	**22.24**	**22.27**	**22.66**		**21.57**
SE noon		10am	noon	E 1.30pm	NW 11.30am		SW noon
		22.21	**22.25**	**22.28**			
		SW noon	W 12.30pm	E 3pm			
		22.30					
		E 10.30am					

Note
18 out of 51 (35%) mention direction of view. Of the 18, 11 (61%) are pure sky

Table 13
Mean monthly air temperature at Somerset House, London 1820–22

	J	F	M	A	M	J	J	A	S	O	N	D
1820	33	38	42	50	53	57	61	60	56	48	43	41
1821	39	37	44	52	51	55	59	63	61	52	49	46
1822	41	45	48	48	57	64	64	63	57	53	50	38

October 1820 was not a particularly warm month and Table 10 shows that the maximum temperatures for 17 and 25 October 1820 were in the low fifties Fahrenheit. Constable's hands must have been cold for those 1820 studies! However the temperatures were warmer for most of the rest of his sky studies. For instance September 1821 was a comparatively warm month averaging 61°F. Using weather records recorded by Luke Howard[34] it is possible to see what was the maximum temperature on each day of the sky studies. This maximum temperature is given for each dated study in Table 10, and the averages for each month (taken from just the days he produced the sky studies) are given in Table 11a. It can be seen that Constable preferred warm days when the maximum temperature was at least well into the sixties Fahrenheit. For example the average maximum temperature of the thirteen studies made in September 1821 was 68°F; also note that the study done on 2 November 1821 was a warm day with a maximum temperature of 63°F.

The pure sky study dated 18 April (R22.30A) and catalogued by Reynolds in 1996 as produced in 1822 is most unusual, assuming that the date has been correctly transcribed. The size is unusually small for a pure sky study and gives no clue as to the year. The weather evidence gives some support for 1822, as shown in Appendix 1.

2.6.2 The hour of painting (Table 11b)

The hour of painting is of vital interest and tells a fascinating story. Table 11b shows the timing of forty-eight out of the fifty-four studies, most to the nearest half hour. Constable was therefore extremely diligent in giving the time of the studies, which was important to him for a number of reasons. Firstly the hour relates to the position of the sun and hence the lighting of the picture. This is especially important for the pure sky studies as there are no shadows on the landscape from which to estimate the time. Even when painting in the open air with his friend John Dunthorne, according to Lucas, they would paint one view at only a certain time each day. When the shadows changed they postponed working on a particular study until the same hour the following day. Table

10 clearly shows that noon was Constable's preferred hour, with a quarter (25%) of the studies completed at this time. Noon is an excellent time to paint skies in that the sun is at its highest in the sky to the south, casting the smallest shadows of the day, and moving shadow is less pronounced either side of noon. In *English Landscape Scenery*, when discussing *Stoke by Neyland, Suffolk* (Plate 16), Constable remarks on 'the solemn stillness of Nature in a Summer's Noon ... and the sun shining full on the south side of the Church.'[35] 'Nature in a Summer's Noon' would be an appropriate subtitle for many of Constable's works.

Secondly all of the pure sky studies were painted between 10am and 3pm, apart from one (R22.22), which was painted at 5.30pm. Eleven of the seventeen pure sky studies were painted between 11am and 1pm, suggesting that Constable was looking to perfect the noon sky. Many of Constable's finished works represent noon; for example *The Hay Wain* (Plate 38) was originally entitled *Landscape: Noon* when he sent it to exhibition, and *The Cornfield* (Plate 48) also represents noon. This is therefore important new evidence that the pure sky studies were stimulated by a desire to improve the skies of his large finished works.

Thirdly Constable built up a selection of skies at all times of the day from 5.30am, at dawn, through to sunset. There is at least one study for each hour so that whatever time Constable wanted to represent he had a sky to refer to. Whether this was a conscious decision on his part, or whether circumstances just led to this complete coverage is impossible to tell. Whatever the reason it is remarkable that he recorded the hour so religiously, which again confirms his desire to achieve scientific accuracy in his work.

In the letterpress written in 1833/34 to accompany *Summer Morning* Constable wrote:

> *Nature is never seen, in this climate at least, to greater perfection than at about nine o'clock in the mornings of July and August, when the sun has gained sufficient strength to give splendour to the landscape, 'still gemmed with the morning dew', without its oppressive heat, and it is still more delightful if vegetation has been refreshed with a shower during the night.*[36]

This perfection did not inspire any of the sky studies documented to be painted at exactly 9am but there is one study at 8.30am and four at 10am (the most painted hour apart from noon). The reference to recent rain leads on to the next section which looks at references to past weather.

2.6.3 References to past weather (Table 12a)

Past weather is mentioned in nine out of the fifty-one weather inscriptions, of which eight refer to previous rain. Eight of these nine are of 1821 so it would appear that Constable was more concerned to note earlier rainfall when engaged in studies of sky and landscape, as opposed to pure sky studies, most of which were made during 1822. This is not surprising since, as already discussed, Constable liked to paint the landscape after rain, and the sky colours are not influenced by recent rain to the same degree as are landscape colours. Nevertheless the current sky is always a consequence of recent weather, and Constable was no doubt aware that rain cleans the air and improves visibility as well as freshening the vegetation. As Ruskin wrote in *Modern Painters V* some years later: 'Every colour, wet, is twice as brilliant as it is when dry.'[37]

The recording of the past weather again confirms that Constable was interested in portraying 'episodes' of weather in his works rather than just a moment in time.

2.6.4 References to future weather (Table 12b)

Constable makes eleven references to future weather of which eight mention rain and the other three refer to the fact that the days turned out well: 'The day beautiful at noon plain blue sky' (R21.39), 'turned out a may day' (R21.58) and 'grand all the afternoon and sunny' (R22.25). These references to future weather show Constable's interest in predicting how the weather was likely to change. Again, his scientific–empirical approach of keen observation would have enabled him to see if there was any common appearance of the sky that led to rain or shine. Two of the annotations refer to both past and future weather (R21.49 & R22.25), amounting almost to a weather diary.

Table 14
Wind directions at Stratford recorded by Howard

	N	NE	E	SE	S	SW	W	NW	Variable
1820									
October	3	5	2	2	3	7	2	7	-
1821									
July	3	1	2	3	2	4	6	9	1
August	1	3	6	1	3	7	2	8	-
September	1	1	1	2	-	9	7	7	2
October	2	2	1	5	1	11	1	8	-
Total	7	7	10	11	6	31	16	32	3
1822									
July	3	-	-	2	2	11	3	8	2
August	1	1	4	1	-	4	9	11	-
September	3	9	4	1	-	5	1	7	-
October	-	1	3	8	1	10	2	4	2
Total	7	11	11	12	3	30	15	30	4

Note
Stratford is 8 miles east of Hampstead

2.6.5 *Quoted wind direction (Table 12c)*

More than two-thirds of the sky study inscriptions (71 per cent) mention the wind direction, of which westerly winds dominated. Indeed twenty-eight of the thirty-six that mention wind direction (79 per cent), note a wind from the westerly quarter, from south west through to north west. This is the prevailing wind direction, and weather records for nearby Stratford (see Table 14) show that during the months of July, August, September and October in 1821/22 the recorded wind was from the westerly quarter for just over 60 per cent of those days. Howard records that south-west and north-west winds were more frequent than westerly winds but there is a margin of error regarding the exact direction. If we look at this period as a whole then it appears that Constable may have deliberately chosen to paint on those days when there was a westerly wind. On average about three out of five days had westerly winds in the period under consideration, whereas four out of five of Constable's annotations state a westerly wind. Such days would have produced more of Constable's favourite cumulus clouds, despite his determination to represent typical English weather and climate.

The last three annotations in 1822 recorded an easterly wind showing fair weather cumulus clouds. The other wind directions get little mention although Table 14 shows that all of them occurred on several days in both 1821 and 1822.[38]

2.6.6 *Quoted wind speed (Table 12d)*

Constable's use of a form of the Beaufort wind scale in twenty-six of the fifty-one weather inscriptions has already been mentioned above. Table 12d shows that Force 3 – a gentle wind speed – was the most common one to be mentioned. Working in the open air on Hampstead Heath would leave Constable exposed to the full force of the wind, and one would suppose that a strong wind might hinder his work. Fifteen of the studies were done in winds of Force 3 or less but eight were done in Force 5 or Force 6. Moreover Constable used the terms 'windy' and 'very brisk' on a further three occasions. The wind did not seem to put him off his skying, indeed it encouraged him by carrying the clouds quickly over the Heath, giving movement to the scene.

2.6.7 *Quoted direction of view (Table12e)*

In some of Constable's Hampstead sky studies it is possible to tell the direction of view from the painting itself – for instance the church at Harrow is a familiar beacon (e.g. R21.44, R21.49). He did not need to state the direction of view for such studies. Of the fifty-one weather inscriptions he mentions the direction of view in eighteen of them of which twelve relate to pure sky studies. It is not easy to work out the direction of view in a pure sky study, unless the position of the sun and time of day are evident. Table 12e shows that ten of the directions of view are towards the south-east quadrant following the sun in the late morning. Table 12e also shows the time at which the studies were painted and the wind direction, when given. This confirms that most of these studies towards the south-east quadrant were done around noon. The wind direction is also given in thirteen of these studies. It is interesting to compare the direction of view with the wind direction. Did Constable prefer to paint these open air studies into the wind, or with the wind at his back, or at right angles to the wind? Table 15 shows the direction of view and the wind direction for these thirteen studies.

It can be seen that seven of the thirteen studies were painted at right angles to the wind, and that on most of those occasions the wind was Force 5 or 6. This would allow Constable to watch a panorama of clouds moving quickly past. For instance, on 28 September 1821 (R21.57) he wrote: 'looking North West windy from the S.W. large bright clouds flying rather fast'. On two occasions the study was painted into the wind, and in the case of the 31 September study (R22.30) the easterly wind was recorded as gentle. This 31 September study is interesting because the cloud perspective is unusual. The clouds appear to rise steeply at an alarming and apparently impossible angle. However the fact that the study is painted into the wind means that the visible streets of cumulus clouds would be moving directly overhead and would give an impression similar to that observed by Constable. On the four other occasions the wind was at 135 degrees, which is half way between being at right angles to the wind and having the wind behind. The study painted on 31 August 1822 (R22.22) could be an example of the wind being behind the painter, but the inscription is not clear: 'Large clouds to the Eastward – light wind [?West]'. Howard recorded a west wind for that day, but it is not clear whether the view is to the east, or whether there were just large clouds to the east. The picture is consistent with the opinion that the view is to the east with the sun and wind behind Constable.

It would seem therefore that Constable preferred to paint at right angles to the wind, particularly for the pure sky studies. It must be noted, however, that if Constable was looking to the south, towards the noon-day sun, then the frequent westerly wind would be at right angles to the view irrespective of the cloud perspective. The wind direction and angle of view are very important in trying to understand the perspective of the sky studies.

Table 15
Direction of view versus wind direction

Study	*Direction of view*	*Wind direction*	*Angle*	*Comments*	*Wind speed*
21.52	**North**	**West**	**90**	**Right angles**	**F6**
22.45	North	South east	135		
22.10	North east	North west	90	Right angles	
22.21	**East**	**South West**	**135**		**F3**
22.30	**East**	**East**	**0**	**Into wind**	**F3**
22.23	**South east**	**West**	**135**		**Very brisk**
22.25	**South east**	**West**	**135**		**F5**
21.48	South	West	90	Right angles	F5
22.27	**South**	**East**	**90**	**Right angles**	**F5**
22.28	**South**	**East**	**90**	**Right angles**	**F5**
22.66	**South west**	**North west**	**90**	**Right angles**	**F2**
21.41	West	West	0	Into wind	
21.57	**North west**	**South west**	**90**	**Right angles**	**Windy**

Note
Bold denotes a pure sky study

2.6.8 Summary of interpretations of the 1820/22 sky study weather inscriptions

This detailed analysis of Constable's weather inscriptions on the fifty-one surviving sky studies has enabled much new light to be shed on Constable's meteorological understanding and the way in which he used this knowledge to paint his skies. The main findings are as follows:

- September was the most popular month for his sky studies (35 per cent of all sky studies were made in this month) followed by July (25 per cent). He normally liked the air temperature to be well into the sixties Fahrenheit.

- He painted a selection of cloud studies at virtually every hour from dawn to dusk to provide an hourly catalogue of skies.
- His preferred hour was noon with twelve sky studies, followed by 10am with four studies. There are also nine evening/sunset studies.
- All but one of the pure sky studies were painted between 10am and 3pm.
- Nine inscriptions refer to past weather of which eight refer to previous rain.
- Eleven inscriptions refer to future weather of which eight refer to rain later.
- Of the thirty-six studies that mention the wind direction, twenty-eight refer to westerly winds (SW + W +NW), i.e. about four out of five. This is a greater proportion of westerlies than actually occurred: records show that westerlies actually occurred in the relevant months on approximately three days out of five.
- Constable was fully familiar with a form of the Beaufort wind scale and used the appropriate terminology on twenty-three studies. Altogether wind speed was mentioned on twenty-six studies, i.e. half.
- Of the eighteen studies which give the direction of view, twelve are pure sky studies. Of the thirteen studies that give both the direction of view and the wind direction, seven show that Constable painted at right angles to the wind, and two studies were painted into the wind. The direction in which he painted in relation to the wind direction is very important in trying to understand the cloud perspective in the studies.

The annotations to the sky studies are therefore an extremely valuable source of information regarding Constable's meteorological knowledge and the purpose of the sky studies. They suggest that the single most important reason for the pure sky sky studies was for Constable to perfect the noon skies of his six-footers.

2.7 Constable's annotations to Forster's book

Thomas Forster (1789–1860) was a brilliant young writer and dilettante natural scientist, who became a friend of Luke Howard, and published the first edition of his book *Researches About Atmospheric Phaenomena* when he was just twenty-four years old. It was one of the first meteorological texts to deal with explanations rather than just descriptions of the physical phenomena of the atmosphere. It was written in a non-technical style to describe the concepts of meteorology to the intelligent reader as well as to provide useful summaries of atmospheric phenomena for other scientists. As such, although it is a 'text book' in physical meteorology dealing with the common weather events experienced in Britain, it would also have been of great interest to anyone curious about the weather.

Forster's book appeared in three editions. The first edition was published in June 1813 by Underwood at seven shillings.[39] It devoted a major part of the first chapter to Howard's cloud classification. The second edition, 'corrected and enlarged with a series of engravings, illustrative of the modifications of the clouds, etc.' was published two years later in 1815 by Baldwin at a cost of ten shillings and sixpence. The third edition appeared in 1823, published by Harding, Mavor, and Lepard at fifteen shillings, containing also a Calender of Nature based on Forster's own observations, from 1818 onwards, at Hartwell in Sussex. The book was popular and highly regarded as its run of three editions in ten years shows. In the introduction to the third edition Forster wrote: 'Two large impressions of this work having been sold, the Author has yielded to the solicitations of his friends in preparing for the press a third', but there is no record of how large were the sales of previous editions. As a general text book on atmospheric phenomena it had no equal in the English language until Howard himself published *Seven Lectures on Meteorology* in 1837.

Constable owned a second-hand copy of the second edition. This came to light when books from Constable's library, which are still in the Constable family collection, were catalogued in the early 1970s.[40] The inside cover of Constable's copy is inscribed 'Constable' and also '6/- Published at 10/6 scarce' (the latter phrase does not appear to be in Constable's hand). It was probably written by a bookseller and confirms that Constable's copy was bought second-hand. It was indeed published at ten shillings and six pence, and was presumably out of print by 1823 when the third edition emerged.

Two hypotheses therefore present themselves as to when Constable acquired the book: the first is that the book was bought second-hand some time before 1823; the second is that Constable did not buy the book until much later, in the late 1820s or early 1830s by which time probably all editions were scarce. We can only speculate as to which is correct. In the British Museum duplicate book sale at Sotheby's on 21 May 1818 a copy of the first edition of Forster's book was sold for one shilling, which hardly suggests that the first edition was a rare book at that time. At a similar sale on 27 February 1831 a first edition again fetched only two shillings and sixpence, while a second edition sold for nine shillings. Thus the second edition was selling at just below its original cost and at three shillings more than Constable's copy. If bought before 1823, the book would still be quite new, although not necessarily in good condition. If bought much later, its condition might have deteriorated sufficiently to place it at a price one third cheaper than the second edition sold by the British Museum.

Constable was friendly with the Carpenters, who were booksellers and publishers in Old Bond Street, London. James Carpenter and his son William supplied books to Constable for many years. It seems that William Carpenter, as well as appreciating Constable's art, also had an interest in clouds, for Constable wrote to him in 1833:

> *Dear Carpenter ... Your remark about the purple in the sky put me to a sad plunge (for it was quite just). It has caused me to go all over it again, and the divil of a tug I had with it, but it is now less objectionable. I have now got some light in my eyes, and some wind in my face. I am sure you will like it better. What a glorious morning is this for clouds.*[41]

It is not clear which painting Constable is referring to, but Forster's book would have been of great interest to both William Carpenter and Constable. Unfortunately there is no record of a sale.

It is not therefore possible to state exactly when Constable acquired his copy of Forster's book. By 1821 Constable was in his mid-forties and showed himself to be fully abreast of meteorological terminology through his letters and the annotations to his sky studies. There is every reason to believe that, in his search for inspiration to paint skies the way he wanted to, he would seek out a meteorological text to help him. The cloud sketches in Forster's book are crude but nevertheless would help Constable to understand Howard's classification better. His contacts with the Carpenters, who supplied him with many second-hand books, could well have produced Forster's book at a time when Constable was actively engaged in mental anguish about his skies. In making all his sky studies of that year, he would be constantly thinking, talking, writing and possibly reading about skies. Constable may well have bought the book in the autumn of 1821 or early 1822, which might then have sparked the large number of pure cloud studies of that year.

If we accept the fact that Constable bought the book second-hand, then we might ask whether or not he wrote all the annotations. Certainly no-one has expressed any doubts and the handwriting, in pencil, has been identified as Constable's.[42] On pages vii and viii of the Preface, a line is drawn down the right-hand margin and over the page, to mark the following paragraph:

> *Meteorology considered as a subject of amusement seems to have some advantages over many other pursuits; in as much as it may be studied and will afford interest in places unfavourable*

to the cultivation of other sciences. The botanist, who delights in the diversification of nature exhibited in the endless variety of the forms and colours of flowers; or the naturalist, who finds amusement in contemplating the habits of animals, and the adaptation of the structure of each to its mode of life, cannot indulge their inclination except in habitable countries, or where the vegetation and life abound. But on the barren mountain's rugged vortex, in the uniform gloom of the desert, or on the trackless surface of the ocean, we may view the interesting electrical operations which are going on above, manifested in the formation and changes of the clouds, which bear water in huge masses from place to place, or throw it down in torrents on the earth and waters; and occasionally creating whirlwinds and water spouts; or producing the brilliant phaenomena of meteors and of lightening; and constantly ornamenting the sky with the picturesque imagery of coloured clouds and golden haze. The atmosphere and its phaenomena are everywhere, and thunder rolls, and rainbows glitter in all conceivable situations, and we may view them whether it may be our lot to dwell in the frozen countries of polar ice, in the mild climates of the temperate zone, or in the parched regions which lay more immediately under the path of the sun.

This passage would surely appeal to Constable – someone who rarely wandered out of south-east England. It would content him to know that nearly all atmospheric phenomena are likely to be experienced at any one location, given sufficient time. Hampstead Heath provided the venue for all the sky studies of 1821/22.

A short line in the margin of page x picks out the following sentence: 'The heads of the ancient Greek philosophers are of a remarkably fine form for intelligence.' Constable had been interested in physiognomy since as early as 1793, when he acquired Lavater's book on the subject.[43]

A line in the right hand margin of page xii is found against the following paragraph:

But the stream of time is a fluctuating torrent, and intellectual excellence seems to flourish at alternative periods. Shortly after learning again began to flourish, and the energies of the human mind again exerted themselves according to the particular genius of individuals, there appeared those who delighted in aerial phaenomena, and Saussure, De Luc, Bertholon and others at length roused the attention of mankind to the production of our atmosphere.

Constable appears interested in the reawakening of interest in meteorology, as well as other natural sciences. His Hampstead lectures on the rise of landscape art, pick out the 'particular genius of individuals' that paved the way to scientific understanding.[44]

The last three lines of a sentence occupying the whole of page xiv are marked by Constable:

The ruins of stupendous cities once the ornament of the east; the numerous fortifications, walls, temples, aqueducts, and other works of art, now nothing but the desolated habitations of wild animals, and the traces left of sciences which, like fruitless flowers, bloomed in the spring of time only to decay, are monuments of human fatality which must impress reflecting persons with gloomy notions of the instability of society, and incline us to fear that, in spite of all the efforts of genius and of art of modern times, the light of knowledge which rose in the east, and civilized the oriental nations, will set on the western parts of the world, and leave us ere long a monument to future ages of the fluctuating nature of human perfection, unless by a strict attention to the improvement of the physical organization of our species, conjoined with the adoption of some general plan of education superior to any hitherto enforced, we should permanently improve the moral and intellectual character of future generations, without which all the scientific records imaginable would be to them only as cyphers scrawled on the barrenness of intellect.

This sentence is echoed by Constable in his descriptions of *Old Sarum* (1829; plate 57 in this volume) in *English Landscape Scenery*, and in the notes accompanying *Stonehenge* (exhibited 1836; Plate 63 in this volume).[45]

The rest of the annotations relate to the meteorological text. On page 9, under the heading 'Of the Cirrus', Constable has written 'doubtful' in the margin against the following sentence: '[T]he long continued appearance, and the multiform and everchanging configuration of this (the cirrus) and the other modifications, unattended by rain, and accompanied by dry, variable, and generally easterly winds is indicative of a very peculiar state of the electric atmosphere.' Constable's remark seems to be directed towards the last phrase; in other words he doubts whether the conditions outlined are 'indicative of a very peculiar state of the electric atmosphere'. Meteorological theory was preoccupied at that time with the effect of atmospheric electricity on precipitation and cloud form.[46] Howard in his description of cirrus in 1833 stated that 'the upward direction of the fibres, or tufts of this cloud is found to be a decided indication of the decomposition of vapour preceding rain: the downward as decidedly indicating evaporation and fair weather. In each case they point towards the place of the Electricity which is evolved all the time.'[47] It is very difficult to understand today the importance that atmospheric electricity was given within meteorological theory at the beginning of the nineteenth century. It was quite common to use a rod of iron and pith balls to measure atmospheric electricity accompanying various weather conditions. Howard devotes a chapter of *The Climate of London* to observations of atmospheric electricity.[48] The 'peculiar state of the electric atmosphere' referred to by Forster probably means that both positive and negative charges were observed accompanying 'fair weather' cirrus on different occasions. Constable may have been concerned that Forster was linking stable weather conditions with apparently unstable electrical conditions, or he may not have been convinced that atmospheric electricity was as important as Forster makes out.

On page 9, under the heading 'Of the Cumulus' a whole phrase is written by Constable in the margin opposite the beginning of the section which states: 'The cumulus is a convex aggregate of watery particles increasing upwards from a horizontal base.' Unfortunately it cannot be deciphered as the pencil appears to have been washed off – but it probably referred to the mention of the horizontal base which is often a key feature of a cumulus cloud. (At some time the whole book appears to have been immersed in water or perhaps drenched by a heavy shower.) Nevertheless the annotation shows Constable's interest in cumulus – perhaps his favourite cloud. In the right-hand margin there is a line against the following sentence: 'It is commonly of a dense structure, formed in the lower atmosphere and moving along in the current of wind which is next to the earth.' Constable was no doubt familiar, from his keen observations and days as a windmiller, with wind shear and the common phenomena of clouds at different heights moving in different directions, the small cumulus tending to move in the same direction as the wind close to the ground.

The next sentence is marked with a double line and a word which cannot be read is found in the margin: 'Its first appearance is generally a small irregular spot, which becomes the nucleus on which it forms.' Howard's cumulus clouds were what we would probably call 'fair weather cumulus' today (Plate 10). If they grew larger they were classed as cumulostrati as long as they did not produce precipitation, or nimbus if they did. The lifespan of a typical 'fair weather cumulus' is about half an hour, making it a particularly difficult cloud to paint.

A line in the right-hand margin of pages 10 and 11 appears against the following paragraph describing the formation of cumulus:

> *The sun's rays warming first the surface of the earth, and their radiation causing warmth to be propagated upward, this warmth converts water on the earth's surface into vapour, which rises and exerts its electrical force on that which the nocturnal decrease of temperature had not decomposed, and which therefore remained diffused.*

> *The latter, in passing through the atmosphere to give place to that from below, changes its climate, arrives in a colder air, and is thereby decomposed and thrown into a state of visible cloud.*

This explanation was written at a time before the concept of thermals – the upward convection of moist air – was suggested by Brandes in 1820.[49] Constable was obviously interested in the processes leading to the formation of cumulus clouds, although it is doubtful that Forster's poor explanation would have been of much inspiration to him. Badt denies that an interest in atmospheric physics would affect Constable's painting of clouds,[50] but Constable never painted a cumulus cloud when the other painted weather elements were not conducive to its formation.

These notes and markings by Constable in the section 'Of the Cumulus' confirm his interest in that cloud type, and demonstrate conclusively that he knew that the cloud he perhaps painted most often was called cumulus.

On page 12, under the heading 'Of the Stratus', a line in the right-hand margin picks out the following two sentences: 'It may properly be called the cloud of the night, as it frequently makes its appearance about sunset, and disappears soon after sunrise. When ascending in the atmosphere, it often seems at a certain elevation to take the irregular hemispherical form and become a cumulus.' In the margin is written 'but not in [bad?] weather'. Constable is here questioning a confusion in Howard's classification, in which only advection and radiation mist or fog are identified as stratus. It often occurs under anticyclonic conditions associated in summer with anything but bad weather. The low-lying cloud that is almost identical in appearance but accompanies 'bad weather',[51] would today also be called stratus, or stratus fractus, if not precipitating, or nimbostratus if precipitating. These clouds are formed in very different weather conditions, usually associated with frontal systems accompanying depressions. Confusingly, Howard would have called low-lying, non-precipitating clouds (not of advectional or radiational origin) cirrostratus, or nimbus if precipitating. In Howard's classification, cirrostratus is an all-embracing term for layer clouds. The confusion was removed by redefining stratus in 1887 to include all cloud below one kilometre.[52] Thus Constable, on the basis of his keen observations of the atmosphere, points to an area of confusion in Howard's classification.

On page 14, a line in the right-hand margin is made against 'The fine mists which creep, as it were, along the valleys of a summer's evening, are generally white, and, when seen at a distance by moonlight, have a very fanciful appearance. They are strikingly contrasted to the yellow fogs of November.' Constable was probably interested in the different colouring of summer stratus and winter smog (the word 'smog' – a mixture of smoke and fog was not defined until 1906). Interestingly, Constable never painted smog in his views of London, restricting his outdoor painting to the seasons other than winter.

In the top margin of page 19, under the heading 'Of the Cirrostratus' is written 'heat, wind[s?] electricity moisture', a list of the meteorological factors that, taken together, Constable would have believed to control cloud formation. These words are not directly linked to the text, but suggest that Constable was jotting down his general thoughts about cloud formation as he read. This again confirms that Constable was very interested in the processes of cloud formation and not just their form.

The paragraph immediately following is almost encircled by Constable, one phrase being underlined twice. The underlined phrase reads: 'All clouds are capable of becoming brighter and darker, according to their relative position with respect to the sun.' In the margin Constable has written 'as seen opposite or under the sun'. Constable is pointing out that the position of the observer in relation to the sun is also important. To paint realistic cloud colours, according to the position of the sun and the aspect of a scene, is extremely difficult, especially if the relative positions are changing because of a strong wind. Clouds also control the lighting of the landscape below. Constable's interest emphasises his determination to capture a fleeting moment on canvas; the lighting of the landscape and clouds often changes very quickly, especially in the windy skies Constable so loved to paint.

On page 23, under the heading 'Of the Cumulostratus', Forster observes that the cumulostratus sometimes 'overhangs a perpendicular stem, and looks like a great Mushroom'. Alongside this phrase Constable wrote 'it is only [caps with?] a mushroom in thunder'. Here Constable is agreeing with Forster that cumulostrati produce thunder, which is not the case. He is confusing the 'mushroom'-shaped cumulostratus (Plate 11), which Howard defined as forming from the spreading out of the top of a cumulus cloud, often in the evening when convection has ceased, with the 'anvil' or 'crown of cirrus' that is the hallmark of Howard's nimbus or thunderstorm cloud (cumulonimbus in present day terminology). The main distinction is that the 'mushroom' is composed entirely of supercooled water droplets, whereas the 'anvil' is much higher and is composed of ice crystals, giving it a more fibrous appearance than the mushroom. (Two excellent photographs to distinguish the 'mushroom' and the 'anvil' are given in Plates 10 and 11.) Howard's distinction between cumulostratus and nimbus is confusing because he failed to take into account their differing heights, nor did he realise that cirrus clouds are composed of ice crystals.

Beside the statement under the heading 'Of the Nimbus' on page 24 – 'No cloud effuses rain until it has previously undergone a change sufficiently remarkable to constitute it a distinct modification, to which the term nimbus has been properly applied' – Constable wrote 'This is not correct electrical fluid will convert an [...?] without an [...?]'. Although two key words cannot be read, Constable would appear to contend that 'electrical fluid' will produce rain without a change in the shape of the cloud. Constable was correct in that it is true that several cloud types, including cumulus, can produce rain, but he was incorrect, as we know today, to state that rain is produced by an 'electrical fluid'. (In those days atmospheric electricity was widely considered as a fluid.) Howard himself wrote in 1833 of the importance of atmospheric electricity as 'one of the most universally diffused, most active and most useful fluids in nature', but he regarded electricity as 'a secondary agent ... in the production of rain ... which modifies the effect of the two grand predisposing causes – a falling temperature and the influx of vapour.'[53] Howard was right that atmospheric electricity is a secondary factor and we know today that it does play an important role in the coalescence of water droplets. Constable, on the other hand, appears to regard 'electrical fluid' as a possible primary cause of rain, which although being incorrect does demonstrate that Constable had sufficient meteorological confidence to disagree with Forster.

Having described all the different cloud types Forster then summarises his conclusions in section IX of the first chapter. A line in the right-hand margin of page 27 emphasises the following paragraph:

> *That cumuli are the immediate result of this process; and that in the evening, when the heat is diminished, the air deposits its vapour again in the form of dew, which gravitates to the ground, becoming more dense as it approaches the earth, because the lower atmosphere is not the coolest; and finally lodges on the surface of the herbage, or of the ground, where it awaits the reascending sun to be again evaporated.*

A water cycle linking two of his favourite elements – dew and cumulus – no doubt appealed to Constable. This annotation shows that Constable was interested in the physical causes of dew as well as its visual appeal.

On pages 28–9, Forster uses the conclusion from Howard's article on clouds that had been published in Rees's *Cyclopedia* in 1807:

> *We shall conclude with a brief review of the modifications according from the STRATUS, formed by the condensation of vapour or its*

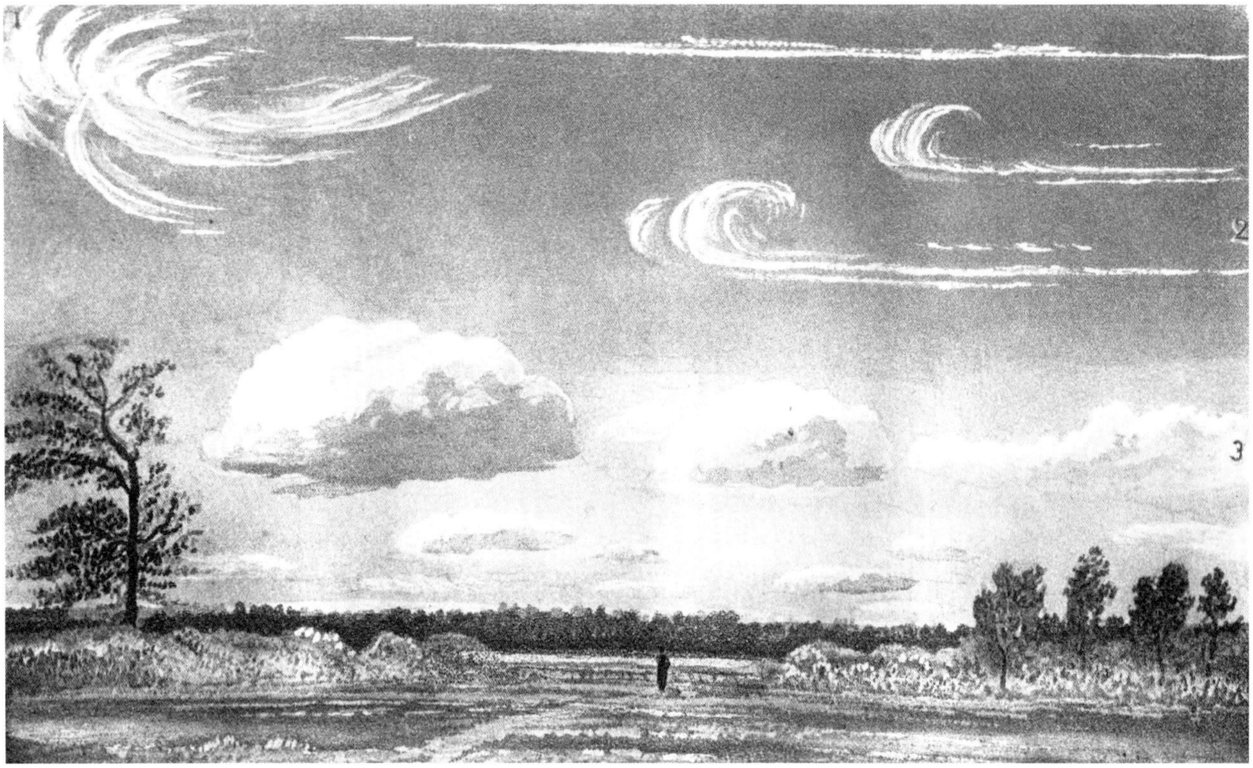

Plate 8 Cloud studies by Thomas Forster, taken from the second edition of his book *Researches about Atmospheric Phaenomena*

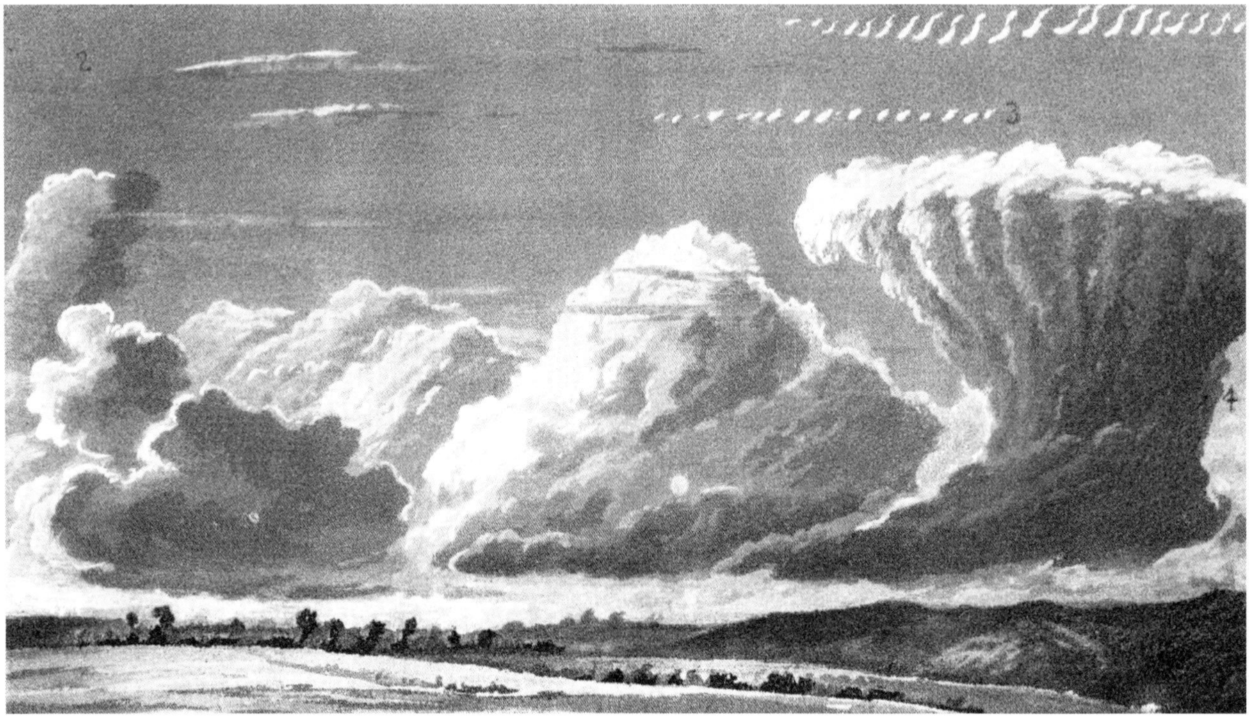

Plate 9 Cloud studies by Thomas Forster, taken from the second edition of his book *Researches about Atmospheric Phaenomena*

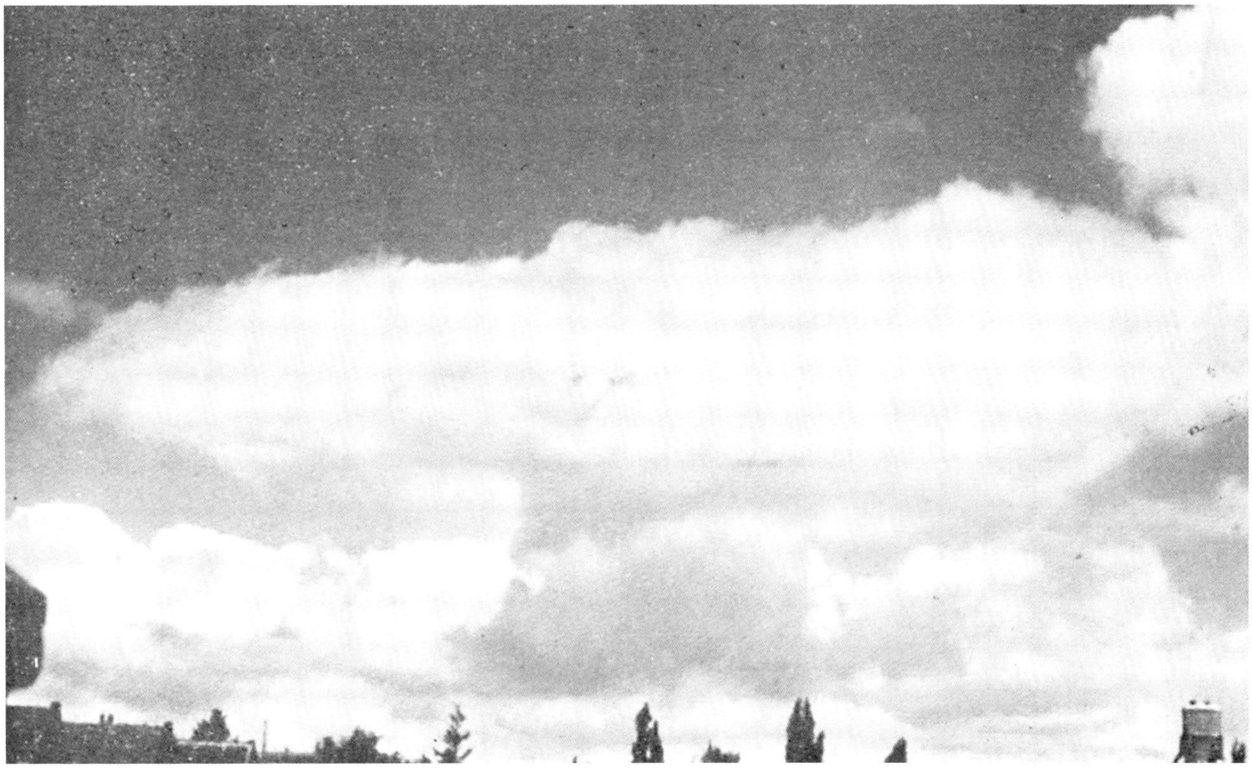

Plate 10 Stratocumulus from spreading out of cumulus. Photo: A. J. Aalders, Bussum, Netherlands. Reproduced courtesy of the Royal Meteorological Society

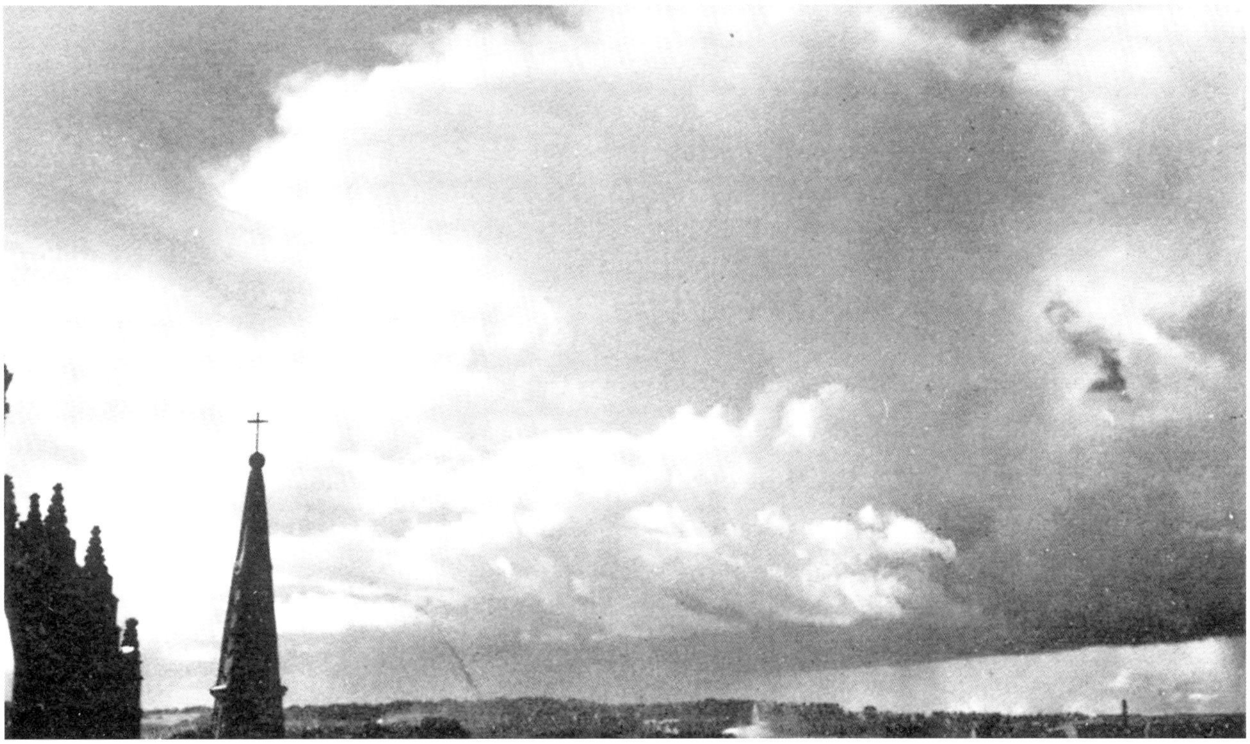

Plate 11 Cumulonimbus with anvil. Royal Meteorological Society (Clarke Collection)

escape from the surface to the CUMULUS, collecting its water in the second stage of its ascent, both probably existing by virtue of a positive electricity. From there proceeding through the partially conducting CUMULO-STRATUS the CIRROSTRATUS and CIRROCUMULUS; the latter positively charged, and considerably retentive of its charge; the former less perfectly insulated, and, perhaps, conducting horizontally; we arrive thus at the region where the CIRRUS light and elevated obeys every impulse or invitation of that fluid, which, while it finds a conductor, ever operates in silence; but which embodied and insulated in a denser collection of watery atoms, sooner or later bursts its barrier, leaps down in lightening, and glides through the NIMBUS from its elevated station to the earth.

Constable marked this passage with a line down the right-hand margin. Here is conclusive proof that, at some time, Constable was familiar with Howard's entire cloud classification.

At the bottom of page 30 Constable wrote 'not so' against the first two sentences of the following paragraph:

M. De Luc asserts that clouds are not the constant result of evaporation from the earth. He accounts for them by supposing that the air is decomposed by the sun's rays, so as to deposit aqueous particles, which become clouds. If this be admitted to take place, it does not argue against the ascent of vapour: and whether the watery particles arise immediately from the ground, or are deposited by the air, they may equally be supposed capable of becoming cloud, when operated upon by the nubific principle which is believed to be electrical, indeed, these two processes may co-operate to the production of clouds, so that, if this hypothesis be advanced against Mr Howard's theory it cannot be regarded as constituting a valid objection.

As Forster said in his preface, De Luc was a powerful voice in meteorology, and Forster attempts to iron out an apparent contradiction between the two theories of cloud formation discussed, no doubt, in an attempt to quell criticism of Howard's work. Against the second part of the paragraph, at the top of page 31, Constable has written in the right-hand margin: '[....?] as Howard's'. The first word cannot be read, but taken with the 'not so' on the previous page, Constable seems to dismiss De Luc's theory, and support Howard's. A sensible decision as De Luc's theory had already been dismissed by most meteorologists. The fact that Constable actually wrote Howard's name affords further proof that he was not only aware of Howard's cloud classification but also of his theories on the origins of clouds and precipitation.

On page 50 in the section 'Of the Varieties of the Cirrus' are the words: 'unusual motion of cirrus clouds ... "as if every particle was alive"', at the side of which, according to Leslie Parris and Conal Shields,[54] Constable wrote, 'this also happens in [cumulus?] thunder clouds diverging [moisture?]'. (The first insertion and question mark are my own.) The interpretation of the word 'cumulus' is doubtful, not only because the word is not written clearly, but also because if Constable had gleaned anything from Howard's classification, he would not have associated cumulus with thunder. An accompanying pencil sketch appears to depict swiftly 'growing' thunder clouds. Constable's use of the phrase 'thunder cloud' confirms that he had his own simple colloquial names for clouds. He would find it difficult to marry his phrase with Howard's term 'nimbus', which was also applied to other clouds that produced rain.

On page 52, in section II, 'Of the Varieties of the Cirrocumulus', a line in the right-hand margin picks out the following paragraph:

The permanent features of any cloud should be distinguished from those which are only transitory, or which the cloud exhibits in the progress

> *of its change from one modification to another. I have before noticed that in the change from the cirrus to the cirrocumulus, a number of appearances present themselves, which cannot be referred to either. They generally, however, end in a determinable modification, which I call its permanent form; and in which it generally remains for some time, and then evaporates, or changes again.*

This paragraph would be important for Constable as a painter determined to capture on canvas the essential and distinctive qualities of a cloud type. The paragraph also emphasises that identifying clouds is not always a simple task, and Constable would probably have been reassured to read that Forster occasionally experienced difficulties!

On pages 60–1, in Section IV, 'Of the Varieties of the Cumulus', a line is drawn in the right-hand margin against:

> *It is curious to watch the formation of cumuli in a morning, and trace them, when it is possible, from the minute specks of cloud which, here and there, seems to form out of the atmosphere, to those large masses which move majestically along in the wind, and convey water from place to place for the irrigation of the earth. In fair weather, soon after sunrise, a small cloud appears; this increases, others form near it, and they fall into one another as if attracted: a large mass is at length upraised, and then all the smaller ones which form in its neighbourhood are soon lost, while the large one is augmented; and the spectator, though he seldom sees it in actual congression, feels no doubt that the disappearance of the smaller, and augmentation of the larger cloud, is owing to the larger mass having attracted the smaller into itself. It becomes a question however, why the small clouds are lost to appearance before they are quite drawn into the larger one? Possibly when the small cloud is very near, or most of its vapours drawn away, the rest rush with a velocity into the larger; as a magnet, when it has approached a larger within a certain distance, is forcibly and suddenly attracted to the latter. When these ephemeral mountains of electrified vapour have increased much, as they do towards the middle of the day; large ones often inosculate, and form dense and extensive irregular masses.*

Constable wrote in the margin against the last sentence: 'but the formation generally evaporates in the middle of the day'. This lengthy account describes the formation of what today would be called cumulus streets, in 'fair' weather when convection is limited, which may sometimes merge into stratocumulus sheets. Constable adds the general observation that such clouds must eventually evaporate, as their average life is only an hour or two. In fair weather Constable notes that generally these clouds evaporate by midday. Both Forster and Constable were avid watchers of the sky, and Constable shows that his powers of observation were on a par with Forster's. In this case Forster's explanation – likening clouds to magnets – is rather bizarre.

Chapter II examines in more detail the various cloud types and then Constable's annotations to the text, which have been quite frequent up to this point, cease. It appears that Constable was only really interested in Forster's interpretation of Luke Howard's cloud classification, which is covered mostly in the first chapter which runs from page 1 to page 40. Forster suggests his own cloud names to go alongside Howard's Latin names, but Constable, together with the rest of the world, seems to have ignored them! Forster's names are rather forgettable apart from the obvious 'raincloud':

Howard	**Forster**
Cirrus	Curlcloud
Cumulus	Stackencloud
Stratus	Fallcloud
Cirrocumulus	Sondercloud
Cirrostratus	Wanecloud
Cumulostratus	Twaincloud
Nimbus	Raincloud

Chapter II goes on to discuss rain, cloud colours, cloud heights and cloud buoyancy as well as rainbows and halos. These subjects would also have interested Constable and it is interesting to speculate that perhaps the annotations were the work of one session, and page 61 was as far as he got; or perhaps Constable did not think he had much to learn on these topics from Forster.

However, there are two further small, but interesting, annotations towards the back of the book. On page 161, in Chapter IV, entitled 'Of The Indications Of The Future Changes Of The Weather' or 'Of Prognostics' for short, and in the section on 'Proverbs relating to the Months and Seasons', Forster has taken an extract from Chaucer's 'Canterbury Tales', one line of which reads 'When the clouds are upon the hills, they'll come down by the rills'. An 'X' has been placed alongside this line, and at the bottom of the page Constable has written: 'X cumulostrati'. This interpretation is not at all clear, and considering that Constable's only meeting with mountain weather was during his Lake District trip in 1806, it is strange that he has picked out this line. Howard's cumulostrati heralded a worsening of the weather, and on page 162, Forster relates 'the well known rules of the Shepherd of Banbury'. Constable has also written 'cumulostrati' against the following line: 'Large clouds like rocks, forebode great showers'. This interpretation is much better. Indeed Howard says of cumulostratus that 'it is among the regular harbingers' of 'thunderstorm' and 'the cumulostratus affords a general doubtful prognostic'.[55] Constable was undoubtedly interested in 'prognostics' from his windmiller days, and this is born out by the annotations to his sky studies, as already discussed.

Summarising what Constable's annotations to Forster's book tell us about Constable's meteorological understanding, the following conclusions can be drawn:

- The fact that Constable has written 'cumulostrati' and Howard's name demonstrates that he was familiar with current meteorological theories.
- He was sufficiently familiar with meteorological theories to pick out ambiguities in Howard's classification, and also to disagree with certain of Forster's conclusions.
- He was completely familiar with Howard's classification of clouds at some stage of his life.
- He demonstrates an interest in the physical processes that generate the different cloud types, particularly cumulus, and also in the formation of dew.
- The detailed and careful annotations show that Constable only studied the sections of the book that directly related to Howard's classification, and suggest that he had not studied Howard's cloud classification previously.
- He had some difficulty marrying his own colloquial cloud classification with Howard's cloud classification.
- He also noted sections that would help him as a painter, relating to cloud form and the interplay between the position of the sun in the sky – the position of the clouds – and the lighting of the landscape.

Thus the annotations to Forster's book show that Constable's meteorological knowledge was considerable and demonstrate his desire to understand meteorological processes in order to improve his painted skies. Badt's theories that it was Luke Howard's publication of *The Climate of London* in 1818–20 that introduced Constable to Howard's cloud classification, and that Constable would not be interested in atmospheric processes are therefore unlikely. Badt quite rightly points out that Howard's classification of clouds, based on visual observations, was a first step in the development of meteorology:

> *Now it is important to realise that it was precisely this first stage in the scientific development of meteorology which became important for the painters and poets; it was the kind of scientific work which remains within the scope of simple first-hand observation. What Howard and Forster produced in the way of scientific explanations based on the theories of their time,*

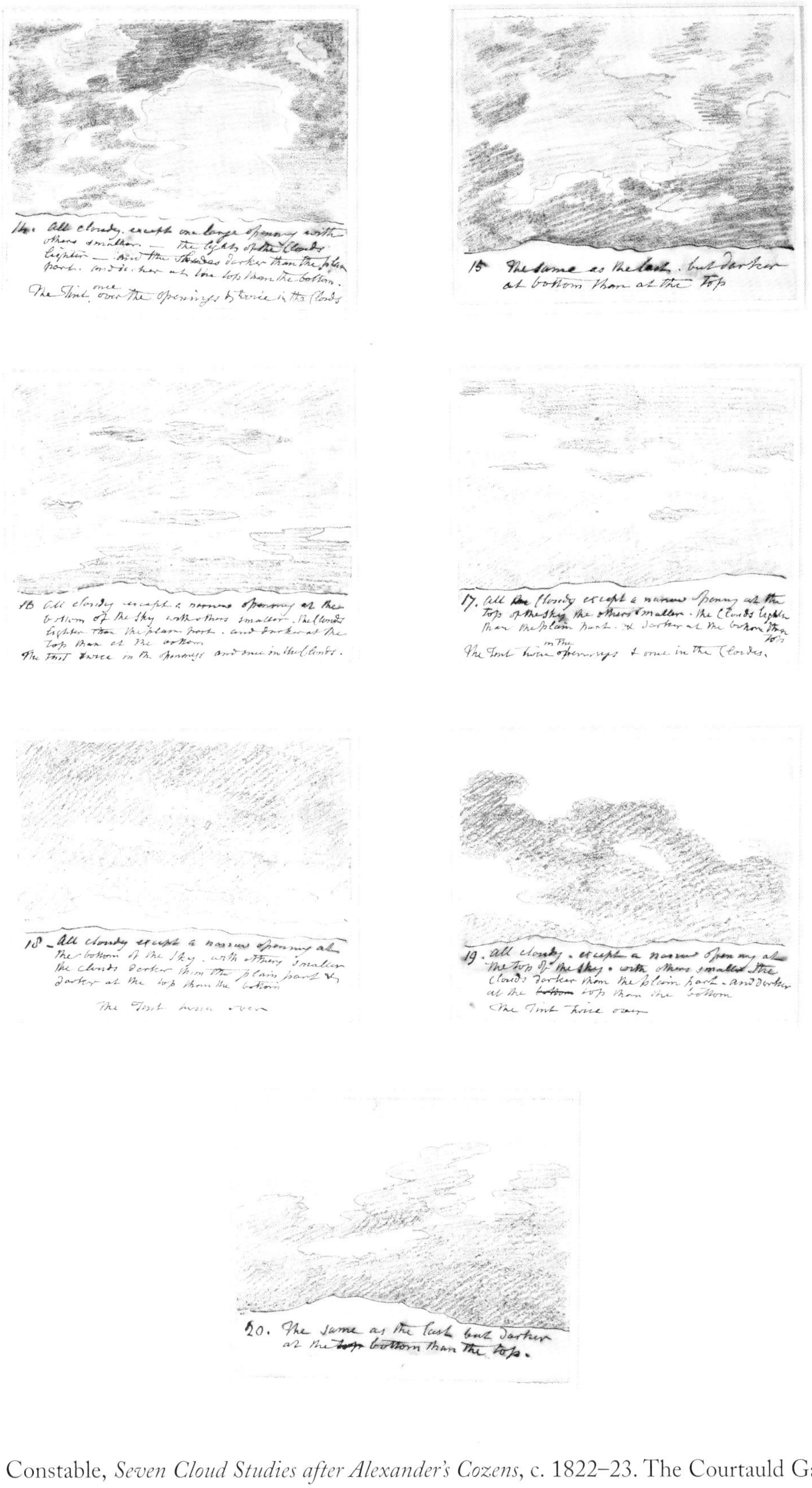

Plate 12 John Constable, *Seven Cloud Studies after Alexander's Cozens*, c. 1822–23. The Courtauld Gallery, London

> *by reference to invisible factors, forces and laws, was of no more fruitful interest for Goethe than it was for Constable. But in their striving towards order and intelligibility in the empirical sphere the poet and painter were on common ground with the scientists.*[56]

This is no doubt true for other poets and painters but not so for Constable. He was interested in the formation of clouds and the current theories of rain. This interest was important to him in his quest to make his skies dynamic, so that the weather he portrayed was conducive to the appearance of the painted clouds and vice versa. Constable also wanted to harmonise his skies with his landscapes and create a freshness of look and a consistent wind that matched the sky.

2.8 Copies of Cozens' skies and other drawings

Constable copied, in pencil, twenty skies from Alexander Cozens' treatise, *A New Method of Assisting the Invention in Drawing Original Compositions of Landscape*, written c. 1785 (see Plate 12). The 1976 Constable exhibition catalogue[57] suggests that these copies may have been made during Constable's skying period of 1821/22. However the skies are pure fiction and as far as cloud classification is concerned they are completely unidentifiable. It is therefore surprising that Constable should have gone to such great lengths to copy out twenty skies. Nevertheless Constable had a great respect for Cozens, as is discussed in Chapter 4. More recently it has been suggested that Constable made these copies whilst staying with Sir George Beaumont during a visit to Leicestershire in 1823, when it is known that he copied another set of Cozens' schematic designs. The paper used for Constable's copies is watermarked 1822.[58] Even though Constable most likely copied these skies in 1823, he would probably have been aware of their existence much earlier. As Fleming-Williams points out, Beaumont, an early mentor of Constable's, was a pupil of Cozens at Eton.[59] Moreover Fisher would have been fully familiar with Cozens' works and methods of teaching. The sky drawings tell us little of Constable's meteorological understanding, only that he was so determined to improve his painted skies that he was willing to try anything! The copies were seemingly drawn quickly and are two dimensional. They are rather suggestive of a 'White Sheet' which should not have appealed to Constable. He may have been more interested in the inscriptions that accompany Cozens' skies since he took the trouble to copy these using pen and ink. The inscriptions relate to the position of the clouds and their lighting; for instance, the drawing labelled number 18 states: 'All cloudy except a narrow opening at the bottom of the Sky. with others smaller the clouds darker than the plain part & darker at the top than the bottom. The Tint twice over.'

On paper watermarked 1817, but probably drawn in the early 1830s, Constable produced an ink drawing of a dramatic sky accompanied by, or indeed inspired by, a passage from Robert Bloomfield's *The Farmer's Boy* which was first published in 1800.[60] Plate 13 shows a typical Constable sky full of chiaroscuro. The verse reads:

> *With saunt'ring step he climbs the distant stile,*
> *Whist all around him wears a placid smile;*
> *There views the white-rob'd clouds in clusters driven,*
> *And all the glorious pageantry of Heaven.*
> *Low, on the utmost bound'ry of the sight,*
> *The rising vapours catch the silver light;*
> *Thence Fancy measures, as they parting fly,*
> *Which first will throw its shadow on the eye,*
> *Passing the source of light; and thence away,*
> *Succeeded quick by brighter still than they.*
> *Far yet above these wafted clouds are seen*
> *(In a remoter sky, still more serene,)*
> *Others, detach'd in ranges through the air,*
> *Spotless as snow, and countless as they're fair;*
> *Scatter'd immensely wide from east to west,*
> *The beauteous 'semblance of a Flock at rest.*
> *These, to the raptur'd mind, aloud proclaim*
> *Their MIGHTY SHEPHERD's everlasting Name.*

No doubt Bloomfield was one of Constable's favourite poets, expressing in words the exact sentiments that Constable attempted to express in his paintings and drawings. The poem describes cumulus clouds driven across the sun in rapid succession, with a bed of altocumulus above stretched calmly across the sky. The poem also reminds us of the religious symbolism of the sky which was also important to Constable. It is written in the bible that Christ had said 'Hereafter shall ye see the son of man sitting on the right hand of power and coming in the clouds of Heaven.'[61] The awesome power of the atmosphere and man's inability to do anything to control it, able only to observe it, make the sky a powerful symbol of God and heaven. The poem above demonstrates that Constable was inspired by poetic references to the sky as well as by more scientific approaches.

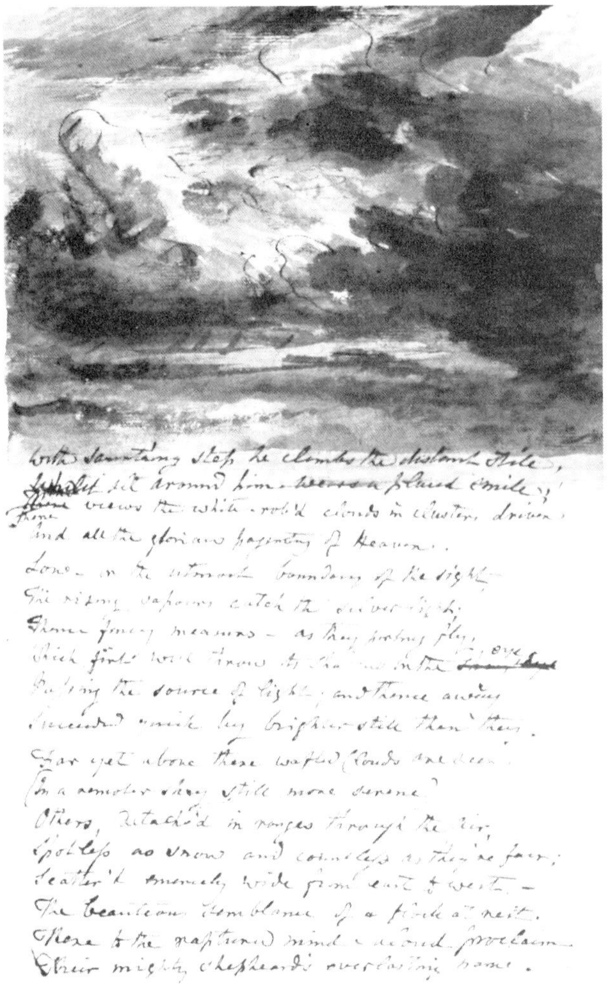

Plate 13 John Constable, Sketch accompanying passage from Robert Bloomfield's *The Farmer's Boy*

Accompanied by an adapted quotation from Burns, Constable also produced two atmospheric pen and ink drawings which Reynolds dates as 1832:[62]

Around me scouls the Wintry sky
That blast each bud of hope and joy
Nor Shelter, Shade, nor home have I

Reynolds compares the tempestuous nature of the drawings with the gloom that filled Constable's mind around the time of the deaths of two of his closest friends, Fisher on 25 August 1832, and John Dunthorne on 2 November 1832.

2.9 Constable's enigmatic rainbow

Constable's rainbows are almost as well known as his clouds, but whereas clouds are present in some form almost every day in England, rainbows are seen much less frequently. Thus there is no 'rainbow period' in Constable's works similar to his 'skying period' of 1820/22. However Schweizer[63] suggests that at some time between 1827 and 1831 Constable began to study the science behind the production of rainbows, knowledge of which emerges clearly in the text accompanying *Stoke by Neyland, Suffolk* in *English Landscape Scenery*, and in a series of rainbow diagrams drawn probably in 1833. Schweizer goes so far as to state that rainbows came to be regarded by Constable as his 'personal emblem': 'Constable's use of the rainbow as a personal emblem reached an important point in 1831 when he included it in his painting of *Salisbury Cathedral from the Meadows*, the most monumental and dramatic rendering of this natural spectacle ever to appear in his art.'[64]

Constable both painted rainbows from nature which were meteorologically accurate and used them for artistic effect in situations which could never occur in nature, such as in the 1831 painting of *Salisbury Cathedral from the Meadows* (Plate 59) and *Stoke by Neyland* (Plate 14) in *English Landscape Scenery*. However Constable was aware of the fact that a rainbow cannot be seen once the sun is higher in the sky than 42 degrees, which it is in both these examples. This enigma is difficult to explain. Why should Constable be such a perfectionist with regard to the weather in his paintings – his wind and clouds and the harmonic lighting of his landscapes – and yet be content to introduce a meteorologically impossible rainbow to a painting? We shall attempt to answer this question as we examine Constable's knowledge of the rainbow. Firstly we should remind ourselves what Constable wrote in that famous letter to Fisher of 23 October 1821:

> *The sky is the source of light in nature – and governs everything.... Their difficulty in painting both as to composition and Execution is very great, because with all their brilliancy and consequence – they ought not to come forward or be hardly thought about in a picture – any more than extreme distances are – But these remarks do not apply to phenomenon – or what the painters call accidental Effects of Sky – because they always attract particularly.*[65]

Thus the rainbow and other effects such as crepuscular rays were given a special exemption by Constable, and although a rainbow cannot 'come forward' in a picture Constable makes it clear that if he introduces such an effect he wants it to attract attention.

The rainbow would certainly have been an appealing emblem for Constable, representing on the one hand the symbolism of hope and grace and on the other the crowning glory of his beloved chiaroscuro. Landow warns that the rainbow is a problematic image in art with its religious overtones as the seal of the covenant between God and man:

> *Turner, who spans the Romantic and early Victorian years both spiritually and chronologically, finally tells us that to see Nature's rainbow as an emblem of hope is itself one of the great fallacies of hope: it is to believe, as Grimshaw and Linnell apparently did, that God marked Nature with signs for man's sake, and to believe that man will find in Nature meanings that he himself has hidden there – and find them true. Like Tennyson and Browning, Turner realises that the 'thoughtful eye' demanded by Fairburn can no longer see in this optical phenomena an unambiguous Covenant-sign. Like these poets, he transforms the rainbow into a powerful image of man's problematic relation to problematic Nature.*[66]

Similarly Constable used the rainbow to his own ends to symbolise problems rather than solutions, particularly in *Salisbury Cathedral from the Meadows*, in which it has been suggested that the rainbow symbolises not only the problems facing the Church of England at the time, but also the problems in his own life.[67]

Schweizer has attempted to show diagrammatically how the rainbow in *Salisbury Cathedral from the Meadows* defies meteorological science.[68] He calculates that the top of the bow subtends an angle of 38 degrees (see Figure 13) which is close to the maximum possible angle of 42 degrees, produced when the sun is at the horizon. From the illumination of the landscape – the diagonal rays of sunlight falling on to Fisher's house – and the apparent height of the sun, Schweizer calculates the angle to be 64 degrees. However, one should be wary of assessing the height of the sun from depicted crepuscular rays which, although they originate from the sun, are not an accurate guide to its height in the sky. Crepuscular rays can be viewed obliquely and hence the sun could be at an angle much lower than 64 degrees.

If one looks at the shadow on the old fence post in the bottom left-hand corner of *Salisbury Cathedral from the Meadows* (Plate 59), the geography and the illumination of the cathedral

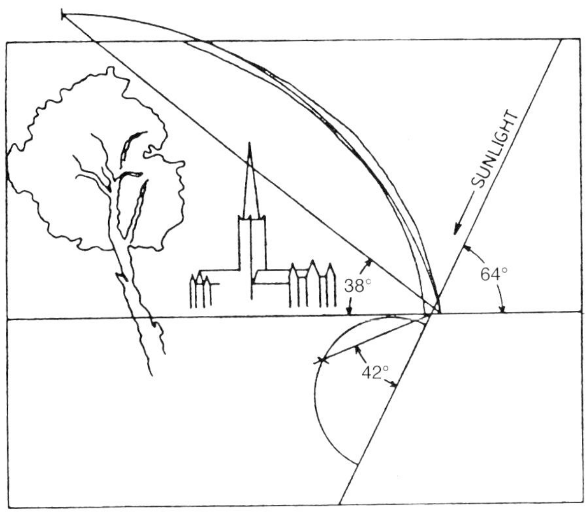

Figure 13 Rainbow angle from Constable's *Salisbury Cathedral from the Meadows*, 1831

suggests that the sun has reached an angle just north of west in the sky, which in the middle of August would happen between 6pm and 7pm. By that time the height of the sun in the sky is about 15 degrees which would mean that the rainbow would have a height of about 27 degrees in the sky, which is still significantly smaller than that observed. The rainbow arches protectively just behind the cathedral and, in this case, is not the rainbow that the artist would see but the bow that someone standing in the meadow on the right would see. Schweizer assumes that the rainbow is in the plane of the picture but it is in fact coming out of the picture at a shallow angle. The lighting of the landscape suggests that the sun is to the right of the picture and not, as it should be, behind the observer. Nevertheless the view of the rainbow is not as impossible as Schweizer suggests. The view of the cathedral over the River Avon is from the north west at Long Bridge, and the picture was entitled *Summer Afternoon – A Retiring Tempest* by Constable when he exhibited it in Worcester in 1836. It is not clear why Constable chose to add the rainbow to a painting in which the sun is not directly behind the viewer. Certainly in his notes accompanying *Stoke by Neyland* in *English Landscape Scenery* Constable was aware of the fact that a rainbow must always 'be parallel with the plane of the picture'. It would appear therefore that Constable was quite happy to use an amount of 'poetic licence' for his 'accidental Effect of Sky'; but nonetheless the meteorological conditions with the late afternoon thunderstorm and the flashes of lightning are certainly conducive to the formation of a rainbow. However in order to produce a complete bow as seen over the cathedral the rain would have to have been falling right across the picture from the dark cloud at the top of the picture. The evidence seems to point, therefore, to the fact that the rainbow and the lightning were added very late in the painting of the picture. None of the surviving sketches for the finished work contained a rainbow or lightning, although the plate in *English Landscape Scenery* entitled *Salisbury Cathedral* has a double rainbow which may be based on an untraced sketch of the cathedral. When the painting was exhibited at the Royal Academy in 1831 it was accompanied by the following misremembered quotation from Thomson's *Seasons*:

> *As from the face of Heaven the scatter'd clouds*
> *Tumultuous rove, th' interminable sky*
> *Sublimer swells, and o'er the world expands*
> *A purer azure.... Through the lighten'd air*
> *A higher lustre and a clearer calm,*
> *Diffusive tremble; while, as if in sign*
> *Of danger past, a glittering robe of joy,*
> *Set off abundant by the yellow ray,*
> *Invests the fields, and nature smiles reviv'd.*[69]

Cormack cautions that one should not try to read too much into the symbolism of any of Constable's paintings but then suggests that:

> *The painting could be construed as an allegory of Constable's own life , as the passage he quoted from Thomson refers to nature's rejuvenation after the death of Celadon's lover, Amelia. But his picture is, nevertheless, restless and worrying for other reasons ... the passage of the Reform Bill that had particularly upset Fisher and*

> *Constable in March 1831 ... the lightning flashes around the tower could be taken as attacks on the body of the church. The rainbow, the quotation, and the image of the spire thrusting through the dark clouds to the pure 'azure', suggest the stability of the church and happier times to come.*[70]

Constable's sky had moved beyond realism into the realm of symbolism.

Table 16 shows the dates and times (GMT) when a rainbow is not visible in England, and that the maximum height of the sun in England at 52 degrees north is approximately 62 degrees. On 21 June, when the sun climbs to its highest point in the northern hemisphere summer, a rainbow is not visible in England from about 8.30am until 3.30pm. On the other hand on 21 March and 21 September a rainbow is possible at any point during the day.

Table 16
Approximate height of rainbow at noon for different months and latitudes

	SE. England (52 degrees north)		*N. Italy (44 degrees north)*	
	Height of sun	*Height of rainbow*	*Height of sun*	*Height of rainbow*
21 January	17 deg.	25 deg.	27	15
21 February	27	15	38	4
21 March	38	4	46	*
21 April	50	*	56	*
21 May	58	*	65	*
21 June	60	*	68	*
21 July	58	*	65	*
21 August	50	*	56	*
21 September	38	4	46	*
21 October	27	15	38	4
21 November	17	25	27	15
21 December	13	29	23	19

* = Rainbow below horizon, and therefore not visible

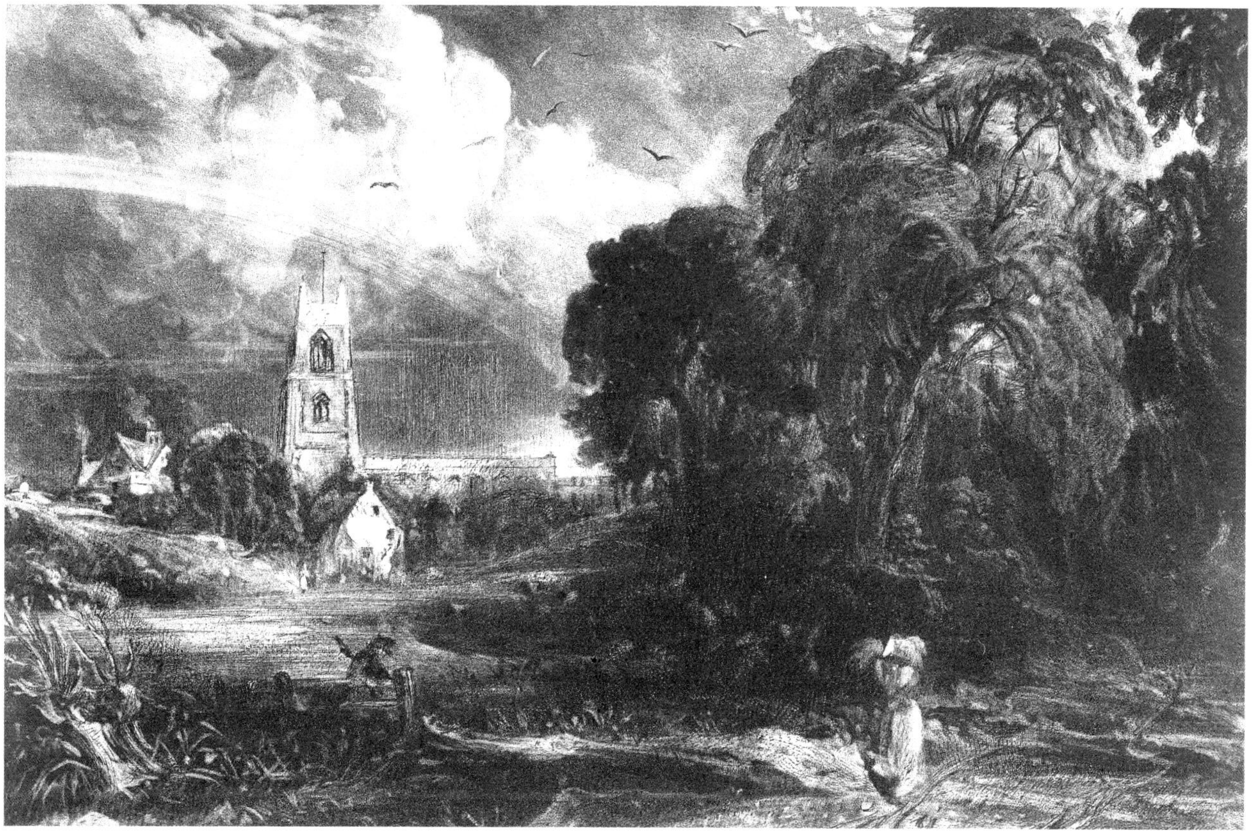

Plate 14 David Lucas, John Constable's *Stoke by Neyland*, Suffolk. Engraving, 1833. V&A Picture Library

Let us now consider what Constable understood about the formation of rainbows. In *English Landscape Scenery*, plate 7, *Stoke by Neyland*, depicts a rainbow arching over the village church at noon (Plate 14). The text states:

> *The solemn stillness of Nature in a Summer's Noon, when attended by thunder clouds, is the sentiment attempted in this print; at the same time an endeavour has been made to give an additional interest to this Landscape by the introduction of the Rainbow, and other attending circumstances that might occur at such an hour. The effect of light and shadow on the sky and landscape are such as would be observed when looking to the northward at noon; that time of day being decidedly marked by the direction of the shadows and the sun shining full on the south side of the church.*[71]

The angle of the rainbow in the mezzotint is about 20 degrees which would mean that for the rainbow to appear at noon the date would have to be in late January. This can hardly be called summer!

Constable goes on to show however that he is fully aware of the importance of the time of day and day of the year in controlling the visible portion of a rainbow, and offers the following valuable advice to other landscape painters about the formation and form of rainbows:

> *Of the rainbow – the following observations can hardly fail to be useful to the Landscape Painter. When the Rainbow appears at Noon, the height of the sun at that hour of the day causes but a small segment of the circle to be seen, and this gives the Bow its low or flat appearance: the Noon-day bow is therefore best seen 'Smiling in a Winter's day,' as in the summer, after the sun has passed a certain altitude, a Rainbow cannot appear.*

The 20 degree rainbow in the plate certainly does appear flattened but it is strange that Constable uses the plate to typify a 'Summer's Noon'. It is probable that Constable did not realise that in southern England it is impossible at noon to see a bow at all from the beginning of April until the first week of September. I have been unable to trace a table or diagram, published in Constable's time, such as Table 16, which sets out such dates.

Constable then importantly observes 'that a Rainbow can never appear foreshortened, or be seen obliquely, as it must be parallel with the plane of the picture, though a part of it only may be introduced'. This would be useful advice for other artists who might be tempted to paint a rainbow sideways on. Nevertheless if Constable could 'cheat' on nature and alter the rainbow angle to suit his purpose, why shouldn't other landscape painters also alter the angle of view for effect?

Constable then discusses why the bow sometimes appears imperfect due to intervening cloud: 'nor can a Rainbow be seen through any intervening cloud, however small or thin, as the reflected rays are dispersed by it, and are thus prevented from reaching the eye; consequently the Bow is imperfect in that part'. The beauty of the rainbow is praised:

> *Nature, in all the varied aspects of her beauty, exhibits no feature more lovely nor any that awaken a more soothing reflection than the Rainbow, 'Mild arch of promise'; and when this phaenomenon appears under unusual circumstances it excites a more lively interest. This is the case with the 'Noon-tide Bow,' but more especially with that most beautiful and rare occurrence, the 'Lunar Bow.'*

The lunar bow is rare and occurs when a full moon takes the place of the sun. Although, because of the lower level of illumination, the lunar bow appears white it is in reality the same colour as a normal rainbow as moonlight is merely reflected sunlight. Perhaps Constable also regards his portrayal of a noon-time bow as exciting because of its rarity.

The next section continues 'The morning and evening Bows are more frequent than those at noon, and are far more imposing and attractive from their loftiness and span; the colours are also more brilliant, "Flashing brief splendour through the clouds awhile."' He then goes on to discuss multiple bows:

> *For the same reason the exterior or secondary Bow is at these times also brighter, but the colours of it are reversed. A third, and even fourth Bow, may sometimes be seen, with the colours alternating in each; these are always necessarily fainter, from the quantity of light lost at each reflection within the drop, according to the received principle of the Bow.*

It was not until much later that it was widely appreciated that in fact the third and fourth bows are bows (circles) around the sun, and it is not until the fifth bow that the rainbow is to be found in the sky away from the sun. Boyer suggests that Halley (1656–1742) was the first to calculate this:

> *Halley seems to have been the earliest to carry through to the end the calculations on the tertiary rainbow; and the result must have been a surprise. He found that the third rainbow arc has an angular radius of 40° 20', and that it should appear not in the part of the heavens opposite the sun, but as a circle around the sun itself. For at least two thousand years men had been looking for this arc in the wrong part of the sky!*[72]

The third bow and the fourth bow are difficult to see not only because of their faintness, but also because we have to look towards the sun, which is swamped by skylight. Also it is likely that in many cases a different shower of rain from the one producing the primary and secondary bows is required which may indeed prevent the primary and secondary bows being visible. Constable's reference to the third and fourth bows is therefore misguided, but even today few people realise this error.

Constable concludes his discussion of the theory of rainbows by alluding to the discrepancy between Newton's seven prismatic colours of the rainbow (heptachromatic) and the three-coloured rainbow that many artists use (trichromatic).[73] He also discusses the fact that the sky on the inside of a bow is lighter than the sky on the outside. As discussed in Chapter 1, the area between the primary and secondary bows is called Alexander's Dark Band:

> *Perhaps more remains yet to be discovered as to the cause of this most beautiful Phenomena of Light, recent experiments having proved that the primitive colours are further refrangible. Though not generally observed, the space within the Bow is always lighter than the outer portion of the cloud on which it is seen. This circumstance has not escaped the notice of the Poet, who with that intuitive feeling which has so often anticipated the discoveries of the Philosopher, remarks:*
>
> > *'And all within the arch appeared to be*
> > *Brighter than that without.'*

Yet more detailed evidence of Constable's understanding of the formation of rainbows is given in the four rainbow diagrams shown in Figures 14–17. These were probably part of Constable's notes on skies that he mentioned to George Constable in 1836 which he might put together to give a lecture. The diagrams show several important things; firstly, that Constable was fully aware of the principles of reflection and refraction leading to the formation of the primary and secondary bows as shown in Figure 14. Secondly, he knew the rainbow angles for the primary and secondary bows, as written out in Figure 14. Thirdly, in Figure 16, he lists the seven prismatic colours and draws three areas over the top to suggest the three primary colours and also writes that 'there is no limit to the number of prismatic colours' suggesting that he was aware of the problems of defining Newton's seven colours. Fourthly, Figure 17, if held upside down, shows how a full circular bow may be seen by an observer

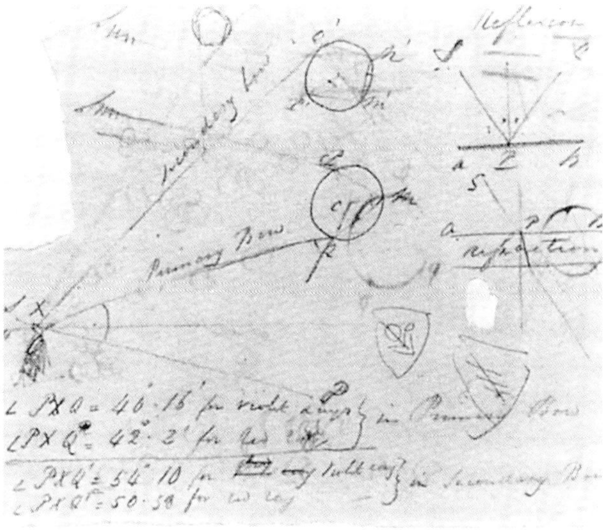

Figure 14
Constable's rainbow diagrams – recto of sheet A

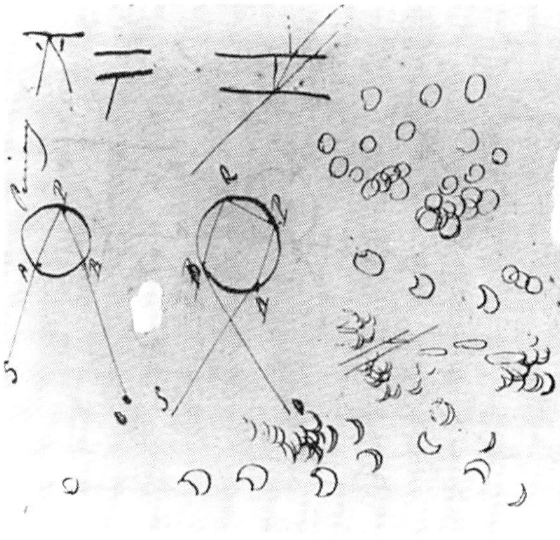

Figure 15
Constable's rainbow diagrams – verso of sheet A

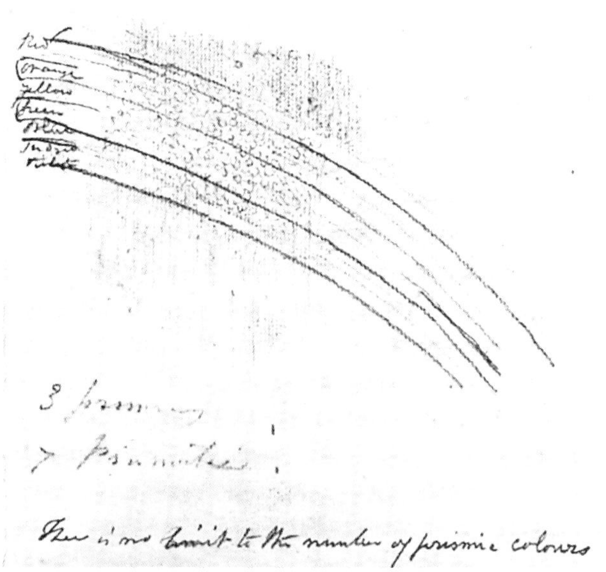

Figure 16
Constable's rainbow diagrams – recto of sheet B

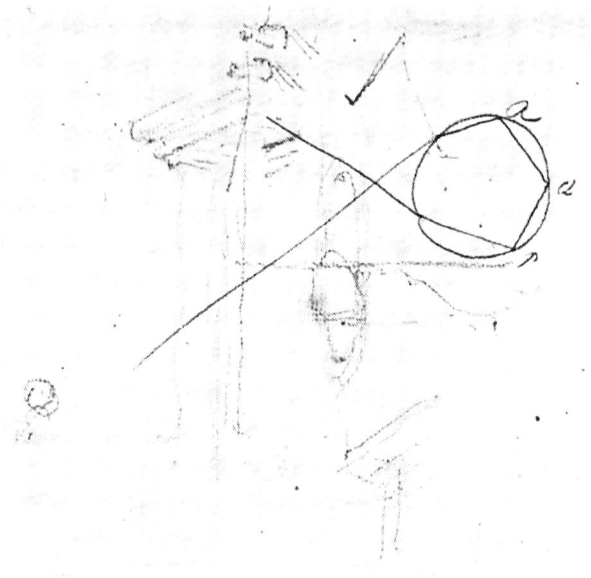

Figure 17
Constable's rainbow diagrams – verso of sheet B

on top of a hill. Fifthly, Figure 15 shows crescent-shaped raindrops which echo his friend George Field's views expressed in his 1835 book *Chromatography*.[74] Field believed that raindrops become lenticular in form as they fall through the atmosphere due to atmospheric friction. Schweizer suggests that the source for Constable's rainbow diagrams is not clear and suggests that perhaps Charles Boner, the teacher he hired for his children who was also mathematically trained, may have helped him.[75]

In total, therefore, Constable was well aware of the fundamental contemporary principles of rainbow formation. The influence that this had upon his painting of rainbows is discussed in detail by Schweizer who argues that from the rainbow diagrams it should have been clear to Constable that 'the width of the secondary arc of a rainbow is theoretically twice as wide as the primary arc, and that the width of the dark band of sky that separates the outermost band of red in the primary arc from the innermost red of the secondary arc is slightly less than three times the width of the secondary arc itself.'[76] This type of information would have been of great practical guidance to a landscape artist and Schweizer surmises that Constable's *London from Hampstead with a Double Rainbow* (Plate 61) – a watercolour painted a few months after he exhibited *Salisbury Cathedral from the Meadows* at the Royal Academy – showed that he was fully aware of it. Certainly the secondary bow is wider (about 1.6mm compared to 1.3mm), but only by about 23 per cent. The distance between the two bows (about 3.6mm) is about 2.25 times the width of the secondary bow.[77] This suggests that Constable painted the double bow by eye rather than by rule, but nevertheless his recently acquired knowledge would help him to confirm the theories he had studied: that the secondary bow is wider and that the colours are reversed.

Interestingly this double rainbow picture also shows converging rays of light which Fleming-Williams compares to Leslie's description of such a phenomena described to him by Constable:

> *I remember that he pointed out to me an appearance of the sun's rays, which few artists have perhaps noticed, and which I never saw given in any picture, excepting in his Waterloo Bridge. When the spectator stands with his back to the sun, the rays may be sometimes seen converging in perspective towards the opposite horizon. Since he drew my attention to such effects, I have noticed very early in the morning the lines of the rays diminishing in perspective through a rainbow.*[78]

Light rays that converge opposite the sun are called anticrepuscular rays, but they are rarely seen. When such anticrepuscular rays happen to intercept a rainbow the result is what is called a 'rainbow wheel' and Lynch and Livingston state that *London from Hampstead with a Double Rainbow* (1831) (Plate 61) contains a 'nice rainbow wheel'.[79] It could be that Constable was the first person to notice such effects and that Leslie's recollections are the first published observations of anticrepuscular rays and the rainbow wheel.

Constable's knowledge of the rainbow may be summarised as follows:

- He was aware of the rainbow angles of the primary and secondary bows.
- He recognised that the colours of the secondary bow are reversed.
- He realised that the height of the bow in the sky varies with time of year and time of day.
- He realised that a rainbow cannot be viewed obliquely or foreshortened and that in a painting of a rainbow the sun must effectively be directly behind the viewer.
- He knew that a rainbow cannot be seen through cloud.
- He was aware of the existence of the 'lunar' rainbow.
- He was aware of the debate between Newton's seven-coloured rainbow and the more common artistic perception that the bow is made up of just three primary colours.
- He was aware of the darkened area between the primary and secondary bows.
- From his rainbow diagrams it is clear that Constable was aware that the secondary bow is wider and fainter than the primary bow.
- His observations of anticrepuscular rays and the rainbow wheel may be the first documented evidence of such effects.

Just as he had done with clouds, Constable studied the available scientific literature on rainbows, studied actual rainbows in the sky and consulted with his friends to enable him to understand the form and formation of rainbows. Although the primary source of his scientific knowledge is not known, the extent of his rainbow knowledge is remarkable.

2.10 *English Landscape Scenery*

Constable began to plan the publication of *English Landscape Scenery* in 1829, at the age of fifty-three. He wanted to encapsulate his entire life's work in a published series of mezzotints and, as Reynolds points out, the choice of regional landscapes was overshadowed by the choice of the weather reproduced in the plates: 'Constable's main preoccupation was with the cloudscape and the light, features which he included in the term "chiaroscuro of nature" which the mezzotints were designed to embody.'[80]

In Constable's second edition of *English Landscape Scenery* published in 1833 he added a number of commentaries to some of the mezzotint plates and changed the full title to *Various subjects of Landscape, characteristic of English Scenery, principally intended to mark the Phenomena of the Chiar'Oscuro of Nature*. Constable defined chiaroscuro as 'that power which creates space; we find it everywhere and at all time in nature; opposition, union, light, shade, reflection, and refraction, all contribute to it'.[81] This definition is also summed up in the quotation he used in the description of *Spring*:

> *...light and shade alternate, warmth and cold,*
> *And bright with dewy clouds, and vernal show'rs,*
> *And all the fair variety of things.*

This, thought Constable, typified the English countryside, and he wanted to capture in the mezzotints 'one brief moment caught from fleeting time' as he stated in the introduction. The skies of most of the plates are full of wind and rain, with Constable's favourite cumulus and nimbus clouds taking prominence because they were the most suitable clouds to produce the chiaroscuro effect Constable was seeking, to produce 'light and shade alternate'. The text of *Spring* is very revealing in describing the importance of clouds to Constable in producing heightened chiaroscuro:

> *This plate may perhaps give some idea of one of those bright and animated days of the early year, when all nature bears so exhilarating an aspect, when at noon large garish clouds, surcharged with hail or sleet, sweep with their broad cool shadows the fields, the woods, and hills; and by the contrast of their depths and bloom enhance the value of the vivid greens and yellows, so peculiar to this season; heightening also their brightness, and by their motion causing that playful change, always so much desired by the painter.*

Constable then attempts to explain the formation of such clouds, but his vocabulary is descriptive rather than meteorological:

> *The natural history ... of the skies above alluded to, which are so particularly marked in the hail squalls at this time of the year, is this:- the clouds accumulate in very large and dense masses, and from their loftiness seem to move but slowly: immediately upon these large clouds appear numerous opaque patches, which, however, are only small clouds passing rapidly before them, and consisting of isolated pieces, detached probably from the larger cloud. These floating much nearer the earth, may perhaps fall in with a stronger current of wind, which as well as their comparative lightness, causes them to move with great rapidity: hence they are called by wind-millers and sailors 'messengers,' being always the forerunners of bad weather.*

Forster also discusses these clouds, which are called 'scud' clouds in his second chapter, section XIII entitled 'Of the fragments of Nimbi called Scud'.[82] These clouds were not classified by Howard. Constable goes on to discuss how these scud clouds can have different colours according to their relative position:

> *They float about midway in what may be termed lanes of the clouds; and from being so situated, are almost uniformly in shadow,*

> *receiving only a reflected light from the clear blue sky immediately above, and which descends perpendicularly upon them into these lanes. In passing over the bright parts of the large clouds, they appear as 'darks'; but in passing the shadowed parts they assume a grey, a pale, or lurid hue.*

The scud clouds are not clearly visible in the plate but the text demonstrates how Constable liked to back up his powers of observation with explanation.

The text accompanying *Stoke by Neyland, Suffolk* (Plate 14) contains a long fascinating account of the rainbow, which was discussed in the last section. It begins: 'The solemn stillness of Nature in a Summer's Noon, when attended by thunder clouds, is the sentiment attempted in this print.... The effect of light and shadow on the sky and landscape are such as would be observed when looking to the northward at noon.' *A Sea Beach Brighton* also has a stormy sky: 'It is intended in this print to give one of those animated days when the masses of clouds, agitated and torn, are passing rapidly'. *Old Sarum* likewise is accompanied by thunder: 'Sudden and abrupt appearances of light, thunder clouds, wild autumnal evenings, solemn and shadowy twilights, ... with variously tinted clouds, dark, cold, and grey, or ruddy and bright, with transitory gleams of light.' This obsession with stormy skies has been linked to Constable's state of mind at the time after the death of his wife in 1828, and certainly the mezzotint medium allowed him to stress the contrast between light and darkness, shadow and sunlight.

The evidence of Constable's meteorological understanding from *English Landscape Scenery* confirms that he was interested in atmospheric processes as well as cloud form. His explanations are descriptive but he was writing for a general audience.

This chapter has examined the direct evidence in Constable's writings, annotations and pictures which demonstrates his meteorological understanding, together with the writings of others such as Leslie and Lucas about Constable. Other less direct evidence, such as the effect of Hampstead Heath, has also been discussed. It is clear that Constable had a remarkable knowledge of contemporary meteorological science and used this to great advantage in his art. No other artist of his age, or since, has succeeded in representing the sky with such scientific truth. This is not to imply that Constable's meteorological knowledge and vocabulary was perfect, or that he was averse to introducing 'special effects' in his skies if it suited him, as we shall see again in Chapter 3, but that he achieved a unique harmony of landscape art and contemporary meteorological science.

One further possible important influence on Constable's skies which has not yet been considered is that represented by the skies of other artists. These will be considered in Chapter 4.

Notes

1 C. R. Leslie, *Memoirs of the Life of John Constable*, 2nd edn (London: Longman's, Brown, Green and Longman's, 1845), p. 93.

2 Ibid., p. 307.

3 Conal Shields and Leslie Parris note that Constable was probably influenced by the teachings of Francis Bacon and his followers. Baconianism was popular in scientific circles at the beginning of the nineteenth century. Shields, C. & Parris, L. John Constable (London: Tate Gallery, 1969), p. 8. Ibid., pp. 333, 355.

4 C. Klonk, *Science and the Perception of Nature: British Landscape Art in the Late Eighteenth and Early Nineteenth Century* (London: Yale University Press, 1996), p. 198.

5 Keats, quoted in K. Badt, *John Constable's Clouds* (London: Routledge & Kegan Paul, 1950), p. 102.

6 See Badt, *John Constable's Clouds* for a fascinating discussion of the role of art and science at the beginning of the nineteenth century, and how this relates to the romantic movement.

7 Ibid.

8 L. Hawes, 'Constable's sky sketches', *Journal of the Warburg and Courtauld Institutes* XXXII (1969): 344–65.

9 J. E. Thornes, 'Constable's clouds', *Burlington Magazine* CXXI (1979): 697–704.

10 R. Wailes, *The English Windmill* (London: Routledge & Kegan Paul, 1954), p. 93.

11 Ibid., p. 110.

12 Hawes, 'Constable's sky sketches', p. 352.

13 Leslie, *Memoirs of the Life of John Constable* 1845, p. 4.

14 Ibid., 1845, p. 5.

15 Ibid., 1845, p. 350.

16 Taken from E. H. Gombrich, *Art and Illusion*, 5th edn (London: Phaidon, 1977), p. 271.

17 See B. A. Boudreau, 'John Constable's 1821 and 1822 cloud studies: the artist as a scientist', *Weather* 53 (1998): 357–62.

18 R.B. Beckett, *John Constable's Discourses* (Ipswich: Suffolk Records Society, 1970), p. 74.

19 L. Howard, *Barometrographia* (London, 1847).

20 Leslie, *Memoirs of the Life of John Constable* 1845, pp. 78–9.

21 G. Reynolds, *The Later Paintings and Drawings of John Constable* (London: Yale University Press, 1984), p. 72.

22 R. B. Beckett, *John Constable and the Fishers* (London: Routledge & Kegan Paul, 1952), p. 78.

23 Leslie, *Memoirs of the Life of John Constable* 1845, p. 91.

24 See Appendix 3.

25 See Appendix 3.

26 Leslie, *Memoirs of the Life of John Constable* 1845, p. 104.

27 Beckett, *John Constable and the Fishers*, p. 101.

28 For an interesting account of the development of the Beaufort wind scale see L. G. Garbett, 'Admiral Sir Francis Beaufort and the Beaufort scales of wind and weather', *Quarterly Journal of the Royal Meteorological Society* 52(218) (1926): 161–72.

29 Reynolds, *The Later Paintings and Drawings of John Constable*. The equivalent numbers in Hoozee, *L'opera completa di Constable* (Milan: Rizzoli Editore, 1979) are also given in Reynolds. In 1996 Reynolds published *The Early Paintings and Drawings of John Constable* (London: Yale University Press, 1996).

30 J. E. Thornes, 'The weather dating of John Constable's cloud studies', *Weather* 34 (1978): 308–15.

31 J. Constable, *English Landscape Scenery* (London, 1830), 'Spring'.

32 J. Constable, *English Landscape Scenery*, 2nd edn (London, 1833), introduction.

33 The mean monthly temperature is calculated from the daily means of the maximum and minimum recorded air temperature. These temperatures were published by J. Glaisher in the *Philosophical Transactions Part II* (1849) and are for Somerset House in central London. The weather data was published by Luke Howard in *The Climate of London* (London, 1833, 2nd edn). These temperature data are also representative of Hampstead where it may have been one or two degrees cooler due to the higher altitude.

34 Luke Howard, *The Climate of London*, 1833 edition.

35 Constable, *English Landscape Scenery*, 1830 edition, *Stoke by Neyland, Suffolk.*

36 J. Constable, *English Landscape Scenery*, 1833 edition, notes to *Summer morning*.

37 J. Ruskin, *The Works of John Ruskin*, edited by E. T. Cook and A. Wedderburn, 39 vols. (London: Library Edition: 1903-12), *VI*, p. 298.

38 In discussing the 'natural history' of *Stratford Mill* (Plate 36) with David Lucas, Constable stated 'that the inclination of the trunks of the main group of trees away from the river showed the direction of the prevailing wind'. R. B. Beckett, *John Constable's Correspondence*, 6 vols, vol. 4, *Patrons, Dealers and Fellow Artists* (Ipswich: Suffolk Records Society, 1966) p. 417.

39 The cost of each edition is included to provide a clue as to when Constable acquired his copy.

40 L. Parris, C. Shields and I. Fleming-Williams (eds) *John Constable: Further Documents & Correspondence*, [*JCFD&C*] (London: The Tate Gallery and the Suffolk Records Society, 1975) p. 44.

41 R.B. Beckett, *John Constable's Correspondence*, vol. 4, p. 146.

42 L. Parris et al., *JCFD&C* (p. 44) do not express any doubts.

43 The book is listed in L. Parris et al., *JCFD&C* (p. 32) as part of the Constable family collection.

44 R.B. Beckett, *John Constable's Discourses*, p. 28.

45 The text for *Old Sarum* in *English Landscape Scenery* is given in full in Beckett, *John Constable's Discourses*, p. 24. Constable's thoughts are remarkably similar to Forster's:

> *The present appearance of Old Sarum – wild, desolate and dreary – contrasts strongly with its former greatness. This proud and 'towered city', once giving laws to the whole kingdom – for it was here our earliest parliaments on record were convened – can now be traced but by vast embankments and ditches, tracked only by sheepwalks: 'The plough has passed over it'.*

Constable's notes accompanying *Stonehenge* state:

The mysterious monument of Stonehenge, standing remote on a bare and boundless heath, as much unconnected with the events of past ages as it is with the uses of the present, carries you back beyond all historical records into the obscurity of a totally unknown period.

46 See W. G. K. Middleton, *A History of the Theories of Rain* (London: Oldbourne History of Science Library, 1965), p. 111.

47 Luke Howard, *The Climate of London*, 1833 edition, p. xlii, footnote.

48 Ibid., p. 137.

49 H. Brandes first 'recognised that cumulus clouds were formed as a result of the convection upwards of moist air' in 1820. See J. A. Day and F. H. Ludlam, 'Luke Howard and His Clouds', *Weather* 27 (1972): p. 454.

50 Badt, *John Constable's Clouds*.

51 'Bad weather' is defined by the British Meteorological Office in *Cloud Types for Observers* (London: HMSO, 1962), p. 11, as 'the conditions which generally exist during precipitation and a short time after'.

52 See R. Abercromby 'Suggestions for an International Nomenclature of Clouds', *Quarterly Journal of the Royal Meteorological Society* 13 (1887): p. 62.

53 Luke Howard, *The Climate of London*, 1833 edition, p. lxxii.

54 L. Parris et al., *JCFD&C*, p. 45.

55 L. Howard, 'Clouds'. In Rees's *Cyclopedia* (1807), p. viii.

56 Badt, *John Constable's Clouds*, p. 63 – these thoughts are echoed by Klonk, *Science and the Perception of Nature: British Landscape Art in the Late Eighteenth and Early Nineteenth Century* (London: Yale University Press, 1996), in her definition of 'phenomenalism'.

57 *Constable: Paintings, Watercolours and Drawings*, bicentenary exhibition catalogue compiled by Leslie Parris, Ian Fleming-Williams and Conal Shields (London: Tate Gallery Publishing, 1976), p. 128

58 Reynolds, *The Later Paintings and Drawings of John Constable*, p. 129, 23.55–23.74.

59 I. Fleming-Williams, *Constable and His Drawings* (London: Philip Wilson, 1990), p. 284.

60 Tate Gallery, *Constable: Paintings, Watercolours and Drawings*, p. 111, 'Winter', lines 245–62.

61 Matthew XXVI, 64.

62 Reynolds, *The Early Paintings and Drawings of John Constable*, p. 252 and plate 1434.

63 P. D. Schweizer, 'John Constable, rainbow science, and English color theory', *The Art Bulletin* LXIV(3) (1982): p. 427.

64 Ibid., p. 425.

65 See Appendix 3.

66 G. P. Landow, 'The rainbow: a problematic image'. In U. C. Knoepflmacher and G. B. Tennyson, *Nature and the Victorian Imagination* (Berkeley: University of California Press, 1977): 341–69.

67 See M. Cormack, *Constable* (Oxford: Phaidon, 1986), p. 205.

68 Schweizer, 'John Constable, rainbow science, and English color theory', p. 426.

69 Reynolds, *The Later Paintings and Drawings of John Constable*, p. 225.

70 Cormack, *Constable*, p. 205.

71 A. Wilton, *Constable's English Landscape Scenery* (London: British Museum, 1979), p. 38.

72 C. B. Boyer, *The Rainbow from Myth to Mathematics* (New York: Yoseloff, 1959), pp. 249–50.

73 For full discussions of this dilema see Schweizer, 'John Constable, rainbow science, and English color theory', p. 431, and M. Kemp, *The Science of Art* (New Haven: Yale University Press, 1990), part III, pp. 259–322.

74 G. Field, *Chromatography; or, a Treatise on Colours and Pigments* (London, 1835), p. 233.

75 Schweizer, 'John Constable, rainbow science, and English color theory', p. 430.

76 Ibid., pp. 427–30.

77 These measurements are taken from the original which is located in the British Museum Print Room.

78 Fleming-Williams, *Constable Landscape Watercolours and Drawings* (London: Tate Gallery, 1976), quoting from Leslie, *Memoirs of the Life of John Constable* 1845, p. 310.

79 D. K. Lynch and W. Livingston, *Color and Light in Nature* (Cambridge: Cambridge University Press, 1995), p. 107.

80 G. Reynolds, *Constable: The Natural Painter* (St. Albans: Panther Books, 1976), p. 117.

81 Quoted in Wilton, *Constable's English Landscape Scenery*, pp. 7–8.

82 T. Forster, *Researches about Atmospheric Phaenomena*, 3rd edn (London, Harding, Mavor and Lepard, 1823), p. 76.

CHAPTER THREE

Evolution of the skies in Constable's art

A fresher gale
Begins to wave the woods and stir the stream

I shall now look in detail at the developments and changes that took place in Constable's skies as his career developed. Indeed, just as Damisch[1] uses clouds to help to unravel the history of landscape art up to the end of the nineteenth century, so we can use Constable's skies to help trace the evolution of his art. Implicit in this review is the notion that Constable's skies improved steadily through his career, becoming gradually more realistic, up to and beyond his skying period of 1820–22. The increasing confidence with which Constable introduced the wind into his canvases, as his career progressed, provides useful evidence for the chronology of his works; moreover the gradual improvement in skill that Constable developed in the painting of his skies means that the skies can be used, in conjunction where appropriate with historical weather records, to help to date certain works.

Reynolds does not believe that, in general terms, it is possible to date Constable's works in terms of development: 'We cannot say of him, as we can of many major painters, that his production displays an undeviating and unreversed progression from an earlier to a later manner, and that any specific piece can be placed at a definite point on this ascending curve.'[2] Constable's skies however, do appear to follow a linear, undeviating and unreversed progression as his career develops. Shirley's biography of Constable, *The Rainbow*, published in 1949, interestingly divides Constable's life into a number of linear phases based on the time within an imaginary day.[3] If one were to create a similar imaginary day based on the interpretation of developments in Constable's skies the years would be remarkably similar to Shirley's division of Constable's life, but not quite the same. This parallel between Constable's life and his skies should not surprise us, for to Constable the sky was 'the chief organ of sentiment'. His skies followed his moods – as he said after his wife had died in 1828: 'can it be wondered that I paint perpetual storms?'

I have modified Shirley's scheme slightly and added the appropriate Beaufort wind speed for added effect to give the following divisions for this chapter:

Dawn in the valley	1776–98	Calm
Sunrise	1799–1811	Light air
Morning	1812–16	Slight breeze
Late morning	1817–20	Gentle breeze
High noon	1821–22	Moderate breeze
Afternoon	1823–28	Fresh breeze
Sunset	1829–32	Strong breeze
The valley in shadow	1833–37	Near gale

Badt points out the difficulty of dividing Constable's works into the traditional four groups into which most painters' works can be divided – the first drafts, the sketches, the studies and the finished works.[4] Badt therefore divides Constable's works into four other groups: the pencil studies and sketches; the landscape sketches in oil (rarely in watercolours); the finished oil paintings usually intended for exhibition; and finally the sky/cloud studies which, he argues, form a special group of their own. This classification is not all embracing but does provide an initial framework within which to discuss the works that will be examined in this chapter.

Constable's pencil studies and sketches do not usually contain much information about the sky and therefore they will not be discussed in great detail. There are some notable exceptions however and these will be examined where appropriate. There are also many drawings that use other media, such as pen and ink, or combinations of pencil, pen and grey wash, some of which contain skies of interest.

The landscape sketches in oil, especially those that were made in advance of the big 'six-footers', enabled Constable to experiment with the composition of the proposed finished work. In some cases the vitality and freedom, the expressiveness and feelings contained in these sketches has made them even more prized than the finished works that followed them. However the skies in these sketches are often unrecognisable in form, and, as Badt explains, 'In these sketches the clouds are not so much represented as merely indicated; they have no definite natural forms but are either wildly scampering ribbons or patches, wreaths, or balls and lumps of white and grey, which simply suggest the shapelessness, the changeability and indefiniteness of clouds driving across the sky.'[5] These skies are wonderfully impressionistic, but will not be discussed in detail unless there is an obvious change in mood, caused by the sky, between the sketches and the finished work.

The watercolour sketches are important, because, by definition, it is so much easier to express a transient moist sky in watercolour than in oil. It is surprising, therefore, that Constable did not use watercolour more often. There were two distinct watercolour periods: firstly up to 1806 and then from 1830 onwards. Ian Fleming-Williams points out that Constable's first experiments with watercolour coincided with the first major exhibition of The Watercolour Society in London in 1805.[6] It is almost certain that Constable attended this exhibition where many of the exhibits had weather-related titles such as *A Partial Shower, Sunshine and Distant Rain* and *Still, Warm Evening*. Constable's watercolours at this time, especially those of 1806 produced in the Lake District, will be examined in detail for their weather content. There was then a long gap until 1830 when Constable suddenly switched to using watercolours for all his outdoor painting. Constable exhibited four watercolours in the 1832 exhibition, and three of them received a favourable review from the *Literary Gazette*: 'Nos. 632, 643, 644. J. Constable, R.A. – Under these numbers we have a church, a mill, and a farmhouse, making a trio of rural associations at once picturesque and pleasing. Need we add, that they sparkle and glitter with the *dew* of Mr. Constable's pencil? Indeed, as water-colours, so they ought.'[7]

The finished oil paintings, which were produced in the studio using traditional techniques, are most clearly influenced by the Dutch, Flemish and Italian schools of landscape painting. They are very different from the landscape oil sketches and, as Badt suggests, 'these pictures are silent, calm, deeply considered, and in them feeling is controlled by thought'.[8] The skies in these finished works are probably the most realistic in all landscape art, and they show a clear progression in naturalistic quality throughout his life. They are the main subject of discussion in this chapter and it will be shown that the skies of Constable's finished landscapes were transformed by the skying period of 1820/22 such that the sky of *The Hay Wain* is the first of Constable's skies to approach what he was trying to achieve.

The sky studies, almost exclusively of 1820/22, will be examined in detail. I agree with Badt that these studies are unique and should be looked at as a separate group. Why did Constable feel the need to produce this remarkable series of studies, and why did he start to annotate them with detailed weather notes, as already shown in Chapter 2? How do they relate to the rest of Constable's art? These, and other questions, will be tackled in the section 'High noon' below.

3.1 Dawn in the valley 1776–98: calm

Although very few paintings and sketches survive from this period, his time working for his father, and training for part of that time as a windmiller, would have taught Constable much about the workings of the weather, as discussed in the last chapter. His friendship with Sir George Beaumont began to develop and Constable, at the impressionable age of eighteen, was introduced by him to Claude, Cozens and Girtin. Constable spent as much time as he could painting in the fields and woods with John Dunthorne, the local plumber and glazier, but there are few signs in the works that survive of Constable's impending genius, nor of his interest in the sky. His family were reluctant for Constable to pursue a career as an artist, but they did allow him to have painting lessons and associate with local and London-based artists. Later in life, in a letter to John Fisher in 1821, Constable recalls that it was the scenes of his boyhood that made him a painter and that 'I had often thought of pictures of them before ever I touched a pencil'.[9]

Constable had no formal drawing lessons and the turning point in his artistic education happened almost by chance. In 1796 he went on a business trip to Edmonton, just outside London, and became acquainted with the portraitist, engraver, topographer and part-time drawing master John Thomas 'Antiquity' Smith, and the professional artist John Cranch. These two friendships gave Constable what he needed most – pragmatic advice on both the theory and practice of art. Smith, in particular, provided Constable with the confidence to indulge his feelings and find beauty in paintings of nature, although Constable also copied artists such as Jacob Ruisdael at this time. Constable was no child genius, as were Girtin and Turner. He had to struggle to learn the rudiments of the profession, and indeed later in life he wrote 'The art requires a long apprenticeship, being *mechanical* as well as intellectual' and also that the art of seeing nature 'is a thing almost as much to be acquired as the art of reading the Egyptian hieroglyphics'.[10]

At this early age Constable was very familiar with the tall dynamic skies of his native Suffolk but he had not yet attempted to paint them. He had acquired however the basic skills of painting and a love of nature that was to serve him well in later life.

3.2 Sunrise 1799–1812: light air

In 1799 Constable went up to London and through his acquaintance with Joseph Farington, the academician and diarist, he managed to gain admittance as a probationer at the Royal Academy School. There then followed a period of tuition and copying from the old masters, and from Jacob Ruisdael, already his favourite artist. He became a full student at the Academy by the end of 1799 and built up a series of friendships with artists and dealers. In one of his letters to Dunthorne, probably in his first winter in London, he shows his affection for the sky. 'I paint by all the daylight we have, and that is little enough. I sometimes see the sky, but imagine to yourself how a pearl must look through a burnt glass.'[11] The smoke from a million domestic and industrial fires in London's winter air produced the burnt glass effect. Constable's reference to the sky as a 'pearl' shows his astute observation and love of the unpolluted air of Suffolk.

The next few years saw Constable journeying between London and Suffolk. He would spend as much time as he could and most of the summers in East Bergholt, which he still regarded as his home. His first exhibit at the annual Royal Academy exhibition was in 1802, the year when he wrote the famous phrase 'There is room enough for a natural painter' in a letter to Dunthorne.[12] This letter, as well as spelling out Constable's determination to become a professional landscape painter, is full of statements that shaped the rest of his career:

> *For the last two years I have been running after pictures, and seeking the truth at second hand. I have not endeavoured to represent nature with the same elevation of mind with which I set out, but have rather tried to make my performances look like the work of other men.... There is little or nothing in the exhibition worth looking up to. There is room enough for a natural painter. The great vice of the present day is bravura, an attempt to do something beyond the truth.*

Constable's exhibit at the 1802 exhibition was called *Landscape* but he was very disappointed that another of his submissions, possibly entitled (according to Leslie) *Flatford Mill*, was rejected. Leslie records that Constable took one of his rejected pictures to show Benjamin West, the then President of the Academy. The following extract from Leslie is worth repeating in full:

> *'Don't be disheartened, young man, we shall hear of you again; you must have loved nature very much before you could have painted this.' He then took a piece of chalk, and showed Constable how he might improve the chiaroscuro by some additional touches of light between the stems and branches of the trees, saying, 'Always remember, Sir, that light and shadow never stand still.' Constable said it was the best lecture, because a practical one, on chiaroscuro he ever heard. Mr West, at the same time, said to him, 'Whatever object you are painting, keep in mind its prevailing character rather than its accidental appearance (unless in the subject there is some peculiar reason for the latter) and never be content until you have transferred that to canvas. In your skies, for instance, always aim at brightness, although there are states of the atmosphere in which the sky itself is not bright. I do not mean that you are not to paint solemn or lowering skies, but even in the darkest effects there should be brightness. Your darks should look like the darks of silver, not lead or of slate.' This advice was not addressed to an inattentive ear.*[13]

This lesson must have made a deep impact on Constable in that he could tell such an exact story to Leslie. The advice regarding the painting of skies and chiaroscuro would be music to his ears, and this letter is a clear forerunner of Constable's famous 'skies' letter written to Fisher in 1821. (See Appendix 3.) It must have sown the seed in Constable's mind that 'the sky is the source of light in nature, and governs everything'. Also it taught Constable that the dynamic forces in nature that produce the light and the wind are more important than the static 'objects' of nature. Thus 'the prevailing character' of the sky is more important than 'its accidental appearance'. It is ironic that Constable mostly painted 'the prevailing character of the sky' during his career, yet his skies were criticised more than Turner's who preferred to mostly paint the sky's 'accidental appearance'.

Constable returned to the Stour valley in the summer of 1802 and set about putting his new 'charter' into practice. He painted real views, such as *Dedham Vale* (Plate 15) and *A Lane near Dedham* without any of the 'bravura' he so despised. However the skies in these two pictures are disappointing. The clouds are distant and two dimensional and they resemble more that 'white sheet drawn behind the objects' than real skies. It would be a long time, almost another twenty years, before Constable mastered his skies.

This initial, intensive period of outdoor work in 1802 was not repeated for some years. In April 1803 Constable spent nearly a month at sea on the East Indiaman *Coutts* before it sailed to China, and of the voyage he wrote to Dunthorne: 'I saw all sorts of weather. Some the most delightful, and some as melancholy. But such is the enviable state of a painter that he finds delight in every dress nature can possibly assume.'[14] This is an interesting observation and shows that Constable found

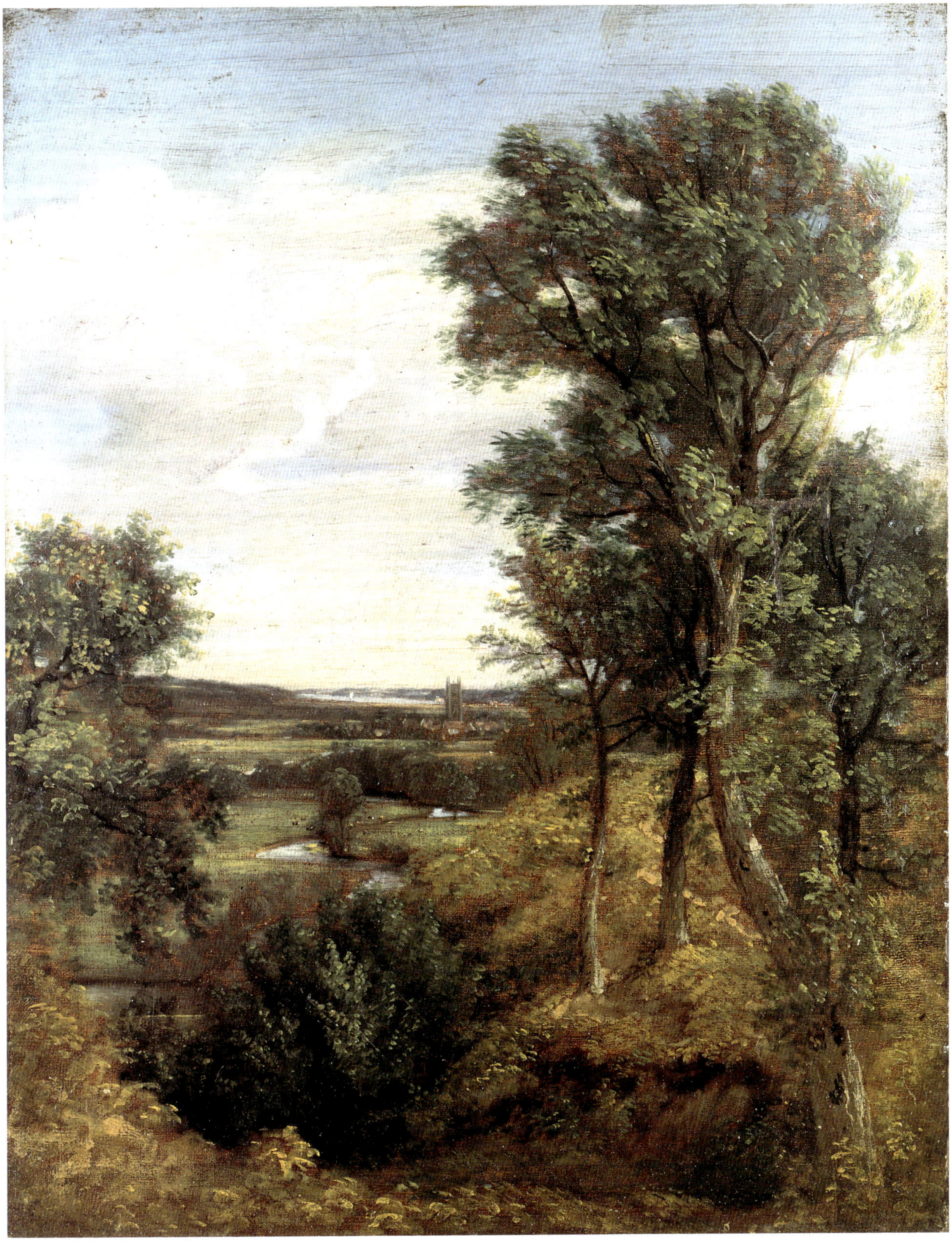

Plate 15 John Constable, *Dedham Vale*, 1802. V&A Picture Library

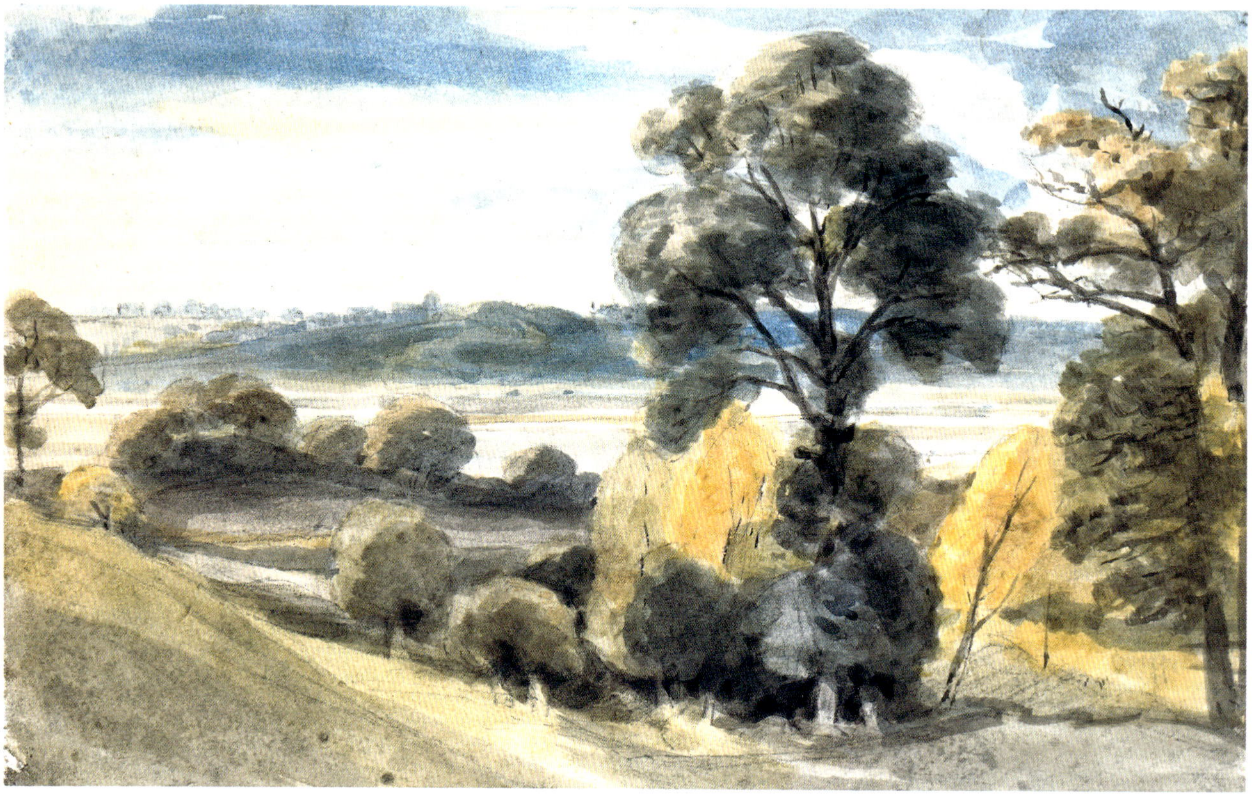

Plate 16 John Constable, *Stour Valley*, 1805. Private collection

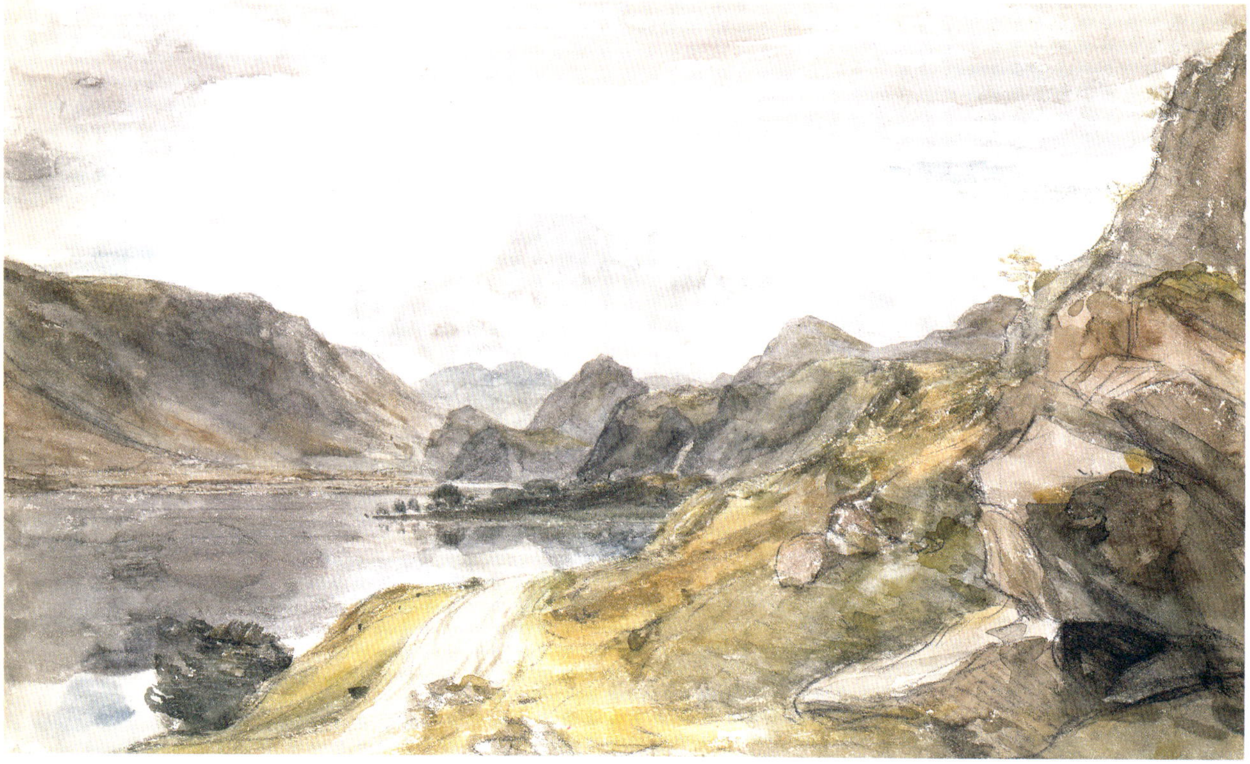

Plate 17 John Constable, *Derwentwater*, 1806. Private collection

delight in all weather situations. The analogy of the sky being represented as 'dressing' nature, and therefore changing nature's moods, is a good one.

The first known drawing of a rainbow by Constable has been dated by Reynolds at somewhere between 1800 and 1805.[15] The drawing is in black and white and shows a complete bow over East Bergholt Common.

In 1805 Constable annotated a watercolour view entitled *Stour Valley* (Plate 16) with the words: 'Nov' 4. 1805 – Noon very fine day the Stour'. This is the earliest known weather-related inscription made by Constable and shows his keen attention to detail in explaining the lighting of the landscape. The date and the time of day are explicitly determined by the low angle of the sun and the cool sunlight. The weather statement that it was a 'very fine day' implies that the sky was mostly clear with little cloud and bright sunshine. The sky in the picture is just an impression, there are no recognisable clouds. The long shadows point to the north so the view is to the east.

Another watercolour dated November 1805, entitled *Vale of Dedham*, has a piece of paper framed with the drawing on which is written 'a very fine morning'. Constable had already started to note the weather conditions, as well as the date and time, a habit he continued on his Lake District tour of 1806. In total Constable stayed seven weeks in the Lake District, producing at least ninety-five drawings and watercolours from 1 September through to 19 October. Several of these drawings had weather inscriptions, such as *Derwentwater* (Plate 17) which is inscribed on the back in pencil: 'Sep. Noon 1806 about 2 o clock the clouds had moved off [?to] the left and left a very beautiful clear effect on all the Distances ... the heavy clouds remained edged with light'. The sky in this picture is one of the most realistic of his works to that date. The clouds do appear to have some three-dimensional character and there is the beginning of cloud perspective. The weather throughout his Lake District tour was mostly cloudy and wet, but, as Fleming-Williams points out, Constable did not start to annotate the drawings until he arrived in the more mountainous area to the north of the lakes.[16] There then followed a series of annotations in quick succession:

21 September:	*...stormy with slight rain*
	Stormy Day – noon
22 September:	*...very stormy afternoon*
? September:	*Noon ... about 2 o clock the clouds had moved off [to?] the left and left a very beautiful clear effect on all the Distances ... the heavy clouds remained edged with light*
25 September:	*fine clouday day tone very mellow*
27 September:	*twilight – after much rain*
1 October:	*Evening after a fine day*
	Evening after a shower
2 October:	*morning previous to a fine day*
	twylight after a very fine day
4 October:	*Noon Clouds breaking away after rain*
	Dark Autumnal day at noon ... the effect exceedingly terrific
6 October:	*Stormy Evening*
? October:	*10 oclock a very still fine morning*

The cloudy wet weather was of course typical for the Lake District at that time of year. Already Constable shows that he is interested in the changing weather, and that he wants to remind himself of the time of day that the picture represents, and what the weather had been like before and after he painted the picture. These annotations are not as detailed as they were to become on his 1821/22 sky studies, but interestingly are similar to the rather brief 1820 weather annotations he made (shown in Table 10 in the previous chapter). By 1820 though he had started also to note the wind speed and direction using a form of the Beaufort scale. The Lake District inscriptions do not mention the wind direction, although they do include the word 'stormy' several times, which implies strong winds. The Beaufort scale was only formally conceived in 1805 but a similar scale had been used by sailors since the middle of the eighteenth century. Constable would have been familiar with nautical terms from his connections with his father's boats and also from the month he spent on board ship in 1803. However, Constable does not appear to have mentioned the wind speed and/or direction on any of his pictures until the inscriptions of October 1820.

Leslie was not impressed by Constable's Lake District work, observing that: 'They abound in grand and solemn effects of light, shade, and colour, but from these studies he never painted any considerable picture.... I have heard him say the solitude of mountains oppressed his spirits.'[17] Ian Fleming-Williams suggests however, that the grey overcast skies would have focused Constable's powers of observation due to the enforced use of scotopic vision ('the vision supplied by cells in the retina that respond only to tonal differences, to shades of grey'), which reduces the detail and colour in poor light.[18] Fleming-Williams regards Constable's view of *Borrowdale, Twilight* (Plate 18) as an excellent example of scotopic vision and certainly the view shows perfect use of aerial perspective without recourse to detail. Fleming-Williams goes on to state that: 'It is in watercolour drawings such as this that we first see signs of the future Constable, the truly great landscape painter.'

The Lake District pictures certainly provided ample dynamic skies for Constable to paint or draw. His annotations to several of the sketches show that he was keenly interested in the weather and its effect on the lighting of the landscape, as well as in the painting of the mobile skies. He succeeded in improving the portrayal of clouds – as in *Derwentwater* (Plate 17) – and in the portrayal of aerial perspective – as in *Borrowdale, Twilight* (Plate 18). Thus the Lake District visit was very important in the development of Constable's skies. It was some time however before his skies painted in oil achieved the realism of these watercolour skies.

Constable's first 'pure sky' study has been dated at 1806; it is a pastel drawing on brown paper inside the back cover of an 1806 sketchbook now at the Louvre (RF08700). There was some doubt about whether or not this drawing had been added to the 1806 sketchbook at a later date but Reynolds establishes that it was originally facing another drawing in the sketchbook and therefore it certainly is of 1806.[19] Although there is a small strip of land along the bottom of the drawing it is essentially a 'pure sky' study; however the sky is difficult to interpret and the clouds are indistinct.

All the oils he exhibited in 1807 and 1808 at the Royal Academy and at the British Institution were Lake District scenes in which the sky was still little more than a backcloth. He failed to produce in oil the success of the dynamic watercolour skies. By 1808 it appears that Constable had begun producing oil sketches out of doors for the first time and on 1 August 1809 he painted a 'finished' oil picture, *Malvern Hall from the Lake*, outdoors in a single day. The afternoon sky, with the sun going down over the trees, is given some perspective by the radiating light, but the clouds are indistinct. *Malvern Hall from the South-West*, painted on the same visit to Solihull, has an interesting sky. Parris and Fleming-Williams state that the painting is 'remarkable for its lowering sky' which is unusual for this period in Constable's sky development.[20] The broken sheet of stratocumulus with small gaps to the blue sky beyond is more typical of a decade later in the *Weymouth Bay* (Plate 28) mould where the clouds appear to be too brown and too heavy.

Dedham Vale (Plate 19), painted in 1810, depicting an early morning mist lying in the valley bottom, was the first of several sketches for *Dedham Vale: Morning* exhibited at the Royal Academy in 1811, which shows gentle morning sunshine illuminating the landscape. The sky is still distant and two dimensional in both pictures, although the attempt to show the early morning stratus being burnt off by the sun is engaging. Constable, throughout his career, was interested in the changing light conditions at different times of day and year. This painting is his first attempt to

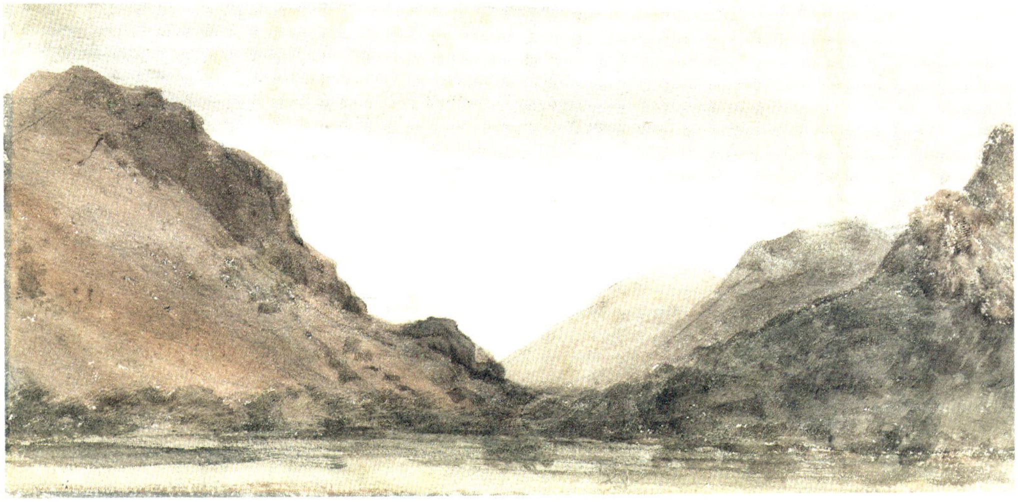

Plate 18 John Constable, *Borrowdale, Twilight*, 1806. Private collection

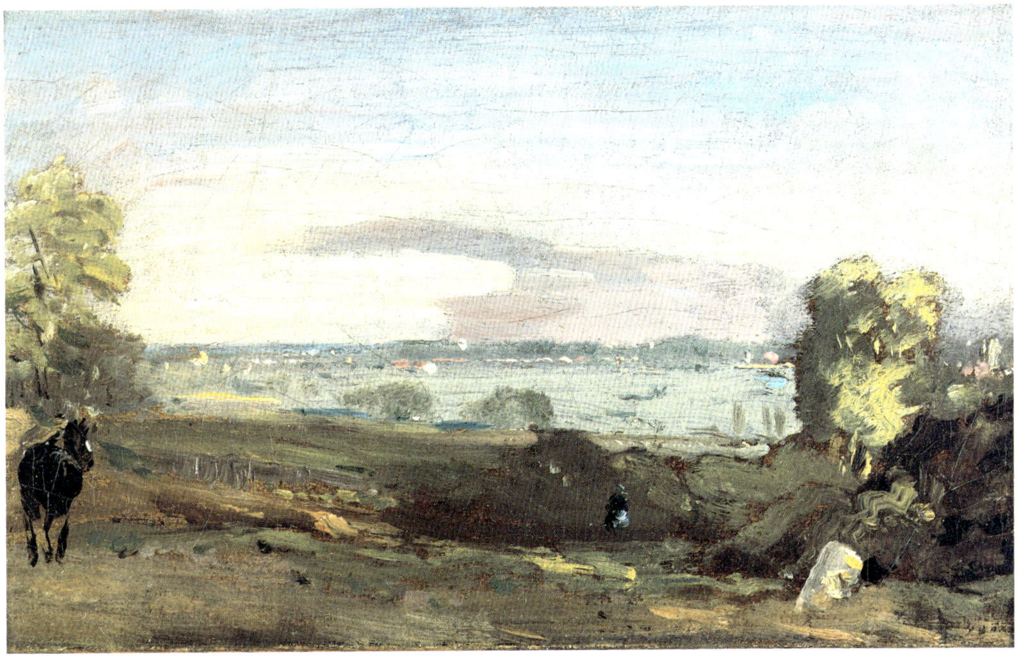

Plate 19 John Constable, *Dedham Vale*, 1810. Private collection

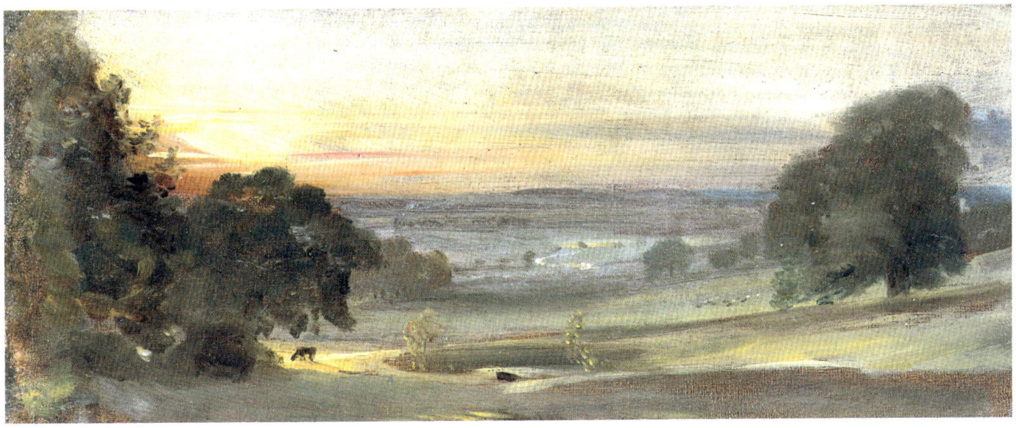

Plate 20 John Constable, *The River Stour at Sunset*, 1809. Private collection

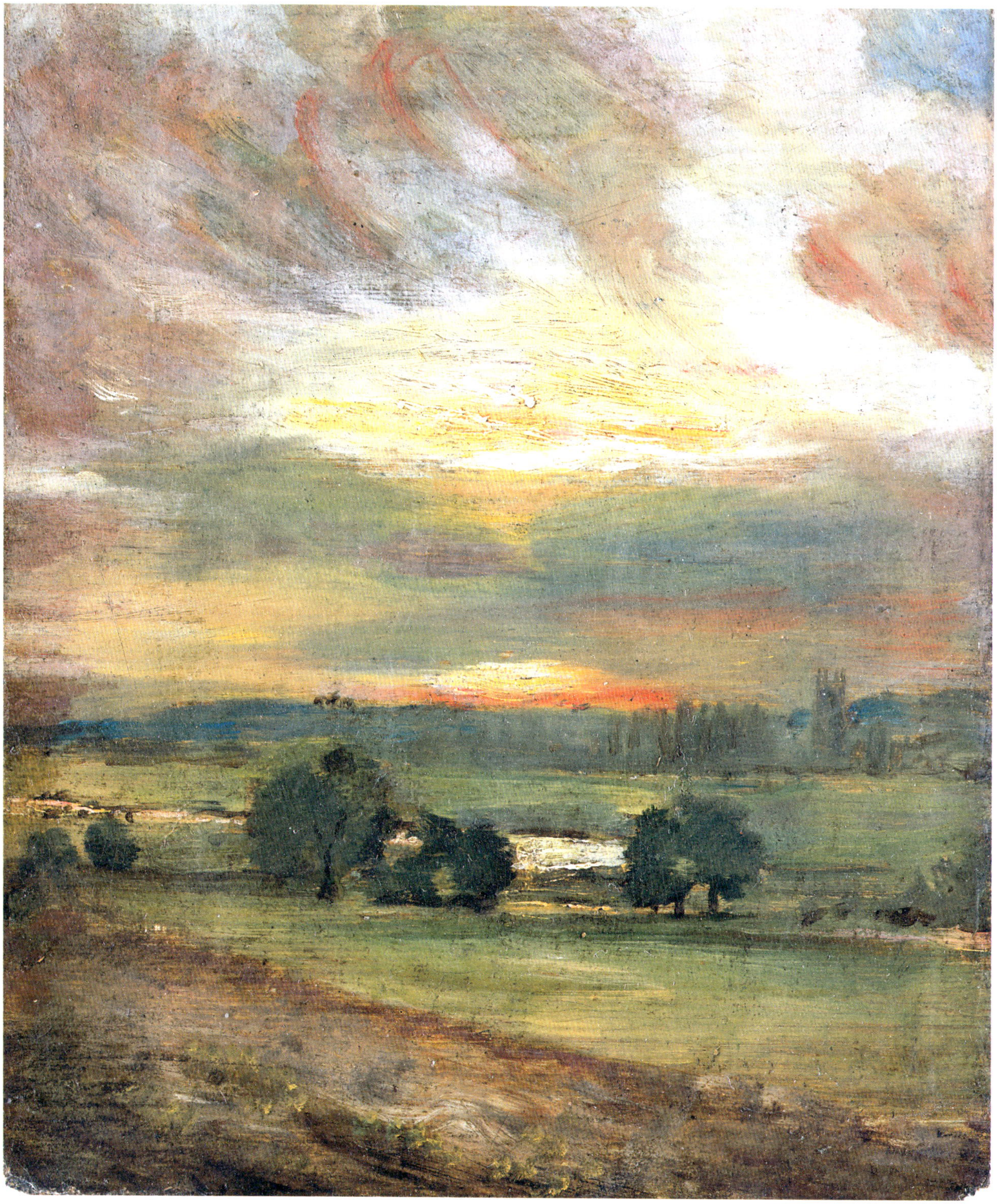

Plate 21 John Constable, *The Valley of the Stour, Sunset,* 1812. Private collection

capture the magic of an English country morning when the glow of sunrise is just departing.

In Chapter 4 we shall examine how the vivid sunrises and sunsets in some of Turner's work might have been influenced by volcanic eruptions, especially the 1815 eruption of Tambora. Lamb has published tables of volcanic eruptions that are likely to have affected the earth's climate for 1500–1968.[21] Table 5 (Chapter 1) gave further examples of volcanic eruptions in Constable's lifetime. In Constable's early boyhood in the years 1783–85 there were several significant eruptions in Iceland, Japan and Italy (Vesuvius) that caused the sun to be dimmed all over Europe. In Norfolk in 1783 it was reported that the sun remained coppery coloured until it was 20 degrees above the horizon. Coloured sunsets also attracted notice but Constable would have been too young to have been influenced by these significant events. The next volcanic eruption that received attention in England was in 1808 (in the Azores) when Luke Howard noted the abnormal brilliance of the twilight on 6 May 1808. As a result of the Mount Etna eruption of 1809 Howard reported a rose-coloured haze over the sky at twilight at Plaistow in London on 1 and 2 April 1809. Constable's oil sketch *The River Stour at Sunset* (Plate 20) dated at 1809 depicts a spectacular sunset. Another eruption in the Azores on 31 January 1811 led to unusually highly red-coloured skies over London on 3 and 8 February 1811 and again from mid June in every month until December 1811. Vesuvius also erupted again in 1811 and Howard recorded red twilights on 12, 15 and 19 October 1811. There was a violent eruption in St. Vincent (West Indies) in April 1812 and Howard noted an unusually coloured twilight on 8 May 1812 and during every month until the end of October 1812. Thus there were likely to have been heightened sky colours throughout this period of 1808–12, and there were many more important eruptions right through to the end of the century.

It is clear that the sunrises and sunsets of this period were notable for their increased redness. Since we can date many of Constable's pictures exactly it is interesting to compare his sunsets and sunrises with this volcanic record. For instance the Dedham Vale sunrises painted outdoors in 1810 all show a rose-coloured glow that culminated in *Dedham Vale: Morning*. From 1810 onwards the outdoor oil sketch began to play a more important role in his art. Did Constable merely faithfully portray the heightened sunrise colours, or was it the brilliant sunrises that attracted him to this theme? There is another vivid sunrise in *The Rectory from East Bergolt House,* also painted in 1810 and dated 30 September.

By the end of this era of 'sunrise' and experimentation Constable had achieved the peace and stillness of the early sunny morning but had not yet portrayed the world of movement or attempted to get the wind to blow in his oil paintings.

3.3 Morning 1812–16: slight breeze

Even more vivid skies, this time in the form of sunsets, were painted by Constable in 1812 – *A Hayfield behind West Lodge* (4 July), *Fields behind West Lodge, Sunset* (7 July) and *The Valley of the Stour, Sunset* (31 October, Plate 21). This collection of sunsets following the series of sunrises in 1810 suggests that Constable was building up his collection of studies at different times of day. The scientific approach of creating a dated collection of experiments in light and colour at different times of the day in order to explore how the light and colour of the sky affected the lighting and colours of the landscape was unique, and was later an important influence on the Impressionists, especially Monet.

Constable's first known painted rainbow was in 1812 with a study in oil entitled *Landscape with Double Rainbow* (Plate 22) which is dated 28 July 1812. On 22 July he had written to his wife, Maria, 'How much real delight have I had with the study of landscape this summer! either I am myself improved in the art of seeing nature ... or nature has unveiled her beauties to me less fastidiously'.[22] Constable's repertoire of sky effects was growing as he observed nature more closely. The double rainbow must be an early morning or late

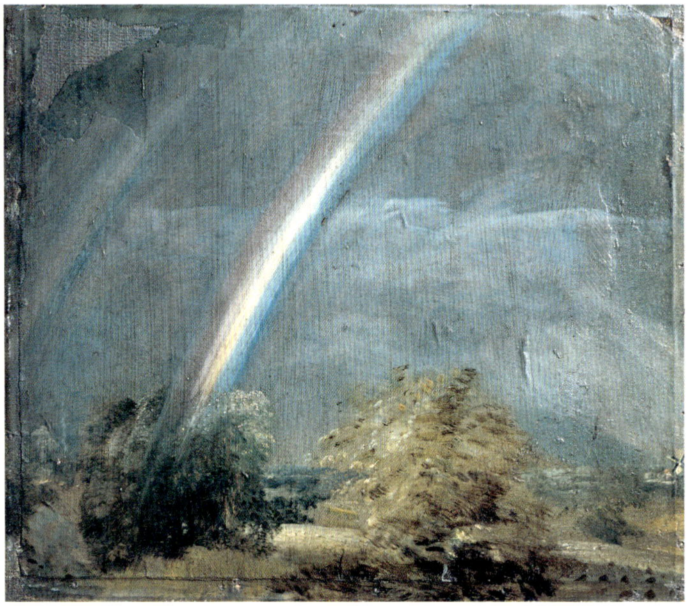

Plate 22 John Constable, *Landscape with Double Rainbow*, 1812. V&A Picture Library

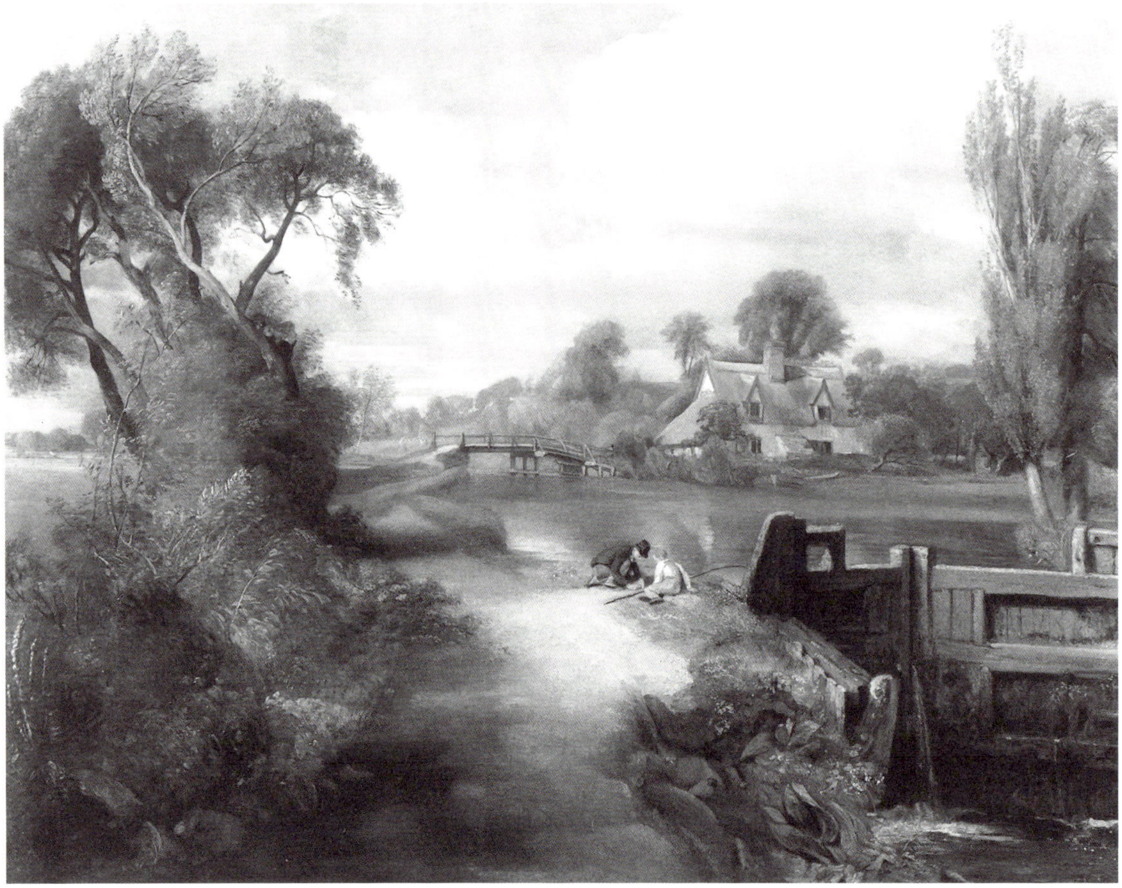

Plate 23 John Constable, *A Lock on the Stour*, 1813. Anglesea Abbey, The Fairhaven Collection (The National Trust). Photograph: Courtauld Institute of Art

afternoon scene as at that time of year, in July, the rainbow disappears between about 10am and 4pm. This double rainbow was painted well before Constable studied the theories of rainbow formation, as discussed in Chapter 2. Indeed it is not clear from the painting that the colours are reversed in the secondary bow, as they should be, nor that the secondary bow is twice the width of the primary bow. Probably he painted the secondary bow from memory rather than from observation, as often the secondary bow is only visible for a short length of time.

On 1 October 1812 Constable painted another rainbow in *Willy Lott's House with a Rainbow*. This time there is no sign of a double bow but the rainbow colours are more vivid. There are three bold colours: red, yellow and blue which show that Constable at this stage adopted the conventional artist's view of the rainbow as trichromatic (consisting of three colours) rather than Newton's heptachromatic view (seven colours).

This was a period of intense experimentation in Constable's life which resulted for the first time in natural colours appearing on his canvases. The skies are still quiet, but the light is more natural and the clouds are becoming three dimensional. If we look at the finished skies, for example, the sky of the 1813 *A Lock on the Stour* (Plate 23), the depicted clouds are undoubtedly cumulus, but they are still distant and one has to infer that similar clouds to the left of the picture are creating the sunshine and shade seen in the foreground. The sky and cloud colours are more realistic than hitherto but the scene is still static. The sky in *Malthouse Field, East Bergholt* (Plate 24), attributed to 1814, is ambitious with a lane of recognisable cumulus clouds running from the centre to the left of the picture giving some feel of perspective. In the 1814 *Landscape: Ploughing Scene in Suffolk (A Summerland)* there is a significant attempt to give the clouds perspective but the sky and the landscape are hardly linked and seem almost to

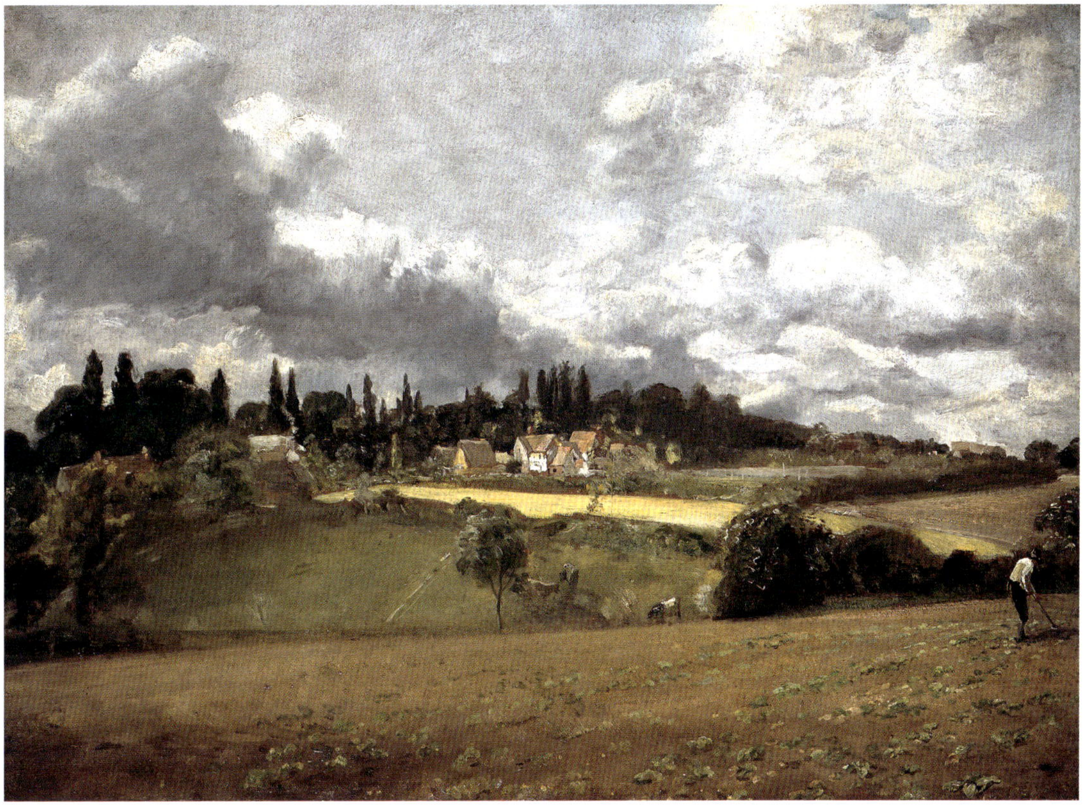

Plate 24 John Constable, *Malthouse Field, East Bergholt*, 1814. Private collection

belong to two separate paintings.[23] The sky of the 1815 *Golding Constable's Kitchen Garden* (Plate 25) is also still distant and although the fair weather cumuli are three dimensional and the cloud colours are realistic with their darkened bases, the sky is again separate from the landscape and the cloud shadows are out of sight.

One of the more interesting skies of this period appears in *Stoke by Nayland* (Plate 26) painted in oil on 30 July 1816. Here Constable has succeeded in giving depth to the sky, and the dark base of the cumulus street seen to the right of the tall tree suggests that the clouds are much closer than a similar street of cumulus above the horizon. Nevertheless there is no real harmony between the sky and the landscape. The sky is very bright and one would expect the landscape to be brighter too. This cannot be said of the sunlight in *Wivenhoe Park* (Plate 27) which is remarkably bright and warm but the clouds are distant and static and rather too heavy. The cloud perspective is impossible to untangle. The perspective in the landscape is superb, but as the eye travels across the lake to the house the clouds appear to rear up behind it in an almost vertical sky.

After Constable finally married Maria in October 1816 his landscape subjects began to broaden in scope and for the first time he painted coastal scenes. The two oil sketches entitled *Weymouth Bay* may well have been painted whilst on their six-week honeymoon at Osmington, near Weymouth. The larger of the two (Plate 28) has a huge enigmatic sky with streets of cumulus clouds climbing at 45 degrees over the horizon. Tyldesley, a meteorologist, writes about this painting:

> *By good fortune, I saw a sky very similar to the one Constable painted over this part of the Dorset coast on the afternoon of 4 August 1966. On that*

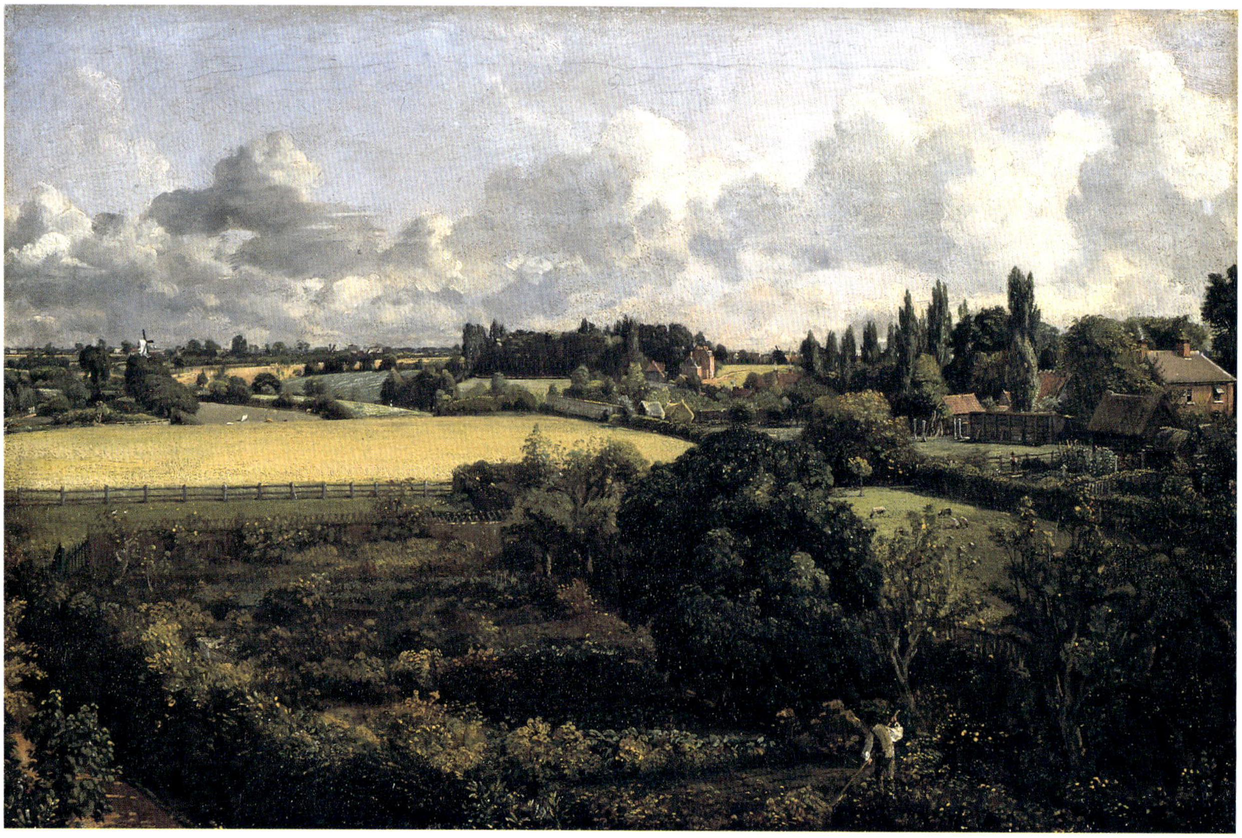

Plate 25 John Constable, *Golding Constable's Kitchen Garden*, 1815. Ipswich Borough Council Museums and Galleries

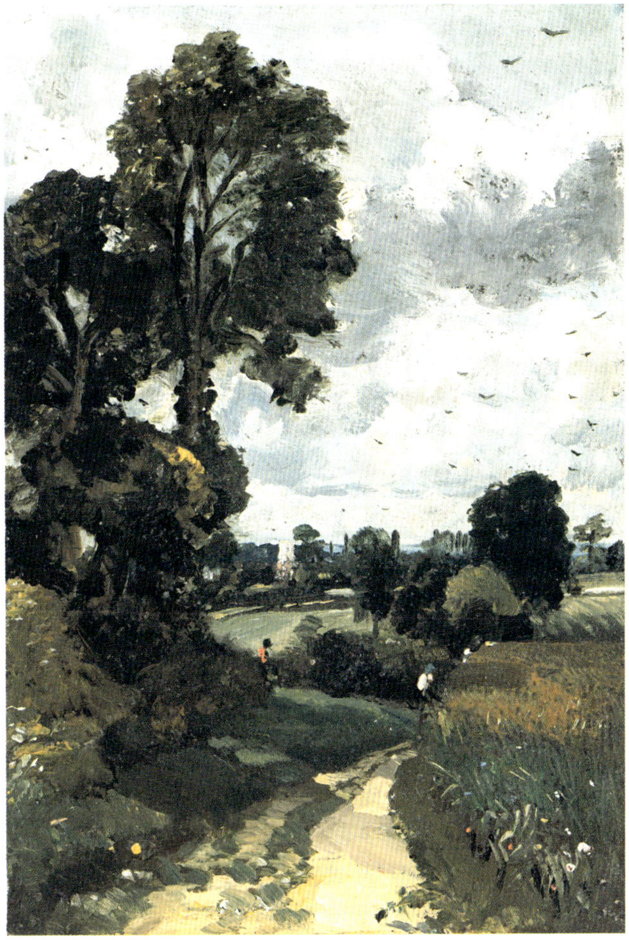

Plate 26 John Constable, *Stoke by Nayland*, 1816. Private collection

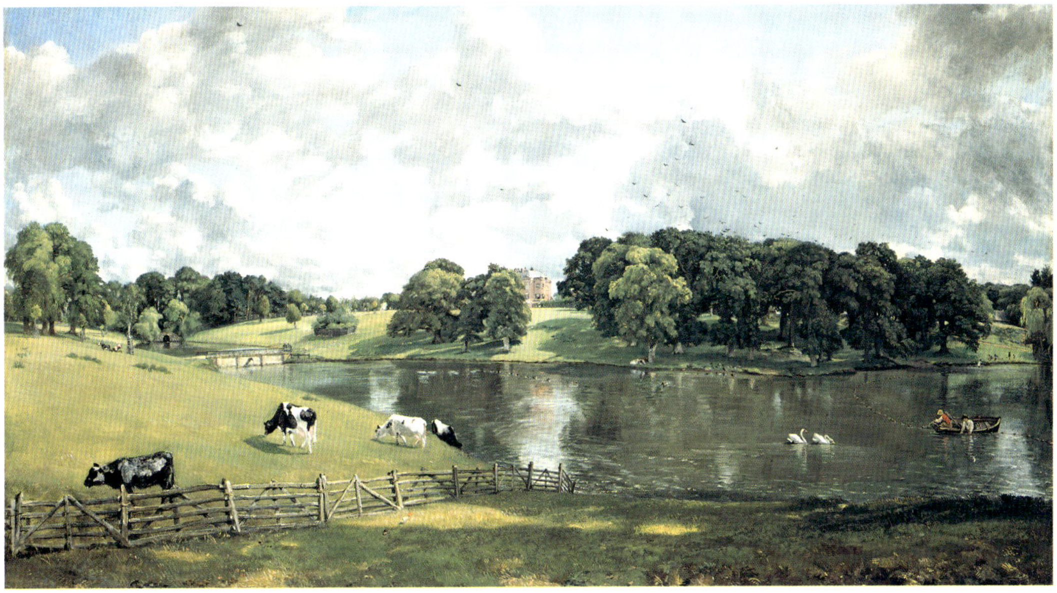

Plate 27 John Constable, *Wivenhoe Park, Essex*, 1816. National Gallery of Art, Washington, Widener Collection. Photograph copyright 1999 Board of Trustees, National Gallery of Art, Washington

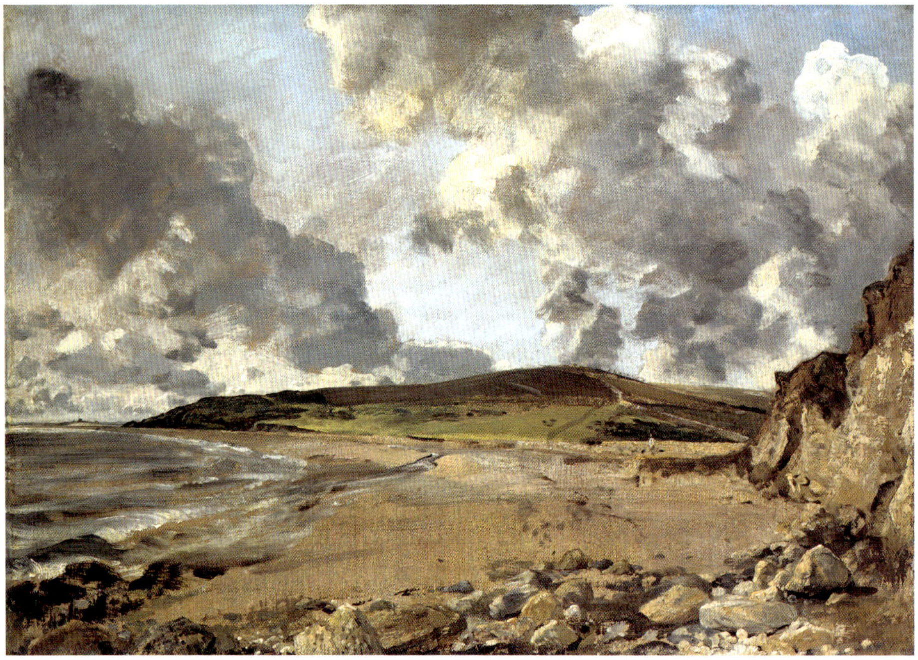

Plate 28 John Constable, *Weymouth Bay, with Jordan Hill*, 1816. National Gallery, London

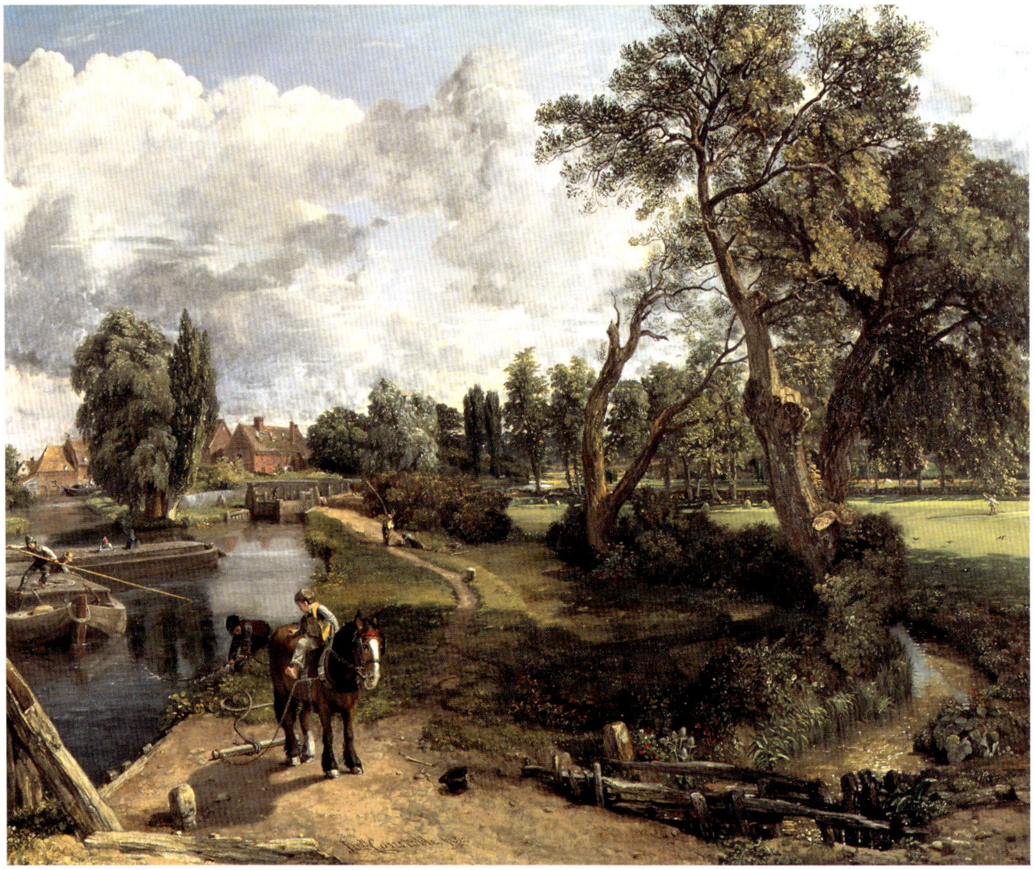

Plate 29 John Constable, *Scene on a Navigable River (Flatford Mill)*, 1817.
Copyright Tate Gallery, London 1998

day a depression was over the North sea, and in its rear an unstable west-north-westerly airstream covered the South Coast. Convective cloud was forming over points of high land around Weymouth, and streaming out over the sea in long lines almost parallel to the coast, forming a series of irregular cloud streets. Once over the sea, further vertical development was arrested by the lower surface temperature, so that each line of cloud thinned and finally dissolved well out to sea. The air was exceptionally clear, and a visibility of over 25 miles was reported from Portland throughout the afternoon.

This experience helps in appreciating what Constable saw, and why he had difficulty in rendering it in paint ... the farthest point of land in the painting is about 3 miles away, so that with a visibility of over 25 miles, there would be very little scope for such a conscientiously literal artist as Constable to employ any of the devices of aerial perspective.[24]

The cloud perspective, therefore, is not that unrealistic in *Weymouth Bay*, and Constable is not afraid to make his clouds obtrusive. The colouring of the clouds and their shapes are reminiscent of *Wivenhoe Park* but the effect is to make the clouds appear much too dense and heavy. Indeed the main cloud street on the right looks almost like a monster peering over the scene. In his famous skies letter of 1821 Constable wrote 'Certainly, if the sky is obtrusive, as mine are, it is bad; but if it is evaded, as mine are not, it is worse; it must and always shall with me make an effectual part of the composition.'[25] Up to this point in Constable's career his skies had not been obtrusive, they resembled more 'a white sheet drawn behind the objects'. From this point on Constable struggled to give his skies more prominence without being obtrusive – a difficult task.

Thus in this productive experimental period Constable's skies had progressed to become three dimensional with realistic perspective and form. Constable's favourite cloud – the cumulus – emerges to dominate his skies and to give his landscapes light and shade, sunshine and shadow. Most of the skies are still motionless and frozen in time but there are signs of movement in the trees and a slight breeze is developing.

3.4 Late morning 1817–20: gentle breeze

The year 1817 is seen as a watershed in Constable's career. His marriage shifted his attention from his parents' home in Suffolk to his new married life in London. *Flatford Mill* (Plate 29), which was exhibited at the Royal Academy exhibition of 1817, was the forerunner of his six-foot canvases that began with *The White Horse* (Plate 34) exhibited in 1819. This meant that everything had to be scaled up, including the sky. In *Flatford Mill* the sky is again distant and the clouds play no part in the lighting of the landscape. The form of the clouds has improved slightly but the problem of sky perspective has been avoided. Nevertheless the sky has progressed from *Wivenhoe Park* in that the three-dimensional form of the cumulus towers is more convincing and the clouds appear lighter and less dense.

The 1817 version of *A Cottage in a Cornfield* is easily distinguished from the version exhibited in 1833 by the sky (Plates 30 and 31). The 1817 version has an uninspiring sky with no perspective and no cloud form, whereas the 1833 painting has a powerful, dynamic sky, three dimensional in perspective, which Bonacina described as follows: 'In the *Cottage in a Cornfield* (V&A) we find a still scene of fierce noon-day heat in July or August, and get a powerful impression of fast growing cumulus clouds. That lonely cottage by the ripening corn will hardly escape a crashing storm that afternoon!'[26] Nothing approaching such a description could be written of the 1817 version. This is a clear case of how the sky can help to date some of Constable's works. Leslie Parris and Ian Fleming-Williams have postulated that much of the 1833 exhibited version was painted on the spot in 1815 and then 'licked up' in March 1833.[27] It is possible that the sky was also 'licked up' in 1833 as will be discussed in section 3.8 below.

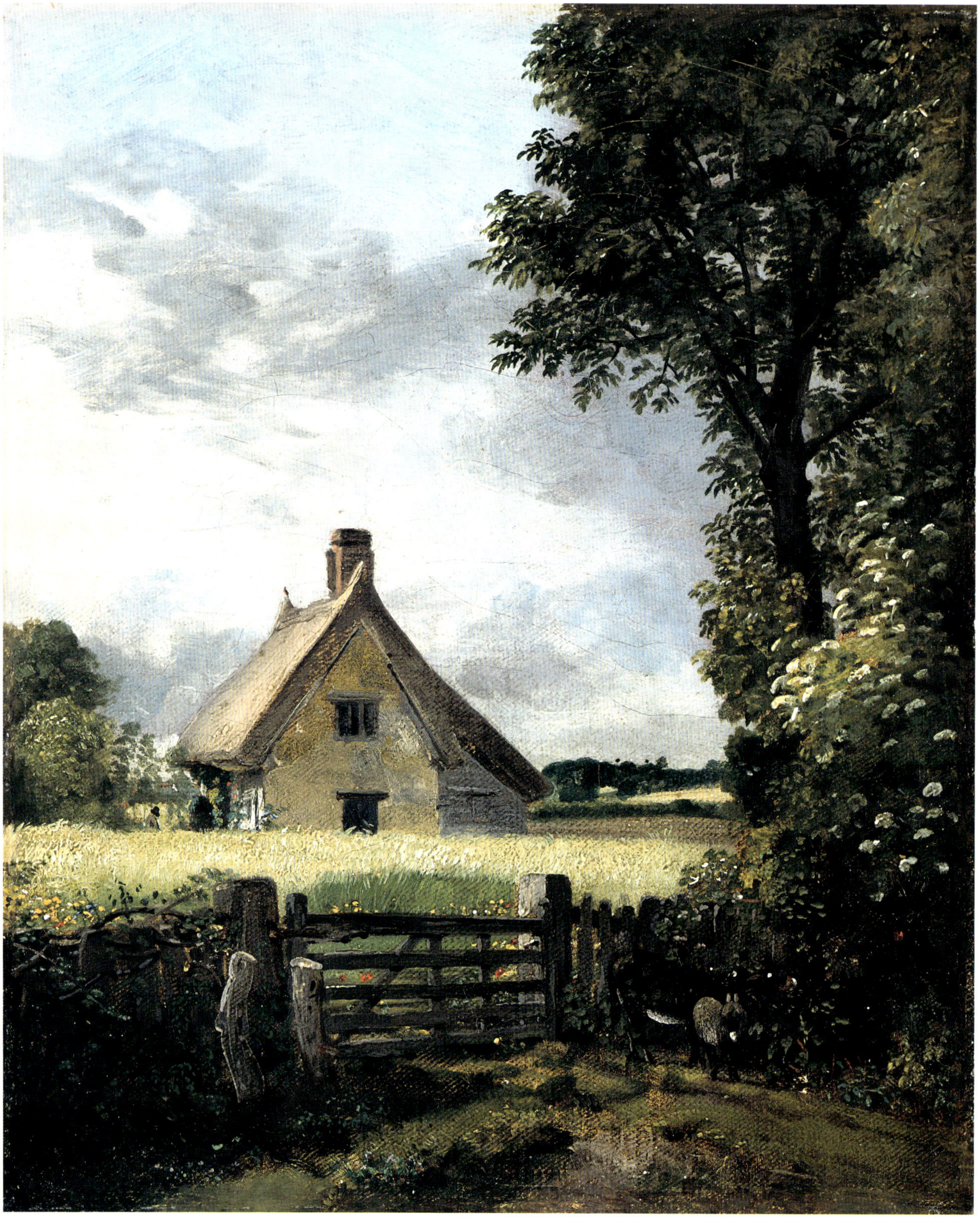

Plate 30 John Constable, *A Cottage in a Cornfield*, 1817. The National Museum of Wales

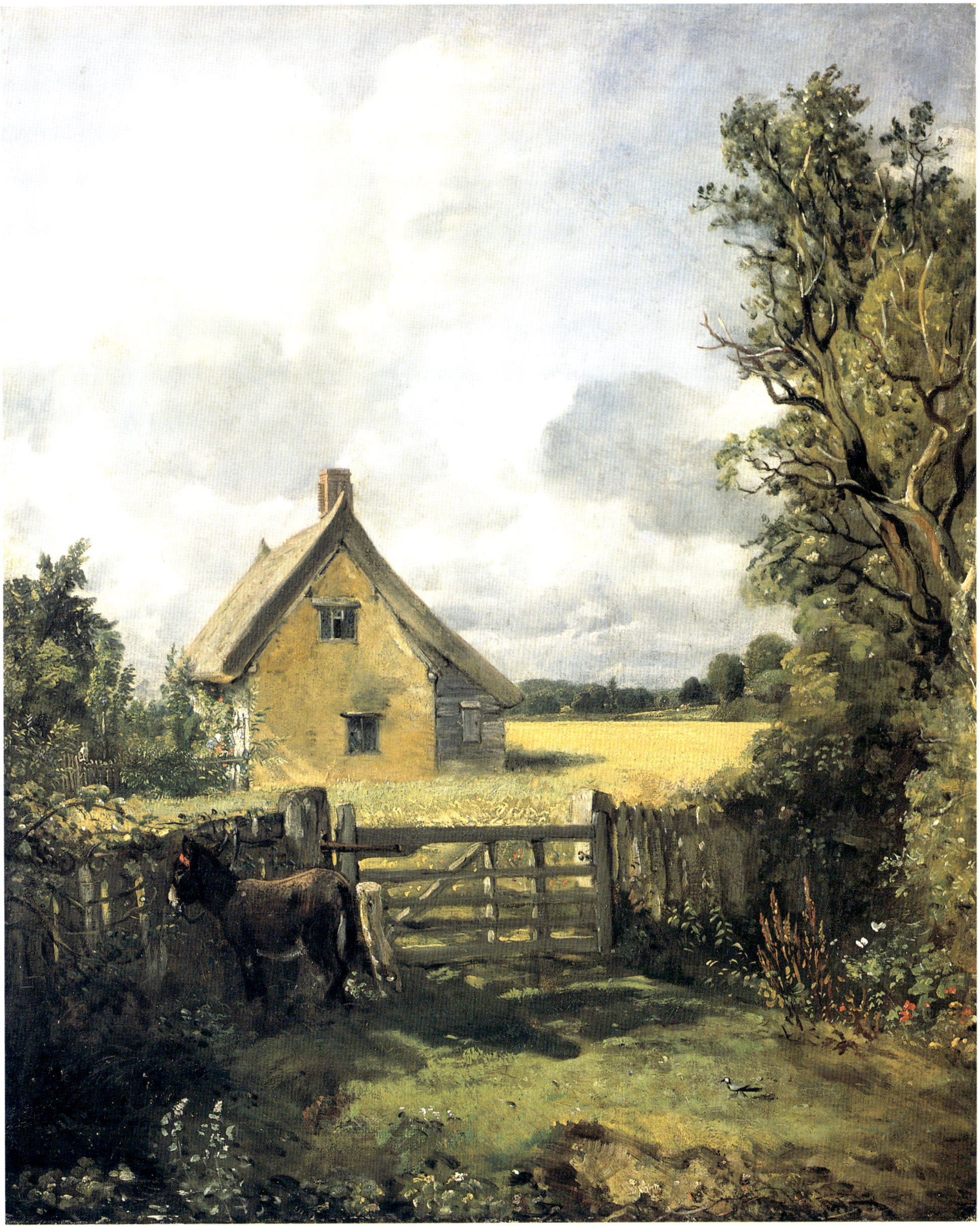

Plate 31 John Constable, *A Cottage in a Cornfield*, 1833. V&A Picture Library

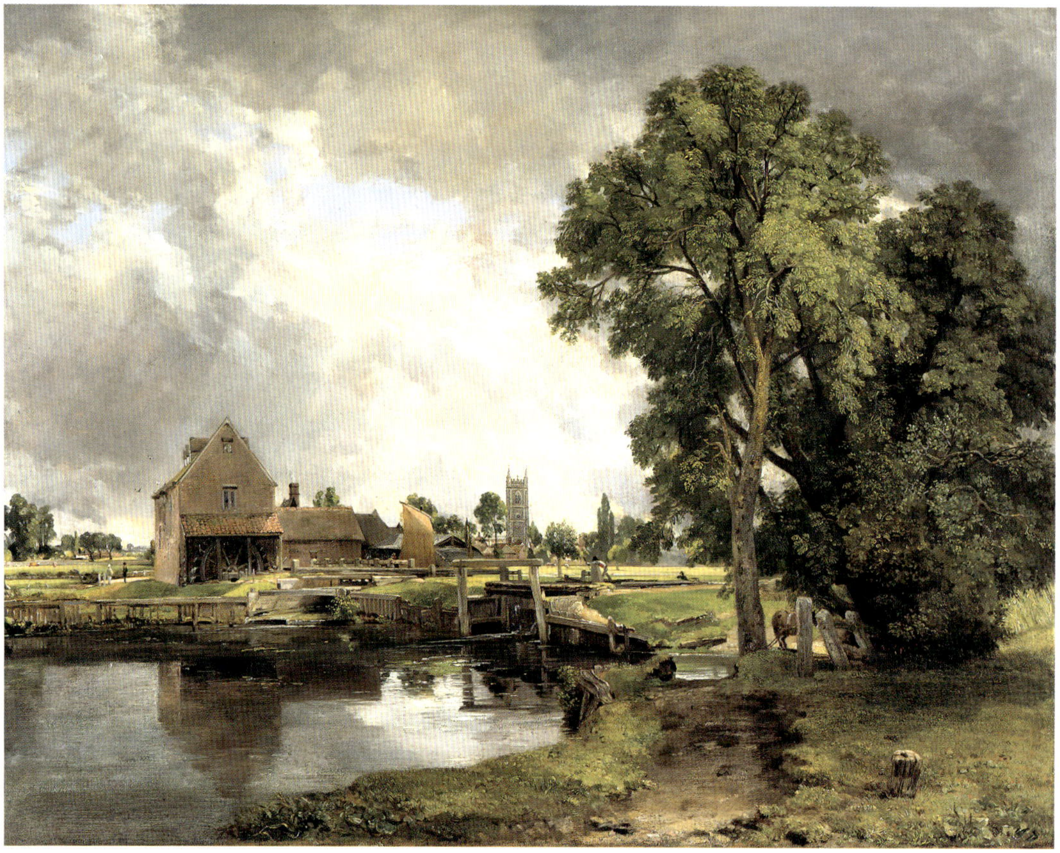

Plate 32 John Constable, *Dedham Lock and Mill*, 1819[?] Private collection

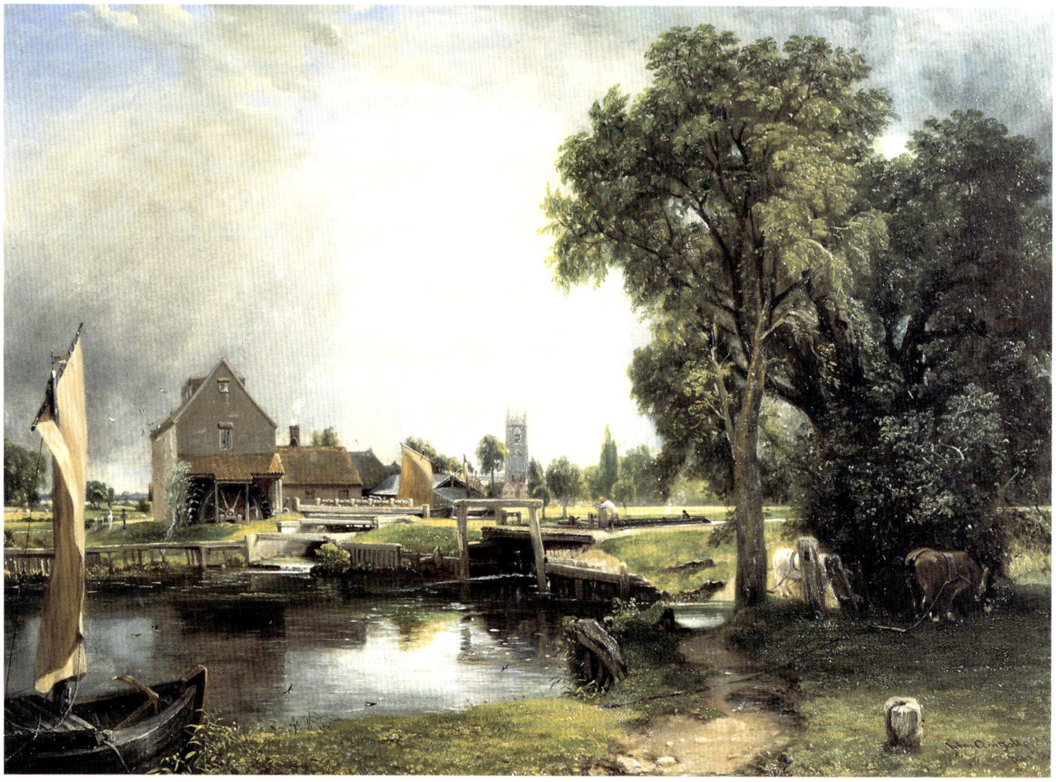

Plate 33 John Constable, *Dedham Lock and Mill*, 1819[?] V&A Picture Library

The skies of the various versions of *Dedham Lock and Mill* are intriguing. The version from a private collection (Plate 32), catalogued as no. 94 by Parris and Fleming-Williams,[28] has been the subject of debate as to whether it was exhibited in 1819 at the British Institution as *A Mill*. Parris and Fleming-Williams think that it was the 1819 exhibit, whereas Reynolds in his 1984 catalogue believes that it is a later copy of the painting that was exhibited. The sky is far superior to the skies in the other versions of *Dedham Lock and Mill* (Plate 33). There is no other sky with this dynamism and perspective until after the skying period of 1820/22. The crepuscular rays of sunlight illuminating the mill from the patch of blue sky above is much more in keeping with later work.

The White Horse (Plate 34), exhibited at the Royal Academy in 1819, was the first of Constable's six-footers and Leslie claims it was 'the most important picture, to Constable, he ever painted'.[29] The size of the painting meant that it was too large to work out of doors and so it was painted in the studio. It was a success with the critics and was instrumental in Constable being elected as an Associate of the Royal Academy that year. The sky is similar to *Flatford Mill* – the clouds are detailed but distant. There is some attempt to bring the base of a cloud overhead in the top left corner, and there is an attempt to depict cumulus streets in the centre of the sky but the overall impression of the sky is still rather subdued.

Two sky studies made with crayons on blue paper are dated 9 July 1819. There are also another five similar drawings catalogued by Reynolds. These drawings show that Constable was beginning to think hard about improving his skies. I have not seen the originals but the copies in Reynolds' catalogues suggest that they lack the perspective of the 1820/22 studies and there are no weather inscriptions.

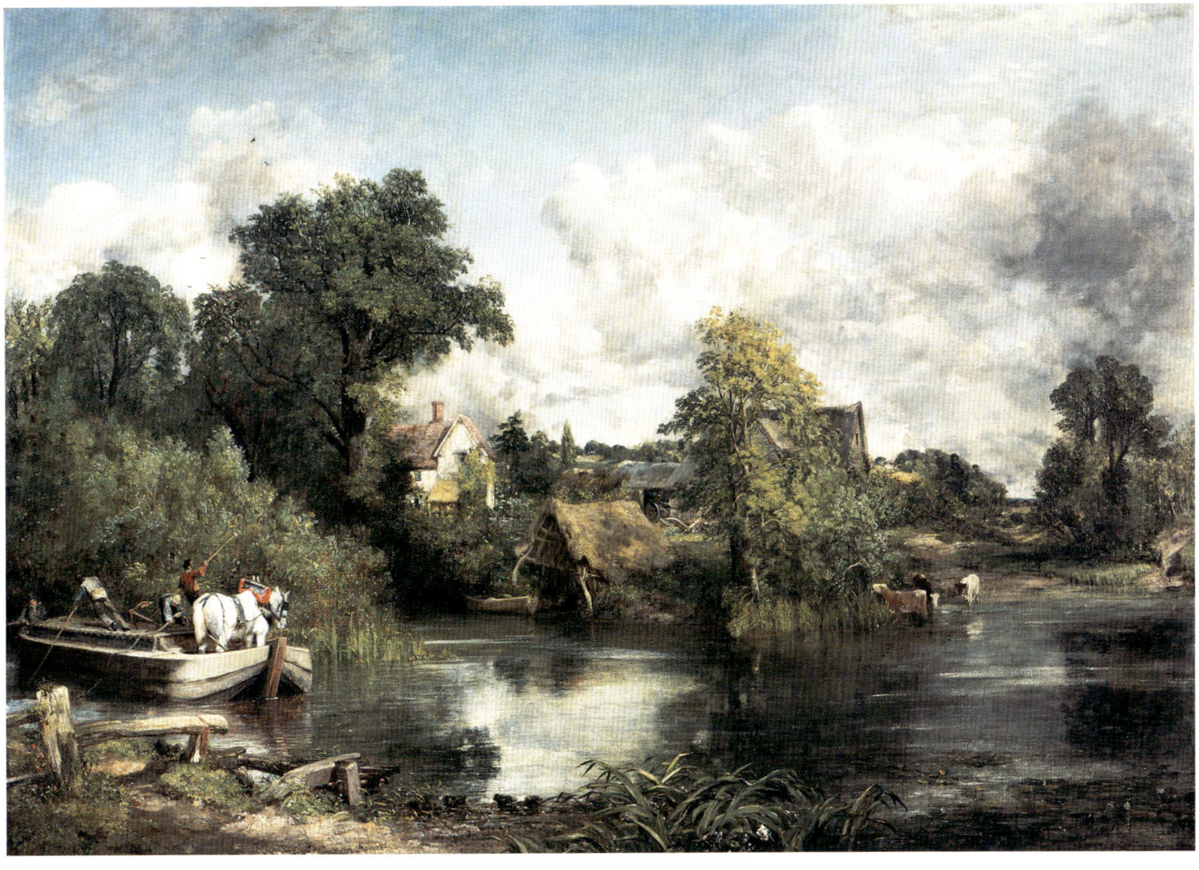

Plate 34 John Constable, *The White Horse*, 1819. Copyright The Frick Collection, New York

Branch Hill Pond (Plate 35) is inscribed 'End of Octr. 1819', and is the earliest dated oil sketch painted at Hampstead. The sky is much more dynamic than any other picture up to that date with a heavy shower in the distance and slanting light, but the sky is impressionistic rather than realistic. This contrasts with the quiet distant clouds of *Stratford Mill* (Plate 36), exhibited in 1820 and bought by Fisher for his lawyer John Tinney. Criticisms of the sky in *Stratford Mill* were relayed by Fisher to Constable, which sparked the 23 October 1821 skies letter from Constable back to Fisher. The criticisms have already been discussed in Chapter 2 (section 5), but basically Tinney would probably have preferred a blue sky. The clouds have more perspective than in *The White Horse* and also the cloud colours are fresher. William Carey, an art critic, writing in *The British Freeholder* on 1 July 1820 commented as follows on the weather depicted in *Stratford Mill*: 'We may suppose it a day after recent rain, and the sky is not yet wholly cleared up. The light upon the clouds is well diffused, and the general effect powerful and commanding; but it would be still better if the pencilling was not too busy and flickered in expressing the motion of the air, in some parts near the horizon.' Constable's skies were beginning to attract critical attention but Constable had not yet achieved the atmospheric effect that he wanted.

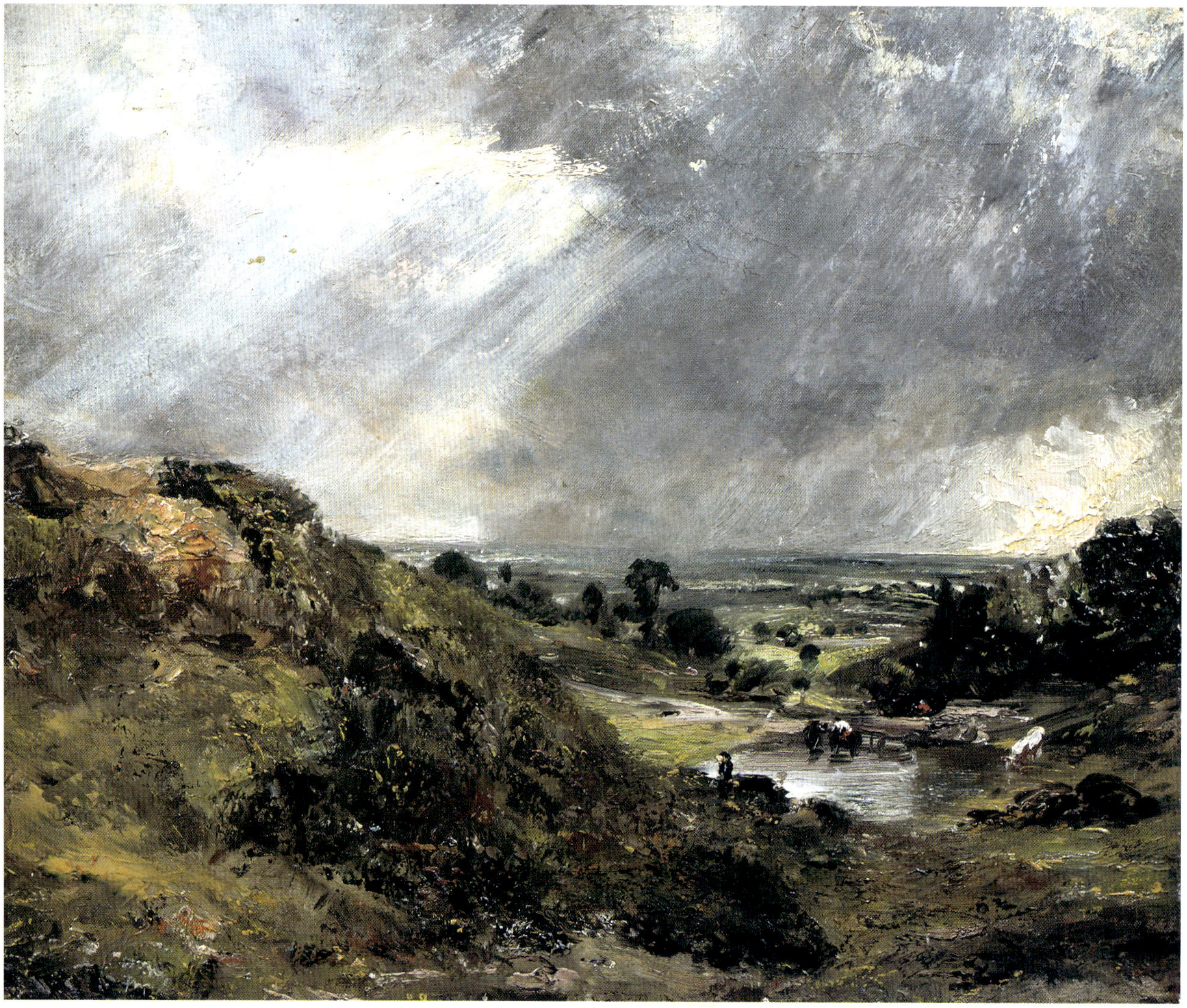

Plate 35 John Constable, *Branch Hill Pond*, 1819. V&A Picture Library

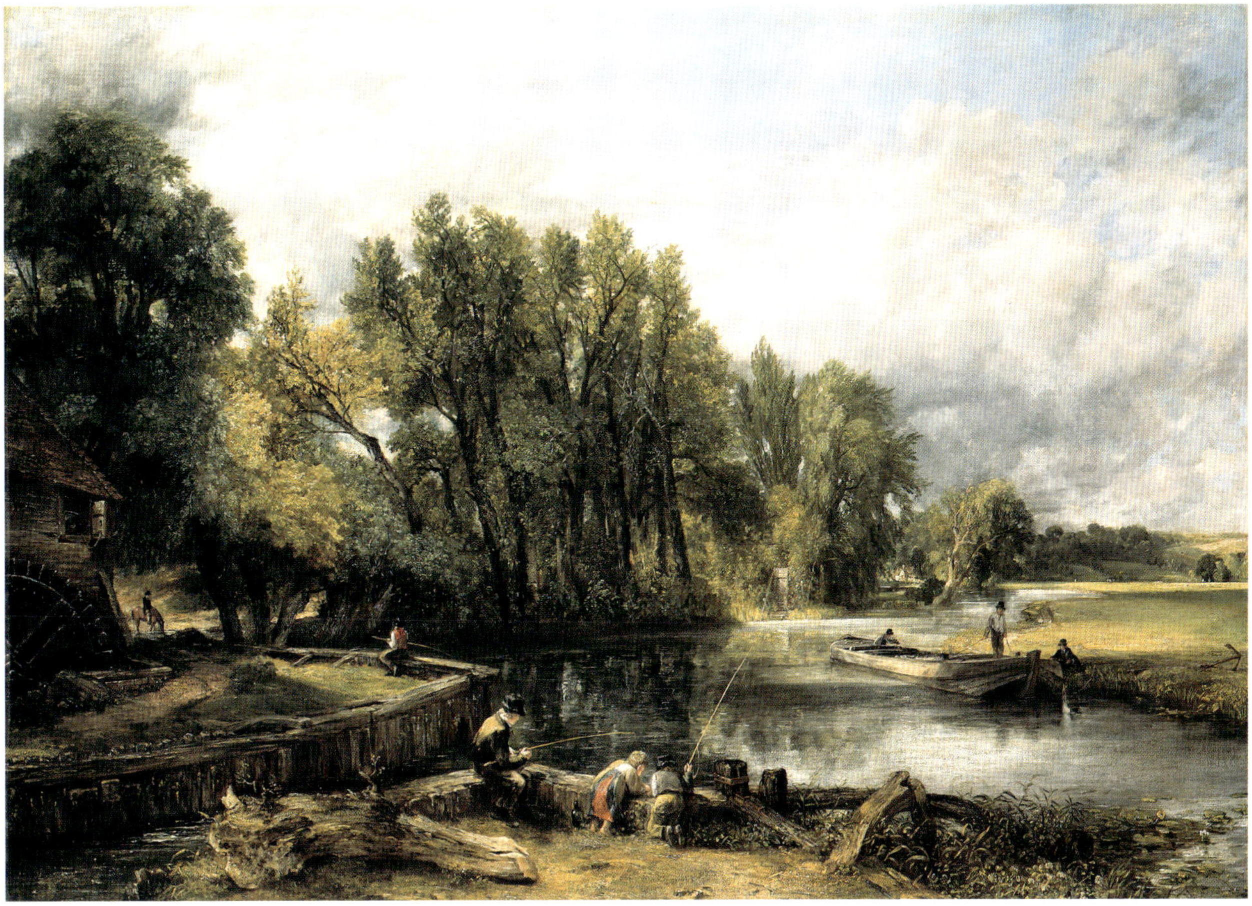

Plate 36 John Constable, *Stratford Mill*, 1820. Copyright National Gallery, London

In October 1820 Constable suddenly embarked upon his remarkable series of sky studies painted on Hampstead Heath. This intensive skying period was to last for two years in which time he painted well over one hundred sky studies. At least four sky studies inscribed with the full date and brief weather notes were painted in October 1820. These studies differ from the 1821/22 sky studies in that they are smaller and the inscriptions are generally shorter (see Table 10); also they are all late afternoon/evening views.

Luke Howard's weather notes tally very closely with Constable's inscriptions.[30] On 17 October Howard notes 'very tempestuous night, with frequent showers' the wind being from the south west, backing to west by 18 October. Constable's inscription reads 'Hampd. 17th October 1820 Stormy Sunset. Wind. W.'. This is the earliest known of Constable's painted oil landscapes to have a weather inscription. The painting is known as *Sketch at Hampstead: Stormy Sunset* (Plate 88) and is very similar to the sketch made just over a week later entitled *Hampstead Heath: Evening*. For 25 October Howard notes 'Cloudy' with a north-west wind. Constable's inscription 'Hampstead Heath – fine evening [...] wind N W October 25 1820' is comparable and the sketch depicts a similar sunset.

The sketch dated 28 October, but without the year, was given as 1821 in my 1978 catalogue,[31] but Reynolds dates it as 1820 (R20.82). The sketch is of a much more vivid red sunset, with the sun at the centre of the picture (Plate 89). The sky is a great deal more spectacular than the three earlier 1820 studies and indeed there were several reports of exceptional sunset colours in London in July and

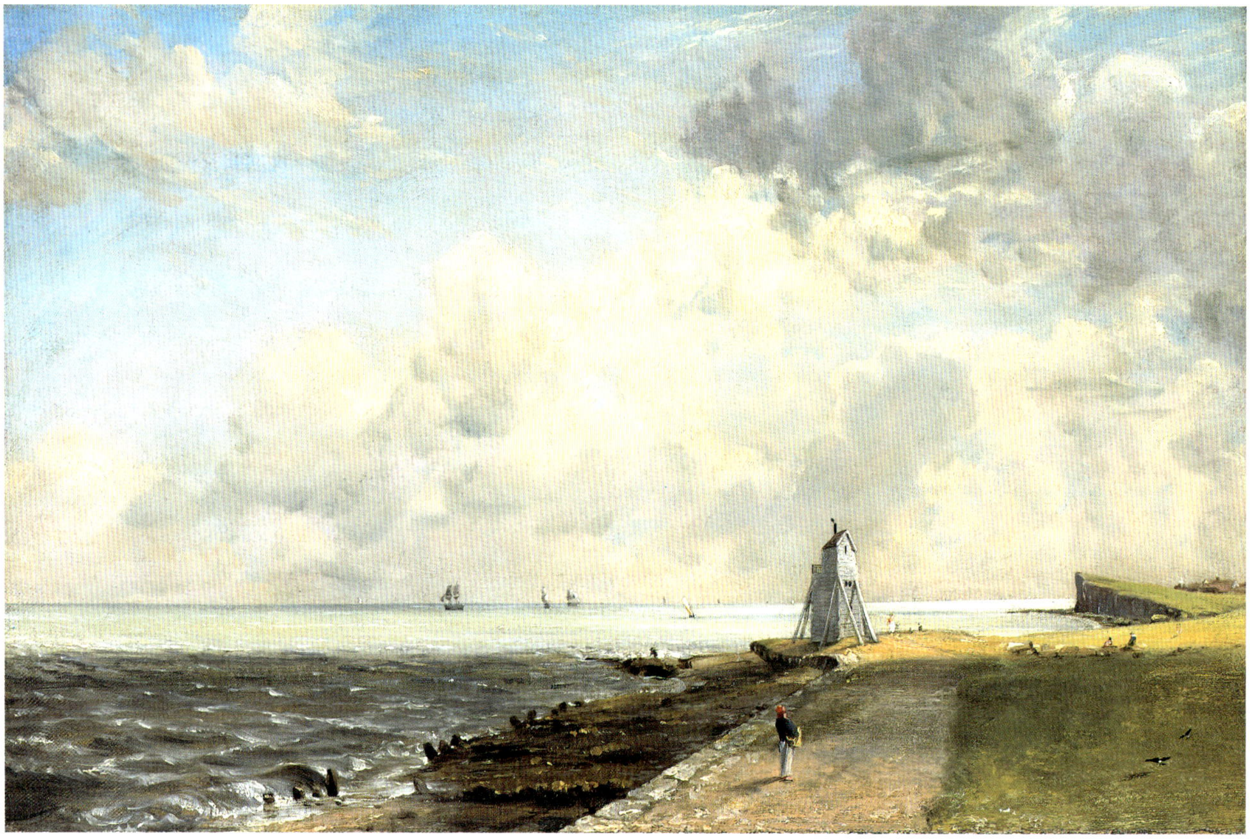

Plate 37 John Constable, *Harwich Lighthouse*, 1820. Copyright Tate Gallery, London 1998

August 1821 due to the eruption of the volcano Kluchev in Eastern Russia earlier in the year.[32] Constable's inscription '28th Octr. fine Evening Wind Gentle at S.W.' ties in better with 1821 as Howard also records a south-west wind, whereas in 1820 Howard recorded a north-west wind. As stated in Appendix 1 this picture could be either 1820 or 1821 but because of its small size it has been catalogued as 1820.

At the Royal Academy in 1820 Constable exhibited *Stratford Mill* together with a view of *Harwich Lighthouse* (Plate 37). This latter seascape proved to be popular and Constable made several versions of it, so that it is not possible to know which was the exhibited version. However the sky in the Tate Gallery version is more in keeping with Constable's other skies at this time – the clouds are distant and indistinct. The sky in the Mellon Center version, although identical in form, is much more dynamic and the lighting is more realistic which suggests that it was made later than the Tate version. Unusually Constable used the same sky, at least in outline, in the *Yarmouth Jetty* compositions of 1822–23 in which the sky is more similar to the Yale version of *Harwich Lighthouse* than to the Tate version. Thus it is likely that the Tate version of *Harwich Lighthouse* was exhibited at the Academy in 1820 and that the other versions were painted at a similar time to the *Yarmouth Jetty* paintings.

By the end of 1820 Constable had already started to paint sky studies inscribed with the weather conditions but the skies of his finished pictures were still disappointing.

3.5 High noon 1821–22: moderate breeze

This period in Constable's life has become known as his 'skying period' and the famous sky studies have already been discussed in some detail in Chapter 2. It remains, however, to discuss the impact of this 'skying period' on Constable's finished works and indeed why Constable embarked upon such a detailed programme of sky sketching. The arguments of Badt and Hawes have already been briefly referred to in Chapter 2 but will now be examined in detail.

Badt made much of the possible intellectual stimulus that Luke Howard's cloud classification would have had for Constable at a time when Constable was struggling to harmonise his skies with the landscape in his six-footers. Constable's annotations to Forster's book, discussed in detail in Chapter 2, showed that he was fully familiar with Luke Howard's cloud classification at some time in his life. He may well have bought his second-hand copy of the second edition of Forster's book published in 1815 sometime before 1823 when the third edition came out, or he may have bought it much later in the 1830s. Luke Howard's own book, *The Climate of London*, was first published in parts between 1818–20 and may have attracted Constable's attention. Badt was convinced that it was Howard's book rather than Forster's that provided the key stimulus:

> *And it was this book of Howard's which probably – almost certainly – spurred Constable to the most intensive study of the sky and to the creation of these special cloud pictures, the same which had the effect for Goethe of 'limiting the indefinite, the unstable and the unattainable', and which 'gave him a thread on which to hang his numerous isolated observations in a sensible and illuminating way'.*

Certainly either of these books would have given Constable more confidence, providing as they did a basic understanding of the formation and life history of clouds, to make his skies both realistic and dynamic.

Hawes on the other hand stresses the environmental influences upon Constable's atmospheric understanding and doubts that Howard's cloud classification would have had much impact in comparison, for instance, with Constable's experience as a windmiller. He lists a number of other factors which he considers most relevant to Constable's Hampstead series of sky studies:

> *I Life-long Dedication to Open-air Sketching – including sporadic sky sketching from 1806 (if not earlier). The Hampstead series falls within the artist's most intensive phase of outdoor oil sketching: 1820–25*
>
> *II Early Experiences as a Windmiller – when he made his 'earliest studies and ... observations'.*
>
> *III Some awareness of Earlier Sky Sketches – whether by Claude, Van de Velde the Younger, A. Cozens, J.R. Cozens, Joseph Wright, William Crotch or Turner.*
>
> *IV Turner's Skies: 1817–19 – including the unprecedentedly extensive series of sixty-five watercolour studies in the 'Skies' sketchbook of c. 1817–18, and the notable skyscapes in two large oil paintings: Raby Castle (1818) and Entrance to the Meuse (1819).*
>
> *V The Environment of Hampstead Heath – a 'natural observatory', and the locality of the 1821–22 sky series. (Artist first paints there in 1819).*
>
> *VI Criticism of the Sky in Certain Exhibited Works: 1819–21 – as indicated in two letters of 1821 and by remarks in two critical journals, respecting The Mill (1819), Stratford Mill (1820) and The Hay Wain (1821).*
>
> *VII Convictions about the Crucial Role of the Sky in Landscape and its Difficulties of Execution – stated in a letter of 1821 (in the context of 'Skying').*
>
> *VIII Art Theory – passages advocating on-the-spot sky sketching, in widely available treatises by De Piles, Gilpin, Taylor and Richter.*
>
> *Possible Indirect Relevance: Some awareness of contemporary meteorological classifications,*

gained some time before 1836 via Thomas Forster's book (1813), a more palatable study than Howard's forbidding two-volume work (1818–20), the greater part of which comprises tedious tabulations.[34]

Hawes continues:

No one of these factors, taken alone, adequately accounts for the studies; but taken together and seen as converging stimuli, I believe they bring us appreciably closer to an understanding of how and why Constable's dazzling eruption of sky sketches came about.

Hawes goes out of his way to dismiss Badt's theory but he has missed the point himself in several instances. For instance it was those 'tedious tabulations' in a later edition of Howard's *Climate of London* that has enabled detailed comparisons to be made between Constable's inscriptions on the sky studies and the actual weather conditions that prevailed in London. Moreover the influence of Turner's skies and the skies of other artists mentioned was likely to have been small, as will be discussed in the next chapter. It is therefore just as easy to argue that Howard's influence was primary and that all the empirical and environmental factors that Hawes itemises were secondary. In reality it is safer to assume that all these influences were important and that no one factor dominated.

By 1821 Constable was in his mid-forties and at the peak of his career when he painted *The Hay Wain* (Plate 38, exhibited as *Landscape: Noon*) which was the first of his finished pictures to achieve the harmony that Constable wanted in his sky – the harmony to bind the landscape and the noon sky together, to achieve consistent light and convincing

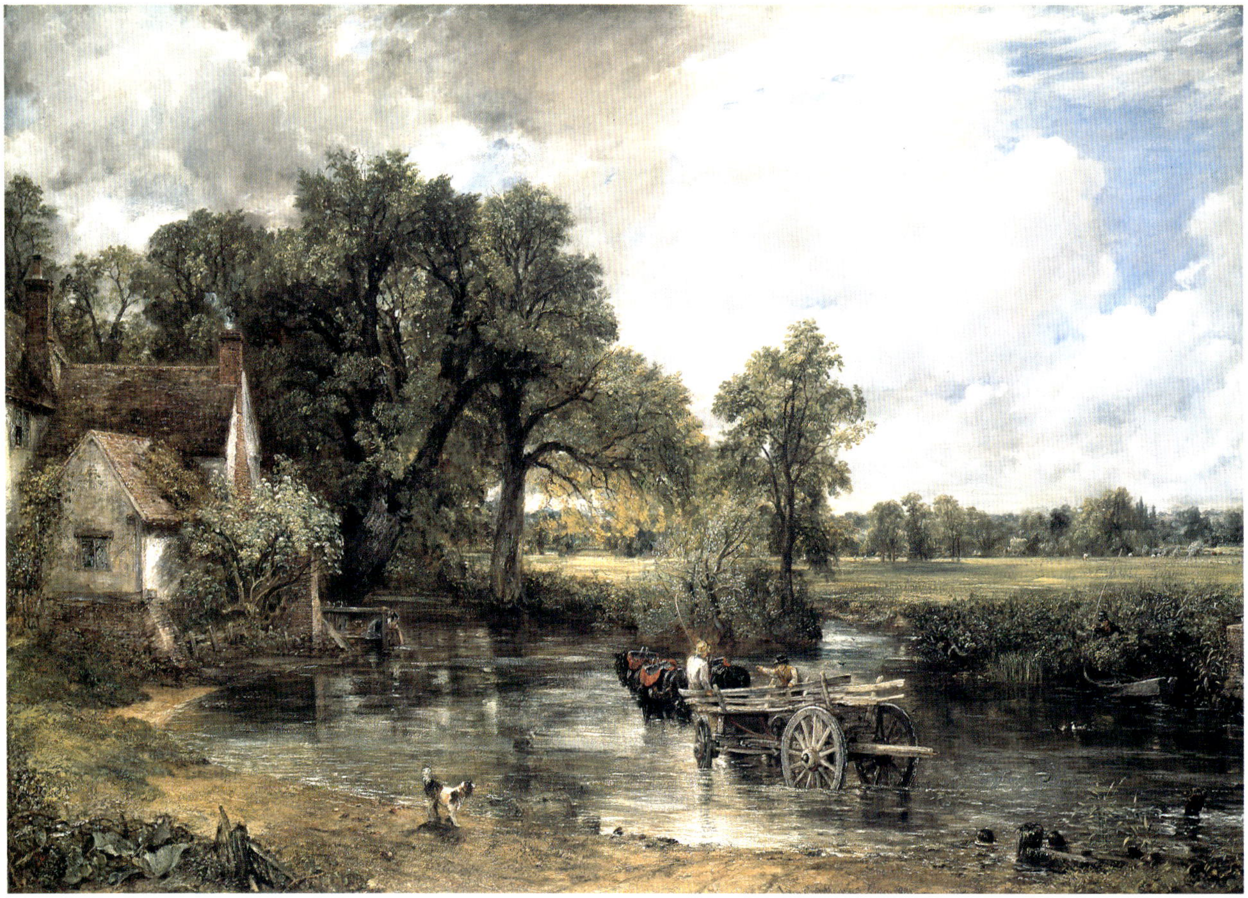

Plate 38 John Constable, *The Hay Wain*, 1821. Copyright National Gallery, London

cloud form and perspective. Thus *The Hay Wain* represents a significant watershed in Constable's sky painting. Constable's skies during and after 1821 are demonstrably superior to all his skies before 1821. The achievement of balanced light gives a freshness and realistic feeling to his later studies that is almost entirely lacking before 1821. This freshness was noted by the art critic Robert Hunt writing in *The Examiner* on 27 May 1821:

> *Landscape: Noon – is a picture by Mr Constable, which we think approaches nearer to the actual look of rural nature than any modern landscape whatever. An able judge of Art who saw and admired it with us, thought it a little mannered from a certain sparkle there is over it. We do not think so, but granting the objection to be just, it is a mere slight flaw in a diamond, for what an open air and fresh and leafy look it has with its cottage and foreground so brightly and yet so modestly contrasting their reddish hue with the green and blue and yellow tints of the trees, fields, and sky – a sky which for noble volume of cloud and clear light we have never at any time seen exceeded except by Nature.... We challenge the Dutch masters to shew us anything better than this.*[35]

Other critics were not so flattering; another review of *Landscape: Noon* in the *Repository of Arts* in June 1821 stated that 'His dark clouds impart too much of their sombre hue to his trees'.[36]

It would appear therefore that Constable's main aim in retouching the painting was to remove some of his 'white spots' that were meant to represent the refraction of the sun's rays through water droplets or dew on the vegetation. When the sun shines on a landscape after rain, or early in the morning when the dew is still fresh, the droplets do appear to sparkle, giving an extra beauty to the landscape; moreover the flickering light through the trees as the wind blows the branches to and fro suggests movement. Constable attempted to paint these marvellous effects with mixed success. His technique of using white spots of paint to represent the sparkle was appreciated by Hunt but was heavily criticised by others. For instance the review of *Landscape: Noon* in *Bell's Weekly Messenger* on 28 May 1821 stated:

> *There is a style of execution in this gentleman's productions which do not accord with our ideas of imitating nature. We do not object to his selection of scenery; they are in general very beautiful – the present picture is particularly so. But why all that excess of piebald scambling [sic] in the finishing, as if a plasterer had been at work where the picture hung, and it had received the spirits of his brush? The Artist may say, 'I intend what I paint always to be viewed from a certain distance, you will then get rid of my white spots.' This is certainly an affectation and trickery of art unknown to our best painters; – for instance, if we approach near a Claude, a Both, a Ruysdael, or a Poussin, and examine almost with a microscopic-eye, we see the effects of nature undisguised in all her enchanting forms, and admire the simplicity of the pencilling in all her features.*[40]

Constable was to be criticised for his 'white spots' for many years to come. The *Bell*'s reviewer was the first of many to complain that Constable, having produced what they thought to be a beautiful picture, perversely spoiled it when applying his finishing touches and those final glazes called scumbling. Constable was determined however to represent the wet sparkle of the landscape after rain or dew and this was his way of achieving it.

It is interesting that in relation to the earlier 1820 painting of *Stratford Mill* Robert Hunt stated that 'We may suppose it a day after recent rain, and the sky is not yet wholly cleared up.' As far as *The Hay Wain* is concerned, however, the time is noon in July or August and any early morning dew would long since have evaporated. The clouds suggest from their depth of convection that they have not yet produced rain, but that showers will surely follow in the afternoon. Hence the landscape and the vegetation would be dry, especially as there is a gentle breeze blowing from right to left, from the west, across the picture, as shown by the smoke from the chimney on the cottage. The cumulus clouds are arranged in 'streets' parallel to the westerly airstream as would be common at that time of year. Hence there would be no need to 'add sparkle' to the picture due to recent rain but the movement of the trees in the breeze would require the presence of some sparkle. For whatever reason Constable decided to 'put out certain catching lights', when he did 'more to it'. The full-size sketch for *The Hay Wain* (Plate 39) is much cloudier than the finished picture and therefore again perhaps suggests that Constable may have altered the sky after his skying experiences to achieve the existing harmony between the sky and the landscape.

Sarah Cove describes graphically how Constable used a palette knife to add what was also known as 'Constable's snow':

> *The Hay Wain ... shows the 'finishing' technique Constable developed to depict fleeting effects of light, movement and texture. Using a palette knife he applied stiffly textured white and coloured specks over the surface of the picture. The Academician Solomon Hart described this process in his Reminiscences: 'Calling upon Constable one day, I found him with a palette-knife, on which was some white, mixed with a viscous vehicle, and upon which he touched the surface of a beautiful picture he was painting. Upon expressing my surprise, he said "Oh! my dear Hart, I'm giving my picture the dewy freshness"... [H]e contended that the apparent*

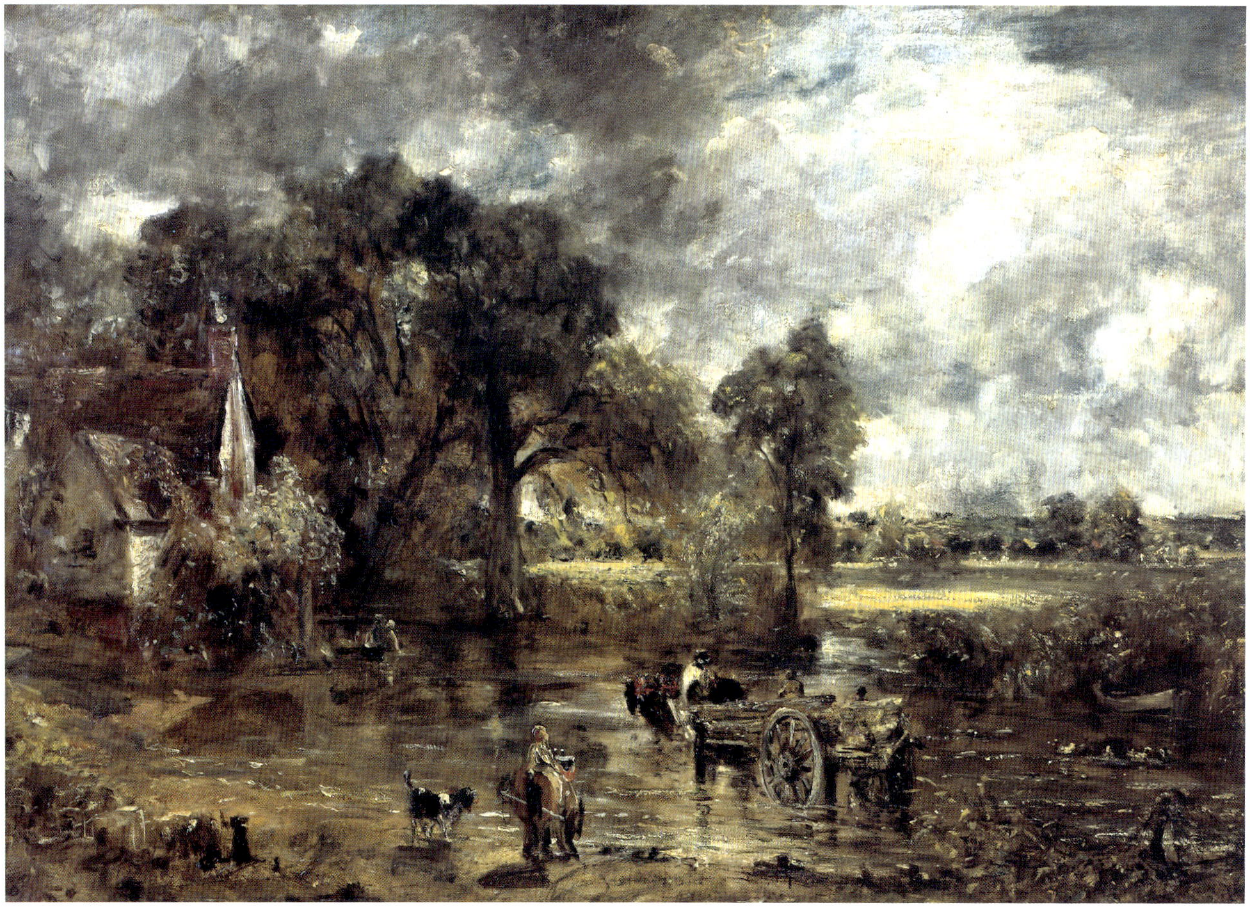

Plate 39 John Constable, Sketch for *The Hay Wain*, 1821, V&A Picture Library

> *crudeness would readily subside, and that the chemical change which would ensue in a short time would assume the truthful aspect of nature'.*[41]

Constable was expecting the polluted London air to darken the white specks, but when the paintings were exhibited the chemical process had not yet had time to take place. Presumably therefore Constable attempted to darken some of these white specks in *The Hay Wain* himself.

Constable also exhibited with *Landscape: Noon* a painting entitled *A Shower*. The present whereabouts is unknown but it received a favourable report in *The Morning Review* on 1 June 1821: '*A Shower*, by J. CONSTABLE, A., is admirable for its fidelity and truth. The lucid appearance of the clouds, and the seeming reality of the descending shower, cannot be exceeded. The hues and tones of verdure, both near and distant, at such a moment, have been most carefully observed and are happily expressed.'[42]

There are twenty-six dated sky studies, with weather inscriptions, attributed to 1821 and twenty-four attributed to 1822 that are known to exist today (see Table 10). Together with the four for 1820 this makes a total of fifty-four dated sky studies of which fifty-one have weather inscriptions. The first was produced on 17 October 1820 and the last on 31 September (1 October) 1822. Appendix 1 compares the weather inscriptions with the historical weather records for all the dated sky studies and shows that there is a very close agreement between them. Indeed, using historical weather records, the author has found it possible to realistically date fifteen studies that have incomplete dates.[43] Appendix 1, which is an updated version of my 1978 catalogue, contains details for fifty-four sky studies (the original catalogue contained details for thirty-six sky studies).

The fifty-four studies that are examined in detail in Appendix 1 probably represent less than half of the sky studies that Constable produced in this period. On 20 September 1821 he wrote to Fisher that: 'I have likewise made many *skies* and effects.... We have had noble clouds & effects of light & dark & colour – as is always the case in such seasons as the present.'[44] Again to Fisher on 7 October 1822 Constable wrote: 'I have made about 50 careful studies of *skies* tolerably large, to be careful.' The average size of the 1821 sky studies is about 250mm x 300mm (10 x 12 inches) whereas the typical size of the 1822 studies is almost twice as big at 280mm x 480mm (10 x 24 inches). Indeed three of the surviving 1822 studies are about 480mm x 580mm (20 x 24 inches) which is four times as big as the 1821 studies. These sizes are easy to explain in terms of fractions of a 20 x 24 inch sheet. Figure 18 shows how such a sheet could be divided up. Thus the 1821 sky studies were mostly on sheets a quarter the size and the 1822 studies were mostly on sheets half the size, and a few on whole sheets. The reason for this scaling-up in 1822 is linked to Constable's desire to paint skies of a comparable size to the skies in his six-foot canvases. As discussed in Chapter 2 it is interesting that most of the 'pure sky' studies painted in 1822 were done close to noon; an attempt to master the sky at the time of day often favoured by Constable (as in *Landscape: Noon*). The studies were all painted in

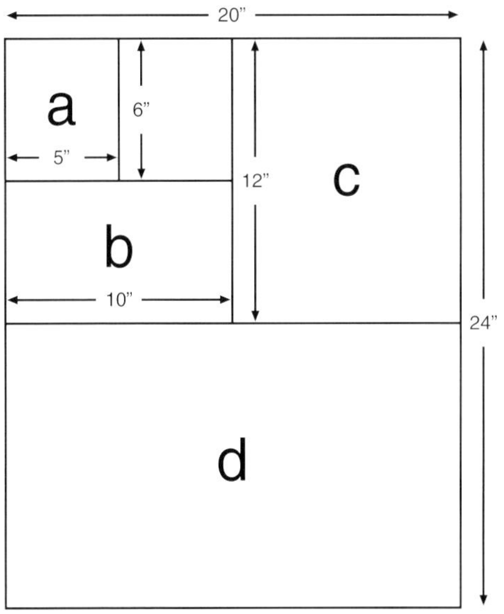

Figure 18 Sheet of paper cut by Constable for sky studies (Adapted from S. Cove, 'Constable's oil painting materials and techniques')

Hampstead, mostly on Hampstead Heath, and were produced in about an hour, as can be deduced from the inscriptions. How Constable succeeded in producing such detailed and realistic skies in such a short time, and with such dynamic ever-changing weather conditions, is still not fully appreciated.

Of the fifty-four sky studies detailed in Appendix 1, nineteen (35 per cent) are classified as 'pure sky' studies; in other words those in which there is no landscape present in the study (apart from the study dated 28 September 1821 that does have a very thin strip of landscape along the bottom, but has been classified as 'pure sky'). These 'pure sky' studies are mostly full of cloud and are remarkable experiments in cloud form, light and dark shading, cloud perspective and colour. Most are views just above the horizon, such as both the studies dated 5 September 1822 (Appendix 1 Nos 48 & 49). Others represent more elevated views up into the sky such as 27 August and 31 August 1822 (Appendix 1 Nos 46 & 47). Indeed the 27 August study makes you feel as though you are up flying amongst the clouds!

There are many other sky studies that have survived but do not have weather inscriptions, and indeed some of them do not have any inscription at all. It is a difficult task to separate those that were definitely painted by Constable from those painted perhaps by his sons, other artists or imitators. Appendix 2 lists sixty-eight sky studies in oil that are similar in style to the 1820/22 series but have no inscription by Constable. Hoozee and Reynolds have both attempted a preliminary sorting out of the genuine from the dubious.[45] Hoozee's study, dated 1979, lists only twenty-six of these additional sixty-eight sky studies as being by Constable. Hoozee's analysis was re-examined in detail by Reynolds in 1984 who lists forty-seven of the sixty-eight studies as genuine, as shown in Appendix 2. This is probably excessive and demonstrates the problem of authenticating such works. If Reynolds is correct then these forty-seven sky studies should be added to the fifty-four sky studies of Appendix 1 to give a total of 101 (of which thirty-nine are 'pure sky') known sky studies by Constable. Even so it is likely that there are many sky studies still to be found. The list of authenticated sky studies in Appendix 2 contains only three more large 1822-sized 'pure sky' studies (R22.17: 472 x 584mm, R22.54: 292 x 482mm & R22.58: 247 x 470mm) taking the total known to about eighteen out of the fifty that Constable said he had made 'tolerably large, to be careful'.

One of the sky studies considered genuine by both Hoozee and Reynolds (Hoozee 358 & Reynolds 22.59) is called *Study of Cirrus Clouds* (Plate 40) which, although it is of an unusually small size (114 x 178mm), has been attributed to 1822. On the reverse of the painting, inscribed in ink, is the word 'cirrus', but it is difficult to read because over the top of the word someone else has written 'Painted by John Constable R.A.'. If it is the word 'cirrus', and it is indeed in Constable's own handwriting, then this is further important evidence that Constable was fully familiar with Luke Howard's cloud classification by 1822. The small nature of the picture however suggests that it could have been painted much later in Constable's career and is therefore not conclusive proof of this. The painting is a superb rendering of cirrus clouds with small tufts of cumulus below.

This collection of so many sky studies is unique in art. They have become sought after as pictures in their own right and stand alone as exceptional representations of the daily weather conditions in those years: a pictorial weather diary. The skies in them are instantly recognisable – far removed from the studio studies he made for his finished works. As shown in Chapter 2 the sky studies were made at all times of day and in a variety of weather conditions. Constable systematically collected, using a scientific approach, a selection of skies that would enable him to produce a scientifically correct natural sky that blended perfectly with his chosen landscape scene. The sky studies, as such, were valuable raw material for the skies of his finished works, and yet there is no evidence that Constable used any of these sky studies directly in his finished works. The experience gained in painting so many skies was used to further his meteorological understanding as to how typical skies were generated and how they evolved. As Leslie Parris and Ian Fleming-Williams state, 'it is Constable's ability to differentiate in paint a variety of cloud types, to suggest the pace and direction of movement and to give them convincing three-dimensional forms without losing their lightness and brightness that speaks most for his understanding'.[46] This gave him the confidence to paint convincing skies in his finished works that he could manipulate to harmonise perfectly with the scene.

One might expect that as a result of this enormous set of sky studies that Constable would have fundamentally changed the way that he painted his skies and his sky palette. However in painting the 'noble clouds & effects of light & dark & colour' it appears that Constable was able to adapt his existing palette to achieve his aims. Cove gives a table of all the pigments used by Constable between 1802 and 1837. There does not appear to be any significant change around 1821/22.[47]

Cove also describes how Constable would have gone about his outdoor sketching at this time. First of all Constable made up a quantity of suitably primed paper supports from 20 x 24 inch sheets of a rough 'brown' woven paper. He then used a fine 'tissue' paper, or Japanese paper, over the top to give a smooth surface. The paper was mostly primed with pinks and browns. His palette for these skying sessions was reduced to just a few colours to produce the required shades of blue and grey. All the materials were carried in a sketching box which Constable would rest on his knees and adjust the lid to act as a support. The angle of the lid could be varied by using a metal 'stay' on the side.

Constable made up his own paint from pigments bought in powder form. Prussian blue was the commonest colour used by Constable for the sky. This was mixed with lead white and charcoal black to produce the required shades of blues and greys. Constable also used red lake and vermilion to add warmth to the colours, although

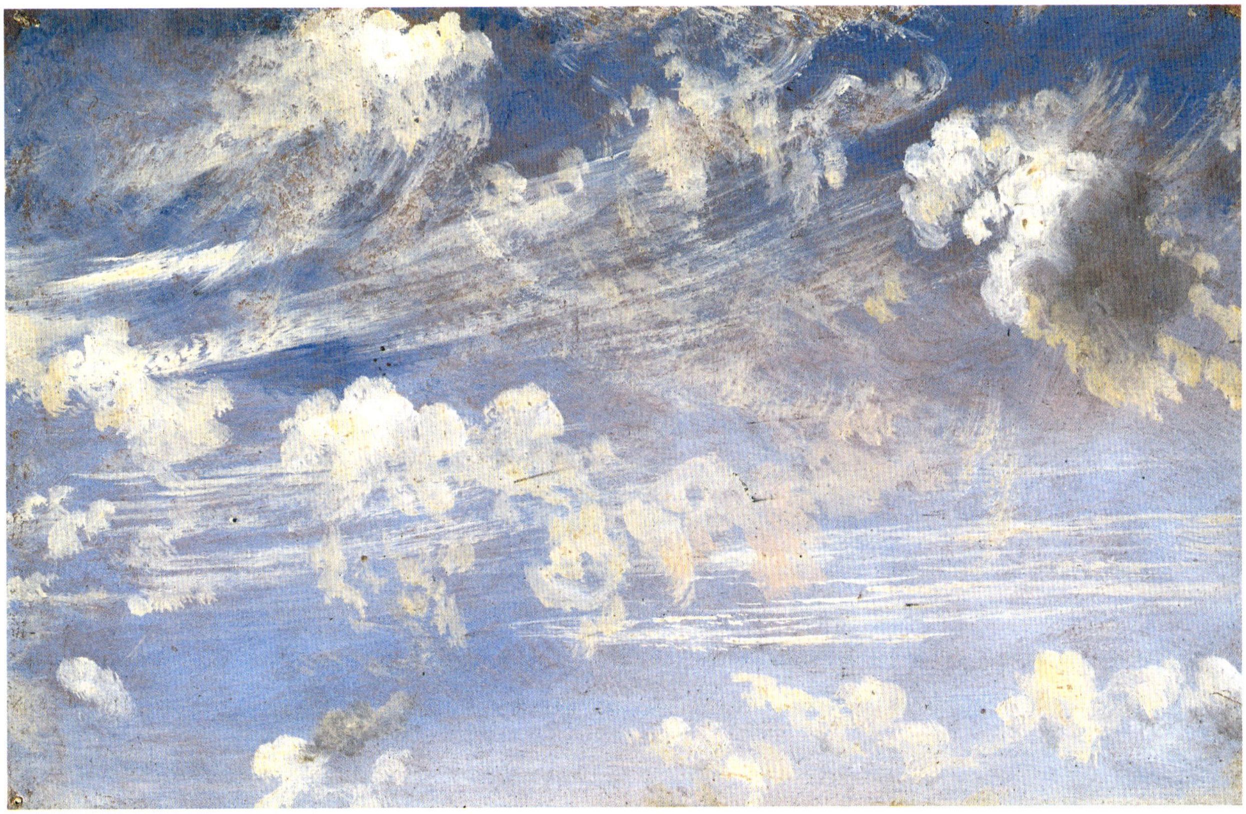

Plate 40 John Constable, *Study of Cirrus Clouds*, 1822[?]. V&A Picture Library

interestingly he did not use vermilion in 1822 according to Cove. Ultramarine was also used by Constable for the final touches to a finished sky but it was, and still is, very expensive as it is made from the semi-precious stone lapis lazuli. It is unlikely, therefore, that he used ultramarine in his sky studies. However it was known at the time that by mixing prussian blue with a small amount of red lake, ultramarine could be nearly achieved.

The technique of painting the rapidly changing sky, quickly mixing the appropriate paints and applying few, accurate brush strokes was very different from the way that Constable painted the sky in his finished works. In the studio the sky would be built up gradually over a number of days as separate layers of paint were added:

> *The system with which Constable painted a 'finished' work changed relatively little from 1802 to the mid-1820s.... The first layer of paint applied to the surface was the 'dead-colouring' of the sky. This was laid on with a large brush, using thin washes consisting mostly of lead white and prussian blue, around contours roughly corresponding to the intended outline of trees and horizon.... Constable used the warm colour of the priming to add depth to the sky by varying the thickness of the brushstrokes. In this way he created a range of effects that cannot be obtained by painting a blue or grey layer directly over a white ground.... The 'dead-colouring' of the sky would have taken very little time to paint and it was then left to dry before the rest of the landscape was begun.... Walnut oil ground with mastic resin and sugar of lead was recommended for 'dead-colouring' the sky as it would dry in 'about two hours'. Constable may have begun several paintings in a day or had them at different stages and worked on them sequentially.... In the 'second painting' of the sky the main cloud formations were worked up using several layers of semi-opaque greys, blues and pinks scumbled over each other to create depth. Highlights were applied in stiffer white paint.... Constable carried out the glazing and 'finishing' only when the painting was properly dry.... To 'sweeten' the colour in the bluest areas of the sky and along the horizon, a scumble of the expensive blue pigment ultramarine (lapis lazuli) was laid on, followed by a scumble of vermilion over the whites of the clouds.*[48]

This procedure seems perfectly to explain the colours of the clouds in the finished works up to 1820, but from *The Hay Wain* onwards it appears that Constable stopped using pinks and vermilion in particular in his skies, thus creating a much more natural look to the clouds. More research is required to confirm this hypothesis that the sky colours Constable used changed as a result of his skying period.

Constable would go up onto Hampstead Heath and sometimes he would paint two or three skies in one day. For instance on 27 September 1821 he painted three sky studies (Appendix 1 Nos 20, 21 & 22) at 10am, noon, and at 4pm. The sky studies would take some days to dry once he had got them home, and some of the inscriptions were probably added back in the studio once the paintings had dried.

In 1822 Constable sent *View on the Stour near Dedham* (Plate 41) to the Royal Academy as his six-foot canvas. The sky is not as perfect as that of *Landscape: Noon* but it is still superior to that of *Stratford Mill* in that the cloud perspective is better. The cumulus streets are almost identical in angle to those in *Landscape: Noon*, but they are not as fresh and natural.

The period 1821/22 was therefore the most active with regard to Constable's sky paintings and radically improved the quality of his finished skies. His improved scientific understanding of the dynamics of the sky, gained through direct observation and experiment, is evident in all his later skies.

The influence of these remarkable sky studies is to be found much further afield than in his own paintings. They represent the beginning of a remarkable shift in the role of clouds in landscape art, and they are also part of a revolution in romanticism. As already stated, the fact that by 1856

Ruskin was to write that 'if a general and characteristic name were needed for modern landscape art, none better could be invented than "the service of clouds"' speaks volumes for the impact that Constable in particular had upon skies in landscape art, by making the sky for other artists as well as himself: the 'chief organ of sentiment'.

Constable was also at the forefront of the demythologising of clouds as religious images. As will be discussed in Chapter 4, up to the turn of the nineteenth century clouds were what separated man from divinity, and it was sacrilegious to view them as just another part of nature. Both Shelley, in his poem *The Cloud* (1820), and Constable, in his sky/cloud studies, were especially revolutionary in their 'angel's eye' view of the sky. This is hardly surprising for an atheist like Shelley who revelled in flaunting such sacrilege, but it is surprisingly radical for Constable, known for his conservative views. Constable's sky studies were made on Hampstead Heath, which is elevated naturally above the surrounding landscape, but in some of them he took himself much higher into the clouds. Moreover Constable kept his sky studies largely private, whereas Shelley's poem was published to the world. It is no wonder that Constable's clouds in his finished works caused a greater stir than one might expect today. It was also in keeping that the Bishop of Salisbury should be worried by the 'dark cloud' that Constable was to paint over his cathedral in 1823.

The viewpoint in Constable's studies and finished pictures had been firmly on the ground up to this period, and the horizon had been at the traditional eye-level. Up until 1822, Constable

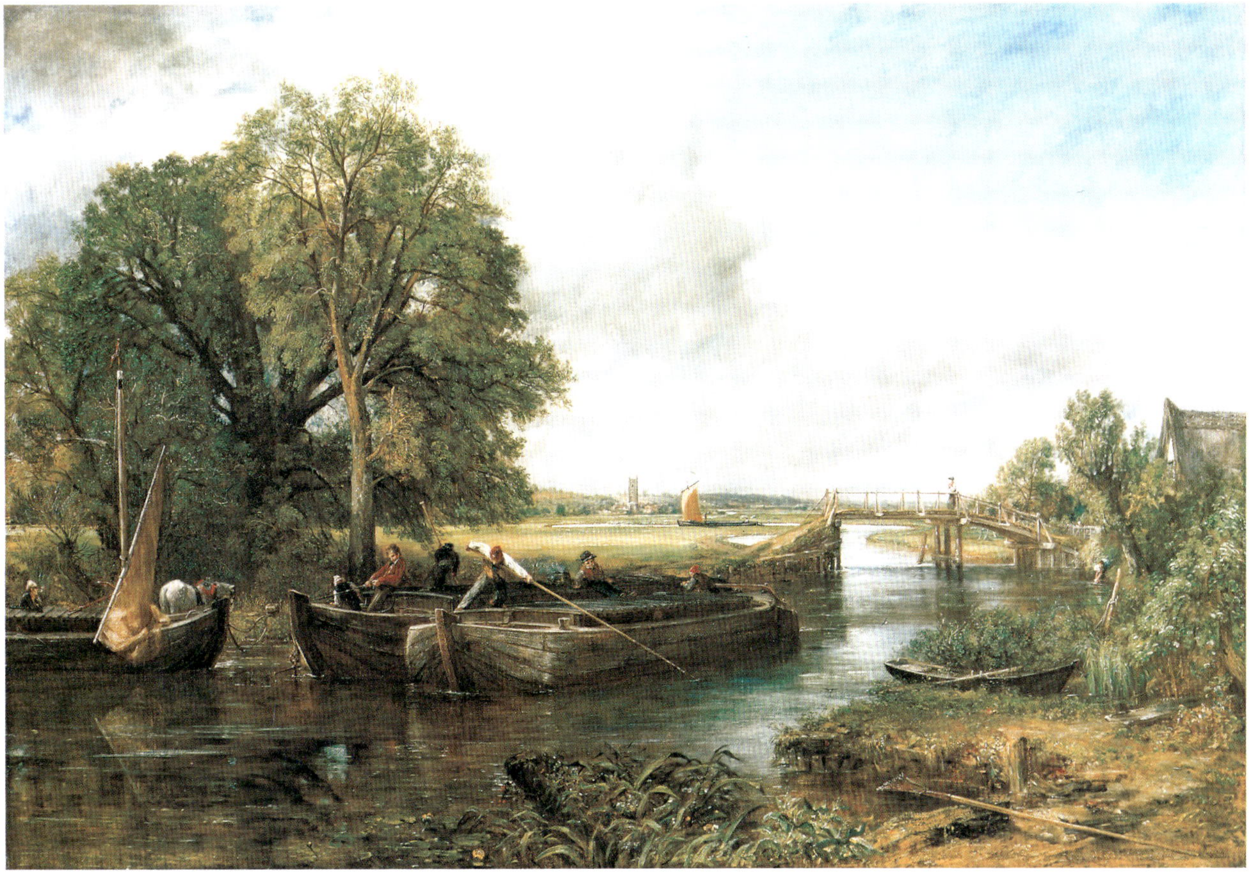

Plate 41 John Constable, *View on the Stour near Dedham*, 1822. Courtesy of the Huntington Library, Art Collections, and Botanical Gardens, San Marino, California

had restricted his views to a three-mile radius in the Stour Valley. The sky studies were therefore a release, allowing him the freedom to paint without the restriction of the horizon. He could paint the sky as he might write a poem, unrestricted by convention, expressing his vision in oil rather than in words. The clouds were his 'poetry in motion' and he achieved what Kenneth Clark has called 'the romantic conjunction of science and ecstasy'.[49]

3.6 Afternoon 1823–28: fresh breeze

Salisbury Cathedral from the Bishop's Grounds (Plate 42) was Constable's main submission to the Royal Academy exhibition in 1823. This picture has been seen as a turning point in Constable's technical development,[50] both from the point of view of painting the exacting detail of the cathedral and from the successful use of warmer colours such as red, green and gold without sacrificing harmony.

The sky in the painting was the subject of much correspondence between Constable and Fisher. The dark cloud over the cathedral was copied from the original sketch done by Constable of the same view in 1820. The exhibited picture was the result of a commission from the Bishop. Constable wrote to Fisher on 9 May, after the opening of the Academy exhibition:

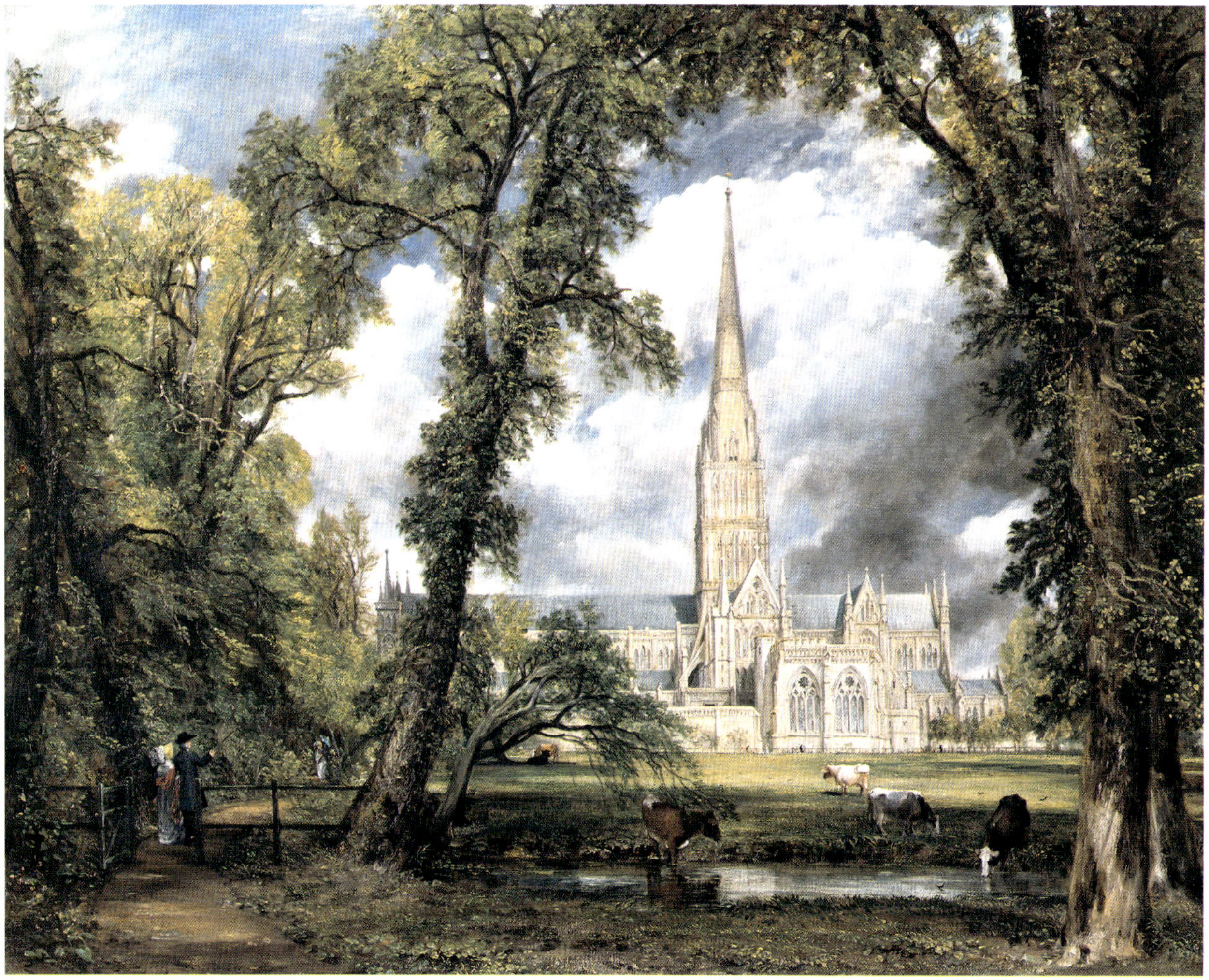

Plate 42 John Constable, *Salisbury Cathedral from the Bishop's Grounds*, 1823. V&A Picture Library

My Cathedral looks very well. Indeed I got through that job uncommonly well considering how much I dreaded it. It is much approved by the Academy and moreover in Seymour St. (that is, by the Bishop and his family) though I was at one time fearfull it would not be a favourite there owing to a dark cloud – but we got over the difficulty.... It was the most difficult subject in landscape I ever had on my easel. I have not flinched at the work, of the windows, buttresses, &c, &c, but I have as usual made my escape in the evanescence of the chiaroscuro.[51]

Constable was mistaken in thinking that the Bishop was happy with the 'dark cloud'. Fisher wrote to Constable on 16 October 1823 reporting the Bishop's views. '[If] Constable would but leave out his black clouds! Clouds are only black when it is going to rain. In fine weather the sky is blue'.[52] The Bishop must nevertheless have been impressed with the painting of the cathedral for he commissioned Constable to paint another version for the marriage of his daughter Elizabeth, but 'I wish to have a more serene sky' he wrote. Fisher wrote to Constable on 2 October 1823 'The

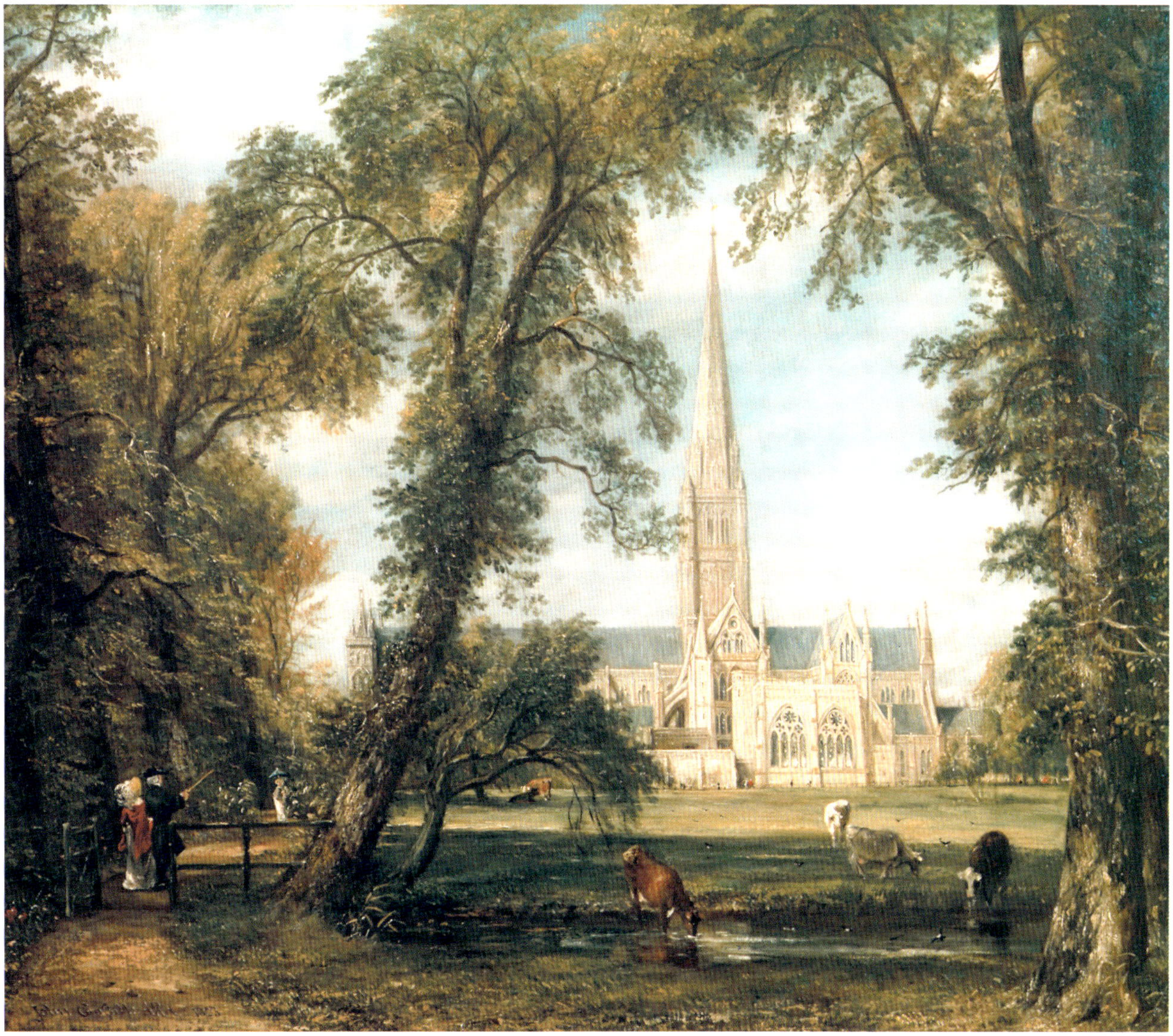

Plate 43 John Constable, *Salisbury Cathedral*, 1823. Courtesy of the Huntington Library, Art Collections, and Botanical Gardens, San Marino, California

Bishop ... hopes that you put your *marriage* picture of Salisbury into a little sunshine'. The new version is indeed less cloudy and the cathedral is bathed in sunlight (Plate 43), but the overall effect is much less dramatic than the original. The 'dark cloud' continued to annoy the Bishop and eventually in July 1824 he returned the picture to Constable for alteration. Constable's response was to paint another version, which unfortunately was not completed until after the Bishop's death. Constable sold the original to Fisher, but bought it back from him in 1829, and then it remained in Constable's possession until he died.

Fortunately Constable was immune to the constant criticism of his skies; he was strong willed enough to ignore these critics and he continued to paint the skies of his finished works as he wanted them. Constable also still occasionally added weather inscriptions to sketches, for instance on a sketch of Hampstead on 9 August 1823: 'Sunset over Harrow. From Hampstead Heath. Saturday August 9. 1823. Stormy evening after a fine day. it rained all the next day.' This is the only weather inscription of 1823 and has not therefore been included as part of his skying period of October 1820 to October 1822.

The sky in *The Lock* exhibited at the Academy in 1824 is mature and fresh. Constable wrote to Fisher on 13 April 1825 'My Lock is now on my easel. It looks most beautifully silvery, windy & delicious…'.[53] The portrayal of wind is suggested by the wind-driven clouds and the shimmering trees.

In May of 1824 Constable moved his family to Brighton in the interests of Maria's health. Many coastal scenes now appear in Constable's work but 1824 was most notable for the gold medals that Constable was awarded by Charles X in Paris for *The Hay Wain* and *View on the Stour*.

One of the most impressionistic of Constable's coastal skies is that of *Seascape Study with Rainclouds* (Plate 44) that has been dated at some time between 1824 and 1828. The dramatic portrayal of the low horizon, the pitch-black sea, the swarthy exploding cumulus shower, the pouring rain with the shaft of sunlight and the illuminated cumulus towers behind, encapsulates in one scene the full glory of the hydrological cycle. This is one of the most expressionistic and powerful of all Constable's sky studies.

The numerous studies of Brighton Beach and the neighbouring coastline that Constable produced in 1824 were sometimes accompanied by inscriptions that added more than just the date and time. For instance:

> *... tide receeding left the beach wet – ...Brighton July 19 Evg.,.. Very lovely Evening – looking eastward – cliffs & light off a dark (?grey) effect – background – very white and golden light. (R24.11)*
>
> *Beach Brighton 22d July, 1824 Very fine Evening. (R24.14)*
>
> *Brighton July 27th 1824 very fine morning after rain (R24.15)*
>
> *Early morning after wet night (R24.35)*

The weather inscriptions are not as detailed as those of 1821/22 but Constable is still interested in painting after rain as the last two inscriptions show. *Brighton Beach with Colliers* (Plate 45) contrasts the lightness of the wet beach with the blues of the sea and sky and the black colliers, which heightens the glare of the 'very white and golden light'. This blue evening summer sky has fewer clouds than perhaps any other Constable oil sketch.

Constable was not impressed with Brighton as a place. 'I am living here but I dislike the place ... and the beach is only Piccadilly by the sea-side.' In the same letter to Fisher he wrote of a visit from Brighton to the Devil's Dyke in Sussex: '– perhaps the most grand & affecting natural landscape in the world – and consequently a scene the most unfit for a picture. It is the business of a painter not to contend with nature & put this scene (a valley filled with imagery 50 miles long) on a canvas of a few inches, but to make something out of nothing, in attempting which he must almost become poetical.'[54] Constable did not want to roam the world to paint spectacular

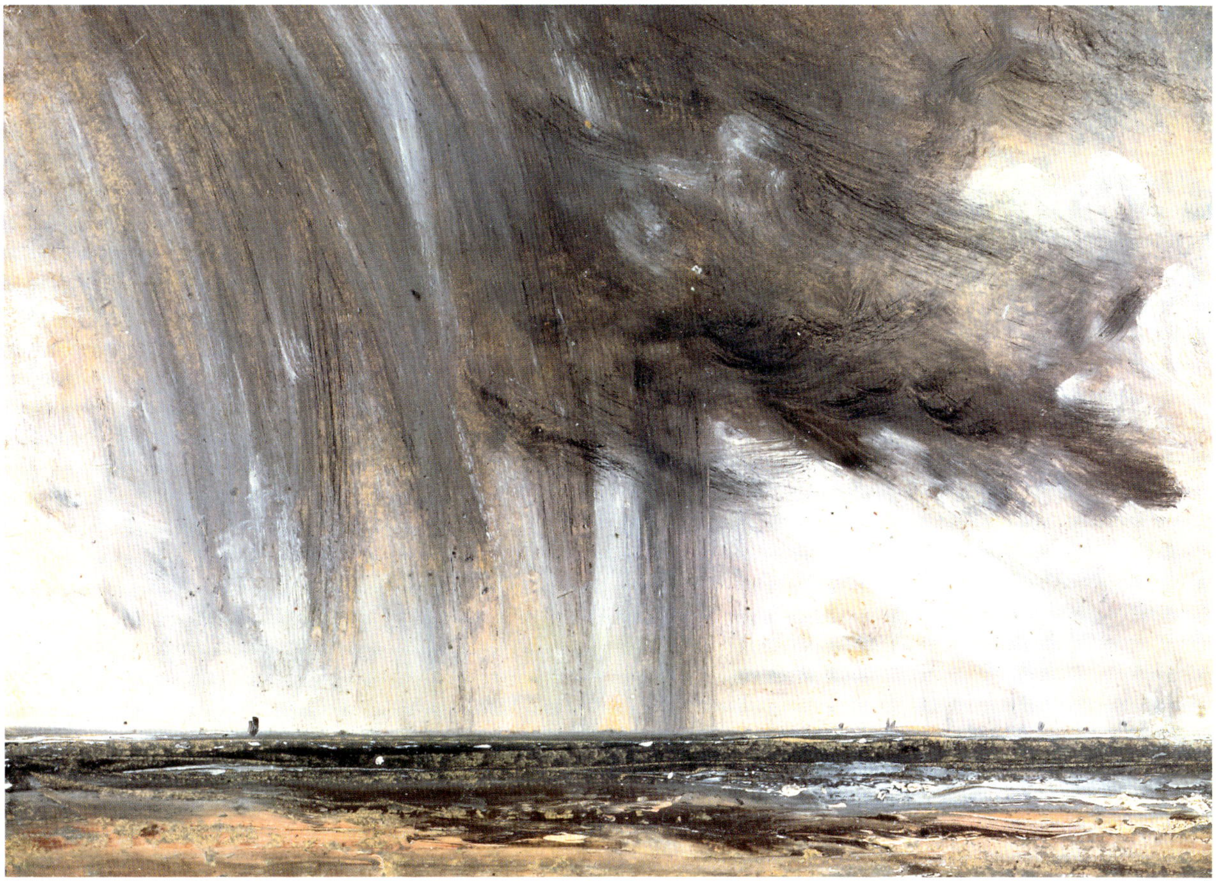

Plate 44 John Constable, *Seascape Study with Rain Clouds*, 1824[?] Royal Academy of Arts, London

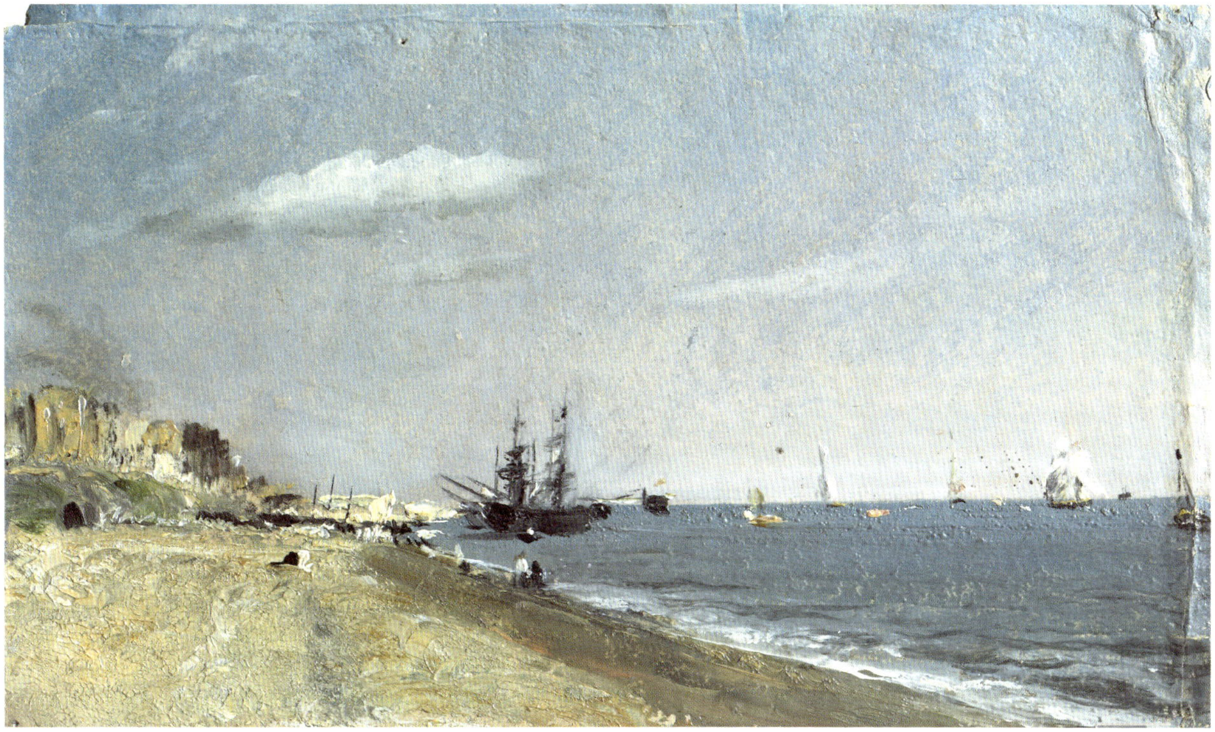

Plate 45 John Constable, *Brighton Beach with Colliers*, 1824, V&A Picture Library

views of nature, nor did he want to battle with nature, to struggle to portray valleys full of imagery. Constable was now content to create new interpretations of his own personal landscapes of Suffolk, Hampstead and Salisbury. Paintings such as *The Lock* were indeed created 'out of nothing' expressing Constable's intensely poetic feelings for one otherwise innocuous canal lock. Similarly Constable's skies were created 'out of nothing' – he could go onto Hampstead Heath and portray in oil a sky that no one else would even notice.

The major painting of 1825 was *The Leaping Horse* (Plate 46), which was the sixth and last of his six-foot canvases of scenes on the Stour painted for the Royal Academy exhibitions. The sky is more overcast than in the previous six-footers and the clouds are of much greater vertical extent. The sky in the full-size sketch, with its huge single cloud, is rather different from the finished painting, but both paintings are full of breeze. Constable referred to the weather in the finished picture as 'blowing'.[55]

The magnificent street of cumulus showers in *Branch Hill Pond, Hampstead Heath* (Plate 47) gives the sky a beautiful three-dimensional feel and totally dominates the picture. The eye is led automatically to the falling rain in the middle distance. Similar streets of cumulus clouds, sweeping from the middle distance to the top left of the sky, feature in several of Constable's works, but this is the finest version. The drawing of a similar sky in *Worthing* dated 22 September 1824 may well have provided the inspiration for this Hampstead sky, as might *Malthouse Field, East Bergholt* (Plate 24).[56]

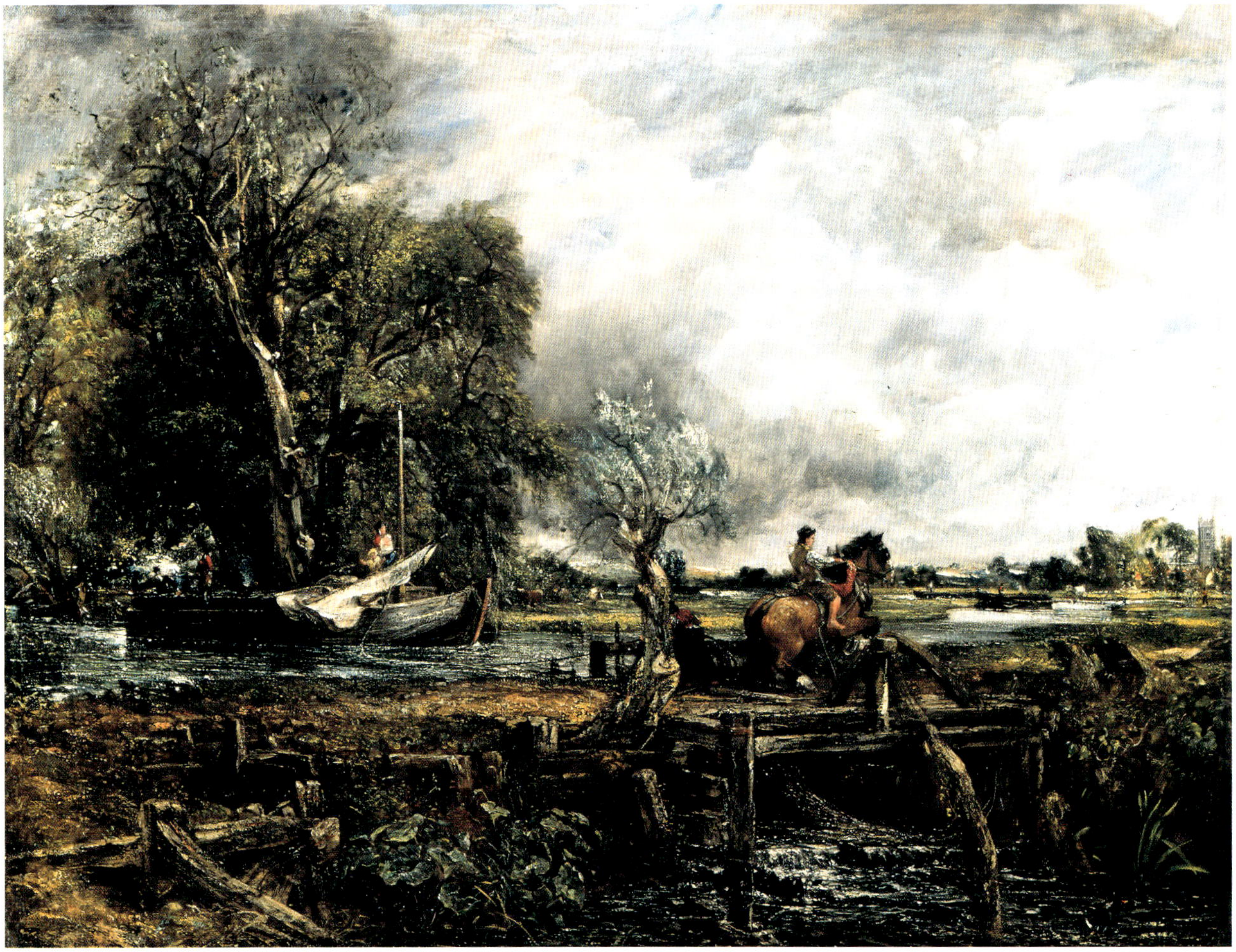

Plate 46 John Constable, *The Leaping Horse*, c. 1824. Royal Academy of Arts, London

Rosenthal writes that *The Cornfield* (Plate 48), exhibited at the Royal Academy in 1826, typifies Constable's picturesque phase which culminated in the 1828 version of the *Vale of Dedham* (Plate 49).[57] Rosenthal identifies a crisis in Constable's East Anglian landscapes that took place over the winter of 1821/22. In the 1810s, he argues, Constable was concerned with recreating the landscapes of a particular place. Realism and exact reproduction of topography and agricultural practice was dominant. After 1822 Constable worked more in the studio and away from the direct experience of nature. Constable's style changed and he became more concerned with the naturalism of sensation. The low viewpoints of *The Lock* and *The Leaping Horse* were more threatening, and Constable started to introduce features into pictures – such as the church in *The Cornfield* – which did not exist. Rosenthal argues that this picturesque approach was not just a ploy to sell his pictures – indeed it made them harder for him to sell because they were so personal to himself – but was a response to the destruction of rural Suffolk as Constable knew it. The picturesque paintings of *The Cornfield* and *Dedham Vale* were nostalgic retrospectives and landscapes of memory. Although this is an interesting theory, Constable's change of style after 1821/22 was also a function of the newly found power that Constable had

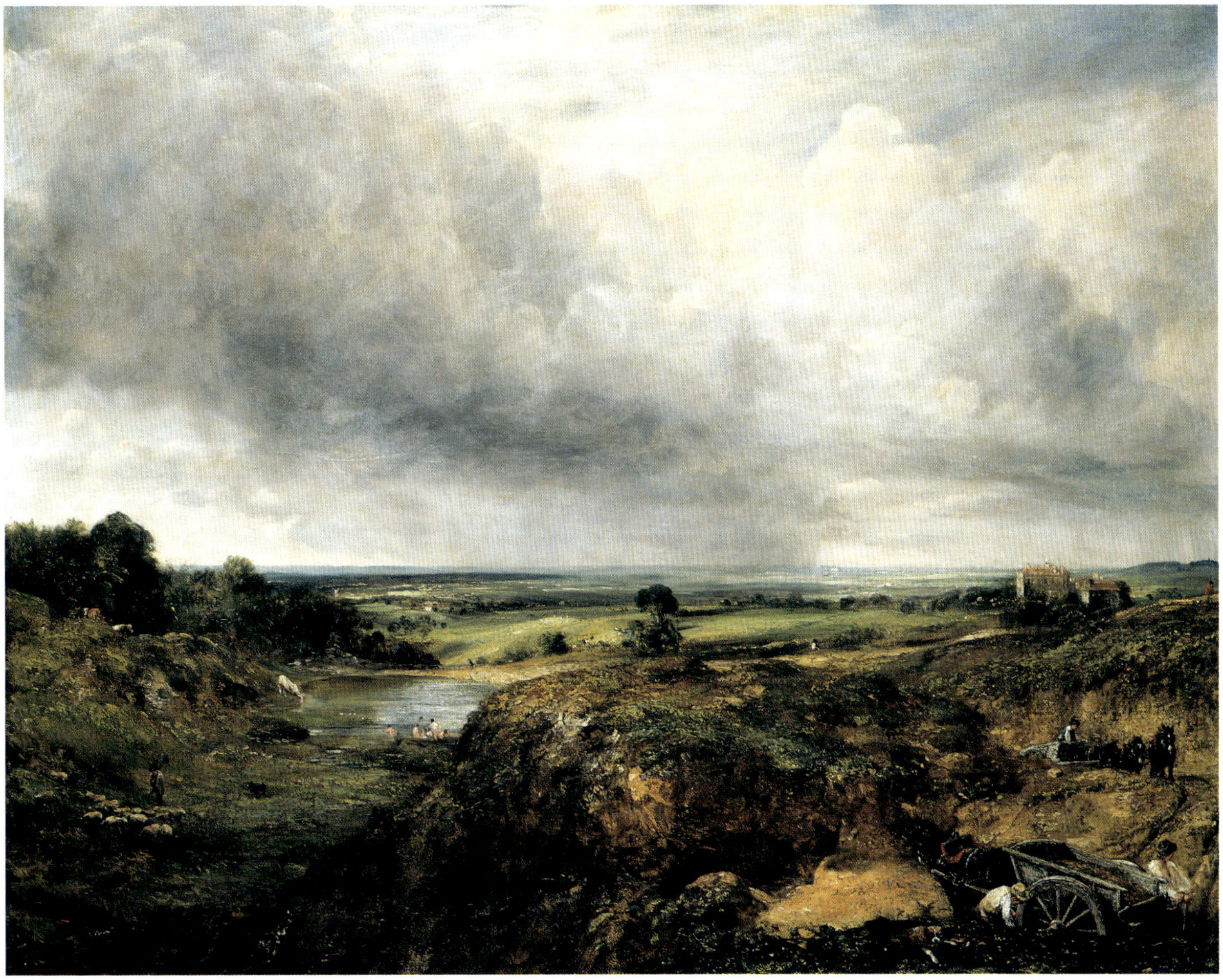

Plate 47 John Constable, *Branch Hill Pond, Hampstead Heath*, 1824–25. Virginia Museum of Fine Arts, Richmond, VA. The Adolph D. and Wilkins C. Williams Fund. Photo: Ann Hutchison. Copyright 1999 Virginia Museum of Fine Arts

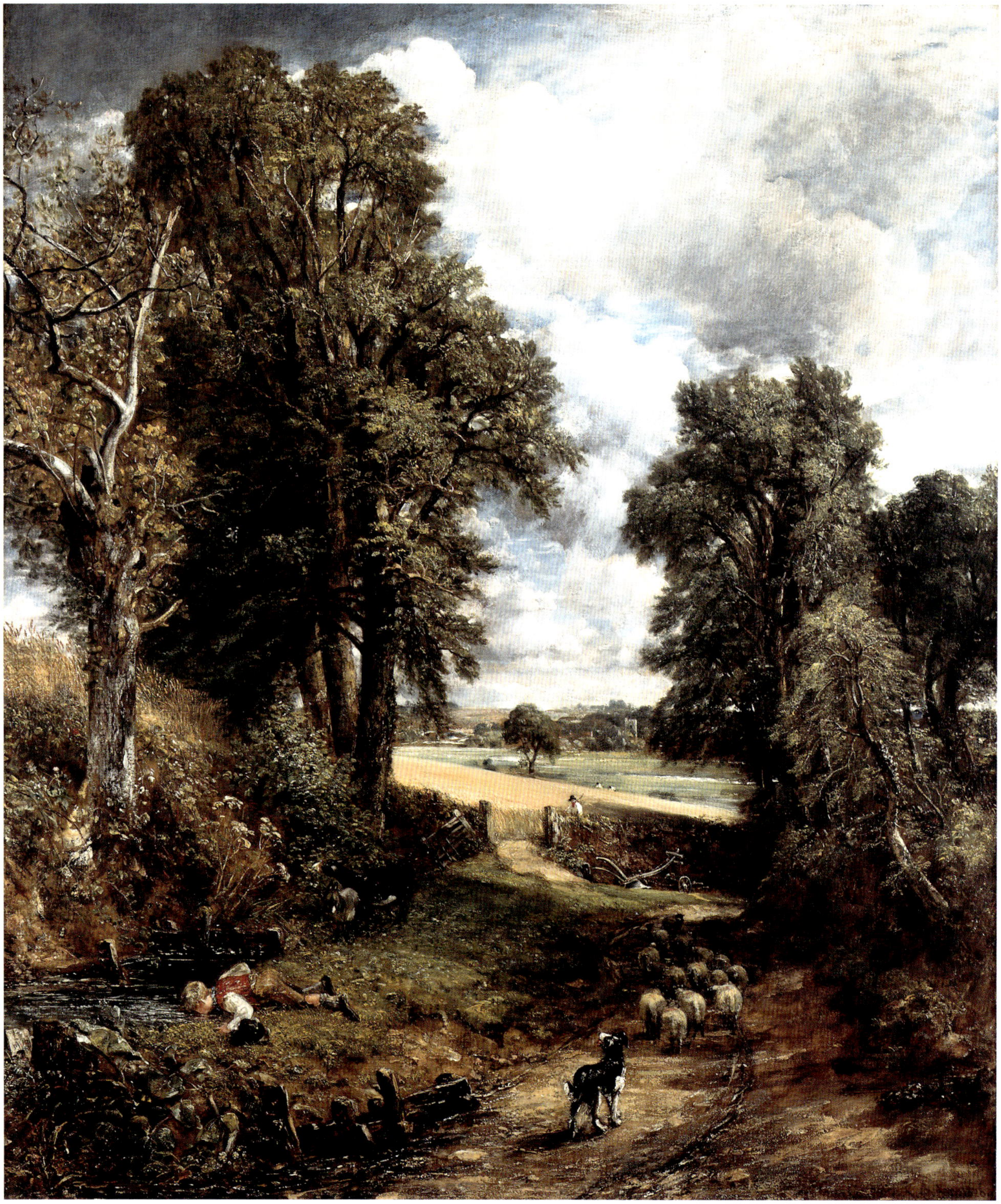

Plate 48 John Constable, *The Cornfield*, 1826. Copyright National Gallery, London

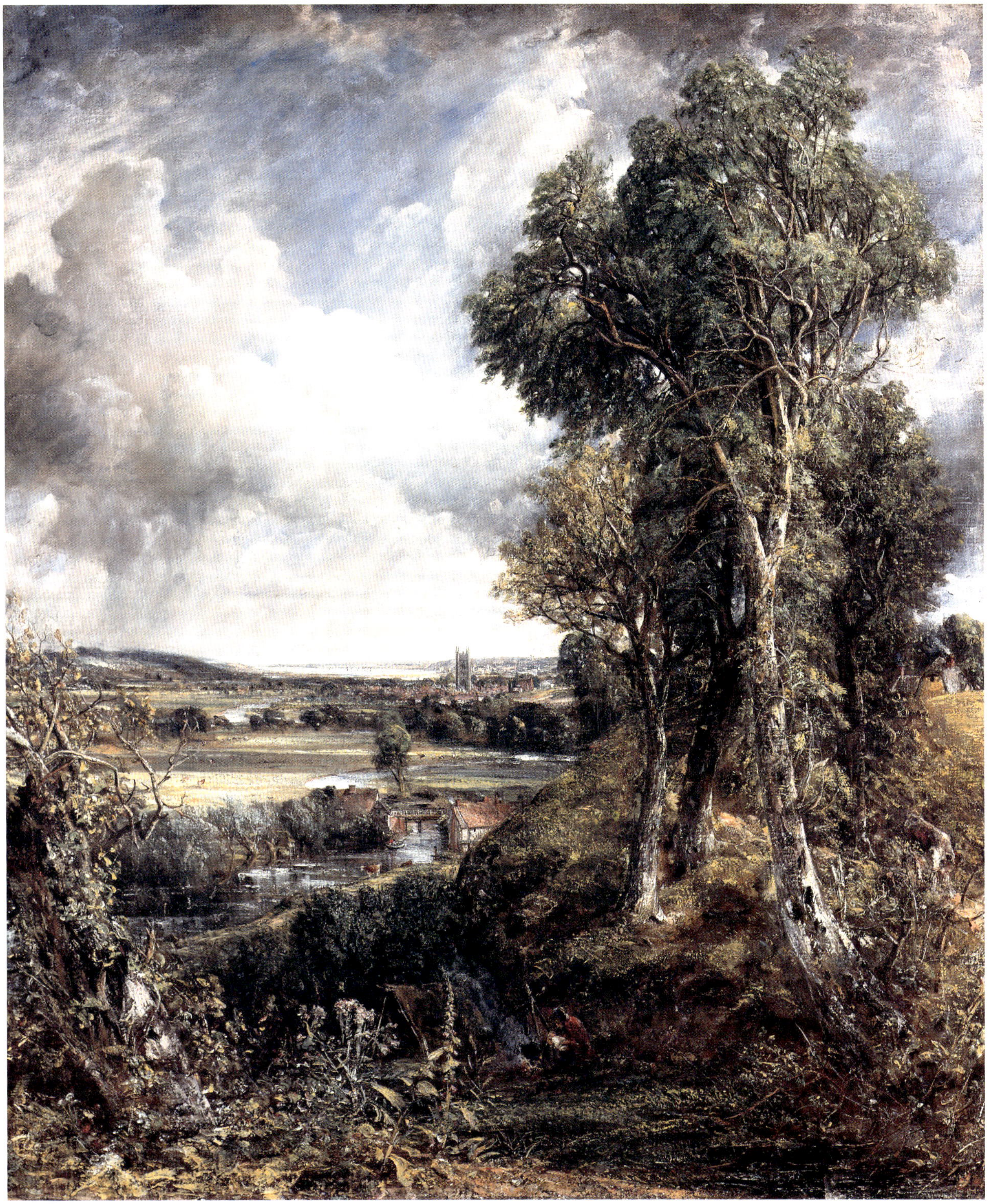

Plate 49 John Constable, *Vale of Dedham*, 1828. The National Gallery of Scotland

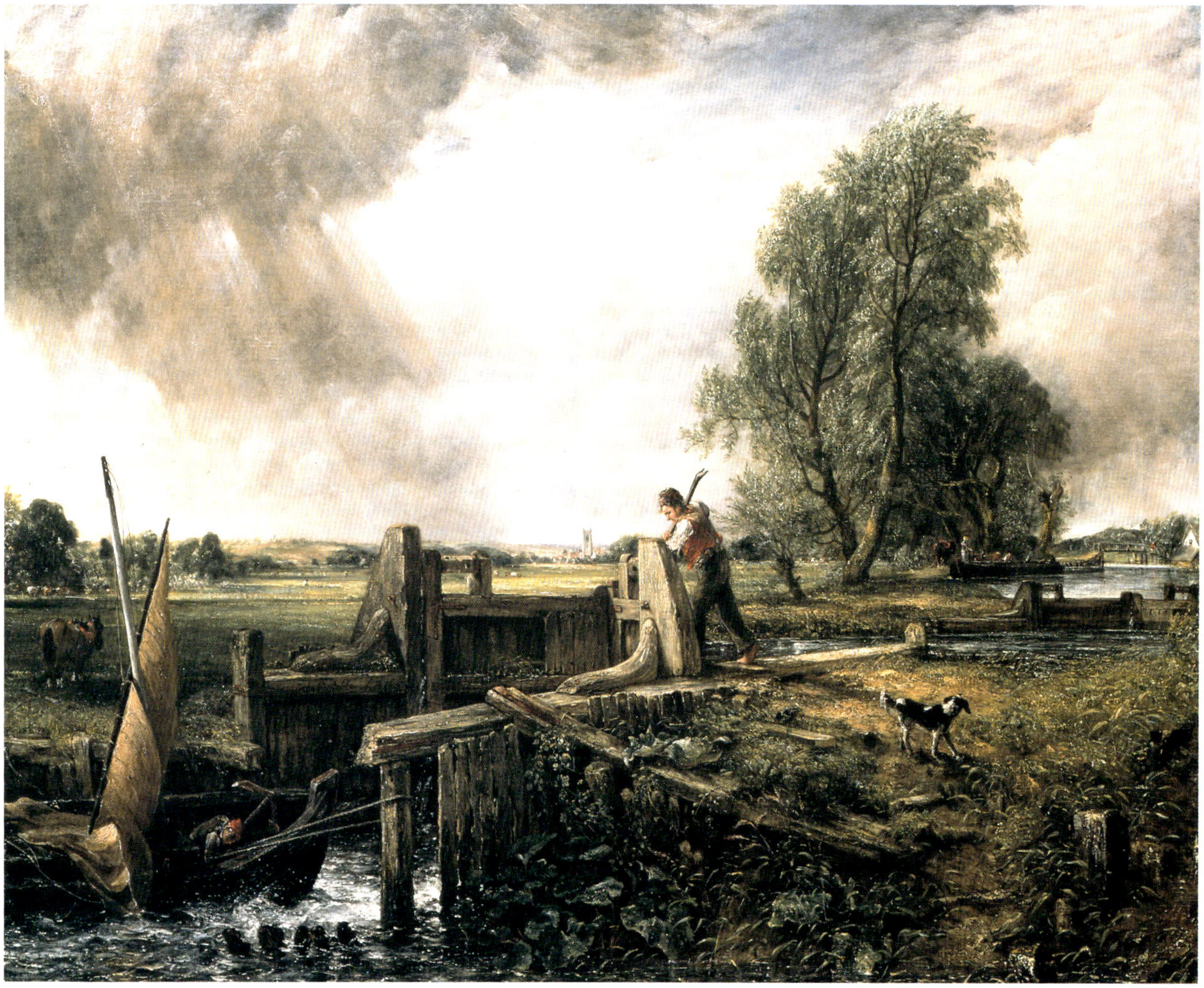

Plate 50 John Constable, *A Boat Passing a Lock*, 1826. Royal Academy of Arts, London

acquired. Just as his understanding of skies had progressed during the skying period to the extent that he could create recognisable, dynamic skies at will, so his ability as a painter had reached its peak. Having mastered the harmony between sky and landscape he moved beyond realism towards idealism. He could create landscapes just as convincing and powerful as his skyscapes.

The Cornfield was exhibited again at the British Institution in 1827, for which Constable added to the title *Landscape: Noon* and also some lines of poetry partly taken from Thomson's *Seasons*:

A fresher gale
Begins to wave the woods and stir the stream,
Sweeping with shadowy gust the fields of corn.

The noon sky is full of fair weather cumulus clouds, the sun high in the sky above the top right of the picture. There is tremendous depth to the sky with row upon row of cumulus to the horizon being blown along in the wind. Constable wrote of the picture to Fisher on 8 April 1826: 'The trees ... are shaken by a pleasant and healthful breeze – "at noon"'.[58]

The painting that Constable chose as his Diploma work in 1829 when he was at long last elected to the Royal Academy was *A Boat Passing a Lock* (Plate 50) painted in 1825. It depicts a heavy shower with a strong wind slanting the rain over a view of the same lock as depicted in *The Lock*, but at a slightly different angle.

The large number of studies of Brighton culminated in *The Chain Pier Brighton* (Plate 51)

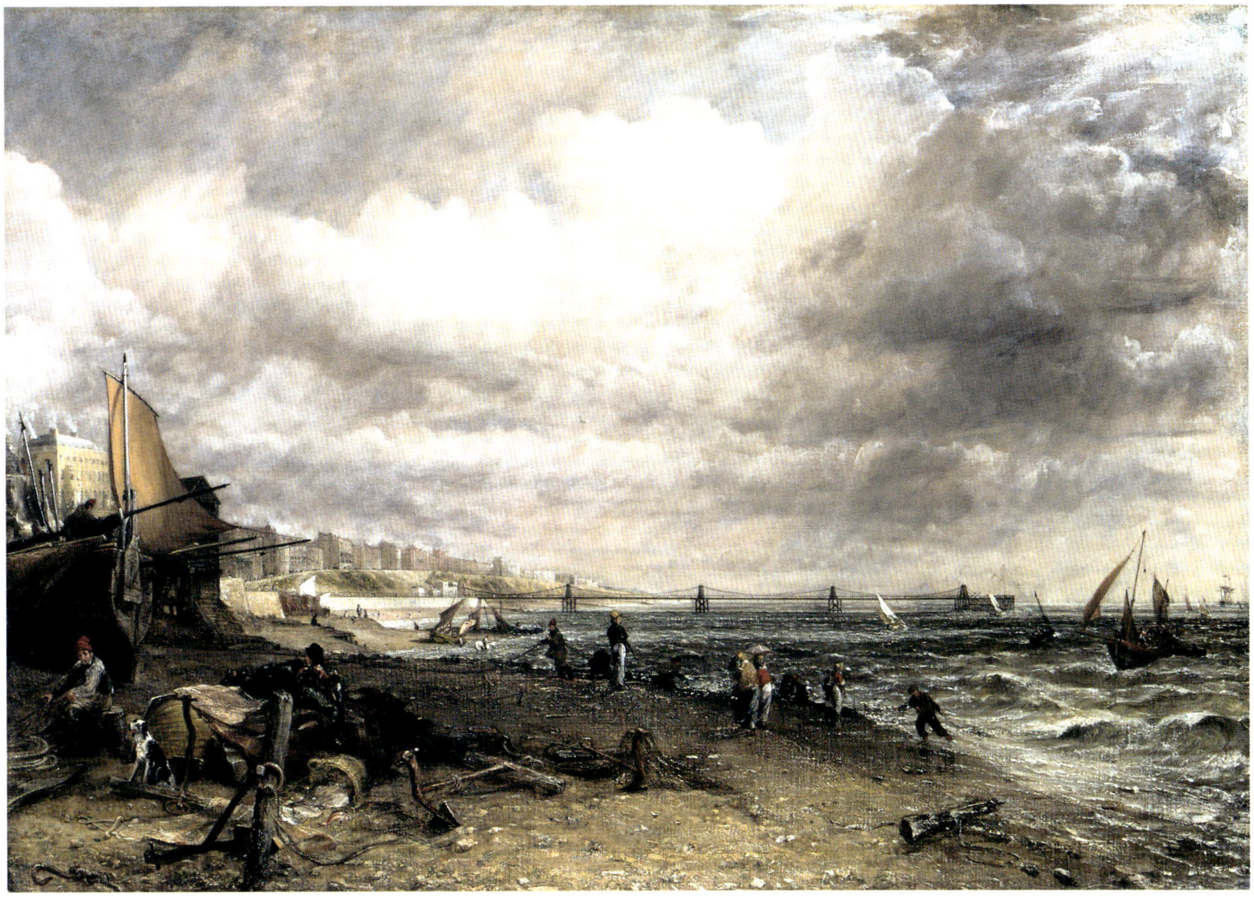

Plate 51 John Constable, *The Chain Pier Brighton*, 1827. Copyright Tate Gallery, London 1998

exhibited at the Royal Academy in 1827. This change of subject from the scenes of Suffolk was welcomed by his friend Fisher. The sky is almost overcast with heavy showers falling from the dark cumulus on the right of the picture and the wind is whipping up the waves. This painting forms the first link between the sky and the changing state of Constable's mind.[59] Fisher wrote to Constable shortly after Maria's death in November 1828: 'I wish if "Brighton" is not out of your possession that you would put it on an easel by your side, Claude fashion, & so mellow its ferocious beauties. Calm your own mind and your sea at the same time, & let in sunshine & serenity.'[60] This sky was the most cloudy of the big finished skies that Constable had exhibited, with only a hint of blue getting through between the clouds. Two of the figures walking along the beach are crouching from the wind, and one of them seems to be carrying an umbrella. The 'ferocious beauty' of the painting, as Fisher called it, derives entirely from the sky which totally dominates the scene. A review in *The Sun* on 8 May 1827 stated: 'Constable's *Chain Pier at Brighton* is marked by this artist's usual strict adherence to nature. The atmosphere possesses a characteristic humidity about it, that almost imparts a wish for an umbrella, so naturally is the illusion preserved.'[61] Another review in *The Examiner* on 1 July 1827 stated that Constable had captured 'the natural look of our English atmosphere, half sullen and half-smiling'.[62]

In a watercolour dated 20 May 1827, entitled *Sky Study with Rainbow* (Plate 52), Constable has depicted a strange yellow bow with the light darker beneath than above the bow. This seemingly inaccurate rendering was contrasted by Schweizer with the much more accurate British Museum watercolour *London from Hampstead with a Double*

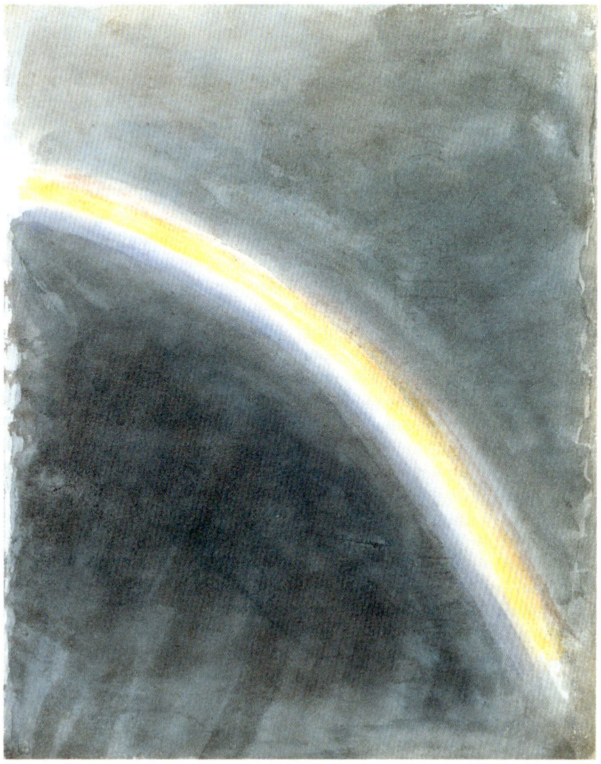

Plate 52 John Constable, *Sky Study with Rainbow*, 20 May 1827. Yale Center for British Art, Paul Mellon Collection (B1975.4.1874)

Rainbow (Plate 61) to show how Constable's meteorological understanding of rainbows had improved between 1827 and 1831.[63] The yellow bow in the 1827 study almost seems to be mixed with white and may be a representation of a fog-bow rather than a rainbow. In reality no one rainbow is like any other and it is possible to get instances where 'the yellow may be very wide' as the meteorologist Tricker mentions in his *Introduction to Meteorological Optics*.[64]

We have already mentioned the picturesque nature of *Dedham Vale* exhibited at the Royal Academy in 1828 together with *Hampstead Heath: Branch Hill Pond* (Plate 53). In the review of the exhibition by *The Sun* on 5 May 1828 it is interesting that it is not clear which painting was being referred to: '*Landscape*, by Constable. – A rich and varied piece of colouring, imbued all over with the qualities of English landscape. A shower has apparently just passed over, and a few flitting clouds throw their flickering light and shades over the country.'[65] The sky so dominates both landscapes that it is almost immaterial which one is being referred to! The sky, the clouds, the sunlight and the atmosphere in the *Dedham Vale* of 1828 is so superior to the 1802 version (compare Plates 15 and 49) that this serves as a perfect example of the tremendous advance in sky painting that Constable had made over that time. Such a comparison brings home yet again his mastery of the sky and light, and the harmonisation of the sky and landscape that he achieved in the 1820s. The sky in the 1802 version looks dull, flat and dead in comparison. The *Hampstead Heath: Branch Hill Pond* sky is similar to the sky of the 1825 versions discussed earlier but the heavy showers in the distance are falling from individual cumulus clouds rather than a street of cumulus clouds as in the 1825 versions.

Constable's seventh child, Lionel Bicknell, was born on 2 January 1828. The year however ended on a tragic note when Maria died on 23 November. Constable was devastated and never ceased to mourn for her until his own death in 1837. Nevertheless he had seven motherless children between the ages of ten months and eleven years to bring up, a responsibility that kept him at his art.

The years between 1823 and 1828 had seen Constable's skies grow more dominating and more full of rain. The wind had freshened and Fuseli's comments reported by Constable in 1823 sum up this period rather well. 'Speaking of me generally [Fuseli] says – I like de landscape – of Constable – but he makes me call for my great coat & particularly he says I am always picturesque – of a fine color – & de lights always in their right places.'[66]

3.7 Sunset 1829–32: strong breeze

The emotion and heartbreak of Maria's death spilled over into Constable's skies, and the ruins of *Hadleigh Castle* (Plate 54) with its huge stormy sky seems very appropriate as his main Royal Academy submission of 1829. The full title given by Constable was

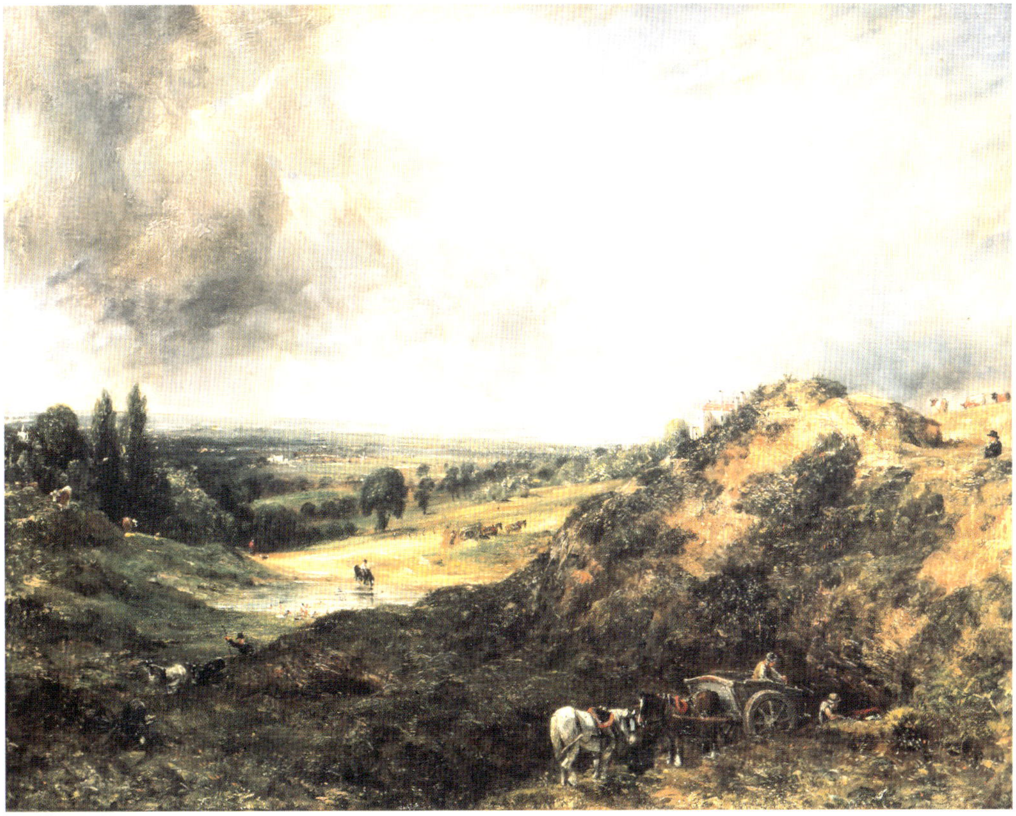

Plate 53 John Constable, *Hampstead Heath: Branch Hill Pond*, 1828. V&A Picture Library

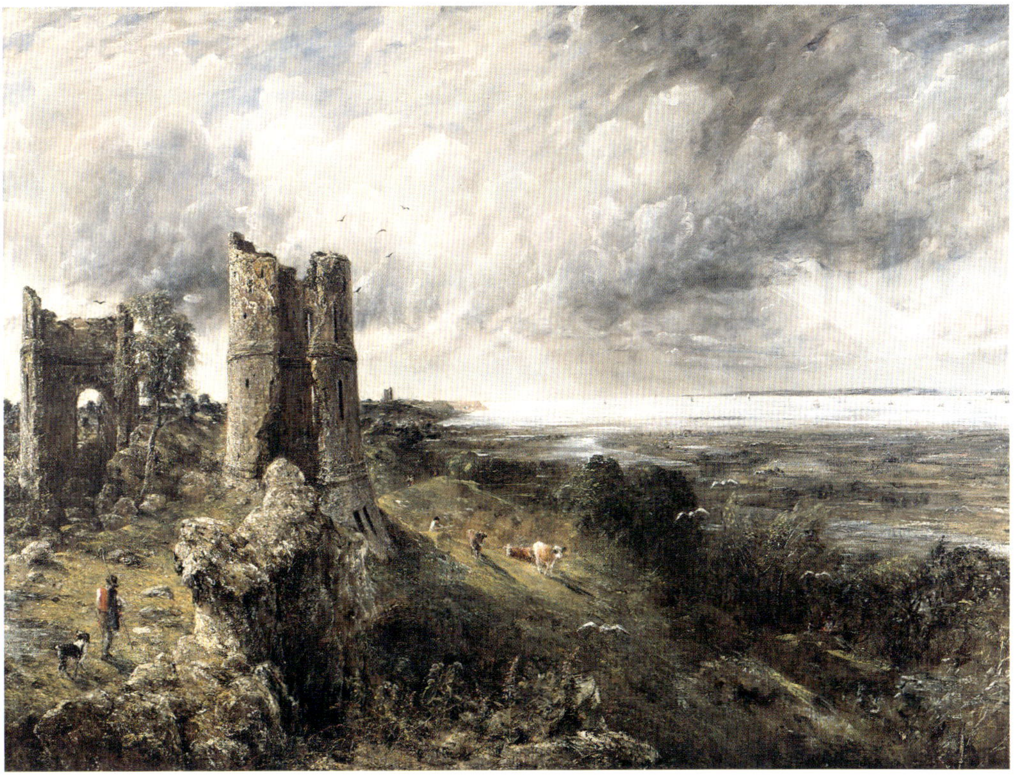

Plate 54 John Constable, *Hadleigh Castle*, 1829.
Yale Center for British Art, Paul Mellon Collection (B1977.14.42)

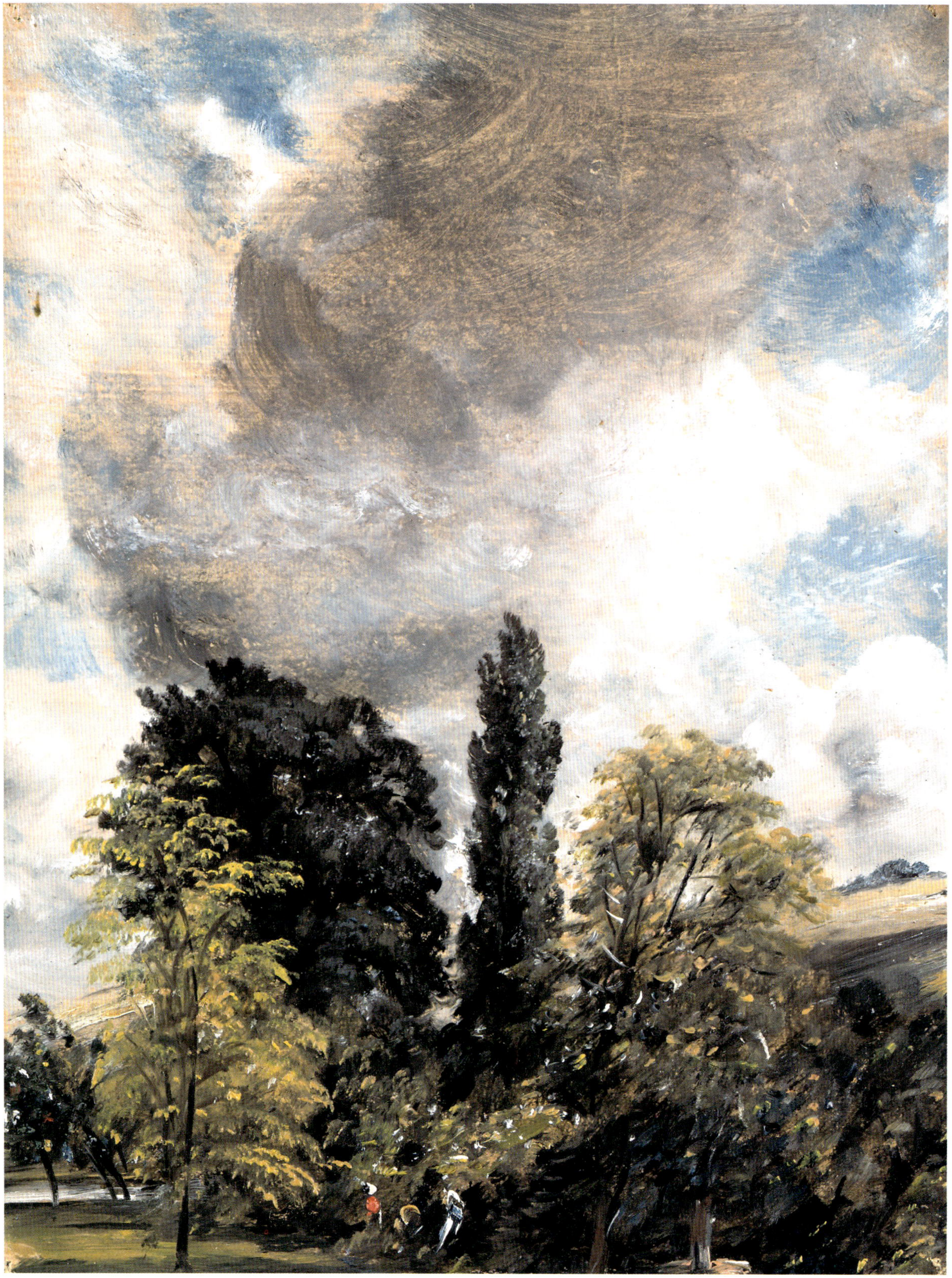

Plate 55 John Constable, *The Close, Salisbury*, 1829. V&A Picture Library

Hadleigh Castle. The Mouth of the Thames – morning after a stormy night, which was accompanied by a quotation from Thomson's *Seasons*:

> *The desert joys*
> *Wildly, through all his melancholy bounds*
> *Rude ruins glitter; and the briny deep,*
> *Seen from some pointed promontory's top,*
> *Far to the dim horizon's utmost verge*
> *Restless, reflects a floating gleam.*[67]

The inscription 'morning after a stormy night' is reminiscent of his 1820/22 cloud studies, as is the sky itself. The huge cumulus, the remnants perhaps of a cumulonimbus, dominates the sky.

On 10 February 1829 Constable was at last elected as a full member of the Royal Academy and he was keen that his first picture before the Academy should be well received. *The London Magazine* in June 1829 said that *Hadleigh Castle* was 'full of power, and truth, and freshness' but went on to criticise its 'silvery effect'.[68] Constable's 'snow' was again under scrutiny but generally the critics were impressed.

In July Constable visited Fisher at Salisbury and produced a number of outdoor oil studies including *The Close, Salisbury* (Plate 55) which is inscribed 'Close – 15 July – 1829 11. o clock noon – Wind S.W – very fine.' The sketch is a superb rendering of the base of a cumulus cloud moving rapidly overhead. More cloud studies were to follow in the summer of 1830. Several of the sketches made at this time, particularly of Harnham Ridge, show a resemblance to the sky studies of 1820/22 and mark a rekindling of Constable's creative urge.

About this time Constable began to work on the first edition of *English Landscape Scenery* which was issued in five parts between June 1830 and July 1832. He engaged David Lucas as engraver and twenty-two plates were published in this first edition. This was the start of an unfortunate saga that lasted until Constable's death. The various editions all failed to sell and Constable lost considerable amounts of money. Despite Constable's loss it is undoubtedly our gain that the artist undertook such a project, as the inscriptions that accompanied many of the prints tell us much of Constable's knowledge at that time. His commentaries on rainbows and clouds have already been discussed in Chapter 2.

The sky is not neglected in any of the mezzotints in *English Landscape Scenery* and Lucas often added more to the sky than appeared in the originals. This is especially true for those originals that were painted before 1820/22; for example the sky of the engraved version of *Lock on the Stour* (exhibited at the Royal Academy in 1813, entitled *Head of a Lock on the Stour. – Rolling Clouds* (Plate 23) and issued in Part 4 of *English Landscape Scenery* (Plate 56, November 1831) is far more dynamic and natural than the original. Indeed all the mezzotints are remarkably atmospheric, which speaks highly of the technique and is probably the main reason that Constable chose this medium. The beautiful renditions of the skies by Lucas, following Constable's detailed instructions, should also be praised.

The 1829 painting of *Old Sarum* (Plate 57) is a fitting accompaniment to *Hadleigh Castle* as an expression of Constable's feelings at that time. In the text accompanying the mezzotint of *Old Sarum* written in 1833/34 he states:

> *The subject of this plate ... is grand in itself, and interesting in its associations, so that no kind of effect could be introduced too striking, or too impressive to portray it; and among the various appearances of the elements, we naturally look to the grander phenomena of Nature, as according best with the character of such a scene. Sudden and abrupt appearances of light, thunder clouds, wild autumnal evenings, solemn and shadowy twilights, 'flinging half an image on the straining sight,' with variously tinted clouds, dark, cold, and gray, or ruddy and bright, with transitory gleams of light, even conflicts of the elements, to heighten, if possible, the sentiment which belongs to a subject so awful and impressive.*[69]

The sky and atmosphere dominate and control the scene, and both the original painting and the

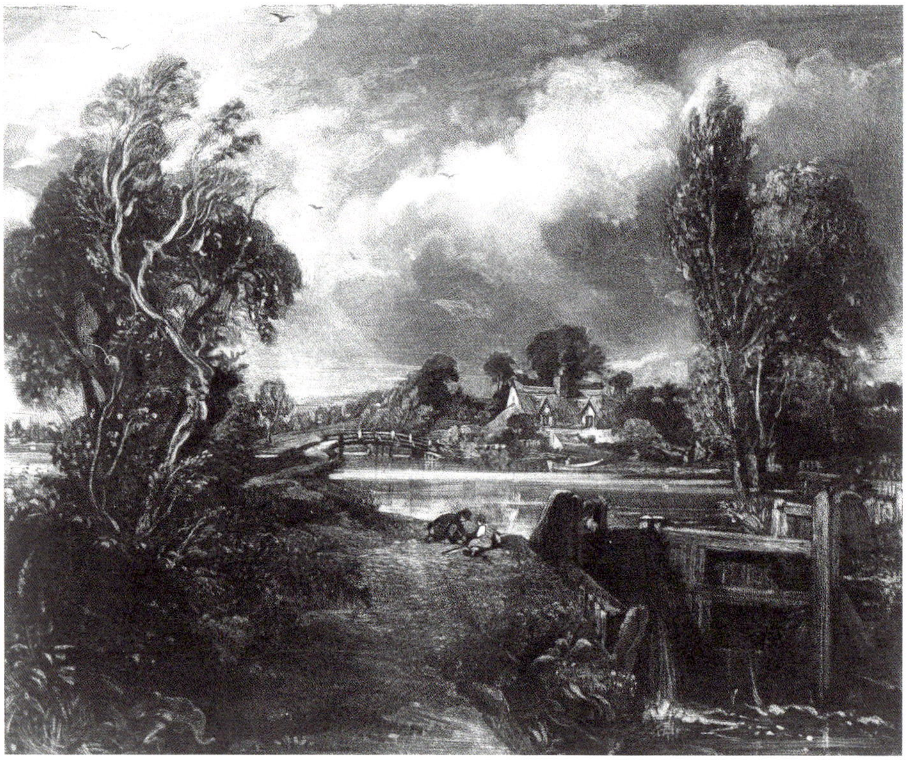

Plate 56 David Lucas, John Constable's *Lock on the Stour*, Suffolk. Engraving, 1833. V&A Picture Library

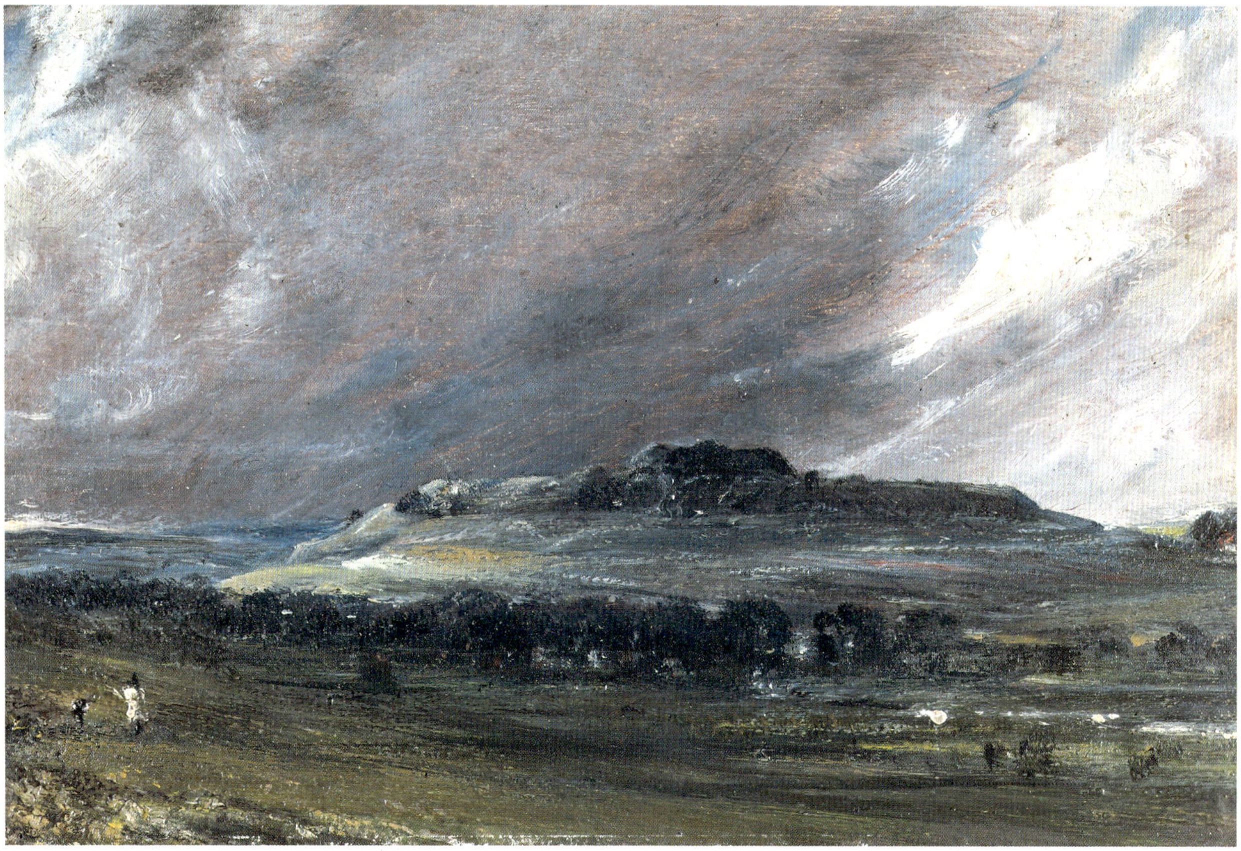

Plate 57 John Constable, *Old Sarum*, 1829. V&A Picture Library

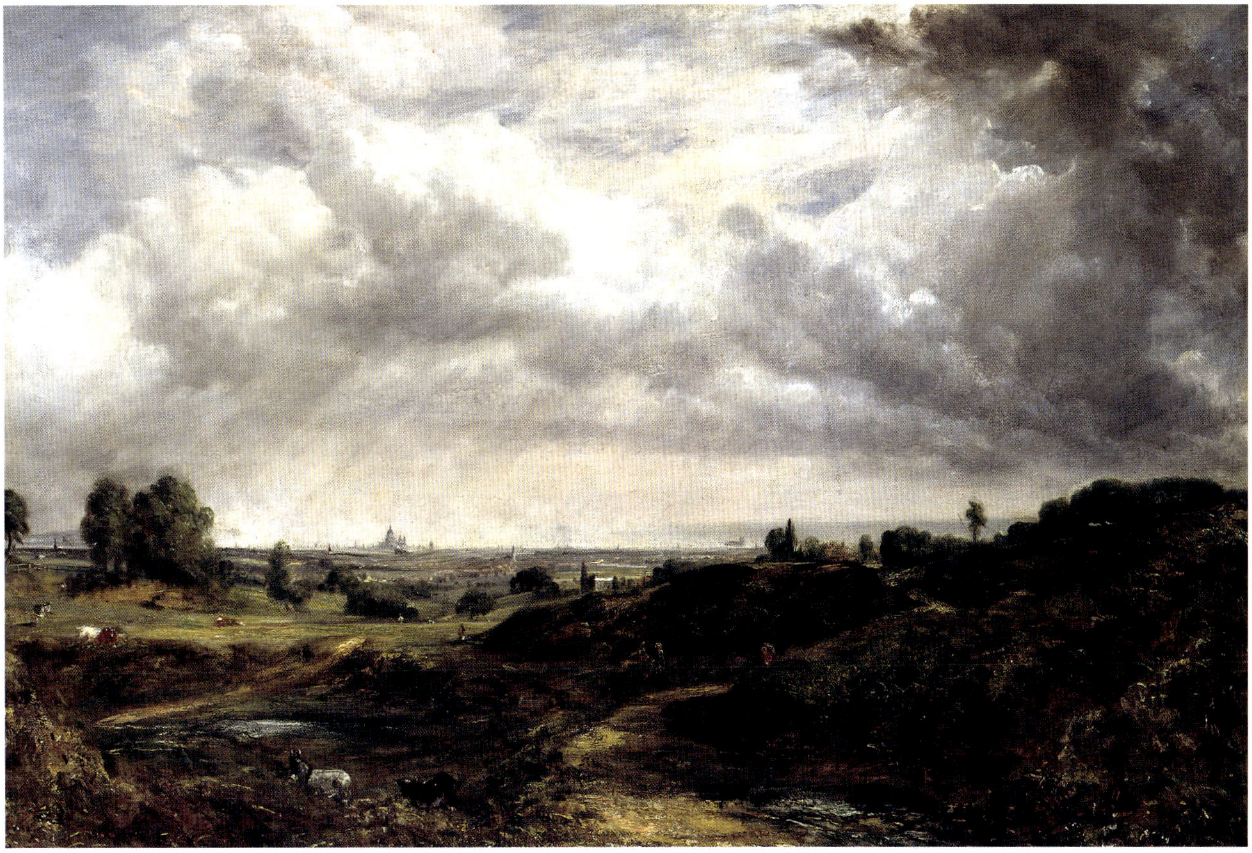

Plate 58 John Constable, *Hampstead Heath*, 1830. Glasgow Museums: Art Gallery and Museum, Kelvingrove

mezzotint succeed in portraying the awesome power of nature.

Helmingham Dell, exhibited at the Royal Academy in 1830, is unusual in that the sky is almost absent, but the sky in *Hampstead Heath* (Plate 58), also exhibited, is as full of light and threatening clouds as ever. Mrs A. M. Constable, in her description of this painting for her list of loans to the South Kensington Museum in 1880, calls it 'Hampstead Heath, supposed to be the best sky ever painted by Constable'.[70] In the summer of 1830 Constable returned to Hampstead Heath to produce a number of new sky studies, although this time in watercolour. Again he began to inscribe some of them on the back:

> *noon. Augt 28 1830 Hampd.*
> *about 11 – Noon – Sepr 15 1830. Wind – W.*
> *Hampstead, drawing Room 12. oclock noon Sept. 1830*

It was as if he was recharging his sky 'batteries' ready for his most complicated sky yet, that exhibited in *Salisbury Cathedral from the Meadows* (Plate 59) in 1831. (The enigmatic rainbow in this painting has already been discussed in Chapter 2.) The sky is so powerful and controversial that the critics were harsh:

> *but the sky is in a state of utter derangement.*[71]

> *A very vigorous and masterly landscape, which somebody has spoiled since it was painted, by putting in such clouds as no human being ever saw.*[72]

> *This will be a good picture in the days to come. At present it is too immediately after the rain, and everything is so vivid and bright, that it seems to touch the eye. The clouds are too theatrically stormy and rain-full.*[73]

> *The inky clouds, and the shower of meal that*

seems to be falling in the foreground, destroy the keeping and natural effect. Mr. CONSTABLE once painted with equal truth and freshness, but he sacrifices these real qualities to a trick of art.[74]

What season of the year is intended to be depicted? ... from the face of that scene, the snow seems melting away; the lightning is glaring, not flashing through the trees; and all the winds of heaven seem hurling the clouds about in every imaginable form and confusion; and yet out of this chaos of the elements, a picture is presented to us which is impossible to pass by without admiration.[75]

The clouds seem to be pouring down rain of a plum colour, plentifully speckled with flakes of snow.[76]

..it is presumed, from the lines quoted from Thomson, to represent the clearing up of a shower; but there is nothing like a clearing up about it.[77]

The remarkable thing about all these reviews is that they are preoccupied with the sky, and hardly mention the cathedral itself. Constable was aware of the criticism and in a letter to Leslie on 2 June 1831, having read the review in *The Library of the Fine Arts*, he wrote, 'they speak ... perhaps fairly, of my "Chaos" as they term the Salisbury. They say (after much abuse & faults), "it is still a picture from *which it is impossible to turn without admiration*".'[78] As stated previously, the rainbow and the lightning were added into the picture by Constable to heighten the effect. That they are meteorologically untenable shows that Constable had broken his own rules for the sky, just as he forsook truth for picturesque landscapes earlier. His poetic licence can be forgiven in that the whole is much greater than the sum of the parts, as the critic quoted above implied. The sky is wrong, but it is magnificent.

Fisher's title for this painting, 'The Church under a cloud', implies all was not well at Salisbury, and the possible symbolism of the sky was discussed in Chapter 2. Essentially Constable's sky in *Salisbury Cathedral from the Meadows* had moved beyond realism into symbolism. However, Constable never again attempted such an allegorical sky.

After thirteen years of marination, Constable finally finished *The Opening of Waterloo Bridge seen from Whitehall Stairs, June 18th 1817* (Plate 60) and sent it to the Royal Academy in 1832. The sky is unusual in that it displays an effect of light whereby the sun's rays are seen converging in perspective towards the opposite horizon. Ian Fleming-Williams suggests that two rapidly drawn pencil studies on the back of *London from Hampstead with a Double Rainbow* (Plate 61) and the watercolour itself, illustrate this effect. Leslie had written:

I regret that among his papers I have not met with the observations on skies and clouds, which he mentions in a letter to Mr. George Constable.[79] *I recollect hearing, at different times, remarks by him on atmospheric effects, but I can scarcely recall any thing he said, with sufficient distinctness to repeat it. I remember that he pointed out to me an appearance of the sun's rays, which few artists have perhaps noticed, and which I never saw given in any picture, excepting in his Waterloo Bridge. When the spectator stands with his back to the sun, the rays may be sometimes seen converging in perspective towards the opposite horizon. Since he drew my attention to such effects, I have noticed very early in the morning the lines of the rays diminishing in perspective through a rainbow.*[80]

This effect, as discussed in Chapter 2, is the exact opposite of crepuscular rays which always converge towards the sun. The observed effect is caused by a gap in the clouds overhead which lets the sun's rays through, at a shallow angle, like a searchlight, but due to perspective the slightly diverging rays actually appear to converge as anticrepuscular rays. When looking at a rainbow the sun is behind you, and light passing through beneath the bow can appear to be converging, giving the impression of a rainbow wheel.

On 25 August 1832 Constable's closest confidant, Archdeacon Fisher, died. Constable wrote to Leslie 'I cannot tell how singularly his death has affected me. I shall pass this week at Hampstead to copy the Winter – for which indeed my mind is in a fit state.'[81] (The copy of Ruisdael's *Winter* will be discussed in detail in the next chapter.) The copy was so good that the owner insisted that Constable should change his copy slightly from the original.

This period of Constable's skies was marked by their increased storminess, and by Constable's enigmatic introduction of atmospheric effects to heighten their drama and mood.

3.8 The valley in shadow 1833–37: near gale

In a note to Leslie at the beginning of 1833 Constable wrote:

> *I have laid by the Cenotaph for the present. I am determined not to harass my mind and HEALTH by scrambling over my canvas – as I hitherto have too often done. Why should I – I have little to lose and nothing to gain. I ought to respect myself – for my friends' sake, who love me – and my children. It is time at '56' to begin at least to know 'one's self', – and I do know what I am not ... your regard for me has at least awakened me to believe in the possibility that I*

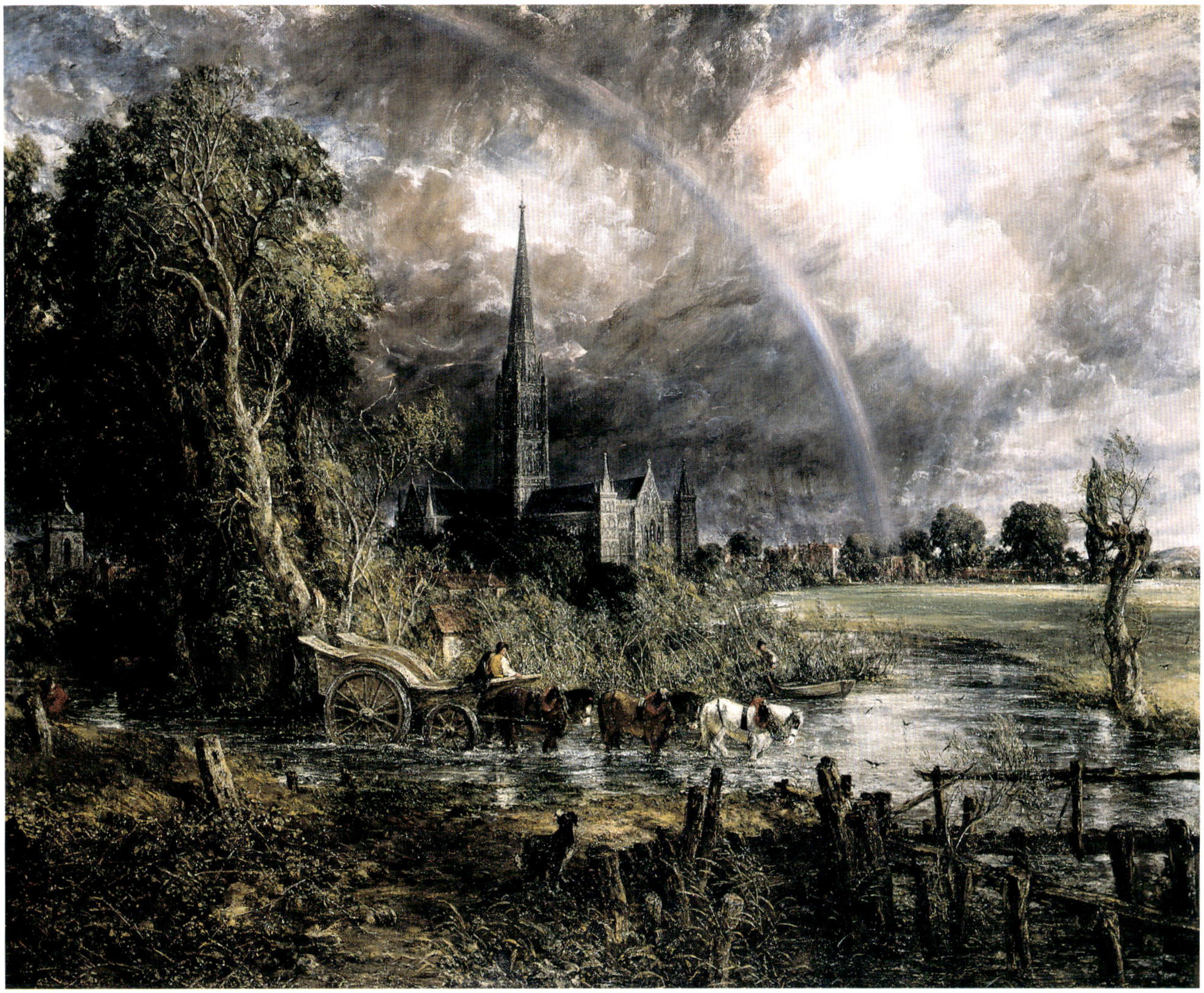

Plate 59 John Constable, *Salisbury Cathedral from the Meadows*, 1831. Copyright National Gallery, London

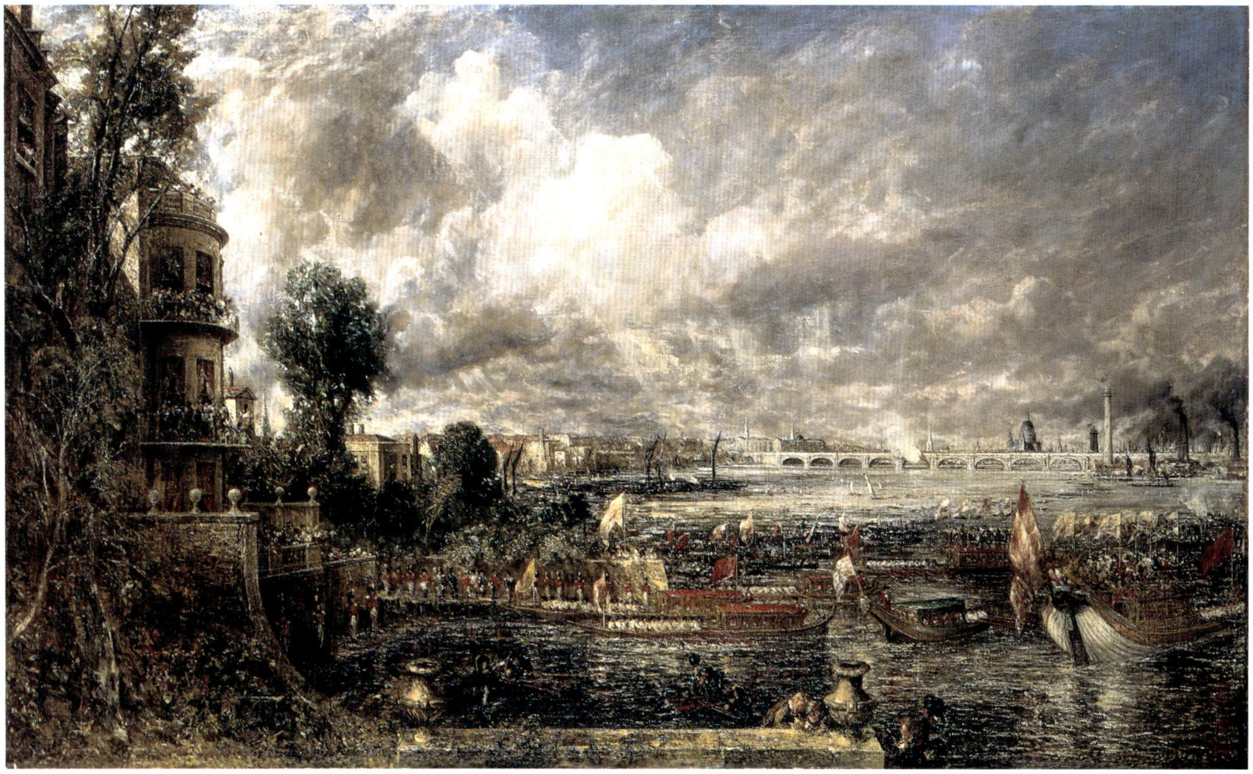

Plate 60 John Constable, *The Opening of Waterloo Bridge*, 1832. Copyright Tate Gallery, London, 1998

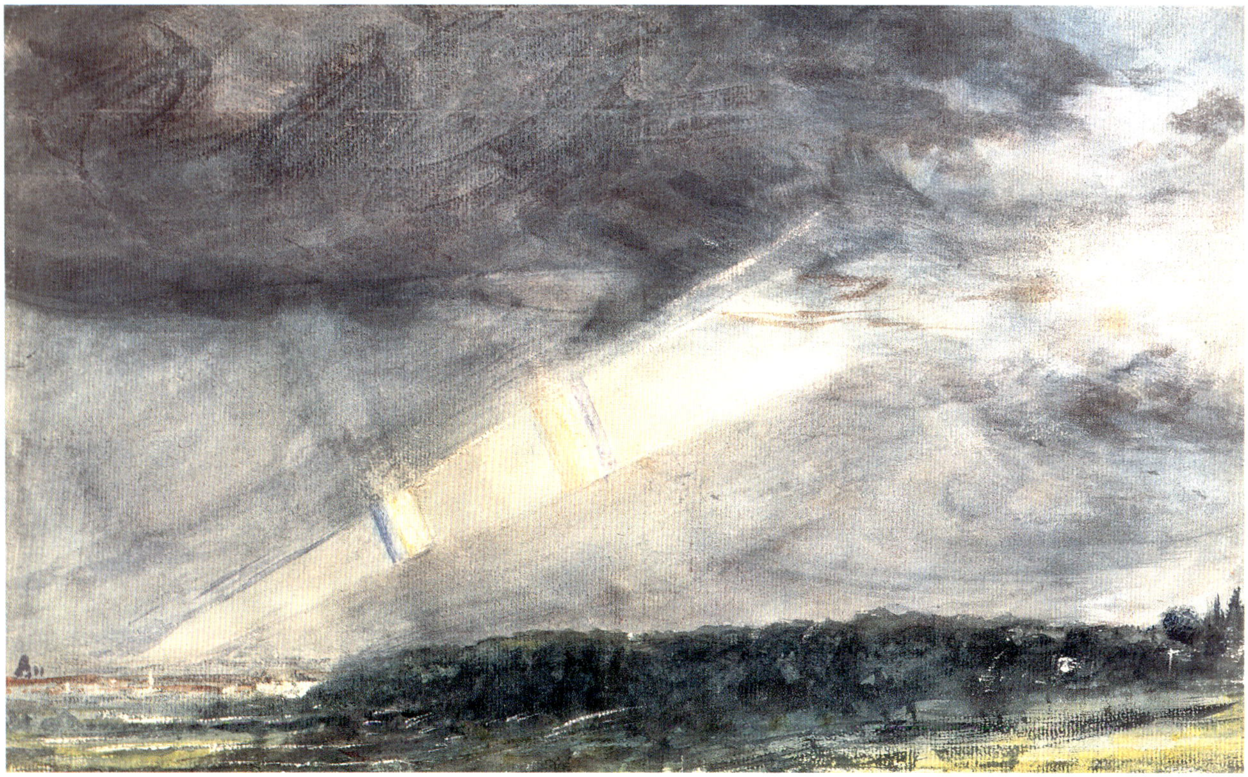

Plate 61 John Constable, *London from Hampstead with a Double Rainbow*, 1831. Copyright British Museum

> *may yet make some impression with my 'light' – my 'dews' my 'breezes' – my bloom and freshness – no one of which qualities has yet been perfected on the canvas of any painter in the world.*[82]

This quotation shows that by the age of fifty-six, Constable was beginning to take things a little easier, but at the same time he still had high hopes for his 'light', 'dews' and 'breezes'. *The Cenotaph* was finally exhibited in 1836, but the main exhibit of 1833 at the Royal Academy was *Englefield House, Berkshire* which was not well received by certain individuals at the Academy. Shee, the President, rather mockingly said that it was 'only the picture of a house',[83] to which Constable replied that it was 'a picture of a summer morning, *including* a house'. The critics responded to Constable's desire not to 'scramble over' the picture; for instance *The Morning Post* stated on 8 May 1833:

> *We have seen nothing to compare with this from the hand of Mr C. for a long time. There is so much freshness and truth, and such a mass of bright but sober colour, that it is quite a gem in its way. Mr. CONSTABLE has evidently forgotten to put on his last layers of whitewash with which he generally compliments his finished pieces. We hope he has lost the brush.*[84]

Constable also exhibited *A Cottage in a Cornfield* (Plate 31) which was discussed briefly earlier when comparing it to the 1817 version. The sky in the 1833 exhibited picture is vastly superior. This suggests three scenarios: firstly that Constable repainted the sky in 1833 when he repainted the tree on the right hand side; secondly that the sky was originally painted in 1815 and is a remarkable precursor of his later skies (as Paris and Fleming-Williams[85] suggest); and thirdly that the whole painting was executed in 1833 (as Reynolds[86] suggests). It is clear from a close examination of the original painting at the Victoria and Albert Museum that the sky has been repainted around the tree in the top right hand corner of the picture, but it is not possible to arrive at a satisfactory conclusion. Further research is required, for instance to assess whether or not Constable used any synthetic aquamarine on the sky, a colour that was not available before 1828.

In 1833 Constable published a second edition of *English Landscape Scenery* with the new title *Various subjects of Landscape, characteristic of English Scenery, principally intended to mark the Phenomena of the Chiar' Oscuro of Nature*, in which the plates were rearranged from the first edition. During 1833 Constable began to write some of the texts that he planned to publish to accompany the plates. On 24 January 1834 he told Leslie that he had 'been busy making a fly leaf to each of my prints ... many can read print & cannot read mezzotint'. (Some of the text relating to skies was discussed at length in Chapter 2.)

The pencil and watercolour sketch *Study of Sky and Trees* has an inscription: '26 Sepr 1833 12 to 1 – noon looking North East' but the weather is not mentioned. The *View at Hampstead, looking towards London*, also a watercolour, does have a weather inscription on the back, 'Hampd December 7, 1833 3 oclock – very stormy afternoon – & High Wind'. The dark sky almost obscures St. Paul's on the horizon.

An interesting anecdote about *Cock Point, near Folkestone* 1833 is contained in a manuscript that accompanied the loan of the watercolour by Mrs A. M. Constable to South Kensington Museum in 1880: 'Cock Point; in painting this a shower of rain came on, Capt Constable, who was with his father exclaimed, "Oh Papa! this will spoil your picture!" "On the contrary", said John Constable, "it will just give it the effect I want."'

Constable's main exhibit at the Royal Academy in 1834 was a watercolour of *Old Sarum* (Plate 62) as he was too ill to work on any oil paintings in time. The painting is very similar to the 1829 version which was used for the *English Landscape Scenery* plate. The sky is equally stormy, though not so dark, and the base of a rainbow has been introduced on the right-hand edge of the picture.

In these last few years of his life the rainbow was a complicated symbol of Constable's hopes and fears, and appears in several of his paintings.

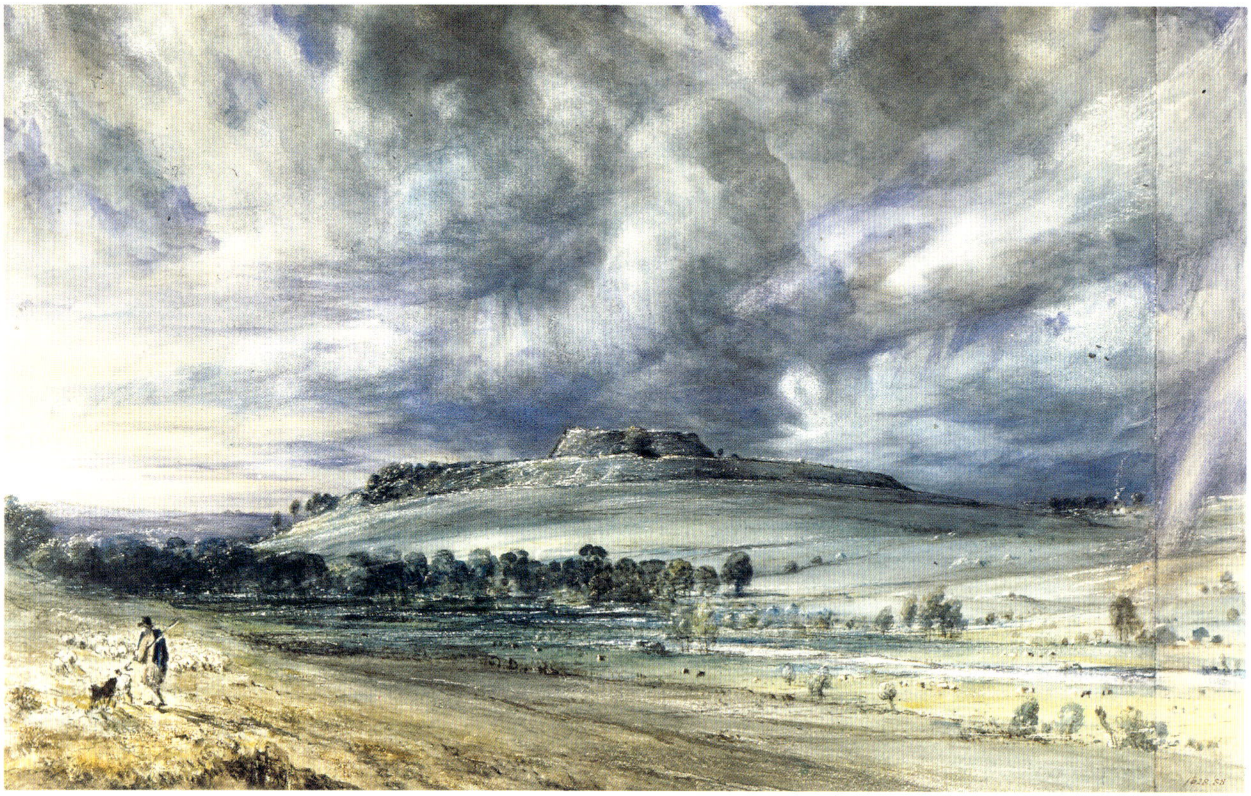

Plate 62 John Constable, *Old Sarum*, 1834. V&A Picture Library

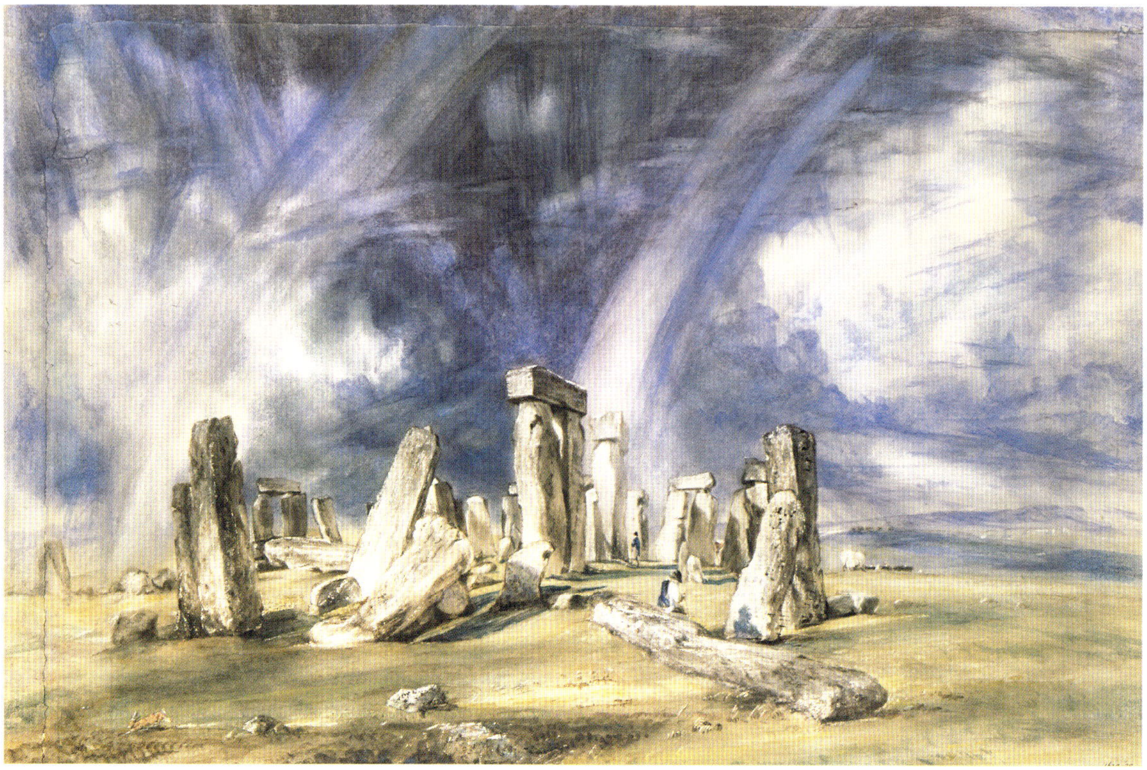

Plate 63 John Constable, *Stonehenge*, 1836. V&A Picture Library

The review in *The Athenaeum* on 8 February 1834 of *A Heath in a Showery Day* exhibited at the British Institution in 1834, and presumably the same painting exhibited in 1833 at the Royal Academy as *A Heath, Showery – Noon*, stated: 'the clouds are like a wet sponge; the ground is soaked, and the air seems filled with moisture: a rainbow bursts through all, and gives a singular splendour to the composition'.[87]

Stonehenge (Plate 63), exhibited in 1836, shows a double rainbow with a powerful vibrant sky that totally dominates the scene. Stonehenge, Old Sarum and Hadleigh Castle are fixed ruins of history, danced upon and eventually torn down by the powers of nature. The rainbow theme continues in *Hampstead Heath with a Rainbow* (Plate 64) and *Cottage, East Bergholt* (Plate 65), both painted in 1836. Constable was also busy transforming the single bow of *Salisbury Cathedral from the Meadows* into a double bow for a mezzotint plate that Lucas was working on.

Why should Constable have become so obsessed with rainbows at this late stage of his career? On 6 September 1835 he wrote to Lucas regarding the rainbow in the mezzotint of the *Salisbury*: 'If it is not exquisitely done, if it is not tender – and elegant – evernescent [sic] and lovely – in the highest degree – we are both ruined. I am led to this having been very busy with rainbows – and very happy in doing them – by the above rules.'[88] The reference to 'the above rules' is not clear but George Field, who was a good friend of Constable, was the designer of the Chromascope, which he claimed 'affords a method by which a rainbow, of any arc or diameter, may be superimposed upon a picture, into which the artist may design to introduce the phenomenon, so as to try its effect, and the best way of producing it'.[89] Lucas reduced the width of the bow when working on the plate which perhaps suggests that some device, or set of rules, had been applied.

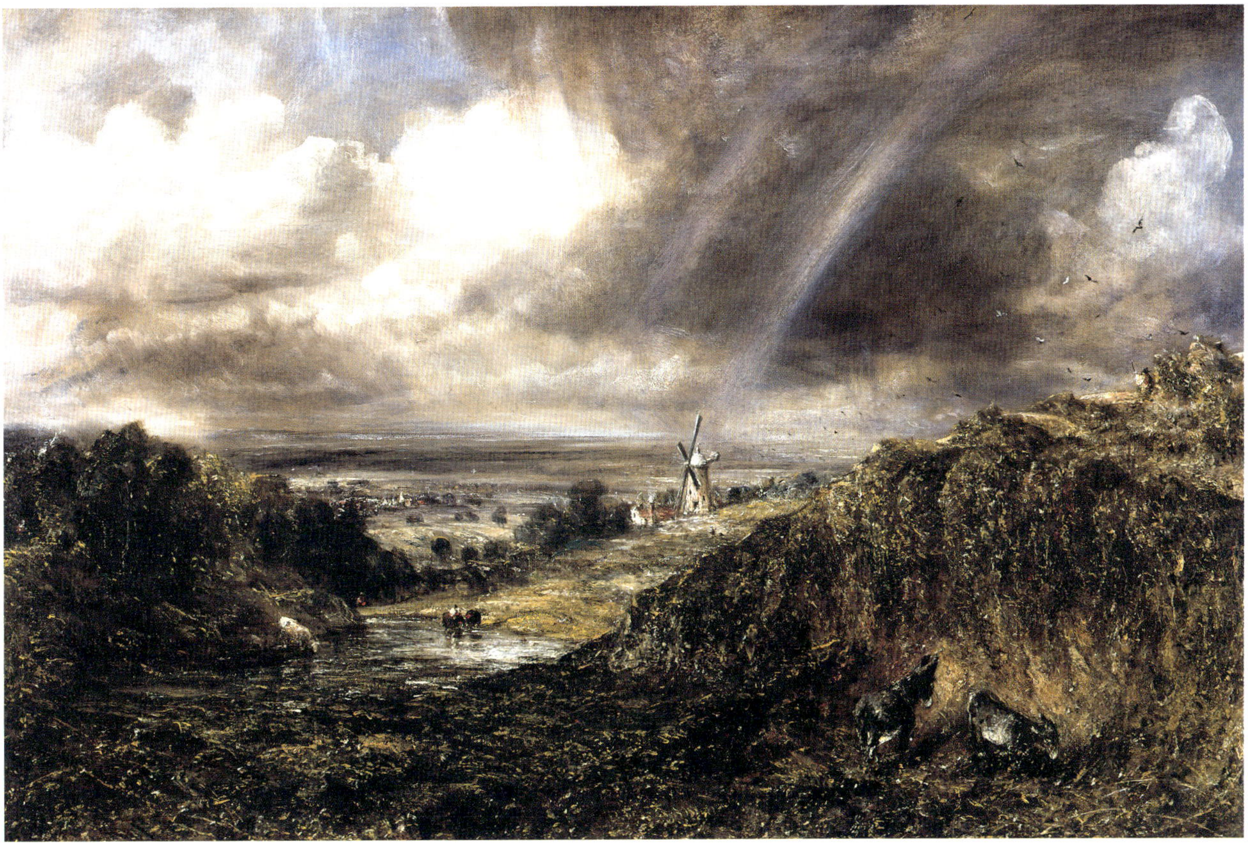

Plate 64 John Constable, *Hampstead Heath with a Rainbow*, 1836. Copyright Tate Gallery, London, 1998

Constable's detailed study of the science of rainbow formation was discussed in Chapter 2 and it would appear that Constable's newly acquired knowledge enabled him to have the confidence to use the rainbow more frequently. For Constable the rainbow epitomised the poetic side of the power of nature. No matter how turbulent the sky, the peace and beauty of the rainbow conveyed God's covenant that man would survive despite the odds. For Constable it gave him faith that his art would survive the flood of criticism that he faced.

Constable's preoccupation with the double rainbow is also interesting. Over the years the rainbow has been used in several different symbolic ways. The biblical interpretation is the symbol of hope and peace after the storm, the bow pointing towards heaven – the covenant between God and mankind. This is the interpretation that most authors have used for Constable's rainbows. However, the rainbow has also been used as a symbol of despair, and of unattainable dreams – the rainbow can never be reached and retreats as you advance towards it; the 'pot of gold' at the end of the rainbow which is tantalisingly close – so near and yet so far. Constable's vision of recognition, fame and fortune for his art was his own tantalising rainbow. Whenever it seemed close, it retreated away again. There is also a further symbolic meaning of the rainbow – the full complete rainbow represents the love and relationship

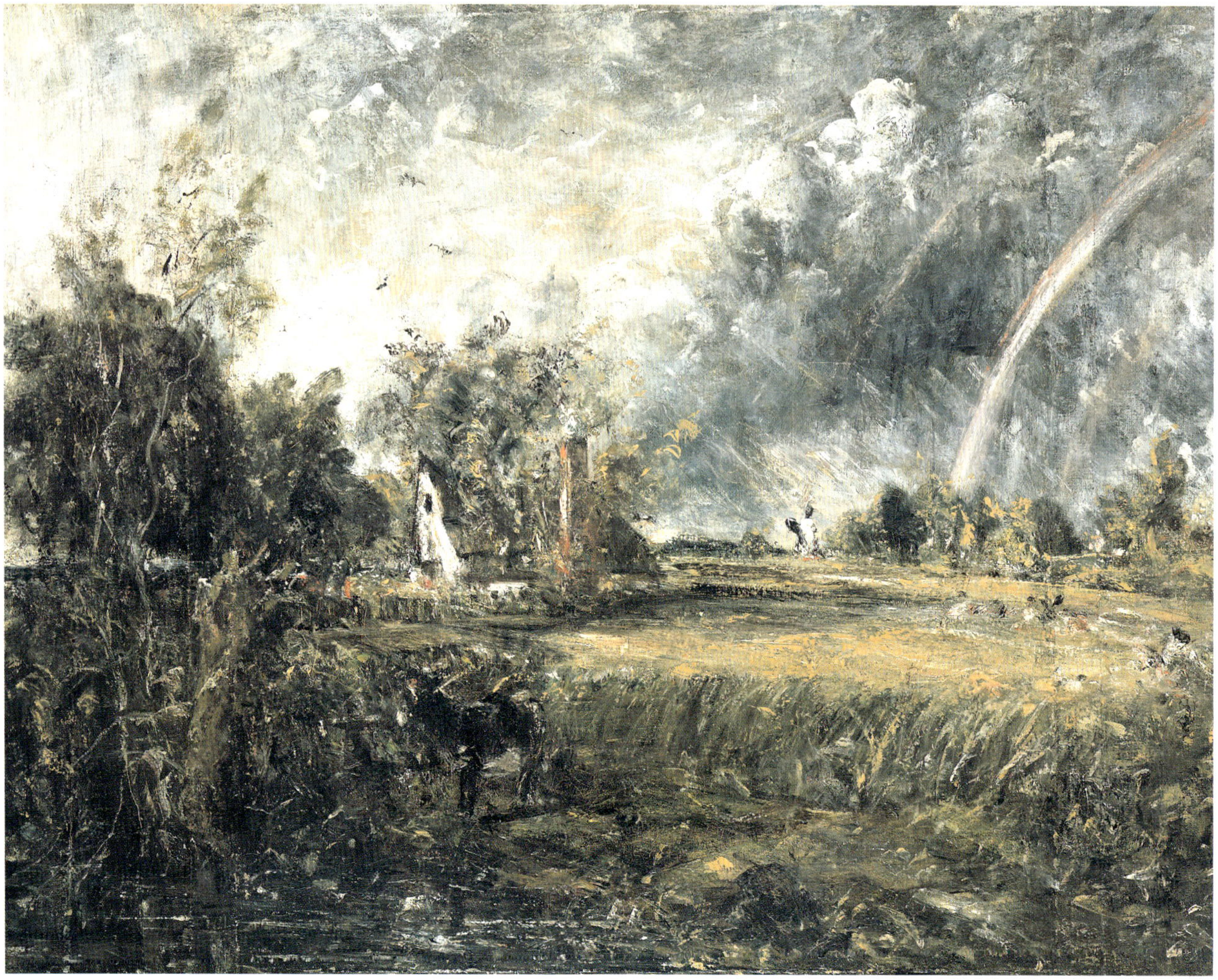

Plate 65 John Constable, *Cottage, East Bergholt*, 1836. Reproduced courtesy of The Board of Trustees of the National Museums and Galleries on Merseyside (Lady Lever Art Gallery)

between two people. You can imagine a rainbow between the heads of two lovers or close friends. If that love or relationship is broken you can only see the fragments of the bows remaining. The double rainbows of *Stonehenge*, *Hampstead Heath with a Rainbow*, and the mezzotint of Salisbury Cathedral may represent the fragments of Constable's bows reaching up to heaven to try to connect with his lost wife Maria and his closest friend John Fisher. It is no surprise that Constable used a copy of Uccello's *Sacrifice of Noah* to illustrate his first lecture on the history of landscape painting at the Royal Institution on 26 May 1836.

Constable died on the night of 31 March 1837 a few weeks before his sixty-first birthday. Although he had achieved some critical acclaim during his lifetime, his tremendous influence on the art of the rest of the nineteenth century was to be unknown to him. His wonderful sky studies would not be seen until much later in the century.

Notes

1 H. Damisch, *Théorie du Nuage: pour une histoire de la peinture* (Paris: Editions du Seuil, 1972), p. 336.
2 G. Reynolds, *The Later Paintings and Drawings of John Constable* (London: Yale University Press, 1984), p. xii.
3 A. Shirley, *The Rainbow – A Portrait of John Constable* (London: Michael Joseph, 1949), p. 228.
4 K. Badt, *John Constable's Clouds* (London: Routledge & Kegan Paul, 1950), pp. 43, 44.
5 Ibid.
6 I. Fleming-Williams, *Constable and his Drawings* (London: Philip Wilson, 1990), p. 60.
7 *The Literary Gazette*, 16 June 1833, p. 378.
8 Badt, *John Constable's Clouds*, p. 45.
9 R. B. Beckett, *John Constable and the Fishers* (London: Routledge & Kegan Paul, 1952), p. 82.
10 The first quotation is from C. R. Leslie, *Memoirs of the Life of John Constable*, 2nd edn (London: Longman's, Brown, Green and Longman's, 1845), p. 303, and was found among Constable's papers; the second from the last lecture at Hampstead, July 1836 (Ibid., p. 359).
11 Ibid., p. 10.
12 Ibid., p. 16.
13 Ibid., pp. 14–15.
14 Ibid., p. 17.
15 G. Reynolds, *The Early Paintings and Drawings of John Constable* (London: Yale University Press, 1996), p. 53, number R03.62.
16 Fleming-Williams, *Constable and his Drawings*, p. 92.
17 Leslie, *Memoirs of the Life of John Constable* 1845, pp. 19–20.
18 Fleming-Williams, *Constable and his Drawings*, pp. 92–3. Fleming-Williams argues (pp. 16–17) that Constable had an unusual width to his vision such that if one compares a Constable landscape with the width of vision that the eye normally takes in (i.e. about 45 degrees), it is usually much wider. He relates this to scotopic vision.
19 Reynolds, *The Early Paintings and Drawings of John Constable*, p. 77, R06.29 (R.35). L. Hawes, in 'Constable's sky studies' (*Journal of the Warburg and Courtauld Institutes* XXXII (1969): 344–65) suggests (p. 352) that another pastel drawing of a 'pure sky' was datable at 1806 but Reynolds suggests 1830.
20 L. Parris and I. Fleming-Williams (eds), *Constable* (London: Tate Gallery, 1991), p. 148.
21 H. H. Lamb, 'Volcanic dust in the atmosphere', *Philosophical Transactions of the Royal Society*, series A, 266 (1970).
22 Leslie, *Memoirs of the Life of John Constable* 1845, p. 37.
23 The sky in this painting has an interesting history. The painting was originally bought by John Allnut from the British Institution Exhibition in 1815. However he was unhappy with the sky and had it repainted by John Linnell. He then regretted his actions and around 1825 he returned the painting to Constable in order to restore the original sky. Constable painted another version instead for Allnut (now owned by the Yale Center for British Art) and kept the original himself. It appears that he never got round to repainting the sky himself and only recently has the original sky been uncovered and restored by the conservator John Bull. Significantly the mezzotint in *English Landscape Scenery* based on the 1814 version of *A Summerland* has a far more dynamic and integrated sky.
24 J. B. Tyldesley, 'Weather in Constable's paintings', *Weather* 23 (1968): 344–8.
25 See Appendix 3.
26 L. C. W. Bonacina, 'John Constable's centenary: his position as a painter of weather', *Quarterly Journal of the Royal Meteorological Society*, 63 (1937): 483–90.

27 Parris and Fleming-Williams, *Constable*, p. 163.
28 Ibid., p. 188.
29 Leslie, *Memoirs of the Life of John Constable* 1845, p. 82.
30 L. Howard, *The Climate of London*, 2nd edn. (London, 1833). The notes for October 14–16 actually read: 'Showery: a little hail: very tempestuous night, with frequent showers'. The next note is for 19 October – 'cloudy'. I am assuming that Howard missed out 17–18 October which should have been inserted after 'hail:'.
31 J. E. Thornes, *The Accurate Dating of Certain of John Constable's Cloud Studies 1821/22 Using Historical Weather Records*, Occasional Paper No. 34, (London: Dept. of Geography, University College London, 1978), p. 15.
32 Reynolds, *The Later Paintings and Drawings of John Constable*, p. 63.
33 Badt, *John Constable's Clouds*, p. 51.
34 Hawes, 'Constable's sky studies', p. 363.
35 Quoted in Judy Crosby Ivy, *Constable and His Critics* (Suffolk: The Boydell Press, 1991), p. 88.
36 Ibid., p. 89.
37 Beckett, *John Constable and the Fishers*, p. 75.
38 See Appendix 3.
39 Ivy, *Constable and His Critics*, p. 41.
40 Ibid., pp. 40–1.
41 Sarah Cove, 'Constable's oil painting materials and techniques'. In Parris and Fleming-Williams, *Constable*, p. 513.
42 Ivy, *Constable and His Critics*, p. 90.
43 See Table 19.
44 Beckett, *John Constable and the Fishers*, p. 78.
45 R. Hoozee, *L'opera completa di Constable* (Milan: Rizzoli Editore, 1979); G. Reynolds, *The Later Paintings and Drawings of John Constable* (London: Yale University Press, 1984).
46 Parris and Fleming-Williams, *Constable*, p. 228.
47 Cove, 'Constable's oil painting materials and techniques', p. 502.
48 Ibid., pp. 511–12.
49 K. Clark, *The Romantic Rebellion* (London: Futura Publications, 1973), p. 275.
50 See, for example, Shirley, *The Rainbow*, p. 117.
51 Beckett, *John Constable and the Fishers*, pp. 122–3.
52 Ibid., p. 144.
53 Ibid., p. 218.
54 Ibid., p. 184.
55 Ibid., p. 97.
56 See also *Malthouse Field, East Bergholt* (Parris and Fleming-Williams, *Constable*, Tate Exhibition no. 37, 1814) and *Worthing* 1824 (Fleming-Williams, *Constable and his Drawings*, p. 203).
57 M. Rosenthal, *Constable* (London: Yale University Press, 1983), p. 171.
58 R. B. Beckett, *John Constable's Correspondence*, 6 vols, vol. 4, *Patrons, Dealers and Fellow Artists* (Ipswich: Suffolk Records Society, 1966), pp. 216–17.
59 The increasing storminess in Constable's later paintings has often been linked to his melancholy state of mind after his wife died. See, for example, M. Cormack, *Constable* (Oxford: Phaidon, 1986), p. 190.
60 Beckett, *John Constable's Correspondence*, p. 241.
61 Quoted in Ivy, *Constable and His Critics*, p. 122.
62 Ibid. p. 123.
63 P. D. Schweizer, 'John Constable, rainbow science, and English color theory', *The Art Bulletin* LXIV(3) (1982): 427.
64 R. A. R. Tricker, *Introduction to Meteorological Optics* (New York: Elsevier, 1970), p. 169.
65 Ivy, *Constable and His Critics*, p. 127.
66 Quoted in Ivy, *Constable and His Critics*, p. 141.
67 Thomson's *Seasons*, (London, 1744), pp. 165–70.
68 Ivy, *Constable and His Critics*, p. 135.
69 Taken from David Hill, *Constable's English Landscape Scenery* (London: The Promotional Reprint Company, 1992), p. 106.
70 See Reynolds, *The Later Paintings and Drawings of John Constable*, p. 219.
71 *The Morning Herald*, 3 May 1831; Ivy, *Constable and His Critics*, p. 150.
72 *The Times*, 6 May 1831; Ivy, *Constable and His Critics*, p. 150.
73 *The Athenaeum*, 14 May 1831; Ivy, *Constable and His Critics*, p. 150.
74 *The Spectator*, 21 May 1831; Ivy, *Constable and His Critics*, p. 152.
75 *Library of the Fine Arts*, 1 June 1831; Ivy, *Constable and His Critics*, p. 152.
76 *The Englishman's Magazine* 1 June 1831; Ivy, *Constable and His Critics*, p. 153.
77 *The Metropolitan*, 1 June 1831; Ivy, *Constable and His Critics*, p. 153.
78 Leslie, *Memoirs of the Life of John Constable* 1845, p. 209.
79 The letter to Mr. George Constable states: 'My observations on clouds and skies are on scraps and bits of paper, and I have never yet put them together so as to form a lecture, which I shall do, and probably deliver at Hampstead next summer. If you want anything more about atmosphere, and I can help you,

write to me. Foster's is the best book; he is far from right, still he has the merit of breaking much ground.' Leslie, *Memoirs of the Life of John Constable* 1845, p. 281.

80 Ibid., p. 310.

81 Beckett, *John Constable and the Fishers,* p. 280.

82 Leslie, *Memoirs of the Life of John Constable* 1845, p. 238.

83 Reynolds, *The Later Paintings and Drawings of John Constable*, pp. 245–6.

84 Ivy, *Constable and His Critics*, p. 172.

85 Parris and Fleming-Williams, *Constable*, p. 165.

86 Reynolds, *The Later Paintings and Drawings of John Constable*, p. 246.

87 Ivy, *Constable and His Critics*, p. 183.

88 Beckett, *John Constable's Correspondence*, p. 421.

89 Quoted in John Gage, *Colour and Culture* (London: Thames and Hudson, 1993) p. 114.

Chapter Four

The influence of art and science on Constable's skies

Light – dews – breezes – bloom – and freshness;
not one of which has yet been perfected on the canvas of any painter in the world.[1]

It is now necessary to try and put Constable's skies into context. How do they compare with the skies of other artists both before and during his lifetime? How did Constable relate to contemporary art theory and meteorological science? Chapter 2 examined the direct influences on Constable in his painting of skies, but in order to assess how innovative Constable's skies are we also need to examine the importance of other influences.

The first half of the above quotation from Constable is often used to encapsulate his own art. Constable undoubtedly thought that what he was trying to achieve on canvas – 'Light – dews – breezes – bloom – and freshness' – had not yet been achieved by any other artist in the world. Therefore one could argue that he had little to learn about these phenomena from the works of other artists. Indeed Constable always endeavoured to paint from nature without regard for other artists, but inevitably his extensive knowledge of the old masters and the Dutch seventeenth-century landscape artists meant that it was almost impossible for him 'to forget that I have ever seen a picture' when painting.[2] It is easy to be critical of the skies of many artists when comparing them to real skies, as the artist's intention was often not to mirror nature but to use the sky as a sympathetic or symbolic backcloth to a landscape. Very few artists – Turner being a great exception – based the skies of their finished works on direct open-air studies. As we have seen in the last chapter even Constable did not copy any of his 1820/22 sky studies directly into a sky of a finished work – at least, none of the surviving sky studies are mirrored in any of his finished works. Constable's 'finished' skies were painted from his imagination but his remarkable understanding of the atmosphere gave him sufficient confidence to 'fly' and to paint the ephemeral sky in four dimensions.

It was, therefore, Constable's intention to paint real, dynamic English skies and we have to be careful when examining the skies of other artists to distinguish those with a similar mission. Hence when examining the skies of other artists the following guidelines will normally be used to assess them: the way that they cope with sky colours: the shape, perspective and colours of their clouds; the portrayal of light and air; the consistency of the lighting of the landscape with the position, or the inferred position, of the clouds and the sun; the use of optical effects such as rainbows etc.; and, finally, the general realism/naturalism of the sky. It is therefore my intention to look at the skies of Constable and other landscape painters through the eyes of a meteorological observer rather than those of an art historian.

4.1 A brief history of skies in landscape art

The sky is an integral part of every landscape painting, and even if the sky cannot be seen directly in a picture the lighting of the landscape is controlled by it. It is therefore remarkable that there have been relatively few studies of the history of skies in landscape painting. Constable, in his lecture at Hampstead in June 1833,[3] attempted to give an account of the origins of landscape painting, going back to the Italian painters Cimabue (c. 1240–1302) and Giotto (c. 1266–1337). Constable inferred that early paintings of biblical scenes of the crucifixion, with a stormy or clearing sky behind the cross, probably represented the origins of the sky in landscape painting.

Kurt Badt briefly mentions the transformation of clouds in art from religious symbols to natural phenomena. He is highly critical of the clouds of the old masters, from Durer (1471–1528), Leonardo (1452–1519) and Titian (1487–1576) to Rubens (1577–1640), Nicolas Poussin (1594–1665) and Claude (1600–82) whom he believes painted clouds as isolated formations. Badt credits the Dutch seventeenth-century painters, especially Cuyp (1620–91) and Ruisdael (1628/29–82), with being the first to paint clouds that were integrated into an overall landscape.[4]

Louis Hawes attempts to trace skyscapes produced by artists before Constable and goes as far back as a cloud study attributed to Claude. Hawes argues that quite realistic cloud studies were produced by several artists, including Willem van de Velde the Younger (1633–1707), Alexander Cozens (1717–86), Joseph Wright (1734–97), William Crotch (1775–1847) and Valenciennes (1750–1819); all before Luke Howard's cloud classification was published in 1803.[5] The majority of these studies are little more than aids to memory, however, and cannot be compared with the dynamic and meteorologically accurate sky studies of John Constable.

Hubert Damisch, the French art historian, has produced the most comprehensive review of the symbolism of clouds in art in his book *Théorie du nuage. Pour une histoire de la peinture.* Unfortunately this book has not been translated into English and has therefore been largely ignored in the sky debate. Damisch examines the changing functions of clouds in paintings since the Middle Ages:

> *From the Middle Ages to the end of the nineteenth century the cloud haunted the skies of Western paintings. Not just a decorative object, the cloud constituted one of the elements of pictorial semiotics, a graph whose functions varied over time. Originally used, like theatre machinery, as a way of incorporating the sacred into the real (the Ascension of Christ, mystical visions), clouds played a more ambiguous role during the Renaissance when the demands of perspective ensured conformity: clouds were then used to conceal the unrepresentable nature of infinity at the same time as pointing to it, thus ensuring the paradoxical balance of a pictorial institution which was also a scientific phenomenon.*[6]

4.2 From the beginnings of art to the end of the sixteenth century

Stanley Gedzelman, an American meteorologist, has produced a brief outline of sky and cloud painting prior to the publication of Luke Howard's cloud classification in 1803.[7] Gedzelman claims that all known cloud types appear in landscape paintings painted between about 1425 and 1675. However he does not discuss Badt's and Damisch's point that most, if not all, such clouds were painted mechanistically, in isolation, and although they may be recognisable they rarely harmonise with the depicted weather and the lighting of the landscape.

The chronology of sky painting outlined by Gedzelman begins about 8000 years ago in Turkey

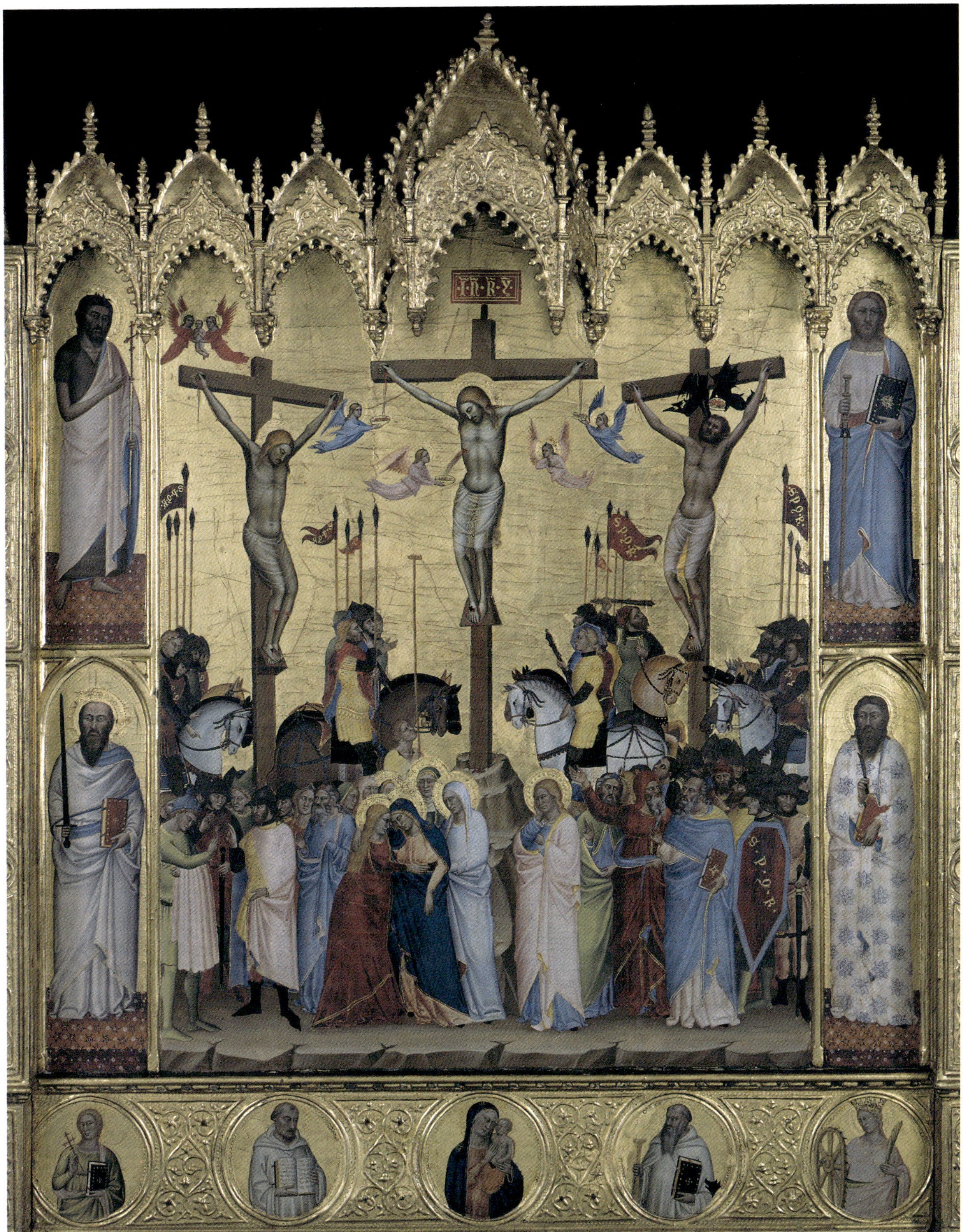

Plate 66 Attributed to Jacopo di Cione, *The Crucifixion.* Copyright Tate Gallery, London, 1998

where a painting has been found of the eruption of a volcano accompanied by an amorphous cloud mass and what appears to be lightning bolts. The first painting of a rainbow yet discovered was found in the Tassili Mountains of the Central Sahara – thought to be produced about 5500 years ago when the Sahara still had green grasslands. Some Egyptian hieroglyphics appear to denote clouds and rainstreaks, but clouds have not yet been observed in Egyptian art. Excavations of the Minoan civilisation based at Mycenae in Greece have discovered the earliest recognisable cumulus clouds decorating a dagger and a gold cup. Aerial perspective is apparent in a mural found in the tomb of Philip II of Macedon dated about 330BC. There is also evidence that the Romans were familiar with aerial perspective and that the colour of the sky is lightest at the horizon in several Roman murals.

Early Christian paintings were influenced by biblical references such as Christ's statement that 'Hereafter shall ye see the son of man sitting on the right hand of power and coming in the clouds of Heaven' (Matthew XXVI, 64). Clouds had therefore to be included in any representation of heaven. However after the fall of the Roman Empire and throughout the Middle Ages it was normal for the sky to be painted in gold. As Gedzelman states, 'the sky was typically eliminated and replaced by a popular convention in the form of a gold curtain, which symbolized the presence of divinity and removed from scenes all

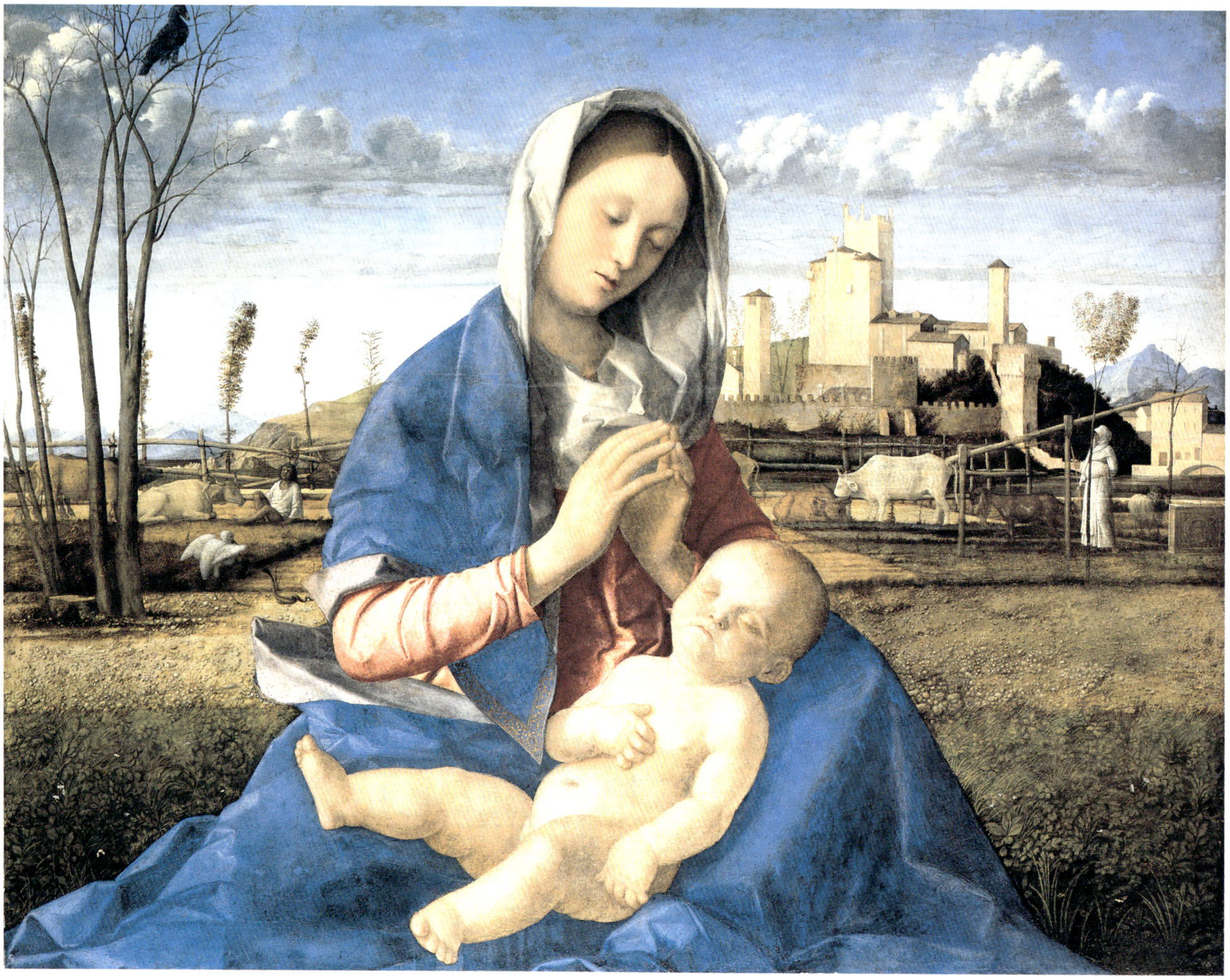

Plate 67 Giovanni Bellini, *Madonna of the Meadow*, 1505–16. Copyright National Gallery, London

suggestions of the time and space frame of this world. Golden skies became so fashionable in the waning years of the Middle Ages that clouds almost disappeared entirely from Gothic Art' (see Plate 66).[8]

Gradually blue sky began to appear in religious paintings and illuminated manuscripts so that by the middle of the fifteenth century artists such as Giovanni Bellini (c. 1430–1516) were painting beautiful topographic skies as idyllic backgrounds to paintings such as the *Madonna of the Meadow* (Plate 67). It was common for the painted skies to be resplendent with representations of heaven such as Garofalo's (1481–1559) *Saint Augustine with the Holy Family and Saint Catherine of Alexandria.*

The works of the Flemish painter Jan van Eyck (c. 1390–1441) stand out at this time for their truth to nature. Not only was he a master of aerial perspective but also he produced painstakingly accurate skies. Gedzelman discusses at length the sky of *The Crucifixion* dated at about 1435 (see Plate 68) which he suggests contains possibly four different identifiable cloud types: cumulus, altocumulus lenticularis, cirrus uncinus and cirrocumulus lacunosis. He also claims that the painting is meteorologically consistent with the biblical account in that it represents a dramatic clearing after a slow-moving cold front has recently passed. This interpretation is by no means far fetched and such a sky might often have been observed by Jan van Eyck after the passing of a thunderstorm accompanying a cold front in his native Low Countries. Another early crucifixion scene that contains a clearing sky after 'the storm' is that by the Italian artist Fra Angelico (c. 1387–1455) entitled *Descent from the Cross* (c. 1443). The identifiable cumulus cloud is too small to be a representation of the cumulonimbus cloud which produced the storm, but the sky is nevertheless realistic in form if not in process.

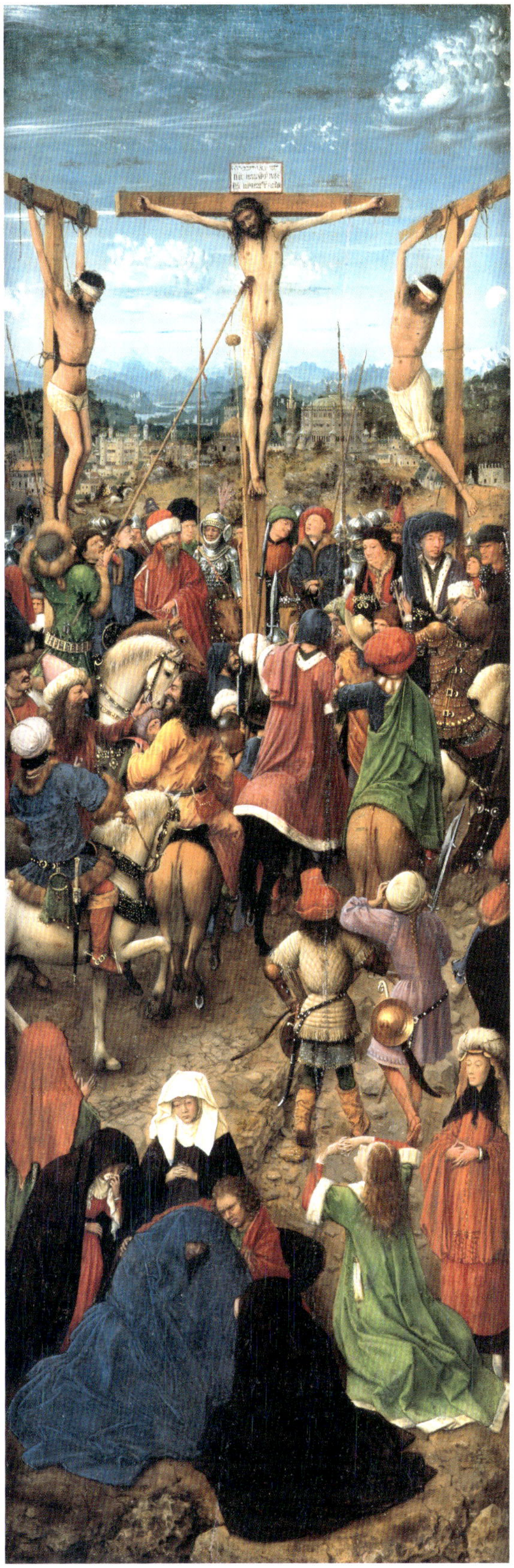

Plate 68 (right) Jan van Eyck, *The Crucifixion*, The Metropolitan Museum of Art, Fletcher Fund, 1933. (33.92a). Photograph Copyright 1998 The Metropolitan Museum of Art, New York

The fifteenth century, therefore, produced the first realistic skies painted with any recognisable precision. Generally the skies are idealised with individually sculptured clouds, high visibility and a passable attempt at aerial perspective. Religious symbolism in the sky was still important but as the century went on the representations of heaven and other religious symbols began to decline. Giovanni Bellini's *The Agony in the Garden* (c. 1460) depicts the pre-dawn sunlight illuminating the bases of distant, possibly cumulus, clouds. There is also a small angel standing on a cloud in the top right of the picture. In this example the angel looks out of place, as though it has been added to the painting rather than the picture being dominated by the symbolic figure.

The development of an understanding of scientific perspective in the fifteenth century, initially by Brunelleschi and Uccello in Florence, had helped artists to control their landscapes but did not help in the painting of skies. The laws of mathematics could not be applied to the ephemeral sky. It is unlikely therefore that Constable would have learnt much about the painting of skies from these fifteenth-century works of art, if indeed he was familiar with them.

The sixteenth century saw greater experimentation and freedom of expression, including for the first time the depiction of mists and storms and optical effects such as rainbows. Leonardo da Vinci's (1452–1519) drawing *The Deluge* is a skyscape of fantasy. In his *Treatise on Painting* Leonardo suggests that clouds can be a source of inspiration to generate new ideas for landscapes.[9] He thought of clouds as random, chaotic forms that could be used as models for rugged mountain scenery. Kenneth Clark suggests that Leonardo's drawings of deluges represent more than his imagination at play, and suggests that the violent storms that sometimes hit Florence aroused his emotions. Clark goes on to suggest that the Deluge drawings 'record one of Leonardo's deepest intuitions, that the forces of nature are totally out of our control, and may easily destroy our fragile civilisation'.[10] Constable did not mention Leonardo in his Hampstead lectures but he was certainly familiar and impressed with Leonardo's *Treatise on Painting*, and Ian Fleming-Williams has shown that Constable adapted Leonardo's method for tracing landscapes on glass.[11] An intriguing question is whether or not Constable ever thought of experimenting with this technique for painting skies. It is unlikely that Leonardo's views on using clouds, and cloud-like shapes, to stimulate ideas for landscapes would have meant much to Constable. It is interesting though that these ideas were taken up by Alexander Cozens (1717–86) whose skies Constable copied, as already mentioned in Chapter 3.

Leonardo wrote: 'If you look at some old wall cover'd with Dirt, or the odd Appearance of some streak'd Stones, you may discover several Things like Landskips, Battles, Clouds, uncommon Attitudes, humerous Faces, Draperies Ec. out of this confused Mass of Objects, the Mind will be furnished with abundance of Designs and Subjects perfectly new.'[12] Leonardo was also attracted by wind and by storms. He describes in great detail how a storm should be depicted:

> *First show the clouds scattered and torn, and flying with the wind, accompanied by clouds of sand blown up from the seashore, and boughs and leaves swept along by the strength and fury of the blast.... Make the clouds driven by the impetuosity of the wind and flung against the lofty mountain-tops, and wreathed and torn like waves beating upon rocks.*

He goes on to state how the Deluge should be portrayed: 'Darkness, wind, tempest at sea, floods of water, forests on fire, rain, bolts from heaven, earthquakes and ruins of mountains ... lightning from the clouds illuminating everything.'

The most important Venetian painter of the sixteenth century was Titian (1487–1576), whose landscapes were certainly appreciated by Constable. Titian's skies are often striking and he developed a particular skill for composing mountains and clouds together. Constable, in discussing Titian's *St. Peter Martyr* painted in about 1525, states that: 'the background of which, although not the model, may be considered as the foundation of all the styles of landscape in every school of Europe in the following century ... and the time verging towards the close of day, as we may judge from the level and placid movement of the clouds on the deep blue sky'.[13] Gedzelman

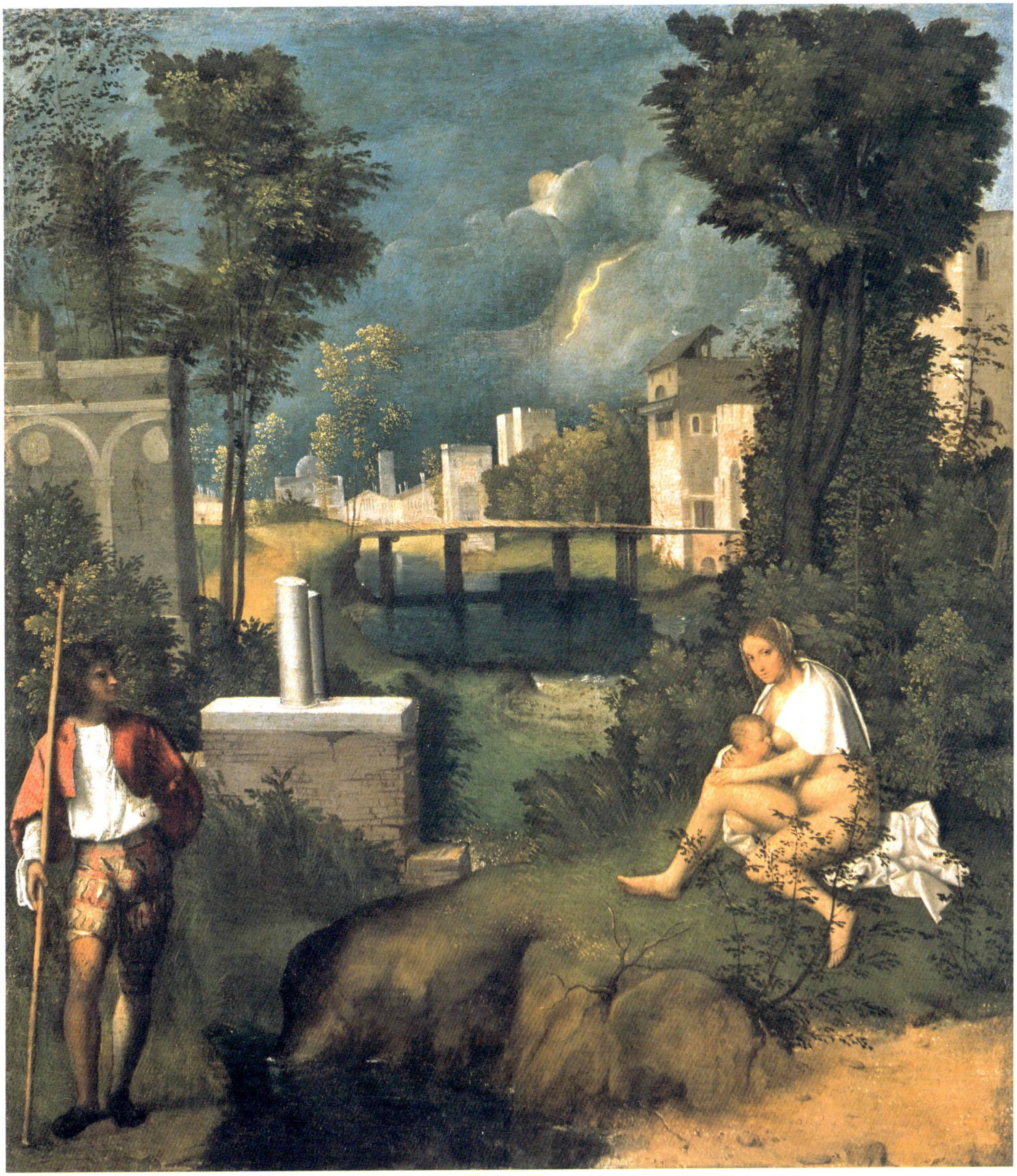

Plate 69 Giorgione, *La Tempesta*, (1503–05). Gallerie del'Accademia, Venice. Photo copyright Osvaldo Böhm

however argues that Titian had a negative effect on sky painting, not for his portrayal of majestic cumulus clouds but for his extensive use of nondescript layer clouds (altocumulus) with scarlet fringes if the sky was meant to be at sunrise or sunset. Gedzelman complains that this method of filling large areas of the sky with tinged altocumulus 'is well suited to covering large areas of canvas with a minimum of time, effort, and understanding'.[14] Titian's great influence on other artists and their patrons meant that too many canvases adopt Titian's monotonous sheets of layer cloud. Constable's admiration of Titian was great but in his many references to Titian, Constable never praises his skies.

Giorgione (c.1477–1510) was a contemporary of Titian in Venice where both of them were pupils of Giovanni Bellini. Constable mentions Giorgione in his first lecture at Hampstead before going on to discuss Titian's *St. Peter Martyr* at great length. It is not known whether Constable was aware of Giorgione's *La Tempesta* (Plate 69), the composition of which has intrigued art historians for centuries. Of interest here is the portrayal of the lightning bolt in the top centre of the picture. Today we are used to seeing time-exposure photographs of lightning with several dramatic forked strokes: Giorgione's short burst of lightning looks unreal and unfinished, as if it should be connected to the ground. Before the days of photography artists had to rely on their own experiences of nature's effects or copy the renditions of others. I have already quoted in section 2.3 the description by Constable of Cuyp's painting *Thunderstorm over Dordrecht* (Plate 78) in which he says 'the lightning descends to the earth … with a glide that is so much like nature that I wish I had seen it before I sent away my "Salisbury"'.[15] Indeed the Cuyp rendition of lightning is far more bold and direct and true to nature than Constable's rather subdued lightning in *Salisbury Cathedral from the Meadows* (Plate 59). Constable's lightning is closer to Giorgione's in *Tempesta* than to Cuyp's in *Thunderstorm over Dordrecht*.

The skies of Pieter Bruegel the Elder (1520?–1569) are often overcast and grey but they bear little resemblance to Titian's layers of altocumulus. Whereas Titian's skies look manufactured, Bruegel's are more realistic and there is a better balance of light. Bruegel painted several series of the four seasons, and his winter scene *Hunters in the Snow* (1565) (Plate 70) has been suggested by Hubert Lamb to be a response to one of Europe's worst winters in 1565.[16] The sky is covered with stratus which is coloured a dark green, the same colour as the frozen ponds below. In these conditions the light which reaches the surface arrives from almost all directions with an unusual absence of shadows. Paintings of snow-covered landscapes are almost absent before 1565 and this exceptionally cold winter. Burroughs points out that, before Bruegel, winter was never painted as cold and snowy, and our traditional 'White Christmas' scene was totally absent.[17] Bruegel painted several winter scenes but they were almost all done in 1565: *A Winter Landscape with Skaters and Birdtrap*, *The Massacre of the Innocents*, *The Adoration of the Magi in the Snow* and *The Numbering at Bethlehem* created a whole new view of the Christmas scene. In *The Adoration of the Magi in the Snow* Bruegel depicts snow falling from a featureless veil of nimbostratus. Bruegel's accurate depictions of seasonal activities have been used as evidence for the onset of the Little Ice Age that set in soon after 1550. His representation of *Hunters in the Snow* (January); *A Dark Day* (February or March), *Haymaking* (June or July), *The Harvest* (July or August) and *The Return of the Herd* (November) show a climate with colder winters and cooler, gloomier springs and autumns than today.

Kenneth Clark calls Bruegel 'the one master of naturalistic landscape who comes between Bellini and the seventeenth century'.[18] The *Hunters in the Snow* has become the classic snowscene, not just for other artists to emulate but also for the general public. Clark goes on to compare it with Handel's *Messiah* and *Pilgrim's Progress* in having instant widespread popular appeal. Bruegel's snowscenes were an inspiration for the next hundred years as

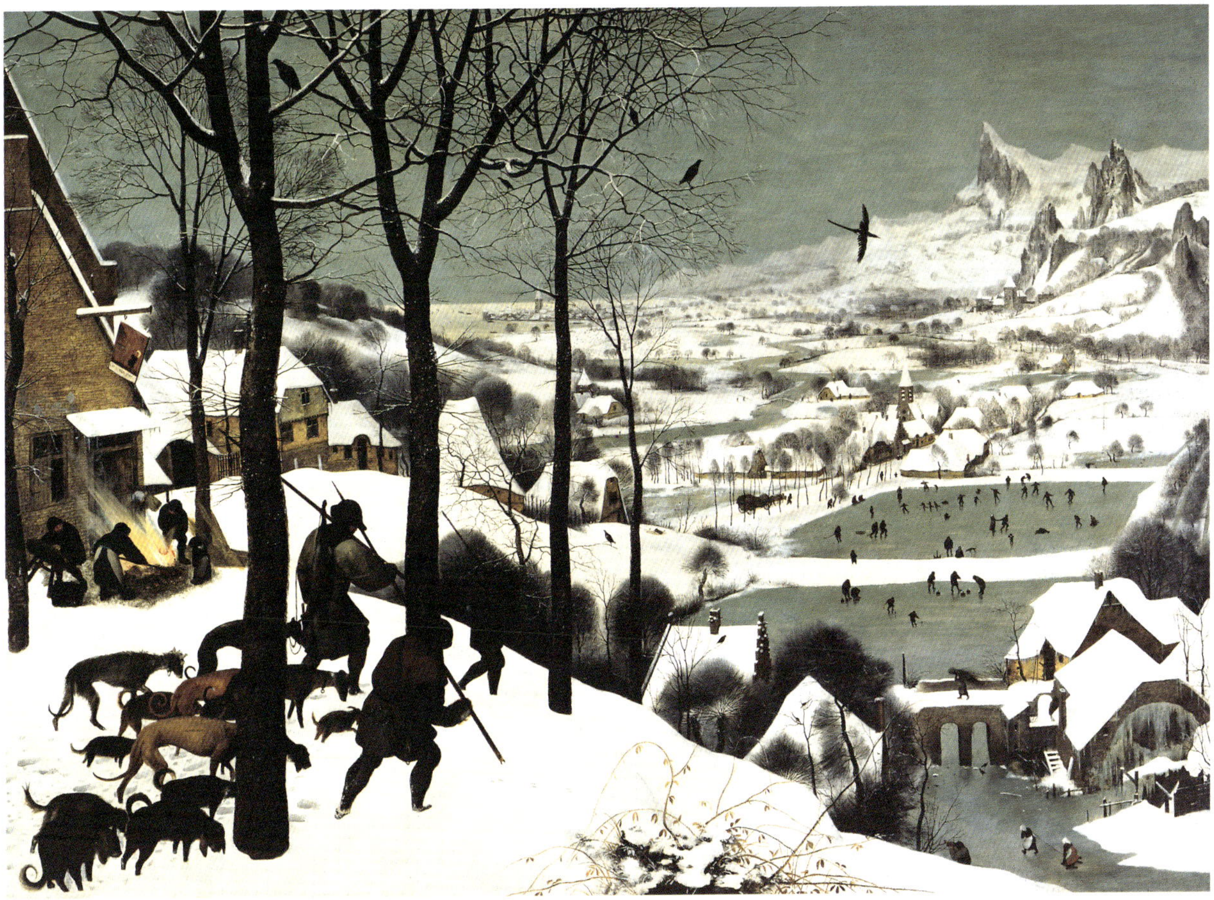

Plate 70 Pieter Bruegel, *Hunters in the Snow*, 1565. Kunsthistorisches Museum, Vienna

snowscenes became popular in Flemish and then Dutch art. Many Christmas cards are adorned with winter scenes painted in the century between 1565 and 1665.

Despite Bruegel's success and his truth to nature Constable does not mention him at all in his lectures on landscape. Perhaps Constable's preference for spring, summer and autumn meant that Bruegel's most famous winter landscapes were of little interest to him. Certainly the overcast, rather gloomy winter skies would not attract Constable's attention.

Thus the skies of paintings up to the end of the sixteenth century would not have interested Constable greatly. Certainly by this time aerial perspective had already been achieved and most cloud forms had appeared somewhere in paint, but Constable's skies benefited most from lessons to be learnt from seventeenth-century skies.

4.3 The painted skies of the seventeenth century

It was not until the seventeenth century that the sky began to inspire artists for its own sake. As Clark observes, 'Brunelleschi's attempts to reduce nature to terms of measurement had been defeated by the sky; and it was the sky which inspired those Dutch painters who first made an impression of landscape their whole subject.'[19] This section will look in detail at the skies of Aelbert Cuyp (1620–91), Jacob van Ruisdael (c. 1628–82), Meindert Hobbema (1638–1709) and others, and their likely influence upon Constable's skies. The sky was also important to other seventeenth-century artists, many of whom clearly influenced Constable, such as Peter Paul Rubens (1577–1640), Nicolas Poussin (1594–1665), Claude Lorrain (1600–82), Rembrandt (1606–69) and Gaspard Poussin (1615–75). Interestingly the influences are distinctly Dutch, Flemish and French rather than Italian, although Claude for one spent much of his time in Italy. Italian skies are very different to the cloudier northern skies painted by the Dutch and Flemish, and not surprisingly Constable's very 'English' skies are much closer to those of the Dutch artists than any others.

4.3.1 Peter Paul Rubens (1577–1640)

> *I mean, indeed, more than the rainbow itself, I mean dewy light and freshness, the departing shower, with the exhilaration of the returning sun, effects which Rubens, more than any other painter, has perfected on canvas.*[20]

Rubens is undoubtedly one of the greatest artists of the seventeenth century and one of the leading landscape painters of all time, and Constable had considerable respect for him. The skies in most of Rubens' many commissioned portraits and religious scenes are not of much interest, but later in his career when he retired to the manor house of Het Steen near Antwerp he indulged in painting the surrounding landscape for his own pleasure. In his lecture at Hampstead in June 1833 Constable bubbles over with enthusiasm for Rubens' landscapes:

> *In no other branch of the art is Rubens greater than in landscape; – the freshness and dewy light, the joyous and animated character which he has imparted to it, impressing on the level monotonous scenery of Flanders all the richness which belongs to its noblest features. Rubens delighted in phenomena – rainbows upon a stormy sky, – bursts of sunshine, – moonlight, – meteors, – and impetuous torrents mingling their sound with wind and wave. Among his finest works are a pair of landscapes, which came to England from Genoa, one of which is now in the National Gallery.*[21]

Constable also delighted in atmospheric phenomena, but he learned more from Rubens than just atmospheric effects. The pair of

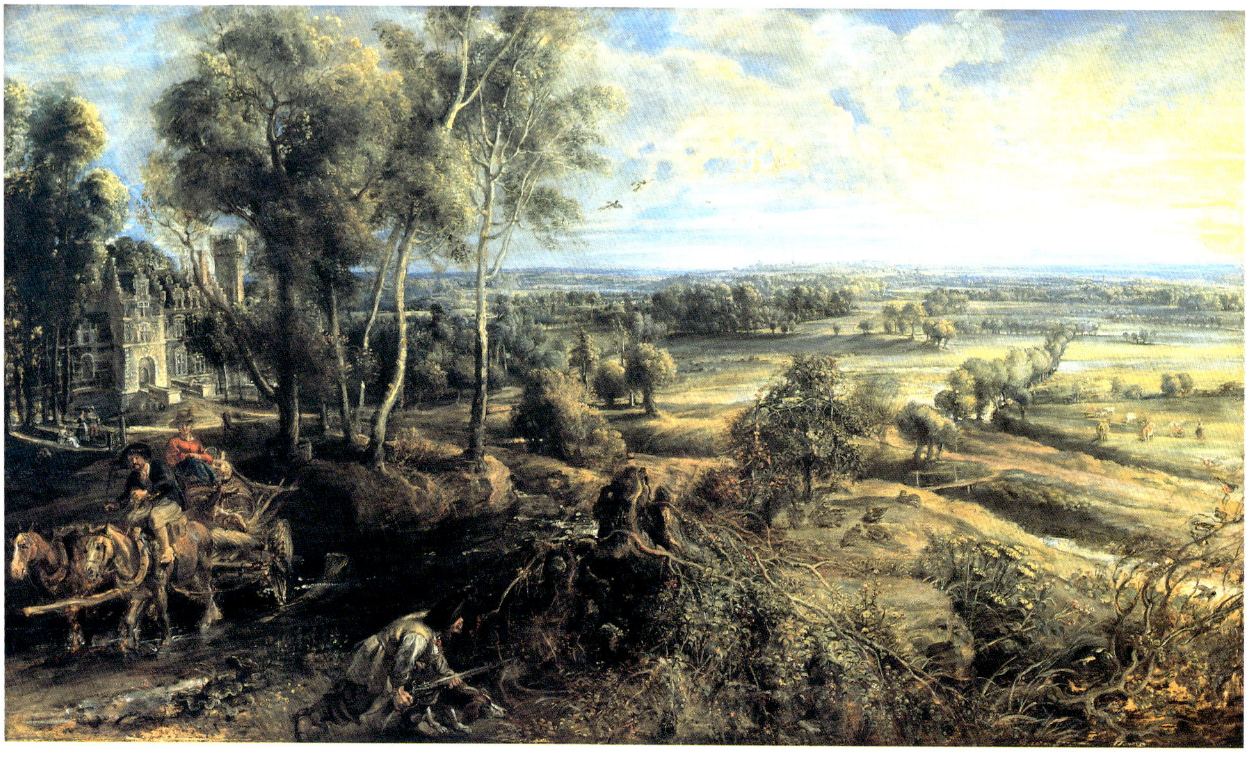

Plate 71 Peter Paul Rubens, *An Autumn Landscape*, 1636. Copyright National Gallery, London

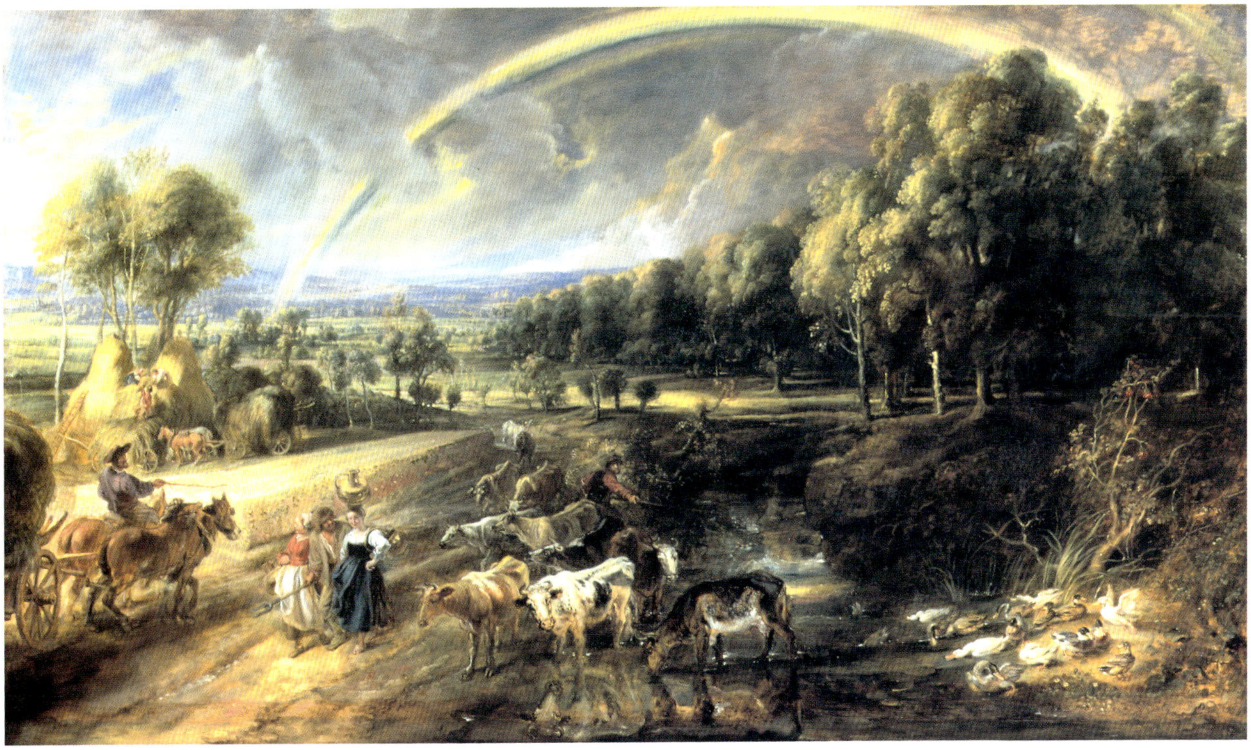

Plate 72 Peter Paul Rubens, *Landscape with a Rainbow*.
Reproduced by permission of the Trustees of the Wallace Collection, London

landscapes that Constable refers to are *An Autumn Landscape* (Plate 71), which was given to the National Gallery by Constable's friend and patron Sir George Beaumont in the 1820s, and *Landscape with Rainbow* in the Wallace Collection. Constable certainly studied *An Autumn Landscape* when it was in Sir George Beaumont's collection, and it has been linked in composition to *The Hay Wain*. Both paintings employ a house on the left and open landscape on the right with a similar group of trees in between. However the skies are totally different. Rubens' sky is interesting and contains some beautiful altocumulus clouds but it has no unity. The sun is rising in the east casting a golden glow beneath the observed clouds. Above the sun, 'there is a patch of altocumulus consisting of a series of ordered ranks and rows crossing at 90 degrees – the first convincing painted example of a mackerel sky'.[22] That is about the only good thing one can say about the sky. The sky in the centre of the painting is virtually unclassifiable with a surprising number of holes or gaps in the clouds. Whereas the landscape retreats for miles into the picture and the aerial perspective is superb, the sky perspective is weak. There is little attempt to bring the clouds overhead. The sky in the upper left-hand corner is different again and much darker. Also the colour of the visible sky appears to get lighter rather than darker towards the top of the picture. Hence the sky is a great disappointment in comparison to the detailed landscape. Rubens' detail in the landscape is exceptional and his handling of the early morning autumnal atmosphere is brilliant. The lighting of the landscape – the feeling of 'freshness and dewy light' is most sensitive and observant. Hence Constable had much to learn from Rubens' composition, light and atmosphere but almost nothing to learn from Rubens' clouds and sky colours. If we look at the sky of *The Hay Wain* in comparison we see that not only does it maintain the freshness and atmosphere of the Rubens, but it is also far superior in terms of the clouds and the cloud perspective. However, considering that Rubens painted *An Autumn Landscape* nearly 200 years before

Constable painted *The Hay Wain,* it is a remarkably atmospheric landscape.

The other landscape praised by Constable – *Landscape with a Rainbow* (Plate 72) – is equally full of atmosphere and sunlight, with a double rainbow. For his third lecture at The Royal Institution in June 1836 Constable chose this painting as marking one of four memorable points in the history of art. The rainbow is remarkable in exhibiting a supernumerary bow below the primary bow, possibly for the first time in landscape art. This shows Rubens' keen attention to detail and astute observation. However the colours of the bows and the lighting of the landscape have been the subject of much discussion and Rubens has been accused of a lack of detailed observation by both Ruskin and Turner. Ruskin says that the primary bow is: 'a dull blue, darker than the sky, in a scene lighted from the side of the rainbow. Rubens is not to be blamed for ignorance of optics, but for never having so much as looked at a rainbow carefully.'[23]

The lighting is certainly unrealistic: the sun should be at right angles to the bow behind the observer. The colours of the bow are difficult to justify but then Rubens was painting at a time when Descartes was only just working out his mathematical explanation of the rainbow. Rubens was more interested in the brilliant effect that the rainbow lent the painting than he was in meteorological accuracy. Certainly the rainbow is delicately painted but the passing storm clouds are rather indistinct, and even obscure the rainbow, in a very unrealistic way, on the left-hand arch. As with *An Autumn Landscape* the aerial perspective and feeling of distance in the landscape is real, the sense of atmosphere is real, but the clouds and the lighting of the landscape are not.

Rubens' influence on Constable's skies is thus confined to the former's portrayal of delicate atmosphere, dewy light and brilliant rainbows. Rubens taught Constable very little about the colour of the sky, the form and dynamics of clouds, and the harmony between the position of the clouds and the sun and the lighting of the landscape.

4.3.2 Nicolas Poussin (1594–1665)

Nicolas Poussin was one of the most influential French artists of the seventeenth century although he worked in Rome for most of his life. He has been described as an intellectual painter who created erudite pictures with beautifully ordered compositions. Sir George Beaumont, Constable's friend and patron, owned the painting *Landscape with Man Washing his Feet at a Fountain* (Plate 73). Constable wrote that it was 'the most affecting picture I almost ever stood before'. On 20 September 1821, when Constable was in the midst of his 1821 sky studies, he wrote to Fisher:

> *I have likewise made many skies and effects; we have had noble clouds and effects of light and dark and colour, as is always the case in such seasons as the present ... there is a noble N. Poussin at the Academy, a solemn, deep, still summer's noon.... Through the breaks in the trees are mountains, and the clouds collecting about them with the most enchanting effects possible.*[24]

The sky in this picture is only a small part of the composition but the clouds are disappointing despite Constable's glowing description of them. The colour of the sky is too uniform a blue and the cumulus clouds in the distance are two-dimensional. Nevertheless Poussin does attempt to bring the clouds overhead in quite a convincing way, and the painting is full of atmosphere and freshness which would appeal to Constable. The blueness of Poussin's skies is almost a trade mark and is a reflection of the bright blue Italian skies. Unfortunately Poussin rarely changes the blue across the sky and hence it can look artificial. In many of his landscapes the sky is very much a backcloth to the picture and two-dimensional clouds are all too common.

Constable was also impressed with Poussin's rendering of *The Deluge* (Plate 74). He stated in his lecture at Hampstead in June 1833: 'in the awful sublimity of the conception of his picture of Winter, generally known as the Deluge, he has surpassed every other painter who has attempted the subject'.[25] Kenneth Clark is also impressed by *The Deluge*, stating that 'perhaps the most astonishing proof of Poussin's powers is to be found in the *Winter (The Deluge)*, where he has given a romantic subject the logic and consistency of his great classic designs without sacrificing its dramatic force'.[26] The pouring rain and the flash of lightning are certainly impressive but not particularly realistic. Turner thought that the painting was a tame performance.

Constable had more to say about *The Deluge* in his third lecture at the Royal Institution in June 1836:

> *The good sense of Poussin, which was equal to his genius, taught him that by simplicity of treatment, the most awful subjects may be made far more affecting than by overloading them with imagery.... But of this picture Fuseli says truly, 'It is easier to feel than to describe its powers. We see the element itself, and not its image. Its reign is established, and by calm degrees ingulfs the whole. It mocks the food it feeds on. Its lurid haze has shorn the sun of his beams. Hope is shut out, and nature expires!'*[27]

The Deluge certainly has its admirers but the sky does not give the painting its power, but rather its atmosphere. In summary, then, although Constable was a great admirer of Nicolas Poussin he would

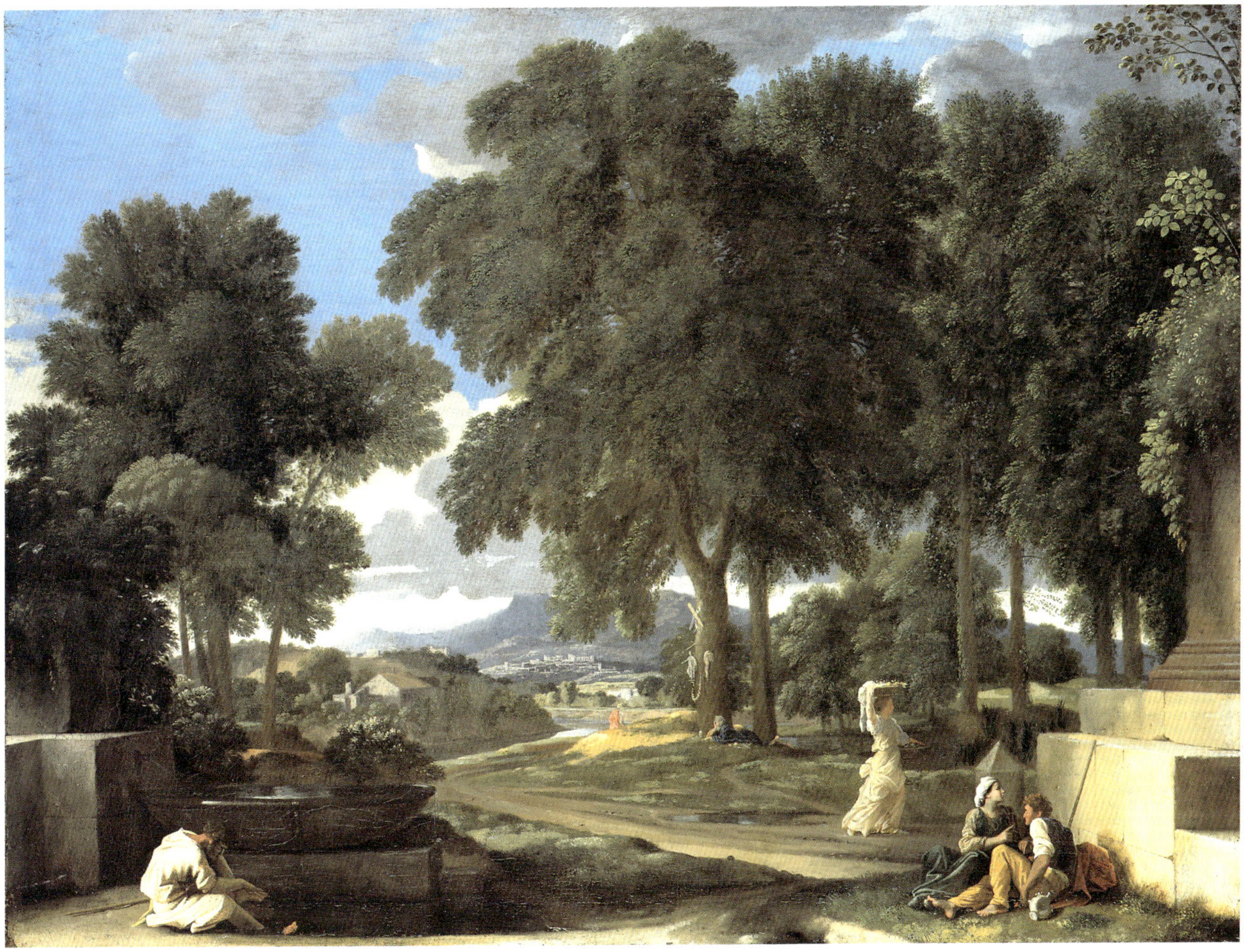

Plate 73 Nicolas Poussin, *Landscape with Man Washing his Feet at a Fountain.* Copyright National Gallery, London

not have learned much from his skies. The freshness, the light and the atmosphere in the landscapes could have given him some inspiration, but less than he might have drawn from Rubens' creations.

Gaspard Poussin (1613–75) was the brother-in-law and pupil of Nicolas Poussin and, according to Constable, 'his style [is] for the most part compounded from that of his brother-in-law and Claude Lorrain. Perhaps his best works are his storms.'[28] Ruskin did not appreciate the skies of either of the Poussins, stating in *Modern Painters* that 'with the Poussins ... their skies are systematically wrong'.[29]

4.3.3 Claude Lorrain (1600–82)

Claude Lorrain, although born in France, spent most of his working life in Italy. He was a passionate observer of light and was not afraid to show the sun itself in pictures as a central unifying element. He made a considerable number of outdoor drawings of sunrises and sunsets. Constable wrote more about Claude in his many writings than any other artist. Leslie writes that Constable was first introduced to Claude at the house in Dedham of the mother of Sir George Beaumont. (Sir George often carried with him, when travelling, Claude's *Landscape with Hagar and the Angel*).

In October 1823 Constable went to stay with Sir George, by now his friend and patron, at Cole-Orton Hall in Leicestershire. He stayed for more than five weeks, which was the longest he ever stayed away from his wife and children. This was at a time before Sir George donated his collection to the National Gallery (in 1826), and Constable spent considerable time copying the Claudes in the

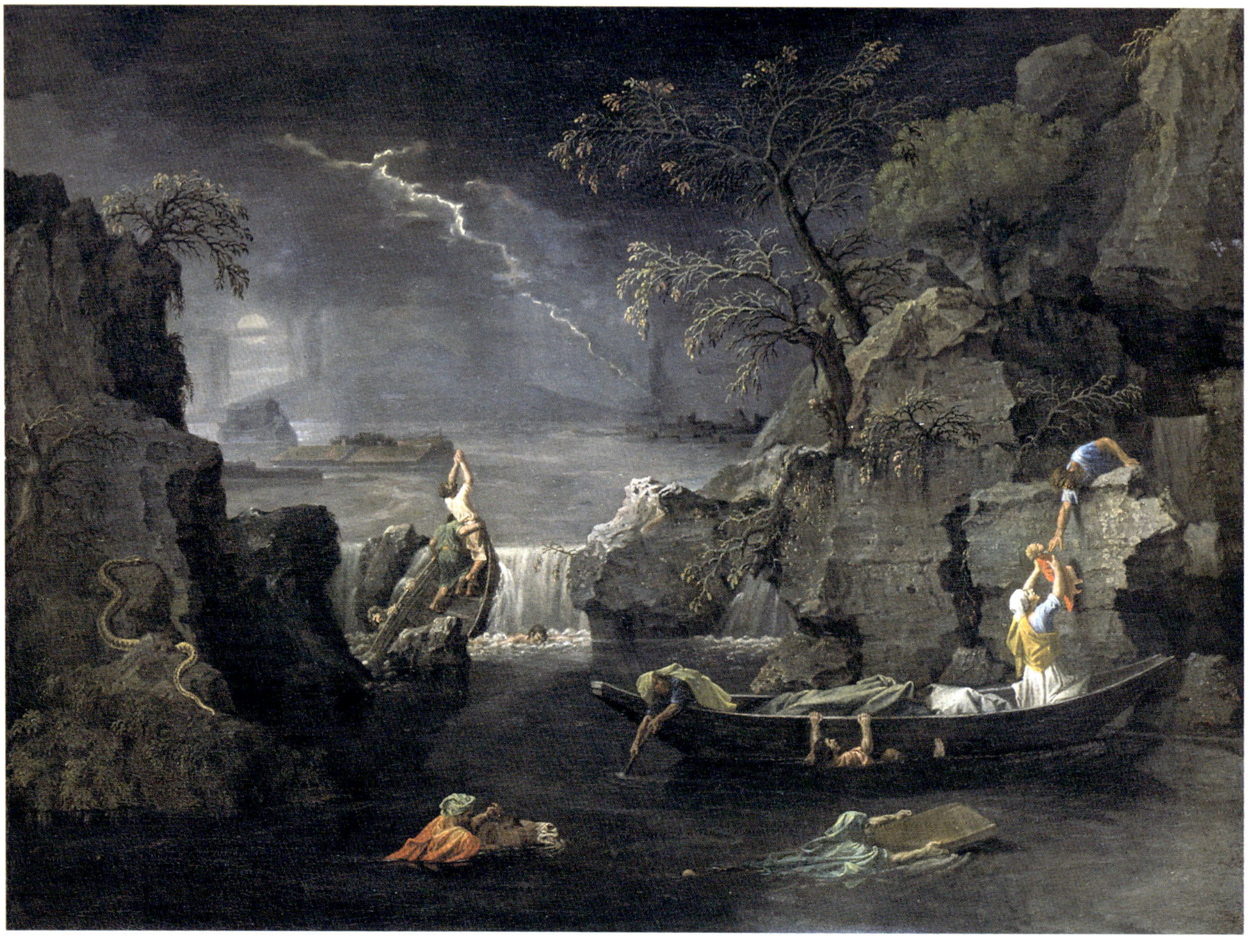

Plate 74 Nicolas Poussin, *L'Hiver ou le Déluge*. Musée du Louvre. Copyright Photo RMN

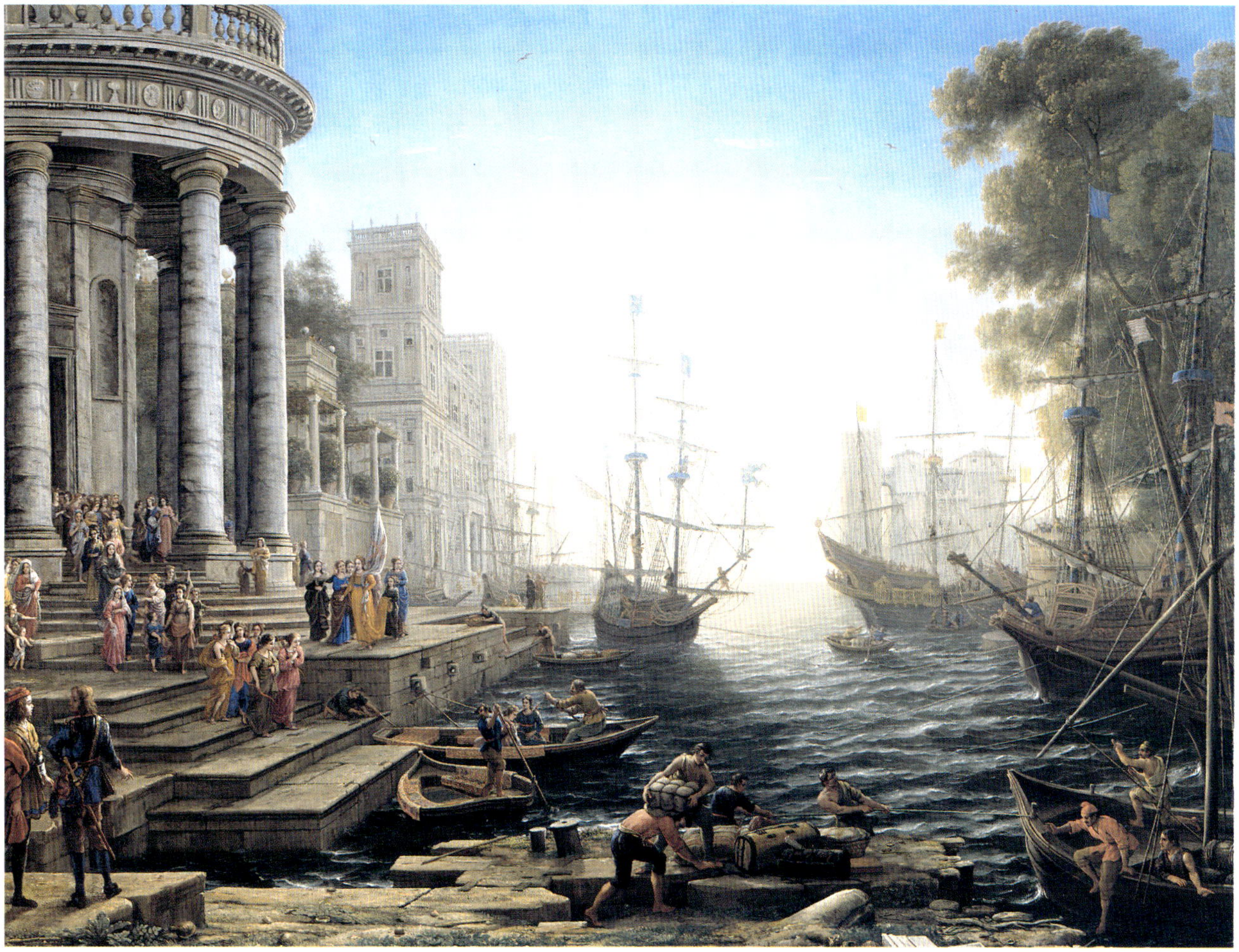

Plate 75 Claude Lorrain, *The Embarkation of Saint Ursala*, 1641. Copyright National Gallery, London

collection. In the letters to his wife and to Fisher at the time he constantly writes excitably about the Claudes and some of the other paintings:[30]

> *Only think, I am now writing in a room full of Claudes ... Wilsons, and Poussins.... I have copied one of the small Claudes; a breezy sunrise, a most pathetic picture [Landscape with the Death of Procris]. Perhaps a sketch would have served my present purpose, but I wished for a more lasting remembrance of it; and a sketch of a picture is only like seeing it in one view; it will not serve to drink at again and again. I have likewise begun the little grove by Claude; a noon-day scene 'which warms and cheers, but which does not inflame or irritate'. [Landscape with a Goatherd and Goats]*
>
> *I am now going to breakfast before the 'Narcissus' of Claude. [Landscape with Narcissus and Echo]. How enchanting and lovely it is; far, very far surpassing any other landscape I ever beheld.*
>
> *I do not wonder at your being jealous of Claude ... but the Claudes, the Claudes, are all, all, I can think of here...*

In his second lecture in June 1836 at the Royal Institution Constable tells us in great detail that 'Brightness was the characteristic excellence of Claude; brightness, independent of colour, for what colour is there here? (Holding up a glass of water)'.[31] Constable then goes on to discuss the lighting of *The Embarkation of Saint Ursala* (Plate 75). 'The St. Ursala, in the National Gallery, is probably the finest picture of *middle tint* in the world. The sun is rising through a thin mist, which, like the effect of a gauze blind in a room, diffuses the light equally ... in no other picture have I seen the evanescent character of light so well expressed.' Thus Constable was considerably influenced by the light in Claude's paintings, as well as by the composition of the pictures. Claude taught Constable 'the calm sunshine of the heart', the wonders of mist and sunrise and the glow of sunset, but Claude had little to teach Constable about wind and rain and clouds. The Italian skies, light and atmosphere could not be more different from the moist cloudy skies of England.

4.3.4 Rembrandt (Harmensz van Rijn) (1606-69)

Rembrandt was seen in his youth as the Dutch answer to Rubens. He soon moved beyond the emulation of Rubens however and established a remarkable reputation of his own. 'His stated preference for "nature" above artistic tradition and his excessive use of chiaroscuro ... what classicists saw as faults became sterling recommendations to 19th-c. Romantics'.[32] Rembrandt was primarily a history painter, though he is just as well known for his portraits and self-portraits. His landscapes are not as well known but Constable admired Rembrandt's painting

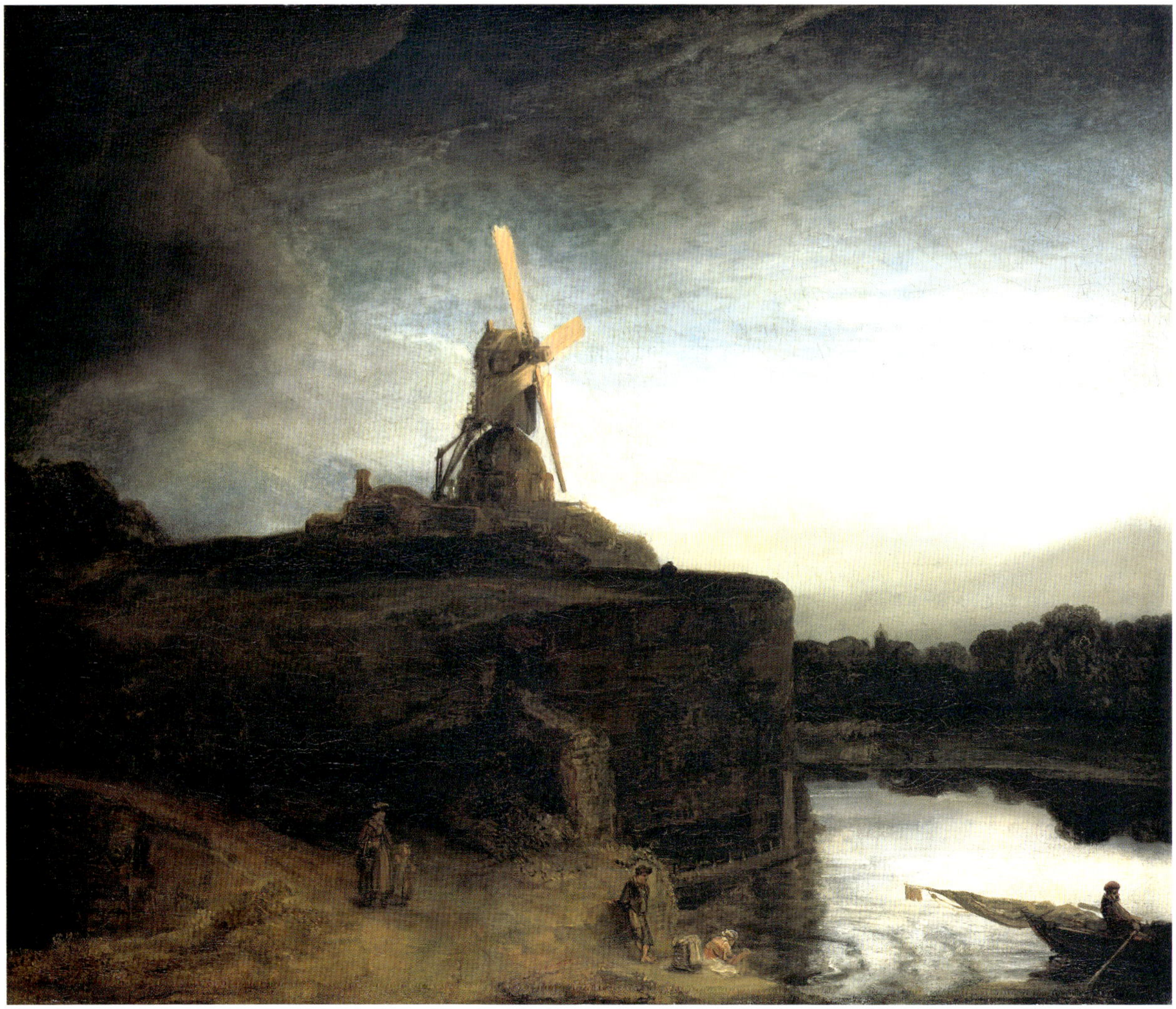

Plate 76 Rembrandt van Rijn, *The Mill*, 1645/1648. National Gallery of Art, Washington, Widener Collection. Photograph copyright 1999 Board of Trustees, National Gallery of Art, Washington

entitled *The Mill* (Plate 76) which he described in detail in his third lecture at the Royal Institution. (This was another of the four memorable points in the history of landscape art identified by Constable.) 'Rembrandt's "Mill" is a picture wholly made by chiaroscuro; the last ray of light just gleams on the upper sail of the mill, and all other details are lost in large and simple masses of shade. Chiaroscuro is the great feature that characterises his art.'[33] Constable wrote elsewhere 'The most perfect of all masters of real chiaroscuro are Claude and Ostade. The chiaroscuro of Rembrandt is decidedly an artificial feature in his works; he painted expressly for it; it was his own peculiar language, and used by him to express the sentiment.'[34]

Constable's frequent reference to the importance of chiaroscuro in his own work has already been discussed, and undoubtedly Rembrandt's excessive use of light and shade in his landscapes acted as a warning to Constable to be more restrained. However it was probably Rembrandt's landscape drawings that most impressed Constable. As Clark notes:

> *Rembrandt ... was one of the most sensitive and accurate observers of fact who has ever lived.... In his landscape drawings of the 1650s, every dot and scribble contributes to an effect of space and light.... The white paper between three strokes of the pen seems to be full of air.... Yet when he came to paint he felt that all these observations were no more than the raw material of art. For him, as for Rubens, landscape painting meant the creation of an imaginary world, vaster, more dramatic and more fraught with associations than that which we can perceive for ourselves.*[35]

Constable was well aware of Rembrandt's powers of observation and ability to capture such observations on paper. In a letter to Fisher on 20 September 1821 Constable writes:

> *I have likewise made many skies and effects – for I wish it could be said of me as Fuseli says of Rembrandt, 'he followed nature in her calmest abodes and could pluck a flower on every hedge – yet he was born to cast a steadfast eye on the bolder phenomena of nature'. We have had noble clouds & effects of light & dark & color – as is always the case in such seasons as the present.'*[36]

This association of 'noble clouds and & effects of light & dark & color' with Rembrandt is hardly surprising but shows the importance that Constable placed on the lighting of the landscape and the consistency that must be achieved with the sky. Rembrandt gave Constable the confidence to portray the landscape and the sky as he saw it.

4.3.5 Salvator Rosa (1615–73)

Salvator Rosa came to be regarded as a hero of the romantic artists of the late eighteenth century and early nineteenth century for his flamboyant landscape style that was in direct contrast to the classical landscapes of Claude and the Poussins. Constable certainly must have been aware of the skies in Salvator's landscapes as he mentions him in his famous 'skies' letter of 23 October 1821: 'Sir Joshua speaking of the landscapes of Titian, of Salvator, and of Claude, says: "Even their *skies* seem to sympathise with their subjects."'

In Constable's lecture at Hampstead in 1833 he describes Salvator's art as 'wild and terrific in his conceptions of natural scenery', and indeed Salvator is credited with starting the vogue in the eighteenth century for 'sublime' and 'picturesque' landscapes. In *Landscape with Tobias and the Angel* (Plate 77) Salvator's sky is certainly wild with cumulus-like streets actually crossing over each other in mid-air – an effect which is totally impossible in nature. Constable would have perhaps appreciated the dramatic lighting of Salvator's landscapes but would not have been impressed with his clouds.

4.3.6 Aelbert Cuyp (1620–91)

Cuyp painted a great variety of subjects including seascapes and landscapes. It has been suggested that his *Landscape with Horseman and Peasants*, which was acquired by the Earle of Bute in the 1760s, began an interest amongst British collectors and as a consequence many of his best works were brought to Britain. Constable would therefore have been familiar with several of Cuyp's landscapes. Constable admired Cuyp's portrayal of weather and light. He wrote: 'Chiaroscuro is by no means confined to dark pictures; the works of Cuyp, though generally light, are full of it.'[37]

Cuyp's landscapes and seascapes are dominated by the sky as one would expect from a Dutch landscape artist. He painted all the moods of the atmosphere from the gentle sunlight in *Landscape with Horseman and Peasants*, to thunderstorms and lightning flashes in *The Maas at Dordrecht in a Storm*, and *Thunderstorm over Dordrecht* (Plate 78).[38] The influence of Cuyp's skies on Constable went beyond the influence of the skies of Rubens and Claude. Cuyp painted real weather in landscapes similar to those beloved by Constable. Cuyp was the first of several Dutch seventeenth-century artists to have a significant effect on Constable's skies.

4.3.7 Jacob van Ruisdael (1628/29–82)

> *I have seen an affecting picture this morning by Ruysdael; it haunts my mind, and clings to my heart, ... the whole so true, clear, and fresh, and as brisk as champagne; a shower has not long passed.*[39]

Jacob van Ruisdael is regarded as one of the world's finest landscape painters and his influence on others, including in England Gainsborough and

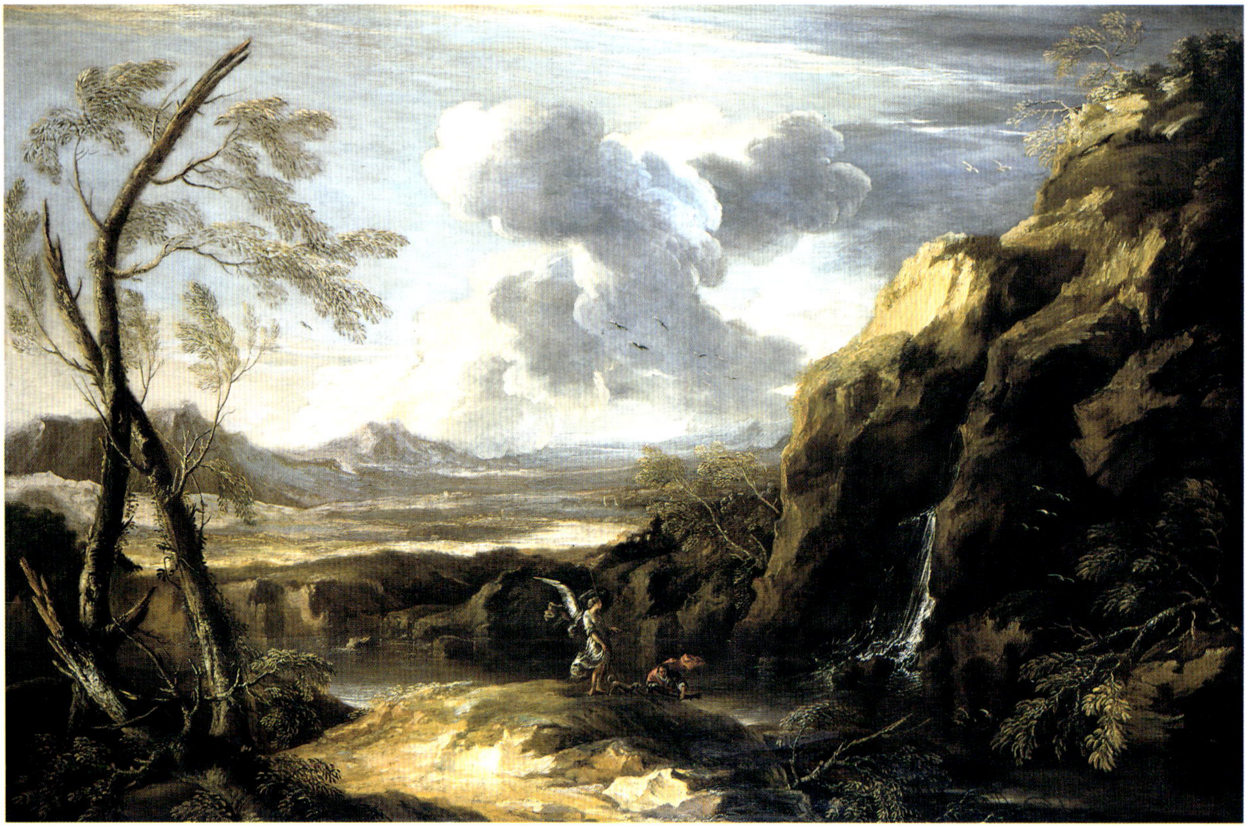

Plate 77 Salvator Rosa, *Landscape with Tobias and the Angel*, 1660–73. Copyright National Gallery, London

Turner as well as Constable, was enormous. Ruisdael came from an artistic background in the city of Haarlem where local tradition has it that landscape painting for its own sake first began in the late fifteenth century. Isaack Ruisdael, Jacob's father, was an art dealer and landscape painter himself although none of his paintings have survived. His uncle, Salomon van Ruysdael (c. 1600–70), was also a very well-respected landscape painter, and his son Jacob Salomonsz van Ruysdael (1629/30–81) became a landscape painter, although of lesser note. Apparently the brothers Isaack and Salomon originally had the surname de Gooyer but changed their names after moving to Haarlem. They seem to have decided to vary the spelling of their new surname to help distinguish between them. Isaack used the spelling Ruisdael and Salomon signed himself Ruysdael. Their respective sons, both called Jacob, continued their fathers' names.

As can well be imagined, there have been problems in interpreting which Ruisdael, Jacob Salomon Ruysdael or Jacob Ruisdael, influenced Constable the most. In Leslie's biography of Constable he confuses the issue by only referring to Jacob Ruysdael! He undoubtedly meant Jacob Ruisdael. (Leslie also wrote: 'I remember being greatly struck by a small picture, a view from Hampstead Heath, which I first saw at *Ruysdael House*, as Mr Fisher called his residence in Keppel Street.'[40] The first mention of 'Ruysdael House' was in 1817 when Constable first moved in to No. 1 Keppel Street in London. Fisher actually addressed two letters, the first to Reysdale House

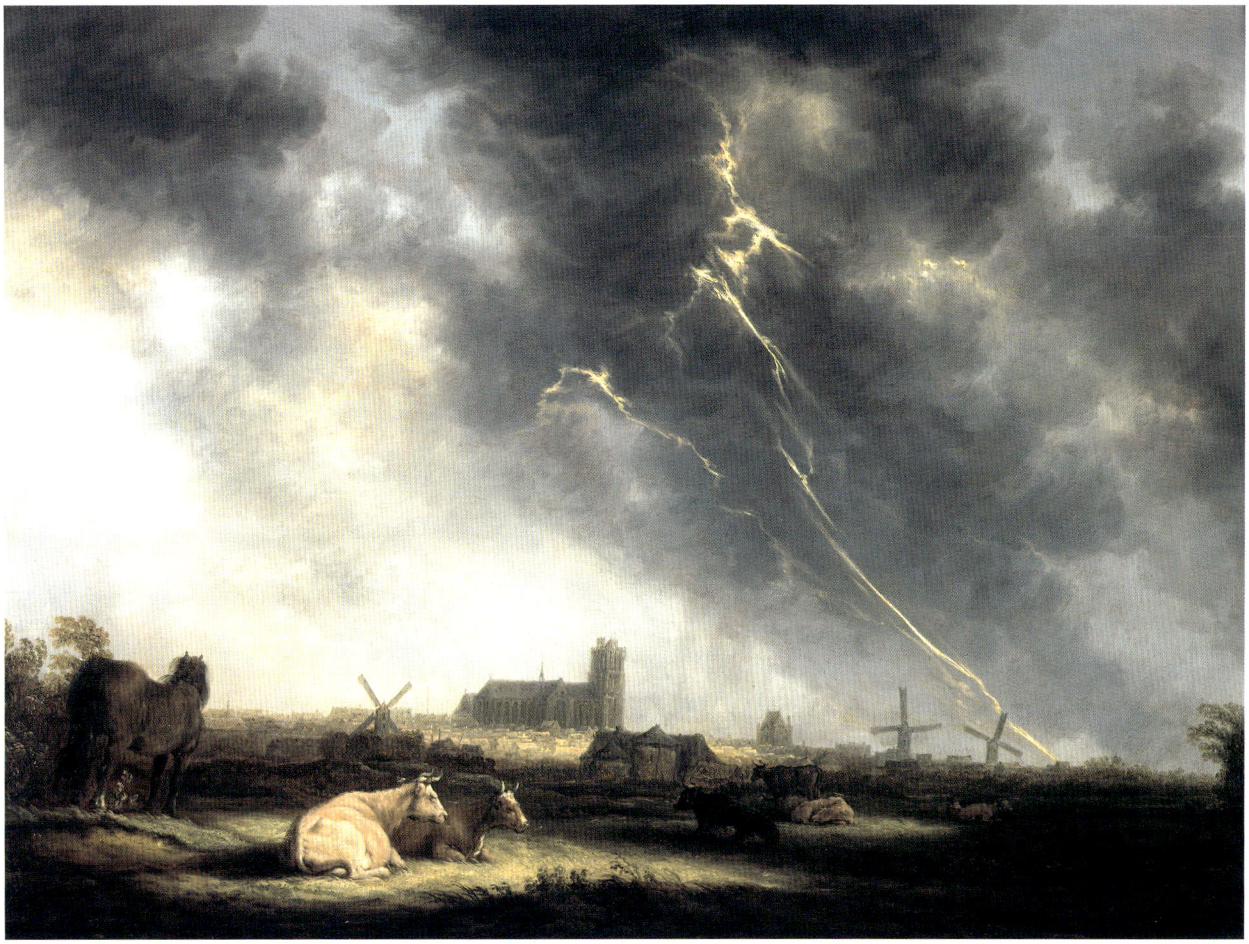

Plate 78 Aelbert Cuyp, *Thunderstorm over Dordrecht*, c. 1645. Foundation E. G. Bührle Collection, Zurich

and the second to Ruysdale House in 1818.) Constable too was confused between the works of Salomon and Jacob. As early as 1797 Constable wrote to John Smith, his friend and early mentor, about an etching of a cottage he had made, 'I think the Cottage something in the style of Solomon Rysdeal. am I right.' Ian Fleming-Williams thinks that he was not right and that the cottage was in the style of Jacob rather than Salomon. He points out that Constable, at his death, owned three of Jacob's etchings, one of which, *The Little Bridge*, was probably the one that Constable was referring to in his letter.[41] It is safe to assume, therefore, that Leslie's references to Ruysdael in his memoirs of Constable are all in fact to Jacob Ruisdael.

In another letter to Smith earlier in 1797 Constable writes: 'I have a mind to copy one of Ruysdael's etchings. I have seen it at your house where there are two trees standing in the water.'[42] These early copies of Ruisdael would not have influenced Constable's skies but show that Constable was already very much enamoured with Ruisdael's art. Smith had probably recommended Ruisdael to Constable, but it was not until he went up to London, as a student at the Royal Academy, that Constable first saw any of Ruisdael's finished works. Having just settled into his accommodation in Cecil Street he wrote to his friend John Dunthorne: 'I shall begin painting as soon as I have the loan of a sweet picture by Jacob Ruysdael to copy. Since I have been in town I have seen some remarkably fine ones by him, indeed I never saw him before.'[43] (This last reference to having never seen Jacob Ruisdael before presumably means that he had never appreciated the quality in his works before.) It is not known which Ruisdael he eventually copied, but he soon wrote to Dunthorne that 'I have finished my copy from Ruysdael, all but the glazing, which cannot be done till the picture is dry.'[44] The picture was clearly an inspiration to Constable, for in 1819 he wrote to Fisher, 'I should hardly like to part with my copy of Ruysdael; its being an old school exercise (of which I have too few), gives it a value to me beyond what I could in conscience ask for it.'[45]

Constable was becoming increasingly associated with Ruisdael, and the first critical comparison was probably made by a reviewer writing in *The Literary Gazette* on 3 July 1819. In commenting on *A Scene on the River Stour (The White Horse)* the reviewer wrote 'This choice falls happily on the picturesque, and the river scene is clothed, like the pictures of Ruysdael and Hobbima, with a rich variety of forms.'[46] This comparison is repeated by *The Literary Gazette* on 6 May 1820 when discussing *Landscape (Stratford Mill)* and *Harwich (Harwich Light-house)*: 'The interest of this, as well as of all the works of this artist, arises from its truth and locality. But it is truth and locality as given by a Ruysdael or a Hobbima, not the every day representation of pictorial scenery.'[47] *The Observer* on 25 June 1821, when commenting on *The Hay Wain* (or *Landscape, Noon* as it was then known), wrote 'There is much skill shewn in this performance, of which Ruysdoen has evidently been the model.'[48] On 28 May 1821 the *Bell's Weekly Messenger* complained of 'white spots' on *Landscape, Noon*, and went on 'This is certainly an affectation ... if we approach near a Claude, a Both, a Ruysdael, or a Poussin ... we see the effects of nature undisguised.'[49]

Ruisdael's landscapes are full of all the elements that would attract Constable – cornfields, windmills, watermills, rivers and skies. In his third lecture at the Royal Institute in 1836 Constable spells out his attraction to Ruisdael's skies:

> *The landscapes of Ruysdael present the greatest possible contrast to those of Claude, showing how powerfully, from the most opposite directions, genius may command our homage. In Claude's pictures, with scarcely an exception, the sun ever shines. Ruysdael, on the contrary, delighted in, and has made delightful to our eyes, those solemn days, peculiar to his country and to ours, when without storm, large rolling clouds scarcely permit a ray of sunlight to break the shades of the forest. By these effects he enveloped the most ordinary scenes in grandeur, and whenever he has attempted marine subjects, he is far beyond Vandervelde.*[50]

Constable showed two copies of Ruisdael pictures during this third lecture, and Leslie's accounts of what Constable said about them include the weather. Constable's description of the first copy, which was apparently borrowed from James Uwins, went as follows:

> *The subject is the mouth of a Dutch river, without a single feature of grandeur in the scenery; but the stormy sky, the grouping of the vessels, and the breaking of the sea, make the picture one of the most impressive ever painted.*
>
> *'It is the Soul that sees; the outward eyes*
> *Present the object, but the Mind descries,'*
>
> *We see nothing truly till we understand it. An ordinary spectator at the mouth of the river which Ruysdael has here painted, would scarcely be conscious of the existence of many of the objects that conduce to the effect of the picture; certainly not of their fitness for pictorial effect.*[51]

It is not certain which Ruisdael picture Constable was referring to; it could have been something similar to *Vessels in a Breeze* (Plate 79), now in the National Gallery. This painting is full of wind and changing light and a sky full of heavy showers. It is very appropriate that Constable made his famous statement, 'We see nothing truly till we understand

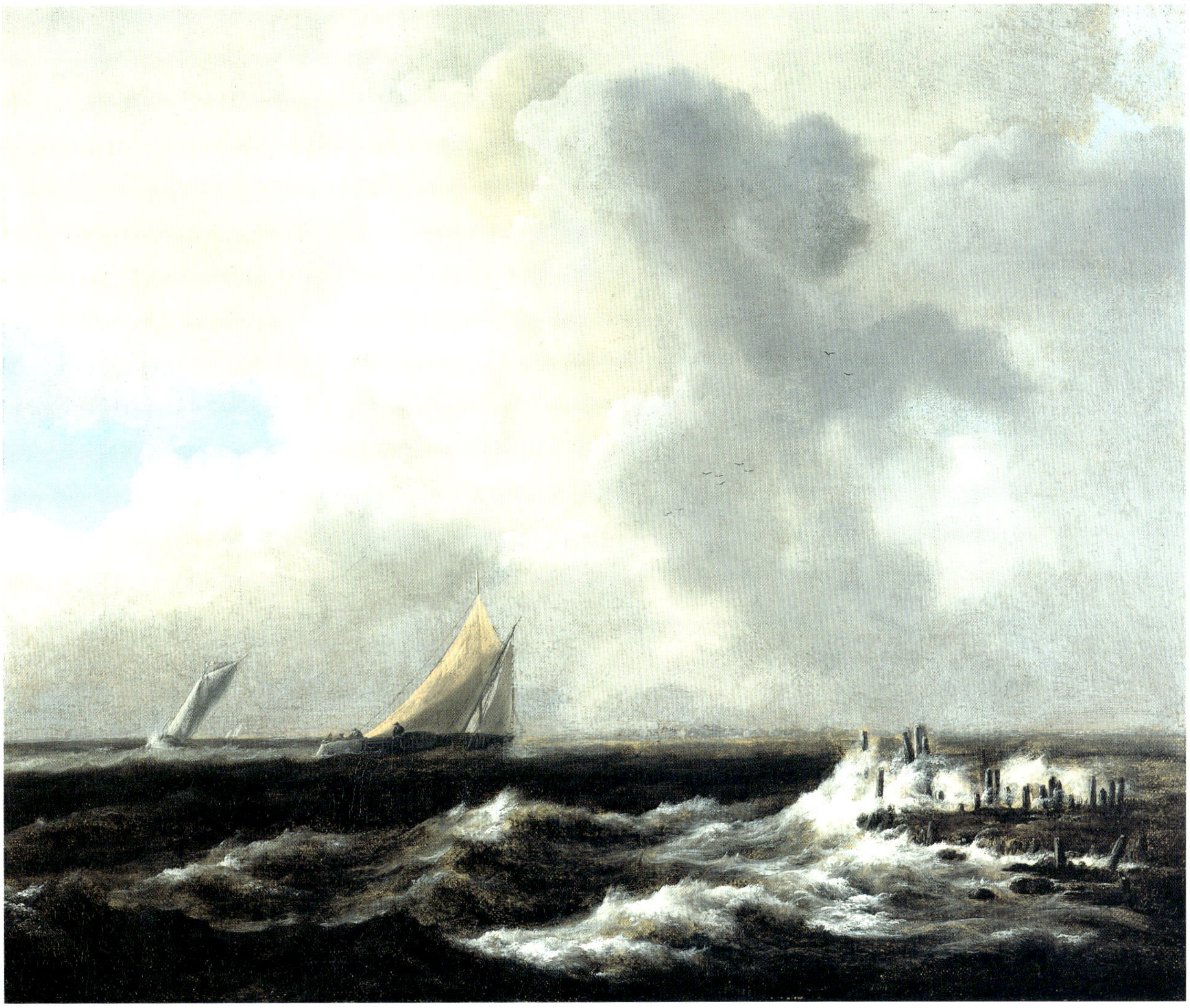

Plate 79 Jacob Ruisdael, *Vessels in a Breeze*. Copyright National Gallery, London

it', about a picture by Ruisdael, whose paintings are dominated by the sky, atmosphere and diffuse light.

The second Ruisdael that Constable showed was undoubtedly his own version of *Winter Landscape* (Plate 80) which he copied in 1832.[52] Constable's description of the painting is remarkable and illustrates both the respect that Constable had for Ruisdael and the detailed knowledge Constable possessed about changes in the weather.[53] There are few other artists apart from Constable who painted pictures from which the weather both before and after the scene can be inferred with such accuracy. Just as Constable had said about the previous Ruisdael that an ordinary spectator would scarcely be conscious of what was going on, this is also true of *Winter Landscape*. Constable wanted his audience to appreciate his own paintings for possessing such qualities.

Constable's skies are even more powerful than Ruisdael's. Not only does Constable achieve movement and time in his skies but also truth to nature. Ruisdael's clouds, although grand and three-dimensional, are rarely real, and the lighting in most of his landscapes does not harmonise with the sky. Nevertheless Ruisdael's landscapes are full of grandeur on account of their noble skies, as Constable noted above, and the reason Fisher called No.1 Keppel Street 'Ruysdael House' is

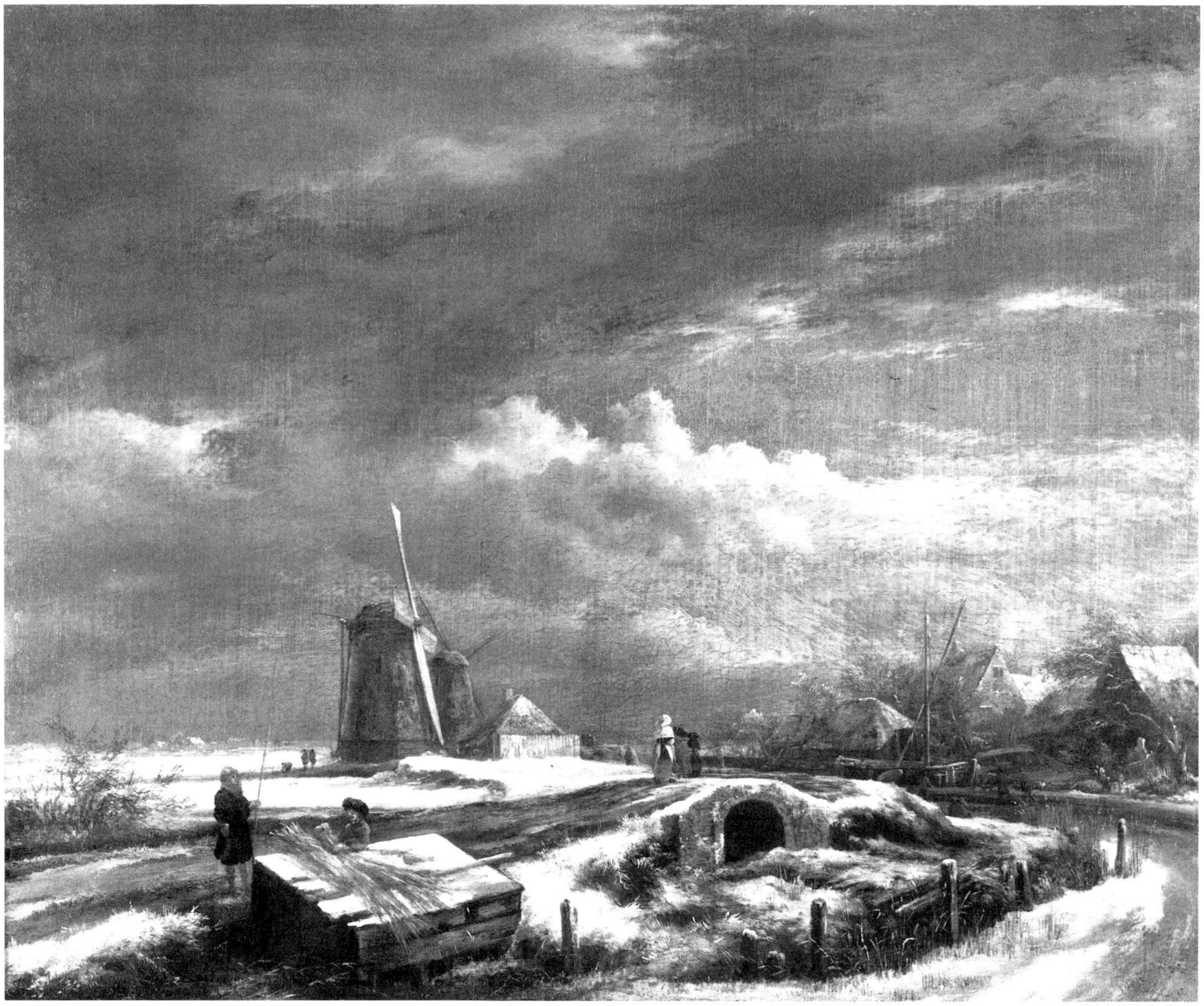

Plate 80 Jacob Ruisdael, *Winter Landscape*.
The John G. Johnson Collection, Philadelphia Museum of Art

because of the grandeur of the skies of Constable's paintings. The brightness of the skies in Ruisdael's paintings contrasts so dramatically with the shade of the landscape that if you walked into a room of Ruisdaels the first thing that would strike you is their cloudiness – the same sensation as one has with Constable.

Constable admired Ruisdael throughout his career and continued to copy his paintings. Although Constable did not replicate exactly the compositions there are some similarities, for example between Ruisdael's *A Landscape with a Cornfield* and Constable's *Hampstead Heath with the House called 'The Salt Box'* as pointed out by Cormack.[54] However Constable never 'used' any of Ruisdael's skies in his works, as it would be out of the question to place a sky from another time and place onto any of his landscapes. Constable was quite capable of creating his own skies that were entirely suited to the time and place of his composition.

4.3.8 Philips Koninck (1619–88), Meyndert Hobbema (1638–1709) and Willem van de Velde (1633–1707)

Koninck was probably a pupil and friend of Rembrandt. He is best known for his panoramic landscapes such as *Landscape with a Road by a River* (Plate 81). The landscape is reminiscent of Rubens, retreating for miles into the picture with clear aerial perspective. The sky is almost a cloudscape in itself taking up some three-fifths of the picture, but there is no linkage between the sky and the landscape, both stand alone. There is a freshness about the picture but the clouds are impossible. Koninck has meant to represent cloud streets (cumulus streets) running from left to right across the picture but they resemble more the smoke from a bonfire. The perspective is wrong and the vertical extent of the clouds is too shallow; also the blue sky colours do not appear to whiten sufficiently close to the horizon. Nevertheless, it is still a remarkable attempt to depict cumulus streets; even Constable did not attempt such a difficult task. Koninck was not mentioned in Constable's landscape lectures, but Constable must have been aware of his impressive panoramas. The flat horizons, which are a signature of Koninck's work, mean that his skies are almost a precursor to Constable's sky studies of 1820–22. If the sky of *Landscape with a Road by a River* is looked at with the landscape removed it resembles Constable's sky studies in form. However this is the only similarity as Koninck's skies are distant and static.

Hobbema was a pupil and friend of Jacob van Ruisdael and became the leading Dutch landscape painter towards the end of the seventeenth century. His landscapes are much quieter than Ruisdael's and lack their dynamic quality. The clouds are much more distant and less threatening. Hobbema's landscapes are nearly always occupied by trees, but his skies are bright and the atmosphere is usually full of light. In a letter to Fisher on 17 November 1824 Constable wrote: 'Change of weather and effect will always afford variety. What if Vander Velde had quitted his sea pieces, or Ruysdael his waterfalls, or Hobbema his native woods. The world would have lost so many features in art.'[55] Constable hoped that he would be remembered for his skies and changing weather, just as Hobbema is remembered for his woodlands. However, he is rather dismissive of Hobbema in a letter to Leslie in 1832: 'Hobbema, if he misses colour, is very disagreeable, as he has neither shapes nor composition.'[56] This is also true of his skies and Constable would have learnt little from them.

Willem van de Velde the Younger was the leading marine painter in Holland in the second half of the seventeenth century. His father Willem van de Velde the Elder (1611–93) was also a marine painter and he brought his son to live in Britain in 1672 and entered the service of Charles II. Father and son often worked together with the father responsible for the draughtsmanship and the son for the colouring. Constable was well aware of Van de Velde's work and indeed copied at least two of his sea-pieces that were exhibited at the British Institution in 1819.[57] Interestingly Constable also noted the dimensions of at least eight of the paintings exhibited, including three by Van de Velde, three by Ruisdael and one by Hobbema. Intriguingly he noted the height of the horizon of the three Van de Veldes. Fleming-Williams suggests that this might be linked to a work he was currently engaged on. However it is also likely that Constable was surprised that the horizon in Van de Velde's pictures is so low and that the skies are consequently so large. Van de Velde's skies are manufactured and static and when he does attempt to portray a storm at sea, for instance *Three Ships in a Gale*, the clouds lose their form in a mass of two-dimensional darkness. Van de Velde may have encouraged Constable not to be afraid of using a low horizon when required, but the form of his clouds and the lack of perspective would not have inspired the form or process in any of Constable's skies.

4.4 Eighteenth-century skies in England – Richard Wilson (1713/14–82), Alexander Cozens (1717–86), Thomas Gainsborough (1727–88) and Thomas Girtin (1775–1802)

In Constable's lecture at Hampstead in 1833, having discussed the important role of Rembrandt in landscape painting and mentioned the significance of Ruisdael and Cuyp, he then identified a decline in landscape painting:

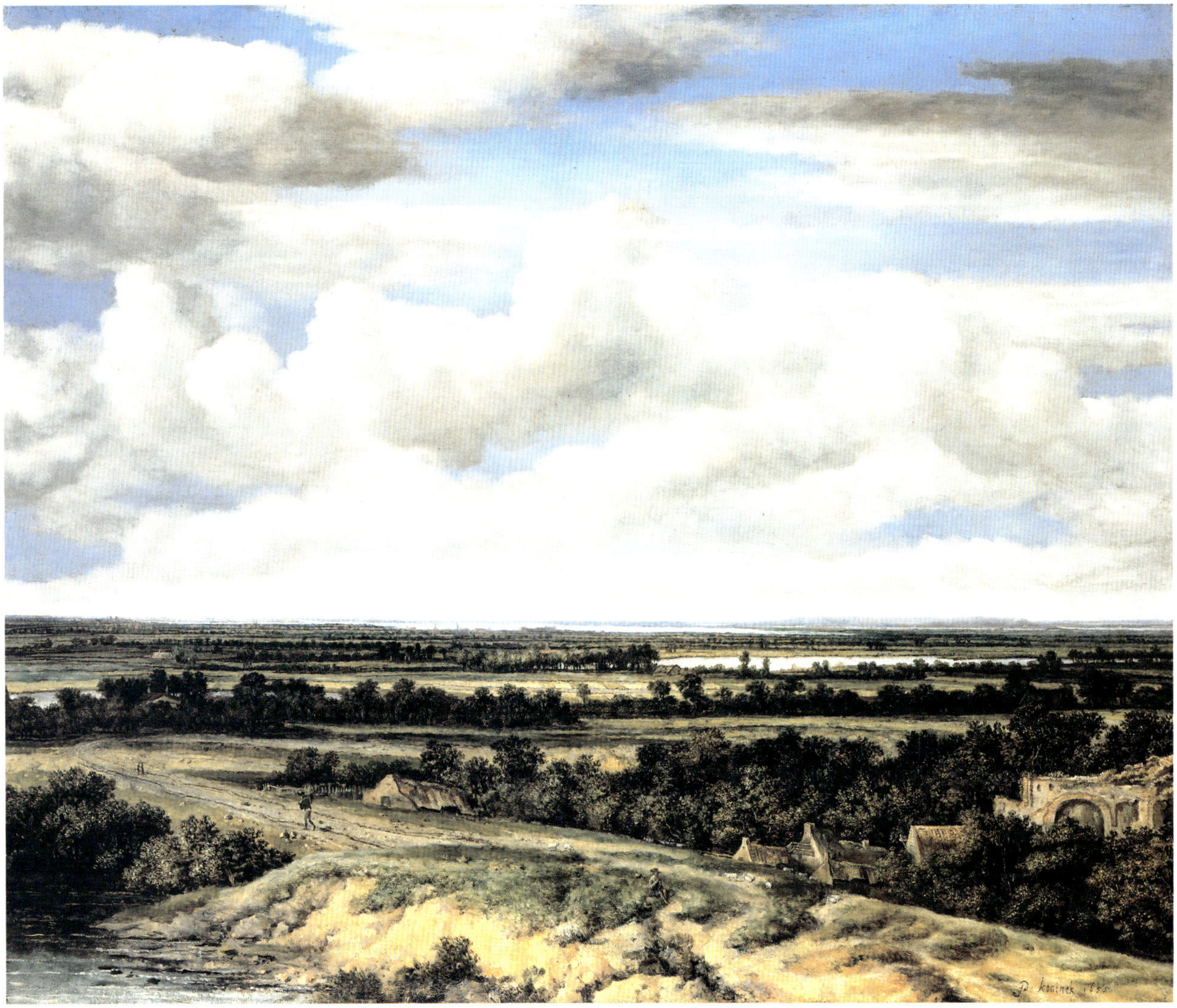

Plate 81 Philips Koninck, *Landscape with a Road by a River*, 1655. Copyright National Gallery, London

> *On the death of these great men Landscape rapidly declined; and during almost the whole of the succeeding century, little was produced.... From this degraded and fallen state it is delightful to say that landscape painting revived in our own country, in all its purity, simplicity, and grandeur, in the works of Wilson, Gainsborough, Cozens, and Girtin.*[58]

Richard Wilson has been variously called 'the father of British landscape painting' and 'the English Claude' (despite the fact that he was born in Wales). He moved to London in about 1729 and was a pupil of the portrait painter Thomas Wright. He then moved to Italy where he was encouraged to turn to landscape painting by Zuccarelli (1702–88) and Vernet (1714–89), two well-respected landscape painters of the day. Whilst in Italy he was also inspired by Claude and the Poussins, and when he returned to England in 1756/57 he continued to paint views of Italy as well as views of England and Wales. His pictures are unusual in that they often have a seemingly Italian sky above an English or Welsh landscape, as mentioned in Chapter 1. *The River Dee, near Eaton Hall* (Plate 1) is a classic example, with a golden sky much more reminiscent of Venice than of Chester. His skies are full of light but they are often hazy and his clouds are static, distant and lacking in form. Nevertheless Wilson was admired by Constable for being true to nature, albeit Italian nature. Constable had been aware of Wilson's work from his early acquaintance in 1795 with Farington, who had been a pupil of Wilson. In 1799 he wrote to Dunthorne mentioning that he had copied two Wilsons, and he continued to speak of Wilson warmly throughout his life; for instance in 1823, in the same letter to Fisher in which he laments that he will never see the Italian landscapes that inspired Wilson and Claude, he goes on to write:

> *I went to the gallery of Sir John Leicester, to see the English artists. I recollect nothing so much as a solemn – bright – warm – fresh – landscape by Wilson, which still swims in my brain like a delicious dream. Poor Wilson. Think of his magnificence, think of his fate. But the mind loses its dignity less in adversity than in prosperity. He is now walking arm in arm with Milton -& Linnaeus. He was one of the great appointments to shew to the world the hidden stores and beauties of Nature. One of the great men who shew to the world what exists in nature but which was not known till his time.*[59]

It is as if Constable was writing his own epitaph, as he probably expected by this time to die in poverty and relative obscurity as Wilson had done. (The reference to Linnaeus is an interesting one in that Luke Howard based his cloud classification on the Linnean system and Constable obviously had great regard for Linnaeus to link him with Milton and Wilson. This tends to confirm Constable's likely respect for Luke Howard's cloud classification.) Wilson's skies are enigmatic, and although Constable found Wilson's landscapes to be bright, warm and fresh the skies are very similar to Claude's and would not have helped Constable's skies in terms of clouds, but they would in terms of light and freshness in the atmosphere.

Alexander Cozens was probably the first English artist to draw skies, and both he and his son John Robert Cozens produced drawings called *The Cloud*, both of which have a topographical rather than a natural feel to them. The painting *After Rain* (Plate 82) by Alexander Cozens, produced nearly fifty years before Constable's cloud studies, is, however, remarkable. The natural colour of the sky, the three-dimensional realism of the retreating thunderstorm, the brightness of the sunlight on the cloud edges, the dark fragmented stratus overhead, and the fallen tree struck by lightning encapsulate the awesome power and the beauty of the atmosphere. Constable would have been impressed that both artists devoted such time and energy to clouds. As already discussed in Chapter 2, Constable copied a series of twenty skies produced by Alexander Cozens in his treatise *A New Method of Assisting the Invention in Drawing*

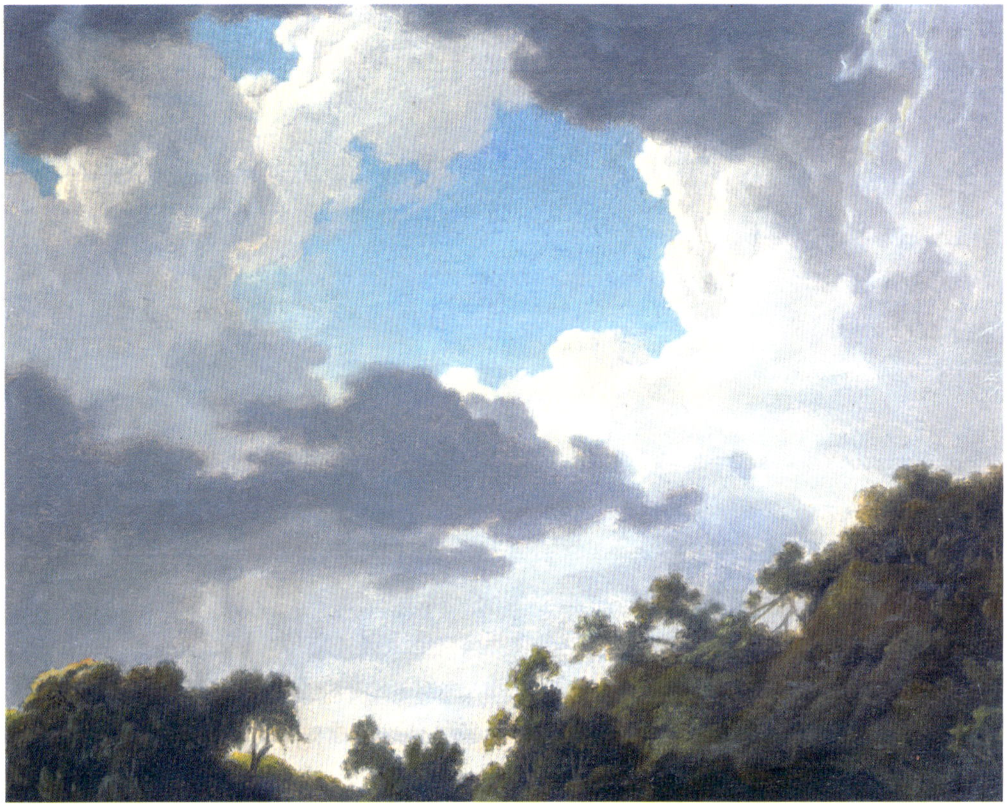

Plate 82 Alexander Cozens, *After Rain*. Private collection

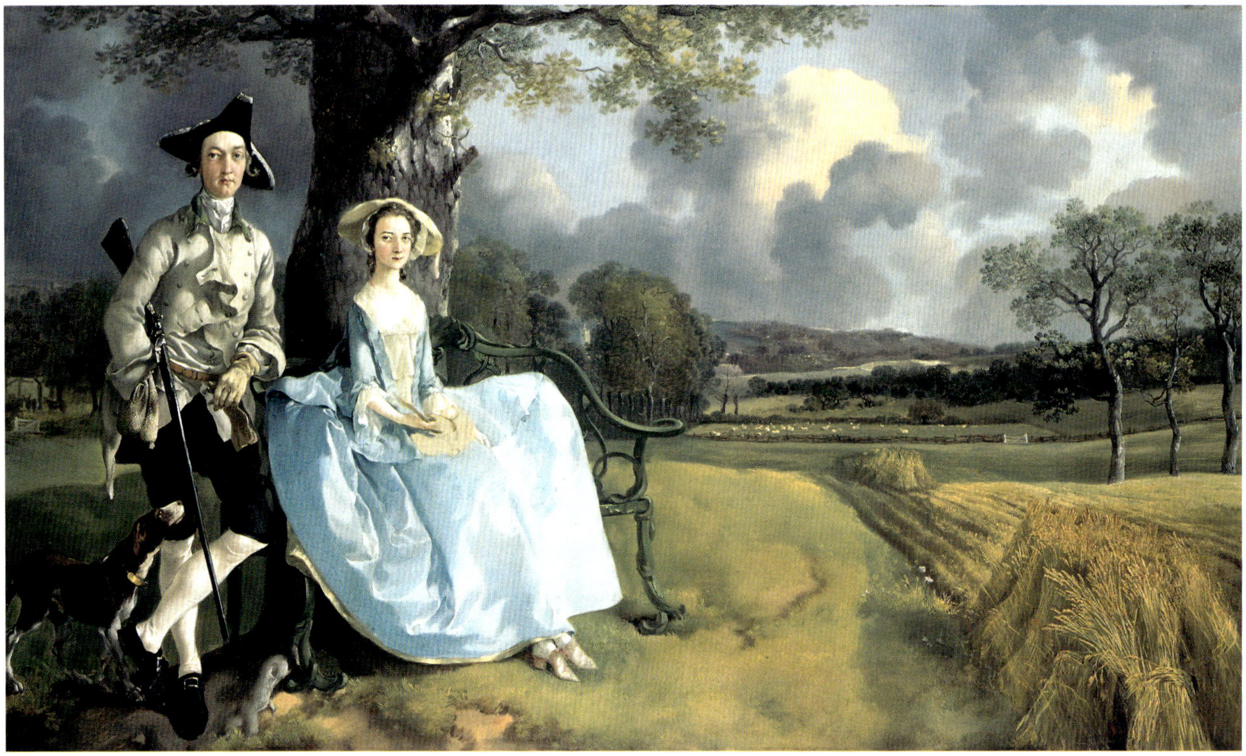

Plate 83 Thomas Gainsborough, *Mr and Mrs Andrews*, 1750. Copyright National Gallery, London

Original Compositions of Landscape (1785–86). These skies were unlikely to have provided any stimulus to Constable other than that he experimented with them and, like any true scientist, having tested Cozen's hypothesis by copying them, he rejected them.

Thomas Gainsborough was always inclined towards landscape painting and included extensive views in some of his portraits, such as *Mr and Mrs Andrews* (Plate 83). This particular painting contains exquisite detail within the landscape but the clouds are very poorly represented. It would appear that there is a large bonfire on the horizon and that black smoke is rising up from it. Gainsborough also often painted stormy skies in the background of his portraits but they are usually two-dimensional and serve merely to contrast with the colours of the sitter. There is little consistency between the lighting of his landscapes and the position of the clouds or the implied position of the sun in the sky. Constable was more interested in Gainsborough's trees and hedges. Gainsborough was born at Sudbury, which is only about fourteen miles from Bergholt. His early landscapes were based on the scenery of the river Stour just as Constable's were many years later. Gainsborough lived for a time in Ipswich and Constable wrote to his friend Smith from Ipswich in 1799: 'I fancy I see a Gainsborough in every hedge and tree'.[60]

In a letter to Leslie in 1834 Constable recalls a previous visit to Petworth when 'The Gainsborough was down.... I placed it as it suited me, and I cannot think of it even now without tears in my eyes. With particulars he had nothing to do; his object was to deliver a fine sentiment, and he has accomplished it.'[61] Leslie also tells us that several fine studies by Gainsborough were hung in Constable's parlour. In the fourth lecture at the Royal Institution in 1836 Constable again praises Gainsborough's art: 'The landscape of Gainsborough is soothing, tender, and affecting. The stillness of noon, the depths of twilight, and the dews and pearls of the morning, are all to be found on the canvases of this most benevolent and kind-hearted man.'[62] Thus Constable saw gentle calm weather in Gainsborough's landscapes, be it the dews of early morning or the stillness of the noon or twilight.

Thomas Girtin was introduced to Constable at the very beginning of his artistic career. Sir George Beaumont owned about thirty watercolours by Girtin and he advised Constable to study them 'as examples of great breadth and truth'. As Leslie comments, 'their influence on him may be traced more or less through the whole course of his practice'. Sir George also introduced Constable to Claude, and Leslie writes that 'it was fortunate for him [Constable] that he began with Claude and Girtin'.[63]

Girtin's skies use the medium of watercolour to advantage and he paints large rolling cumulus clouds, as in *Kirkstall Abbey*. More interesting is a pure cloud study made by Girtin in 1794. This study predates Constable's pure sky studies by a quarter of a century. The sky was never forgotten in Girtin's huge number of paintings created over such a short lifetime. His portrayal of lightning in *Dunstanborough Castle, Northumberland, in a Thunderstorm* is as good as any up to that time. His *Landscape with Stormy Sky*, one of his last works, is as vibrant and true as any of Constable's paintings of rain or showers. Constable would certainly therefore have been inspired by such works if he had seen them, but on the other hand some of Girtin's skies are not so perfect and sometimes the attempted streets of cumulus clouds resemble those of Koninck and Gainsborough, as, for example, in *A View on the Wharfe, near Farnley, Yorkshire* which depicts a real 'bonfire' as well as clouds resembling smoke.

4.5 Nineteenth-century skies – Joseph Mallord William Turner (1775–1851)

Turner was born in London, the year before Constable; by the age of fifteen he was already exhibiting at the Royal Academy, and by 1802 he had become a full Academician. In 1811 he gave his first lectures as Professor of Perspective, though that did not stop him talking about everything else as well as perspective. In one lecture he spoke of the advantages of the British climate for landscape artists:

In our variable climate where [all] the seasons are recognisable in one day, where all the vapoury turbulence involves the face of things, where nature seems to sport in all her dignity and dispensing incidents for the artist's study … how happily is the landscape painter situated, how roused by every change in nature in every moment, that allows no languor even in her effects which she places before him, and demands most peremptorily every moment his admiration and investigation, to store his mind with every change of time and place.[64]

These words could easily have been written by Constable and, as Wilton observes in his biography of Turner,[65] Constable expressed similar sentiments in his Introduction to the 1833 edition of *English Landscape Scenery*: 'England, with her climate of more than vernal freshness, and in whose summer skies, and rich autumnal clouds, the observer of Nature may daily watch her endless varieties of effect'.[66]

Constable goes on to state that he is trying in *English Landscape Scenery* to give 'to one brief moment caught from fleeting time' a lasting and sober existence. Constable then compares two approaches of artists trying to achieve distinction in their art:

In Art as in literature, there are two modes by which men endeavour to attain the same end, and seek distinction. In the one, the Artist, intent only on the study of departed excellence, or on what others have accomplished, becomes an imitator of their works, or he selects and combines their various beauties; in the other he seeks perfection at its PRIMITIVE SOURCE, NATURE. *The one, forms a style upon the study of pictures, or the art alone; and produces, either 'imitative', 'scholastic', or that which has been termed 'Eclectic Art'.*[67]

It is very likely that Constable would have included Turner in the 'eclectic art' category despite Turner's astute observations of nature. There is a great difference between Turner's sketchbooks, such as the *Skies* sketchbook c. 1818/19, which certainly does 'seek perfection at its primitive source, nature', and his finished works, which are often sublime creations of contrived suggestive scale and variations in light which combine to produce a landscape of grandeur.

Constable was obviously more aware of Turner's exhibited works and undoubtedly admired him and his art even if he didn't always understand why Turner should receive so much public recognition and acclaim. In 1812, in a letter to Maria his future wife, Constable wrote about Turner's landscape *Snow Storm: Hannibal and his Army Crossing the Alps* (Plate 84), 'It is so ambiguous as to be scarcely intelligible in some parts (and those the principal), yet as a whole, it is novel and affecting.'[68] The storm effects in this painting are typical of many of Turner's skies – full of the power of nature, dwarfing the futile efforts of mankind. Using the atmosphere as a symbol of the power of nature is a theme which returns again and again in Turner's art. David Cox (1783–1859) was later to do the same, but to a more limited extent. Constable's skies are also dynamic, but in a natural, typical way. Constable's skies were only used symbolically in his later years, reflecting partly his own depressed feelings. Turner used his skies to reflect universal feelings.

The sky effects in the 'Hannibal' were supposedly seen by Turner in Yorkshire whilst visiting his friends the Fawkes:

'One stormy day at Farnley,' says Mr [Hawkesworth] Fawkes, Turner called to me loudly from the doorway, "Hawkey – Hawkey! – come here – come here! Look at this thunder-storm! Isn't it grand? – Isn't it wonderful? – Isn't it sublime?"

'All this time he was making notes of its form and colour on the back of a letter. I proposed some better drawing-block, but he said it did very well. He was absorbed – he was entranced. There was the storm rolling and sweeping and shafting out its lightning over the Yorkshire

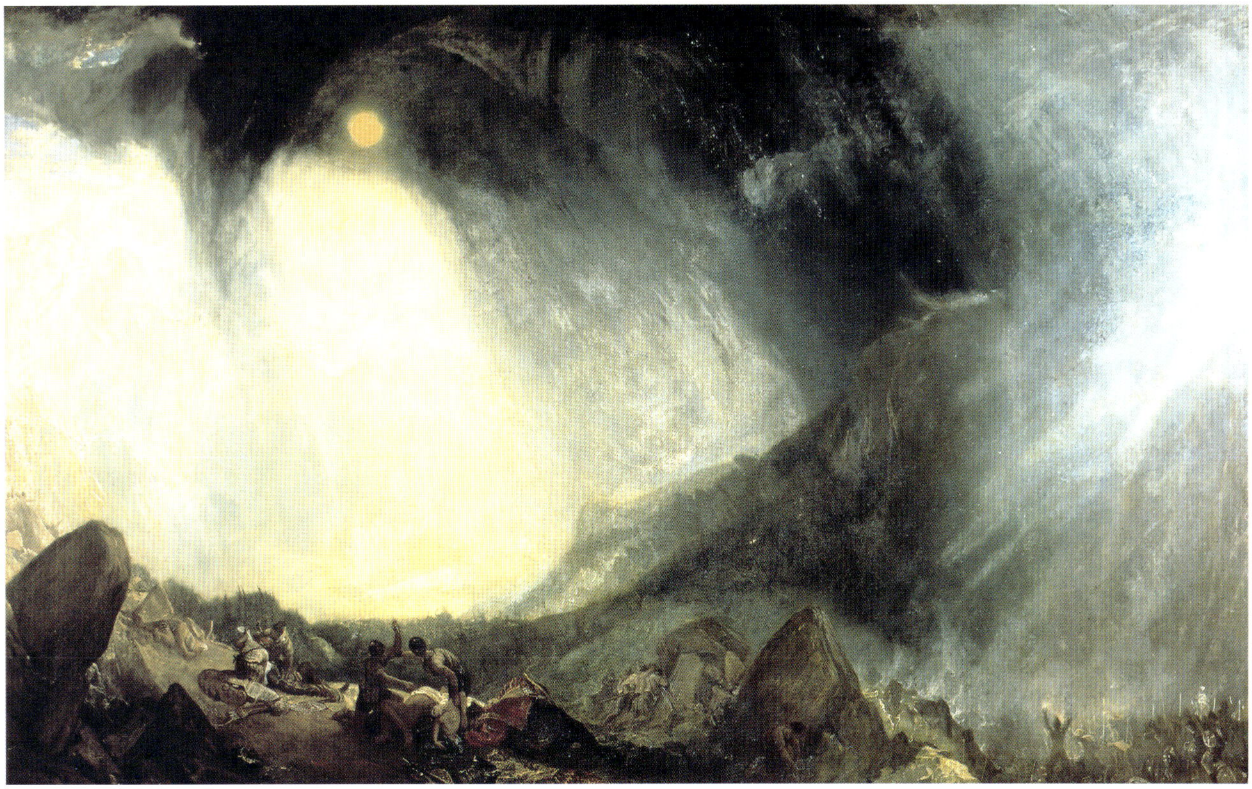

Plate 84 Joseph Mallord William Turner, *Snow Storm: Hannibal and his Army Crossing the Alps* (exhibited 1812). Copyright Tate Gallery, London 1998

> *hills. Presently the storm passed, and he finished. "There," said he, "Hawkey; in two years you will see this again, and call it Hannibal Crossing the Alps."'*[69]

Turner had a fantastic memory for detail and always had a number of grand themes in his mind to which he mentally attached the right sky.

In another one of his letters to Maria, Constable wrote in 1813, 'I dined with the Royal Academy last Monday in the Council room. It was entirely a meeting of artists (none but the members and exhibitors could be admitted), and the day passed off very well. I sat next to Turner.... I was a good deal entertained with Turner. I always expected to find him what I did. He has a wonderful range of mind.'[70] In commenting on the Academy exhibits in 1828 Constable writes: 'Turner has some golden visions, glorious and beautiful; they are only visions, but still they are art, and one could live and die with such pictures.'[71] Of the 1836 Academy exhibits Constable writes: 'Turner has outdone himself; he seems to paint with tinted steam, so evanescent and so airy. The public think he is laughing at them, and so they laugh at him in return.'[72]

It is clear that Constable had considerable respect for Turner's art, but it is also plain that Constable felt that his own mission was totally different to Turner's. Constable's skies therefore owe little, if anything, to Turner. Turner's mastery of light was for the purpose of the Sublime. Turner's glorious sunsets and grandeur storms (the phantasmagorical skies) are at the opposite end of the spectrum from Constable's typical English noon skyscapes. Constable was unlikely to have seen any of Turner's studies of clouds and hence there is little in Turner that would have influenced Constable's skies. Turner was much more interested in the interplay between the atmosphere and sunlight and how he could use this to heighten the effects of his landscapes and seascapes. Constable rarely painted the atmosphere at all but concentrated on the clouds and the sky. The visibility in Constable's landscapes is nearly always very good, such that the horizon can be clearly seen; he rarely paints mist or fog. Turner on the other hand delighted in mist and fog which often blot out the horizon and sky in his paintings. Their skies therefore are almost mutually exclusive and both are wonderful in their own way.

Louis Hawes, in his discussion of the motivation for Constable's cloud studies of 1820–22, places great emphasis on the probable importance of Turner's skies to Constable in the period 1817–19, particularly the sky sketchbook and two exhibited works: *Raby Castle* (1818) (Plate 85) and *Entrance to the Meuse* (1819). Hawes admits however that it was very unlikely that Constable would ever have seen Turner's sky studies, and that even if he did they were 'albeit very rough studies ... and in thin water colour'.[73] The sky of *Raby Castle*, which was exhibited at the Royal Academy in 1818, Hawes argues, is 'probably the most illusionistic sky found in any of Turner's large pictures, and may well have had a certain impact on Constable, inviting him to consider the sky on a more monumental scale and to give it still greater luminosity'. Interestingly Hawes thinks that Turner's sky studies, carried out just before Turner painted *Raby Castle*, were part of the reason for its 'illusionism'. The sky in *Raby Castle* is impressive but it is distant, unique and almost overcast and creates few shadows and little chiaroscuro on the landscape. The clouds in Constable's *Flatford Mill, on the River Stour* (1817), one of his first 'six-footers', are also distant but are much more recognisable than Turner's. Even though the clouds do not come overhead Constable implies that there are many breaks in the clouds which mean that the sun can get through to give the contrasting sunlight and shade. Although Constable was not happy with the skies

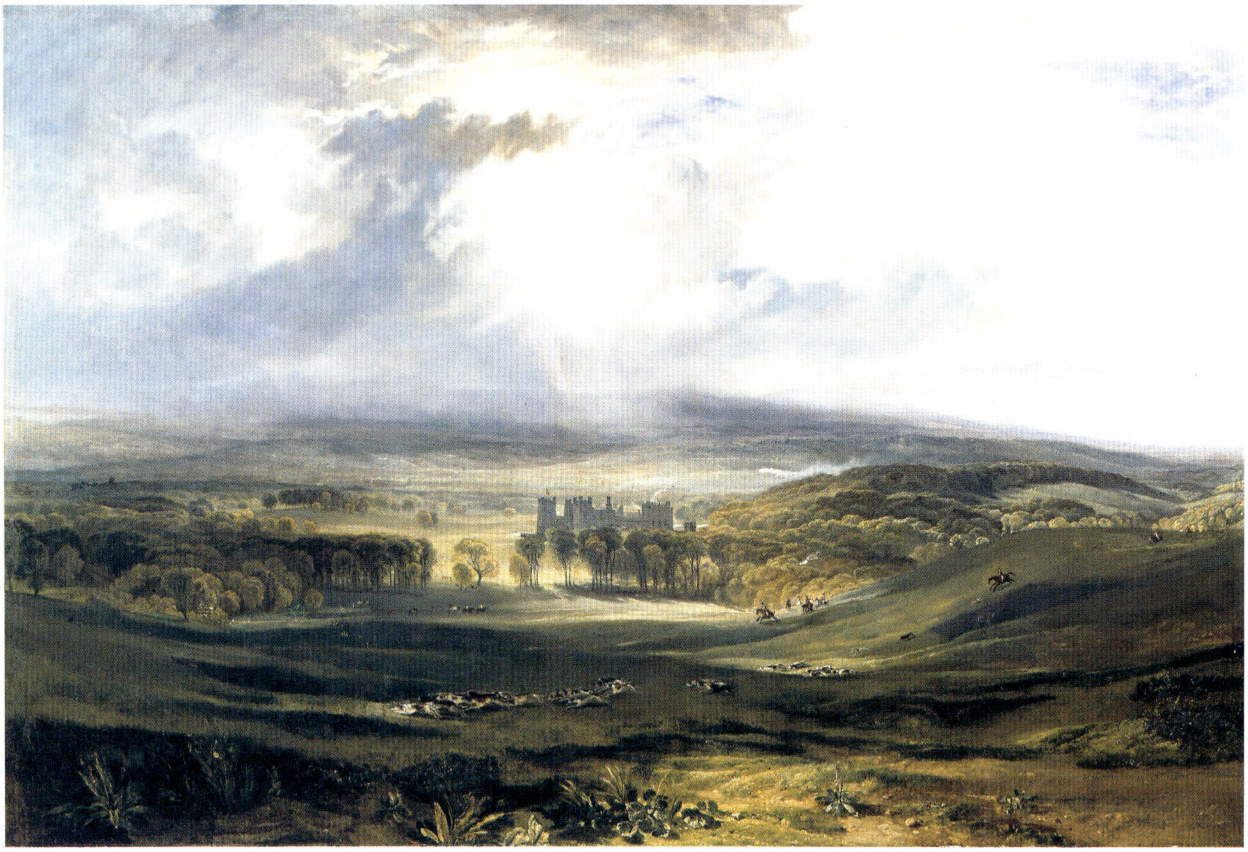

Plate 85 Joseph Mallord William Turner, *Raby Castle*, 1818. The Walters Art Gallery, Baltimore

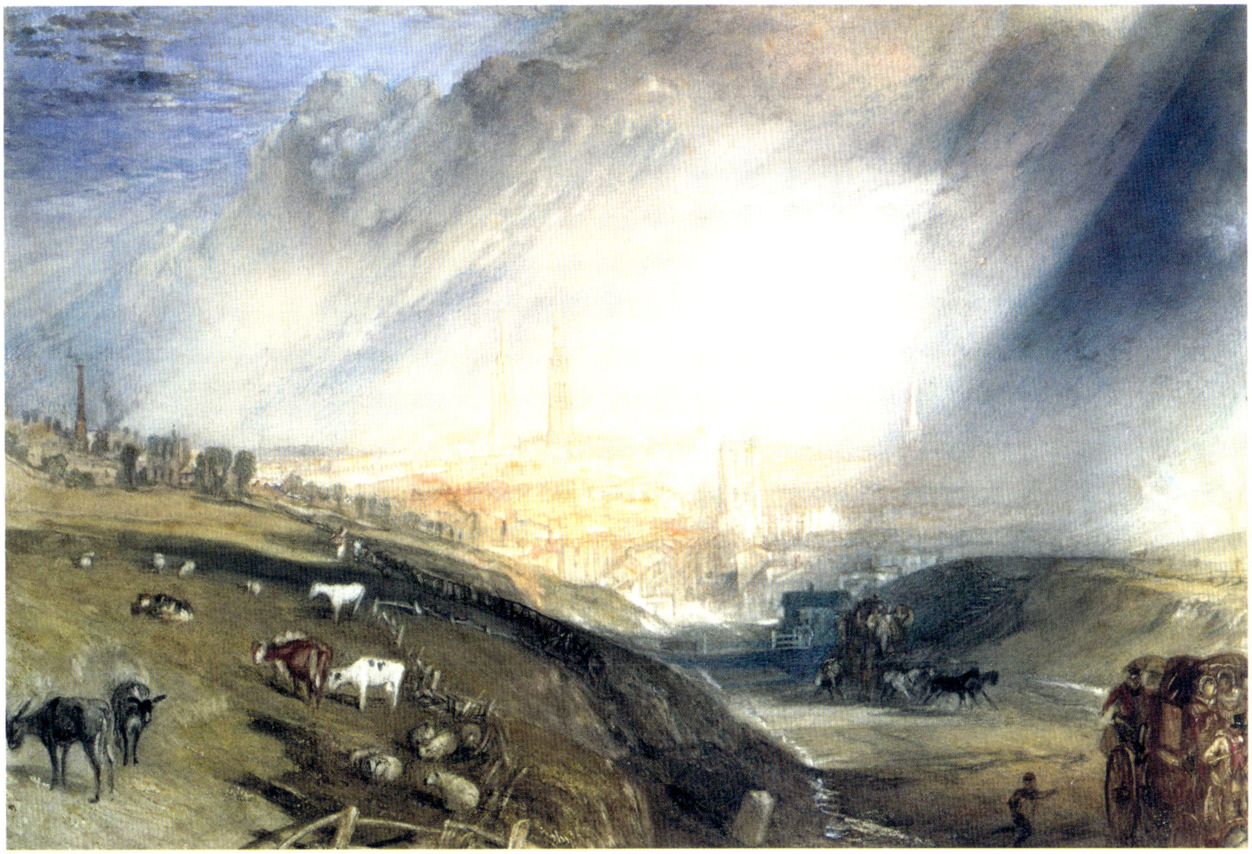

Plate 86 Joseph Mallord WilliamTurner, *Coventry*, c. 1832. Copyright British Museum

of the early 'six-footers', in that the sky was still a backcloth to the picture, it is unlikely that Turner's *Raby Castle* would have helped him.

The sky in Turner's marine painting *Entrance to the Meuse,* which was exhibited at the Royal Academy in 1819, is, according to Hawes, 'the most imposing sky he ever attempted in a large canvas.... The rich array of cloud forms are diversified to an unprecedented extent, providing a kind of anthology of his favourite kinds of clouds – and perhaps for this reason does not resemble nature to the extent we found in *Raby Castle.*' Again, although Constable would probably have admired *Entrance to the Meuse*, it is unlikely that it would have helped him in his quest to 'conquer all difficulties'. It is known that Turner and Constable were table mates at the 1820 Academy dinner and it is quite likely that they discussed the problems of sky painting as it was on both their minds. Perhaps there is a small chance that Turner did mention to Constable his sky sketchbook and that this may have sown a seed in Constable's mind which contributed to the beginning of his sky studies in October 1820.

One of the most impressive of Turner's skies to my mind is that in the watercolour *Coventry,* painted c. 1832 (Plate 86). It represents powerfully and dramatically the back end of the passage of a cold front across the city, with heavy rain to the south east and clearing skies from the north west with the sunlight bursting through. Such a scene is based on Turner's fantastic visual memory rather than on any understanding of meteorology. Typically if Constable had painted a similar scene it would have had a totally different sky, more like *The Hay Wain*; but Constable too produced more impressionistic skies, such as in the beautifully expressive *Seascape Study with Rain Clouds* (Plate 44) which symbolises the hydrological cycle in one canvas.

Turner's vivid sunsets are one of his many trademarks, and Seibold has shown how the effect of volcanic dust from volcanic eruptions such as the Mt Tambora eruption in 1815 probably heightened the sunset colours at the time.[74] If an eruption is sufficiently powerful, material can penetrate the stratosphere and move very quickly around the globe. The residence time in the stratosphere can be several years before eventually settling out. The first half of the nineteenth century was a period of considerable volcanic activity, particularly after about 1808 (see Chapter 1, Table 5). Notable colourful sunrises and sunsets were recorded regularly by Luke Howard in London. Seibold shows how the vivid sunset in Turner's *Petworth Park: Tillington Church in the Distance* (1828) is indicative of volcanic dust in the stratosphere. She also points out that the sun should be below the horizon to give the observed effect and puts this down to Turner's frequent use of artistic licence. Turner was an astute observer of atmospheric effects but he was not afraid to exaggerate or stylise them in his paintings in order to increase the visual impact.

The skies of other artists painting at the same time as Constable, who exhibited at the beginning of the nineteenth century, will not be discussed here as it is unlikely that any of them influenced Constable's skies to any great extent; rather the reverse. Ruskin's statement in 1856 that 'if a general and characteristic name were needed for modern landscape art, none better could be invented than "the service of clouds"',[75] implies that skies began to dominate landscapes. The likely reasons for this include the impact of Luke Howard's cloud classification on art and science in general in the first half of the nineteenth century, and the obsession of many of the romantic poets[76] with the sky, as well as the importance of the skies in Turner's and Constable's paintings. The skies of David Cox (1783–1859), for example *Sun, Wind and Rain* (1845) and *Crossing the Sands* (1848), exhibit the freshness of Constable's skies. Other landscape artists, such as Bonington (1802–28), Palmer (1805–81), De Wint (1784–1849) and Delacroix (1798–1863), produced impressive skies that may have been influenced by Constable.

4.6 Johan Christian Dahl (1788–1857) and the Dresden School

Dahl, a contemporary of Constable, was the first Norwegian landscape painter to achieve international renown, although he spent much of his working life in Dresden. He was a friend of Caspar David Friedrich (1774–1840), himself an interesting interpreter of skies. Both Dahl and Constable insisted on studying nature directly and both produced remarkable outdoor studies which have become as popular as their finished works. Although there is no evidence that Dahl and Constable knew of each other's work it is remarkable that Dahl produced a series of sky studies at about the same time that Constable produced his. Badt argues that this coincidence must have been sparked by Luke Howard's cloud classification.[77] Dahl was aware of the very different skies he encountered in the many countries he painted in. The rainy climate and mountain-ridden skies of Norway, the tall skies of the flat countryside of Denmark, the continental skies of Dresden in Germany, and the misty, hot skies of Naples in Italy were used by Dahl to identify the geography of his scenes. Bang, in her study of the life and works of Dahl, suggests that it is likely that Carus introduced Dahl to Luke Howard's cloud classification in the 1820s.[78] She does not think, however, that Dahl was interested in the scientific explanation of clouds:

> *Dahl's interest in clouds and weather was primarily the consequence of his wish to give a thorough characterization of a given region.... His feeling that grey weather was more characteristic of Norway than sunny, warm tones had therefore little to do with Howard's system of clouds ... he could change the actual shape of clouds observed in order to heighten the pictorial expression. In this he followed the tradition of Claude and Valenciennes and came close to the strict formal accentuation of clouds found in Friedrich's works.... Dahl's cloud studies were not the result of an interest in the natural*

sciences. They were, like all his nature studies, the result of his painterly delight and response to visual stimuli.

Certainly Dahl's cloud studies lack the realism of Constable's skies. There are eleven of Dahl's pure sky studies in the Gothenburg Museum of Art that were painted in oil at some time in the 1820s. They have been compared with Constable's sky studies, but none of them suggest movement or possess any dynamic quality. They are beautiful studies of light and colour but they do no more than confirm Bang's statements above (see Plate 87).

The fascinating debate opened by Badt considers the influence of Howard on Goethe, the poet and philosopher, and Carus in Germany, who then tried to influence Dahl, Friedrich and other Dresden landscape painters. It is interesting that Howard's remarkable influence on Goethe did not in fact manifest itself in the works of the Dresden artists. Friedrich turned down Goethe's request for him to paint a series of cloud studies to illustrate Goethe's treatise on Howard's cloud classification 'replying that to force the free and airy clouds into a rigid order and classification would for him signify the overthrow of landscape art'.[79]

If Constable had seen the skies of the Dresden artists, he would probably have admired them but it is unlikely that he would have learned anything from them.

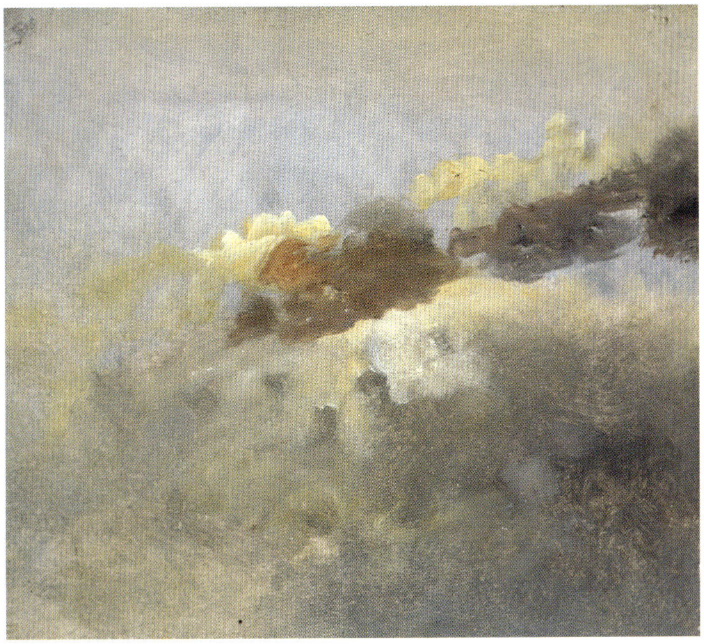

Plate 87 Johan Christian Dahl, *Cloud Study*. Göteborgs Konstmuseum, Göteborg. Photo: Ebbe Carlsson

4.7 Landscape painting, artistic style, science and skies

When the Royal Academy was founded in 1768, landscape painting was considered to be a minor branch of the art of painting. Indeed, at that time, when history painting was at the top of the scale, landscape painting was firmly at the bottom. This is not to say that landscape painting was ignored; there was considerable respect for the idealised landscapes of the old masters such as Claude, the Poussins, and the Dutch and Flemish seventeenth-century artists. Indeed there were also hierarchies within landscape painting, such that 'historic' or 'ideal' landscapes were at the top and 'realistic' or 'topographic' landscapes were at the bottom.

By the turn of the century this situation had altered little and Constable's attempts to paint real English landscapes impressed few in the art world at the time; artists and art critics alike shared this same perception of the artistic hierarchy. It is never easy to classify a landscape artist or painting into an artistic style. Terms to define styles of landscape painting developed over time and attempted to describe the feel of a landscape painting and explain the symbolism of the figures portrayed within the landscape. Terms such as 'the Picturesque', 'the Sublime', 'Romanticism', 'Naturalism', 'Realism', 'Topographic', 'the Ideal', 'Historic', 'Phenomenalism' have all been applied to landscape art produced before or during Constable's time.

It is even harder to apply these terms to the sky. What is an 'Ideal' sky, or an 'Historic' sky? Can we imagine a grand distant thunderstorm that could be called picturesque, or can we call a lashing gale at sea sublime? The cloud studies of Luke Howard are certainly topographic and the portrayal of thunderstorms in scenes of the crucifixion could be called historic. Are Constable's skies 'picturesque', as Fuseli said?'[80]

I shall not enter this debate as to how best to describe Constable's work and skies other than to note that it is difficult to comprehend how artists could use their imagination to invent skies in the same way as they invented landscapes. However, most of these artistic styles, apart perhaps from 'topographic' and 'realist', required the artist to use his or her imagination to compose the sky. Hence most artists created 'ideal' clouds to suit the composition, and were not worried about whether the sky looked realistic as long as it was not obtrusive. Certainly even Constable would never have considered submitting a skyscape as a finished work, and he regarded his Hampstead studies as experiments for his own use. Today Constable's sky studies hang alongside his finished works and are regarded as just as important by most art historians. This transformation of attitudes did not happen quickly but came with, amongst other things, the gradual acceptance of new movements in art such as Impressionism. At the beginning of the twentieth century, the definition of a finished work evaporated and art became free from the shackles of convention.

Constable succeeded in turning landscape art quite literally on its head, although full recognition of his achievements came well after his death. Instead of the landscape dominating the picture, as it had for virtually all artists before him, he made the sky 'the keynote, the standard of scale and the chief organ of sentiment'. Constable strove to provide a scientifically accurate harmony between the sky and the landscape, which he achieved for the first time in *The Hay Wain* in 1821. To accomplish this he turned to nature rather than to the skies of other artists. His sky studies of 1820–22 were his experiments and the finished works during and after this time were the products.

> *The importance of the sky-studies of the early 19th century is the new freedom of expression, a freedom which was based on a more or less total knowledge of the subject-matter. Study and almost scientific observation of the physical phenomena of motion and light result in a deep understanding of atmospheric phenomena. With this knowledge and understanding the artist is in a position to create more freely, to summarise and to extract. 'La vérité', the truthfulness, is not related to the object any more but to the motivating powers. As a result of this 'the spectator might remark: "How absolutely true to type, how well I know this kind of troubled sky" – a replica of which in nature he has never seen at all'*[81]

Gradually at the beginning of the nineteenth century landscape painting began to gain acceptance:

> *Early in the nineteenth century it was recognised that the status of landscape painting was changing. This change happened quickly. The fabulous successes of Turner took place only thirty years after the failure of Wilson; and in the course of the century landscapes which at least purported to be close imitations of nature, came to hold a more secure place in popular affection than any other form of art. A peaceful scene, with water in the foreground reflecting a luminous sky and set off by dark trees, was something which everyone agreed was beautiful, just as, in previous ages, they had agreed about a naked athlete or a saint with hands crossed on her bosom.*[82]

This revolution in artistic taste was championed by Constable, though like many revolutionaries his genius was not recognised until well after his death. It is no coincidence that this move towards naturalism/realism took place at a time when scientific method was busy classifying nature. Wordsworth and other romantic poets such as Shelley used science to help explain or express their feelings about nature. Classification concerned itself with minute detail and botanists were finding their science, just as Constable was finding his art, under every hedge. Similarly Howard found reward in naming every common cloud in the sky. This was an exciting time for discovery in both art and science and the interplay between them was strong. It was still expected that a gentleman should be educated in both the arts and the sciences, and it was typical for individuals like Goethe, Howard and Ruskin to write and publish scientific papers as well as poetry and prose. Indeed Erasmus Darwin, the grandfather of Charles Darwin, wrote up some of his scientific work in the form of poems. To give a flavour of the contemporary understanding of meteorology and its importance as a science and for art, the meteorological writings of John Ruskin (1819–1900) and Luke Howard (1772–1864) will now be examined.

Luke Howard was a contemporary of Constable's, but Ruskin was only eighteen when Constable died in 1837. Nevertheless by that time Ruskin had already written an unpublished article in defence of Turner, following a critical review in *Blackwood's Magazine* in 1836. Ruskin's first edition of *Modern Painters* was published in 1843 when he was just twenty-four years old. His knowledge of landscape art in the first half of the nineteenth century was at least as great as that of any other of his time. I make no apologies therefore for quoting several passages from Ruskin, although he often criticised Constable as we shall see.

In Chapter 1 we noted that Ruskin described 'modern' landscape art as being 'for the service of clouds'.[83] *Modern Painters*, published in five volumes over seventeen years, was originally written in defence of Turner's landscapes, but also shows emphatically that Ruskin recognised the importance of the sky in landscape painting. He wrote in 1856, when discussing 'modern' landscape art,

> *We turn our eyes, therefore, as boldly and as quickly as may be, from these serene fields and skies of medieval art, to the most characteristic examples of modern landscape. And, I believe, the first thing that will strike us ... is their cloudiness.*
>
> *Out of perfect light and motionless air, we find ourselves on a sudden brought under sombre skies, and into drifting wind; and, with fickle sunbeams flashing in our face, or utterly drenched with a sweep of rain, we are reduced to track the changes of the shadows on the grass, or watch the rents of twilight through angry cloud.*[84]

Ruskin was not particularly pleased with this development and agreed with Aristophanes, who called clouds 'great goddesses to idle men', for the deep shadows created by clouds sometimes enabled artists to avoid having to draw or paint details.[85] Nevertheless Ruskin used Howard's cloud classification extensively in his criticisms of landscape paintings, although his understanding of contemporary meteorological theories was far from complete.[86]

In the first half of the nineteenth century both art and science became preoccupied with clouds. The romantic poets wrote about them, artists painted them, and scientists observed them and tried to understand them. Compared to other sciences such as botany, biology, chemistry, geology and physics, meteorology was a late developer, mainly because of the difficulties of measuring the atmosphere above the earth's surface. Hence some romantics turned to clouds as symbols of change and unaccountableness in a world of increasing scientific order; others like Shelley and Constable used Howard's classification as a paradigm to test. The famous debate between Keats and Wordsworth as to whether or not science was the enemy of poetry and destroyed the wonder of nature was typical of a resistance to science that has always been present.

David Knight discusses the relationships between romanticism and the sciences at the turn of the nineteenth century and concludes that there was as much overlap between them as there was distance. Biographies of famous scientists of that era such as Humphry Davy (1778–1829), Michael Faraday (1791–1867) and Alexander von Humboldt (1769–1859) would not be complete without reference to their involvement with the romantic movement. Similarly the works of artists such as Goethe (1749–1832), Coleridge (1772–1834), Shelley (1792–1822), Turner (1775–1851) and Constable (1776–1837) cannot be discussed without reference to contemporary science. Charlotte Klonk refers to this period as a brief moment of balance before the concerns of science and art diverged.[87]

By 1800 the distinction between the arts and the sciences was certainly blurred. One difference was that scientists relied upon reason for explanation whereas artists relied upon more practical skills developed through habit and 'rule of thumb' and handed down. Using this distinction meteorology was both an art and a science at this time. On the one hand complicated theories had been developed to try to explain the behaviour of the atmosphere, but on the other hand weather forecasting still depended upon weather 'lore' such as 'red sky at night, shepherds' delight'. The complicated theories were often not based upon observation, but rather upon supposition. As Knowles Middleton observes:

> *By the year 1800, our subject [theories of rain] was in a peculiarly unsatisfactory condition. Most of the ideas that have since proved fruitful, such as the formation of ascending currents and the cooling of air by ascent, had been almost forgotten; and ideas with little or no future had taken their place.... The eighteenth-century habit of system-building ... was only just beginning to be replaced by an appropriate humility in the face of experimental data – or the lack of them.*[88]

Indeed it was still possible, by careful observation, to contribute to the advancement of meteorology without any formal training in the subject, especially as many of the so-called experts were wrong. Hence the contributions of Luke Howard, who knew more about Latin than meteorology, have been much more influential than the work of De Luc (1727–1817), who was the foremost atmospheric scientist of his day. Equally the observations of artists such as Turner and Constable have to be taken as seriously as those of contemporary scientists and meteorologists.

The so-called 'Age of Enlightenment' after the Middle Ages produced meteorological instruments such as thermometers and barometers, and, indeed, it was very fashionable for country gentlemen to make observations concerning temperature and precipitation in their diaries; but there was very little co-ordination of results or linking of theories as to how pressure, temperature, rainfall and clouds might be related. Howard's classification of clouds, first published in 1803, was a revelation – bringing order and understanding to a hitherto confused science. However it was no more than a classification – it did not explain the formation of clouds or precipitation. Clouds and rain were still 'unaccountable' until well into the twentieth century.

Although Howard's lasting influence is undoubtedly upon meteorology[89] his influence on art was equally great in the first half of the nineteenth century, not just in Britain but across the rest of Europe and North America as well.[90] Goethe wrote his poem 'To the Honoured Memory of Howard' in 1820:

> *To find yourself in the Infinite,*
> *You must distinguish and then combine;*
> *Therefore my winged song thanks*
> *The man who distinguished cloud from cloud.*[91]

4.8 Meteorological science through the eyes of Luke Howard

The best account of Howard's life was written by Howard himself, in a brief autobiographical letter requested by Goethe. It is surprising that a copy of the letter has survived but it reveals that Howard was born in London in 1772 (just four years before

Constable), which means that he lived to the ripe old age of ninety-two. His father, Robert Howard, was a successful manufacturer of iron and tin goods, and accumulated considerable wealth. Howard was brought up as a Quaker, and went to school near Oxford. He recollected in the letter: 'For myself ... I learned more Latin than I have ever since ... been able to unlearn, but in mathematics I was so neglected that ... I have never succeeded in making my way in them.'[92] At fifteen he became an apprentice chemist, a profession he became successful in, eventually setting up several companies with friends. His ideas for the names of clouds had first stirred as a schoolboy but it was not until he was in his late twenties that he actually wrote the *Essay on the Modification of Clouds* which was first published in 1803.[93] In his letter to Goethe he writes:

> *My friend William Allen and myself belonged to a select philosophical society which met together in London every fortnight during the winter; every member was obliged in turn to produce an essay for examination, or pay a fine. In consequence of this obligation, I found myself induced to lay before the society, among other smaller original papers, The Essay on The Clouds.*[94]

The essay was published in parts in *Tilloch's Philosophical Magazine* – the editor of which was also a member of the Askesian Society. Howard's first scientific paper on pollen analysis had been published in 1800 in the Transactions of the London Linnean Society, so he was well aware of the Linnean classification of plants. The cloud classification was, it seems, an immediate success and, together with his other meteorological writings, led to his election as a Fellow of the Royal Society in 1821.

An attempt by the French scientist Lamarck to classify clouds was published in 1802 and is shown in Table 17. The classification was published in French and relates mostly to cloud shapes, but even the French appear to have ignored it.

Table 17
Lamarck's cloud classification

List of cloud types	*Rough translation*
1 brumeux	thick fog, haze or mist
2 en voile	overcast
3 en lambeaux	shreds of clouds
4 boursouflés	puffs of cloud
5 en barres	bars of clouds
6 en balayures	thin bars of cloud
7 pommelés	dappled with small clouds
8 attroupés	flocks of clouds
9 coureurs	running clouds
10 groupés	group of clouds
11 de tonnerre	thunder clouds

Howard has been called 'the father of meteorology' because his comprehensive scientific daily recordings of weather in the London area from 1801 to 1841, and his prolific meteorological writings, transformed the science of meteorology. However, although Howard's cloud classification has largely survived to the modern day, his other theories have not. For instance, as Knowles Middleton comments in his book *A History of the Theories of Rain*, 'Luke Howard deserves and receives our lasting gratitude for producing the first useful classification of cloud-forms, but he was not competent enough in the exact sciences to make any notable contribution to the theory of rain.'[96]

In his book *The Climate of London* published in 1818[97] Howard recognised for the first time that cities alter the local climate. In *Seven Lectures on Meteorology* published in 1837 (the year Constable died) he attempted to summarise the state of meteorological theory as it then was. In the preface he gives his reason for writing the lectures as being 'to present in a familiar and intelligible way the facts and principles of this art and study [meteorology]; now becoming also a science'.[98] The contents of each lecture were as follows:

Lecture First	Constitution and properties of the Atmosphere.
Second	Constant and variable winds, climates and seasons.

Third	Cycles of temperature; increase and decrease of the heat through the seasons; mean and extreme temperatures of the years, months, and climate.
Fourth	The Barometer, its principle, construction and variations; relation of these to the weather and seasons; Evaporation and the Hygrometer; Rain, and its proportions in different seasons, etc.
Fifth	The Clouds: their varieties or modifications of form and structure; the manner of their production, suspension, and resolution into invisible vapour, or descent in rain, snow, or hail: Thunderstorms and their effects: Whirlwinds, Water-Spouts.
Sixth	Electricity of the Atmosphere, and of clouds – especially of the Rain-Cloud: sparks from showers: corposants; manner of the formation of rain, hail and snow – the avalanche – dew and hoar-frost: the iris, corona, halo: the anthelion, parhelion, paraselene: the Rainbow and Meteorological Glory.
Seventh	Colour of the sky, Cyanometer: Night, twilight, daylight: shooting stars and fiery meteors; Meteorolites or stars falling through the air: Refraction by the air, its curious effects: Ignis fatuus, so called; Aurora borealis: conclusion of the course.

He systematically goes through all the atmospheric phenomena, much as Aristotle had done before him. His analysis is, for the most part, descriptive, but he does attempt to explain processes according to accepted theories where he can. For instance his explanations of condensation and evaporation take account of the law of partial pressures proposed by his lifelong friend John Dalton, but he does not close the door on the chemists' view that water was held in solution by the atmosphere. At the end of the first chapter he contemplates what life would be like without an atmosphere: 'No refreshing breezes, no blue skies alternating with kindly showers, no waving branches and rustling leaves: none of the beauty and variety of summer clouds, no rainbow, no rain!'

Meteorological science was very much in its infancy, as Howard implies. The laws of physics and chemistry had yet to be applied in full to the atmosphere. It was not until nearly 100 years later that physico-mathematical models were developed to explain the workings of the atmosphere and the formation of precipitation. For instance the theory of rain proposed by the celebrated Scottish geologist James Hutton in 1784 (the Huttonian Theory) was purely qualitative and completely wrong but was still published in the *Encyclopaedia Britannica* as late as 1824.[99] Howard demolished the theory in the second edition of *The Climate of London* published in 1833.[100] However he was not able to suggest a better theory, most of his comments on the formation of rain relating to the electrification of clouds, which is very much a secondary factor.

Howard's cloud classification had a tremendous influence on the arts as well as upon the science of meteorology. Goethe had been a keen observer of the atmosphere all his life. Howard's classification, which appeared when Goethe was seventy-three, moved him sufficiently to write a series of poems in gratitude to him:

But Howard gives us with his clear mind
The gain of lessons new to all mankind;
That which no hand can reach, no hand can
clasp
He first has gained, first held with mental grasp.
Defined the doubtful, fix'd its limit-line,
And named it fitly. – Be the honour thine!
As clouds ascend, are folded, scatter, fall,
Let the world think of thee who taught it all.[101]

Later Goethe wrote of himself in his diary:

Disciple of Howard, strangely
You look around and above you every morning
To see whether the mist falls or rises
And what clouds are showing.[102]

Howard also inspired Shelley's poem 'The Cloud' which systematically describes each of Howard's cloud types:[103]

NIMBUS	I wield the flail of the lashing hail, And whiten the green plains under, And then again I dissolve it in rain And laugh as I pass in thunder.
CUMULUS	I bear light shade for the leaves when laid In their noon-day dreams
STRATUS	From my wings are shaken the dews that waken The sweet buds every one.
CIRRUS	That orbed maiden with white fire laden, Whom mortals call the moon, Glides glimmering o'er my fleece like floor By the midnight breezes strewn
CIRROCUMULUS	When I widen the vent in my wind built tent Till the calm rivers, lakes and seas Like strips of the sky fallen through me on high Are each paved with the moon and these.
CIRROSTRATUS	I bind the sun's throne with a burning zone And the moon's with a girdle of pearl

The only cloud type that Shelley does not describe is cumulostratus, which is interesting in that is the only cloud type defined by Howard that has not survived.

It is clear then that Howard's cloud classification had a remarkable effect on both the arts and the sciences in the first half of the nineteenth century, not just in the United Kingdom, but across the civilised world. It is no surprise to find therefore that John Constable was also perhaps influenced and inspired by Howard's classification. Both of them moved to London to pursue their chosen careers but there is no evidence of them knowing each other personally, although that does not rule out such an acquaintance. The Royal Society and The Royal Academy of Arts were located next to each at Somerset House and it is therefore possible that they might have met there at some time.

Howard has left a remarkable series of cloud studies, some of which were used by him to illustrate the different cloud types. Plate 4 shows sketches of stratus, cumulus and cirrus. Howard was modest about the quality and usefulness of the sketches that accompanied the *Essay on the Modification of Clouds*. In reproducing this essay, without the prints, in the second edition of *The Climate of London* in 1833 he wrote:

> *In my first publication on clouds, I was induced by a supposed necessity arising from the novelty of the subject to add to the definitions a set of plates, of the several modifications. I have now decided to omit these representations: being satisfied, both by reflection and experience, that the real student will acquire his knowledge in a more solid manner, by observation of nature, without the aid of drawings, and that the more superficial are liable to be led into error by them.*[104]

However another set of prints accompanied the 1837 *Seven Lectures in Meteorology*, some of which are reproduced in Day and Ludlam's 1972 publication, 'Luke Howard and his clouds: a contribution to the early history of cloud physics'.[105] There is a collection of fifty-one of Howard's drawings, mainly in pencil and wash, which were bequeathed to the Royal Meteorological Society and which are held by the Science Museum.

4.9 John Ruskin and the role of skies in landscape painting

As the most influential art criticism of the nineteenth century, Ruskin's writings represent a fascinating yardstick against which to judge Constable's skies. Yet Ruskin's writings are full of inconsistencies. On the one hand he wanted to develop an objective, scientific, visible framework for examining and comparing paintings, but on the other hand he believed that form was more important than process, and that the moral meaning of a work of art was overwhelmingly more important than its scientific truth.[106]

Badt recognises that in championing Turner, Ruskin's position 'was a queer contradiction':

> *Ruskin tried with all the means at his disposal to establish the 'Truth' and the fidelity to nature in Turner's works and to praise these qualities as their special value. It is obvious that this attempt inevitably led him into great difficulties about the idea of truth in art. He had undertaken to prove too much – Turner's landscapes do not correspond of course in any way to those conceptions of nature which were generally felt to be 'true' conceptions. For, whatever element of reality was in fact contained in these pictures, they did not exist originally in the sphere of truth at all, as truth was already coming to be understood at that time. That is to say, the pictures were not subject to the principles of objectivity, normality and the typical.*
>
> *What Ruskin was looking for (or imagining that he had discovered) in Turner was in fact achieved, unnoticed by him, in another current of the Romantic Revival. Other poets and painters were attempting, by methods quite different from those of Turner and from a different intellectual angle, to be truthful in art, i.e. to bring their own feelings to terms with the scientifically verifiable conceptions of nature and reality, to check the validity of their own purely subjective feelings by bringing them into line with general experience and to extend their intuitive abilities by testing them against the results of scientific research.*[107]

Certainly the paintings of John Constable and the cloud poems of Shelley were scientifically constructed and can be regarded as forms of experimental science. Badt concludes that Howard's cloud classification provided the results of scientific research, a paradigm for Constable and Shelley to experiment with. Classification is only the first stage in the development of a science – the qualitative inventory stage. Ruskin's science rarely gets beyond this stage: there are few attempts to correlate his findings statistically, and his attempts at scientific explanation are usually wrong or confused. Nevertheless Ruskin's powerful vision of the sky, as expressed in his writings and drawings throughout his life, are unique. His attempts to assess the 'truth' of skies and clouds in landscape painting are biased by his own cantankerous views and yet they still provide many fascinating insights into nineteenth-century art criticism. In *Modern Painters* Ruskin presented the most comprehensive review of the atmosphere in landscape painting ever written. There are still many lessons to be learned from his writings on the atmosphere today. For instance he believed that 'every class of rock, earth, and cloud, must be known by the painter, with geologic and meteorologic accuracy'.[108] He continues in a footnote:

> *Is not this, it may be asked, demanding more from him than life can accomplish? Not one whit. Nothing more than knowledge of external characteristics is absolutely required; and even if, which were more desirable, thorough scientific knowledge had to be attained, the time which our artists spend in multiplying crude sketches, or finishing their unintelligent embryos of the study, would render them masters of every science that modern investigations have organised, and familiar with every form that nature manifests.*

The level of understanding, according to Ruskin, required by the art critic to assess the sky of a landscape painting was described at the beginning of Chapter 1.

Ruskin attempted to assess landscape art by looking at the number of great ideas that a painting conveys; the greatest art being that which conveys the largest number of great ideas to the spectator, and the greatest artist the one who conveys the most great ideas in the sum of his paintings. The five ideas of 'Power, Imitation, Truth, Beauty and Relation' present a very useful and comprehensive framework which, although Ruskin often abused it in favour of his hero Turner, has not been surpassed. To illustrate what Ruskin meant by these five ideas let us consider in more detail than in Chapter 1 how he would assess a landscape painting using this scheme.

By 'power' Ruskin means a measure of excellence; the finish, the style, the dexterity of the artist's touch, the depth, the colour, the tone etc. must be of the highest quality. By 'imitation' he is referring to the faithfulness of the painted objects to the original. This of course requires trickery of the eye and brain; to create for the spectator the pleasurable illusion that what is in the picture is real, it is not paint on canvas, or chalk on paper. Whereas 'imitation' refers to the material constituents of the picture, 'truth' refers to the faithfulness of the imitation to nature. A tree may look realistic in a painting, and be a perfect imitation of a tree, but only if it is identifiable as an oak tree or an elm can it be said to represent 'truth'. Similarly with clouds, the clouds must be identifiable if they are to represent 'truth'. Ruskin also emphasises that there is a moral 'truth' as well as a material 'truth'. He sees clouds as symbolising nourishing rain for the rivers and crops, or damaging storms, or the resting place of imaginary gods. This 'truth' is much more value-laden than scientific truth and therefore potentially very restricting. This does perhaps go some way towards explaining Ruskin's disdain for Constable's landscapes which were painted to represent nature as well as to symbolise it. The idea of 'beauty' was also a moral one for Ruskin; beauty was not in the eye of the beholder for him. At the time of writing *Modern Painters I* he was deeply religious and saw the landscape as the handiwork of God. He saw beauty as something that could not be explained by intellect, and that everything in nature had beauty, if it had not been spoiled by man. Finally, the idea of 'relation' was meant by Ruskin to represent the intellectual challenge of the painting – the success of the artist in putting across a powerful intellectual message. Great art can summarise the mood of a nation or inspire great thoughts in the beholder or challenge the intellect to unravel its meaning.

Ruskin's new paradigm for the assessment of art was an immediate success. Like all new paradigms it challenged old beliefs whilst retaining a core of good practice. It provided a new set of intellectual tools to enable an analysis of 'modern' art and it also provided a new set of terminology for art critics to use. Ruskin became world famous as an art critic and was appointed the first Slade Professor of Fine Art at Oxford in 1869. Ruskin's paradigm had no room for Constable's 'unfinished' rural landscapes, often painted for their own sake. It was not until the Impressionists turned art criticism upside down towards the end of the nineteenth century that Constable's art was widely acclaimed.

Nevertheless it is useful to examine Ruskin's writings on the sky in order to assess the contemporary atmospheric issues that Ruskin thought worthy to discuss in reviewing landscape art; for example:

> *With them (the old masters), cloud is cloud, and blue is blue, and no kind of connection between them is ever hinted at. The sky is thought of as a clear, high, material dome, the clouds as separate bodies suspended beneath it; and in consequence, however delicate in tone their skies may be, you always look at them, not through them .....If you look intensely at the pure blue of a serene sky, you will see that there is a variety and fulness in every repose. It is not flat dead colour, but a deep, quivering, transparent body of penetrable air, in which you trace or imagine short falling spots of deceiving light, and dim shades, faint veiled vestiges of dark vapour ... whereas, with all the old landscape painters except Claude, you may indeed go a long way before you come to the sky, but you will strike hard against it at last.*[109]

Naturally Turner's skies are praised at length by Ruskin. 'His blue is never laid on in smooth coats, but in breaking, mingling, melting hues, a quarter of an inch of which, cut off from all the rest of the picture, is still *spacious*, still infinite and immeasurable in depth.'[110] Indeed Turner's skies are impressive in the way that they blend together the sky and the atmosphere. For Turner the atmosphere was never invisible, he always gave it depth and space as Ruskin asserts. Constable's skies are different in emphasis to Turner's. Essentially

Constable's skies are very British, with low and medium level clouds, freshness and breeze. Rarely is the atmosphere itself visible in Constable's paintings. Turner's skies, on the other hand, are often all atmosphere – a stormy mixture of sky, cloud and wind that are difficult to untangle. Constable's skies are much more recognisable and typical.[111]

In *Modern Painters V*, in the chapter entitled 'The Cloud-Flocks', Ruskin makes the only attempt I have ever seen published, even to this day, to illustrate cloud perspective.[112] The 'Cloud-Flocks' are the clouds of Ruskin's upper region defined in *Modern Painters I.* His power of observation is illustrated by an occasion one winter morning when he recorded approximately 50 000 separate cloud segments (probably altocumulus) arranged in ranks across the sky. His attempts at drawing up a set of rules for cloud perspective did not please him. Indeed, when later in life he was proposing to use this chapter for the second part of *Coeli Enarrant*,[113] he was going to withdraw the perspective section because he had 'never heard any one express the slightest interest, or intimate that they had put them to any use'.[114]

Damisch criticises Ruskin's analysis of perspective in that it failed to break away from conventional pictorial perspective, but rather forces nature to submit to it.[115] Figures 19 and 20 represent an increasing complexity of perspective from the point of a single observer standing at ground level, and fitted into a rectangle – the conventional frame shape for a picture. Nevertheless because of their unique nature it is worth quoting some extracts from Ruskin's description of these diagrams. First he discusses Figure 19 which represents rectilinear perspective:

> *In order to simplify it, let us assume that the under surfaces of clouds are flat, and lie in a horizontal extended field. This is in great measure the fact, and notable perspective phenomena depend on the approximation of clouds to such a condition … the three figures represent limiting lines of sky perspective, as they would appear over a large space of sky. Supposing that the breadth included was one-fourth of the horizon, the shaded portions of the central figure represent square fields of cloud, and those in the upper-most figure narrow triangles, with their shortest side next us, but sloping a little away from us.*
>
> *In each figure, the shaded portions show the perspective limits of cloud-masses, which, in reality, are arranged in perfectly straight lines, are all similar, and are all equidistant from each other … confusion in aspect is induced by the*

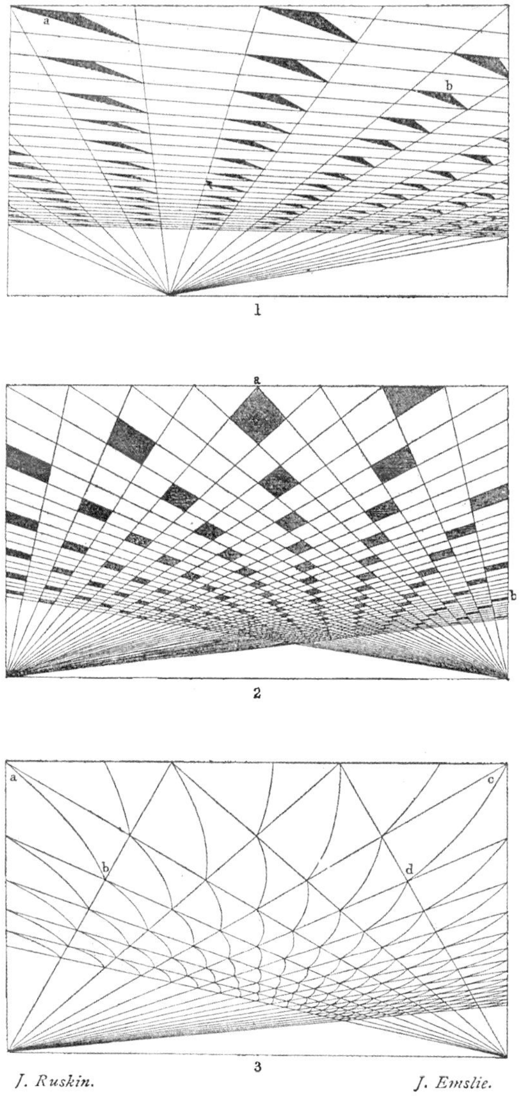

PLATE LXIV.

CLOUD PERSPECTIVE (RECTILINEAR).

Figure 19 Ruskin's rectilinear cloud perspective

apparent change caused by perspective in the direction of the wind. If Fig.3 [the lower diagram of Figure 19] be supposed to include a quarter of the horizon, the spaces, into which its straight lines divide it, represent squares of sky. The curved lines, which cross these spaces from corner to corner, are precisely parallel throughout; and, therefore, two clouds moving, one on the curved line from 'a' to 'b', and the other on the other side, from 'c' to 'd', would in reality, be moving with the same wind in parallel lines.[116]

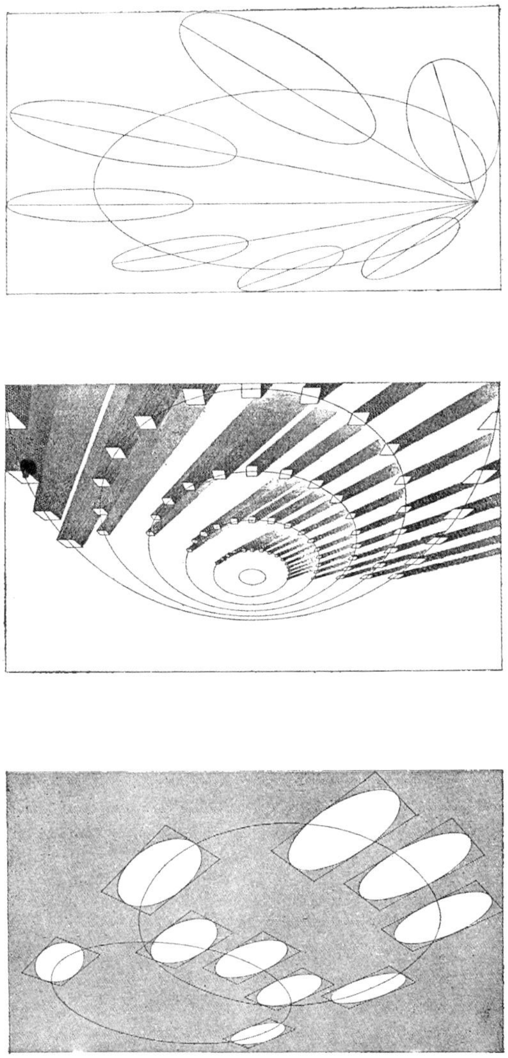

J. Ruskin. *J. Emslie.*

PLATE LXV.

CLOUD PERSPECTIVE (CURVILINEAR).

Figure 20 Ruskin's curvilinear cloud perspective

As discussed in Chapter 1, rectilinear perspective is not really appropriate for skies, and, coupled with the rigid assumptions made by Ruskin, such perspective drawings are limited in value, but could certainly be used to help paint lanes or streets of cumulus clouds. They do however provide a valuable insight into the difficulties of cloud perspective. Ruskin recognises this and continues:

> *Sky perspective, however, remains perfectly simple, so long as it can be reduced to any rectilinear arrangement; but when nearly the whole system is curved, which nine times out of ten is the case, it becomes embarrassing. [Figure 20 middle diagram] represents the simplest possible combination of perspective of straight lines with that of curves, a group of concentric circles of small clouds being supposed to cast shadows from the sun near the horizon.... And in these Figures [Figure 20], which, if we look up the subject rightly, would be but the first and simplest of the series necessary to illustrate the action of the upper cirri, the reader may see, at once, how necessarily painters, untrained in observance of proportion, and ignorant of perspective, must lose in every touch the expression of buoyancy and space in sky. The absolute forms of each cloud are, indeed, not alike, as the ellipses in the engraving; but assuredly, when moving in groups of this kind, there are among them the same proportioned inequalities of relative distance, the same gradated changes from ponderous to elongated form, the same exquisite suggestions of including curve; and a common painter, dotting his clouds down at random, or in more or less equal masses, can no more paint a sky, than he could, by random dashes for its ruined arches, paint the Coliseum.*

Ruskin's thoughts on the colours of the sky and cloud perspective give a fascinating view of the limited amount of meteorology that had permeated art criticism in the nineteenth century. When one considers that Ruskin went far beyond any other art critic of his time in his discussion of skies we can appreciate that the preoccupation of landscape art with clouds in the early part of the nineteenth century was not driven by art criticism but by inspiration on two fronts – those who saw clouds as the last bastion of unaccountableness, and those who were experimenting with the new paradigm presented by Luke Howard.

Thus the sky and studies of the sky inspired both artists and scientists in the first half of the nineteenth century. Indeed this was the golden period as far as the importance of skies in landscape painting is concerned. Meteorology as a science was still in its infancy, describing weather phenomena successfully but explaining them unsuccessfully. Most meteorological phenomena were still a mystery, although simple descriptive physics was able to explain straightforward things like the formation of cumulus clouds and rainbows. Howard's cloud classification was a crucial catalyst for both art and science, showing that the seemingly infinite variety of cloud form could be grasped by those who chose to study it. Just like Newton's explanation of the rainbow, it empowered a giant leap forward for art and science.

Notes

1 C. R. Leslie, *Memoirs of the Life of John Constable*, 2nd edn (London: Longman's, Brown, Green and Longman's, 1845), p. 238.
2 Ibid., p. 307.
3 Ibid., p. 320.
4 K. Badt, *John Constable's Clouds* (London: Routledge & Kegan Paul, 1950).
5 L. Hawes, 'Constable's sky sketches', *Journal of the Warburg and Courtauld Institutes* XXXII (1969): 344–65.
6 This is a translation of the sleeve notes from H. Damisch, *Théorie du Nuage: pour une histoire de la peinture* (Paris: Editions du Seuil, 1972).
7 S. D. Gedzelman, 'Cloud classification before Luke Howard', *Bulletin of the American Meteorological Society* 70(4) (1989): 381–95.
8 Ibid. p. 383. Also it must be noted that in the Middle Ages blue was a very expensive pigment and was mostly reserved for the Virgin's cloak.
9 Leonardo da Vinci, *A Treatise on Painting* (English translation) (London, 1721).
10 K. Clark, *Landscape into Art* (London: John Murray, 1976), p. 93.
11 I. Fleming-Williams, *Constable and His Drawings* (London: Philip Wilson, 1990), p. 119.
12 Quoted in ibid., p. 281.
13 Leslie, *Memoirs of the Life of John Constable* 1845, p. 323.
14 Gedzelman, 'Cloud classification before Luke Howard', p. 389.
15 Leslie, *Memoirs of the Life of John Constable* 1845, p. 257.
16 H. H. Lamb, 'Britain's changing climate', *Geographical Journal* 133 (1967): 445–66.
17 W. J. Burroughs, 'Winter landscapes and climatic change', *Weather* 36 (1981): 352–7.
18 Clark, *Landscape into Art*, p. 56.
19 Ibid., p. 61.
20 Leslie, *Memoirs of the Life of John Constable* 1845, p. 346.
21 Ibid., p. 329.
22 Gedzelman, 'Cloud classification before Luke Howard', p. 392.
23 J. Ruskin *The Works of John Ruskin*, edited by E. T. Cook and A. Wedderburn, 39 vols. (London: Library Edition: 1903-12), *Works XXII*, p. 212.
24 Leslie, *Memoirs of the Life of John Constable* 1845, pp. 90–1.
25 Ibid., p. 327.
26 Clark, *Landscape into Art*, p. 138.
27 Leslie, *Memoirs of the Life of John Constable* 1845, pp. 345–6.
28 Ibid., p. 327.
29 Ruskin, *Works III*, p. 348.
30 Leslie, *Memoirs of the Life of John Constable* 1845, pp. 117–25.
31 Ibid., p. 338.
32 Quoted in *The Thames and Hudson Dictionary of Art and Artists*, revised edition (London: Thames and Hudson, 1994), p. 302.
33 Leslie, *Memoirs of the Life of John Constable* 1845, pp. 346–7.
34 Ibid., p. 300.

35 Clark, *Landscape into Art*, pp. 60–1.
36 Beckett, *John Constable and the Fishers* (London: Routledge & Kegan Paul, 1952), p. 78.
37 Leslie, *Memoirs of the Life of John Constable* 1845, p. 347.
38 See section 2.3 for a discussion of the lightning in *Thunderstorm over Dordrecht.*
39 Leslie, *Memoirs of the Life of John Constable* 1845, p. 176.
40 Ibid., p. 78.
41 Fleming-Williams, *Constable and His Drawings*, p. 45.
42 Leslie, *Memoirs of the Life of John Constable* 1845, p. 8.
43 Ibid., p. 9.
44 Ibid., p. 10.
45 Ibid., p. 80.
46 J. Crosby Ivy, *Constable and His Critics* (Suffolk: The Boydell Press, 1991), p. 83.
47 Ibid., p. 84.
48 Ibid., p. 90.
49 Ibid., p. 89.
50 Leslie, *Memoirs of the Life of John Constable* 1845, pp. 348–9. For a discussion of light in Ruisdael's paintings see Walford, E. J. *Jacob van Ruisdael and the Perception of Landscape*, (Yale: Yale University Press, 1991), pp. 146–7.
51 Ibid., pp. 349–50.
52 See L. Parris, I. Fleming-Williams and C. Shields, *Constable* (London: Tate Gallery, 1976), p. 169 entry 292.
53 See section 2.3 for the description.
54 M. Cormack, *Constable* (Oxford: Phaidon, 1986) p. 247, note 22.
55 Leslie, *Memoirs of the Life of John Constable* 1845, p. 143.
56 Ibid., pp. 221–2.
57 See Fleming-Williams, *Constable and His Drawings*, p. 165.
58 Leslie, *Memoirs of the Life of John Constable* 1845, p. 329.
59 Beckett, *John Constable and the Fishers*, p. 125.
60 Leslie, *Memoirs of the Life of John Constable* 1845, p. 10.
61 Ibid., p. 255.
62 Ibid., p. 354.
63 Ibid., p. 6.
64 Quoted in A. Wilton, *The Life and Work of J. M. W. Turner* (London: Academy Editions, 1979), p. 107.
65 Ibid., p. 133.
66 Taken from A. Wilton, *Constable's English Landscape Scenery* (London: British Museum, 1979) p. 24.
67 Ibid.
68 Leslie, *Memoirs of the Life of John Constable* 1845, p. 32.
69 Quoted in L. Parris, *Landscape in Britain* (London: The Tate Gallery, 1973), p. 90.
70 Leslie, *Memoirs of the Life of John Constable* 1845, p. 47.
71 Ibid., p. 180.
72 Ibid., p. 277.
73 Hawes, 'Constable's sky sketches', p. 356.
74 U. Seibold, 'Meteorology in Turner's paintings', *Interdisciplinary Science Reviews* 15 (1990): 77–86.
75 Ruskin, *Modern Painters III, Works V*, p. 318.
76 J. Drummond Bone, 'Clouds in the poetry of four romantics: Wordsworth, Byron, Shelley and Keats'. (Coventry: Coventry City Art Gallery, 1976).
77 Badt, *John Constable's Clouds*, p. 37.
78 M. L. Bang, *Johan Christian Dahl – Life and Works*, 3 vols. (Oslo: Norwegian University Press, 1987), vol. 1, pp. 68–71.
79 Quoted in ibid., p. 79.
80 See the end of section 3.6.
81 Taken from Thomas Werner, 'Cloud study and the artists'. (Coventry: Coventry City Art Gallery, 1976), p. 8.
82 Clark, *Landscape into Art*, p. 147.
83 Ruskin, *Modern Painters III, Works V*, p. 318.
84 Ibid., p. 317.
85 Aristophanes, *The Clouds*, ~423 BC, ed. K. J. Dover (Oxford: Clarendon Press, 1968).
86 D. Cosgrove and J. E. Thornes, 'Of truth of clouds; John Ruskin and the moral order in landscape'. In Pocock (ed.), *Humanistic Geography and Literature* (London: Croom Helm, 1981).
87 D. Knight, 'Romanticism and the sciences'. In A. Cunningham and N. Jardine (eds), *Romanticism and the Sciences* (Cambridge: Cambridge University Press, 1990), p. 345. C. Klonk, *Science and the Perception of Nature: British Landscape Art in the Late Eighteenth and Early Nineteenth Century* (London: Yale University Press, 1996).
88 See W. E. Knowles Middleton, *A History of the Theories of Rain* (London: Oldbourne History of Science Library, 1965).
89 See J. A. Day and F. H. Ludlam, 'Luke Howard and his clouds: a contribution to the early history of cloud physics', *Weather* 27 (1972): 448–61; and B. J. R. Blench, 'Luke Howard and his contribution to meteorology', *Weather* 18 (1963): 83–92
90 J. E. Thornes, 'Luke Howard's influence on art and literature in the early nineteenth century', *Weather* 39 (1984): 252–5.

91 Reproduced in Badt, *John Constable's Clouds*.
92 It is reproduced in A. W. Slater, 'Luke Howard, F.R.S. (1772–1864) and his relations with Goethe', *Notes and Records of the Royal Society*, 27(1) (1972): 119–40.
93 L. Howard, 'On the modification of clouds', *Tilloch's Philosophical Magazine* (1803): published in 3 parts in vols 16(62): 97–107, 16(64): 344–57, 17(65): 5–11, later published in its entirety in 1804 as *Essay on the Modification of Clouds*, (London).
94 A. W. Slater, 'Luke Howard, F.R.S. (1772–1864) and his relations with Goethe'.
95 L. Howard, 'Account of a microscopical investigation of several species of pollen'. In *Transactions of the Linnean Society* (London,1800), p. vi.
96 W. E. Knowles Middleton, *A History of the Theories of Rain*, p. 148.
97 L. Howard, *The Climate of London*, 2 volumes (London, 1818).
98 L. Howard, *Seven Lectures on Meteorology* (Pontefract, 1837).
99 In Supplement to the 4th, 5th, and 6th Editions of the *Encyclopaedia Britannica*, (Edinburgh, 1824), vol. 5, 359–60.
100 L. Howard, *The Climate of London*, 2nd edn, 2 vols. (London, 1833), vol. 1, p. 124.
101 Reproduced in D. Scott, *Luke Howard* (York, England: William Sessions Ltd., 1976), p. 26.
102 Quoted in Badt, *John Constable's Clouds*, p. 15.
103 For a full discussion see J.E. Thornes, 'Luke Howard's influence on art and literature in the early nineteenth century', *Weather* 39 (1984): 252–5.
104 Howard, *The Climate of London*, 2nd edn.
105 Day and Ludlam, 'Luke Howard and his clouds: a contribution to the early history of cloud physics'.
106 Ruskin, 'Lectures on landscape', delivered at Oxford in the Lent term, *Works XXII*, p. 18.
107 Badt, *John Constable's Clouds*, p. 7.
108 J. Ruskin, *Modern Painters I*, 2nd edn, *Works III*, vol. 1, preface, p. 38.
109 J. Ruskin, *Modern Painters I*, *Works III*, p. 347. Ibid.
110 Ruskin, *Modern Painters I*, *Works III*, p. 347.
111 Constable's favourite cloud is undoubtedly cumulus, whereas Turner preferred cirrus or cumulonimbus.
112 Ruskin, *Modern Painters V*, *Works VII*, pp. 144ff.
113 Ruskin published the first part of what was to be a series entitled 'Coeli Enarrant – studies of cloud form and of its visible causes' in *Coeli Enarrant* (London: George Allen, 1885). The second and subsequent parts were never published.
114 Ruskin, *Modern Painters V*, *Works* VII, p. 133.
115 Damisch, *Théorie du Nuage: pour une histoire de la peinture*, p. 253.
116 Ruskin, *Modern Painters V*, *Works VII*, pp. 153ff.

Chapter Five

A fusion of art and science

I have done a good deal of skying – I am determined to conquer all difficulties and that most arduous one among the rest.

It was Constable's willingness to invest time in understanding meteorological theory as well as in sketching the sky that led to him mastering the art of painting skies. He successfully turned art theory on its head and showed that the sky is the 'key note', the 'standard of scale' and the 'chief organ of sentiment' in a landscape painting. There is still much research to be done but this book has attempted to provide a meteorological framework for the analysis of landscape skies that allows Constable's skies to be assessed objectively as well as appreciated subjectively.

The hypothesis to be tested was that a knowledge of meteorological science enabled Constable to significantly improve his art. This is contentious ground. The relationship between art and science at the beginning of the nineteenth century has received increasing attention in recent years, but this debate is still relatively young. As with all research this book has raised as many questions as it has provided answers.

Constable was interested in the weather even before he began to paint. The flat, gently rolling landscape of Suffolk was often crowned with towering skies. His experience working amongst his father's windmills and boats led him to be aware of the ever-changing weather and gave him a basic sky vocabulary. He became aware for instance, of 'messenger' clouds and had already been on duty 'skying' out for severe weather and shifting winds that might damage the windmills. Already he was probably aware of the sailors' jargon for wind speed that was later formalised into the Beaufort wind scale. By the time he went up to London in 1799 to be admitted as a student to the Royal Academy he was twenty-two years old. He wrote of London: 'I sometimes see the sky, but imagine to yourself how a pearl must look through a burnt glass.' The comparison of the sky with a pearl was an early indication of Constable's precocious feelings for the sky.

His first dated weather notes were written on the back of a study completed in 1805: 'Nov'4. 1805 – Noon very fine day the Stour'. This brief annotation was followed by many more on his Lake District excursion of 1806. Quite why he started this sensible habit of annotating his studies with the date, time and weather notes is not known, but it shows his remarkable attention to detail and his wish to both understand the evolution of the current weather and the subsequent development of the sky beyond his captured scene.

Constable then struggled to perfect his canvas skies. He wanted to catch a second in time that encapsulated not only the prevailing weather conditions but also the previous and future weather: the sky, the clouds, the wind, the temperature, the wet grass and the dew all had to harmonise in order to mirror nature. His move to Hampstead in 1819 reawoke those towering

Suffolk skies as he stood above London seemingly level with the clouds. It wasn't until 1821 that he achieved this harmony for the first time in *The Hay Wain* (Plate 38). The two-year period from October 1820 until October 1822 was a remarkable time when Constable produced well over 100 studies in which the principal theme was the sky. He experimented with different times of the day, different directions of view, different wind speeds and direction, and then in a fascinating departure from traditional landscape painting he left the landscape behind and turned his eyes solely to the sky. His big skyscapes of 1822, painted mostly around noon, are unique in landscape art. Constable, with his assured knowledge of meteorology, from the pinnacle of Hampstead Heath, engulfed himself in the clouds. His accurate studies match almost perfectly the contemporary weather records. How he managed to achieve such truth, time after time, in just an hour on Hampstead Heath, is remarkable. Working in oils in the open air with the wind blowing at his paper, and sometimes drops of rain falling on his studies – he must have been mesmerised by the sky before him. And yet he was able to capture those momentary glimpses of shape, process, colour and meteorological truth.

As the 1820s progressed the skies of Constable's finished works became cloudier and windier until *The Chain Pier Brighton* (Plate 51) in 1827 was the first to have an almost overcast sky full of heavy showers. The skies became even stormier, culminating in *Hadleigh Castle* (Plate 54) in 1829, expressing the emotion and heartbreak of his wife Maria's death. Constable then goes beyond meteorological truth and sensationalises the sky of *Salisbury Cathedral from the Meadows* (Plate 59) in 1831 and attempts to include anticrepuscular rays in *The Opening of Waterloo Bridge seen from Whitehall Stairs, June 18th 1817* (Plate 60). The final years are no less emotional with the daunting sky of *Old Sarum* (Plate 62) in 1834, and the double rainbow in *Stonehenge* (Plate 63) in 1836, symbolising the loss of his dearest love, Maria, and his closest friend, John Fisher.

Constable had achieved mastery of the sky. He could portray a complete repertoire of English weather, although undoubtedly his favourite clouds were cumulus and cumulonimbus – the convective clouds that provide the squally spring hail, the heavy summer showers and the autumnal rainbows. But Constable was not just a painter of clouds. His beloved morning dew and his wet leaves and grass after rain are reminders of events which preceded the scene portrayed. Perhaps Constable's greatest challenge, however, was the portrayal of wind: that invisible mystery which rocks the trees and hurries those moist cloud cargoes across the sky. It is the portrayal of wind, or the lack of it, that tells the evolving story of Constable's skies most clearly. Constable's skies in his finished works begin in calm quiet weather. There is hardly a breath of wind in *Dedham Vale: Morning*, 1811. Slowly the leaves begin to flutter in *Stoke by Nayland* (Plate 26) and the rigid clouds begin to move in *Weymouth Bay* (Plate 28) both of 1816. The wind is still a gentle breeze in *Stratford Mill* (Plate 36) of 1820, but in the sky studies of 1820–22 the trees are beginning to sway and the clouds to dance. A fresh breeze blows through *The Cornfield* (Plate 48) and a strong breeze races the clouds across *Old Sarum* (Plate 62). The near-gale winds that rage as the thunderstorms echo around *Stonehenge* (Plate 63) finally subside as the double rainbow signals the end of the storm in *Hampstead Heath with a Rainbow* (Plate 64).

By the time Constable gave his lectures, starting in 1833, to the Literary and Scientific Society of Hampstead, his meteorological knowledge was probably on a par with any of the scientists who were present. His understanding of Luke Howard's cloud classification; his annotations to Forster's book and his knowledge of cloud formation that allowed him on occasion to disagree with Forster; his understanding of the formation of rainbows given in *English Landscape Scenery;* his rainbow diagrams; his practical painting skills and astute observations of the atmosphere meant that he was probably the most meteorologically aware landscape artist of all time. The scientific truth of his painted skies is unsurpassed.

The intellectual arguments of Kurt Badt as to whether or not Constable was inspired by Luke Howard's *Climate of London* to embark on the sky studies of 1820–22 are irrelevant. Constable's skies evolved in a clear and logical way from the start of his career until the end. Hawes was right to emphasise that there are a host of other reasons as to why Constable produced those unique sky studies. Hopefully what this book has shown is that Constable achieved this perfection in his skies through long periods of experimentation, copious sky sketching, and by studying what had been written by contemporary scientists and meteorologists about skies.

This book presents considerable new evidence by which to gauge the quality of Constable's skies. The detailed analysis of Constable's dated weather inscriptions has shown that he systematically produced a series of sky studies that covered all times of the day, were meteorologically accurate, and were clustered around noon. The 'pure' sky studies in particular were painted close to noon to help Constable complete his large skies in the favoured noon settings of his finished works. The accuracy of the sky studies is such that it is possible to date with some certainty, using historical weather records, fifteen studies where the date has previously been in doubt. The linear development of Constable's skies through his career is in stark contrast to the development of his landscapes, which are much more difficult to date. The skies present a vital clue to the dating of such works as *Dedham Lock and Mill* (Plates 32 and 33) and *Cottage in a Cornfield* (Plates 30 and 31). The gradually increasing wind in Constable's paintings and his use of a form of the Beaufort wind scale show his evolving skills at mastering such an ephemeral force. This is not to imply that his meteorological knowledge was perfect: we know that he was not averse to introducing special atmospheric effects when it suited him. However his knowledge of contemporary meteorological science enabled him to achieve a unique harmony between the sky and the landscape. No other artist, before or since, has consistently succeeded in representing our English weather on canvas with such scientific accuracy and truth to nature.

APPENDIX 1

Towards an accurate dating of certain of John Constable's sky studies 1820/22

I Introduction

In August 1978 the present author published an occasional paper entitled *The accurate dating of certain of John Constable's cloud studies 1821/22 using historical weather records.*[1] The paper examined thirty-six sky studies that the author was able to trace at that time, all of which were inscribed with weather notes by Constable. These weather notes were compared with contemporary historical weather records for the London area and were found to be in very good agreement. For nine of these sky studies that were only inscribed with the day and the month, it was then possible to date them as either 1821 or 1822 using the historical weather records.

Since 1978 several other inscribed sky studies have been identified, including four dated October 1820. In Chapter 3 it was shown that in total fifty-four dated sky studies have now been identified of which fifty-one have weather-related inscriptions. Several important publications have also emerged since 1978, including Hoozee's 1979 *L'opera complete di Constable*[2] and Reynolds' 1984 and 1996 catalogues.[3] There are now fifteen sky studies for which only an incomplete date is given. Of these, eleven give the day and the month but not the year, and parts of the date are missing for the other four. Section IV below shows that the historical weather records enable all fifteen to be dated with some certainty.

This Appendix contains, therefore, an updated and expanded version of my 1978 paper, including a description of the meteorological content of each sky study and, where possible, a copy of the study.

II Method of analysis

In order to justify the use of historical weather records to help date the appropriate sky studies, it must first be shown that the weather notes on the studies accurately dated by Constable correspond to the historical weather records. I have therefore compiled a catalogue of the 1820/22 cloud studies, based on sources available in Britain. Of the fifty-four dated sky studies that have been documented (see Table 10), thirty-six sky studies are accurately dated and with weather notes. Three of the sky studies are accurately dated but contain no weather inscription, and the remaining fifteen studies have weather inscriptions but were not accurately dated by Constable. It is proposed to use historical weather data to attempt to accurately date these fifteen sky studies.

III Historical weather records

Standardised meteorological records were not begun in Britain until 1841. Hence we have to rely upon respected records kept by individuals in the London area. Although I have been unable to trace a reliable weather diary covering 1820/22 kept by anyone living in Hampstead, other records for London exist. The most reliable weather record is that kept by Luke Howard, published in *The Climate of London*.[4] It covers the period from 1806–30 and contains continuous daily observations of wind direction, atmospheric pressure, maximum temperature, minimum temperature, and rainfall, as well as a brief comment on the day's weather, principally taken at Stratford – a suburb of London eight miles to the east of Hampstead (Figure 21). The weather on Hampstead Heath would hardly differ from that at Stratford in the Lea/Thames Valley, although the showery weather loved by Constable could well have been more frequent at Hampstead due to the relief. To give an extreme example: in the Hampstead storm of summer 1975 more than 150mm of rain fell over parts of Hampstead, whilst Stratford remained almost dry.

In order to check Howard's data, other available weather records have also been extracted for the London area. They come from a ring of sites to the south of Hampstead (see Figure 21), and although they are not considered by the Meteorological Office to be as reliable as Howard's records, they do provide a worthwhile check for consistency, as well as snippets of useful information over and above that provided by Howard. It is remarkable how similar the observations are. They comprise:

- Cary in the Strand (five miles south of Hampstead)
- Rev. Cowe in Sunbury (sixteen miles to the south west)
- Hoy in Kew (eight miles to the south west) (1821 only)
- Belville in Greenwich (ten miles to the south east)

The details relating to these observations are given later. Unfortunately none of the weather observers recorded wind speed, so it is not possible to check the accuracy of Constable's portrayal of wind speed, for which he used an early version of the Beaufort wind scale (see Chapter 2, section 2.6).

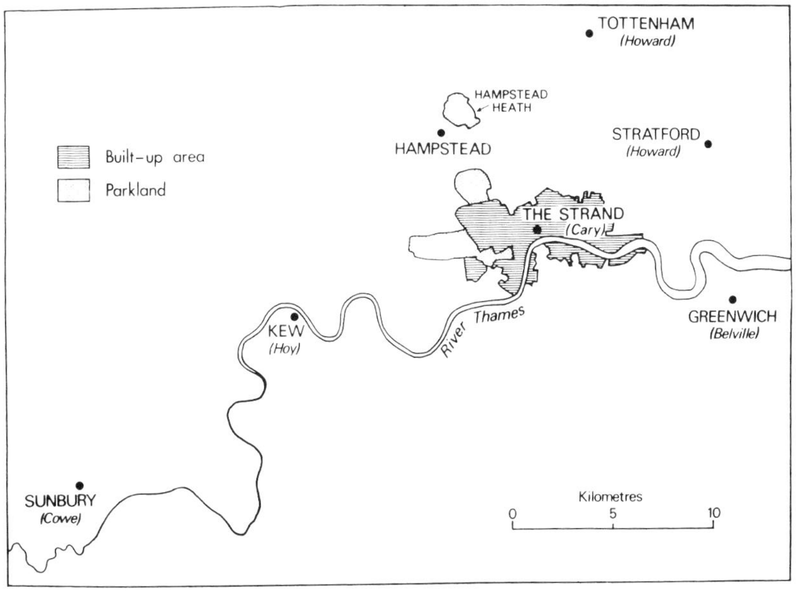

Figure 21 Historical weather record sites (1820–22) in relation to Hampstead Heath

IV Comparison of Constable's weather notes with the historical weather records

The agreement is remarkably good considering the differing purposes for which the weather notes were being made. Constable's notes were to remind him, in sensual terms, of the weather that generated his skyscapes, whereas Howard and the others were recording the day's weather to provide a factual record. The catalogue below lists for each skyscape Constable's weather notes and the historical weather data for that day, together with a brief comparison of the two and an estimate of the agreement on a four-point scheme: excellent, very good, good and poor. Of the thirty-six accurately dated studies with weather notes, nine show excellent agreement, fifteen very good, eleven good, and only one poor. The following lists the studies in each category. (Numbers refer to my numbering of the studies below).

Excellent:	8, 9, 12, 13, 23, 25, 40, 52, 53
Very good:	3, 5, 6, 14, 19, 24, 27, 30, 32, 37, 38, 48, 49, 50, 51
Good:	1, 2, 15, 16, 20, 22, 29, 34, 36, 45, 47
Poor:	26

It is not always possible to match the observations exactly, but the agreement is sufficiently good to suggest that Constable's weather notes and skyscapes are meteorologically accurate within a relatively small band of error. The weather inscription on only one study has a poor agreement with the observed weather conditions. Therefore, we may confidently use the weather notes provided by Constable to attempt to date the fifteen sky studies that are not accurately dated.

V The problem of dating

Reynolds has made the best attempt to date by year as many of Constable's works as possible, including all of the sky studies catalogued here.[5] As he states, however, he had problems in placing Constable's works into chronological order: 'The arrangement of the entries in a chronological sequence does not imply the claim that each single work can be securely dated within a particular year. It is often peculiarly difficult to date individual examples on purely stylistic grounds. Constable's ingenuity in technique was accompanied by the capacity to revert to earlier methods when he chose.'[6]

In the next section it will be assumed that the fifteen sky studies that we are attempting to date belong to the period between October 1820 and October 1822. The historical weather records will be compared to Constable's weather notes and a conclusion drawn. How big an assumption is it that all of the fifteen studies were painted in this two-year window?

Firstly, all the studies considered are in oil; this distinguishes them from the only other set of Constable paintings that contain weather notes – the watercolours painted during Constable's visit to the Lake District in 1806. I have been able to trace only a limited number of other oil sky studies that are accurately dated outside 1820/22 and contain weather notes, and only one that was made at Hampstead (on 9 August 1823). The two sky studies made at Hampstead much later are both watercolours:

> about 11 – Noon – Sepr 15 1830. Wind – W.
> Hampd December 7, 1833 3 oclock – very stormy afternoon – & High Wind

Hence it appears that to assume that all of the oil sky studies accompanied by weather information are from the period 1820/22 is valid, particularly when supported by the evidence provided by the size of the studies. Beckett writes: 'A certain uniformity of measurements indicate that Constable kept by him a stock of sheets of stout paper cut up into suitable sizes. Dated examples of 1821 measure about 25 x 30cm while those of 1822 ... are of larger size, about 28 x 48cm or even 48 x 58cm. There are also a large number of much smaller cloud studies, none of which is dated; some of them may have been done several years later.[7] That the studies of 1822 were on the whole larger is certainly borne out by Table 19 which shows that, for the sky and landscape studies, whereas the typical size of the 1820 studies was about 140 x 200mm and those of 1821 was about 240 x 300mm, those of 1822 were close to 250 x 380mm. The 1822 pure sky studies were even bigger, averaging 360 x 500mm. The 1821 pure sky studies were of similar size to the 1821 sky and landscape sketches. Moreover, Constable, in a letter to Fisher on 7 October 1822, stated: 'I have made about fifty careful studies of *Skies*, tolerably large to be careful.' Leslie also refers to the size of the 1822 studies: 'Twenty of Constable's studies of skies made during this season are in my possession, and there is but one among them in which a vestige of landscape is introduced. They are painted in oil, on large sheets of thick paper, and all dated, with the time of day, the direction of the wind, and other memoranda on their backs.'[8]

It is sometimes suggested that all of Constable's pure sky studies date from 1822; in fact this is not so. Table 19 shows that at least three pure sky studies were dated, with weather notes, in 1821.

VI Weather dating

This catalogue contains the historical weather records for the fifteen cloud studies dated below in Table 18. A full discussion of dating is given in the catalogue entry for each study below.

Table 18
The dating of fifteen sky studies with incomplete dates

Number	Constable's date	Size (mm)	Assigned year	Certainty
(4)	*28th Octr.*	159 x 203	1820	Probably 1820
(7)	*19th July*	145 x 325	1821	Certainly 1821
(12)	*August 1821*	250 x 298	1821	14 August 1821?
(11)	*September 3d.*	241 x 298	1821	Certainly 1821
(17)	***Septr 13th.***	248 x 303	1821	Certainly 1821
(18)	*Sepr. 24th*	248 x 305	1821	Certainly 1821
(21)	*27 Sept*	248 x 292	1821	Certainly 1821
(28)	*Oct. 30th*	241 x 266	1821	Most likely 1821
(31)	***April 18th***	145 x 220	1822	Most likely 1822
(33)	***28th July***	290 x 480	1822	Most likely 1822
(35)	*2(?) July 1822*	311 x 521	1822	Most likely 29 July 1822?
(39)	*July*	247 x 400	1822	15–18? July 1822?
(43)	***Sunday 11 to 12***	Unknown	1822	18 August 1822?
(46)	***27 Augt***	475 x 575	1822	Certainly 1822
(54)	***31st Sepr***	480 x 590	1822	Certainly 1 October 1822

Note
Pure sky studies given in bold

Table 19
Date and size of each sky study classified into 'sky and landscape' or 'pure sky'

SKY AND LANDSCAPE (=35)

1820 (=4

	Date	Size (mm)
(1)	17.10.20	127 x 171
(2)	18.10.20	197 x 318
(3)	25.10.20	140 x 245
(4)	28.10.20?	159 x 203
	Mean size (mm)	**156 x 234**

1821 (=23)

	Date	Size (mm)
(5)	14.07.21	254 x 274
(6)	18.07.21	Unknown
(7)	19.07.21?	145 x 325
(8)	19.07.21	241 x 292
(9)	25.07.21	167 x 222
(10)	?.08.21	250 x 298
(11)	03.09.21?	241 x 298
(12)	10.09.21	216 x 292
(13)	10.09.21	248 x 302
(14)	11.09.21	242 x 298
(15)	12.09.21	241 x 298
(16)	12.09.21	241 x 292
(18)	24.09.21?	248 x 305
(20)	27.09.21	165 x 310
(21)	27.09.21?	248 x 292
(22)	27.09.21	235 x 286
(24)	02.10.21	245 x 298
(25)	09.10.21	247 x 292
(26)	12.10.21	247 x 285
(27)	13.10.21	248 x 298
(28)	30.10.21?	241 x 266
(29)	31.10.21	260 x 325
(30)	02.11.21	248 x 298
	Mean size (mm)	**233 x 293**

1822 (=8)

	Date	Size (mm)
(32)	04.07.22	321 x 495
(34)	29.07.22	292 x 241
(35)	29?.07.22	311 x 521
(36)	30.07.22	242 x 298
(37)	31.07.22	165 x 298
(38)	31.07.22	162 x 305
(39)	?.07.22?	247 x 400
(44)	25.08.22	266 x 482
	Mean size (mm)	**250 x 380**

PURE SKY (=19)

1821 (=3)

	Date	Size (mm)
(17)	13.09.21?	248 x 303
(19)	25.09.21	212 x 290
(23)	28.09.21	255 x 305
	Mean size (mm)	**238 x 300**

1822 (=16)

	Date	Size (mm)
(31)	18.04.22?	145 x 220
(33)	28.07.22?	290 x 480
(40)	01.08.22	305 x 508
(41)	01.08.22	472 x 584
(42)	12.08.22	254 x 222
(43)	18?.08?.22?	Unknown
(45)	26.08.22	Unknown
(46)	27.08.22?	475 x 575
(47)	31.08.22	470 x 580
(48)	05.09.22	370 x 490
(49)	05.09.22	298 x 483
(50)	06.09.22	Unknown
(51)	06.09.22	300 x 500
(52)	21.09.22	287 x 483
(53)	21.09.22	305 x 492
(54)	31.09.22?/01.10.22?	480 x 590
	Mean size (mm)	**347 x 483**

VII Historical weather records (2)

A. LUKE HOWARD, *The Climate of London*, 2nd edn, 3 vols (London, 1833).

Volume 3 contains observations for Stratford 1819–30, and occasional notes for Tottenham, where Howard worked, are also included. Howard made most of his observations at 9am for the previous day. The wind direction was based on his memory of the direction over the previous twenty-four hours: 'but with due reference to the present state of wind vane'. Maximum and minimum temperatures were recorded with two thermometers, the second acting as a back-up if the first was faulty. There were no problems with thermometer number 1 during the period we are interested in and therefore the maximum temperature from thermometer 1 is used below. Rainfall was the total from 9am the previous day, and the comments were based on his memory of the previous day's weather. The pressure values are an average of the daily maximum and minimum. Figure 22 shows a sample extract for October 1821.

1821.		Wind.	By Clock.		Temp.		T. No. 2.		Evap	Rain, &c.	Hygr. at 9 a. m.
			Max.	Min.	Max.	Min.	Max.	Min.			
10 mo. Oct.	1	NW	30·13	29·70	65°	43°	66°	45°	—		
	2	NW	30·13	29·80	61	44	64	46	—		
	3	SW	29·80	29·40	68	60	69	61	—	26	
	4	S	29·90	29·25	65	43	62	44	—	91	
	5	NW	30·03	29·90	58	43	58	41	47		
	6	W	30·06	30·00	65	53	67	51	—		
	7	SW	30·05	29·90	67	51	67	50	—	5	
	8	NW	30·28	29·90	63	33	65	34	—	12	
	9	SW	30·27	30·00	60	35	58	33	—		
	10	SE	30·00	29·62	61	41	61	39	35		
	11	SE	29·88	29·50	58	46	61	45	—	—	
	12	NW	30·35	29·80	58	39	60	41	—		
	13	N	30·38	30·30	60	33	62	40	—		
	14	SE	30·30	30·23	61	46	60	40	—	18	
	15	NE	30·23	30·13	54	32	56	33	—	3	
	16	N	30·17	30·10	58	36	56	34	—		
	17	NW	30·10	29·86	61	45	58	43	—		
	18	SW	29·86	29·81	57	45	62	47	35	—	
	19	NW	29·81	29·00	66	46	56	43	—		
	20	SW	29·10	28·78	57	40	57	38	—	26	
	21	NW	29·11	29·06	52	46	52	43	—	27	
	22	SW	29·30	29·10	56	42	56	38	—	4	
	23	SE	29·45	29·10	53	35			—	15	
	24	SW	29·95	29·45	51	38	53	34	—	1	
	25	SW	30·04	29·94	53	42	53	40	—	3	
New M.	26	SW	30·17	30·05	58	50	58	48	—		
	27	SW	30·27	30·16	61	54	61	55	—	12	
	28	SW	30·29	30·20	60	31	62	33	—	—	
	29	SE	30·20	30·05	51	34			—		
	30	E	30·06	29·84	57	37	52	36	—		
	31	NE	29·93	29·82	60	46	60	45	46	8	
			30·38	28·78	68	31			1·63	2·51	

Figure 22 Extract from Luke Howard's weather observations (October 1821 – Stratford, London)

B. REV. J. COWE, *Cowe's Meteorological Register* (London, Kenny & Co. Printers, 1889)

Daily records 1795–1839 at Sunbury. The barometer was read at 8am as was the wind direction. It is not clear whether or not this was for the previous day. The maximum temperature must have been for the previous day.

C. MR. CARY *Philosophical Magazine and Journal* (London)

Daily observations were published monthly in the above magazine for The Strand. The temperature noted is that at noon on the day in question. Pressure was measured at 1pm and comments were presumably made on the day's weather in the evening.

D. J. H. BELVILLE *Meteorological Records* 1811–56 at Greenwich. Meteorological Office Archives, Vol. 1: September 1811 – October 1826

Belville's observations are most interesting in that he gives morning and afternoon approximate cloud cover in tenths. The timing of the other observations is not clear, although it appears that pressure was taken at noon when the observations were taken at the Observatory up to the end of 1821. The observations were then taken at Park Row from 1822 until 1825.

E. T. HOY *Weather Diary* kept at SYON HOUSE in Kew (and other places before 1821). July 1771 – March 1822.

The record is a very full one but unfortunately is only suitable for the 1820/21 studies. The wind direction was measured at 8am and the temperature was taken at 3pm.

VIII A catalogue of Constable's accurately dated sky studies and a comparison with historical weather records

Notes

1. The details of each painting are summarised as follows: date; title; owner; size (in mm); materials; classification. Details of exhibitions, exhibition catalogues and any literature which specifically addresses the individual painting are then given in chronological order. Exhibition catalogues and other literature are referred to by author and year: Publication details, where available, are given below.

Auckland (1973), *John Constable: The Natural Painter*, exhibition catalogue compiled by Graham Reynolds (Auckland, Melbourne and Sydney).

Badt, K. (1950), *John Constable's Clouds* (London: Routledge & Kegan Paul).

Baskett, J. (1966), *Constable Oil Sketches*.

Birmingham City Art Gallery (1960).

Boston (1946), *Paintings, Drawings and Prints by J. M. W. Turner, John Constable and R. P. Bonington*, exhibition catalogue (Museum of Fine Arts, Boston).

Burlington Fine Arts Club (1903).

Davies, M. (1959), *National Gallery Catalogues: The British School*.

Detroit and Philadelphia (1968).

Grosvenor Gallery Exhibition (1889). *A Century of British Art from 1737 to 1837*

Herbert Art Gallery, Coventry (1975).

Hoozee, R. (1979), *L'opera completa di Constable* (Milan: Rizzoli Editore).

Leggatt (1952). Summer Exhibition

Manchester (1956), *John Constable 1776–1837*, exhibition catalogue. Introduction by R. B. Beckett (Manchester City Art Gallery).

New York (1983), *Constable's England*, exhibition catalogue compiled by Graham Reynolds (Metropolitan Museum of Art, New York).

Parris, L. (1981), *The Tate Gallery Constable Collection* (London, Tate Gallery).

Paterson (1928).

Reynolds, G. (1960).

(1973), *Catalogue of the Constable Collection in the Victoria and Albert Museum*, 2nd edn.

(1984), *The Later Paintings and Drawings of John Constable* (London: Yale University Press).

(1996), *The Early Paintings and Drawings of John Constable* (London: Yale University Press).

Richmond (1963), *Painting in England, 1700–1850: Collection of Mr and Mrs Paul Mellon*, exhibition catalogue compiled by Basil Taylor, foreword by Leslie Clarke, 2 vols. (Virginia Museum of Fine Arts).

Royal Academy (1934).

(1963), *Treasures of the Royal Academy* catalogue.

(1964/65), *Painting in England, 1700–1850, from the Collection of Mr and Mrs Paul Mellon*, winter exhibition catalogue compiled by Basil Taylor (Royal Academy).

Tate (1976), *Constable: Paintings, Watercolours and Drawings*, bicentenary exhibition catalogue compiled by Leslie Parris, Ian Fleming-Williams and Conal Shields (Tate Gallery).

Thornes, J. E. (1978), *The Accurate Dating of Certain of John Constable's Cloud Studies 1820/22 Using Historical Weather Records*, Occasional Paper No. 34 (London: Dept. of Geography, University College London).

Washington (1969), *John Constable: A Selection of Paintings from the Collection of Mr and Mrs Paul Mellon*, exhibition catalogue. Introduction by John Walker; notes by Ross Watson (National Gallery of Art, Washington D.C.).

Wildenstein (1937), *Catalogue of a Centenary Memorial Exhibition of John Constable, R. A.*, exhibition catalogue. Organised by Percy Moore Turner; foreword by the Hon. Andrew Shirley (Messrs Wildenstein's Galleries). Yale (1965), *Painting in England, 1700–1850, from the Collection of Mr and Mrs Paul Mellon*, exhibition catalogue compiled by Basil Taylor (as for Royal Academy 1964/65) (Yale University Art Gallery, New Haven).

2. The studies are classified as either:

    (a) Pure sky – if no significant landscape or vegetation is visible.
    (b) Sky and landscape (L/S)– if any significant element of landscape or vegetation is visible.

3. Constable's exact inscriptions are not always clear, some commentators differ in interpretation. The version given in Reynolds[9] has been used where possible.

4. In the historical weather notes pressure is given in inches of mercury, temperature in degrees Fahrenheit and rain in inches.

5. The agreement between Constable's inscription and the contemporary weather records for the fully dated sky studies is meant only as a general guide, and is divided into four categories: excellent, very good, good, poor.

(1) 17 October 1820; Sketch at Hampstead: stormy sunset; Plate 88; Victoria and Albert Museum (V&A) (147–1888); 127 x 171; oil on paper or card; sky and L/S; Reynolds (1973, 207), Thornes (1978, 10), Hoozee (1979, 284), Reynolds (1984, 20.77)

Constable's inscription: 'Hampd. 17th October 1820 Stormy Sunset. Wind. W.'

	WIND	*PRES.*	*TEMP.*	*RAIN*	*CLOUD*	*COMMENTS*
Howard (Stratford) (Tottenham)	SW	28.84	56	–	–	On the 17th, a brilliant meteor, about 7, p.m. descending to the NW, followed by a lunar halo.
Belville	WSW	28.72	54	0.21	am 5/10 pm 3/10	very high wind flying(?) clouds
Cary		28.92	54			Fair
Cowe	S	28.84	56			cloudy
Hoy	NW	28.82	51			Rain in the Night, High Wind, & Squally with showers

Comparison: This is the first recorded sky study of the 1820/22 period. The study certainly depicts a stormy-looking sunset with wisps of small cumulus clouds being dragged across the sky by the wind. Howard recorded a westerly wind for 18 October 1821, but there is no direct mention of stormy weather for 17 October. Howard does record 'very tempestuous night, with frequent showers' at about this time but is not specific with the date.

Conclusion: Good agreement

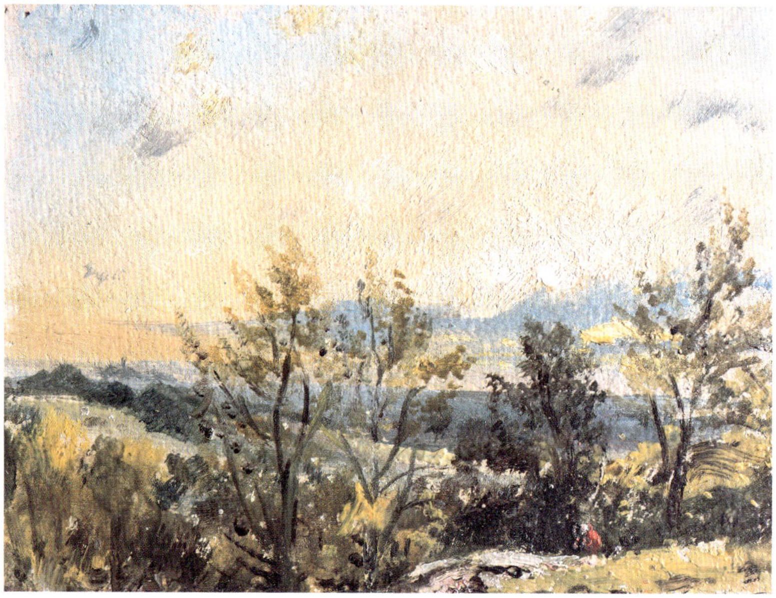

Plate 88 John Constable, *Sketch at Hampstead: Stormy Sunset*, 17 October 1820 V&A Picture Library

(2) 18 October 1820, Hampstead Heath; Plate 89; Private collection; 197 x 381; oil on paper laid on canvas; sky and L/S; Reynolds (1996, 20.78).

Constable's inscription: '18 Oct 1820 – 4 to 5 1/2/ ... wind north west'

	WIND	*PRES.*	*TEMP.*	*RAIN*	*CLOUD*	*COMMENTS*
Howard (Stratford)	W	29.13	54	0.03		
Belville	W	28.92	55		4/10 5/10	Fair
Cary		29.08	52			Fair
Cowe	SW	28.87	56			Fair
Hoy	NW	28.95	52			Cloudy morning: Clear: Cloudy & Some Rain aft.

Comparison: This is another evening sky looking to the west with a shower depicted on the right horizon. The sky is almost overcast and the sun is therefore hidden from view. Howard recorded 0.03 inches of rain which confirms that there were some showers around. Howard recorded a north-westerly wind on 19 October 1820 which suggests that the wind may have been veering towards the north west by the evening of 17 October. Hoy does however record a north-westerly wind.

Conclusion: Good agreement

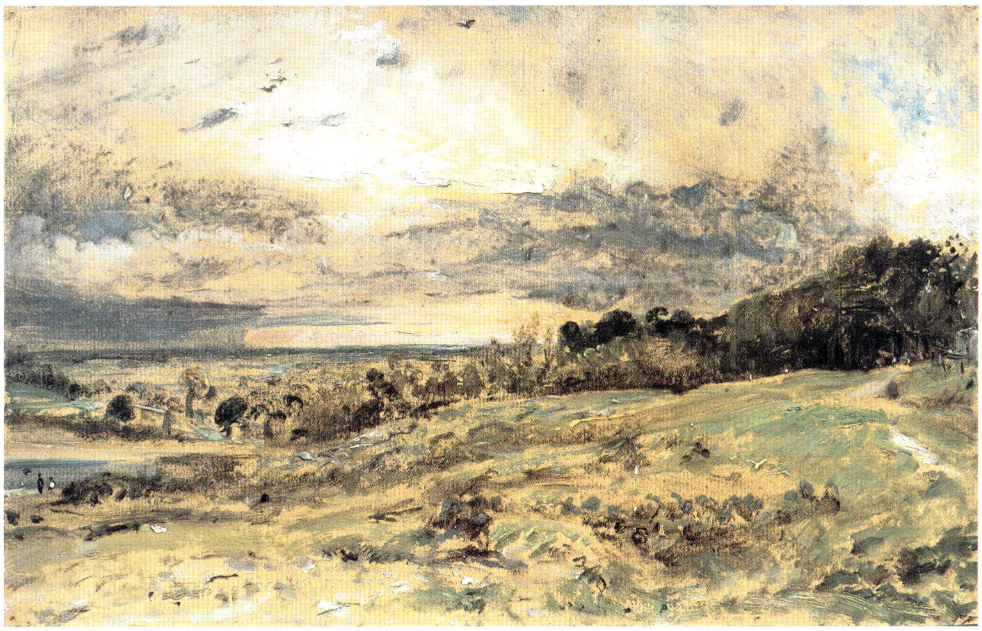

Plate 89 John Constable, *View of Hampstead Heath Looking Towards Harrow*, 18 October 1820
Private collection

(3) 25 October 1820, Hampstead Heath: evening; Private collection; 140 x 245; oil on card; sky and L/S; Hoozee (1979, 286), Reynolds (1984, 20.81).

Constable's inscription: 'Hampstead Heath – fine evening (...) wind N W October 25 1820.'

	WIND	*PRES*	*TEMP*	*RAIN*	*CLOUD*	*COMMENTS*
Howard (Stratford)	NW	29.12	52			Cloudy
Belville	W	29.00	52	0.40	6/10 4/10	Cloudy at times
Cary		29.23	52			Fair
Cowe	W	28.92	53			Fair
Hoy	SW	28.95	51			Cloudy, Aft.Clear

Comparison: This is another sunset scene very similar in style to **(1)** above, but this time the sky is less windy and therefore more serene. Howard's wind direction agrees with Constable's, and Cowe described the day as 'fair'.

Conclusion: Very good agreement

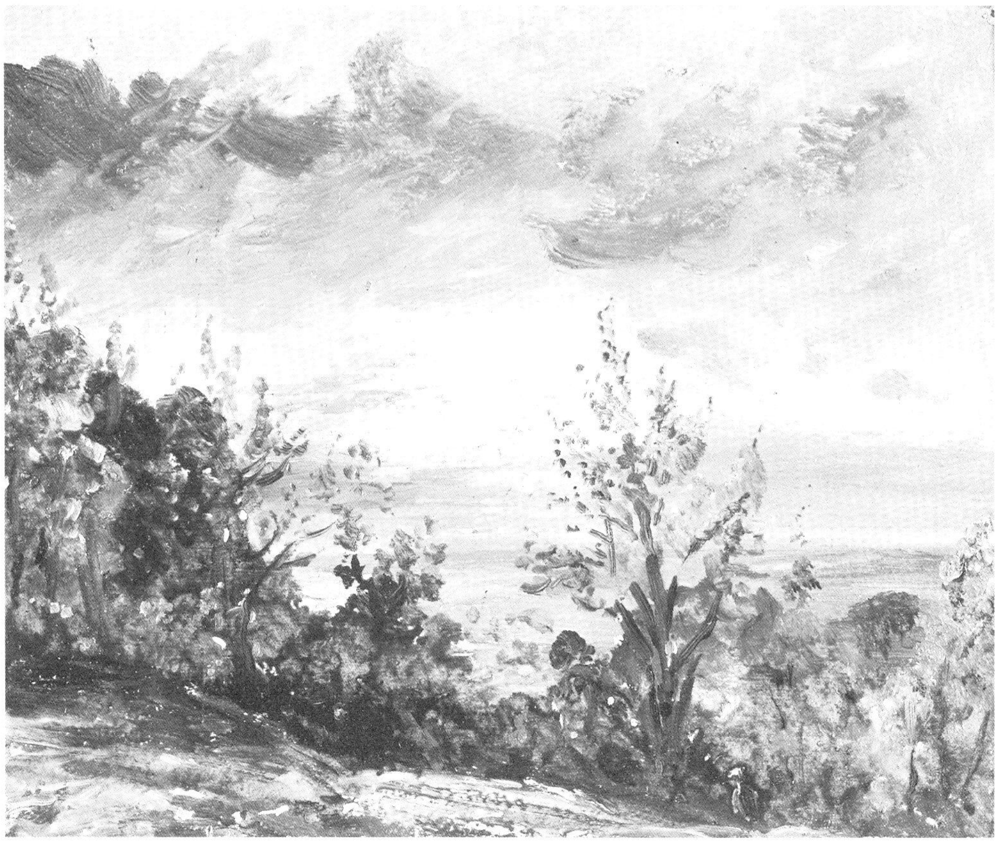

Plate 90 (opposite) John Constable, *Sketch at Hampstead: Evening*, 28 October 1820? V&A Picture Library

(4) 28 October 1820?, Sketch at Hampstead: evening; Plate 90; V&A (159–1888); 159 x 203; sky and L/S; Reynolds (1973, 208), Thornes (1978, 14–15, 30 (study no. 8)), Hoozee (1979, 287), Reynolds (1984, 20.82).

Constable's inscription: '28th Octr. fine Evening Wind Gentle at S.W.'

1820	*WIND*	*PRES*	*TEMP*	*RAIN*	*CLOUD*	*COMMENTS*
Howard (Stratford)	NW	29.48	50			Cloudy
Belville	WNW	29.50	51		2/10 3/10	Fair
Cary		29.70	52			Fair
Cowe	W	29.47		55		Fair
Hoy	NW	29.46	47			Cloudy, Aft. Clear

1821	*WIND*	*PRES*	*TEMP*	*RAIN*	*CLOUD*	*COMMENTS*
Howard (Stratford)	SW	30.25	60			Foggy: drizzling: night clear: a stratus on the marshes.
Belville	SE	30.19	59	0.18	9/10 0/10	Close and damp
Cary	-	30.32	62			Cloudy
Cowe	S	30.08	62			Fair
Hoy	SW	30.10	57			Mostly Cloudy

Comparison: Both Hoozee and Reynolds date this study as 1820. The wind direction points to 1821, although Howard did record a southerly wind on 29 October 1820, so that the wind could have backed to the south-west by the evening of the 28 October. The depicted sunset is much more spectacular than that of 17 and 25 October 1820, and there were several reports of exceptional sunset colours in London in July and August 1821 due to the eruption of the volcano Kluchev in Eastern Russia earlier in the year. Hence there are arguments that point to either 1820 or 1821. Reynolds points out that the study is made in a very similar position to that of the 17 October 1820 study and also it should be noted that the size of the study is smaller than all of the 1821 studies. Thornes (1978) suggests that it was rather cold on 28 October 1820 but the temperature was little different from 17 and 25 October 1820. Overall therefore 1820 seems the more likely year but 1821 cannot be ruled out.

(5) 14 July 1821; View from Hampstead Heath, looking west; Plate 91; Royal Academy (47); 254 x 274; oil on paper laid on canvas; sky and L/S; Manchester (1956, 39), Royal Academy (1963, 226), Auckland (1973, 24), Tate (1976, 194), Thornes (1978, 1), Hoozee (1979, 294), Reynolds (1984, 21.37)

Constable's inscription: 'Hampstead July 14 1821 6 to 7 p.m. N.W. breeze strong.'

	WIND	*PRES.*	*TEMP.*	*RAIN*	*CLOUD*	*COMMENTS*
Howard						
(Stratford)	NW	29.67	72	0.09		Cloudy
(Tottenham)						Fine day – very fine sunset
Belville	SW	29.74	66		7/10 4/10	Cloudy, Hazy
Cary		29.89	67			Cloudy
Cowe	SE	29.78	73			Fine: rain at night
Hoy	NW	29.72	73			Mostly cloudy

Comparison: This is the first study of 1821 with a weather inscription that I have been able to catalogue. All the weather records agree that it was a fine but cloudy day, and both Howard and Hoy record a north-westerly wind. Cowe recorded his south-easterly wind direction at 8am, whereas Howard took the predominant direction for the day. It is not known what period Belville's wind direction, in this case south-westerly, refers to. Howard recorded a southerly wind on 13 July. It is quite possible therefore that the wind was more southerly in the morning, becoming north-westerly in the afternoon or early evening. Howard notes a 'very fine sunset' and Constable depicts a vivid yellow sunset with broken stratocumulus racing across the sky.

Conclusion: Very good agreement

(6) 18 July 1821, Hampstead Heath from under 'The Terrace'; whereabouts unknown; size unknown; oil; Hoozee (1979, 295), Reynolds (1984, 21.38)

Constable's inscription: 'Hampstead Heath from under 'The Terrace'; hot day, noon Painted on the spot 18 July 1821.'

	WIND	*PRES.*	*TEMP.*	*RAIN*	*CLOUD*	*COMMENTS*
Howard (Stratford)	SE	30.12	75			Fine
Belville	NE	30.24	70		3/10 1/10	Fine
Cary		30.36	74			Fair
Cowe	E	30.20	77			Fine
Hoy	SE	30.15	73			Mostly Clear

Comparison: It certainly was a hot day with temperatures well into the mid-seventies. Pressure was high suggesting an anticyclone with warm easterly winds off the continent.

Conclusion: Very good agreement

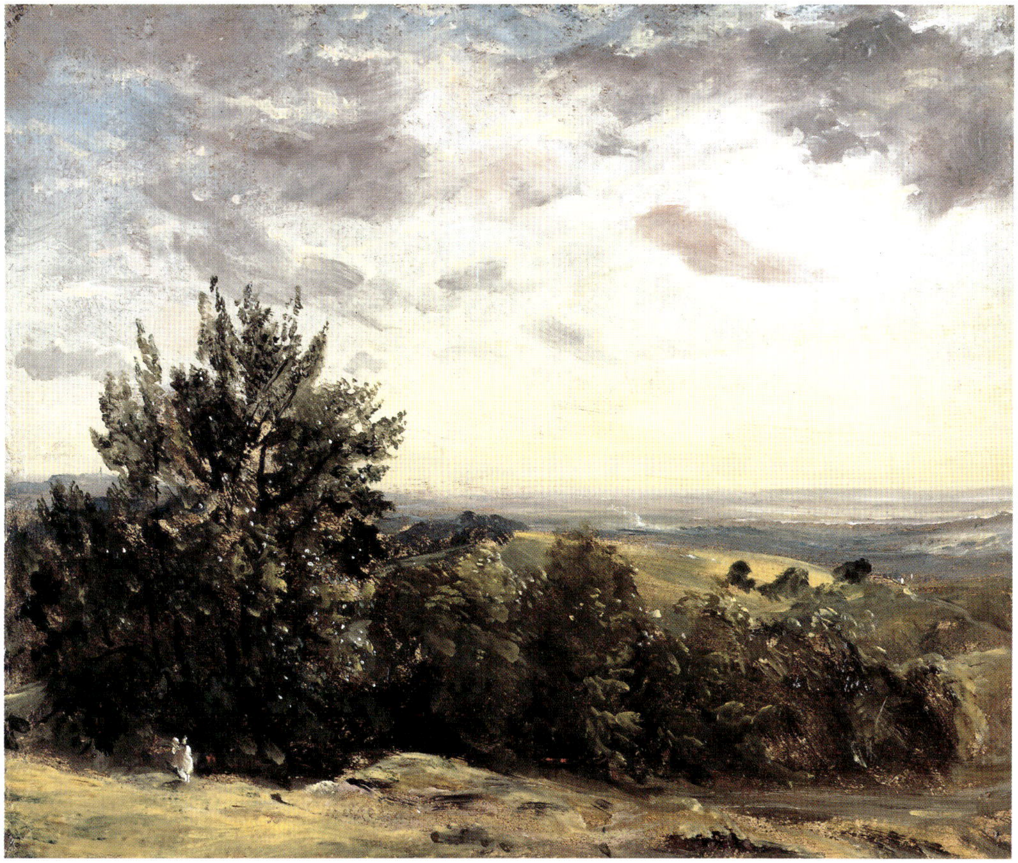

Plate 91 (opposite) John Constable, *Landscape Study: Hampstead Looking West*, 14 July 1821. Royal Academy of Arts, London

(7) 19 July 1820/21?; View over Hampstead Heath, looking east; Plate 92; Yale Center for British Art; 145 x 325; oil on paper laid on panel; sky and L/S; Richmond (1963, 110), Royal Academy (1964/65, 76), Yale (1965, 39), Washington (1969, 37); Thornes (1978, 11, 26), Hoozee (1979, 526), Reynolds (1984, 21.39).

Constable's inscription '1/2p 5 am 19th July looking East. / The day beautiful at noon plain blue sky.'

1821	*WIND*	*PRES.*	*TEMP.*	*RAIN*	*CLOUD*	*COMMENTS*
Howard (Stratford)	E	29.88	78			Fine: some thunder in the evening
(Tottenham)						Very fine and hot day: heavy clouds in the W, which afterwards passed off to northward, where was much brilliant lightning about 9 p.m.: One clap followed, and lightning in other quarters.
Belville	E	29.91	72		1/10 4/10	Very fine: Evn. lightning
Cary		30.08	74			Fair
Cowe	SE	30.06	81			Fine
Hoy	SE	29.98	77			Mostly clear

1822	*WIND*	*PRES.*	*TEMP.*	*RAIN*	*CLOUD*	*COMMENTS*
Howard (Stratford)	SW	29.45	78			Fine
(Tottenham)						Two loud claps of thunder about 4.30 a.m. with heavy rain: showery until about nine.
Belville	SE	29.44	76	0.18	5/10 5/10	Thunder shower at 4 a.m. – dry and cloudy
Cary		29.45	75			Fair
Cowe	S	29.48	75			Fair

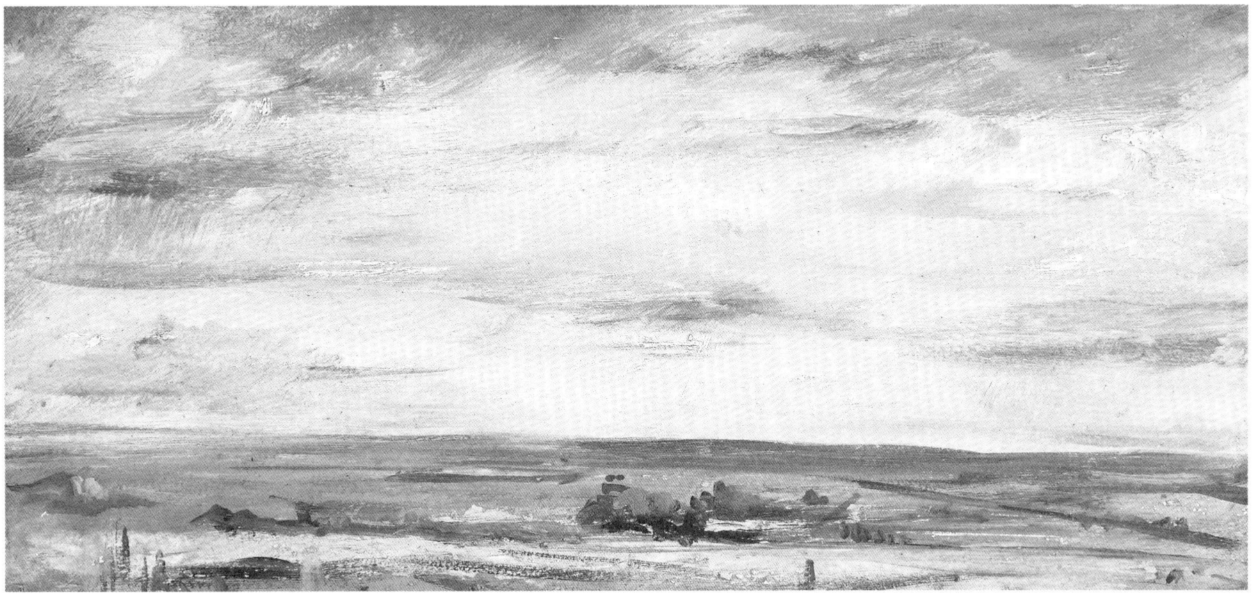

Plate 92 John Constable, *Cloud Study, Early Morning, Looking East from Hampstead*, 1821(?).
Yale Center for British Art, Paul Mellon Collection (B1981.25.117)

Comparison: Constable was certainly in Hampstead during most of July 1821 and other sky studies are dated the 14th (4), 18th (5), 19th (7) and 25th July (8). The inscription ties in well with weather records for 1821. Howard's notes for Tottenham state that it was a very fine and hot day. The evening thunder would not have affected Constable at 5.30am. Temperatures were in the high seventies and it must have been a beautiful hot summer's day, with a build up of thundery activity late in the afternoon. A dating of 1822 is most unlikely in that Howard records at Tottenham for 19 July 1822, 'Two loud claps of thunder about half-past four a.m. with heavy rain: showery till about nine'. Constable could hardly have omitted to mention that! The size of the picture (145 x 325) is unusual as far as his other cloud studies are concerned and gives no clue. The study is of a bright colourful sunrise that Hoozee states is unusual and different from any other Constable study. The fact that it was made so early in the morning, some three hours before the next earliest study (see No. 24 painted between 8 and 9am), suggests reasons for its unusual brightness. A dating of 1821 seems certain.

(8) 19 July 1821, Hampstead Heath, with pond and bathers; private collection, 241 x 292; oil on millboard; sky and L/S; Burlington Fine Arts Club (1903, 24); Hoozee (1979, 296), Reynolds (1984, 21.40)

Constable's inscription: 'Evening of Coronation July 19. 1821. Westward by North – cloudy and tempestuous looking but did not turn out so.'

Comparison: The weather records for 19 July 1821 are given in entry **(7)** above. Howard reported 'Heavy clouds in the West' and that there was thunder and lightning about 9pm in Tottenham. Constable's observation that it was 'cloudy and tempestuous looking but did not turn out so' was no doubt true for Hampstead as the thunderstorms were to the north. The sky in the study certainly looks stormy but it must have been a warm day if people were still bathing in the evening. The maximum temperature was in the high seventies.

Conclusion: Excellent agreement

(9) 25 July 1821, Hampstead Fields, looking west; private collection; 167 x 222; oil on panel; sky and L/S; Reynolds (1984, 21.41)

Constable's inscription: 'July 25. 1821. looking due West Wind to W 5 afternoon sun behind a shower'

	WIND	*PRES.*	*TEMP.*	*RAIN*	*CLOUD*	*COMMENTS*
Howard (Stratford)	NW	29.76	72	0.04		Showery
Belville	WSW	29.66	69	0.23	7/10 7/10	Heavy Showers
Cary		29.85	68			Showery
Cowe	S	29.70	72	0.519		Showery
Hoy	SW	29.50	64			Cloudy some Rain

(Note that the Cowe observations were for the three-day period 23/24/25 July 1821)

Comparison: All of the weather observations refer to showery weather which confirms Constable's inscription. The painting shows a cumulus shower in the middle distance which obscures the visibility.

Conclusion: Excellent agreement

(10) August 1821, View from Hampstead Heath, looking towards Harrow; Plate 93; Manchester City Art Galleries (1917.176); 250 x 298; oil on paper mounted on canvas; sky and L/S; Royal Academy (1934, 685/393), Wildenstein (1937, 58), Manchester (1956, 42), Auckland (1973, 23); Hoozee (1979, 297), New York (1983, 38), Reynolds (1984, 21.44)

Constable's inscription: '5 Oclock afternoon: August 1821 very fine bright & wind after rain slightly in the morning.'

Comparison: The first half of August 1821 was dominated by westerlies and the second half by easterlies. There were several days when it rained, but some of them can be ruled out as Howard recorded that the rain fell in the afternoon e.g. 2 and 11 August. On 12 August Howard recorded 'a few drops of rain' and on 14 August Cowe recorded 'rain am'. From 25 August onwards it rained every day until the end of the month. 14 August is the most likely candidate therefore. The sky in the painting is superb with cirrus aloft and broken stratocumulus at right angles to it below. The sun is obscured by the clouds with shafts of sunlight bursting through.

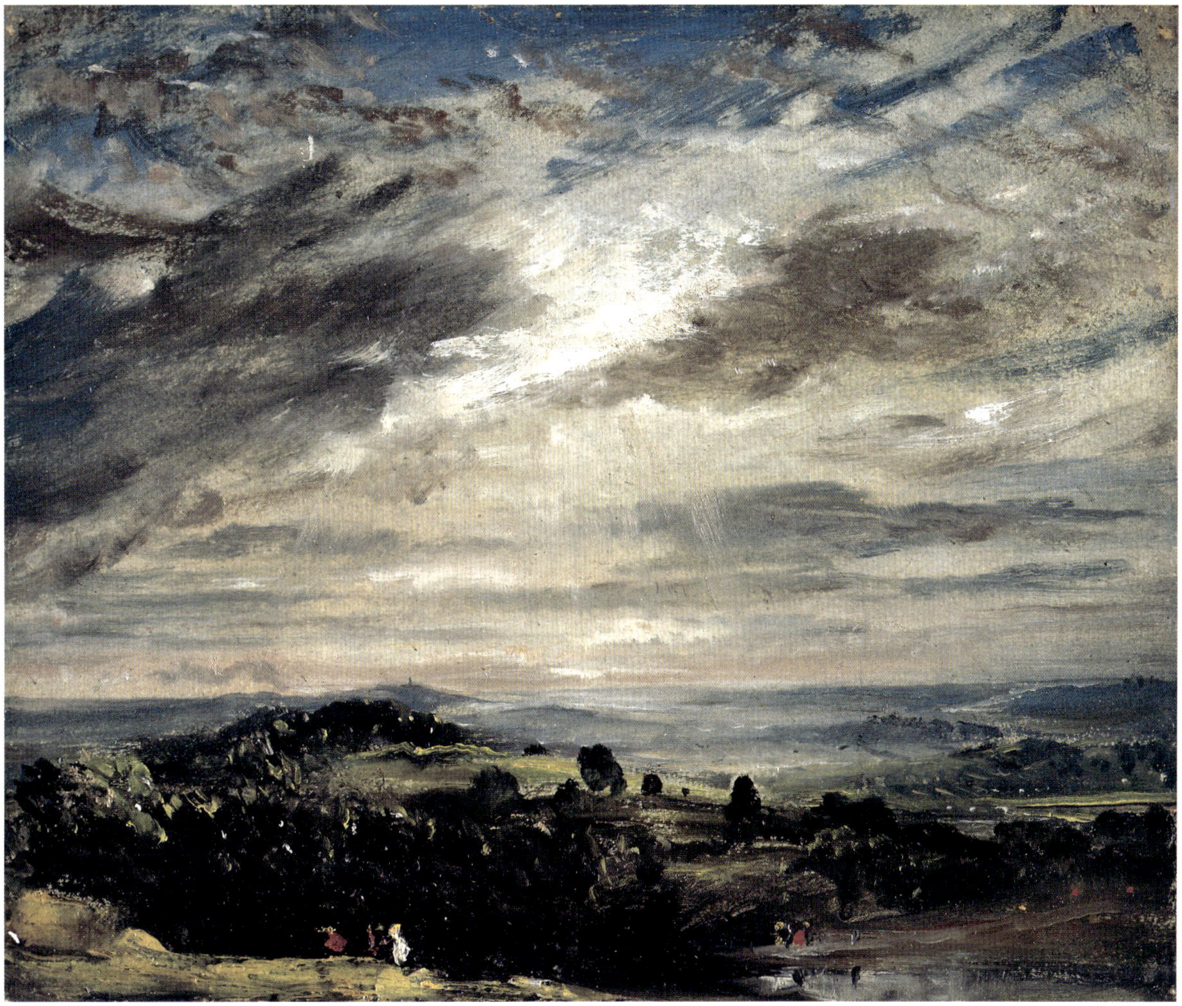

Plate 93 John Constable, *View from Hampstead Heath Looking Towards Harrow*, August 1821. Copyright Manchester City Art Galleries

(11) 3 September 1821? Study of sky and trees; Plate 94, V&A (151–1888); 241 x 298; oil on paper; sky and L/S; Reynolds (1973, 221), Thornes (1978, 13(sketch 4), 28(sketch 4)), Hoozee (1979, 298), Reynolds (1984, 21.45)

Constable's inscription: 'September 3d. Noon. very sultry. with large drops of Rain falling on my palate light air from S.W.'

1821	*WIND*	*PRES.*	*TEMP.*	*RAIN*	*CLOUD*	*COMMENTS*
Howard (Stratford)	SW	29.83	78			Cloudy and fine at intervals
Belville	SW	29.86	72		3/10 7/10	Fine
Cary		30.02	72			Fair
Cowe	SSE	29.58	74			Fair
Hoy	SW	29.82	71			Mostly Cloudy some drops

1822	*WIND*	*PRES.*	*TEMP.*	*RAIN*	*CLOUD*	*COMMENTS*
Howard (Stratford)	NW	29.96	73			Fine
Belville	SW	29.87	68	0.4	3/10 4/10	Fair
Cary		30.01	69			Fair
Cowe	W	29.84	72			Fair

Comparison: There is no doubt that this study was made in 1821; so certain is the Victoria and Albert Museum that this was painted in 1821 that they have inserted 1821 on the frame of the picture. The inscription agrees nicely with the weather data for 3 September 1821. Temperatures were in the mid-seventies and Hoy actually states, 'mostly cloudy some drops' which suggests that although it was cloudy, it was one of those days when 'it was trying to rain but didn't', there not being sufficient depth of convection. The wind appears to have been from the south west also. On September 1822 the wind was more to the north and temperatures not quite so high. The size is also typical of 1821. The sky shows the base of a dark cumulus cloud overhead with some light rain falling from it.

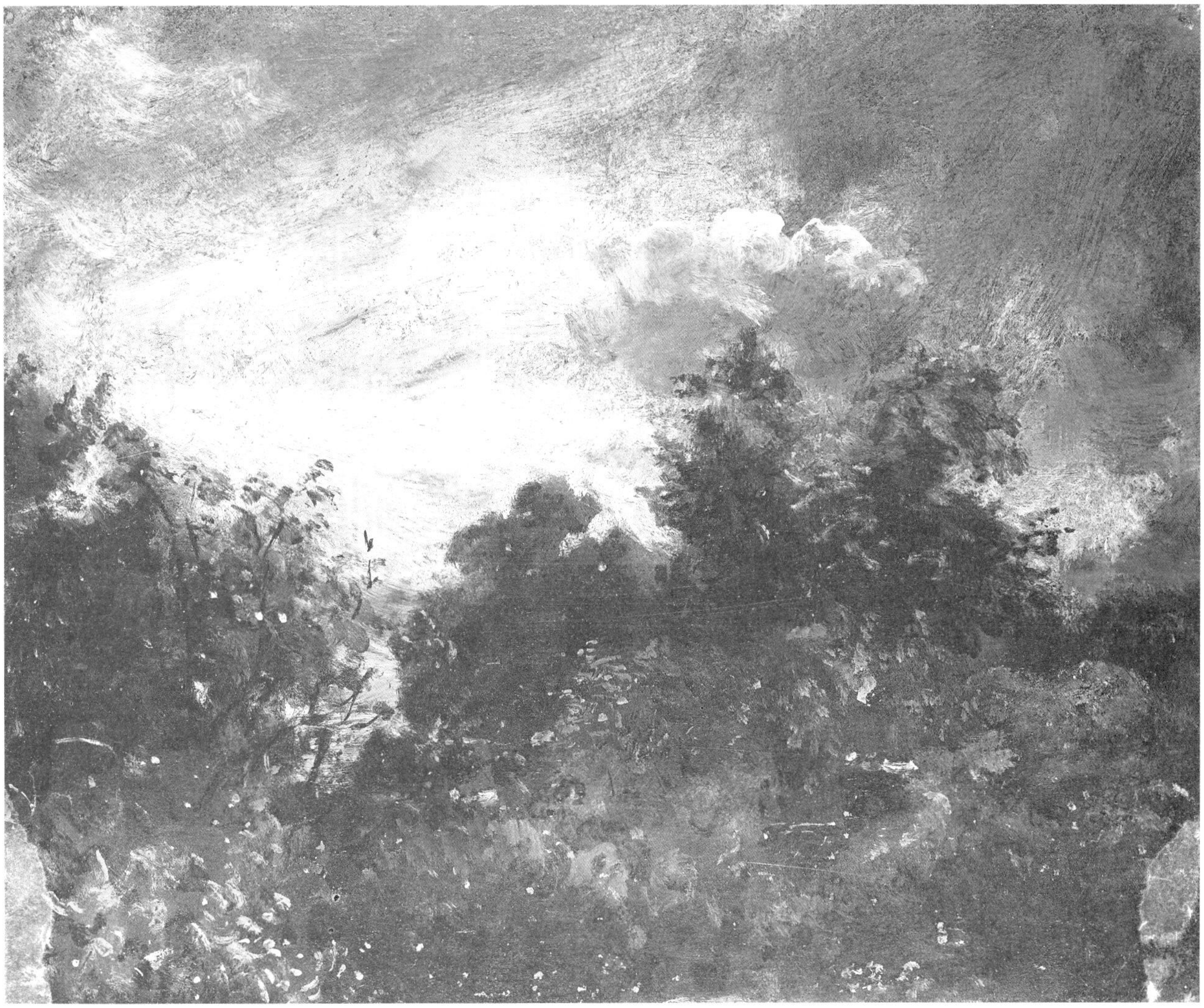

Plate 94 John Constable, *Study of Sky and Trees*, 3 September 1821[?]. V&A Picture Library

(12) 10 September 1821; **Cloud study**; whereabouts unknown; 216 x 292; oil; sky and L/S?; Grosvenor Gallery Exhibition (1889, 280); Reynolds (1973, R222), Thornes (1978, 2), Hoozee (1979, 299), Reynolds (1996, 244)

Constable's inscription: 'Sepr. 10 1821 Eleven o'clock Sultry with warm [?] rain falling large heavy clouds [...?] a heavy downpour and thunder.'

	WIND	*PRES.*	*TEMP.*	*RAIN*	*CLOUD*	*COMMENTS*
Howard (Stratford)	W	29.82	70	0.11		Some thunder about noon: heavy showers; lunar halo.
Belville	SW	29.61	68		7/10 5/10	Thunderstorm between 11 & 12 o'clock
Cary		29.77	66			Showery
Cowe	W	29.58	69			Fine
Hoy	SW	29.55	64			Cloudy aft. clear SW.

Comparison: A study dated 10 September 1821 was exhibited in 1889 at the Grosvenor Gallery; however the above weather inscription appears, crossed out, on the back of the study dated 12 September 1821. Reynolds (1960: 137) states 'The existence of two inscriptions relating to different dates suggests that the artist sometimes wrote these on the backs of his oil sketches later, from rough notes made at the time or from memory'. The thundery activity noted by Howard and Belville must have been to the north and east of the centre of the city as it was noted also by Constable, but not by Cary, Cowe or Hoy.

Conclusion: Excellent agreement

(13) 10 September 1821; Cloud study with tree tops and building; Plate 95; private collection; 248 x 302; oil on paper; sky and L/S; Parris and Fleming-Williams (1991, 119), Reynolds (1996, 21.46)

Constable's inscription: 'Sepr. 10. 1821, Noon. gentle Wind at West. very sultry after a heavy shower with thunder. accumulated thunder clouds passing slowly away to the south East. very bright & hot. all the foliage sparkling (?with the) and wet.'

Comparison: This inscription fits in perfectly with the previous study **(12)** made at 11am. The thunder storm has passed over and the sky is clearing with sunlight bursting through the clouds. Constable states that the wind was from the west but that the thunderstorm passed away to the south east, confirming that he realised that thunderstorms do not move with the ground level wind.

Conclusion: Excellent agreement

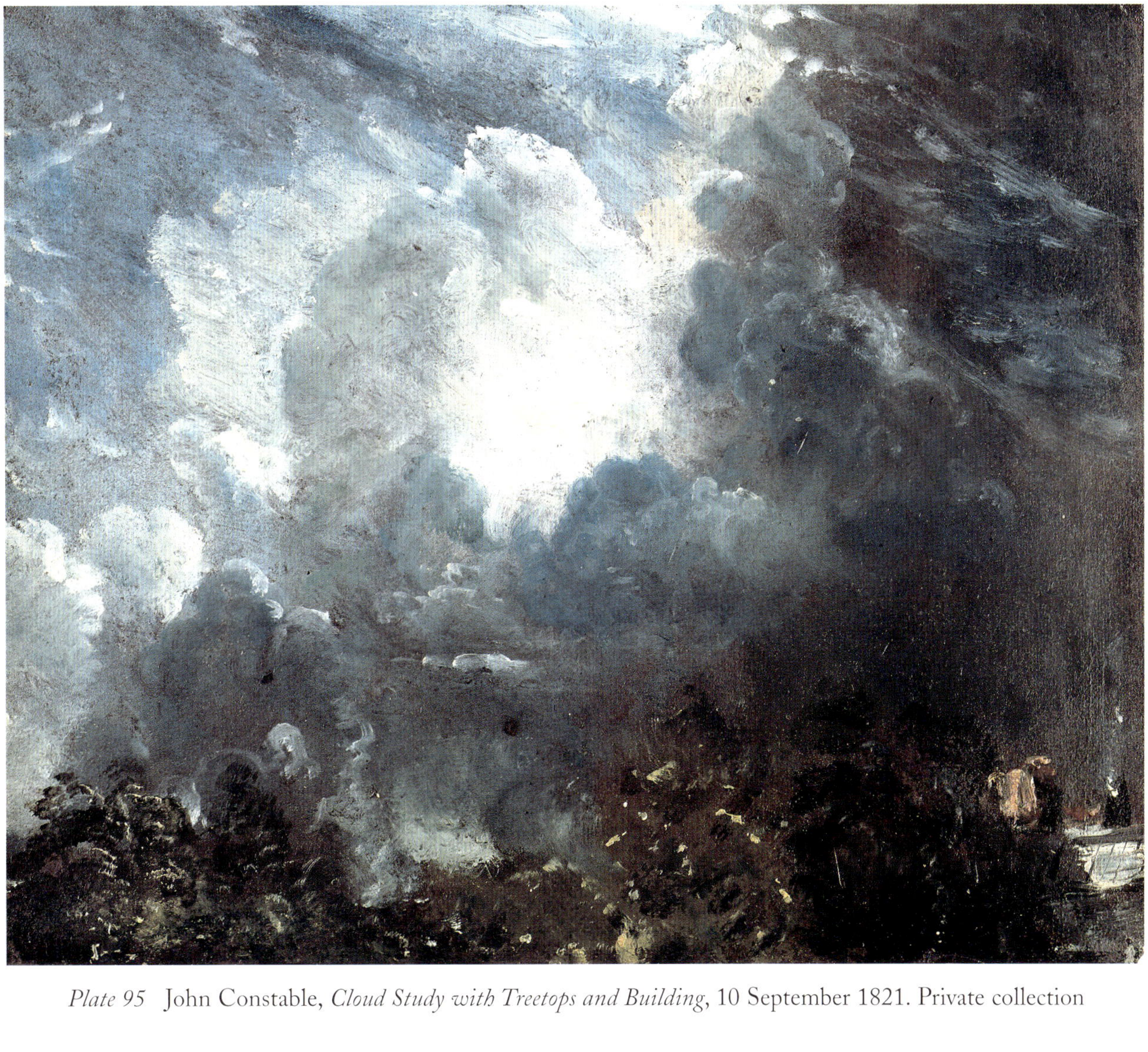

Plate 95 John Constable, *Cloud Study with Treetops and Building*, 10 September 1821. Private collection

(14) 11 September 1821; **Study of clouds at Hampstead; Plate 96**; Royal Academy of Arts (52); 242 x 298; oil on paper laid on board; sky and L/S; Manchester City Gallery (1956, 48), Royal Academy (1963, 224), Detroit and Philadelphia (1968, 126), Thornes (1978, 3), Hoozee (1979, 300), New York (1983, 39), Reynolds (1984, 21.47)

Constable's inscription: Hampstead Sept 11, 1821. 10. to 11. Morning under the sun – Clouds silvery grey on warm ground Sultry. Light wind to the S.W. fine all day – but rain in the night following.

	WIND	*PRES.*	*TEMP.*	*RAIN*	*CLOUD*	*COMMENTS*
Howard (Stratford)	W	29.80	71			Cloudy: fine.
Belville	SW	29.91	66		2/10 4/10	Fair
Cary		30.08	66			Fair
Cowe	W	29.89	70			Fair
Hoy	NW	29.80	60			Cloudy clear

Comparison: The weather data are in very good agreement, suggesting a fine day with some cloud around. The painting is almost a pure sky study but for a clump of trees, and shows 'streets' of small cumulus clouds that are characteristic of a light westerly airstream. The cloud amount in the painting agrees well with Belville's figures showing about 3/10 of cumulus cloud. Temperatures were warm, but not hot. The humidity was probably quite high, shown by the thunderstorm of the previous day, which was why Constable wrote that it was 'sultry'. There is no mention of rain in the night in the weather records, although Howard mentions a showery morning on the 12 September.

Conclusion: Very good agreement

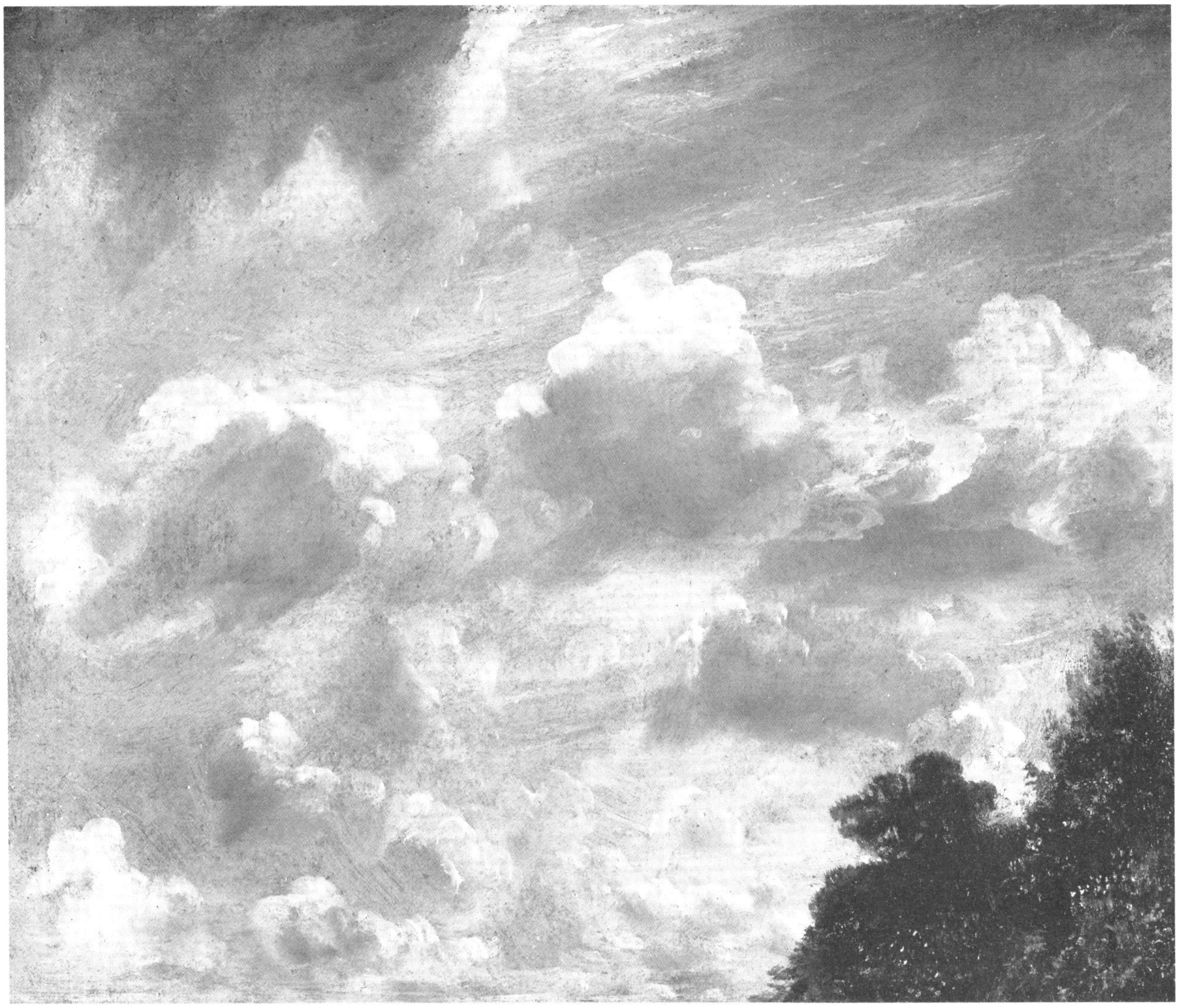

Plate 96 John Constable, *Cloud Study, Hampstead; Tree at Right*, 11 September 1821. Royal Academy of Arts, London

(15) 12 September 1821; Study of sky and trees, with a red house, at Hampstead; Plate 97; V&A (156–1888); 241 x 298; oil on paper; sky and L/S; Reynolds (1973, 222), Thornes (1978, 4), Hoozee (1979, 301), Reynolds (1984, 21.48)

Constable's inscription: 'Sepr. 12 1821. Noon. Wind fresh at West. [three or four words deleted].. Sun very Hot. looking southward exceedingly bright vivid & Glowing, very heavy showers in the Afternoon but a fine evening. High wind in the night.'

	WIND	*PRES.*	*TEMP.*	*RAIN*	*CLOUD*	*COMMENTS*
Howard (Stratford)	SW	29.73	71	.13		Showery morning : cloudy
Belville	SW	29.55	66	.08	8/10 9/10	Heavy rain
Cary		29.68	69			Stormy
Cowe	S	29.58	70	.153		Rain a.m.
Hoy	SW	29.57	64			Mostly cloudy heavy S.W.and some thunder aft.

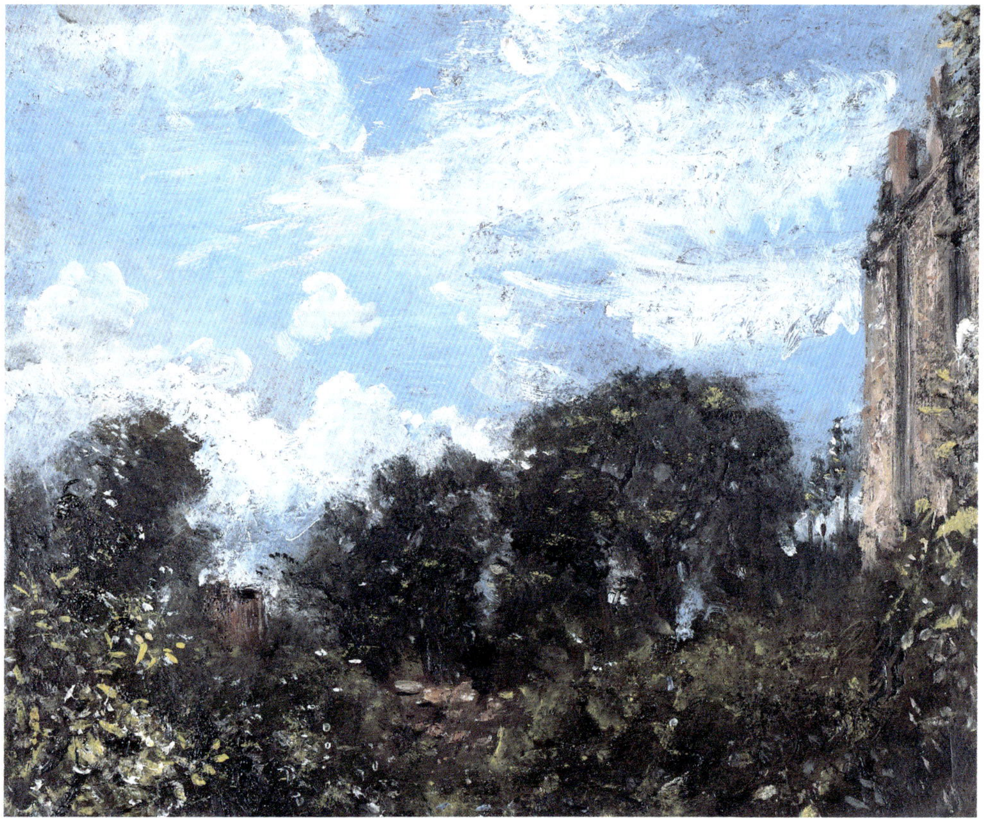

Plate 97 John Constable, *Study of Sky and Trees, with a Red House, at Hampstead*, 12 September 1821. V&A Picture Library

(16) 12 September 1821; Hampstead Heath, looking towards Harrow, at sunset; Plate 98; Private collection; 241 x 292; oil on paper; sky and L/S; Tate (1976, 195); Thornes (1978, 5), Hoozee (1979, 302), Reynolds (1984, 21.49)

Constable's inscription: 'Sepr. 12. 1821. Sun setting over Harrow This appearance of the Evening was [aft?] just after a very heavy rain more rain in the night and a very [light?] wind which continued all the day following – [the 13th] while making this sketch observed the Moon rising very beautifully [in the?] due East over the heavy clouds from which the late showers had fallen., and Wind Gentle ... increasing from the North west. Rather'

Comparison: These two long descriptions of the weather of 12 September are consistent except in the reference to a '[light?] wind' in **(16)** and a 'fresh' wind in **(15)**. I have been unable to check the inscription of **(16)** which may read 'high' rather than 'light', which is more consistent with the rainy south-westerly airstream. Of course the wind may have dropped by the evening and picked up again in the night. The reference to future weather in both accounts suggests that the descriptions were added later, particularly in view of the description of weather on 10 September which appears crossed out on the back of **(15)**. This may have led to some confusion, Constable not being quite sure whether **(15)** was painted on 10 or 12 September. The picture suggests 12 September in that rain could not have been falling at the time of the painting, from that sky. Howard and Cowe specifically refer to rain in the morning which Constable does not mention. Pressure dropped sharply during the day; it is quite possible a depression passed through – warm front in the morning and a vigorous cold front in the afternoon.

Conclusion: Good agreement

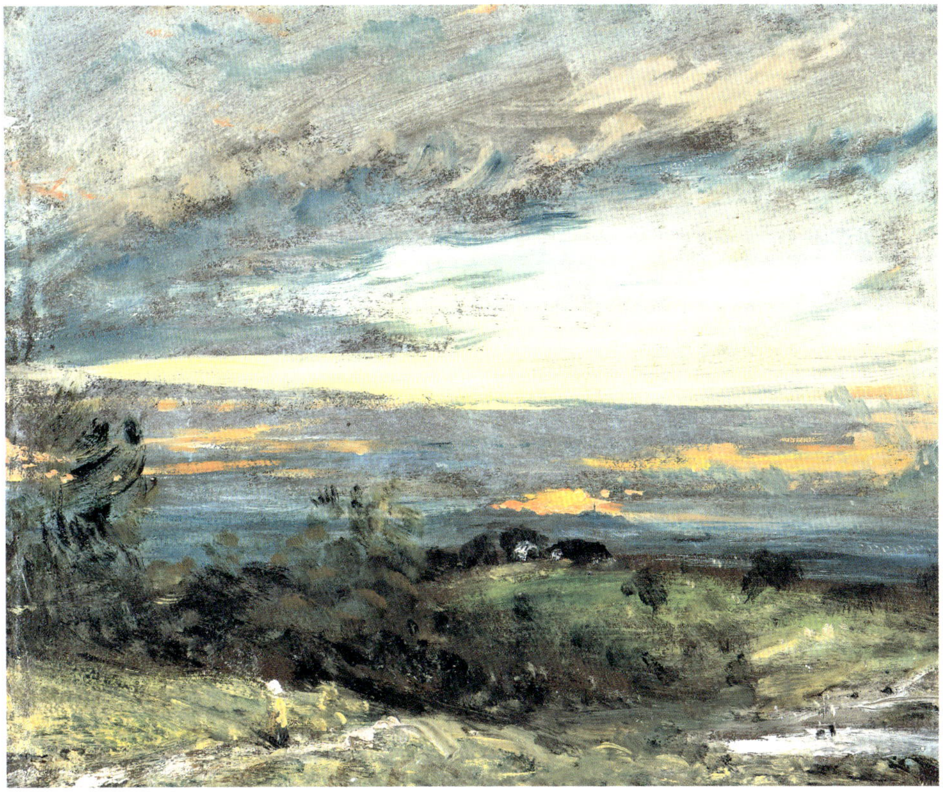

Plate 98 John Constable, *Hampstead Heath, Sun Setting over Harrow*, 12 September 1821. Private collection

(17) 13 September 1821?; Study of altocumulus* clouds; Plate 99; Yale Center for British Art (B1981.25.156); 248 x 303; oil on paper laid on board; pure sky; Washington (1969, 44), Thornes (1978, 13(5)), Hoozee (1979, 346), Reynolds (1984, 21.50)

Constable's inscription: 'Septr 13th. one o'clock. Slight wind at North West, which became tempestuous in the afternoon, With Rain all the night following.'

1821	*WIND*	*PRES.*	*TEMP.*	*RAIN*	*CLOUD*	*COMMENTS*
Howard (Stratford)	NW	29.93	66	.15		Cloudy: rainy night.
Belville	W	29.87	67	.42	5/10 10/10	Cloudy, evening rainy
Cary		30.02	66			Fair
Cowe	SW	29.83	65	.218		Showery
Hoy	NW	29.80	63			Cloudy

1822	*WIND*	*PRES.*	*TEMP.*	*RAIN*	*CLOUD*	*COMMENTS*
Howard (Stratford)	NE	30.12	64			Cloudy and fine
Belville	E	29.94	61	.2	7/10 2/10	Windy and cloudy
Cary		30.10	59			Cloudy
Cowe	E					Fine

* Note that altocumulus was not defined until after 1855 by Renou, the director of French meteorological observatories at the time. Renou was the first to stress the importance of the height of a cloud in its classification. Howard would probably have called it cirrostratus.

Comparison: The weather evidence points clearly to 1821. The north-west wind and Howard's reference to a 'rainy night' fits very closely with Constable's inscription. The fine easterly weather of 1822 does not fit at all. This therefore is the first pure sky study that has been associated with 1821. Constable made two other pure sky studies which are accurately dated 25 and 28 September on very similar-sized paper. All Constable's pure sky studies of September 1822 were done on much larger paper. This study can therefore be accurately dated as 13 September 1821.

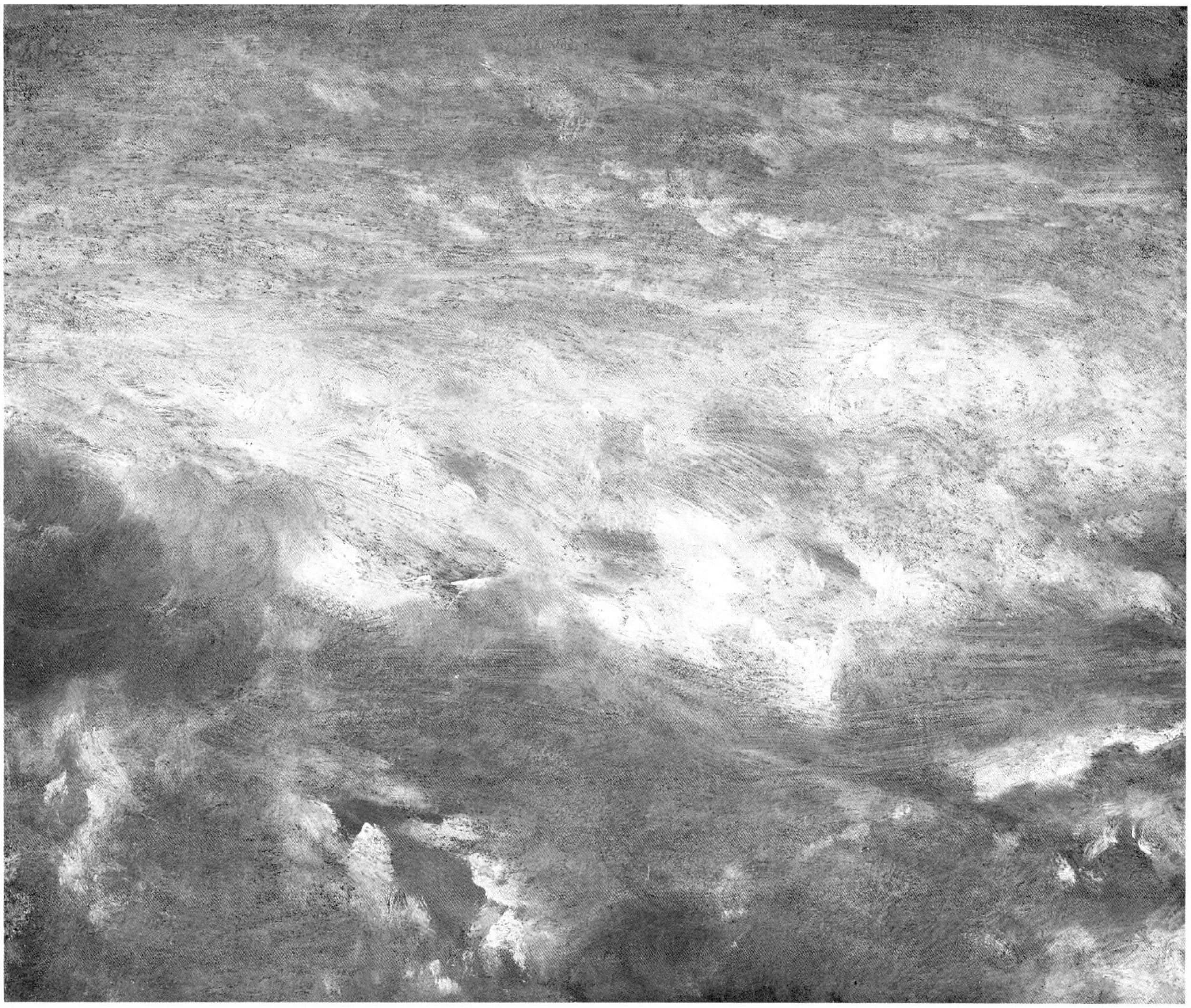

Plate 99 John Constable, *Cloud Study*, 13 September 1821. Yale Center for British Art, Paul Mellon Collection (B1981.25.156)

(18) 24 September 1821?; Study of sky and trees; Plate 100; V&A (167–1888); 248 x 305; oil on paper; sky and L/S; Reynolds (1960, 224), Thornes (1978, 14 (6)), Hoozee (1979, 303), Reynolds (1984, 21.51)

Constable's inscription: 'Sepr. 24th ... 10 o'clock morning wind S.W. warm & fine till afternoon, when it rained and wind got more to the north.'

1821	*WIND*	*PRES.*	*TEMP.*	*RAIN*	*CLOUD*	*COMMENTS*
Howard (Stratford)	W	29.80	66			Overcast
Belville	SW	29.55	67		5/10 8/10	Cloudy Fine night
Cary		29.74	66			Showery
Cowe	SW	29.58	64			Cloudy
Hoy	SW	29.53	63			Cloudy with showers

1822	*WIND*	*PRES.*	*TEMP.*	*RAIN*	*CLOUD*	*COMMENTS*
Howard (Stratford)	NE	29.27	60	.85		Rainy
Belville	NE	29.23	62	36	10/10 10/10	Cloudy
Cary		29.33	59			Showery
Cowe	E	29.42	60	.479		Showery

Comparison: The weather data supports the 1821 dating in that the wind direction is very similar and the temperature is warm for late September. The picture shows the edges of large cumulus clouds conducive to the rain that followed. The 24 September 1822 had an easterly airstream that was much too wet to fit Constable's description. The size also fits in with Constable's other September 1821 studies. The dating of 24 September 1821 is indisputable.

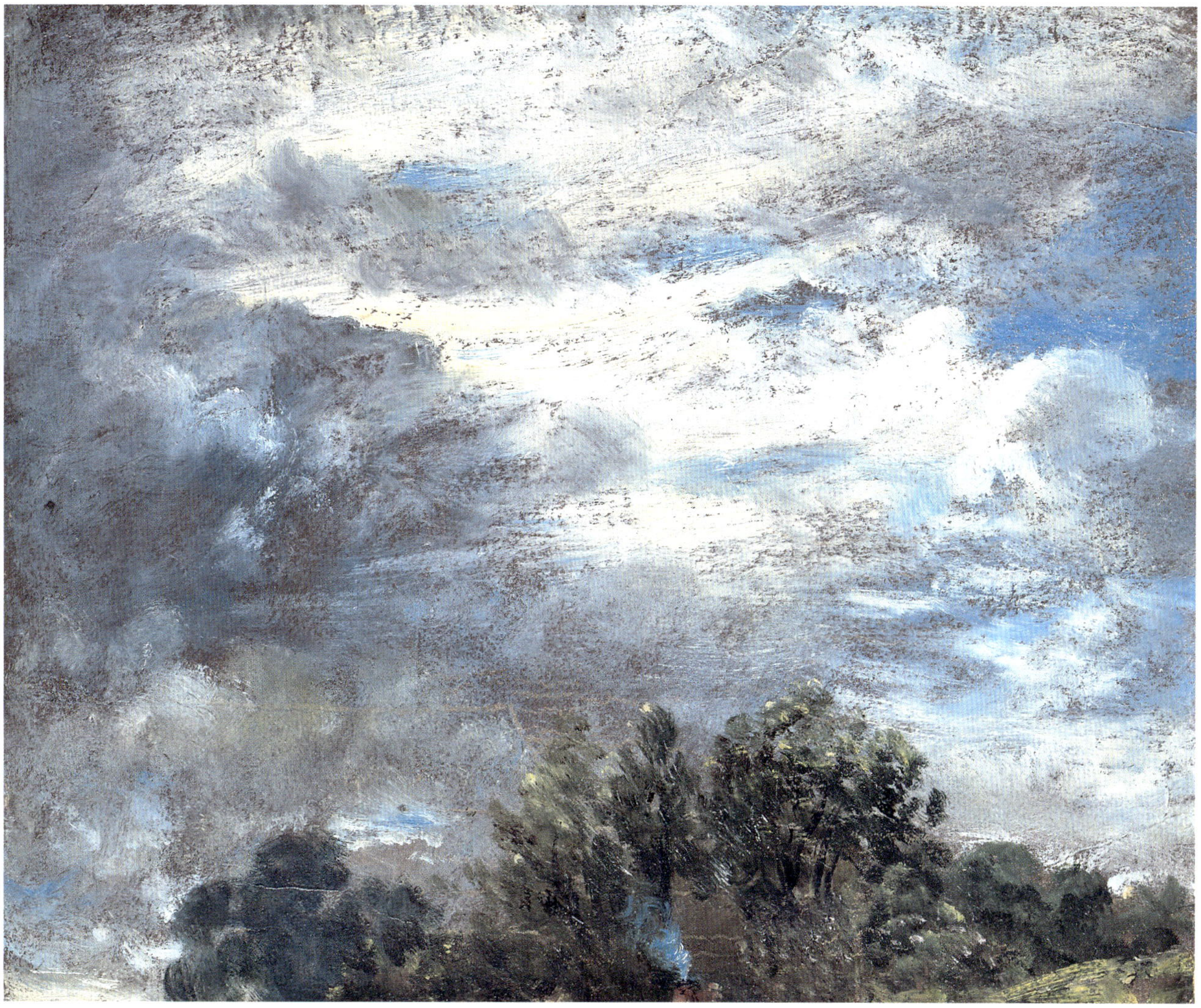

Plate 100 John Constable, *Study of Sky and Trees*, 24 September 1821[?], V&A Picture Library

(19) 25 September 1821; Cloud study: sun bursting through dark clouds; Plate 101; Yale Center for British Art; 212 x 290; pure sky; Washington (1969, 40 Note that the study is upside down in the Washington catalogue); Thornes (1978, 6), Hoozee (1979, 304), Reynolds (1984, 21.52)

Constable's inscription: '25th. Septr 1821 about from 2 to 3 afternoon looking to the north – Strong Wind at west, bright light coming through the Clouds which were lying one on another.'

	WIND	*PRES.*	*TEMP.*	*RAIN*	*CLOUD*	*COMMENTS*
Howard (Stratford)	W	29.98	66			Overcast
Belville	SW	29.91	64	.02	7/10 10/10	Cloudy
Cary		30.04	64			Fair
Cowe	SW	29.87	64			Fair
Hoy	NW	29.88	66			Cloudy morning: aft Cloudy

Comparison: A westerly airstream is confirmed by the weather data and it seems to have been a cloudy but dry day. Constable's picture of an almost overcast sky ties in with Belville's cloud data. The study depicts the bases of several large cumulus clouds that have merged into stratocumulus, with the sun bursting through as the title suggests. Constable's statement that the clouds were 'lying one on another' suggests that there were several layers of cloud at different heights, perhaps a layer of altocumulus above the stratocumulus. This is the second pure sky study identified as 1821.

Conclusion: Very good agreement

Plate 101 John Constable, *Cloud Study*, 1821. Yale Center for British Art, Paul Mellon Collection (B1981.25.147)

(20) 27 September 1821; Cloud study with trees; Plate 102; Yale Center for British Art; 165 x 310; oil on paper laid on board; sky and L/S; Washington (1969, 41), Thornes (1978, 7), Hoozee (1979, 307), New York (1983, 17–19), Reynolds (1984, 21.53)

Constable's inscription: 'Sepr 27th 1821 – 10 morning, fine morning after Rainey night.'

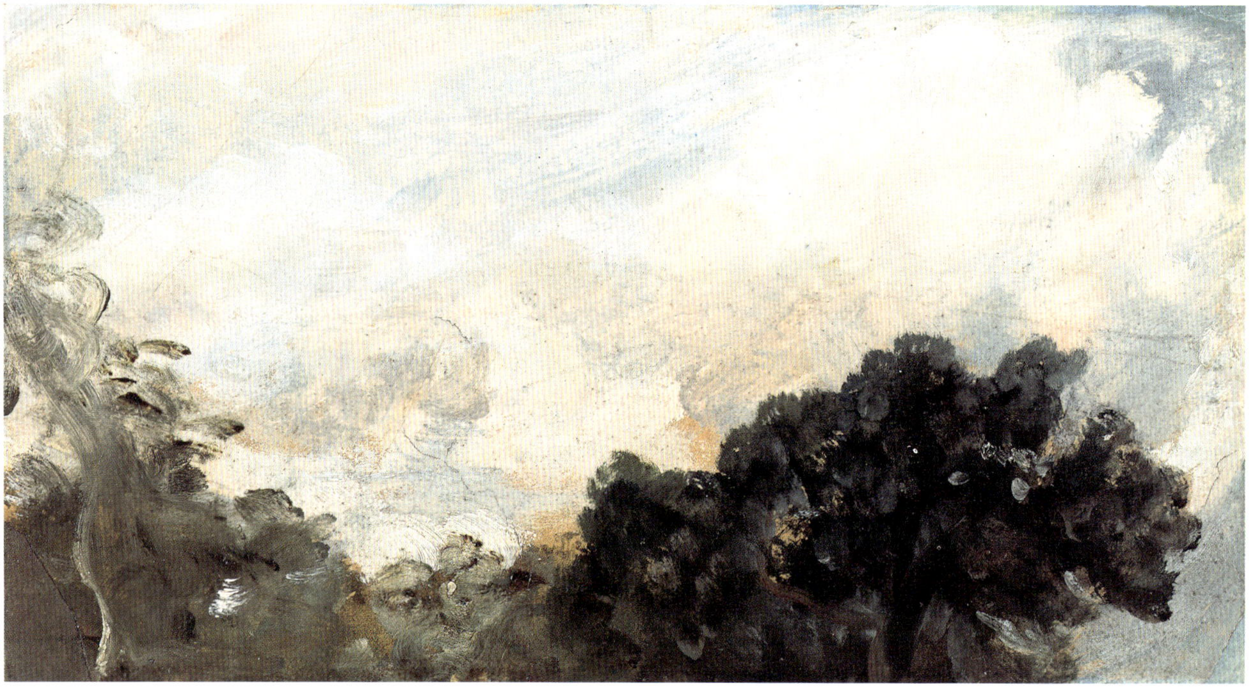

Plate 102 John Constable, *Cloud Study with Trees*, 27 September 1821
Yale Center for British Art, Paul Mellon Collection (B1981.25.152)

(21) 27 September 1821?; Cloud study over an horizon of trees; Plate 103; Royal Academy of Arts (70); 248 x 292; oil on paper laid on board; sky and L/S; Manchester (1956, 51), Royal Academy (1963, 218), Tate (1976, 197), Thornes (1978, 14(7)), Hoozee (1979, 308), Reynolds (1984, 21.54)

Constable's inscription: 'Noon 27 Sept very bright after rain wind West'

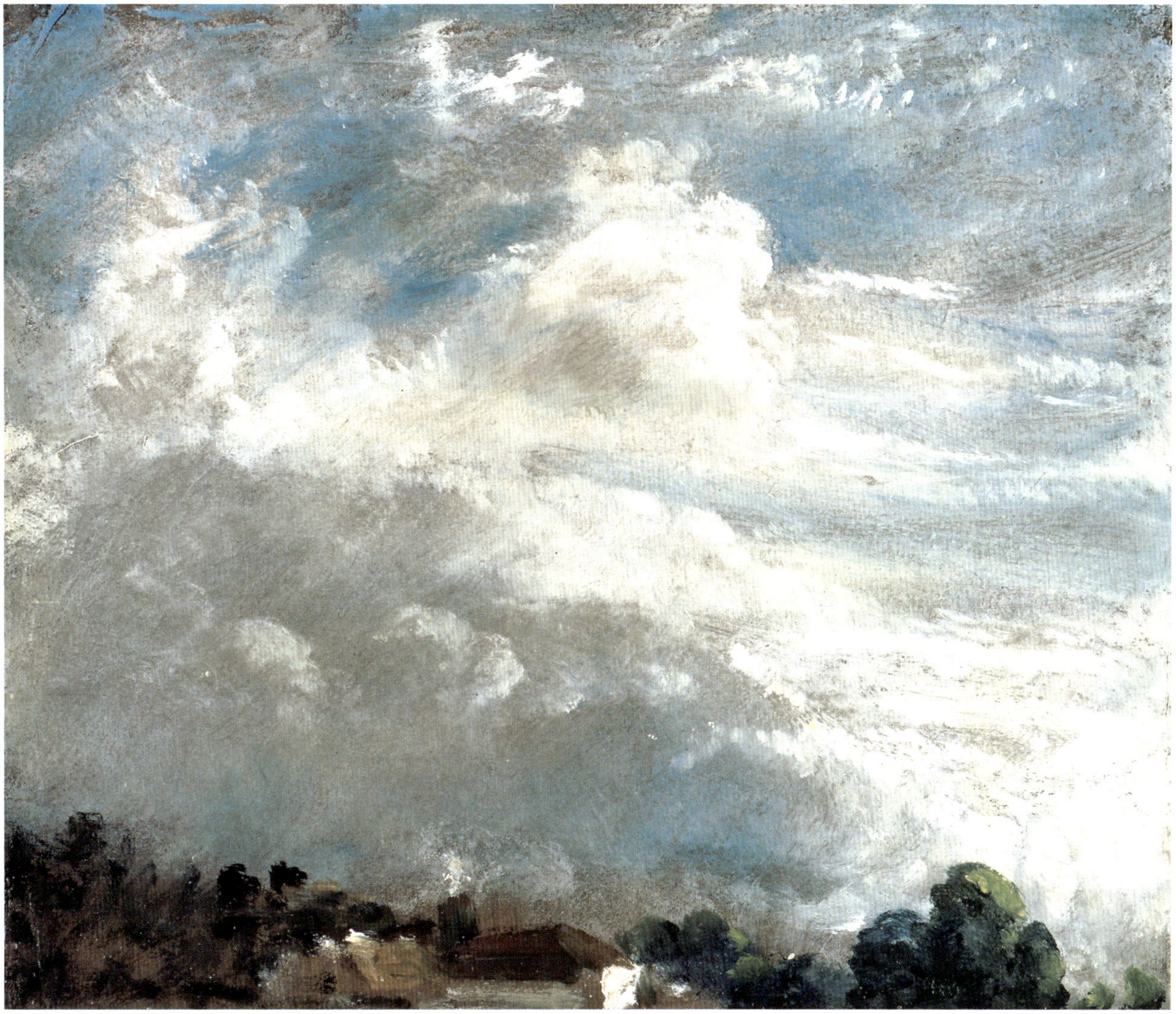

Plate 103 John Constable, *Cloud Study: Horizon of Trees*, 27 September 1821?
Royal Academy of Arts, London

(22) 27 September 1821; Hampstead Heath looking over to Harrow; Plate 104; Royal Academy of Arts (73); 235 x 286; oil on paper laid on board; sky and L/S; Manchester (1956, 43), Royal Academy (1963, 228), Tate (1976, 196), Thornes (1978, 8), Hoozee (1979, 305), Reynolds (1984, 21.55)

Constable's inscription: '4 afternoon 27 Septr 1821 wood bank of Vale very (warm?) & bright after rain.'

1821	*WIND*	*PRES.*	*TEMP.*	*RAIN*	*CLOUD*	*COMMENTS*
Howard (Stratford)	NW	29.88	63			Cloudy
Belville	WSW	29.80	68		9/10 4/10	Cloudy
Cary		29.94	65			Showery
Cowe	SW	29.86	65			Fair
Hoy	NW	29.75	62			Mostly Cloudy Some drops

1822	*WIND*	*PRES.*	*TEMP.*	*RAIN*	*CLOUD*	*COMMENTS*
Howard (Stratford)	N	30.21	58			Bleak
Belville	NE	30.05	57		8/10 7/10	Cloudy
Cary		30.24	57			Cloudy
Cowe	NE	30.01	59			Fair

Comparison: The three studies at 10am, noon and 4pm all mention earlier rain which is not mentioned in the weather records. All three pictures depict large cumulus clouds showing considerable convection that could have led to scattered showers. The reading of 'warm' in **(22)** is not impossible, but seems unlikely in that temperatures remained in the low sixties (apart from that recorded by Belville). The westerly airstream certainly supports the weather depicted. The dating of **(21)** as 1821 seems certain. The wind was from the north and east on that day in 1822, which was described as bleak by Howard. The towering cumulus clouds depicted by Constable are so similar to those displayed in two other studies on 27 September 1821 that this must be of the same day.

Conclusion: Good agreement for **(20)** and **(22)**

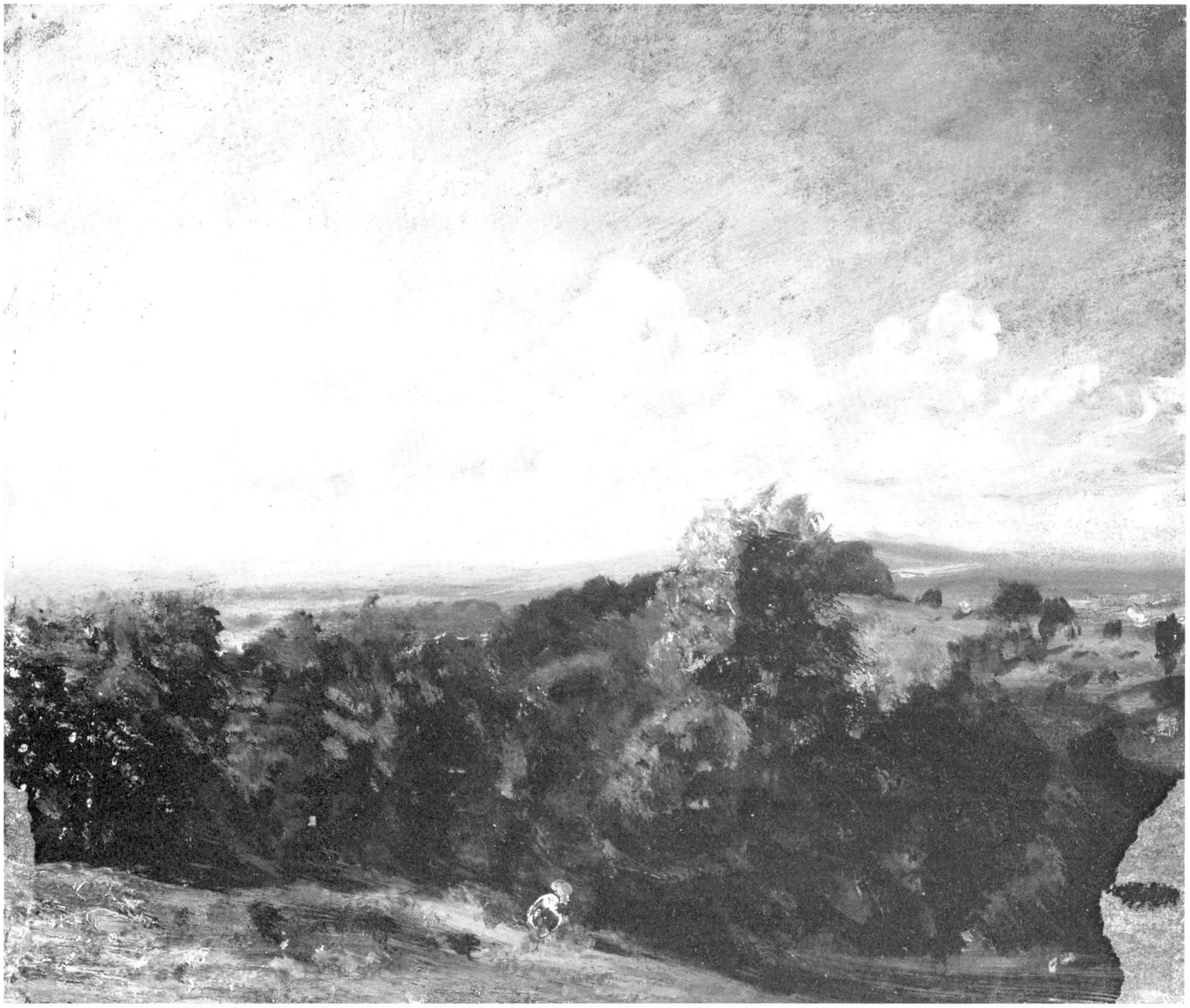

Plate 104 John Constable, *Landscape Study: Hampstead Heath Looking Towards Harrow*, 27 September 1821. Royal Academy of Arts, London

(23) 28 September 1821; **Stratocumulus clouds; Plate 105**; Yale Center for British Art; 255 x 305; oil on paper laid on board; pure sky; Washington (1969, 43), Thornes (1978, 9), Hoozee (1979, 309), Reynolds (1984, 21.57)

Constable's inscription: 'Sep. 28 1821 Noon – looking North West windy from the S.W. large bright clouds flying rather fast very stormy night followed.'

	WIND	*PRES*	*TEMP.*	*RAIN*	*CLOUD*	*COMMENTS*
Howard (Stratford)	SW	29.62	65	.30		Fine: rainy night
Belville	S	29.80	63		5/10 8/10	Wind evening strong
Cary		29.88	65			Fair with high wind
Cowe	SW	29.86	65			Fair: rain at night
Hoy	SW	29.80	60			Mostly Cloudy rain at night

Comparison: Excellent agreement of both wind direction and strength, and also the rainy night to follow. The day was fine but rather cloudy – Constable's painting showing what appears to be an almost overcast stratocumulus sky. It is curious to note that the painting has been titled 'Stratocumulus clouds' when the term 'stratocumulus' was not in use when Constable made the study. (It did not appear until the 1870s.) Howard would probably have called it either extensive cumulus or cirro-stratus. There is a very small strip of landscape along the bottom of the picture, but this can be classified as a pure sky study. This study was dated as 1822 when exhibited in the Grosvenor Gallery in 1889, presumably because it is a virtually a pure sky study. However the weather on 28 September 1822 was cool and fine with north-easterly winds, which is nothing like Constable's inscription. The dating of 1821 is therefore indisputable.

Conclusion: Excellent agreement

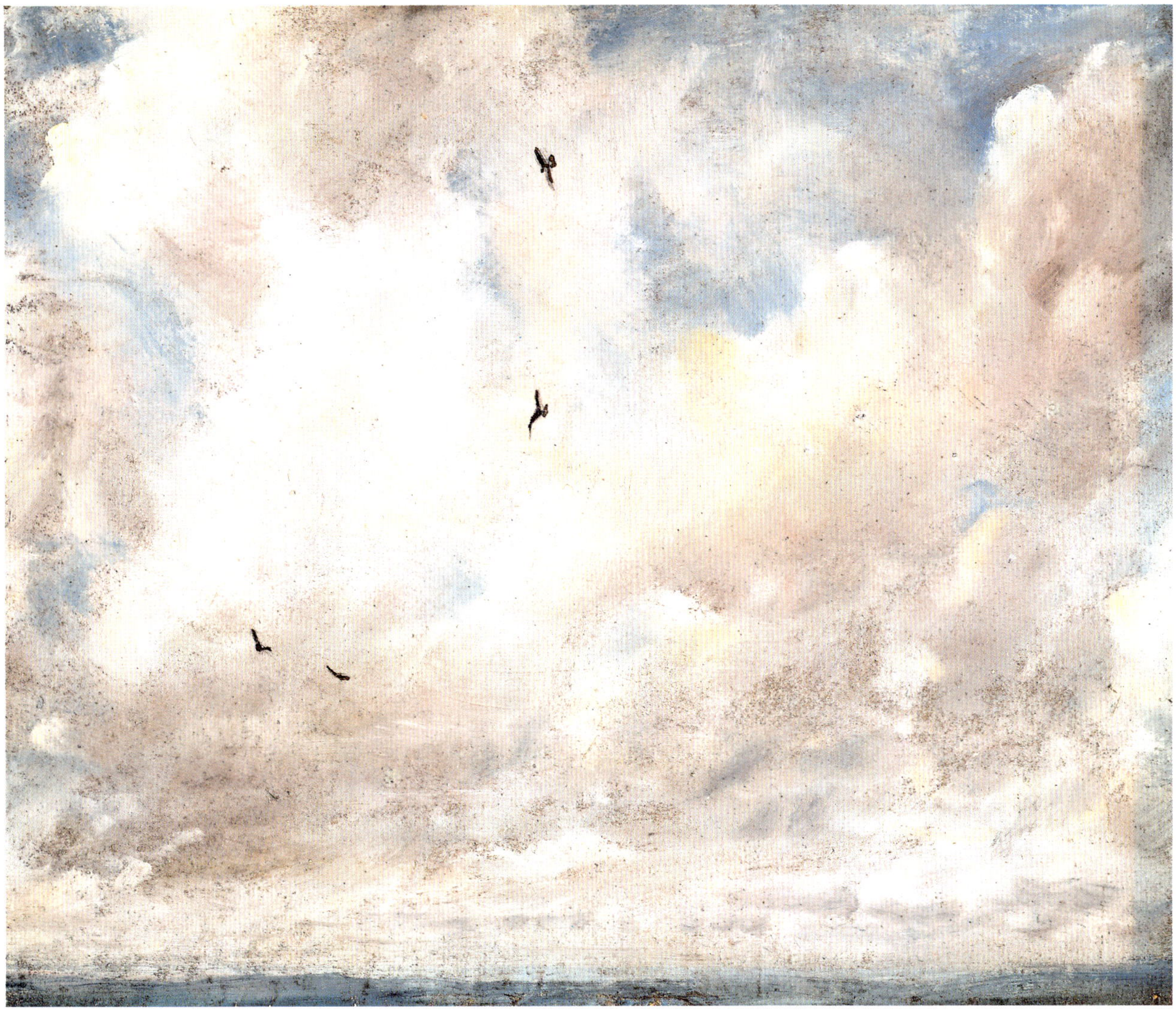

Plate 105 John Constable, *Cloud Study*, 28 September 1821. Yale Center for British Art, Paul Mellon Collection (B1981.25.155)

(24) 2 October 1821; **Study of sky and trees at Hampstead; Plate 106**; V&A (168–1888); 245 x 298; oil on paper; sky and L/S; Reynolds (1960, 226), Baskett (1966, colour plate 15), Thornes (1978, 10), Hoozee (1979, 311), New York (1983, 40), Reynolds (1984, 21.58)

Constable's inscription: 'Ocr. 2d. 1821. 8. to 9. very fine still morning. turned out a may day.'

	WIND	*PRES.*	*TEMP.*	*RAIN*	*CLOUD*	*COMMENTS*
Howard						
(Stratford)	NW	29.96	61			Fine
(Tottenham)						Remarkably fine: brilliant sunset
Belville	SW	30.05	60		3/10 4/10	Fair
Cary		30.20	59			Fair
Cowe	W	29.94	62			Fine
Hoy	NW	29.96	58			Cloudy aft. clear

Comparison: Constable's reference to 'a may day' relates well to the weather records. Although the day was 'remarkably fine' the temperature was on the cool side. The clouds depicted by Constable in the study appear to be cirrus and cirrostratus illuminated by the sun which is still low in the sky.

Conclusion: Very good agreement

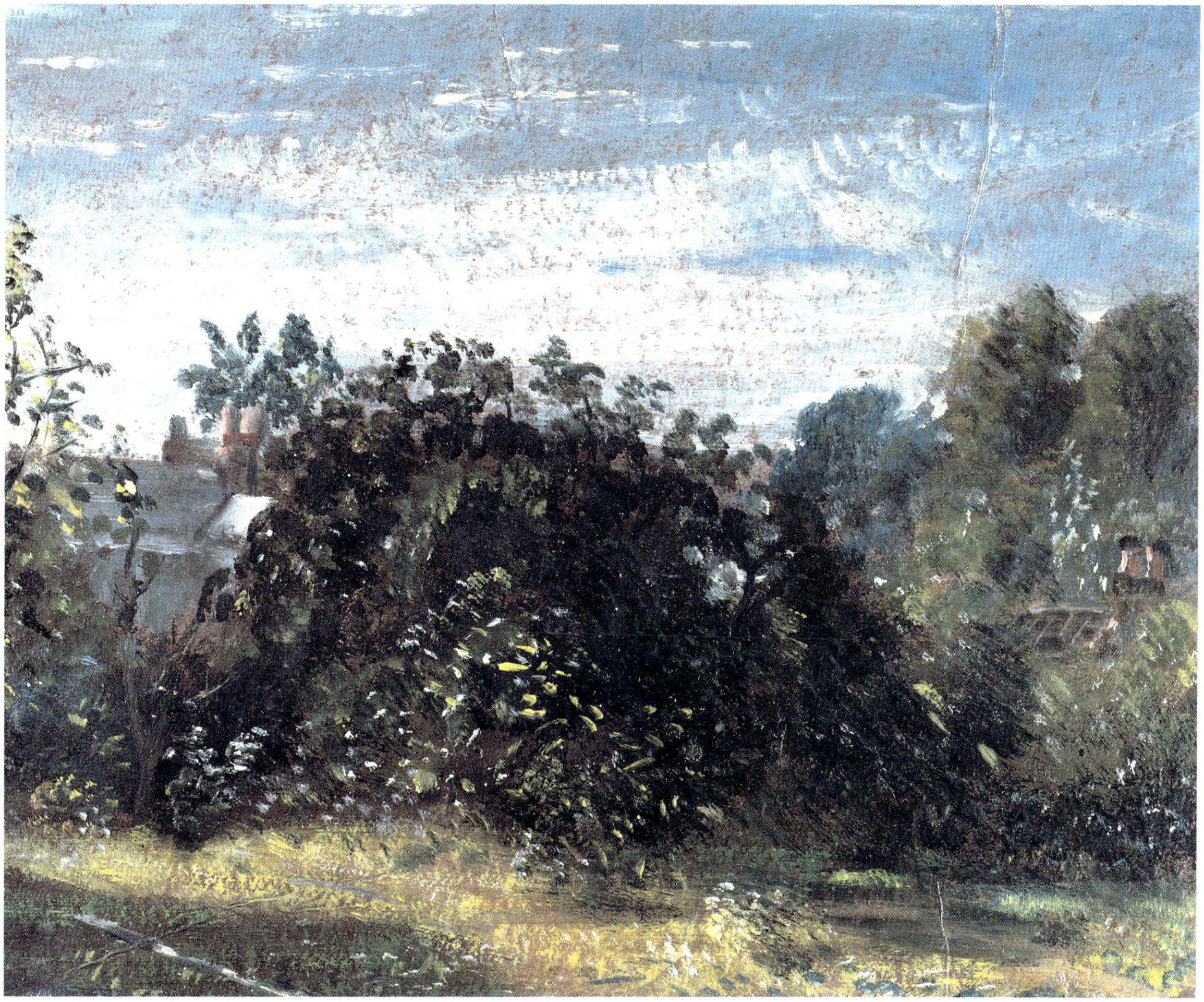

Plate 106 John Constable, *Study of Sky and Trees at Hampstead*, 2 October 1821. V&A Picture Library

(25) 9 October 1821; **A lane through trees**; private collection; 247 x 292; oil on paper mounted on board; sky and L/S; Thornes (1978, 11), Hoozee (1979, 313), Reynolds (1984, 21.59)

Constable's inscription: '9th Octr 1821 Sun hot Wind southern with mist.'

	WIND	*PRES.*	*TEMP.*	*RAIN*	*CLOUD*	*COMMENTS*
Howard (Stratford)	SW	30.12	60			Foggy morning: fine: lunar corona at night.
Belville	SE	30.18	60		2/10 1/10	Fair
Cary		30.35	59			Fair
Cowe	SW	30.15	61			Fine
Hoy	NW	30.12	58			Cloudy mo : clear day

Comparison: There is no direct evidence as to whether or not this study represents a sunrise or a sunset. Both Howard and Constable mention poor visibility which Howard links to the morning, which could suggest a sunrise. It would appear that the picture depicts a misty morning with the sun burning off the low-level stratus. The wind was certainly of southerly origins for three out of the four records. Howard records a north-westerly wind on 8 October, which might explain Hoy's anomaly. Once the mist had cleared it was a fine day, though temperatures remained cool.

Conclusion: Excellent agreement

(26) 12 October 1821, Hampstead Heath, looking towards Harrow; David Goodstein Collection, Los Angeles; 247 x 285, oil on paper laid on millboard; sky and L/S; Leggat (1952, 39), Hoozee (1979, 314), Reynolds (1984, 21.60)

Constable's inscription: 'Very fine evening after a brilliant day, gentle wind South, 12th October, 1821'

	WIND	*PRES.*	*TEMP.*	*RAIN*	*CLOUD*	*COMMENTS*
Howard (Stratford (Tottenham)	NW	30.08	58			Fine *stratus*
Belville	W	29.75	55	0.10	5/10 4/10	Haze
Cary		29.95	57			Fair
Cowe	N	29.64	59			Cloudy
Hoy	NW	29.65	57			Cloudy Morning. Clear Day

Comparison: The wind had been from the south east according to Howard and from the south according to Cowe on 11 October but had obviously turned to the north on 12 October. Thus Constable's inscription does not fit the weather record very well. Howard's description of 'Fine' does not preclude Constable's perception of 'a brilliant day', but it is a poor match. Constable was perhaps enjoying the cool misty mornings and dry clear days even though it wasn't that warm. The other interpretation is that the date is incorrect, though it is not possible to suggest an alternative date. The 2 October did have a 'brilliant sunset' (see **(23)** above) but the wind was more from the west than south.

Conclusion: Poor agreement

(27) 13 October 1821; Hampstead Heath: Branch Hill Pond; Plate 107; V&A (781–1888); 248 x 298; oil on paper; sky and L/S; Reynolds (1960, 227), Baskett (1966, 50 and plate 16), Thornes (1978, 12), Hoozee (1979, 316), Reynolds (1982, 21.61)

Constable's inscription: 'Octr – 13th. 1821. – 4 to 5 afternoon – very fine with Gentle Wind at N.E.'

	WIND	*PRES.*	*TEMP.*	*RAIN*	*CLOUD*	*COMMENTS*
Howard (Stratford)	N	30.34	60			Fine
Belville	E	30.27	55		7/10 4/10	Foggy morning Fine day
Cary		30.39	58			Fine
Cowe	N	30.20	60			Fair.
Hoy	NW	30.12	58			Cloudy & Foggy morning: clear aft.

Comparison: Good agreement between the wind direction and description of the 'fine' day. The sky cleared as the day went on. Constable's study depicts a mostly blue sky with lenses of very thin stratocumulus. A fine though cool October day. Baskett points out that the smoke from the 'Salt Box' chimney shows that the view must be towards the north west as the wind is from the north east.

Conclusion: Very good agreement

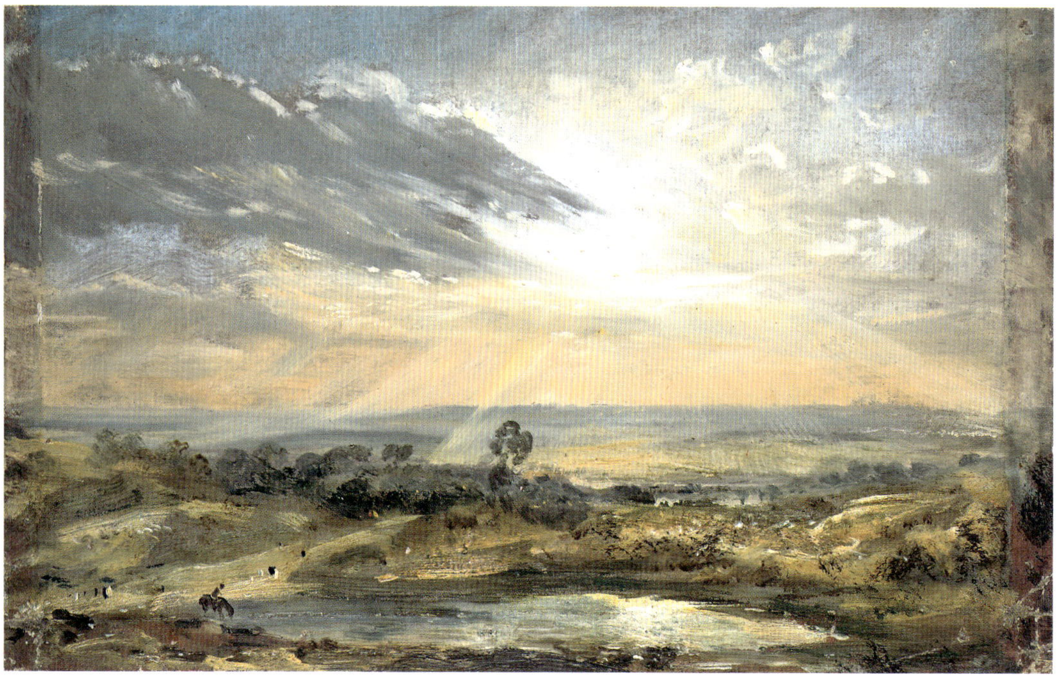

Plate 107 John Constable, *Hampstead Heath: Branch Hill Pond*, 13 October 1821. V&A Picture Library

(28) 30 October 1821?, Hampstead; whereabouts unknown; 241 x 266; oil; sky and L/S?; Grosvenor Gallery (1889, 256), Hoozee (1979, 318), Reynolds (1984, 21.63)

Constable's inscription: 'Hampstead Oct. 30th. very fine – gentle wind at south-west.'

1820	*WIND*	*PRES.*	*TEMP.*	*RAIN*	*CLOUD*	*COMMENTS*
Howard (Stratford) (Tottenham)	SW	29.40	53			Fine
Belville	S	29.51	48		1/10 2/10	Fine pleasant weather
Cary						
Cowe	SW	29.42	55	0.073		Fine, rain at night
Hoy	NW	29.45	51			Mostly Clear

1821	*WIND*	*PRES.*	*TEMP.*	*RAIN*	*CLOUD*	*COMMENTS*
Howard (Stratford)	E	29.95	57			Fine: a *stratus* at night.
Belville	ESE	30.15	61		0/10 0/10	Fog Fair
Cary	-	30.10	52			Fair
Cowe	SW	30.03	59			Fine
Hoy	SE	30.00	50			Cloudy all Day

Comparison: Reynolds dates this study as 1821, presumably because of the size which is more typical of 1821 than 1820. The wind direction of south westerly was recorded by both Howard and Cowe in 1820, whereas in 1821 Howard, Belville and Hoy all recorded easterly winds, although Cowe recorded south westerly. All observers agree that 30 October was a 'fine' day in both 1820 and 1821. The temperature is warmer in 1821, which may be more in keeping with Constable's 'very fine' inscription, but the difference is small. The inscription itself is rather short and is very similar to the inscription of 28 October (4) which might suggest that these two studies are from the same year. However the inscription of 13 October 1821 (27) is also similar in length: '4 to 5 afternoon – very fine with Gentle Wind at N.E.'. Thus, although a dating of 1821 is most likely in view of the size, 1820 is also a possibility.

(29) 31 October 1821; Hampstead Heath, looking towards Harrow; Plate 108; Yale Center for British Art (B1976.7.103); 260 x 325; oil on paper laid on canvas; sky and L/S; Hoozee (1979, 319), Reynolds (1984, 21.64)

Constable's inscription: 'Hampstead 31st Oct. 1821. Very fine afternoon of a beautiful day, it began with rain. Wind fresh from West'

	WIND	*PRES.*	*TEMP.*	*RAIN*	*CLOUD*	*COMMENTS*
Howard (Stratford)	NE	29.87	60	0.08		Fine
Belville	WSW	29.82	54	0.01	7/10 2/10	Damp and cloudy
Cary		29.96	59			Fair
Cary	S	29.82	60	0.099		Fair, rain at night
Hoy	NE	29.76	54			Cloudy all Day some Drops

Comparison: The weather was very warm for the last day of October and Cary confirms the rain in the night before the fine day evolved. Constable's wind direction is similar to that recorded by Belville but different to that by Howard, Hoy and Cary. Howard recorded a south-west wind on 1 November, so the wind direction was obviously changing from easterlies to westerlies. Constable wrote to Fisher on 3 November 'The last day of Octr was indeed lovely so much so that I could not paint for looking.... I made two evening effects.' The second painting has not yet been identified but the Yale picture shows a vivid yellow sunset with scattered cumulus clouds.

Conclusion: Good agreement

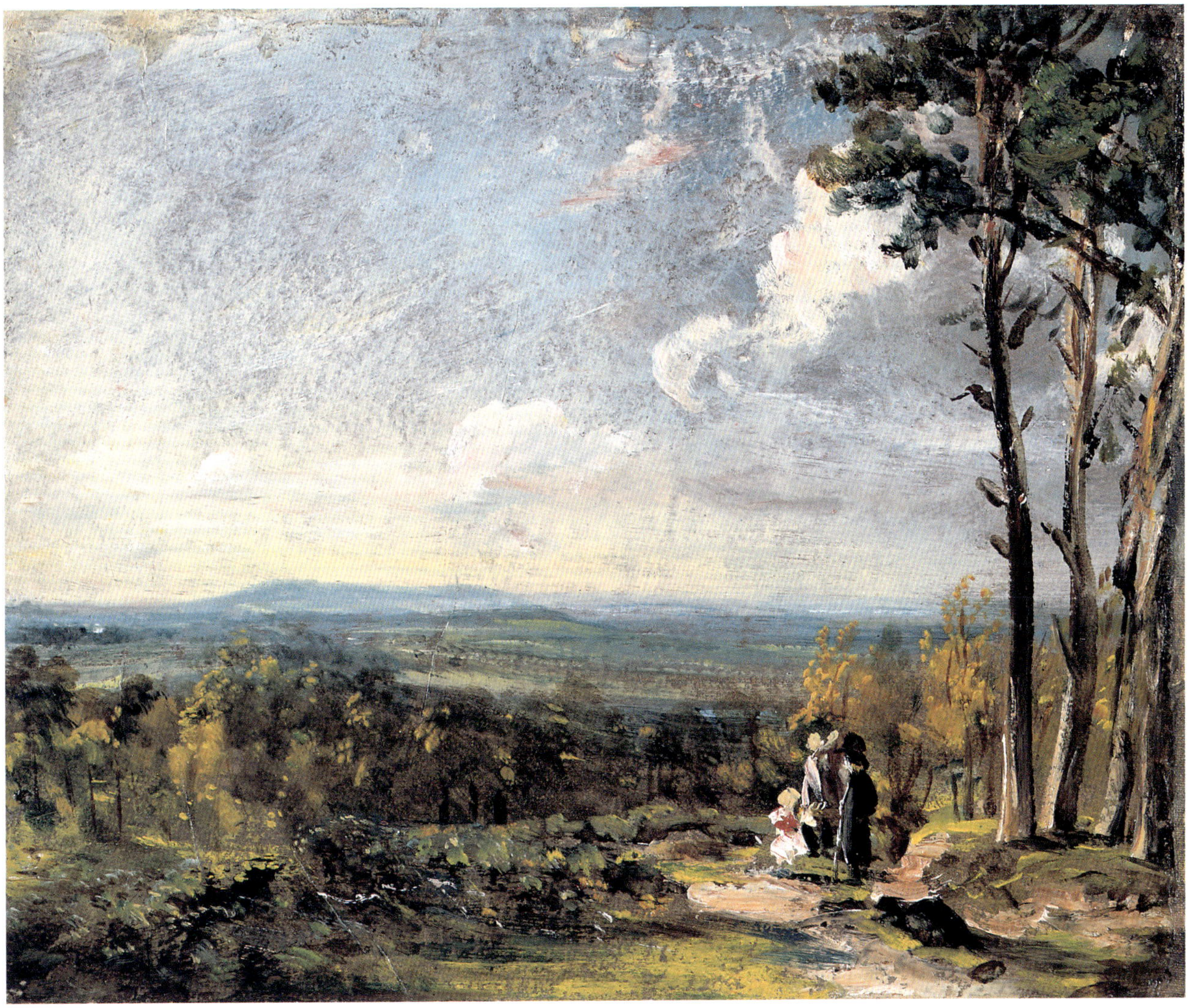

Plate 108 John Constable, *A View on Hampstead Heath with Figures in the Foreground*, 1821. Yale Center for British Art, Paul Mellon Collection (B1976.7.103)

(30) 2 November 1821; A sandbank at Hampstead Heath; Plate 109; V&A (164–1888); 248 x 298; oil on paper; sky and L/S; Reynolds (1960, 228), Thornes (1978, 13), Hoozee (1979, 320), Reynolds (1984, 21.66)

Constable's inscription: 'Novr. 2d 1821. Hampstead Heath windy afternoon.'

	WIND	*PRES.*	*TEMP.*	*RAIN*	*CLOUD*	*COMMENTS*
Howard (Stratford)	W	29.77	63	.13		Cloudy
Belville	SW	29.82	61		5/10 10/10	High wind
Cary		29.93	62			Showery
Cowe	SW	29.81	64	.126		Fair, rain at night
Hoy	NW	29.80	62			Cloudy all day

Comparison: This is not really a skyscape in that most of the picture is taken up by the sandbank. However Constable's mention of a 'windy afternoon' is backed up by Belville, and the part of the sky that is visible appears overcast and 'showery', which Belville's cloud amount for the afternoon – 10/10 – confirms. A warm day for early November which probably explains why Constable was out in the open air. This is the last of the sky studies with weather notes in 1821.

Conclusion: Very good agreement

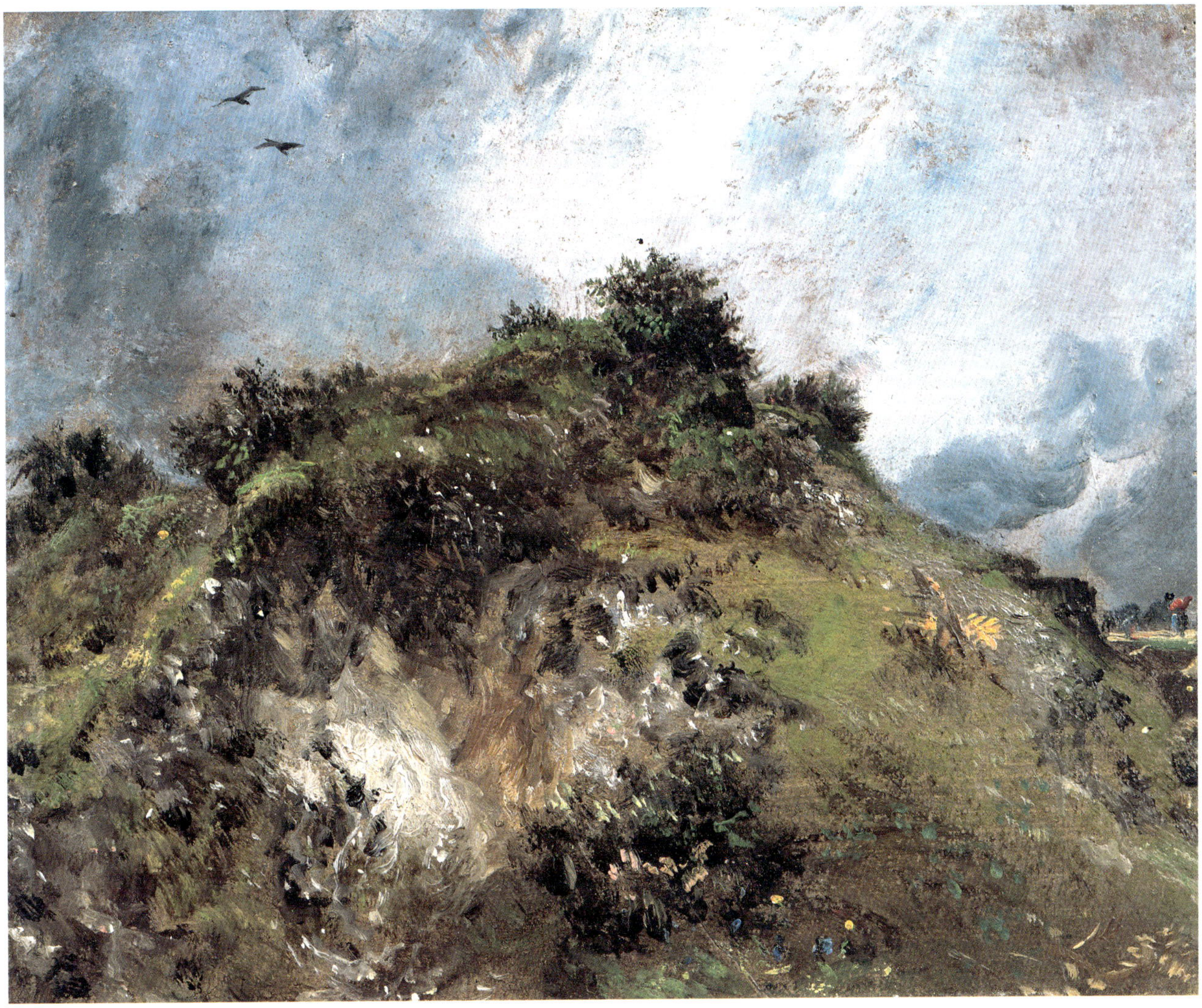

Plate 109 John Constable, *A Sandbank at Hampstead Heath*, 2 November 1821.
V&A Picture Library

(31) 18 April 1822?; Cloud study; private collection; 145 x 220, oil on board laid on panel; pure sky; Reynolds (1996, 22.30A)

Constable's inscription: '.... April 18th [?] Showery Wind N. Easterly'

1820	*WIND*	*PRES.*	*TEMP.*	*RAIN*	*CLOUD*	*COMMENTS*
Howard (Stratford)	SE	30.10	69			Fine
Belville	NE	30.06	66		2/10 1/10	Fine
Cowe	E	30.08	72			Fair
1821	*WIND*	*PRES.*	*TEMP.*	*RAIN*	*CLOUD*	*COMMENTS*
Howard (Stratford)	NW	29.65	62	0.06		Showery: frequent rainbows
Belville	W	29.64	54	0.05	6/10 5/10	Fair flying clouds
Cowe	W	29.54	55			Fair
1822	*WIND*	*PRES.*	*TEMP.*	*RAIN*	*CLOUD*	*COMMENTS*
Howard (Stratford)	N	29.59	56	0.15		Rain
Belville	Variable	29.34	55		10/10 8/10	Light rain
Cowe	E	29.59	63			Showery

Comparison: This is by far the smallest pure sky study that has an inscription, and a dating of 1822 is most probable given the weather data. The study shows a dark cloudy sky with breaks of blue. In 1822 Howard recorded a north wind and Cowe an easterly; also Cowe says it was showery in 1822. Although they all recorded easterly winds in 1820, it would have been too fine.

(32) 4 July 1822; Cloud study; Plate 110; private collection; (64.24); 321 x 495, oil on paper mounted on canvas; sky and L/S; Reynolds (1984, 22.9)

Constable's inscription: 'Hampstead. July 4th, 1822 very fine and hot Wind, W Clouds very high and climbing'

	WIND	*PRES.*	*TEMP.*	*RAIN*	*CLOUD*	*COMMENTS*
Howard (Stratford) (Tottenham)	Var.	29.87	78			Fine A few drops of rain evening: very close night: lightning in the S, about 1 a.m. with showers of rain.
Belville	S	29.89	76		5/10 8/10	Fair
Cary		30.04	76			Fair
Cowe	SW	29.92	77		0.188	Fine, rain at night

Comparison: It was obviously a humid and hot day with temperatures in the upper seventies. The wind direction is confirmed by Cowe as being from the westerly direction and there were thunderstorms in the night following, the 'climbing' cumulus clouds eventually producing rain. The study shows a number of beautifully illuminated cumulus clouds.

Conclusion: Very good agreement

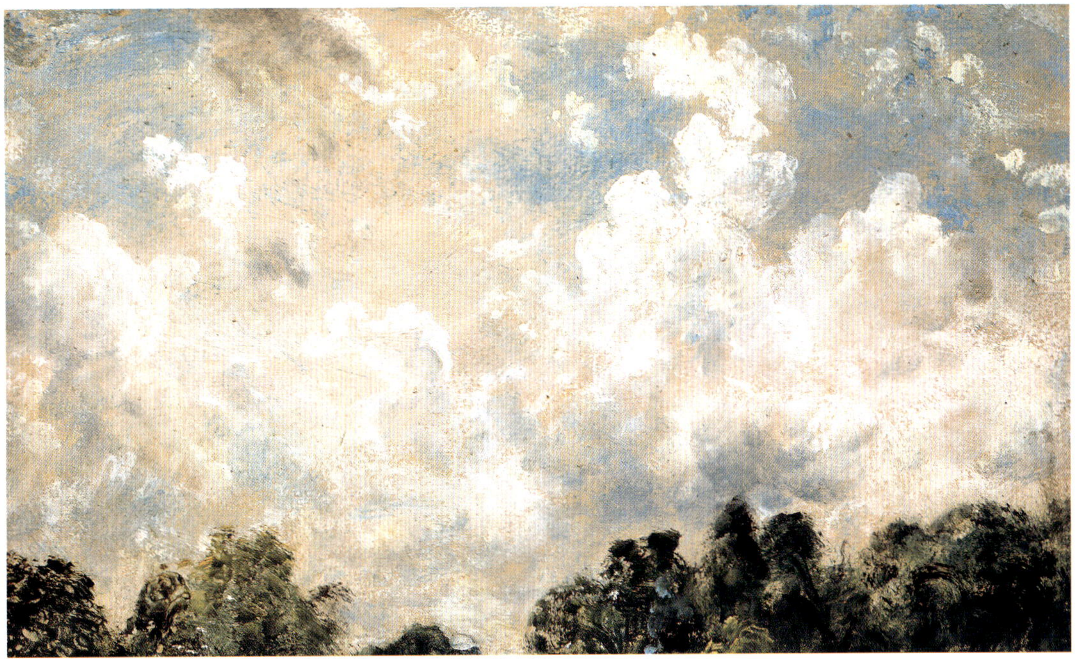

Plate 110 John Constable, *Clouds above Hampstead Heath*, 4 July 1822. Private collection

(33) 28 July 1822?; Study of clouds; private collection, New York; 290 x 480; oil on paper; pure sky; Paterson (1928, 1) Boston (1946, 133), Thornes (1978, 12 (2)), Hoozee (1979, 332), Reynolds (1984, 22.11)

Constable's inscription: '28th July 12 oclock noon. Very fine day, showery and (?) warm No. West under the sun'

1821	*WIND*	*PRES.*	*TEMP.*	*RAIN*	*CLOUD*	*COMMENTS*
Howard (Stratford)	SE	29.92	70			Fine
Belville	W	29.90	68		8/10 5/10	Fair
Cary		29.99	63			Hazy
Cowe	SW	29.85	67			Fair

1822	*WIND*	*PRES.*	*TEMP.*	*RAIN*	*CLOUD*	*COMMENTS*
Howard (Stratford) (Tottenham)	SW	29.43	72	05		Fine Very showery day
Belville	SW	29.46	72	.36	4/10 8/10	Much rain in the night
Cary		29.60	66			Showery
Cowe	S	29.50	68	.104		Showery

Comparison: The inscribed 'No. West' could well mean the direction in which Constable was looking rather than the wind direction, as it doesn't fit either year very well. This is a pure sky study for which Beckett (1961) states, 'Almost certainly of 1822, when Constable was at Hampstead during the last week of July'. The size (29 x 48 cm) is unlike any of his 1821 pure sky studies. The weather data for 28 July 1822 suggests an unstable south-westerly airstream with showers and Howard records a 'very showery day' at Tottenham. The picture itself is of streets of cumulus clouds with blue sky between, which would certainly fit the 1822 evidence. 1821 was fine and had a south-east airstream according to Howard. Cary of the Strand records a 'hazy' day in 1821, which certainly does not correspond to the picture. In view of the other evidence, it seems reasonable to assign this study to 28 July 1822.

(34) 29 July 1822; Distant view of the Grove, Hampstead; Plate 111; Royal Academy (69); 292 x 241; oil on paper laid on canvas; sky and L/S; Manchester (1956, 52), Royal Academy (1963, 213), Tate (1976, 205), Thornes (1978, 15), Hoozee (1979, 333), Reynolds (1984, 22.12)

Constable's inscription: 29 July 1822 looking east 10 in the morning – silvery clouds

	WIND	*PRES.*	*TEMP.*	*RAIN*	*CLOUD*	*COMMENTS*
Howard (Stratford)	W	29.45	74	.14		Showery: some thunder.
(Tottenham)						heavy clouds p.m.: shower evening.
Belville	W	29.44	68	.09	9/10 9/10	Thunder showers
Cary		29.57		70		Showery
Cowe	SW	29.47	74	.216		Showery

Comparison A showery day with, no doubt, many fine large cumulus clouds. A westerly airstream with vigorous convection leading to 'some thunder' according to Howard. Temperature quite warm and pressure low; the picture appears nearly overcast with large 'silvery' clouds.

Conclusion: Good agreement

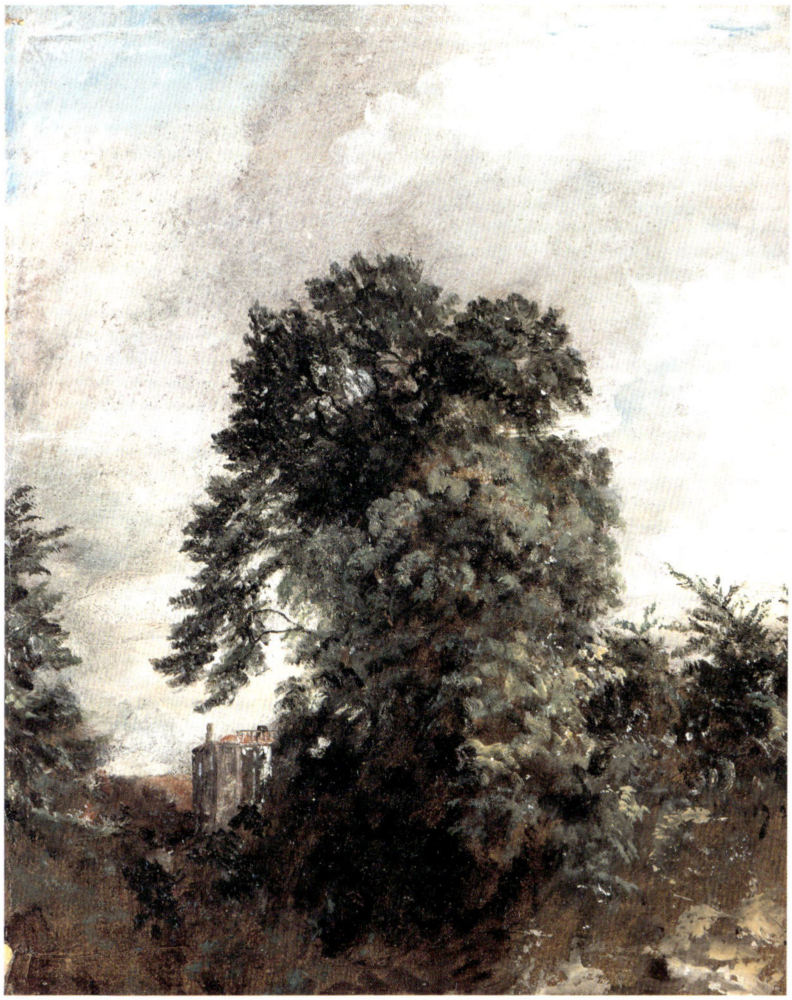

Plate 111
John Constable, *Landscape Study: Tree and Corner House*, 29 July 1822. Royal Academy of Arts, London

(35) 29(?) July 1822; The road to the Spaniards, Hampstead; Plate 112; John G. Johnson Collection, Philadelphia Museum of Art; 311 x 521; oil on paper laid on canvas; sky and L/S; Boston (1946, 132), Tate (1976, 204), Thornes (1978, 14), Hoozee (1979, 331), New York (1983, 42), Reynolds (1984, 22.10)

Constable's inscription: '[Hamp]stead. Monday 2(?) July 1822 looking NE 3 PM (?previous to) a thunder squall wind N West.'

Comparison: In my previous catalogue of 1978 (Thornes 1978) I dated this as 2 July 1822, which was not even a Monday. Reynolds (1984, 22.10) points out that there is a second digit after the 2 which cannot be clearly read. The most obvious date is 29 July 1822, which was a Monday, and means that it was painted later in the same day as **(34)**. For the other Mondays in July 1822 Howard records: 1 July – Stratford: Cloudy – Tottenham: Fine Day; 8 July – Stratford: Cloudy; 15 July – Stratford: Fine – Tottenham: Fine day: heavy clouds ,with a few drops, evening; 22 July – Stratford: Fine. None of these mention thunder, whereas on the 29 July thunder was mentioned by Howard and Belville. The sky in the painting is full of large developing cumulus clouds threatening rain. A dating of the 29 July 1822 is therefore indisputable.

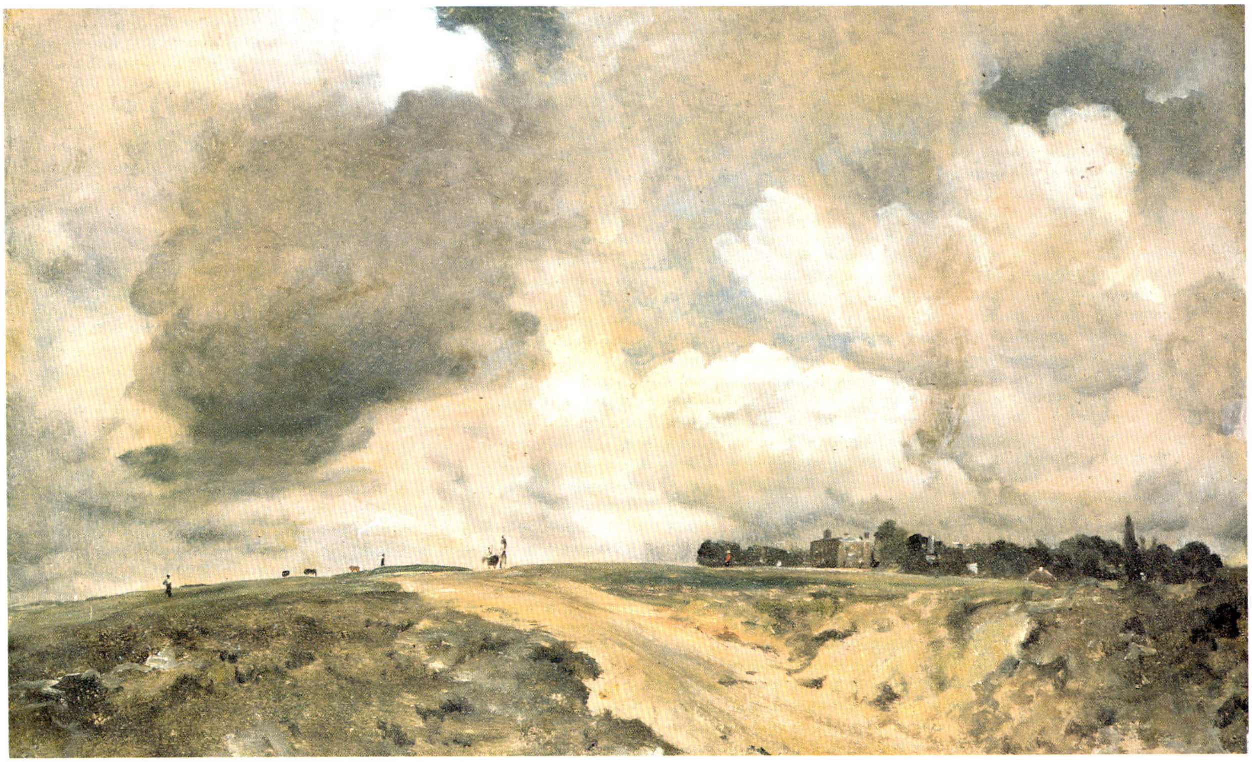

Plate 112 John Constable, *The Road to the Spaniards, Hampstead*, 2 July, 1822.
The John G. Johnson Collection, Philadelphia Museum of Art

(36) 30 July 1822; A view on Hampstead Heath with trees and figures; Plate 113; V&A (165–1888); 242 x 298; oil on blue paper; sky and L/S;. Reynolds (1960, 246), Thornes (1978, 16), Hoozee (1979, 334), Reynolds (1984, 22.13)

Constable's inscription: 'July, 30th 1822. Noon under the Sun.'

	WIND	*PRES.*	*TEMP.*	*RAIN*	*CLOUD*	*COMMENTS*
Howard (Stratford) (Tottenham)	NW	29.57	67			Fine Showers
Belville	NW	29.53	68	.32	4/10 5/10	Cloudy
Cary		29.64	64			Showery
Cowe	W	29.48	68	.193		Showery

Comparison: It is unusual that Howard records a 'fine' day, whereas the others record showery activity. Certainly Constable's picture shows large towering cumulus clouds, which could well have produced heavy but scattered showers. A north-westerly airstream made the day a little cooler than the one before.

Conclusion: Good agreement

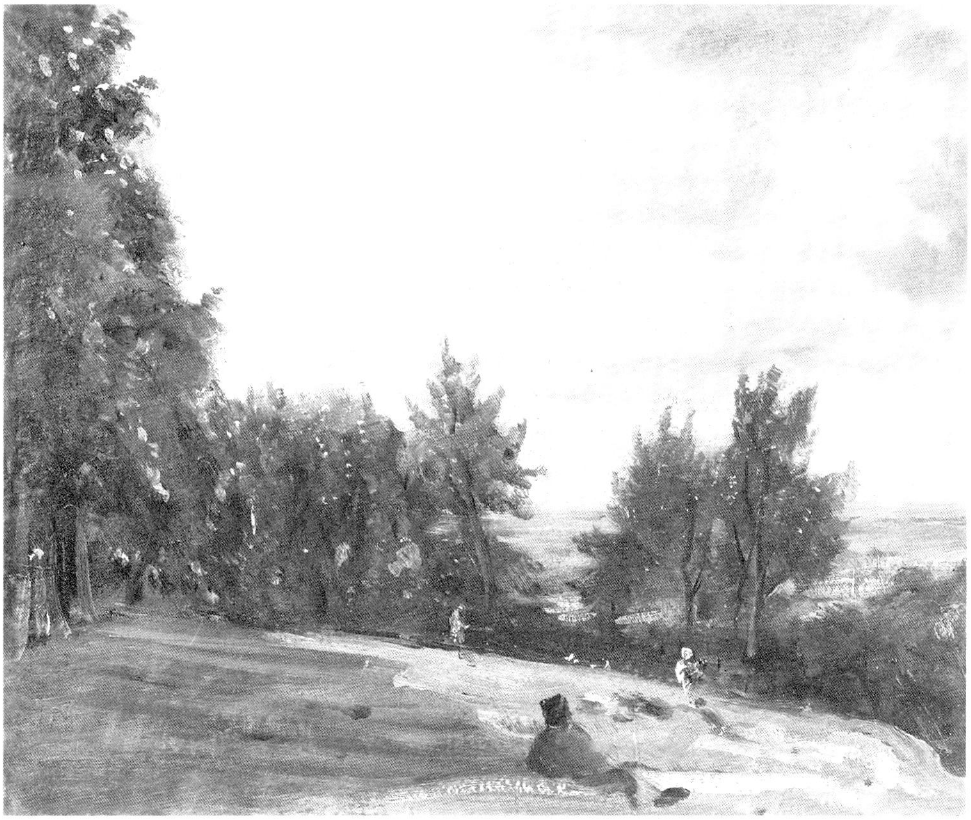

Plate 113 John Constable, *A View on Hampstead Heath*, 30 July 1822. V&A Picture Library

(37) 31 July 1822; A view at Hampstead: evening; Plate 114; V&A (337–1888); 165 x 298; oil on paper; sky and L/S; Reynolds (1960, 247), Thornes (1978, 17), Hoozee (1979, 335), Reynolds (1984, 22.14)

Constable's inscription: 'Evning, 31st July, 1822 Shower Approaching'

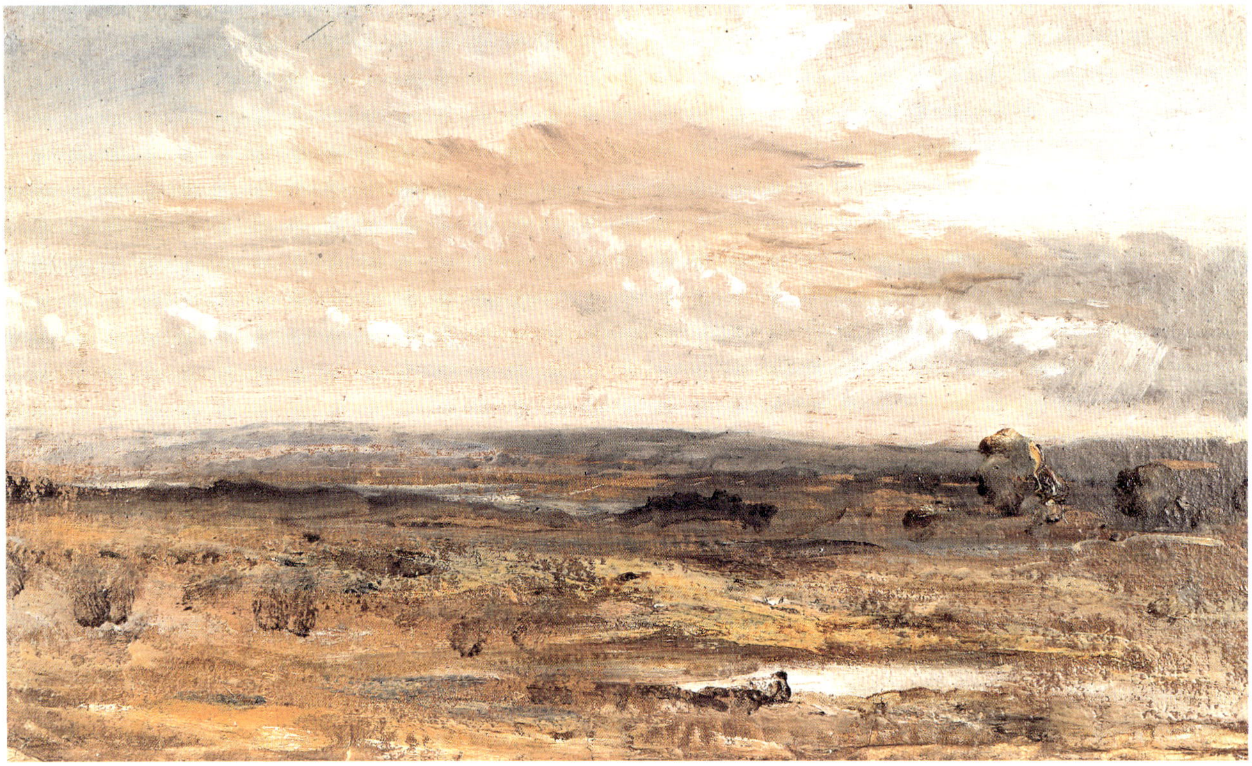

Plate 114 John Constable, *A View at Hampstead: Evening*, 31 July, 1822. V&A Picture Library

(38) 31 July 1922; Hampstead: stormy sunset; Plate 115; V&A (336–1888); 162 x 305; oil on paper; sky and L/S; Reynolds (1960 248), Thornes (1978, 18), Hoozee (1979, 336), Reynolds (1984, 22.15)

Constable's inscription: 'July 31. 1822 Stormy sunset.'

	WIND	*PRES.*	*TEMP.*	*RAIN*	*CLOUD*	*COMMENTS*
Howard (Stratford) (Tottenham)	SW	29.70	75	.26		Showery Showers
Belville	W	29.60	66	.01	7/10 7/10	Cloudy at times shower at 7 p.m.
Cary		29.75	61			Showery
Cowe	SW	29.71	68			Showery

Comparison: Both pictures depict large cumulus clouds with possibly cumulonimbus; (38) has falling rain expressively painted, and both therefore tie in well with the weather record. Howard's temperature seems rather high, but all are in agreement as to the westerly showery airstream. In (37) there is a representation of crepuscular rays pointing back to where the sun is behind the clouds.

Conclusion: Very good agreement

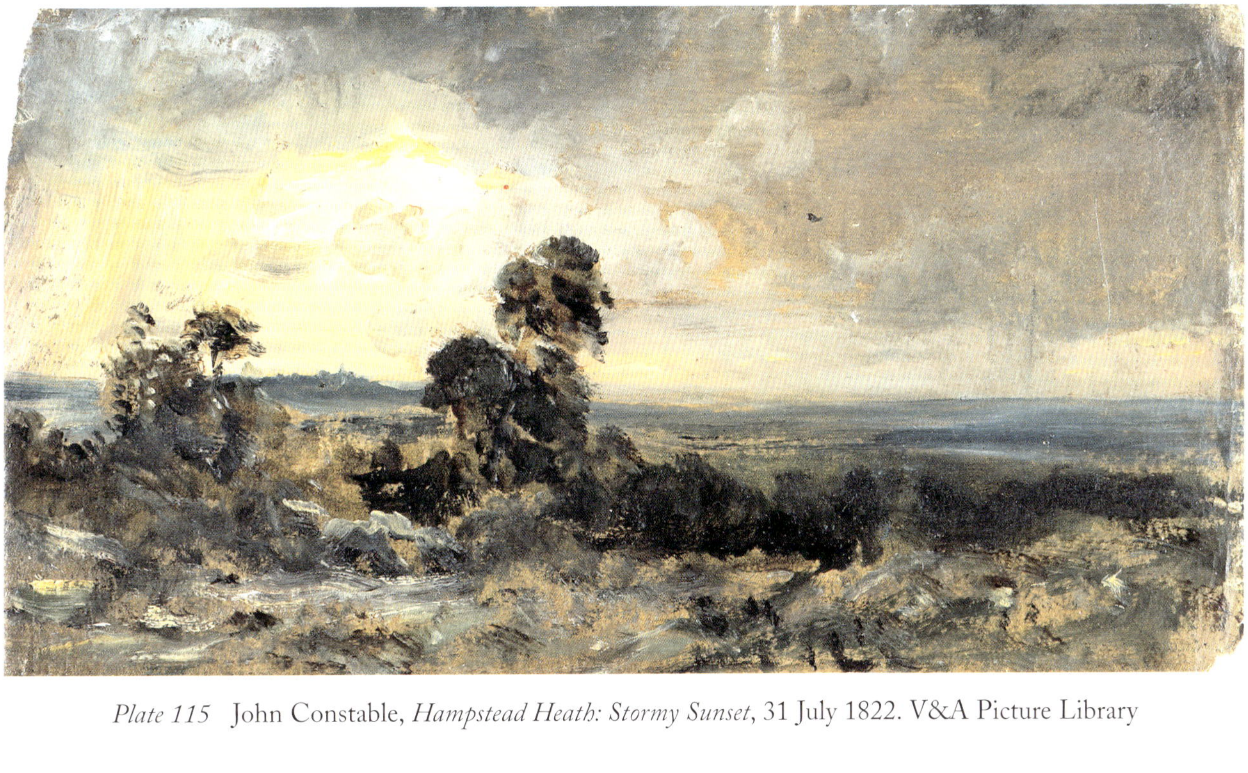

Plate 115 John Constable, *Hampstead Heath: Stormy Sunset*, 31 July 1822. V&A Picture Library

(39) ? July 1822; Hampstead Heath; private collection; 247 x 400; oil on canvas; sky and L/S; Hoozee (1979, 380), Reynolds (1984, 22.45)

Constable's inscription: 'July – noon – Hampstead Heath – looking north – wind South east'

Comparison: The size of this study is bigger than any of the 1821 series but is not typical of the 1822 series either. However the sizes of the 1822 sky and landscape studies did vary considerably. If this is of July 1822 there were two days when Howard recorded a south-east wind: 15 and 18 July. Cowe recorded a south-east wind on 17 July, and Belville on 19 July. The small black and white plate (No. 303a) in Reynolds' 1984 catalogue is difficult to interpret but the sky is lit by the sun behind the artist's back.

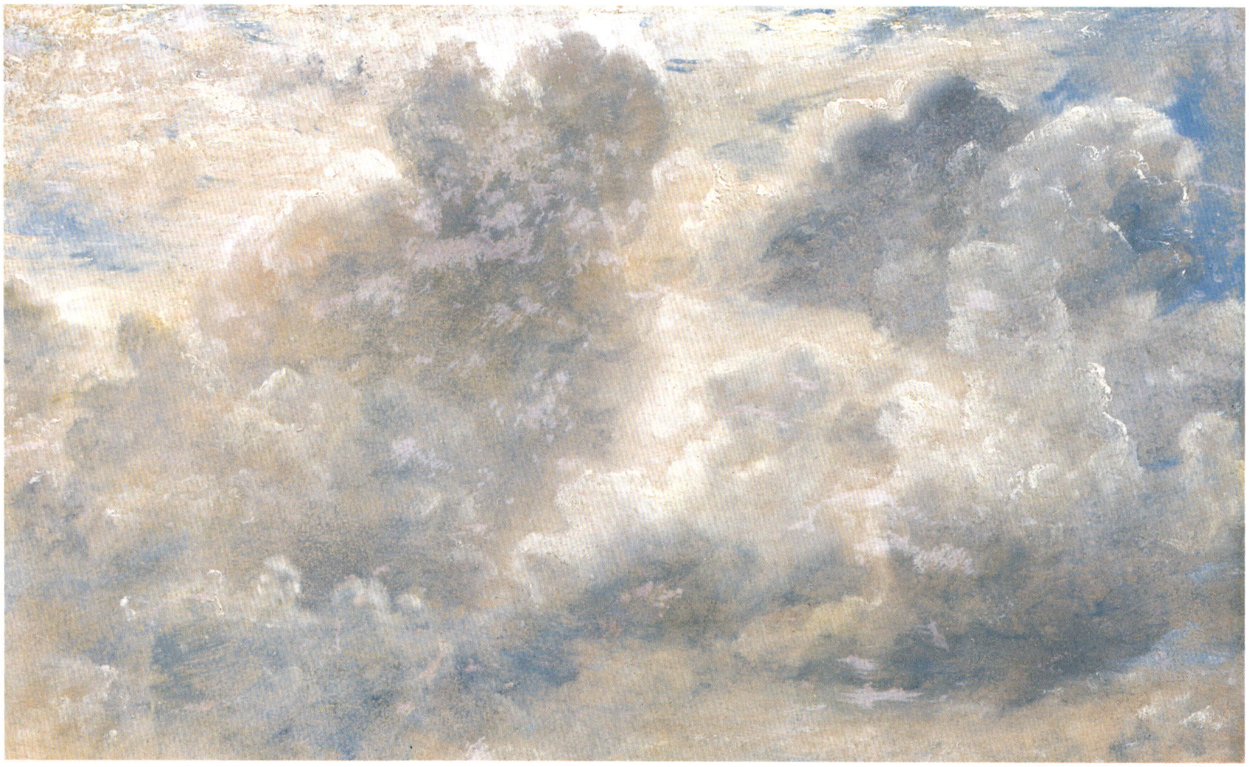

Plate 116 (opposite) John Constable, *Study of Cumulus Clouds*, 1 August 1822.
Yale Center for British Art, Paul Mellon Collection (B1981.25.144)

(40) 1st August 1822; Study of Cumulus Clouds; Plate 116; Yale Center for British Art (B1981.25.144) 305 x 508; oil on paper laid on canvas; pure sky; Badt (1950, plate 5), Guildhall (1952, 46), Manchester (1956, 54), Arts Council (1959, 65), Huntington Art Gallery (1961, 28), Washington (1969, 51), Thornes (1978, 19), Hoozee (1979, 337), New York (1983, 43), Reynolds (1984, 22.16)

Constable's inscription: 'Augt 1. 1822 11 o clock A.M. very hot with large climbing Clouds under the Sun. wind westerly'

	WIND	*PRES.*	*TEMP.*	*RAIN*	*CLOUD*	*COMMENTS*
Howard (Stratford) (Tottenham)	W	29.73	68			Fine Showers part of the day
Belville	W	29.75	65	.11	5/10 7/10	Light showers
Cary		29.88	66			Showery
Cowe	W	29.64	68			Fine

Comparison: This is the first big cloud study accurately dated and 'tolerably large to be careful' that I have come across. The showery unstable westerly airstream evident the three previous days continued, but with fewer actual showers. Could it be that these three days of beautiful clouds helped inspire the large pure cloud studies? The picture is of large towering cumulus clouds – an excellent subject for a pure cloud study.

Conclusion: Excellent agreement

(41) 1 August 1822; Cloud study; whereabouts unknown; 472 x 584; oil; pure sky; Hoozee (1979, 338), Reynolds (1984, 22.17)

Comparison: Although this study does not have a weather inscription the picture itself can be compared with the weather data given for **(40)** above which was painted on the same day. The black and white plate (no. 345) in Reynolds' 1984 catalogue shows the dark base of a cumulus cloud in the centre of the picture, and it could certainly have been painted on the same day as **(40)** although the forms of the cumulus clouds are not as distinct.

(42) 12 August 1822; Cloud study; Dr Charles Warren; 254 x 222; oil; pure sky; Hoozee (1979, 623), Reynolds (1984, 22.18)

Constable's inscription: 'Aug 12. 1822'

	WIND	*PRES.*	*TEMP.*	*RAIN*	*CLOUD*	*COMMENTS*
Howard (Stratford)	SW	29.75	75			Cloudy morning: fine afternoon
Belville	W	29.79	71	0.03	7/10 5/10	Cloudy
Cary		29.43	67			Showery
Cowe	S	29.73	72			Fair

Comparison: Hoozee lists this study as of doubtful origin and certainly the edges of the cumulus clouds are painted in a less distinct fashion than the other sky studies of this time. Reynolds states in his entry for 22.18 'so far as it can be judged from a photograph it looks fully authentic'. The weather data shows that there were cumulus showers around that day and the loose handling of the clouds could just reflect the speed with which Constable was trying to capture the effect he wanted.

(43) 18? August 1822; Study of electric clouds; whereabouts unknown; oil; Leslie (1896, p115), Reynolds (1984, 22.66)

Constable's inscription: 'Sunday, 11 to 12, very fine hot day, wind light at N.W. climbing electric clouds looking S.W.'

	WIND	*PRES.*	*TEMP.*	*RAIN*	*CLOUD*	*COMMENTS*
Howard (Str.)	NW	30.16	80			Fine
Belville	N	30.13	76		5/10 1/10	Mostly Cloudy
Cary		30.24	75			Fair
Cowe	WSW	30.12	84			Fine

Comparison: There are very few Sundays in 1821/22 when Howard records a north-west wind which was also a 'very fine hot day'. Although the inscription refers to 'climbing electric clouds' the actual painting shows fair weather cumulus clouds, although with the temperature in the eighties large 'climbing' cumulus clouds could have developed later in the day without producing any rain. There is no mention of thunder on any Sunday in the periods we are interested in during the summer and autumn of both 1821 and 1822.

(44) 25 August 1822; A view on Hampstead Heath with Harrow in the distance; private collection; 266 x 482; oil on paper laid on canvas; sky and L/S; Manchester (1956, 37), Hoozee (1979, 339), Reynolds (1984, 22.19)

Constable's inscription: 'Hampstead Heath. Sunday Augst. 25, 1822 After Sunset'

	WIND	*PRES.*	*TEMP.*	*RAIN*	*CLOUD*	*COMMENTS*
Howard (Stratford) (Tottenham)	W	29.64	70	.01		Fine Showery day.
Belville	SW	29.65	68	0.06	5/10 6/10	Flying Clouds
Cary		29.79	67			Showery
Cowe	W	29.62	68			Fine

Comparison: Although the inscription does not mention the weather we can compare the study with the weather data. The study shows distant decaying cumulus clouds at the end of the day. This fits in well with the weather data which suggests a showery day. The convection would have ceased by sunset and the sky would be clearing.

(45) 26 August 1822; **Cloud study**; whereabouts unknown; Size unknown; oil on paper; pure sky; Leslie, (1896, 115, footnote), Thornes (1978, 20), Reynolds (1984, 22.20)

Constable's inscription: 'August 26th 1822, noon, under the sun, very hot and bright, looking S.W.'

	WIND	*PRES.*	*TEMP.*	*RAIN*	*CLOUD*	*COMMENTS*
Howard (Stratford) (Tottenham)	NW	29.64	70			Showers Shower p.m.
Belville	SW	29.61	67	.01	4/10 4/10	Flying Clouds
Cary		29.74	69			Fair
Cowe	W	29.60	69		.105	Showery

Comparison: This picture is classed as a pure sky study by Beckett. Again Constable favours a showery westerly airstream, and the sun would appear hot when it shone between the scattered clouds.

Conclusion: Good agreement

(46) 27 August 1822; Cloud study; Plate 117; Tate Gallery (6065); 475 x 575; oil on paper relaid on synthetic board; pure sky; Parris (1981, 22), Davies (1959, 27–28), Tate (1976, 209a), Thornes (1978, 12(3)), Hoozee (1979, 340), Reynolds (1984, 22.21)

Constable's inscription: '27 augt 11, o clock Noon looking Eastward large silvery (clouds?) wind Gentle at S West'

1821	WIND	PRES.	TEMP.	RAIN	CLOUD	COMMENTS
Howard (Stratford)	E	30.01	63	.02		Cloudy
Belville	E	30.00	73*		10/10 9/10	Cloudy with cold wind
Cary		30.18	64			Cloudy
Cowe	E	29.98	63			Cloudy rain at night
Hoy	NE		62			Cloudy all day

* seems rather high

1822	WIND	PRES.	TEMP.	RAIN	CLOUD	COMMENTS
Howard (Stratford)	SW	29.65	71	.21		A thunder-storm about noon: showery
(Tottenham)						Showery through the day: a very dark cloud p.m. followed by a thunder-shower.
Belville	Var	29.63	68		5/10 8/10	Cloudy Thunder storm at 2 p.m.
Cary		29.74	63			Fair
Cowe	S	29.60	65	.209		Showery

Comparison: This pure cloud study, which was exhibited at the Tate exhibition of 1976, would appear to be from 1822 because of its size, which is very similar to the accurately dated pure cloud study of 31 August 1822 **(45)** (475 x 575 cm). The picture depicts large towering cumulus clouds pregnant with rain, which fits in entirely with the weather of 27 August 1822, which was a stormy day with a south-west wind according to Howard. Thunderstorms were rife in the early afternoon. 27 August 1821, on the hand, had an easterly airflow with little rain, just cloud. This study can be dated with certainty as 27 August 1822.

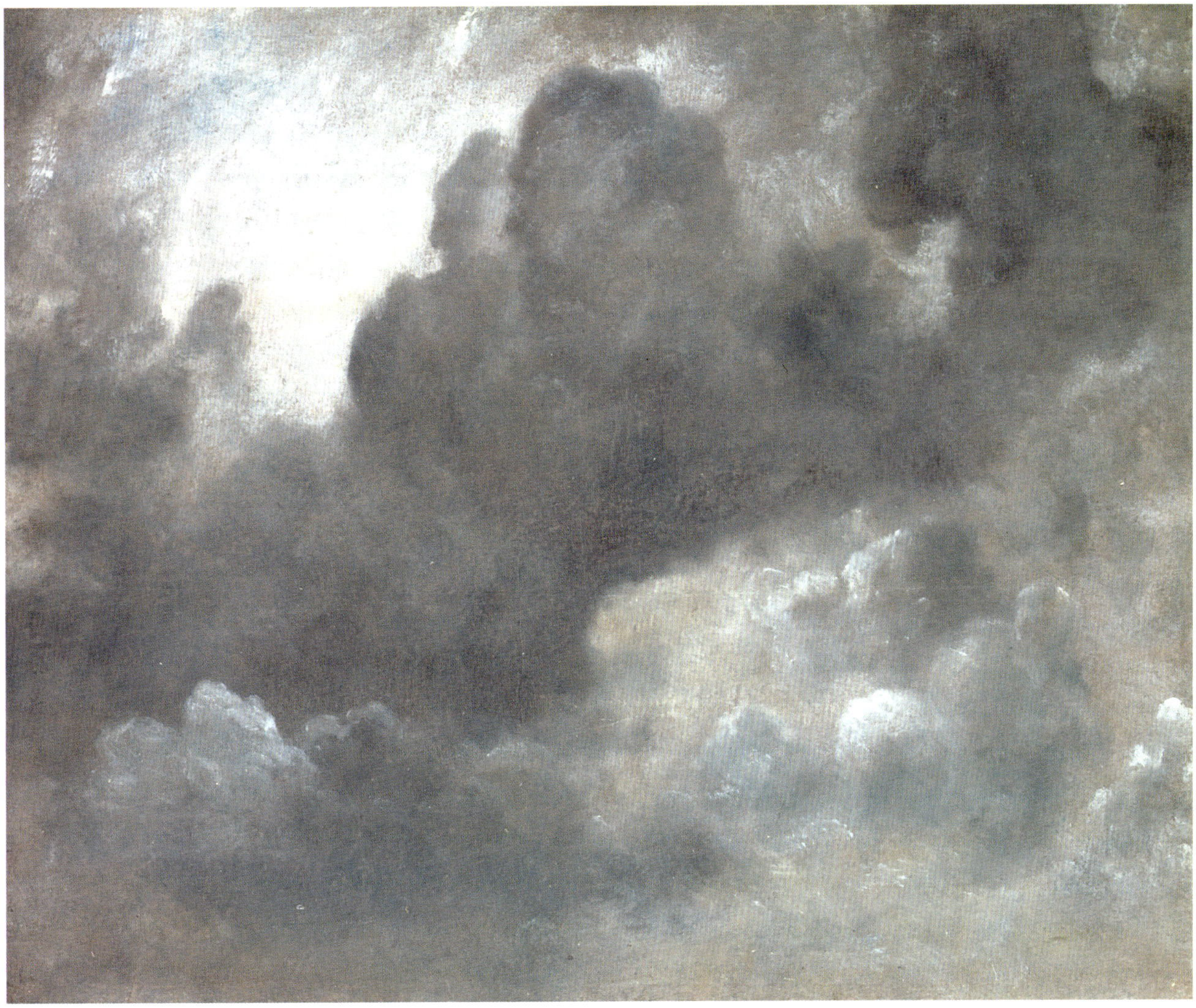

Plate 117 John Constable, *Cloud Study*, 27 August 1822. Tate Gallery, London 1998

(47) 31 August 1822; Cloud study: evening; Plate 118; Birmingham City Museum and Art Gallery (45'29); 470 x 580; oil on paper; pure sky; Paterson (1928, 7) Birmingham City Art Gallery (1960, 33); Thornes (1978, 21), Hoozee (1979, 341), Reynolds (1984, 22.22)

Constable's inscription: '5–6 oclock Eveng Augt 31st 1822. Large clouds to the Eastward – light wind (?west).'

	WIND	*PRES.*	*TEMP.*	*RAIN*	*CLOUD*	*COMMENTS*
Howard (Stratford)	W	30.00	69			Fine
Belville	NW	29.84	66	.08	2/10 3/10	Fair
Cary		29.99	67			Fair
Cowe	SW	29.80	77			

Comparison: Another large pure sky study with streets of cumulus clouds (with not, however, enough vertical depth to produce rain). A westerly airstream yet again, and this time it is Cowe's temperature that seems excessive. The sketch shows the base of a street of cumulus clouds which is running from west to east overhead. The dark cloud in the top centre is the base of the cumulus which comes right over the head of the artist as it should.

Conclusion:
Good agreement

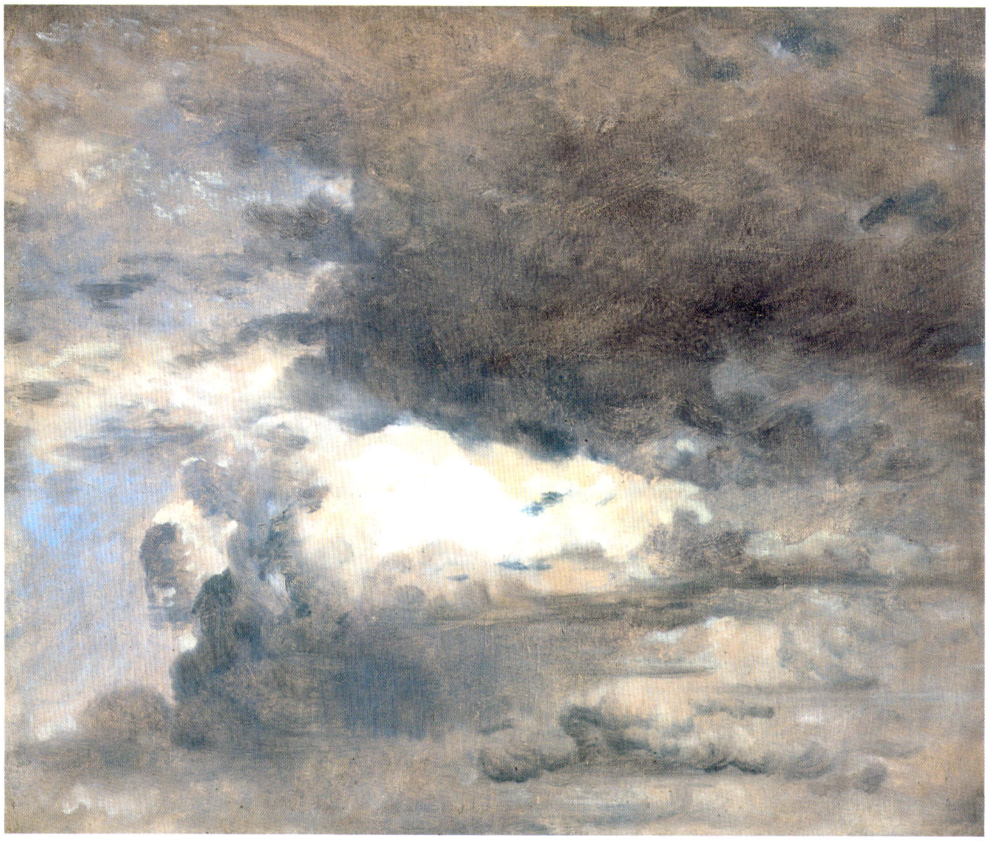

Plate 118 John Constable, *Study of Clouds*, 31 August 1822, Birmingham Museums & Art Gallery

(48) 5 September 1822; Cloud study; Plate 119; National Gallery of Victoria, Melbourne (455/4); 370 x 490; oil on paper; pure sky; Badt (1950, plate 3), Auckland (1973, 27), Tate (1976, 207), Thornes (1978, 22), Hoozee (1979, 342), Reynolds (1984, 22.23)

Constable's inscription: '5th September 1822, 10 o'clock. Morning looking South-East very brisk wind at West, very bright and fresh grey clouds running fast over a yellow bed about half-way in the sky. Very appropriate for the coast at Osmington.'

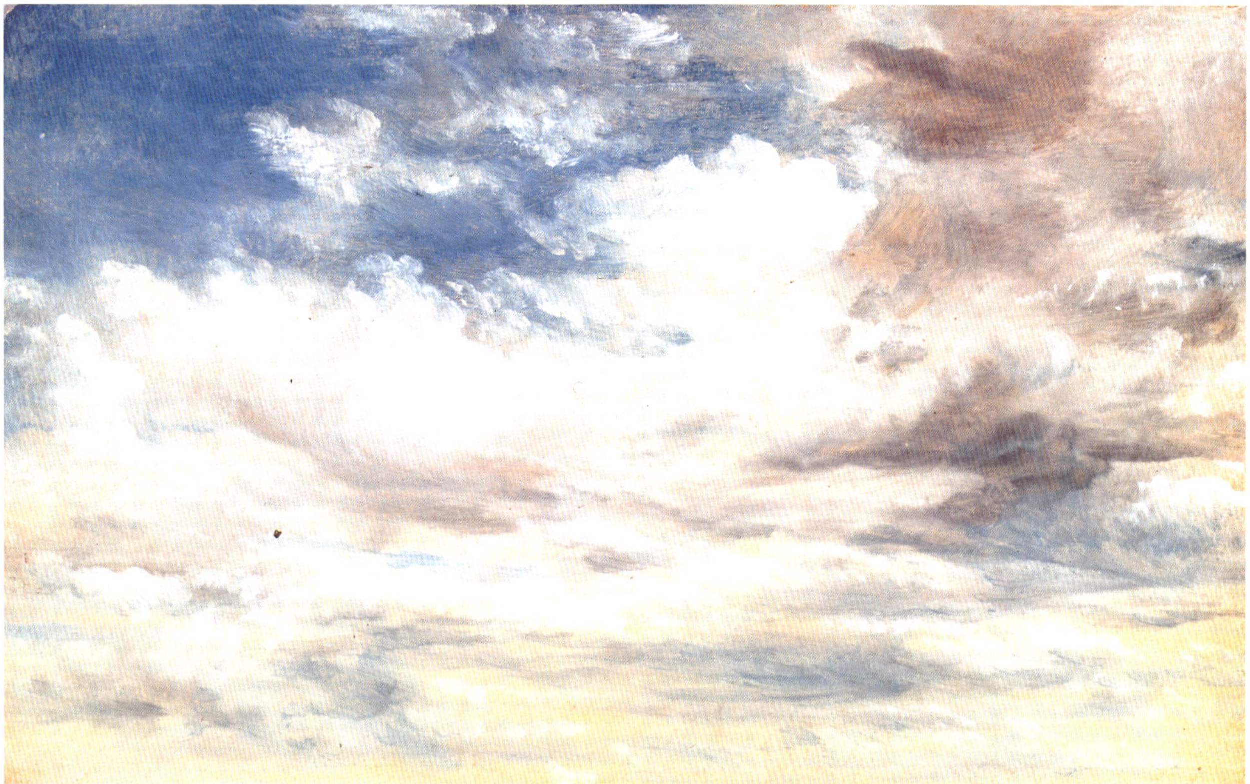

Plate 119 John Constable, *Clouds*, 5 September 1822.
National Gallery of Victoria, Melbourne, Australia (Felton Bequest 1938)

(49) 5 September 1822; Cloud study; Plate 120; V&A (590–1888); 298 x 483; oil on paper; pure sky; Reynolds (1960, 249), Thornes (1978, 23), Hoozee (1979, 343), Reynolds (1984, 22.24)

Constable's inscription: 'Sept. 5. 1822. looking S.E. noon. Wind very brisk. & effect bright & fresh. Clouds moving very fast. with occasional very bright openings to the blue.'

	WIND	*PRES.*	*TEMP.*	*RAIN*	*CLOUD*	*COMMENTS*
Howard (Stratford)	SW	29.80	73			Fine
Belville	SW	29.79	71		7/10 8/10	Wind very high cloudy
Cary		29.91	66			Cloudy
Cowe	W	29.86	70	.06		Fine: rain at night

Comparison: These two studies made in quick succession – 10am and noon – suggest that the sky was to Constable's liking. He mentions that the effect was 'bright and fresh' in both, and also that the clouds were moving very fast. There was a warm westerly airstream with plenty of cloud around – mostly streets of stratocumulus according to the pictures, which were too thin to produce any rain at the time. Belville comments that the wind was 'very high', whipping the clouds across the sky.

Conclusion: Very good agreement

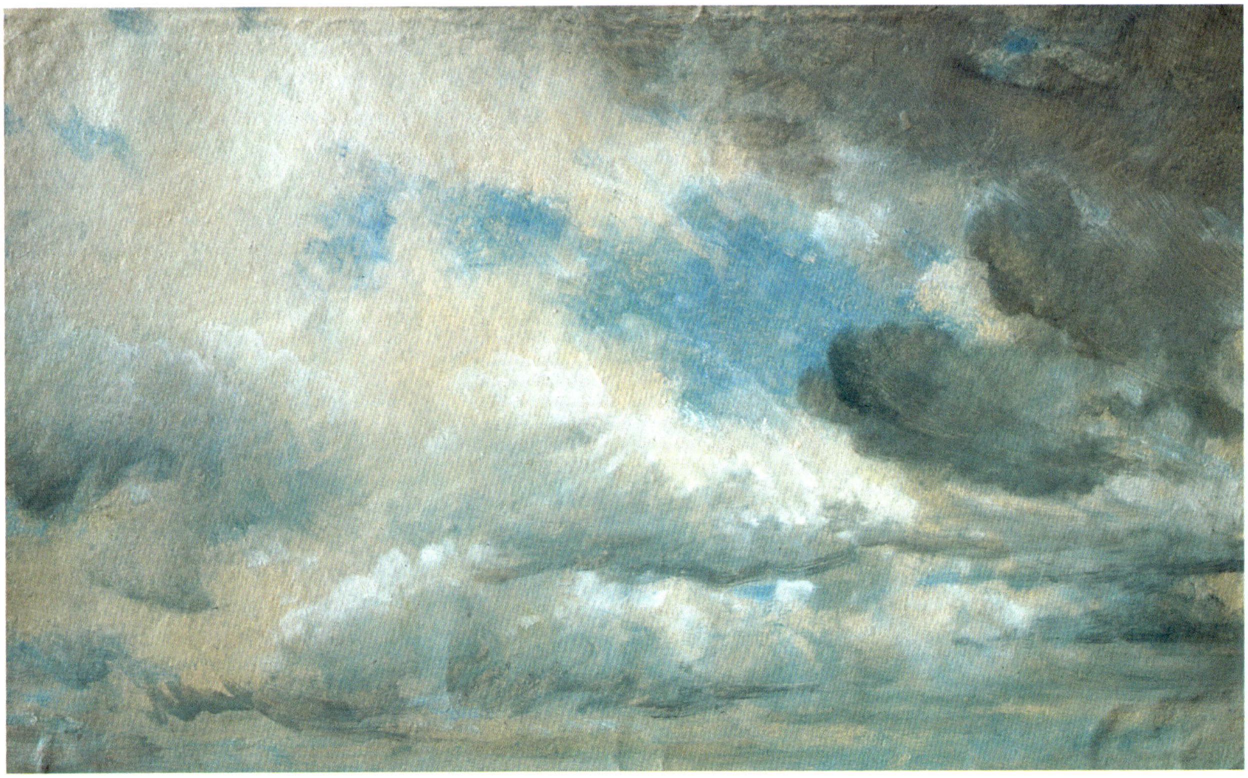

Plate 120 John Constable, *Cloud Study*, 5 September 1822. V&A Picture Library

(50) 6 September 1822; **Cloud study; Plate 121**; private collection; Size unknown; oil; pure sky; Grosvenor Gallery (1889, 313), Thornes (1978, 24), Hoozee (1979, 345), Reynolds (1984, 22.26)

Constable's inscription: 'Sepr. 6. 1822 Noon. Gentle wind at west. hot & fine.'

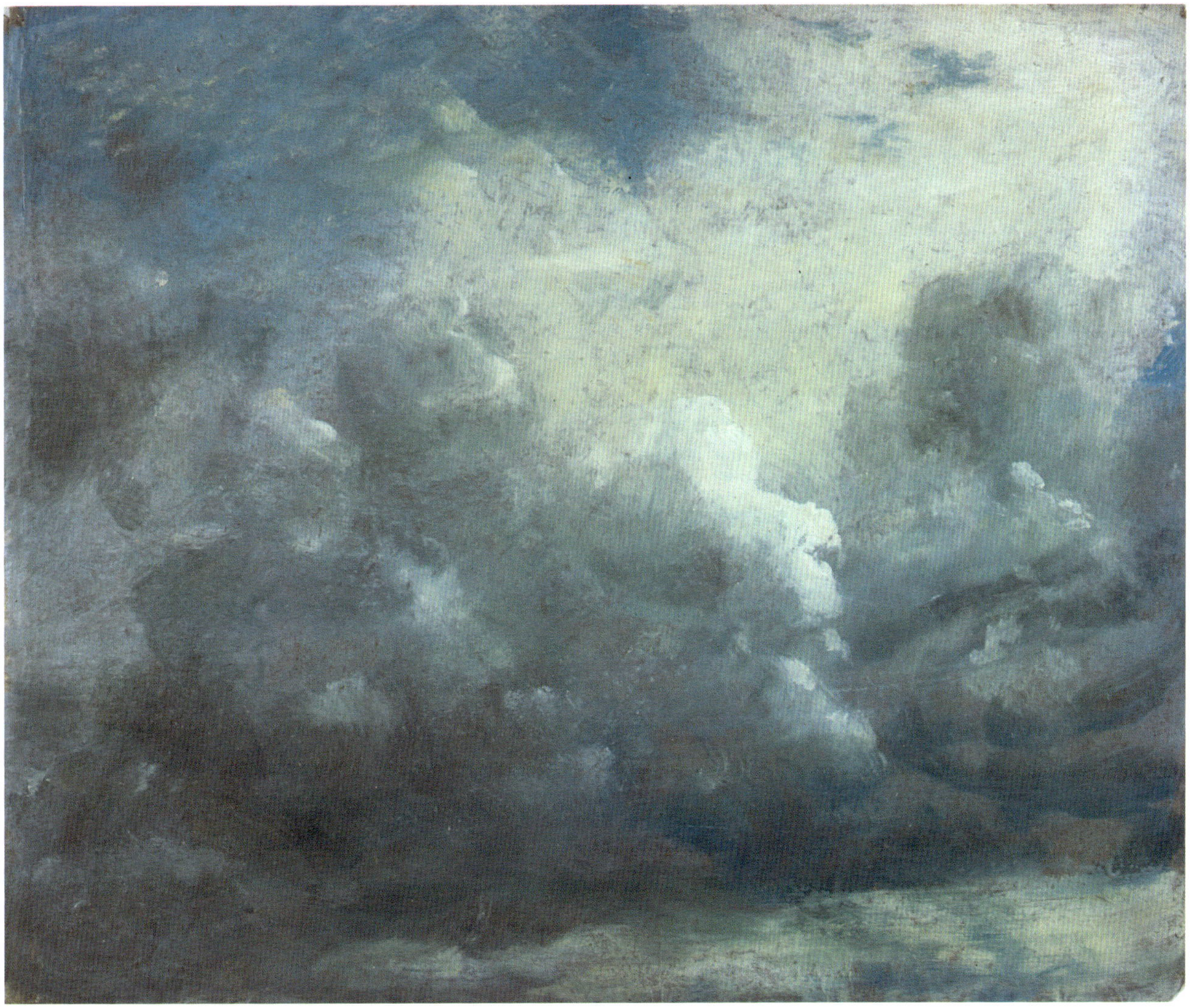

Plate 121 John Constable, *Cloud Study*, 6 September 1822. Private collection

(51) 6 September 1822; Cloud Study; Plate 122; private collection; 300 x 500; oil (?); pure sky; Paterson (1928, 2), Thornes (1978, 25), Hoozee (1979, 344), Reynolds (1984, 22.25)

Constable's inscription: 'Sept. 6th, 1822, looking S.E. – 12 to 1 oclock, fresh and bright, between showers – much the look of rain all the morning, but very fine and grand all the afternoon and evening.'

	WIND	*PRES.*	*TEMP.*	*RAIN*	*CLOUD*	*COMMENTS*
Howard (Stratford)	SW	29.93	72			Fine
Belville	SW	29.77	70		9/10 4/10	Cloudy drizzling rain
Cary		29.87	67			Showery
Cowe	SW	29.78	74			Fine

Comparison: Streets of cumulus are depicted in both **(50)** and **(51)** and appear to have been accompanied by scattered showers. The afternoon seems to have been clearer with less cloud and more sunshine, borne out by Belville's cloud records. The temperature was in the low seventies which, with a gentle wind, would feel hot in the sunshine.

Conclusion: Very good agreement

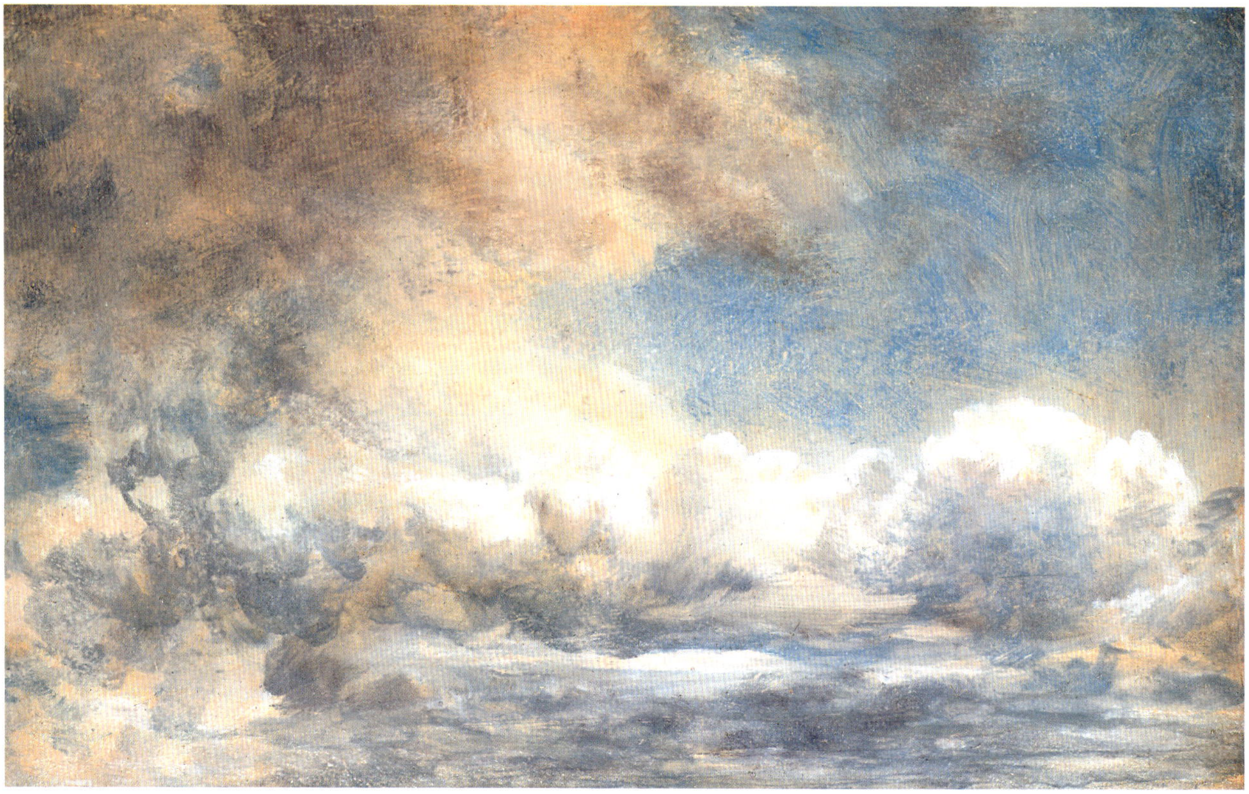

Plate 122 John Constable, *Cloud Study*, 6 September 1822. Private collection

(52) 21 September 1822; Cloud study; Plate 123; Yale Center for British Art (B1981.25.116); 287 x 483; oil on paper laid on panel; pure sky; Paterson (1928, 5), Richmond (1963, 115), Royal Academy (1964/65, 77), Yale (1965, 40), Washington (1969, 52), Thornes (1978, 26), Hoozee (1979, 347), Reynolds (1984, 22.27)

Constable's inscription: 'Sepr. 21. 1822. _ past one o clock. looking south. Wind very fresh at East, but warm.'

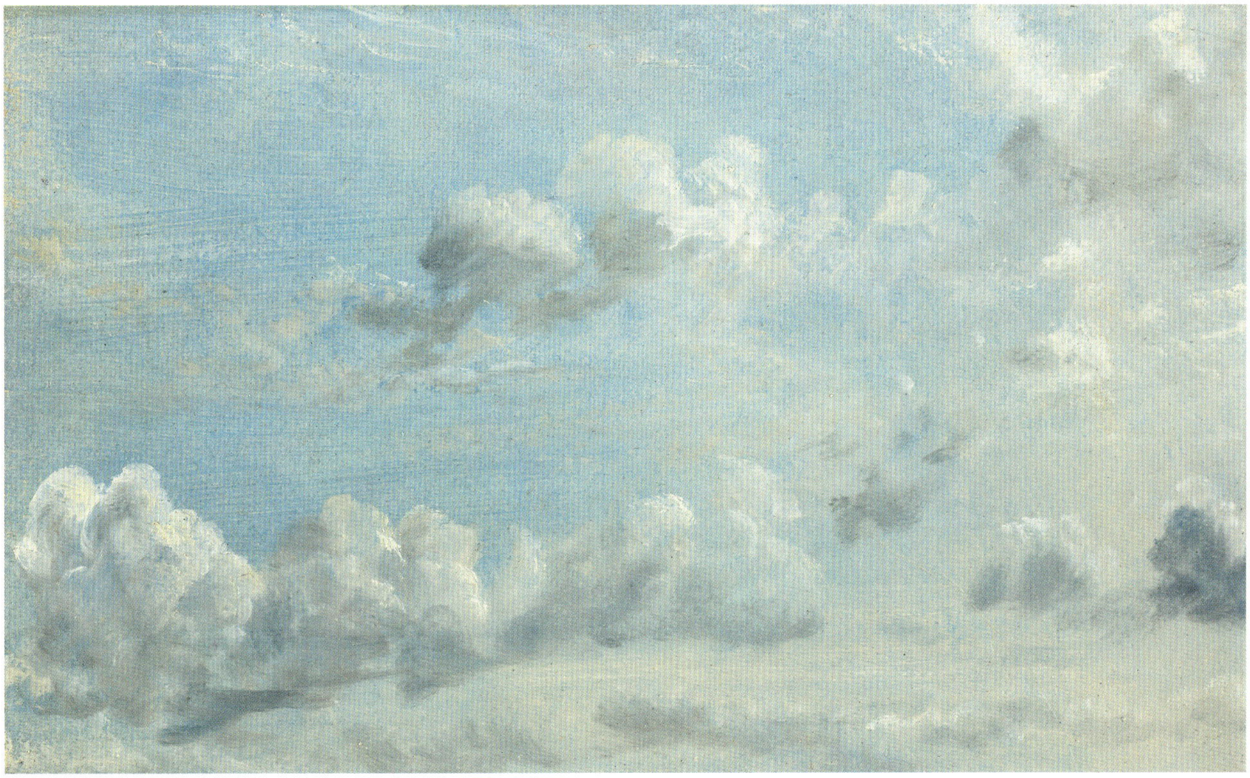

Plate 123 John Constable, *Study of Cumulus Clouds*, 21 September 1822.
Yale Center for British Art, Paul Mellon Collection (B1981.25.116)

(53) 21 September 1822; **Cloud study; Plate 124**; Courtauld Institute Galleries (Witt Collection); 305 x 492; oil on paper laid on board; pure sky; Paterson (1928, 3), Thornes (1978, 27), Hoozee (1979, 348), New York (1983, 44), Reynolds (1984, 22.28)

Constable's inscription: 'Sepr. 21 1822. looking South brisk Wind at East Warm & fresh. 3 oclo afternoon.'

	WIND	*PRES.*	*TEMP.*	*RAIN*	*CLOUD*	*COMMENTS*
Howard (Stratford)	E	29.84	65			Fine
Belville	ENE	29.78	64		3/10 3/10	Flying Clouds
Cary		29.92	60			Fair
Cowe	E	29.80	65	.062		Fine a.m. fair p.m.

Comparison: Two studies in quick succession, but this time unusually with an easterly airstream producing streets of 'fair weather' cumulus. Both pictures are very similar and the agreement of wind direction between Constable and all the weather records is excellent. Constable mentions a 'brisk wind' and a 'fresh wind', not noted in the records, but the general absence of extensive cloud is confirmed by Belville.

Conclusion: Excellent agreement

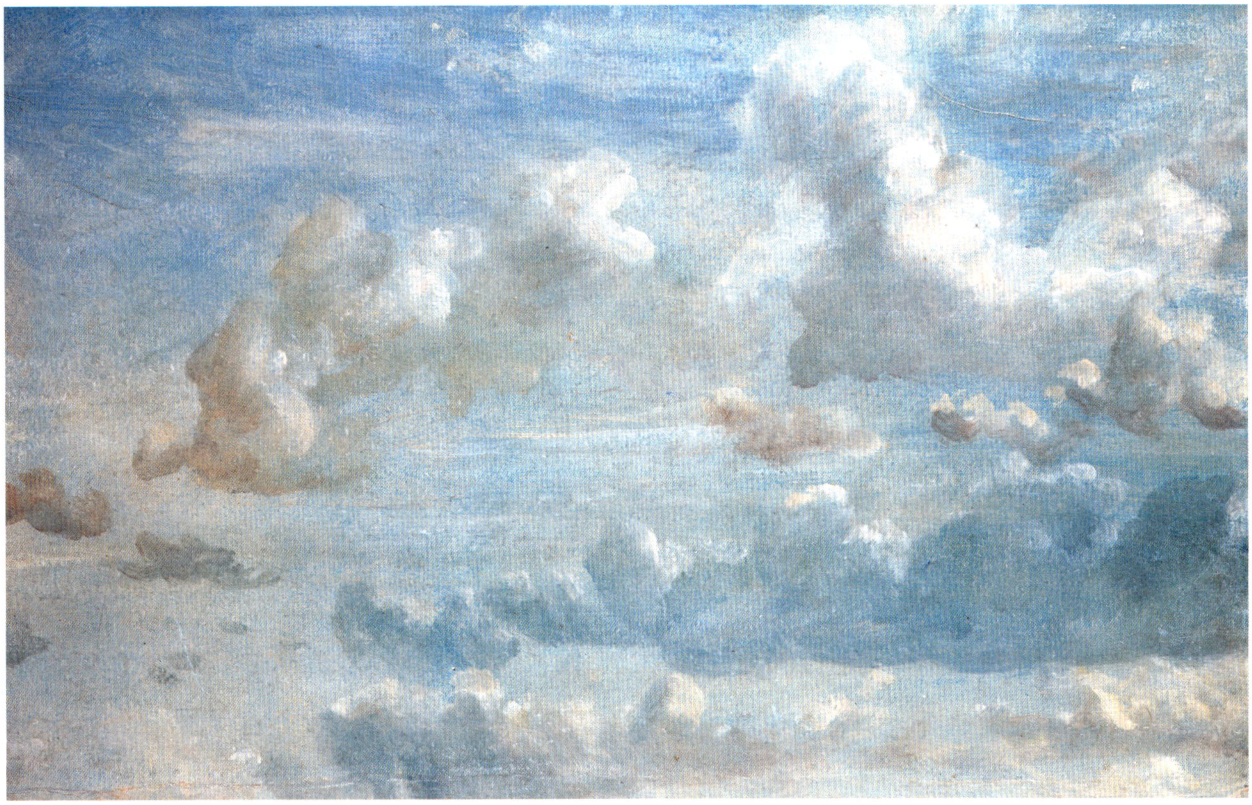

Plate 124 John Constable, *Cloud Study*, 21 September 1822. The Courtauld Gallery, London

(54) 31September (1 October?) 1822?; Cloud study; Plate 125; Ashmolean Museum, Oxford; 480 x 590; oil on paper laid on canvas; pure sky; Paterson, (1928, 6), Badt (1950, Plate 4), Manchester (1956, 55), Herbert Art Gallery, Coventry (1975, 33), Tate (1976, 209), Thornes (1978, 15 (9)), Hoozee (1979, 349), Reynolds (1984, 22.30)

Constable's inscription: '31st Sepr 10–11 o'clock morning looking Eastward a gentle wind to East.'

	WIND	*PRES.*	*TEMP.*	*RAIN*	*CLOUD*	*COMMENTS*
1821 1 October						
Howard (Stratford)	NW	29.91	65			Fine: windy
Belville	W	29.60	63		9/10 4/10	Cloudy
Cary		29.74	65			Showery
Cowe	W	29.59	65			Stormy

	WIND	*PRES.*	*TEMP.*	*RAIN*	*CLOUD*	*COMMENTS*
1822 1 October						
Howard (Stratford)	E	29.67	56			Fine
Belville	E	29.60	60		2/10 8/10	Fine morning cloudy aft.
Cary		29.74	61			Fair
Cowe	E	29.63	64			Fair

Comparison: The peculiar date is not unusual. Apparently, Constable often overran the days of the months. The weather of 1 October 1822 bears out the inscription: the wind was indeed easterly and the weather was fair and reasonably warm for the time of year. The corresponding day in 1821 was 'windy' according to Howard, with a westerly airstream. The evidence points clearly to a dating of 1 October 1822. The painting is unusual in that the clouds appear to rear up at an unusual angle, but this is probably because Constable was painting into the wind and the depicted cumulus streets were moving straight towards him.

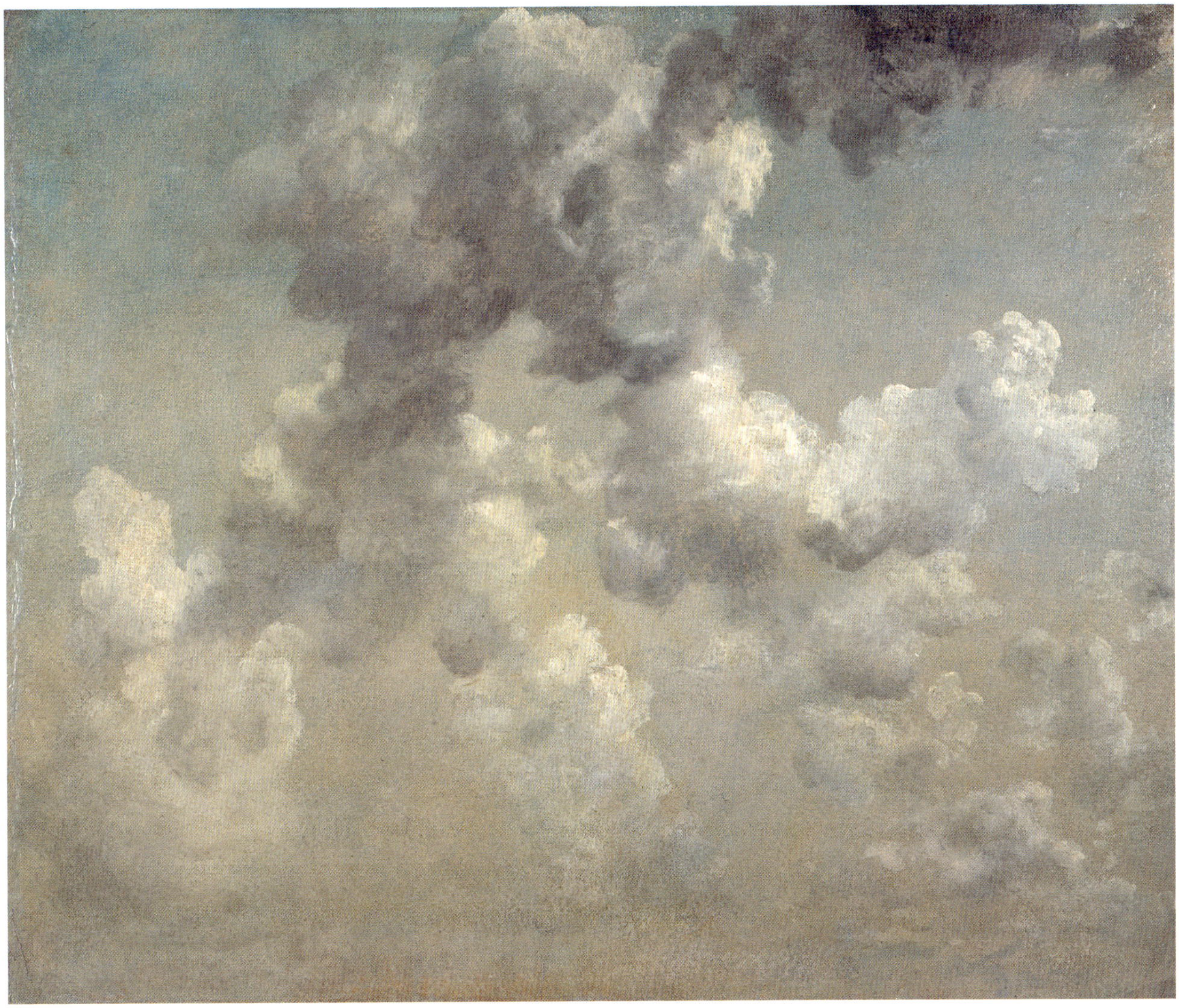

Plate 125 John Constable, *Cloud Study*, 31 September/1 October 1822.
Ashmolean Museum, Oxford

IX Conclusion

This study reaffirms the accuracy with which Constable observed nature. It is only because of Constable's skilful open-air technique, which enabled him to portray a weather scene in less than an hour, that weather dating of the above kind is possible. The painting of clouds is very difficult, as any artist will admit. They are never the same from minute to minute, always changing their form and colour. 'Nature never lets one of the members of even her most disciplined groups of cloud be like another; but though each is adopted for the same function, and in its great features resembles all the others, not one, out of the millions with which the sky is chequered, is without a separate beauty and character.'[10]

List of owners

Victoria and Albert Museum, London (12)	**1, 4, 11, 15, 18, 24, 27, 30, 36, 37, 38, 49**
Private owners (14)	**2, 3, 8, 9, 13, 16, 25, 31, 33, 39, 42, 44, 50, 51**
Yale Center for British Art (8)	**7, 17, 19, 20, 23, 29, 40, 52**
Whereabouts unknown (6)	**6, 12, 28, 41, 43, 45**
Royal Academy, London (5)	**5, 14, 21, 22, 34**
Ashmolean Museum, Oxford (1)	**54**
Birmingham City Art Gallery (1)	**47**
Courtauld Institute, Witt Collection, London (1)	**53**
David Goodstein Collection, Los Angeles (1)	**26**
John G. Johnson Collection, Philadelphia Museum of Art (1)	**35**
Manchester City Art Gallery (1)	**10**
National Gallery of Victoria, Melbourne (1)	**48**
New Orleans Museum of Art (1)	**32**
Tate Gallery, London (1)	**46**

Notes

1 J. E. Thornes, *The Accurate Dating of Certain of John Constable's Cloud Studies 1821/22 Using Historical Weather Records*, Occasional Paper No. 34, (London: Dept. of Geography, University College London, 1978).
2 R. Hoozee, *L'opera completa di Constable* (Milan: Rizzoli Editore, 1979).
3 G. Reynolds, *The Later Paintings and Drawings of John Constable* (London: Yale University Press, 1984); *The Early Paintings and Drawings of John Constable* (London: Yale University Press, 1996).
4 L. Howard, *The Climate of London*, 2nd edn, 2 vols. (London, 1833).
5 Reynolds, *The Later Paintings*; *The Early Paintings*.
6 Reynolds, *The Later Paintings*, p. xii.
7 R. B. Beckett, 'Correspondence and other materials of John Constable', R.A (1961), unpublished manuscript, Victoria & Albert Museum Library; passages quoted contained in vols. XVIII and XIX.
8 C. R. Leslie, *Memoirs of the Life of John Constable*, 2nd edn (London: Longman's, Brown, Green and Longman's, 1845), p. 102.
9 Reynolds, *The Later Paintings*; *The Early Paintings*.
10 J. Ruskin, *Modern Painters I*. In *The Works of John Ruskin*, edited by E. T. Cook and A. Wedderburn, 39 vols. (London: Library Edition: 1903-12), *III*: p. 362.

APPENDIX 2

Sky studies without weather inscriptions attributed to John Constable

There are 68 sky studies listed below. Numbers under Hoozee and Reynolds refer to their cataloguing of the studies.

A) Considered genuine by Hoozee and/or Reynolds

	Hoozee	*Reynolds*	*Size*	*Pure sky*
1)	306	21.99	245 x 298mm	no
2)	321	22.42	295 x 485mm	no
3)	322	21.112	248 x 298mm	no
4)	323	21.111	254 x 298mm	no
5)	338	22.17	472 x 584mm	yes
6)		22.31	?	
7)	350	22.54	292 x 482mm	yes
8)		22.55	198 x 320mm	yes
9)	351	21.120	247 x 302mm	yes
10)	352	21.119	253 x 305mm	yes
11)	353	22.56	229 x 190mm	yes
12)		22.57	265 x 320mm	yes
13)	354	22.58	247 x 470mm	yes
14)	355	21.129	220 x 292mm	yes
15)	356	21.121	241 x 292mm	yes
16)	358	22.59	114 x 178mm	yes
17)		22.60	115 x 150mm	no
18)	359	22.61	152 x 240mm	yes
19)	360	21.107	245 x 292mm	no
20)	379	22.43	245 x 394m,m	no
21)	381	22.44	229 x 190mm	no
22)	383	21.101	251 x 305mm	no
23)	385	21.117	250 x 280mm	no
24)	386	21.103	302 x 238mm	no
25)	389	21.104	355 x 305mm	no

	Hoozee	*Reynolds*	*Size*	*Pure sky*
26)	390	21.108	356 x 302mm	no
27)	534	22.47	328 x 500mm	no
28)	535	22.68	316 x 502mm	no
29)	578	21.123	210 x 285mm	no
30)		22.64	190 x 270mm	yes
31)		22.65	255 x 335mm	yes
32)		22.70	241 x 292mm	no
33)		22.71	200 x 225mm	no
34)		22.72	115 x 150mm	yes
35)		22.73	241 x 292mm	no

(35 in total, of which 15 were pure sky; 19 landscape and sky, and 1 unknown)

B) Considered genuine by either Hoozee or Reynolds

	Hoozee		*Reynolds*	*Size*		*Pure sky*
36)	357	Genuine	-	Dubious	300 x 500mm	no
37)	621	Dubious	22.69	Genuine	260 x 360mm	no
38)	623	Dubious	22.18	Genuine	254 x 222mm	yes
39)	624	Dubious	22.53	Genuine	475 x 575mm	no
40)	626	Dubious	21.125	Genuine	146 x 223mm	yes
41)	627	Dubious	21.126	Genuine	146 x 223mm	yes
42)	628	Dubious	21.127	Genuine	133 x 149mm	yes
43)	633	Dubious	21.128	Genuine	238 x 330mm	yes
44)	645	Dubious	22.62	Genuine	194 x 280mm	no
45)	647	Dubious	21.130	Genuine	210 x 270mm	no
46)	648	Dubious	21.131	Genuine	233 x 305mm	no
47)	649	Dubious	22.63	Genuine	265 x 330mm	no
48)	681	Dubious	21.122	Genuine	193 x 240mm	yes

(13 in total, of which 6 were pure sky and 7 landscape and sky)

C) Considered dubious by both Hoozee and Reynolds

	Hoozee	*Reynolds*	*Size*	*Pure sky*
49)	620	Dubious	177 x 240mm	no
50)	622	Dubious	175 x 230mm	no
51)	625	Dubious	100 x 180mm	no
52)	629	Dubious	165 x 265mm	no
53)	630	Dubious	95 x 140mm	yes
54)	631	Dubious	95 x 140mm	yes
55)	632	Dubious	115 x 152mm	yes
56)	634	Dubious	140 x 190mm	no
57)	635	Dubious	62 x 82mm	yes
58)	636	Dubious	62 x 82mm	yes

	Hoozee	*Reynolds*	*Size*	*Pure sky*
59)	637	Dubious	62 x 82mm	yes
60)	638	Dubious	62 x 82mm	yes
61)	639	Dubious	62 x 82mm	yes
62)	640	Dubious	62 x 82mm	yes
63)	641	Dubious	62 x 82mm	yes
64)	642	Dubious	62 x 82mm	yes
65)	643	Dubious	146 x 230mm	no
66)	644	Dubious	95 x 140mm	no
67)	646	Dubious	210 x 270mm	no
68)	650	Dubious	127 x 190mm	no

(20 in total, of which 11 were pure sky and 9 landscape and sky)

Notes

1. Hoozee numbers greater than 600 are considered dubious.
2. Reynolds only gives a number to those paintings he considers genuine.
3. Of the 68 listed paintings above, 32 are 'pure sky' and 35 are landscape and sky. One is unknown.
4. Of the 68 paintings listed above Hoozee (1979) considers 26 genuine and 32 dubious, and there are 10 he doesn't mention.
5. Of the 68 paintings listed above Reynolds (1984) considers 47 genuine and 21 dubious.
6. Of the the 47 studies considered genuine by Reynolds 21 are 'pure sky' studies.

APPENDIX 3

Letter to John Fisher

The Revd. John Fisher
etc. etc.
Close
Salisbury

Hampstead 23^{d} Octr 1821.

My dear Fisher,

I trust You will pardon this delay of mine in replying to Your last long and very kind letter – I fully expected to have been with You at this time – but I have had many interruptions but what has prevented me has been a good deal of Indisposition in my family. which has made it almost impofsible for me to leave home. Our time expires at this place this month – and when I have settled my family in Keppel Street I shall be able to make You a Visit for a few days. should it be then convenient to You to receive me.

I have not been Idle – and have made more particular and general Study than I have ever done in one summer. but I am most anxious to get into my London painting Room. for I do not consider myself at work without I am before a six foot canvas – I have done a good deal of skying – I am determined to conquer all dificulties and that most arduous one among the rest. and now talking of skies – ~~we cannot but~~

It is quite amusing and interesting to us to see how admirably You fight ~~my~~ their battles You certainly take the best pofsible ground for getting Your friend out of a scrape – "(the examples of the great masters"–) that Landscape painter = who does not make his skies a very material part of his compoisition – neglects to avail himfelf of most of his greatest aids. Sir Joshua speaking of the "landscape" of Titian of Salvator of

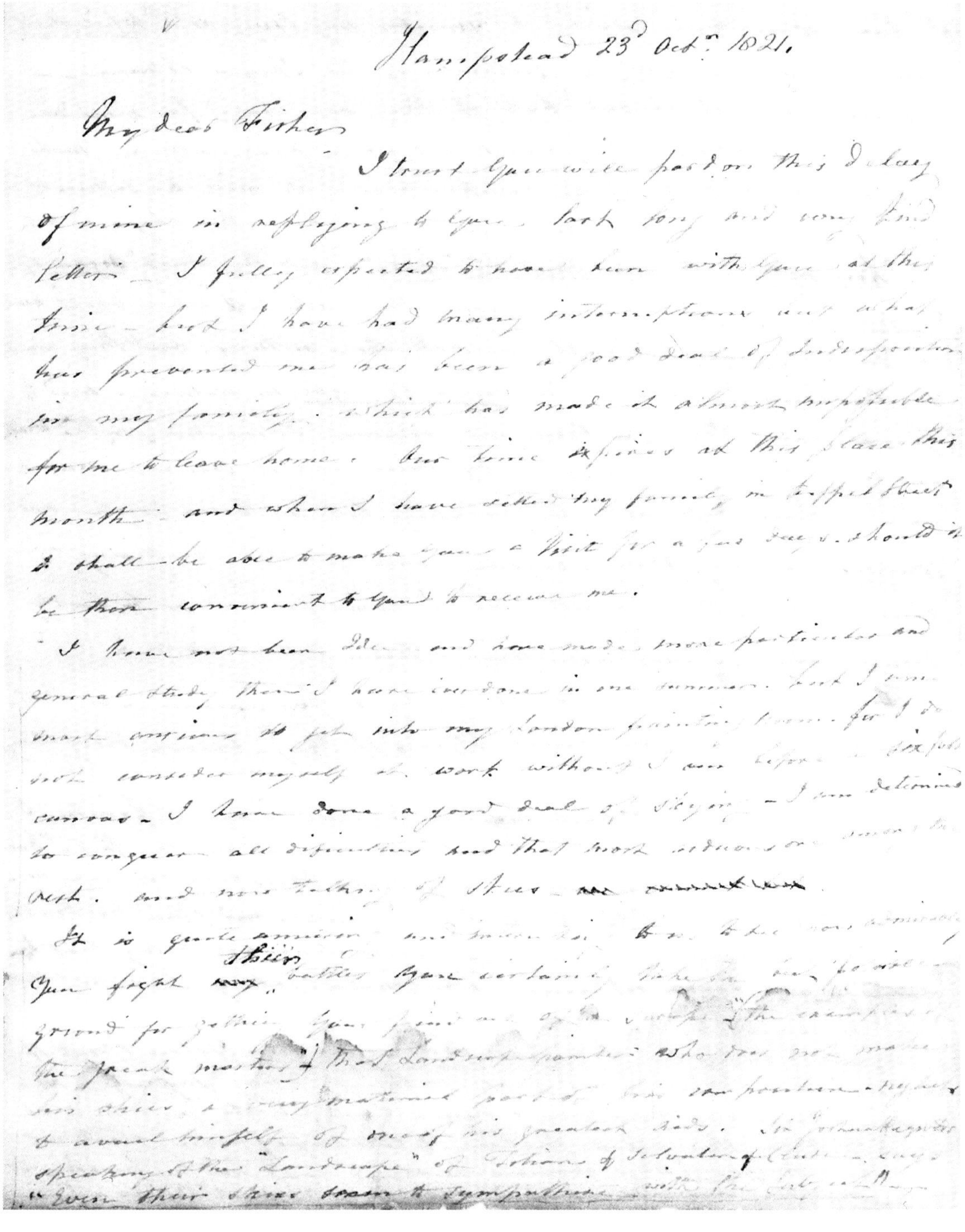

Hampstead 23^d Octr 1821.

My dear Fisher

I trust you will pardon this delay of mine in replying to your last long and very kind letter – I fully expected to have been with you at this time – but I have had many interruptions and what has prevented me has been a good deal of indisposition in my family, which has made it almost impossible for me to leave home. Our time expires at this place this month – and when I have settled my family in Keppel Street I shall be able to make you a visit for a few days, should it be then convenient to you to receive me.

I have not been idle and have made more particular and general study than I have ever done in one summer, but I am most anxious to get into my London painting room, for I do not consider myself at work without I am before a six foot canvas – I have done a good deal of skying – I am determined to conquer all difficulties, and that most arduous one among the rest. and now talking of skies – ~~[illegible]~~

It is quite amusing and interesting to see how admirably you fight ~~my~~ their battles you certainly take the best possible ground for getting your friend out of a scrape (the example of the great masters) That Landscape painter who does not make his skies a very material part of his composition – neglects to avail himself of one of his greatest aids. Sir Joshua Reynolds speaking of the "Landscape" of Titian & of Salvator & Claude – says "Even their skies seem to sympathise with the subject.

Claude – says "Even their skies seem to sympathise with the Subject" – I have often been advised to consider my Skey – as a "White Sheet" drawn behind the Objects" – Cirtainly if the Skey is obtrusive – (as mine are) it is bad. but if they are evaded (as mine are not) it is worse. they must stand and alwa[y]s shall with me make an effectual part of the composition. it will be difficult to name a clafs of Landscape – in which the skeys is not the "key note"– the standard of "Scale" – and the chief "Organ of "Sentiment' – You may conceive then what a "White Sheet" would do for me. impresfed as I am with these notions. and they cannot be Erroneous. the 'skey' is the "source of light in nature – and governs every thing – Even our common observations on the weather of every day – are suggested by them but it does not occur to us – their difficulty in painting both as to composition and Execution is very great. because with all their
in a picture
brilliancy and consequence – they ought not to come forward or be hardly though[t] about. any more than extreme distances are –

But these remarks do not apply to phenomenon – or what the painters call accidental Effects of Skey – because they always attract particularly.

I hope you will not think ~~my~~ I am turned Critic instead of painter. I say all this to You though You do not want to be told – that I know very well what I am about – & that my Skies have not been neglected though they often faild in execution – and often no doubt from over anxiety about them – which alone will destroy that ~~the ease of nat[?ure]~~ Easy appearance which nature always has – in all her movements –
(but he is too far gone)
Again talking of criticism have you seen ~~John Bull~~ of sunday week. Poor Ward will certainly hang himself – as a man (to those who know him) is much liked – but he is not at all pitied in this great picture & Catalogue (for they should not be mentioned apart) it is grevious he should have had the temerity to ~~do it. Haydon has not escaped~~ – meddle with such things – poor Haydon who nobody either pities or likes. has not escaped but though he deserves much he has in this motion – only got the lash by a chance swing of the whip. Jas Ward Esqr R. A. – has been an author before. he wrote an .. account of an old Woman in Staffordshire who lived six months – on counting her fingers & sucking the bed cloths.

How strange it is that we should prefer raising all manner of difficulties in painting – to truth and common sense.

How much I can Imagine myself with You on Your fishing excursion in the new forest. what river can it be. but the ~~Sunds~~ sound of water escaping from Mill dams. So do Willows – Old rotton Banks slimy posts. & brickwork. I love such things – Shakespeare could make anything poetical – he mentions "poor Tom's" haunts among <u>Sheep cotts</u> – & Mills – the Water mist & the Hedge pig: as long as I do paint I shall never cease to paint such Places. they have always been my delight – & I should indeed have delighted in seeing what you describe ~~with You~~ in Your company "in the company of a man to whom nature does not spread her volume or utter her voice in vain".

But I should paint my own places best – painting is but another word for feeling. I afsociate my "carelefs
and I am gratefull
boyhood" to all that lies on the banks of the <u>Stour</u>. they made me a painter that is I had often thought of pictures of them before I had ever touched a pencil. and Your picture is one of the strongest instances I can recolect of it. but I would say no more – for I am fond of being an Egotist. in whatever relates to painting.

Does not the Cathedral look very beautiful amongst the Golden foliage its Silvery grey must sparkle in it. Poor Reed has sent me some copies made at Wilton. The Claude & a V. de Veld – they are very far from bad. and very much better than I expected. I only wanted You to call on him. nothing Else. Your advise. & notice of him could not fail of being of service to him. in a matter in which the World is led by appearances – I hope he is getting a living. he seems industrious I have requested the loan of the little Teniers at the Mifs
handside
Fishers for him to Copy. it is a Good Tone but rather too hot on the Right.

[The rest of the letter is written at the bottom and top of the fourth side of the folded sheet, the side used as a cover with its address to Fisher. Most of the two halves of the original black wax seal are still attached to this 'cover'.]

[at the foot of the page:]

My wife & Children are now quite well. the former & my eldest Boy having been great invalids. We hope sincerely Mrs Fisher & all your Children and relations our good friends at Salisbury are well. is the <u>Portrait</u> of which you make such laughable mention – still running the Gauntlit at the Publick House [?] what can the Good Bishop be about. but You fully account for all the scrape – the worst I should fear is that some of the dignity of his High Station must go with it – but I will say no more – that <u>love of patronage</u> which You mention. brought me known to you. and Your excellent family. & which has brought with it most of the great

[at the top of the page]

blefsings of my life. I long to get to work. I shall do another large Work of my Own. & Sav[iles] picture – but that is a dead pall he is not only a fool. but he is as Crazy as a fool can be.

My last Years work has got much <u>together.</u> this weather has blown & washed the powder off. I do not know what I shall with it. but I love my children to well to expose them to the taunts of the Ignorant. though they shall never flinch from honorable competition I have just paper enough to say adieu – & add my Wife's (who is sitting by me) best regards to Yourself & all family. I am Y[rs] John Constable

Note
This letter was originally transcribed by Ian Fleming-Williams

Bibliography

Abercromby, R. 'Suggestions for an International Nomenclature of Clouds', *Quarterly Journal of the Royal Meteorological Society* 13 (1887).

Aristophanes, *The Clouds*, ~423 BC, ed. K. J. Dover (Oxford: Clarendon Press, 1968).

Aristotle, *Meteorologica*, ~350 BC (London: Loeb Classical Library, 1962).

Badt, K. *John Constable's Clouds* (London: Routledge & Kegan Paul, 1950).

Bang, M. L. *Johan Christian Dahl – Life and Works*, 3 vols. (Oslo: Norwegian University Press, 1987).

Battershill, N. *Painting Skies* (London: Pitman Publishing, 1980).

Beckett, R. B. *John Constable and the Fishers* (London: Routledge & Kegan Paul, 1952).

'Correspondence and other materials of John Constable' (1961), unpublished manuscript, Victoria & Albert Museum Library.

John Constable's Correspondence, 6 vols., vol. 4, *Patrons, Dealers and Fellow Artists* (Ipswich: Suffolk Records Society, 1966).

John Constable's Discourses (Ipswich: Suffolk Records Society, 1970).

Blench, B. J. R. 'Luke Howard and his contribution to meteorology', *Weather* 18 (1963): 83–92.

Bonacina, L. C. W. 'John Constable's centenary: his position as a painter of weather', *Quarterly Journal of the Royal Meteorological Society* 63 (1937): 483–90.

'Landscape meteorology and its reflection in art and literature', *Quarterly Journal of the Royal Meteorological Society* 65 (1939): 485–97.

Bone, J. Drummond 'Clouds in the poetry of four romantics: Wordsworth, Byron, Shelley and Keats'. (Coventry: Coventry City Art Gallery, 1976).

Boudreau, B. A. 'John Constable's 1821 and 1822 cloud studies: the artist as a scientist', *Weather* 53 (1998): 357–62.

Boyer, C. B. *The Rainbow from Myth to Mathematics* (New York: Yoseloff, 1959).

Brimblecombe, P. 'London air pollution', *Atmospheric Environment* 11 (1977): 1157–62.

The Big Smoke – A history of air pollution in London since medieval times (London: Routledge, 1987).

British Meteorological Office, *Cloud Types for Observers* (London: HMSO, 1962).

Observer's Handbook (London: HMSO, 1969).

Burroughs, W. J. 'Winter landscapes and climatic change', *Weather* 36 (1981): 352–7.

Clark, K. *The Romantic Rebellion* (London: Futura Publications, 1973).

Landscape into Art (London: John Murray, 1976).

Constable, J. *English Landscape Scenery* (London, 1830).

English Landscape Scenery, 2nd edn (London, 1833).

Cormack, M. *Constable* (Oxford: Phaidon, 1986).

Cosgrove, D. and J. E. Thornes 'Of truth of clouds; John Ruskin and the moral order in landscape'. In Pocock (ed.), *Humanistic Geography and Literature* (London: Croom Helm, 1981).

Cove, S. 'Constable's oil painting materials and techniques'. In Parris and Fleming-Williams (eds), *Constable* (London: Tate Gallery, 1991).

Cozens, A. *A New Method of Assisting the Invention in Drawing Original Compositions of Landscape* (London, c. 1785).

Damisch, H. *Théorie du Nuage: pour une histoire de la peinture* (Paris: Editions du Seuil, 1972).

Day, J. A. and F. H. Ludlam, 'Luke Howard and his clouds: a contribution to the early history of cloud physics', *Weather* 27 (1972): 448–61.

Field, G. *Chromatography; or, a Treatise on Colours and Pigments* (London, 1835).

Fleming-Williams, I. *Constable and His Drawings* (London: Philip Wilson, 1990).

Constable Landscape Watercolours and Drawings (London: Tate Gallery, 1976).

Forster, T. *Researches about Atmospheric Phaenomena*, 2nd edn (London: Baldwin, Cradock & Joy, 1815).

Gage, J. *Colour and Culture* (London: Thames and Hudson, 1993).

Garbett, L. G., 'Admiral Sir Francis Beaufort and the Beaufort scales of wind and weather', *Quarterly Journal of the Royal Meteorological Society* 52(218) (1926): 161–72.

Gedzelman, S. D. 'Cloud classification before Luke Howard', *Bulletin of the American Meteorological Society* 70(4) (1989): 381–95.

Gilpin, W. *Three Essays on Picturesque Landscape* (London: R. Blamire, 1792).

Glaisher J. *Philosophical Transactions Part II* (1849).

Gombrich, E. H. *Art and Illusion*, 5th edn (London: Phaidon, 1977).

Greenler, R. *Rainbows, Halos, and Glories* (Cambridge: Cambridge University Press, 1980).

Hawes, L. 'Constable's sky sketches', *Journal of the Warburg and Courtauld Institutes* XXXII (1969): 344–65.

Hill, D. *Constable's English Landscape Scenery* (London: The Promotional Reprint Company, 1992).

Hoozee, R. *L'opera completa di Constable* (Milan: Rizzoli Editore, 1979).

Howard, L. 'Account of a microscopical investigation of several species of pollen'. In *Transactions of the Linnean Society* (London, 1800).

'On the modification of clouds', *Tilloch's Philosophical Magazine* (1803): published in 3 parts in vols 16(62): 97–107, 16(64): 344–57, 17(65): 5–11.

Essay on the Modification of Clouds, 1st edn (London,1804).

'Clouds'. In *Rees Cyclopedia* (London, 1807).

The Climate of London, 1st edn, 2 vols. (London, 1818).

The Climate of London, 2nd edn, 2 vols. (London, 1833).

Seven Lectures on Meteorology (Pontefract, 1837).

Barometrographia (London, 1847).

Ivy, J. Crosby *Constable and His Critics* (Suffolk: The Boydell Press, 1991).

Jeffares, B. *Landscape Painting* (Oxford: Phaidon, 1979).

Kemp, M. *The Science of Art* (New Haven: Yale University Press, 1990).

Klonk, C. *Science and the Perception of Nature: British Landscape Art in the Late Eighteenth and Early Nineteenth Century* (London: Yale University Press, 1996).

Knight, D *Romanticism and the sciences*. In A. Cunningham and N. Jardine (eds), *Romanticism and the Sciences* (Cambridge: Cambridge University Press, 1990).

Lamarck, J. *Annuaire Météorologique* (Paris, 1802).

Lamb, H. H. 'Britain's changing climate', *Geographical Journal* 133 (1967): 445–66.

'Volcanic dust in the atmosphere', *Philosophical Transactions of the Royal Society*, series A, 266 (1970).

Landow, G. P. 'The rainbow: a problematic image'. In U. C. Knoepflmacher and G. B. Tennyson (eds), *Nature and the Victorian Imagination* (Berkeley: University of California Press, 1977): 341–69.

Leonardo da Vinci *A Treatise on Painting* (English translation) (London, 1721).

Leslie, C. R. *Memoirs of the Life of John Constable*, 2nd edn (London: Longman's, Brown, Green and Longman's, 1845).

Memoirs of the Life of John Constable, ed. A. Shirley (London, 1937).

Linke, F., *Monthly Weather Review*, 56 (1928), 224–25.

Lynch, D. K. and W. Livingston *Color and Light in Nature* (Cambridge: Cambridge University Press, 1995).
Middleton, W. E. Knowles *A History of the Theories of Rain* (London: Oldbourne History of Science Library, 1965).
Minnaert, M. *The Nature of Light and Colour in the Open Air* (New York: Dover Publications Inc., 1954).
Neuberger, H and M. Neuberger, 'Color memory in cyanometry', *Bulletin of the American Meteorological Society* 24 (1943): 47–53.
Neuberger, H. 'Climate in art', *Weather* 25 (1970): 46–56.
Novak, B. *Nature and Culture* (London: Thames and Hudson, 1980).
Nussenzveig, H. 'The theory of the rainbow', *Scientific American* (April 1977).
Parris, L. *Landscape in Britain* (London: The Tate Gallery, 1973).
Parris, L., C. Shields and I. Fleming-Williams (eds) *John Constable: Further Documents & Correspondence* (London: The Tate Gallery and the Suffolk Records Society 1975).
Parris, L., I. Fleming-Williams and C. Shields *Constable* (London: Tate Gallery, 1976).
Parris L. and I. Fleming-Williams (eds) *Constable* (London: Tate Gallery, 1991).
Rayleigh, Lord 'On the light from the sky, its polarisation and colour', *Philosophical Magazine* 41 (1871): 107–20, 274–9.
Reynolds, G. *Catalogue of the Constable Collection in the Victoria and Albert Museum*, 2nd edn (London: Victoria and Albert Museum, 1973).
Constable: The Natural Painter (St. Albans: Panther Books, 1976).
The Later Paintings and Drawings of John Constable (London: Yale University Press, 1984).
The Early Paintings and Drawings of John Constable (London: Yale University Press, 1996).
Rosenthal, M. *Constable* (London, Yale University Press, 1983).
Ruskin, J. *The Works of John Ruskin*, edited by E. T. Cook and A. Wedderburn, 39 vols. (London: Library Edition: 1903-12)
Coeli Enarrant (London: George Allen, 1885).
Schaaf, F. *Seeing the Sky* (London: John Wiley and Sons, 1990).
Schweizer, P. D. 'John Constable, rainbow science, and English color theory', *The Art Bulletin* LXIV(3) (1982).
Scientific American, *Light from the Sky* (San Francisco: W. H. Freeman and Co., 1980).
Atmospheric Phenomena (San Francisco: W. H. Freeman and Co., 1980).
Scott, D. *Luke Howard* (York, England: William Sessions Ltd., 1976).
Seibold, U. 'Meteorology in Turner's paintings', *Interdisciplinary Science Reviews* 15 (1990): 77–86.
Shields, C. and L. Parris *John Constable 1776–1837* (London: Tate Gallery, 1969).
Shirley, A. *The Rainbow – A Portrait of John Constable* (London: Michael Joseph, 1949).
Slater, A. W. 'Luke Howard, F.R.S. (1772–1864) and his relations with Goethe', *Notes and Records of the Royal Society*, 27(1) (1972): 119–40.
Stringer, E. T. *Techniques of Climatology* (San Francisco: W. H. Freeman & Co., 1972).
The Thames and Hudson Dictionary of Art and Artists, revised edition (London: Thames and Hudson, 1994).
Thomson, J. *Thomson's Seasons* (London, 1744).
Thornes, J. E. 'The weather dating of John Constable's cloud studies', *Weather* 34 (1978): 308–15.
The Accurate Dating of Certain of John Constable's Cloud Studies 1821/22 Using Historical Weather Records, Occasional Paper No. 34 (London: Dept. of Geography, University College London, 1978).
'Luke Howard's influence on art and literature in the early nineteenth century', *Weather* 39(8) (1984): 252–5.
'Constable's Clouds', *Burlington Magazine* CXXI (1979): 697–704.
Tricker, R. A. R. *Introduction to Meteorological Optics* (New York: Elsevier, 1970).
Tyldesley, J. B. 'Weather in Constable's paintings', *Weather* 23 (1968): 344–8.
Wailes, R. *The English Windmill* (London: Routledge & Kegan Paul, 1954).
Walford, E. J. *Jacob van Ruisdael and the Perception of Landscape* (London: Yale University Press, 1991).
Werner, T 'Cloud study and the artists' (Coventry: Coventry City Art Gallery, 1976).
Wilde, O. 'The decay of lying', *The Works of Oscar Wilde*, Golden Heritage Series (Leicester: Galley Press, 1987).
Wilton, A. *Constable's English Landscape Scenery* (London: British Museum, 1979).
The Life and Work of J. M. W. Turner (London: Academy Editions, 1979).

Index

aerial perspective 28, 29–31, 156, 164, 175
air pollution 31, 33–6
Airy, Sir George 47
Alexander's Dark Band 46, 86
Angelico, Fra 157
anticrepuscular rays 45, 88, 142, 200
Aristophanes 19, 187
Aristotle 18, 28, 46, 190
atmospheric perception 19
aurora borealis 45
Bacon, Roger 46
Badt, Kurt 17, 18, 40, 52, 72, 78, 93, 94, 117, 118, 154, 184, 185, 191–2, 201
Bang, M. L. 184–5
Beaufort wind scale 58, 63, 66, 93, 99, 100, 199, 203
Beaufort, Admiral Sir F. 58, 95
Beaumont, Sir George 80, 164, 166, 179
Beckett, R. B. 204
Beethovan, Ludwig van 19
Bellini, Giovanni 157, 158, 160
Belville, J. H. 203, 208
Bertholon 70
Bishop of Salisbury 125–8
Bloomfield, Robert 80
Bonacina, L. C. W. 19, 109
Bonington, Richard Parkes 184
Boner, Charles 87
Bruegel, Peter 160
British Institution 100, 134, 149, 175
British Museum 69
Brunelleschi 52, 158, 161
Burnet, John 40
Burns, Robert 81
Cary, Mr 203, 208
Carey, William 114
Carpenter, James & William 41, 69
Carus, Carl Gustav 52, 184, 185
chiaroscuro 43
Cimabue 154
Clark, Kenneth 126, 158, 161, 165, 169
Claude Lorrain 21, 23, 95, 154, 161, 166–9, 172, 177, 179, 184, 185, 193
climate change 31–3
cloud classification 37–9
cloud colours 39
cloud iridescence 45
cloud perspective 40–1
cloud street 41
Cowe, Rev. 203, 208
Coleridge, Samuel Taylor 188
Constable, George 57, 86
Constable, John
- annotations to Forster's book 68–78
- copies of Cozen's skies 80
- *English Landscape Scenery* 89–90
- meteorological understanding 20, 51–90, 199–201
- rainbow knowledge 81–8, 135–6, 141–2
- scientific approach 51–2
- sky studies 1820/22 58–68, 115–24
- weather inscriptions 58–68
- wind, portrayal of 93, 200
- windmiller days 53–5

Constable, Maria 103, 106, 128, 135, 136, 149, 180, 181, 200
Cove, Sarah 120–4

Cormack, Malcolm 175
Cox, David 19, 42, 180, 184
Cozens, Alexander 22, 80, 95, 154, 158, 176, 177
Cozens, John Robert 177
Cranch, John 95
crepuscular rays 45, 82, 113, 142
Crotch, William 154
Cuyp, Aelbert 54, 154, 160, 161, 170, 176
cyanometer 26
Dahl, Johan Christian Clausen 184–5
Dalton, John 190
Damisch, Hubert 93, 154, 194
Darwin, Charles 187
Darwin, Erasmus 187
Davy, Humphry 188
Delacroix, Eugene 184
De Luc 70, 76, 188
De Saussure 26, 70
De Wint, Peter 184
Debussy, Claude 19
Descartes, René 46, 47, 164
diffraction 45
Dunthorne, John 64, 81, 95, 96, 172, 177
Durer, Albrecht 154
electromagnetic spectrum 23, 24
Eyck, Jan van 157
Faraday, Michael 188
Farington, Joseph 95, 177
Field, George 87, 147
Fisher, John 20, 41, 56, 80, 82, 95, 96, 114, 121, 126–8, 135, 139, 142, 149, 164, 172, 175, 200, 205, 278–82
Fleming-Williams, Ian 80, 88, 94, 99, 100, 109, 113, 123, 145, 172, 176
fog 29, 34, 35
Forster, Thomas 19, 39, 52, 57, 68–78, 89, 117, 200
Friedrich, Caspar David 184, 185
Fuseli, Henry 136, 165, 169, 186
Gainsborough, Thomas 170, 176, 177–9
Gage, John 28
Garofalo 157
Gedzelman, Stanley 37, 154, 157, 159
geometrical perspective 30, 31
Gilpin, Sawrey 22
Giorgione 160
Giotto 154
Girtin, Thomas 95, 176, 177, 179
Goethe, Johann Wolfgang von 52, 185, 187–90
Gombrich, Sir Ernst 54, 55
Halley, Edmund 86
Hampstead & Hampstead Heath 53, 55–6, 66, 70, 90, 114, 115, 121, 124, 125, 141, 199, 203, 204
Hawes, Louis 52, 117, 118, 154, 182, 201
Hobbema, Meyndert 161, 172, 175, 176
Hoozee, Robert 122, 202
Howard, Luke 17, 21, 36, 52, 54, 55, 66, 68–78, 89, 103, 115, 116, 117, 122, 154, 184–91, 196, 200, 203
Humboldt, Alexander von 188
Hoy, T. 203, 208
Hunt, Robert 119
Hutton, James 190
Jacob's ladder 45
Keats, John 52, 187
Kemp, Martin 28
Klonk, Charlotte 51, 188
Knight, David 187
Koninck, Philips 175
Lake District 58, 99, 199
Lamarck, Jean-Baptiste 36, 189
Lamb, Hubert 103, 160
Landow, George 82
landscape art 20
landscape meteorology 18, 19
Leonardo da Vinci 154, 158
Leslie, C. R. 51, 54, 55, 56, 88, 90, 96, 100, 103, 143, 166, 171, 172, 179, 205
Linke scale 27, 28
Linnaeus, Carl von Linne 36, 37, 177, 189
little ice age 32
Lucas, David 53, 90, 139, 147
lunar bow 85
Magritte, René 19
Mediterranean light 26
Middleton, Knowles 188, 189
Mie scattering 24
Milton, John 177
Minnaert, Marcel 25, 47
Monet, Claude 19, 33, 34, 103

Neuberger, H. 26, 27, 28, 31, 32, 33
Newton, Sir Isaac 47, 52, 86, 105, 196
Nussenzveig, H. 46
Ostade, Adriaen van 169
Palmer, Samuel 184
Parris, Leslie 100, 109, 113, 123, 145
perspective 21
phenomenalism 51
Potter 47
Poussin, Nicholas 21, 154, 161, 164–6, 167, 169, 172, 177, 185
Poussin, Gaspard 161, 166, 169, 185
rainbow 23, 28, 46–8, 81–8, 99, 105, 136, 141–3, 147–9, 153, 156
rainbow colours 18, 47
rainbow wheel 88, 143
Raleigh scattering 24
Rees's Cyclopedia 73
reflection 45
refraction 45
Rembrandt, Harmensz van Rijn 43, 168–9, 176
Reynolds, Graham 39, 56, 59, 64, 81, 89, 93, 99, 113, 115, 122, 145, 202, 204
Rosenthal, Michael 131
Royal Academy 95, 96, 100, 109, 113, 116, 124, 126, 130, 134, 136, 139, 141, 142, 185
Royal Institution 51, 54, 149, 167, 169, 179
Royal Meteorological Society 191
Rubens, Peter Paul 21, 40, 154, 161–4, 168, 169, 175
Ruisdael, Isaack 171
Ruisdael, Jacob van 21, 54, 154, 161, 170–6
Ruysdael, Jacob Salomon van 171
Ruskin, John 17, 19, 21, 22, 65, 125, 164, 166, 184, 187, 191–6
Salisbury Cathedral 82, 83, 139, 141–2
Salvator Rosa 21, 23, 169
scattering 45
Schweizer, P. D. 81, 82, 83, 87, 88, 135
Seibold, U. 183, 184
Shelley, Percy Bysshe 19, 125, 186–8, 190–2
Shirley, Andrew 93
sky
  blue 27
  golden 156, 157
  Italian 25
  phantasmagorical 181
skying 22, 199
skyscape 22
sky colours 24–28
Smith, John Thomas 'Antiquity' 95, 172, 179
smog 25
Snell's law 46
Somerset House 62, 64, 191
sun, colour of 44
supernumerary arcs 46
Teniers, David 40
Theodoric of Freiberg 46
Thomson, James 19, 134, 139
Titian, Tiziano Vecelli 154, 158–60, 169
Torin, Captain 58
Tricker, R. A. R. 136
troposphere 28
Turner, Joseph Mallord William 17, 19, 21, 35, 96, 103, 118, 153, 164, 165, 179–84, 187, 192–4
twilight 33
Tyldesley, J. B. 30, 106
Uccello, Paolo 158
Uwins, James 173
Valenciennes 154, 184
Velde the Older, Willem van de 175
Velde the Younger, Willem van de 22, 154, 172, 175–6
Vernet, Claude-Joseph 177
visibility 28, 29, 32, 36
volcanic activity 33, 103, 156, 184
Wagner, Richard 19
Wailes, R. 53
Watercolour Society 94
West, Benjamin 96
Wilde, Oscar 34, 35
Wilson, Richard 25, 26, 167, 176, 177
Wilton, Andrew 180
Worcester 83
Wordsworth, William 186, 187
World Meteorological Organisation 29
Wright, Joseph 154
Wright, Thomas 177
Young, Thomas 47
Zuccarelli, Francesco 177